C R O S S C U R R E N T S

# NTEMPORAR

# ITICAL ISSUES

## OND EDITION

RLTON
SITY OF WESTERN ONTARIO

KER
OLLEGE

D0855202

nada

I(T)P·
International Thomson Publishing
The Trademark ITP is used under licence

© Nelson Canada
A Division of Thomson Canada Limited, 1994

Published in 1994 by
Nelson Canada,
A Division of Thomson Canada Limited
1120 Birchmount Road
Scarborough, Ontario M1K 5G4

**Canadian Cataloguing in Publication Data**
Main entry under title:
Crosscurrents: contemporary political issues
2nd ed.

Includes bibliographical references.
ISBN 0-17-604234-2

1. Canada - Politics and government - 1984-   .*
2. Political culture - Canada. I. Charlton,
Mark William, 1948–   . II. Barker, Paul Frederick, 1953–

FC630.C76 1994      320.971      C94-930230-9
F1034.2.C76 1994

| | |
|---|---|
| **Acquisitions Editors** | Dave Ward and Andrew Livingston |
| **Editorial Manager** | Nicole Gnutzman |
| **Production Editor** | Tracy Bordian |
| **Developmental Editor** | Joanne Scattolon |
| **Art Director** | Liz Nyman |
| **Design** | Liz Nyman |
| **Cover Illustration** | Joe Fleming |

Printed and bound in Canada
1  2  3  4  (WC)  97  96  95  94

**OTABIND**

The pages in this book open easily and lie na...
process. Otabind combines advanced adhesive to
cover to achieve books that last longer and are bo

**Bound to stay open**

# CONTENTS

**INTRODUCTION**　　　　　　　　　　　　　　　　　　　　vii

## PART ONE: Canadian Society and Political Structure

1. **Is dualism still the essential element of Canada's political culture?**　　2

   YES　BRIAN MULRONEY, Dualism in Canada　　4
   NO　WILLIAM THORSELL, Let Us Compare Mythologies　　11

2. **Does multiculturalism weaken Canada?**　　18

   YES　REGINALD W. BIBBY, Is Multiculturalism Tearing
   Us Apart?　　20
   NO　AUGIE FLERAS, Multiculturalism as Society-Building:
   Doing What Is Necessary, Workable, and Fair　　25

3. **Is western alienation justified?**　　43

   YES　DAVID ELTON, The West Wants In　　45
   NO　J.M.S. CARELESS, The Myth of the Downtrodden West　　51

4. **Can native sovereignty co-exist with Canadian sovereignty?**　　62

   YES　JOHN A. OLTHUIS AND ROGER TOWNSHEND, The Case
   for Native Sovereignty　　65
   NO　THOMAS FLANAGAN, Native Sovereignty: Does Anyone
   Really Want an Aboriginal Archipelago?　　70

# PART TWO: The Constitution and Federalism

**5. Should individual rights take precedence over collective rights?** 82

YES PIERRE TRUDEAU, Values in a Just Society 84
NO PAUL MARSHALL, The Importance of Group Rights 90

**6. Is the Canadian Charter of Rights and Freedoms antidemocratic?** 100

YES ROB MARTIN, The Canadian Charter of Rights and
Freedoms Is Antidemocratic and Un-Canadian 103
NO PHILIP L. BRYDEN, The Canadian Charter of Rights and
Freedoms Is Antidemocratic and Un-Canadian:
An Opposing Point of View 108

**7. Should the federal government be strengthened?** 115

YES M.W. WESTMACOTT, Conflicting Constitutional Visions: Is
there a Case for a Strong National Government? 117
NO R.A. YOUNG, What Is Good About Provincial
Governments? 124

**8. Was the Charlottetown Accord good for Quebec?** 137

YES BENOîT BOUCHARD, Good for Quebec 139
NO LUCIEN BOUCHARD, Bad for Quebec 143

# PART THREE: Institutions

**9. Is the prime minister too powerful?** 152

YES DENIS SMITH, Is the Prime Minister Too
Powerful?—Yes 154
NO JOSEPH WEARING, Is the Prime Minister Too
Powerful?—No 160

**10. Do public servants dominate ministers?** 169

YES FLORA MACDONALD, The Minister and the
Mandarins 171
NO DON PAGE, Ministers and Mandarins: Ministers
Must Lead 178

**11. Should party discipline be relaxed?** 192

YES DAVID KILGOUR, JOHN KIRSNER, AND KENNETH MCCONNELL,
Discipline versus Democracy: Party Discipline in
Canadian Politics 194

NO ROBERT J. JACKSON AND PAUL CONLIN, The Imperative
of Party Discipline in the Canadian Political System          201

12. Should Parliament review Supreme Court nominees?          209

YES F.L. MORTON, Why the Judicial Appointment Process
Must Be Reformed          211

NO H. PATRICK GLENN, Parliamentary Hearings for
Supreme Court of Canada Appointments?          219

# PART FOUR: Political Behaviour

13. Are political parties in decline?          230

YES JOHN MEISEL, Decline of Party in Canada          232
NO RONALD G. LANDES, In Defence of Canadian Political
Parties          247

14. Are polls bad for politics?          258

YES JEFFREY SIMPSON, Pollstruck          260
NO MICHAEL ADAMS, Pro Polling          270

15. Should a system of proportional representation be adopted in Canada?          278

YES JOHN HIEMSTRA, Getting What You Vote For          280
NO PAUL BARKER, Voting For Trouble          292

16. Do referendums enrich democracy?          304

YES PATRICK BOYER, Our Democratic Reformation          307
NO MARK CHARLTON, The Limits of Direct Democracy          322

17. Do business groups have privileged access to government?          336

YES WILLIAM D. COLEMAN, One Step Ahead: Business in
the Policy Process in Canada          338
NO W.T. STANBURY, Assessing the Political Power
of Business Interests          347

18. Do the media distort election campaigns?          366

YES DAVID TARAS, Bad Habits and Broken Promises:
The Media and Election Campaigns          368
NO MICHAEL NOLAN, Don't Shoot the Messenger: The
Media and Election Campaigns          381

# PART FIVE: Public Policy

19. Is employment equity fair and necessary? 392

    YES  CAROL AGÓCS, Employment Equity: Is It Needed?
Is It Fair? 394

    NO  JACK ROBERTS, Employment Equity —Unfair 407

20. Is censorship of pornography consistent with liberalism? 419

    YES  LEO GROARKE, Pornography: From Liberalism to
Censorship 421

    NO  WILLIAM WATSON, Pornography and Liberalism 432

21. Should capital punishment be restored? 443

    YES  GEOFF WILSON, The Case for Capital Punishment 446

    NO  ED BROADBRENT, The Case Against Capital
Punishment 453

22. Should universal medicare be preserved? 462

    YES  TAYLOR ALEXANDER, Universal Medicare: Can We
Afford to Lose It? 464

    NO  DOUGLAS J. MCCREADY, Social Justice: Universality
and Health Care in Canada 475

23. Does Canada need an entrenched Social Charter? 493

    YES  R. BRIAN HOWE, The Case for a Canadian Social
Charter 496

    NO  JANET AJZENSTAT, A Social Charter, Eh? Thanks,
but No Thanks 506

24. Does continental free trade benefit Canada? 514

    YES  IAN WOOTON, The Case for a More Liberal Trade
Regime 516

    NO  ANDREW STRITCH, The Costs of Free Trade 525

Appendix: LUCILLE CHARLTON, How to Write an
Argumentative Essay 439

Contributors 546

Contributor Acknowledgments 550

# INTRODUCTION

In the first edition of *Crosscurrents: Contemporary Political Issues,* we stated our desire to develop a collection of readings that would challenge students to think through a number of contemporary political issues, while fostering an understanding of and tolerance for the views of others. To achieve this goal, we felt that a reader structured in the form of debates or dialogues on leading political issues would provide the ideal format. We find it gratifying that a number of our colleagues have shared our goal and have used the first edition in either their introductory political science or Canadian politics courses.

**Changes to this edition.** In preparing a new edition of *Crosscurrents,* we have maintained the basic structure and format of the first volume. The revised text addresses twenty-four issues. For each issue, an introduction provides the reader with the necessary background and places the subject in the context of more general principles of concern to the study of politics. Two essays with conflicting viewpoints are then presented. Finally, a postscript offers a short commentary on the debate and suggests readings that enable students to explore the topic further.

In order to keep abreast with changing political issues, and to respond to the many helpful comments from colleagues who have used the first edition, we have made a number of significant changes to this volume. Twelve of the twenty-four issues are completely new. Twenty-nine of the readings are new, and twenty-two of these have been written especially for this book. The authors of eight of the readings from the first volume agreed to revise their articles, in most cases providing substantially new material. Because of this, we believe that students will find the readings to be much more engaging as the authors enter more directly into debate with one another.

From the comments of the reviewers, it is clear that about half of the instructors using *Crosscurrents: Contemporary Political Issues* do so in a general introductory course while the other half use it in a Canadian politics course. Thus in selecting topics we have tried to maintain the flexibility of the text. We have retained the public policy section, which covers a variety of issues. Those that use the text in an introductory course may find this section more helpful in the early part of the course when dealing with ideologies and concepts relating to rights and the role of the state in society.

**A note for first time users.** In introducing the first edition of *Cross-currents* we set out our rationale for developing a reader employing the debate format. Since its publication we believe that the rationale for using this format for teaching introductory courses is as strong as ever and bears repeating for those who may be using this text for the first time.

There are three good reasons, we believe, for using the debate format. First, studies have shown that students learn and retain more information when they are engaged in an active learning process. Yet, the reality in most Canadian universities is that students in introductory courses face ever larger class sections, which militate against discussion and active student involvement. While students generally come to political science courses with a great deal of interest and enthusiasm, they frequently find themselves slipping into a pattern of simple note-taking and passive learning.

Second, most introductory political science courses must of necessity address abstract principles and concepts, and cover a great deal of descriptive material concerning processes and institutions. At the same time, students come to these courses expecting that they will discuss and debate what is going on in the chaotic world of politics. Unfortunately, it is often difficult for them to relate the debates of everyday political issues to the broader and more abstract principles encountered in their introductory courses. Without a reference point, discussions of contemporary issues may seem more like interesting "current events" digressions with little direct relationship to the overall propositions being dealt with in the lectures.

Third, students frequently bring to their readings an uncritical awe for the authority of the published word. When confronted with a series of readings by the leading authorities on each subject, there is a strong temptation for students to think that the text presents the "final" word on the subject. They assume that further discussion and debate can add little new to the issue.

With these thoughts in mind, we have endeavoured to develop a collection of readings that will serve as a resource for a more interactive style of teaching, whether it be in classroom or tutorial discussion situations or in a more formal debate setting. Because of the flexibility of the format, *Crosscurrents* can be employed in the classroom in several ways.

(i) Some may wish to assign the chapters simply as supplementary readings to reinforce material covered in lectures, and use them as points of illustration in classroom lectures or discussions.

(ii) The readings may be used as a departure point for essay assignments in the course. In order to encourage students to develop their critical skill, they could write an assessment of the arguments and evidence presented in one of the debates. Alternatively, they could select one side in the debate and write an essay developing their own arguments in favour of that view. In order to assist students in such a task, we have included, as an appendix, instructions on writing an argumentative essay.

(iii) Others may wish to use the series of readings as a means of organizing weekly discussion sessions into a debate format. On each topic, two students may be asked to argue the case for one particular side, followed by group discussion. This format requires students to adopt a particular point of view and to defend that position with fellow students. Because the necessary background material is provided with the readings, this format is very easily adapted to large courses where teaching assistants are responsible for weekly tutorial sessions.

## ACKNOWLEDGMENTS

We would like to express our appreciation to the many reviewers who offered very helpful comments and suggestions. We are particularly indebted to those authors who graciously agreed to write original essays or revise earlier ones specifically for this volume, as well as to the authors and publishers who have granted us permission to use their published work. In addition, we want to acknowledge the excellent support of Dave Ward and Joanne Scattolon of Nelson Canada in helping us to bring this project to final completion. Finally, we would be amiss to not mention the patient support of our families who, in their indirect way, have contributed to this volume.

MARK CHARLTON, Langley, B.C.
PAUL BARKER, London, Ont.
October 1993

## ABOUT THE EDITORS

**Mark Charlton** is an Associate Professor of Political Science at Trinity Western University, Langley, British Columbia. Professor Charlton received his Ph.D. in political science from Laval University where he studied as an Ontario–Quebec Fellow. He is author of *The Making of Canadian Food Aid Policy* (1992) and co-editor of *Crosscurrents: International Relations in the Post–Cold War Era* (1993). He has also published a number of articles in *International Journal, Études Internationales,* and the *Canadian Journal of Development Studies.*

**Paul Barker** is an Assistant Professor of Political Science at Brescia College. Professor Barker received his Ph.D. from the University of Toronto. He has written articles on public policy that have appeared in *Canadian Public Administration, Canadian Public Policy,* and the *Canadian Journal of Law and Society.*

# PART ONE

## CANADIAN SOCIETY AND POLITICAL CULTURE

*Is dualism still the essential element of Canada's political culture?*

*Does multiculturalism weaken Canada?*

*Is western alienation justified?*

*Can native sovereignty co-exist with Canadian sovereignty?*

# ISSUE ONE

## Is Dualism Still the Essential Element of Canada's Political Culture?

**YES** BRIAN MULRONEY, "Dualism in Canada," from
Canada, House of Commons, *Debates,* pp. 8400–8405

**NO** WILLIAM THORSELL, "Let Us Compare Mythologies,"
*Report on Business* 6, no. 11 (May 1990): 105–7 and
110–11

In 1867, the Fathers of Confederation faced many challenges, but none greater than the need to deal with the hopes and aspirations of both the French-speaking and English-speaking communities. The dualistic quality of British North America presented John A. Macdonald and his colleagues with the kind of issue that tests the mettle of statesmen. In the case of Canada, the statesmen rose to the occasion, and the solution was federalism. A federal state would allow for the building of a new country while providing the flexibility required for the two founding cultures to pursue their goals.

The task of addressing the issue of dualism did not end with Confederation. Over the years, governments grappled with the problem of striking the right balance between the two elements. If governments were to fail in their efforts, the consensus was that the country would break apart. This gloomy prospect more than anything else seemed to confirm the claim that dualism was indeed at the core of Canada.

Canada has, of course, not remained unchanged since 1867. In the early part of the 20th century, people arrived from countries such as Germany, Poland, and Russia to settle the Prairies. These new Canadians had not played a part in the original founding of Canada, which placed dualism at the centre of things, but they were nonetheless now part of Canada. In more recent years, the numbers of new immigrants from

Asia, Africa, and the Caribbean have swelled. Though not part of the experience of 1867, these immigrants constitute a significant aspect of Canadian life. And then there are those who *were* present in 1867, but who were ignored—the native peoples, who have now begun to establish a presence for themselves.

These developments suggest that, while dualism still captures an important part of Canada, it provides an incomplete picture. There is more to Canada than the two communities of English- and French-speaking citizens. Dualism must now compete with the claims of ethnic groups who make up what is now called multiculturalism. Canada is not a nation of two peoples, but of many peoples. Furthermore, the aboriginal peoples, as they demonstrated during the debate on the Meech Lake Accord, believe that they too constitute a distinct part of what is Canada.

Such arguments, however, may go too far. The definitive test for what is essential to a country is to ask whether a country could survive without one element or another. Canada may, in fact, be more complex than it was in 1867, but some argue that a failure to recognize the primacy of dualism would lead to the country's demise. From this perspective, the survival of Canada as a nation is not dependent upon the strength of multiculturalism or the aboriginal peoples.

In the readings, Brian Mulroney presents the case for dualism as the fundamental quality of Canada. The context for his comments was the Meech Lake Accord and verbal attacks on French-speaking Canadians in parts of Canada in 1989. William Thorsell, editor-in-chief of the prestigious *Globe and Mail*, contends that dualism must now recognize the newer aspects of Canada.

## YES

## Dualism in Canada

*Brian Mulroney*

**Right Hon. Brian Mulroney (Prime Minister) moved:**

That this House reaffirm its commitment to support, protect and promote linguistic duality in Canada, as reflected by this House in the Constitution Amendment, 1987 and the Official Languages Act, 1988.

He said: Mr. Speaker, I rise on this, the twenty-fifth anniversary of the Canadian flag, the universal symbol of Canada, to speak of national unity and linguistic duality.... Every Parliament since Confederation has had to confront the question of Canada's linguistic duality. The members of every Parliament have had to stand up and declare themselves on this very fundamental issue....

It is time for all of us to stand up for Canada again because in recent days we have witnessed regrettable denials of some of Canada's fundamental values. Debate over language has been almost as frequent and fundamental a characteristic as the history of Canada's duality itself. But, with tolerance and respect for one another, we have built a country that has not simply acknowledged its own diversity but thrived on it.

Confederation was the coming together of English- and French-speaking Canadians whom Wilfrid Laurier was later to characterize as the "marble and the oak" of this remarkable home that we now call Canada.

The Fathers of Confederation never suggested in 1867 that building a country in which English and French would both be spoken would in any way or at any time be easy. In fact, they often referred to the difficulties that they knew awaited successive generations of Canadians. They called upon them even then for the foresight, the openness and the tolerance that would be required to bring this great Canadian experiment forward and to enrich it generation after generation. They also understood that this was a fundamental characteristic of the new nation that they were building for a people searching for a new home from countries around the world.

Sir John A. Macdonald said in the Confederation debates in respect of the concept of duality, to paraphrase him in that particular debate in February 1865, 125 years ago just about today, he acknowledged that the easiest and the most efficient way to run Canada would be with a unitary state with one language. He acknowledged that that brought with it great advantages. But as he indicated, the only problem with it is that it would not work. If you adopted that view, there would be no Canada because, as he said, "any proposition which involved the absorption of the individuality of Lower Canada, Quebec at the time, would not be received with favour by her people."

In 1865 he was speaking of the notion of individuality of Lower Canada. Today, the same fundamental meaning finds usage in the word "distinct." It is as true today as it was when Sir John A. Macdonald and Etienne Cartier began the nation-building work of binding this country together with their own hands.

That duality was something that just did not happen. It was acknowledged, reflected upon and deemed by everyone involved as absolutely indispensable, not only to the functioning of Canada, but to the existence of Canada. Macdonald acknowledged time and time again that Canada could not come together without a fundamental acknowledgment of that linguistic duality.

That duality was enriched and strengthened over decades by wave after wave of immigrants from eastern Europe, central Europe and elsewhere, who caused the prairies to bloom and the sovereignty of Canada to extend to the farthest reaches of this continent. It is a safe statement to make today when I say that if Canada as we know it was begun essentially by Scottish Protestants from Ontario and French Catholics from Quebec, it has been immeasurably enriched by people from every country of the world who have now made of Canada a truly modern, tolerant society.

Mr. Speaker, few subjects have so aroused public opinion and stirred such individual passions as the debates over language. But some of the finest chapters in our history were written by those who made the voice of reason prevail, who made tolerance triumph and who wrought the necessary accommodations.

Linguistic duality and the protection of minority language rights are not abstract concepts. They are given life by legislative enactments such as the Official Languages Act. They are given permanence and protection by the Constitution and they are given meaning by the national will of a generous and a tolerant people.

The rejection of minorities is an attack on the nature of Canada. When language becomes a motive for exclusion and fear, it is time for all Canadians who love their country to speak up and speak out. There is no place in Canada for intolerance—although no one would suggest that Canada, or any other country, is absolutely free from it.

The resolution now before the House is an opportunity for all members to speak up and speak out, again, for what is best about Canada. It is an opportunity to send an absolutely unequivocal message, again, of unity and mutual respect. The issue before us is not bilingualism or even, despite claims to the contrary, the expense of bilingualism. The issue before us is simple and important—the will of English- and French-speaking Canadians to continue to live together with mutual respect and fraternity, while honouring our original undertakings to each other and to the whole nation.

It is time to refer back to some of our fundamental values and I think it is also time to try to put this entire issue in some perspective. This is not the first time nor will it be the last time that there have been misconceptions and misrepresentations on the government's policies regarding official languages.

This is not the first time nor will it be the last that certain voices have been heard alleging that the policy constitutes enforced bilingualism. Something is being "rammed down people's throats." Surely that phrase and that expression had to arise in Canada. Only in a country this prosperous and this magnificent would people have the time to worry about expressions like that. Nothing is being forced down anybody's throat, although the concept of enforced bilingualism or a double standard, one for Quebec and another for the rest of the country, has been alleged in this country from the days of the Confederation debates. There have always been voices, fortunately few and far between. But there have always been voices who have tried to trade on this kind of falsehood and distortion that fortunately has been repudiated time and time and time again by this Parliament, regardless of its composition and regardless of the government that happened to be sitting at the right of the Speaker.

There is no better way to bury these damaging misunderstandings than to recall the words of one of the original architects of the original Official Languages Act. In 1974, the Hon. Gerard Pelletier, then Minister of Communications, spoke as follows, and I quote:

—some people were surprised recently by my statements favouring the promotion of an intensely French Quebec. They thought they saw a contradiction with the federal government's official languages policy. But the effort of the federal government in linguistic matters has always been subjected to the most absurd interpretations, the most frequent being that the ultimate objective of the Official Languages Act is to make each and every Canadian citizen bilingual. The facts are diametrically opposed to this fable: one of the effects of this law is to permit anyone to remain unilingual, if that is his wish, in all of his relations with the Government of Canada.

If you want to be bilingual, terrific. If you want to remain unilingual and deal with the Government of Canada, the law was designed in such a way as to make sure that both sides of this great national debate and these two perceptions could be accommodated equally.

What is more appropriate for a country that values its linguistic duality and protects its linguistic minorities in an imperfect nation such as ours? While we have many advantages and many accomplishments, our imperfections show every day of the week. What would be more appropriate than to proceed on a sensitive and delicate issue along the lines that Mr. Pelletier suggested in 1974.

It is time, Mr. Speaker, to remind ourselves what it is like to be a minority and to treat minorities with the same tolerance and generosity of spirit that we would want to be treated with, if our situations were reversed. How else would you treat a minority, except to ask yourselves what would it be like to be a minority and to treat the minority in exactly the same way that you would want you and your family to be treated if the situation were reversed. Surely that is a fundamental concept of social justice in this country.

While we happen to be talking about linguistic minorities, the principle holds true for visible minorities and every minority in Canada who is entitled to be treated with justice and equity and equality at all times and in all circumstances in this country of Canada. It is just these values of tolerance and generosity that will help us face an increasingly competitive and interdependent world.

Mr. Speaker, it is such an obvious advantage, and not a handicap, for Canada to speak the world's two leading languages. Our competitors in Europe often speak three languages fluently and four or even five quite well. Today some Canadians say they are disadvantaged because they want to preserve the integrity of one language. But please, never prevent our young people from learning two languages, because that enriches the whole nation. Linguistic duality lies at the foundation of our country and must be constantly preserved and promoted if we are to progress as a nation.

The British North America Act established rights and obligations respecting the use of English and French in Parliament, the Quebec Legislative Assembly and all the courts of Canada and Quebec. Three years later, these same rights and obligations were extended to the new province of Manitoba. Section 94 of the BNA Act provided that Parliament could make provision for the uniformity of court procedure in Ontario, New Brunswick and Nova Scotia—but not for Quebec whose system of civil law was distinct. English and French were entrenched as the official languages of New Brunswick in 1982. In 1988, we adopted a new Official Languages Act to bring our fundamental language law into line with the Charter of Rights and Freedoms.

In adopting the Official Languages Act in 1969, Parliament had recognized the importance of our linguistic duality. But the 1969 Act, in spite of its achievements, had other shortcomings because it focused on the individual's right to obtain services from the government, not on the vitality of minority communities—and thus was not able to halt the erosion of minorities throughout Canada.

The lesson we have learned over the past twenty years is that the strength of the community is critical and must be fostered if linguistic minorities across Canada are to retain their vitality. This is what inspired the major changes supported by all, or almost all, members of this House barely a year and a half ago. That is why we gave a community orientation to our official languages policy when we adopted the new Official Languages Act....

The federal government has been active over the past years in promoting linguistic minorities. We give considerable financial help to provincial governments to provide minority language education and second language education training and facilities. We assist provinces to make possible a wide, indeed a vast range and array of other provincial services to minority language communities.

In 1988, for example, we signed agreements with the Saskatchewan government to give the Fransaskois greater control over the education of their children. We entered into an agreement with Prince Edward Island on services in French, and another on a school and community centre in Charlottetown. We concluded a Memorandum of Understanding with Nova Scotia on the Collège de l'Acadie. We reached agreements with New Brunswick on school community centres which provide a focal point for the education and cultural activities of the minority community.

We arrived at a framework agreement with Ontario on the promotion of official languages. In 1989, we signed an agreement with Ontario on a Francophone college network, something that the French-speaking Canadians in the province of Ontario had requested for decades. In co-operation with the government of the province of Ontario I was delighted that this Parliament and this government were able to finally meet an historic need which helps build Canadian unity and which represents the very best elements of our society which must be encouraged if Canadian unity is going to be strengthened.

We concluded an agreement with the Yukon on French language services. We entered into an agreement with the province of Quebec, a very important and substantial agreement, on the provision of health and social services to the English-speaking population of that province. On February 2, this year, we signed an agreement with Quebec on official languages and education.

As one can see, there is symmetry and there is balance. There is fairness. There is not a double standard by this Parliament in respect of the application of bilingualism, or in the application of the official languages law. There are imperfections, obviously. But each and every member of this House seeks to eliminate and minimize those imperfections and from time to time as we proceed with improvements and amendments we make it better. When we make it better, we make life a little better for minority communities across Canada.

That, surely, is the principal objective of a sensitive and thoughtful approach to bilingualism and to the fundamental rights and values of minority language communities across this country. They must be able to turn to the Parliament of Canada when in moments of difficulty; and the Parliament of Canada should be able to respond with as much generosity and leadership as this country is capable of.

Mr. Speaker, while we have made important progress over the years to uphold this fundamental characteristic of our nationhood, our history has been marred by troubling and divisive linguistic disputes. We will not tell each other scare stories. These events did not just begin a few weeks ago, in northern Ontario. One has only to recall the controversy over the closing of Catholic schools in Manitoba in 1890, Regulation 17 in Ontario in 1912, which had a devastating effect on that province's francophone community, and the "Gens de l'Air" dispute of 1976.

In 1905, Prime Minister Sir Wilfrid Laurier decided that language rights in Alberta and Saskatchewan, in contrast to the situation in Quebec and Manitoba at that time, should not be entrenched in the Constitution but rather left within provincial legislative jurisdiction. It was, Mr. Speaker, therefore open to Alberta and Saskatchewan in 1988 to override a Supreme Court decision and abolish certain language rights and obligations that they had inherited from the Northwest Territories.

But in 1981, another significant decision was taken, obviously not with this in mind. No one can foresee the future with accuracy, but another significant decision was taken. It was to entrench in the Constitution a notwithstanding clause which permits legislatures to override many of the basic rights and freedoms of Canadians. Because of that clause it was open to Quebec, in enacting Bill C-178 respecting external, commercial signs in 1988, to override freedom of expression provisions of the Canadian Charter.

In all three cases the provincial legislatures used existing powers to limit rights that had been confirmed by the Supreme Court of Canada. In each case the government and, I suppose, most if not all members of the House of Commons and I personally deeply deplore the actions taken. But as has happened over history, it is now left for another day to try and remedy the situation and improve upon minority rights and the status and the state of our bilingual nation and all of the challenges and opportunities it gives to all of us.

We need today through our attitudes, our statements and our actions to arrest this trend and to return to the fundamental concepts as best we can that built this nation....

# Let Us Compare Mythologies

*William Thorsell*

Early in March, Paul Martin Jr., who is for some reason seeking the leadership of the Liberal Party, said this about Canada: "We have declared war on ourselves. We are engaged in a civil war of monumental proportions that simply staggers the mind. East versus West, western alienation against the centre, English versus French—whatever can divide us, we build a monument to it."

Civil war overstates it, but Canada is experiencing doubts about its future that are unparalleled in history. Unparalleled because, unlike the period of the Quebec referendum 10 years ago, the doubts are spread across a broad swath of Canadians, in all sectors of society and all regions of the country. They are unparalleled because, in some particulars, it is difficult to imagine a way to escape them.

How can we explain such angst at a time when Canada's economy is still strong on its feet after seven years of healthy growth and the national government is secure with a second working majority? Does it all come down to our conflict over constitutional negotiations with Quebec—known as the Meech Lake accord? I think not, for while that conflict is serious, the distress of the Canadian people runs too wide and deep to be explained by one variable alone, no matter how important. In many ways, our constitutional conflict is a symptom, not a cause of our problems.

Instead of focusing on specific issues, I want to explore what you might call the atmospherics of Canada's sour mood today—the context. I will argue that Canada's distress in 1990 cannot be understood without appreciating how much the basic moorings of Canada have been loosened by a series of largely unrelated events. We Canadians have experienced the collapse of several major ideals or mythologies that, until recently, helped to sustain Canada's sense of nationhood. The collapse of these ideals signals the death of Canada as we *knew* it, which is obviously very unsettling to many people. I do not think that Canada as we *know* it is therefore dead or doomed, but the question is certainly in the air.

Somewhere in the world today, there may be a country that is not profoundly changing, or that is not at least confused in a sea of change around it. I might have cited such an example of stolidity in Mongolia, until February when *The Globe and Mail's* China correspondent visited that vague and forgotten land only to report that it, too, is riding a crest of social change from green-sequined dancers on local TV to a multi-party system in Ulan Bator.

I am forced, therefore, to cling to Albania, Cuba and the Shining Path guerrillas of Peru as islands of stability in a stream of change—and they are only small islands, surely destined to erode under the insistent pressure that humans feel for individual freedom, the pressure of a global information network and the seductive power of world consumer culture.

Canada, then, is not alone as it grapples with the suddenly shifting foundations of its nationhood and identity. The same forces of globalization that disorient so many other countries are playing themselves out in Canada to the general consternation of its people, most of whom would prefer that the future get back where it belongs. But Canada adds its own disturbances.

Let me march quickly through the main traditional myths of Canadian nationhood—myths well rooted in fact once upon a time, but now detached, more obviously every day, from the realities of life as we experience it. There are dead or dying myths, some more important than others, but few of them publicly recognized by our national leaders as having run their course. I will start with a small and simple one.

MYTH NUMBER ONE   says that Canada is a constitutional monarchy in which the head of state is a king or queen.

Like it or not, this is simply a fiction in the minds of most Canadians who do not conceive of their country as a monarchy, or Elizabeth II as Canada's head of state, or Prince Charles as its king-in-waiting. The deep monarchist sentiments of some Canadians aside—and I fully respect them—this point hardly needs expansion it is so obvious a fact in our national life.

I would go as far as to say that, in the unconscious minds of most Canadians, Canada no longer *has* a head of state. There is only a governor-general representing an anachronism—a shadow symbolizing a memory at the pinnacle of the nation. No leading politician is willing to say it, but the myth of the monarchy is essentially dead, and our failure to admit it leaves our country headless.

MYTH NUMBER TWO   says that Canada is a duality—the product of two founding peoples, English and French, who came together in 1867 to form Confederation "from sea unto shining sea."

This is the core, binding myth of Canadian nationhood, taught in every school (insofar as schools teach history any more). Precisely because this mythology is so fundamental, very few of Canada's leaders, including its academics, artists and journalists, dare to suggest that this ideal has also seen its best day. (I must observe here that academics and journalists are among the most powerful agents of the status quo in any free society, so their conservative role in this case is entirely predictable.) One need only walk awake through the streets and fields of our country to know that the myth of duality, too, is cracking and breaking under the weight of our daily experience.

It is not that duality is untrue, but that it is hopelessly incomplete. Our aboriginal peoples—Inuit, Indian and Métis—challenge the model of two founding peoples that excludes them. They were, after all, here first and there is no logical or moral ground to oppose them on this point. (Members of the government of the Northwest Territories recently dared to ask why English and French were the official languages in the North to the exclusion of native ones.) Less obvious, but just as tenacious, is the historic and growing presence within Canada of other national backgrounds and races who also see themselves as "founding" peoples.

The prairie West was largely settled by the ancestors of its current population a whole generation *after* the original Confederation of 1867. The West was settled, not as a compact between the two founding peoples, but as a compact among many peoples, notably from continental and central Europe. Western Canadians have never been satisfied to see themselves as late arrivals at someone else's party, and who can blame them? The same can be said of hundreds of thousands of recent immigrants from all over the world who are still coming to Canada's major urban centres. More than 50% of our immigrants now arrive from Asia, Africa and the Caribbean.

Canada is not four original provinces frozen in time that can project one moment of their history onto the rest of the land. Canada is 10 provinces, two territories, at least five regions, three city states, many new generations of citizens and continuing immigration from increasingly exotic places in a bewildering flux of time. Canada is alive, and unless we see it as alive, we will not keep it alive.

Still, hardly anyone in a position of national influence dares to acknowledge fully that duality is too narrow and dated a concept to contain the reality of Canada as we actually live it. We have invested too much since the 1960s in the historically limited concept of duality to raise common-sense questions about this without scaring ourselves half to death.

As in the case of the monarchy, the collapse of this myth happens in private hearts long before the public funeral. People in the streets are beginning to recognize that the concept of Canada as a duality is essentially academic in most areas of the country—the word "official" in the phrase "official bilingualism" says it all—but we have not yet created another workable concept to take its place. At the heart of our national mythology, then, we are stuck in the purgatory of pretense that we are something considerably simpler than we actually are. The duality of Canada—which is a truth, but far from the whole truth—is an ideal that is dying on the vine. It leaves our country—which is already headless—drifting without a functioning sense of its own history....

What are our political leaders doing...? For the most part, they are sticking to a rigid strategy of defence. The more Canadians are buffeted by change, the more fervently their leaders exhort them to cling to old verities. Day after day in Parliament, we hear calls from the various political parties to resurrect the mythologies of economic nationalism, Crown corporations, the duality of Canada and official bilingualism as the saviors of Canadian nationhood. An occasional voice even suggests we rally around the Queen, but a rally requires more than a dozen people. None of this addresses what really needs to be done. Indeed, it exacerbates the sense of unreality that already has the nation so much on edge.

A particularly depressing example of this occurred in February when Prime Minister Brian Mulroney threw everything he had into one small drawer of the status quo. He said—and I quote—"Simply put, Canada is the coming together of English- and French-speaking Canadians, and our future lies in the continuing will to live together.... This country will rise or fall on the bilingual nature of its character. What is Canada without it? There's no country; it's like an adjunct of the United States. If you dispose of bilingualism, if you dispose of the protection of minority language rights, then you have dealt a lethal blow to the fundamental tenet of our nationhood."

I believe this is a gross overstatement, indeed, a dangerous gross overstatement. The bilingual nature of Canada is an attractive and important asset, but I don't think most Canadians believe it's the *sine qua non* of national identity. I don't think most Canadians believe, to quote the Prime Minister, that "there's no country" without official bilingualism. There was a country called Canada long before bilingualism appeared as a policy in 1969, and this country is rooted in much broader ground than that. I firmly support official bilingualism at the federal level, but little in our experience over the last 25 years indicates that it is an essential force for keeping Canada together, within Quebec or elsewhere. It's a good and natural policy at the federal level, and a good policy in some provincial arenas, but it simply cannot bear the weight of our nationhood from sea to sea....

I said at the outset that the death of Canada as we *knew* it need not mean the death of Canada as we *know* it. The fundamental threat to Canada is not intolerance—though awful intolerance there be—but hypocrisy. We have nothing to fear from the truth about our national situation and character, but our leaders keep telling us tales. If we stop lying about ourselves, I believe we can get away from warring among ourselves, and go back to our more familiar national wrestling matches. Wrestling matches give us much better odds on settling our problems. And we have reasons to be optimistic about Canada if we have the wits to be frank. Like Sigmund Freud, I believe the truth can set you free.

# POSTSCRIPT

At the beginning of Confederation, the major challenge was dualism. Now, the challenge is different. Canada's leaders still must address the question of dualism, but they must also recognize that this nation is much more complex than it was a century ago. What kind of arrangements will best reflect this new complexity? Can this country be both a duality and a mosaic? If not, does it mean the end of Canada?

Governments have begun to face the new challenge. Policies have been introduced to salve the worries of French-speaking Canadians. Official bilingualism and a series of policies directed toward assisting Quebec reflect the concern over dualism. Similarly, government agencies, such as the federal Department of Multiculturalism and Citizenship, have been established for the purpose of addressing the needs of new Canadians. And the aboriginal peoples, through recent actions, have finally caught the attention of the country. They, too, must be accommodated.

There is, however, evidence that government initiatives of this kind may prove unworkable. The Meech Lake Accord constituted a further attempt to deal with dualism, but failed partly because elements of the new Canada felt that they had been ignored. The 1992 Charlottetown Accord, which also endeavoured to address the issue of dualism, met with defeat as well. It may be increasingly difficult to continue with similar courses of action. Furthermore, founding members of English Canada feel increasingly slighted, and may be unwilling to accept initiatives that confer de facto distinct status on selected groups.

The work of historian Ramsay Cook is a good place to begin understanding dualism and its meaning for Canada. His books on this subject include *Canada and the French-Canadian Question* (Toronto: Macmillan of Canada, 1966), *The Maple Leaf Forever: Essays on Nationalism and Politics in Canada* (Toronto: Macmillan of Canada, 1971), and *Canada, Quebec, and the Uses of Nationalism* (Toronto: McClelland and Stewart, 1986). Donald

Smiley also addresses the question of dualism in his book *The Federal Condition in Canada* (Toronto: McGraw-Hill Ryerson, 1987).

The literature on Canada's aboriginal peoples is growing. *Arduous Journey: Canadian Indians and Decolonization*, edited by Rick Ponting (Toronto: McClelland and Stewart, 1986) investigates the many concerns of natives in Canada. Ponting, along with Roger Gibbins, has also written an introduction to Indian affairs in *Canada: Out of Irrelevance* (Toronto: Butterworths, 1980). On the question of multiculturalism, the Report of the Special Committee on Visible Minorities in Canadian Society, *Equality Now!* (Ottawa: Supply and Services, 1984) provides a good overview of concerns and demands of new Canadians. On the other hand, Reginald W. Bibby, in his book *Mosaic Madness: The Poverty and Potential of Life in Canada* (Toronto: Stoddart, 1990), offers a more critical view of the implications of a "multicultural mosaic."

# ISSUE TWO

**YES** REGINALD W. BIBBY, "Is Multiculturalism Tearing Us Apart?" *Compass* (Jan.–Feb. 1992): 26–28.

**NO** AUGIE FLERAS, "Multiculturalism as Society-Building: Doing What Is Necessary, Workable, and Fair"

Immigration, together with ethnic diversity, has been a component of Canada's history from the very beginning. Nevertheless, the idea of two founding nations has until recently dominated most discussions of Canadian politics. This perception of Canada has gradually changed since the adoption of an official federal policy of multiculturalism in 1971. This change came about, in part, as a result of the public reaction to the Royal Commission on Bilingualism and Biculturalism formed in 1963 by the government of Lester Pearson. Non-British, non-French, nonaboriginal Canadians objected to the notion that Canada was defined as a bilingual and bicultural nation. Are the cultures of other Canadians any less important? Were they second-class citizens in a bicultural society?

The introduction of a policy of multiculturalism in the 1970s was intended to create a sense of inclusiveness while still dealing with the threat of Quebec nationalism. Canada would be a bilingual, multicultural society in which all Canadians could take pride in their cultural identity. Confidence in one's own cultural identity, Pierre Trudeau argued, would promote personal freedom while strengthening national unity (Canada, House of Commons, *Debates*, 1971, p. 8545).

In the 1970s a broad consensus developed among the major political parties that multiculturalism would bring minority ethnic groups into the mainstream of Canadian political life. A federal Department of Multiculturalism and Citizenship was created. Most provinces moved to adopt a variety of multicultural programs and policies. However, since the mid-1980s, the idea of multiculturalism has come under assault. As

18

the proportion of non-Europeans immigrating to Canada has increased in recent years, Canadians have begun to question how a more ethnically diverse population will affect the future of Canada.

Complaints about multiculturalism have taken a number of forms. Some lament that multiculturalism has not lived up to its promises. Multiculturalism has simply drawn attention to various folkloric traditions found within Canada rather than creating a true cultural pluralism. Others suggest that the focus on the cultural side of multiculturalism has tended to gloss over the very real socioeconomic inequalities that exist among ethnic groups within Canadian society. Multiculturalism is thus seen as simply a ploy to co-opt ethnic groups into the political mainstream while ignoring their real needs.

Another line of criticism focuses on the broader impact of multiculturalism on the development of Canadian society as a whole. This argument was best articulated by Reginald Bibby, a sociologist, in his book *Mosaic Madness: The Poverty and Potential of Life in Canada* (Toronto: Stoddart, 1990). Bibby argues that a policy of multiculturalism is symbolic of a trend to promote too much diversity and pluralism in Canada. By focusing too much on our cultural differences and our individual rights, Canadians have lost the sense of what binds them together in collective pursuit. Our politics have come to lack a noble, collective vision that can bind the nation together. In the essay below, Bibby restates for us the essential arguments in his case that multiculturalism is destructive to the nation-building process in Canada.

In the following essay, Augie Fleras, also a sociologist, takes up the complaints against multiculturalism and attempts to refute them. While he admits that multiculturalism has its flaws and at times is "riddled with inconsistencies," Fleras argues that there are no credible alternatives as a basis for society-building in Canada.

# Is Multiculturalism Tearing Us Apart?

*Reginald W. Bibby*

Let's be honest—the reality of grim-faced politicians roaming the country proclaiming the nation's imminent demise tells the story: multiculturalism and bilingualism have failed to bring Canadians together.

The two pivotal policies were aimed at unifying Canada by addressing the demographic diversity of a population that, ancestrally speaking, consisted of a British majority, a large French minority, and people with a wide variety of other national backgrounds. Not flippantly derived, the policies were the product of the exhaustive Royal Commission on Bilingualism and Biculturalism of the 1960s. Bilingualism was an effort to recognize Quebec as an equal partner in Canada; multiculturalism was an attempt to recognize the legitimate place of groups with origins that were other than British or French.

Apart from the question of whether or not multiculturalism specifically is tearing us apart, we at least need to be raising the question of how effective the policy has been in bringing us together.

Let's get one thing straight from the outset: what is at issue here is not the merits of a multicultural society, but rather a policy response to that diversity—namely, multiculturalism. To have reservations about multiculturalism is not to have reservations about a multicultural country. Cultural diversity is potentially an invaluable national resource. A society that is comprised of people who have been exposed to a wide array of lifestyles and social structures, experiences and ideas, values and beliefs is a society that can draw from a significant cultural pool. To subscribe to uniculturalism is not only ethnocentric, but masochistic; a society is deprived of immeasurable benefits. The issue, to repeat, is not diversity but policy.

Canada, in being second only to the United States as the most popular destination of emigrants in modern history, is in the enviable position of having the potential to experience a quality of life matched by few countries. Our large numbers of newcomers, when added to British, French, and native peoples, create an extremely rich cultural pool. The political challenge is to figure out how best to transform our raw resource of cultural diversity into a national asset so that everyone can benefit.

Some observers take the position that optimum social living is almost an inevitable result of diversity. If we protect the individual tiles, the parts will come together somewhat magically to form a beautiful, integrated art-piece. According to such thinking, Canadians seemingly are bound together and enriched by their differences.

Such breezy thinking makes for good after-dinner speeches at cultural events. But, sociologically speaking, it is empty rhetoric. To celebrate differences and minimize commonalities is to fail to realize a basic fact: if a society nurtures diversity, diversity is what it will get. If all that people have in common is their diversity, in reality they have nothing in common at all. Isolated individual tiles, however beautiful, do not a mosaic make.

In sharp contrast to such thinking, sociologists and others find the pattern to be so prevalent as to be virtually axiomatic: in order for groups of any kind to flourish, their members need to have some common goals and agree on some acceptable norms. For collective life at any level to work well, a balance has to be struck between an emphasis on the individual and the group, between an emphasis on individual groups and the overall collectivity. It is true of relationships, families, communities, nations, and for that matter, the world. Needless to say, Canada receives no exemption to the pattern.

The specific contribution of cultural diversity to collective living, rather than being inevitable, seems to be dependent upon at least three key factors. First, people have to have the freedom to retain valued aspects of their former cultures. Newcomers need to know that, this side of the law, those features of their national cultures that they regard as important are welcome in the new setting. Second, new arrivals need to find that their old settings do not count against them. The fact that they have come from Asia or Africa or Europe doesn't matter—they will be treated equitably. Third, and of critical importance, in the interests of the society as a whole, it is essential that opportunities exist for people to share their varied cultures with each other. New arrivals and members of the host society have to interact with one another, reflect and evaluate together, in order that the best features of their cultures can be passed on to everyone. What people want is not mysterious; people everywhere share a desire to experience the best quality of life that is possible. Interaction and evaluation are indispensable to drawing the best contributions from the collective cultural pool.

To the credit of the much-maligned federal government, the policy that was outlined in 1971 addressed each of these key elements. Its major objectives were (1) to permit Canadians who so desired to retain the valued features of their cultural heritages, (2) to assist all Canadians in overcoming cultural barriers to full participation in life—including language, and (3) to promote creative interaction between all cultural groups in the interest of national unity. People of various cultures and ethnic groups, said the prime minister, "will be encouraged to share their cultural expressions and values with other Canadians and so contribute to a richer life for us all." According to the tabled document, "the Government has made it very clear that it does not plan on aiding individual groups to cut themselves off from the rest of society." On the contrary, the government would promote "creative encounters and interchange among all Canadian cultural groups." Presumably "all" meant everyone.

The federal multicultural program deserves some accolades. Over the past two decades, the program has known a measure of success in contributing to the 1971 objectives of preservation and participation. Canadians are certainly more aware of cultural diversity today than they were in the 1970s. The conditions of minorities have become more just and fair. Attitudinally, my ongoing national surveys have found that, despite the claims of accelerated racism, there has been a decrease in prejudice in all regions of the country since the mid-1970s. Blurring the progress picture is the fact that the remaining blatant bigots—about 10 percent of the populace—receive a disproportionate amount of publicity. The multiculturalism program needs to be commended rather than axed for helping to raise the awareness of both cultural diversity and the unacceptability of prejudice and discrimination.

The first two objectives of preservation and participation have also continued to receive the endorsement of the federal government. The Multiculturalism Act of 1988 states that the government is committed to a policy "designed to preserve and enhance the multicultural heritage of Canadians while working to achieve the equality of all Canadians." The twin emphases are further reflected in the four current federal multiculturalism programs.

However, we have a significant problem: the extremely important third objective of stimulating creative interaction between all groups, enabling us to tap our rich national resource of diversity, has seemingly been forgotten. The result? The multiculturalism program has preserved cultures and enhanced participation. But it has not succeeded in bringing Canadians together for the dialogue, reflection, and evaluation that are so essential to producing "a richer life for us all."

The social value of our cultural diversity lies in our being able to reflect together on our rich body of ideas and behaviour, so that we can sort out the true from the trivial, the banal from the best. Through such open and dynamic interchange, we can creatively improve the collective quality of life in the country. Such a milieu, where uninhibited expression and thoughtful discernment ideally are encouraged by governments, schools, the media, religious groups, and our other major institutions, is the key to tapping the collective contributions of diversity.

It's a great dream ... natives, French Canadians, and English Canadians joined by people from around the world, respecting traditions and ideas, yet openly discussing, examining, and selectively adopting them as individuals and as a society ... and thereby enhancing life. Sadly, that dream has been inadequately pursued by the multiculturalism program. In my mind, the failure to emphasize the importance of interaction is the primary reason why multiculturalism has not been particularly successful in bringing Canadians together.

Multiculturalism may be failing to unite us. Has it, though, actually "torn us apart"? That's a stiff charge—but not without some support. There are signs that, in beginning and ending with the first two objectives of the 1971 policy—cultural preservation and equal participation—multiculturalism has inadvertently contributed to division.

To stop at the point of encouraging the preservation of cultural heritages has no particular payoffs for the country as a whole. On the one hand, contrary to stereotypes, it has not been demonstrated that funding contributes to cultural group solidarity at the expense of broader social participation. But that is not to say that "it does no harm" to provide government funds for cultural preservation purposes.

There is good evidence—generated by the Spicer Commission, for example—that, in times of economic strain, such dollar outlays contribute to extremely negative attitudes toward both government and participating cultural groups. And even if grants do not foster in-group solidarity and out-group indifference, during dark days when politicians are claiming we have a serious unity problem, such a program that is aimed at the parts instead of the whole is, to put it mildly, "a hard sell."

In addition to economic and unity concerns, when cultural heritage programs are not tied to some kind of collective purpose, they run the risk of trivializing the social significance of cultural diversity. Multiculturalism becomes synonymous with festivals and food fairs, not to mention paternalistic civic proclamations that acknowledge "the contribution of the multiculturalism community to the community at large."

In short, unless the cultivation of national heritages is designed to contribute to Canadian society as a whole, it is a dubious social venture, with divisive potential.

To stop at the point of stressing the importance of full participation, with the accompanying themes of tolerance and fairness, is to encourage a debilitating preoccupation with discrimination. When social justice becomes our end in all, intergroup relations can become extremely strained and unenjoyable.

Ours is a society where we have become sensitized to be on the lookout for any signs of prejudice or discrimination, with the media playing the role of town crier. Given the ease with which labels such as "racist" and "bigot" can be assigned, it frequently is not wise to speak up in public, let alone speak with each other. I have suggested that acceptable content is frequently limited to the right and the trite—the politically correct and the socially innocuous. Here the important objective of justice ironically has had the function not of bringing Canadians together, but of keeping them apart.

Stripped of the inclination to interact, we find ourselves in the bizarre position of not being able to extract the best from our diverse culture. What we are left with are the consolation prizes of multicultural days and the ongoing admonition to be tolerant.

Multiculturalism, rather than stimulating the kind of intergroup interaction that is so essential to the tapping of our diversity, has inadvertently tended to inhibit it. We are a diverse nation, alive with attitudes and feelings and opinions and beliefs. But the multicultural rules have had the peculiar effect of making it difficult for us to speak with each other, and certainly for us to evaluate the ideas and lifestyles of one another.

The time has come for us to stop wasting our diversity resources. No, the solution does not lie in abolishing the multiculturalism policy and program. We need to continue to encourage newcomers—as well as the people who are already here—to enjoy and cultivate those features of their heritages that they cherish. It also is essential that we ensure that people are not kept from participating fully in Canadian life because of their race or nationality.

But we need to do more. We have to make it possible for Canadians of diverse backgrounds to interact with one another—to speak openly about their differences and concerns, to reflect on their values and dreams, to evaluate the merits of their respective ideas and lifestyles.

Contrary to prevalent rumour, my surveys and the research of others suggest that we have far more in common with each other than we realize. Diversity has limits. We have very similar concerns, values, and hopes. We have much to talk about, much to explore, and much to contribute to one another. Tragically, false stereotypes—perpetuated by geography, the media, and self-serving politicians—are keeping us apart. With or without the help of multiculturalism, it's time to break the silence.

# Multiculturalism as Society-Building: Doing What Is Necessary, Workable, and Fair[1]

*Augie Fleras*

# INTRODUCTION

Canada is currently in the throes of an unprecedented restructuring involving a shift from a predominantly monocultural system to one consistent with pluralist principles and egalitarian practices. As a result, the concept of Canada as a three-nations state[2] is being contested through upheavals in state–minority relations. This transformation is manifest at several levels. The ongoing decolonization of Canada's aboriginal peoples has evolved to the point where the reality of inherent aboriginal self-government cannot be casually dismissed. The proposed renewal in Quebec–Ottawa relations along "distinct society" lines remains a pressing priority. Canada's race relations agenda is being significantly transformed. Efforts to improve majority–minority relations have catapulted the principles and practices of official multiculturalism into the forefront of strategies for managing diversity (Fleras and Elliott 1992). Few Canadians have been untouched by multicultural initiatives in the management of race and ethnic relations. But the threat of a growing backlash against official multiculturalism may deprive Canadians of a key resource in forging the world's first "post-multicultural" society[3] (Fleras 1993).

This paper argues that multiculturalism as official policy and practice has strengthened Canada by shoring up its evolutionary development as a progressive society. Two lines of argument are pursued in defence of this position. First, the paper rejects the proposition that multiculturalism detracts from Canada's growth as a united, distinct, and prosperous society. Criticisms of multiculturalism as "divisive," "regressive," "ornamental," or "impractical" are shown to be unfounded. Second, the paper examines the role of multiculturalism in promoting Canadian unity and national identity. Official multiculturalism will be defended as a means for managing diversity that is necessary, workable, and fair. Finally, the paper argues that nonmulticultural alternatives for managing diversity are no longer viable in a post-multicultural era.

# RETHINKING MULTICULTURALISM—FROM ETHNICITY TO EQUITY

Canada is one of a handful of modern countries—including Australia and New Zealand—in the vanguard for constructing a coherent yet pluralistic society (Hudson 1987; also Pearson 1991; Foster and Seitz 1989). The challenge confronting these liberal democracies is not to be underestimated. Each is expected to forge a progressive yet sovereign entity from disparate parts while not destroying the integrity of the constituent units in the process (Cairns 1993). Over the years, multiculturalism has secured a relatively high profile as a distinctly Canadian strategy for society-building (Fleras 1990). Federal and provincial policies have relied on multicultural principles and practices as a basis for "managing diversity" in a manner both reasonable, fair, and workable. Nevertheless, Canadians remain unclear about what multiculturalism is actually trying to do. In a national survey conducted by the Angus Reid Group (1991) and involving 3,325 Canadians, nearly 38 percent of the respondents knew little or nothing about multiculturalism, or refused to comment.

This public confusion arises because multiculturalism itself has many different levels of meaning. Multiculturalism can be interpreted as: an *empirical fact* (Canada *is* racially and ethnically diverse); as an *ideology* (Canadians tend to value diversity and perceptions of themselves as a tolerant people); as a *policy* (multiculturalism has been officially endorsed as policy at federal, provincial, and municipal levels since the early 1970s); and as a *process* (both politicians and minorities employ multiculturalism as a resource for goal attainment) (Fleras and Elliott 1992). Difficulties also spring from confusing multicultural *ideals* with *practices* ("what it hopes to accomplish and what it has achieved to date"). Likewise, the *intent* of multiculturalism is confused with its *realities* ("what it is trying to do at present" and "what realistically it can attain in a capitalist society").

## Defining Multiculturalism

For our purposes, multiculturalism is defined as a set of principles, policies, and practices for accommodating diversity as a legitimate and integral component of society. Employed in this instrumental sense, the concept of multiculturalism possesses an emphatically political dimension. It consists of formal measures for managing diversity within the framework of societal unity, social equality, and national identity. References to multiculturalism in this paper are directed primarily at official (federal) initiatives unless otherwise stated.

# From Celebrating Differences to Managing Diversity

There is little question that multiculturalism originated and flourished as a political program to achieve political goals in a politically astute manner (Peter 1981). Initially, emphasis was placed on securing Canadian identity and unity through manipulation of national symbols (Breton 1984). Further goals were cultural retention and sharing, as well as the removal of language barriers for ethnic minority participation. As a result, public perceptions of multiculturalism continue to be grounded in images of "celebrating" differences within a "mosaic" framework.

Once a relatively accurate reading of the situation, the folkloric roots of multiculturalism are currently being contested. Multiculturalism for the most part has discarded its ethnicity focus in exchange for the principles of equity and race relations (Fleras 1993). The current emphasis on managing diversity reflects a post-multicultural commitment to antiracism, removal of discriminatory barriers, and institutional accommodation. The discourse on multiculturalism has also outgrown references to the oft-repeated mantra of "mosaic." What is being emphasized instead are images of a "kaleidoscope," with its connotation of asymmetrical parts in constant motion. Table 1 summarizes the evolving paradigm shift regarding multiculturalism's role in the managing of Canada's race and ethnic relations.

**TABLE 1**   SHIFTS IN OFFICIAL MULTICULTURALISM

|  | Celebrating Differences (1970s) | Managing Diversity (1990s) |
|---|---|---|
| Focus | Culture | Structure |
| Frame of Reference | Ethnicity | Equity |
| Mandate | Ethnic symbols (folkloric) | Race relations and antiracism |
| Objective | Individual adjustment | Institutional accommodation |
| Source of Problem | Ethnocentrism | Systemic discrimination |
| Scope | Exclusive | Inclusiveness |
| Means of Solution | Cultural sensitivity | Employment equity |
| Role of State | Passive state involvement | Proactive state involvement |
| Status of Diversity | Sidestream | Mainstream |
| Key Metaphor | "Mosaic" | "Kaleidoscope" |

The inception of the "new multiculturalism" with its post-multicultural emphasis on race relations, institutional accommodation, and equality clearly reflects the restructuring of Canada that is underway. Ethnic and racial diversity is currently upheld as a legitimate and integral component of Canadian society. People of colour are presently in a position to compete as equals without being penalized for who they are. This commitment to accommodation is reflected in the "mainstreaming" of federal, provincial, and municipal institutions to ensure minority access ("openness"), representation ("proportions"), and equity ("equitable treatment"). Such a shift in minority status—from periphery to centre—is but one indicator of how the politicization of official multiculturalism has redefined Canada's distributive ideals in terms of "who gets what." It has also cemented Canada's reputation as the world's first post-multicultural society.

# IN DEFENCE OF MULTICULTURALISM: "WEAKNESS AS STRENGTH"

Those who argue that multiculturalism detracts from what is essential to Canada often resort to a host of criticisms about perceived shortcomings (for an overview, see Stasiulis 1985). This critique portrays official multiculturalism as contrary to the needs of a coherent, prosperous, and united Canada. These criticisms of multiculturalism can be classified into four categories: multiculturalism is (1) "divisive" (undermining Canadian society); (2) "regressive" (defusing minority aspirations and needs); (3) "ornamental" (symbol with little substance); and (4) "impractical" (irrelevant in a capitalist society). This section will examine these criticisms in turn to determine if they stand the test of scrutiny. In exposing many of the fallacies behind the antimulticultural bandwagon, we will also demonstrate how apparent weaknesses of multiculturalism can be interpreted as strengths.

## Cipher or Cement?

Many denounce multiculturalism as an irritant to social unity and national identity. According to this line of thinking, the promotion of multiculturalism runs the risk of "balkanizing" Canada through dismemberment of its constituent units. Construction of a national identity is next to impossible when minorities are encouraged to pursue ethnic "tribalisms" at the expense of citizenship (Bissoondath 1993). A closer inspection of the evidence invites another interpretation.

Multiculturalism originated and continues to exist as an instrument for cementing Canadians into a "distinct society." Multiculturalism is not concerned with the promotion of diversity per se. Even a cursory reading of the Multiculturalism Act of 1988 (or Trudeau's multicultural speech in 1971) should dispel this notion. It is even less concerned with promotion of collective ethnic rights—with or without separate structures, ethnic enclaves, and independent power bases. What government could possibly introduce arrangements for its own self-destruction?

The goals of multiculturalism are firmly fixed on society-building through actions that depoliticize ethnicity as a social force. In place of collective rights and self-sufficient ethnic communities, multiculturalism emphasizes the right of individuals to identify and affiliate with the ethnocultural tradition of their choice—provided this does not violate laws of the land, interfere with the rights of others, or discredit fundamental political/economic institutions. Put bluntly, multiculturalism is *not* about ethnic separatism or divided loyalties. It is about the promotion of *secular tolerance* as a basis for Canadian nationalism and state-building.

To be sure, there is always an element of risk associated with any policy that promotes diversity as means or ends. On certain occasions, minorities may be singled out because of special needs. This preferential treatment is not intended to separate and divide as much as to achieve positive social goals. Nor should the conferral of hyphenated citizenship ("Lithuanian-Canadian") be feared as divisive. A hyphenated identity can be envisaged as two strands of a single Canadian citizenship. The first and *primary* strand involves a non-negotiable commitment to core Canadian values and institutions. The second (and secondary) strand allows an optional identification with the values and symbols of ethnicity.

What about Canadian identity? Does multiculturalism breed a "visionless co-existence" through endless promotion of mindless diversity, as lamented by Reginald Bibby in his acclaimed text *Mosaic Madness?* Perhaps this is so, but an adherence to multiculturalism does not necessarily detract from a coherent Canadian identity. To the contrary, multiculturalism enhances a perception of ourselves as a community that is generally tolerant of diversity. A commitment to multiculturalism (within a bilingual framework) is one of the definitive characteristics that distinguishes Canadians from Americans. Rather than fomenting disunity and dissent, multiculturalism encourages a shared identity within the context of Canada's much vaunted "community of communities" ethic. At the same time it provides the central glue that binds Canadians together through values that furnish meaning, security, and purpose to life (Jamieson 1993).

Those with concerns over multiculturalism as somehow "un-Canadian" have little to fear. Canada's problems have not sprung from too much diversity. Difficulties often arise from insufficient recognition of diversity as necessary and normal. A glance at developments in other parts of the world should confirm this: ethnic strife rarely arises when diversity is encouraged. Conflict flares up when diversity is suppressed or denied full and equal expression in society. Such an interpretation can be applied to Canada. Here the question of unity and state-building extols multiculturalism as the buffer that makes this country safe *for*, but also safer *from*, ethnicity (Moynihan 1993).

It is not multiculturalism but "mono" culturalism that divides and excludes (Mitchell-Powell 1992). Under official multiculturalism, the expression of ethnicity is encouraged, but subordinated to the goals of unity and equality within a framework of diversity. Official multicultural-ism neither divides nor separates since it resolutely rejects an "anything goes" or "everything-as-equally-valid" mentality. The divisiveness within multiculturalism arises from its manipulation by self-serving politicians and minority leaders who have hijacked pluralist principles for ulterior motives.

## Regressive or Progressive?

Multiculturalism has been discredited by some as a regressive tool that distracts minorities from the business at hand. Multiculturalism is said to reinforce class lines, foreclosing minority access to the corridors of power and resources. This notion of multiculturalism as perpetrator of a "vertical mosaic" does not always stand up to scrutiny. First, racial and ethnic minorities are not uniformly marginalized in Canadian society. Certain ethnic groups earn more income than "mainstream" Canadians, while foreign-born Canadians often outperform native-born Canadians in areas such as education (Agocs and Boyd 1993). Other Canadians, of course, are less fortunate, namely, African-Canadians and aboriginal peoples, but their exclusion and exploitation long predated the appear-ance of official multiculturalism.

Second, the explicit intent of multiculturalism is the removal of dis-criminatory barriers that preclude equality. Post-1971 multicultural poli-cies sought to eliminate the cultural fences that create structural barriers to minority participation. Programs and initiatives for "righting past wrongs" are thus directed toward creating greater opportunity structures and equality of outcome.

Multicultural objectives are aimed at replacing the vertical mosaic with a commitment to substantive equality for all. In the past, immi-grants and minorities were expected to conform with the prevailing sys-tem and endure whatever "lumps" they encountered as part of the adjustment process. At present, it is institutions themselves that are under obligation to accommodate diversity. Reforms are focused on rooting out systemic biases related to recruitment, hiring, promotion, and training. While there is little proof yet of dramatic shifts in minority wages or service delivery, the strength of multiculturalism nevertheless resides in its ability to foster acceptance of diversity as normal, necessary, and valuable (McLeod 1987). Multiculturalism also seeks to create a sup-portive social climate where proactive measures for managing diversity can be implemented without public outcries of either encroaching socialism or creeping apartheid.

## Symbol or Substance?

Manoly Lupul (1983) once remarked that multiculturalism is not taken seriously by anyone who is a somebody because it is a frivolous diversion whose value is symbolic rather than substantial. Here the critics got it right—albeit for the wrong reason. There is no question that multiculturalism embraces a restricted ("folkloric"), often symbolic endorsement of ethnoculture. That precisely is the point: multiculturalism is disinterested in preserving the substance of ethnic lifestyles. The prospect of relatively autonomous minority groups—complete with parallel institutions and separate power bases—would infringe on national sovereignty. Instead, multiculturalism endorses a commitment to ethnicity that is symbolic and situational. Minorities are thus entitled to identify and affiliate as individuals with the ethnocultural tradition of their choice. Anything beyond that is "iffy" in locating a working balance between individual and state rights on the one hand, minority versus majority rights on the other.

A framework of national consensus must logically precede a commitment to diversity. Canadian multiculturalism tolerates diversity to the extent that it conforms with the imperatives of capitalism, parliamentary democracy, and liberal individualism. This central framework is critical: an "anything goes" type of accommodation could only incite social chaos and ethnic strife. Accordingly, the limits to tolerance are quite restrictive under these conditions, with an emphasis on the ornamental rather than the operational. Critics may scold multiculturalism for advocating the symbols of diversity over its substance. But their criticism simply chides multiculturalism for something it is neither equipped nor prepared to do. Besides, many Canadians prefer the options of a symbolic ethnicity over the rigours of full-time ethnicity.

## Containment or Cure?

The final criticism of multiculturalism is perhaps the most difficult to refute. Multiculturalism is denounced as impractical and/or irrelevant in a capitalist society. Capitalism by definition creates classes, fosters ethnic and gender cleavages, and encourages endless consumption and consumerism. Nor can it exist apart from the inequities inherent in competitive individualism. Where, then, does multiculturalism fit in a society organized around the pursuit of profit rather than people? Two viewpoints prevail. It could be argued that multiculturalism "lends its weight to the social transformation of capitalism" by establishing "equality rights" as the "antithesis of the inequality wrongs" on which capitalism rests (Robert Needham, pers. comm., May 31, 1993). Alternatively, perhaps, the extent of multiculturalism can only imprint a "human face" upon an essentially exploitative system. This latter interpretation is not intended to downgrade multiculturalism to the level of official "white-wash." To the contrary: multiculturalism as a central feature of Canada has assumed a "life" of its own despite containment by capital or the state. It has evolved in directions never envisaged by the original architects: an overarching framework is now in place that legitimates as normal and necessary the presence of diversity at cultural and institutional levels. What originated as a policy for "European ethnics" is currently intertwined with initiatives for race relations, employment equity, and institutional accommodation. The net effect? The establishment of a policy with a corresponding set of initiatives that strike many as necessary and fair, yet workable within Canada's historical framework. That may not sound like a lot to those with unrealistically high expectations, but the contribution of multiculturalism to Canadian society should not be diminished by unfair comparison with utopian standards.

To sum up: multiculturalism is often criticized as contrary to Canada's best interests. To many it is little more than a government-mismanaged millstone around the collective necks of Canadians. Many of these charges have proven to be groundless. Or they are subject to diverse interpretations. Failure to situate multiculturalism within a society-building framework can also distort interpretations. Finally, the temptation to classify multiculturalism into "either–or" categories overlooks its potential as a weakness or strength, depending on the context.

In short, multiculturalism is not necessarily a weakness that divides, deters, or digresses. At worst, it comes across as a double-edged sword that advances national unity and identity when legitimated, but has a destructive side when denied or manipulated. At best, it furnishes a key "natural resource" for propelling Canada along pluralist lines. This positive role is further advanced by looking at multiculturalism in terms of what is necessary, workable, and fair.

# "DOING WHAT IS NECESSARY, WORKABLE, AND FAIR"

## Multiculturalism as Necessary

Canada constitutes a pluralistic society whose official commitment to multiculturalism is globally admired and occasionally copied (Fleras and Elliott 1992). Entrenchment of multiculturalism on constitutional and statutory levels has placed Canada in the front ranks of countries for the progressive management of race and ethnic relations. No longer a luxury or even an option in light of recent demographic, political, and social upheavals, multiculturalism is now considered a powerful force in coping with the vagaries of uncertainty, change, and diversity. A closer look at the demographic, political, and social changes discloses its potential for society-building.

1. *Changing Demographics.* The proportion of Canadians with some non-French- and non-English-speaking backgrounds now constitutes nearly 45 percent of Canada's population according to the 1991 census data (Statistics Canada 1993). This percentage is likely to increase as the government continues to raise the ceiling on immigration to about 250,000 between 1992 and 1996. Equally significant are the growing numbers of visible minorities. Persons of colour now comprise just over 9 percent of Canada's total population according to preliminary results from the 1991 census, up from the 5.1 percent in 1981. Much of the increase can be attributed to recent changes in immigration patterns between 1981 and 1991 when nearly three-quarters of the immigrants to Canada arrived from nonconventional sources such as Asia and Africa. Just over half of the immigrants and refugees who land in Canada reside in Ontario. Half of these are drawn to the greater Toronto region, with the remaining numbers distributed across other major centres such as Montreal, Vancouver, Winnipeg, and Calgary. These figures alone suggest the necessity for a proactive policy in the multicultural management of diversity.

2. *Political Reforms.* Passage of the Constitution Act, 1982, and the Charter of Rights and Freedoms has elevated public awareness of multiculturalism as a national driving force. No less critical in enhancing the multicultural profile was passage of the world's first Multiculturalism Act in 1988, followed by proclamation of a federal Department of Multiculturalism and Citizenship in 1991. With multiculturalism constitutionally enshrined as a "fundamental characteristic" of Canada, citizens are now better informed, more demanding, and increasingly articulate about their individual rights in a multicultural society. This is especially true of racial minorities, many of whom are less reticent about using the courts to defy practices that contravene the quintessential multicultural right; that is, the right to be the same ("equal") as well as the right to be different.

3. *Social Changes.* Demographic and political changes have ushered in a post-multicultural era in which racial and ethnic minorities are now allowed to compete as equals without being penalized for what they are racially, or what they want to be culturally. Under the terms of the "new mosaic" (see Tepper 1988), ethnoracial diversity is now recognized as a legitimate and integral component of Canada's emergent identity. Nowhere are the changes more manifest than in government initiatives to "mainstream" federal and provincial institutions. Institutions under state jurisdiction must ensure access ("openness" and "inclusiveness"), representation ("based on population ratios"), and equity ("equal treatment") for visible minorities. Failure to comply with these proposals

may result in dismissals of institutional leaders. By prodding Canadian society to respond to the demands of diversity and change, multiculturalism is on the cutting edge of society-building.

## Multiculturalism as Fair

Multiculturalism represents one of the key dynamics shaping recent events in Canada. A profound ideological shift has precipitated a rethinking of Canada's Eurocentrism in terms of what is normal and necessary.[4] In many ways, the shift is comparable with the feminist reordering of a society that historically embraced male privilege and patriarchal priorities. Political discourse is drifting away from a two-nations model of Canada with its adherence to Anglo-conformism and liberal individualism (Abu-Laban and Stasiulis 1992). Acceptance of diversity has evolved to the point where it commands public attention and political concern. Racial and ethnic minorities are now primed to demand—and receive—the same rights as all Canadian citizens, as well as additional considerations for remedying the effects of past discrimination.[5] The fact that many minorities continue to perform poorly on socioeconomic indicators points to discrimination as a contributing factor. Not surprisingly, the energies and resources of multiculturalism are aimed at removing discriminatory barriers—in some cases cultural and attitudinal, in others structural and systemic (Agocs and Boyd 1993).

Promotion of multiculturalism as reasonable and fair is evident in a related way. Canadians as a whole subscribe to a shared value system, including a commitment to the virtues of individual freedom, government intervention for the public good, the spirit of compromise and tolerance, and the ideal of equality. Overt forms of prejudice and discrimination are routinely rejected. Many express discomfort at the presence of discriminatory barriers that inhibit equality and full minority involvement—even if they disagree with the means to dismantle these impediments. An endorsement of multicultural ideals is consistent with egalitarian values (Berry 1993). It also confirms the role of multiculturalism in pursuing what is reasonable and fair through reduction of unjustified inequalities (Berry and Kalin 1993).

## Multiculturalism as Workable

As the cutting edge for social change, multiculturalism has attracted criticism, partly because national shortcomings tend to be magnified around minority relations. At the same time it suffers from highly inflated expectations about what it can or should do. Just as multiculturalism cannot be blamed for all social problems in Canada, neither should it be seen as the all-encompassing solution to problems that rightfully belong to political or economic domains. Rather than a magical formula for success, it is but one component for managing diversity in a context involving the competing demands of individuals, minority groups, and the state.

For political purposes, Canadian society can be envisaged as socially constructed around a series of national compromises. These national compromises range in scope from regional equalization concerns and charter group dynamics, to a perpetual rebalancing of individual and collective rights. In such a system of checks and balances, multiculturalism is aptly suited as a mediator "in-between" opposing ethnocultural forces. As a system of compromises in its own right, moreover, multiculturalism provides a counterbalance for reconciling ambiguities inherent in a diverse and changing society. A capacity for speaking the language of "in-between" enables multiculturalism to secure the priority of the whole without destroying the integrity of its constituent elements. A commitment to multiculturalism furnishes a symbolic rationale for reconciling what otherwise would lapse into dismemberment and chaos. It also steers a path between the conflicting demands of state sovereignty on the one hand versus those of ethnic tribalism on the other (*The Economist* 1993).

The objectives, scope, and limitations of multiculturalism must be clearly articulated if its full potential as "workable" is to be realized. Yet Canadians remain curiously misinformed about what multiculturalism is and how it goes about doing its job. Consider the possibilities for misunderstanding:

- Official multiculturalism is not simply a set of programs for splashing a dash of colour or pageantry into Canada's Anglo-centric agenda. Multiculturalism potentially transforms the national agenda in terms of "who gets what," and "why."

- Multiculturalism is not a coherent set of policies or programs that are fixed in perpetuity. Multiculturalism undergoes renewal and reform through adaptation to political, social, and demographic changes. The open-ended and resilient nature of multiculturalism provides it with the flexibility to shift agendas (for example, from ethnicity to equity) as the context dictates.

- Multiculturalism is not about promoting ethnicity or diversity per se. The focus is on "de-fanging" ethnic differences in a way that eliminates their potential for disruption.

- Multiculturalism does not possess the power or resources to "move mountains." As policy or program, it cannot single-handedly eliminate discrimination or racism. Nor can it automatically improve minority opportunities and life-chances. The strength of multiculturalism resides in its capacity to foster a social climate responsive to nuances in the progressive management of race and ethnic relations.

- Multiculturalism is not about ghettoizing ethnic or racial minorities into isolated enclaves, but about melding differences together into an integrated and viable system. Institutional accommodation and removal of discriminatory barriers are two of the current initiatives for achieving this unity.

- Multiculturalism neither constrains minority aspirations, nor does it lock people of colour into a vertical mosaic. Rather, it provides a rationale for restructuring the social order to improve minority access, equity, and representation.

- Multiculturalism is often associated with several misconceptions that are ripe for debunking. Among these: (a) fact: multiculturalism is *not* expensive (only $1 per year per Canadian in federal expenditures); (b) fact: multiculturalism is *not* divisive (ideally, it seeks to promote unity through preservation, participation, and integration); (c) fact: multiculturalism does *not* detract from national identity (Canada's collective self-image *is* quintessentially multicultural); and (d) fact: multiculturalism is *not* a failure (Compared to what? Better still, consider the paucity of alternatives).

## MULTICULTURALISM: THE CANADIAN WAY

That Canada remains an open, secular, and largely tolerant society is indicative of the extent to which multiculturalism is "working." Some measure of proof is derived from Canada's lofty status (as deemed by various United Nations panels) as a socially progressive society with an enviable standard of living. The fact that Canada has avoided much of the ethnic strife that currently convulses as many as forty-eight countries is further testimony to its resiliency in managing diversity and society-building (*The New York Times* 1993).

Endorsing multiculturalism as a workable alternative for Canada is commendable. But even whole-hearted support is no excuse for glossing over its imperfections. However potent a mechanism for managing diversity, the design and implementation of official multiculturalism is riddled with inconsistencies. Few would deny its capacity for manipulation by politicians and minority leaders for self-serving reasons. Fewer still would dismiss its potential to deter, divide, defuse, or digress. But criticism is one thing: proposals for alternatives to multiculturalism are quite another. Critics may be relentless in their attacks, but the critique is one-sided. Little is offered by way of specifics for a replacement policy. Forced separatism or segregation has long been discredited as an enlightened choice. Other visions are equally vague and unappealing.

Neither assimilation nor integration stand much chance of survival in a post-multicultural era. A much-touted return to "traditional" values as a glue for cementing Canadians into a unified and coherent whole sounds good in theory (Bibby 1990; Bissoondath 1993). In reality, such wishful thinking also may camouflage a "hidden agenda" for the return of immigrant-unfriendly policies.

Multiculturalism remains the policy of choice for a changing and diverse Canada. As philosophy, policy, or practice, it symbolizes an innovative if imperfect social experiment for managing diversity without relinquishing our collective self-image and international reputation as being free, open, and tolerant. Multiculturalism has performed yeoman-like service in revamping Canada from an Anglo-centric outpost, to its much ballyhooed status as a trailblazer in the enlightened management of race and ethnic relations. Under the circumstances, it is not a question of whether Canada can afford multiculturalism. More to the point, Canada cannot afford *not* to embrace multiculturalism in its search for political unity, social coherence, economic prosperity, and cultural enrichment.

## NOTES

1. I would like to thank Professor Robert Needham of the University of Waterloo for numerous helpful comments in the drafting of this paper.

2. Politics in Canada is increasingly premised around a dynamic interplay of three major forces (or "nationalities" if broadly used): namely, aboriginal peoples, French-speaking Canadians centred primarily in Quebec, and the rest of English-speaking Canada (Cairns 1993).

3. The concept of a post-multiculturalism is relatively new. Traditional multiculturalism was concerned primarily with European ethnics and the celebrating of differences through festivals and arts. By contrast, post-multiculturalism revolves around policies and programs for managing race relations through removal of discriminatory barriers and institutional accommodation. Roberta Jamieson (1993:4), the Ombudsperson for Ontario, puts post-multiculturalism into perspective when she describes the new Canada as a "polycultural pluralistic society which regards ethnic, racial, and religious differences as valued, permanent assets which Canada should cherish." Jamieson also remarks that many Canadians have not as yet accepted multiculturalism, let alone moved beyond it.

4. Consult J. Conway, *The West: The History of a Region in Confederation* (Toronto: James Lorimer, 1984).

5. See G.A. Cohen, "Freedom, Justice and Capitalism," *New Left Review* 126 (March/April 1981).

# REFERENCES

Abu-Laban, Yasmeen and Daiva K. Stasiulis. 1992. "Ethnic Pluralism Under Siege. Popular and Partisan Opposition to Multiculturalism," *Canadian Public Policy* 18, no. 4: 365–86.

Agocs, Carol and Monica Boyd. 1993. "The Vertical Mosaic Revisited," in *Social Inequality*, 2nd ed., Jim Curtis (ed.). Scarborough: Prentice-Hall.

Angus Reid Group Inc. 1991. *Multiculturalism and Canadians: Attitude Study, 1991.* National Survey Report submitted to the Department of Multiculturalism and Citizenship.

Berry, John. 1993. "Inter-Cultural Relations in a Multi-Cultural Society." Paper presented at Wilfrid Laurier University, Waterloo, Ontario, April 2.

Berry, John and Rudolf Kalin. 1993. "Multiculturalism and Ethnic Attitudes in Canada: An Overview of the 1991 National Survey." Paper presented to the Canadian Psychological Association Annual Meetings, Montreal, May.

Bibby, Reginald. 1990. *Mosaic Madness.* Toronto: Stoddart.

Bissoondath, Neil. 1993. "A Question of Belonging: Multiculturalism and Citizenship," in *Belonging*, William Kaplan (ed.), pp. 368–87. Montreal and Kingston: McGill-Queen's University Press.

Breton, Raymond. 1984. "The Production and Allocation of Symbolic Resources: An Analysis of the Linguistic and Ethnocultural Fields in Canada," *Canadian Review of Sociology and Anthropology* 21, no. 2: 123–40.

Cairns, Alan C. 1993. "The Fragmentation of Canadian Citizenship," in *Belonging*, William Kaplan (ed.), pp. 181–220. Montreal and Kingston: McGill-Queen's University Press.

*The Economist.* 1993. "Poor Little Devils," May 8.

Fleras, Augie. 1990. "Towards a Multicultural Reconstruction of Canadian Society," *American Review of Canadian Studies* 19, no. 3: 307–20.

Fleras, Augie. 1993. "From Culture to Equality: Multiculturalism as Policy and Ideology," in *Social Inequality in Canada: Patterns, Problems, Policies*, 2nd ed., James Curtis, Edward Grab, and Neil Guppy (eds.), pp. 384–99. Scarborough: Prentice-Hall.

Fleras, Augie and Jean Leonard Elliott. 1992. *Multiculturalism in Canada: The Challenge of Diversity.* Scarborough: Nelson.

Foster, Lois and Ann Seitz. 1989. "The Politicization of Language Issues in 'Multicultural' Societies: Some Australian and Canadian Comparisons," *Canadian Ethnic Studies* 21, no. 3: 55–73.

Hudson, Michael. 1987. "Multiculturalism, Government Policy, and Constitutional Entrenchment—A Comparative Study," in *Multiculturalism and the*

*Charter: A Legal Perspective,* Canadian Human Rights Foundation (ed.). Toronto: Carswell.

Jamieson, Roberta. 1993. "Community, Diversity, Learning—Notes for Remarks." Address to St. Paul's United College 30th Anniversary Celebration, February 24, Waterloo, Ontario.

Jaworski, John. 1979. "A Case Study of Canadian Federal Governments' Multicultural Policies." Unpublished M.A. Thesis, Political Science Department, Carleton University, Ottawa.

Kaplan, William (ed.). 1993. *Belonging: The Meaning and Sense of Citizenship in Canada.* Montreal and Kingston: McGill-Queen's University Press.

Lewycky, Laverne. 1993. "Multiculturalism in the 1990s and into the 21st Century: Beyond Ideology and Utopia," in *Deconstructing a Nation: Immigration, Multiculturalism, and Racism in 90's Canada,* Vic Satzewich (ed.), pp. 359–402. Halifax: Fernwood Press/Social Research Unit, Sociology Department, University of Saskatoon.

Lupul, Manoly. 1983. "Multiculturalism and Canada's White Ethnics," *Multiculturalism/e* 6, no. 3.

McLeod, Keith. 1987. "Introduction," in *Multicultural Education: A Partnership,* Keith McLeod (ed.), pp. vii–xi. Canadian Council for Multiculturalism and Intercultural Education.

Mitchell-Powell, Brenda. 1992. "Color Me Multicultural," *Multi-Cultural Review* 1, no. 4: 15–17.

Moynihan, Daniel Patrick. 1993. *Pandemonium: Ethnicity in International Politics.* New York: Oxford.

*The New York Times.* 1993. "As Ethnic Wars Multiply, U.S. Strives for a Policy," February 7.

Pearson, David. 1991. *A Dream Deferred: The Origins of Ethnic Conflict in New Zealand.* Wellington: Allen and Unwin/Port Nicholson Press.

Peter, Karl. 1981. "The Myth of Multiculturalism and Other Political Fables," in *Ethnicity, Power, and Politics in Canada,* J. Dahlie and T. Fernando (eds.), pp. 56–67. Toronto: Methuen.

Porter, John. 1965. *The Vertical Mosaic.* Toronto: University of Toronto Press.

Sens, Amartya. 1993. "The Threats to Secular India," *The New York Review,* pp. 26–32, April 8.

Simmons, Alan B. and Kieran Keohane. 1992. "Canadian Immigration Policy: State Strategies and the Quest for Legitimacy," *Canadian Review of Sociology and Anthropology* 29, no. 4: 421–52.

Stasiulis, Daiva K. 1985. "The Antimonies of Federal Multicultural Policy and Official Practices." Paper presented to the International Symposium on Cultural Pluralism, Montreal, October.

Statisics Canada. 1993. *Ethnic Origins*. Ottawa: Ministry of Supply and Services.

Tepper, Elliot. 1988. *Changing Canada: The Institutional Response to Polyethnicity. The Review of Demography and its Implications for Economic and Social Policy.* Ottawa: Carleton University Press.

# P⬛S⬛SCRIPT

**W**hat does the future hold for multiculturalism in Canada? Because of the low birthrate and an aging population, most demographic experts contend that Canada needs comparatively high levels of immigration simply for economic reasons. If present trends continue, an increasing number of immigrants will be non-European and nonwhite in origin. Canadians are still uncertain how to respond to these trends. Our ambivalence can be seen in the findings of the Citizens' Forum on Canada's Future, often referred to as the Spicer Commission. The commission found that while Canadians said that they value cultural diversity, they also wanted a single definition of being a Canadian that encompassed all groups. Significantly, the Spicer Commission recommended ending the funding for multiculturalism with the exception of those programs designed to assist in immigrant orientation, reduction of discrimination, and promotion of equality.

Useful background to this issue can be found in Yasmeen Abu-Laban and Daiva Stasiulus, "Ethnic Pluralism Under Siege: Popular and Partisan Opposition to Multiculturalism," *Canadian Public Policy* 18, no. 4 (1992): 365–86. The authors provide some interesting explanations for the growing critique of multiculturalism and review the changing views of both academics and political parties.

A defence of multiculturalism from the government's viewpoint can be found in *Multiculturalism: What is it Really About?* (1991) produced by Multiculturalism and Citizenship Canada. Two recent collections provide additional insights into both the issue of multiculturalism and the role of visible minorities in Canada: see Augie Fleras and Jean Leonard Elliott, eds., *Multiculturalism in Canada: The Challenge of Diversity* (Scarborough: Nelson, 1992) and Daiva Stasiulis, ed., *Visible Minorities and Ethnocultural Groups in Canadian Politics: The Question of Access* (Toronto: Dundurn Press, 1991). A good sense of the sharply divergent views on the impact of multiculturalism on the future of Canada can be found in a collection of conference papers entitled *20 Years of Multiculturalism: Successes and Failures,* edited by Stell Hryniuk (St. John's College Press, 1992). The views range from those of Kas Mazurek, who sees multiculturalism as "a genuinely radical social vision" of Canada, to Richard Ogmundson, a University of Victoria sociologist, who believes the "multiculturalism program to be a form of cultural genocide aimed at the destruction of a pan-Canadian identity."

# ISSUE THREE

**YES** DAVID ELTON, "The West Wants In," in R.D. Olling and M.W. Westmacott, eds., *Perspectives on Canadian Federalism*, pp. 348–51 (adapted)

**NO** J.M.S. CARELESS, "The Myth of the Downtrodden West," *Saturday Night* 96, no. 5 (May 1981): 30–36

In the late 1980s, a new political party, the Reform Party of Canada, emerged in western Canada. Although its leader, Preston Manning, sought to establish a national presence, the party was clearly a creation of the West. And properly so. The Reform Party reflected the continuing concern—rage, one might say—of westerners with policies of the national government. Over the years, a sense of alienation had developed in the West, and the Reform Party was only the latest manifestation of this deeply felt sentiment.

Western alienation is the product of many actions, but its roots are to be found in a set of unpopular policies pursued at the federal level. Federal initiatives in three areas—tariffs, natural resources, and transportation—have been especially grating. For the West, tariffs have historically provided protection for industry located in central Canada. The result is that western Canadians must purchase high-priced goods. Cheaper items are physically only kilometres away in the United States, but they are out of reach.

Similarly, federal resource policies have been seen as denying western interests. First, it was the failure of Ottawa to give the newly created Prairie provinces constitutional authority over their natural resources. The other provinces had been granted such authority, but not the western ones. Finally, in 1930, Ottawa acceded control to the West, but since then the federal government has attempted to exercise control over the resources despite provincial ownership.

Federal transportation policies have further stoked the fires of western alienation. Being landlocked, the West has been forced to rely on rail transportation, and the rail companies have taken advantage of this situation by engaging in discriminatory pricing. In this process, the federal government has aided and abetted rail interests, and contributed to a situation that only further worsens the plight of westerners.

There is, however, evidence that the basis for western alienation may be more apparent than real. The fury of the West is directed against eastern Canada and the federal government, but some suggest that the real enemy is the market. Consider, for instance, the belief that tariffs encourage the development of industry in Ontario. In reality, tariffs provide an incentive for industries to set up in Canada, but the actual decision of where to locate has nothing to do with the federal government and everything to do with market economics. The problem is not federal policy per se, but rather the economic unattractiveness of the Prairies.

Proponents of western alienation may also be accused of presenting half-truths. To be sure, mail rates for some items may be high in the West, but for others they are reasonable and for still others astoundingly low—the Crow's Nest Pass rates for wheat come to mind. As for control of natural resources, it might be argued that the western provinces initially were in no position to exploit them to advantage. Only the federal government had the opportunity to promote the development of these resources. Once the provinces gained maturity, the transfer of authority could be effected.

In the readings, David Elton, president of the Canada West Foundation, an organization that examines issues of interest to the West, argues that western alienation is soundly based. J.M.S. Careless, one of Canada's most eminent historians, contends that western alienation is premised largely on myth.

# YES

## The West Wants In

*David Elton*

"The West Wants In." This is the slogan used by the fastest growing and most popular political party in western Canada in 1990: the Reform Party of Canada. This slogan successfully captures the sentiments of many western Canadians because it simultaneously states a commitment to Canada *and* a desire for fundamental change in the status quo. To understand this mix of pro-Canadianism and western alienation from Canada's national government, it is important to examine the numerous overlapping and at times contradictory public policies and experiences that have shaped the western Canadian mindset.

## NATION-BUILDING

The building of the Canadian Pacific and Canadian National Railways, the creation of the Canadian Broadcasting Corporation (CBC), and the implementation of unemployment insurance, family allowances, old age pensions, and even athletic leagues such as the Canadian Football League (CFL) all played a part in the entrenchment of a strong national identity and attachment to Canada among western Canadians. Of particular relevance to the West was the creation of uniquely western Canadian organizations such as the Canadian Wheat Board and regionally beneficial programs such as the Crow's Nest Pass freight rate and its contemporary equivalent, the Western Grain Transportation Act. The strength of westerners' national ties is evidenced by the extent to which the residents of all four western provinces support national causes, be it serving their country in war, or simply distinguishing themselves from their southern American neighbours, many of whom are physically much closer than are central or Atlantic Canadians.

An examination of values and attitudes towards a wide range of economic, social, and political issues relevant to Canadians also indicates the extent to which the mindset of western Canadians is similar to that of other Canadians. The data collected by national polling organizations indicate not only that western Canadians share many national attitudes and values, but also that differences of opinion within western Canada are often greater than differences of opinion between residents of Canada's west and the rest of the country.

In addition to the development of strong provincial and national ties, a set of regional attitudes and values have also developed that clearly distinguish western Canadians from other Canadians.

# A REGIONAL IDENTITY

At the same time western Canadians were developing the strong provincial and national identity referred to above, a common regional identity was being forged. This sense of regional identity is not based upon a positive reaction to government actions or symbols such as flags and logos; rather it is based upon recurring problems westerners have experienced in seeking to find practical political and economic solutions for dealing with property and natural resource development, the cost of supplies, and the sale of their products.

From early settlement days up to the present, westerners have run up against politically constructed barriers which limit their growth and development with regard to resource utilization, consumption, and the marketing of their products. A brief elaboration of each in turn provides an insight into the national policies which have influenced the development of western Canada's political culture and approach to federal–provincial relations.

# PROPERTY AND NATURAL RESOURCES

When British Columbia entered Confederation in 1871, the province was given the same powers as those extended the four original provinces of Ontario, Quebec, Nova Scotia and New Brunswick; yet the three prairie provinces were denied control over crown lands on the grounds that the national government needed to retain control over crown lands to ensure the orderly flow of immigration into the region. This unequal constitutional treatment of Manitoba, Saskatchewan, and Alberta created considerable friction between the three provincial governments and Ottawa from the outset.[1]

The federal government's decision to retain control over property and natural resources for "the purpose of Canada" (a 19th-century equivalent of the "national interest") was contentious not simply because it smacked of colonialism, but also because it had a direct impact upon the daily lives of residents in the three provinces. Prairie settlers were required to provide roads, schools, and other services commensurate with development without provincial control over land allocations or access to revenues from the sale of crown land. Unlike Canadians in other provinces, who had direct control over the orderly development in their communities, this power rested with distant bureaucrats of the national government. And to add insult to injury, the massive grants of land made by the federal government to the CPR further hampered the provincial governments' ability to deal effectively with local land-use issues.[2]

During most of the first three decades of this century, and particularly during the decade following the First World War, demand for control over property and natural resources was the controversial centrepiece of federal–provincial relations between the three prairie provinces and Ottawa. While the federal government's decision in 1930 to transfer control over property and natural resources to Alberta, Saskatchewan, and Manitoba placed them on an equal footing with British Columbia and the other provinces, Ottawa's unwillingness to treat the three provinces equally was one of the key factors in the development of a legacy of distrust and animosity which has never dissipated.

The contemporary equivalent of the struggle for constitutional control over property is the controversy over the production and sale of oil and gas. Beginning with the federal government's decision to set a ceiling on oil and gas prices in 1973, and culminating with the 1980 National Energy Policy (NEP), federal regulation of this industry has become a vivid symbol of Ottawa's colonial mentality toward western Canada. The central issue was the classic struggle between producers and consumers. Western provinces, primarily Alberta but also British Columbia and Saskatchewan, own the oil and gas resources and thus benefit from sales at international prices. Consumers, most of whom live in Ontario and Quebec, would bear the cost of paying high prices for oil and gas. The federal government's NEP came down in favour of central Canadian consumers at the expense of western Canadian producers.

For western Canadians the NEP was clearly discriminatory in that the federal government was regulating both the export and pricing of oil and gas and yet was leaving unregulated other commodities such as electricity and forestry products produced in Ontario and Quebec. The NEP became "proof positive" of Ottawa's colonial mentality toward western Canada. And, to add insult to injury, when the newly elected Conservative government rescinded the NEP shortly after coming into office, they did so in stages so as to maximize federal revenues, rather than immediately end this most unpopular program.

# TARIFF POLICIES

A second national policy which discriminates against residents of all four western provinces is the national government's tariff policy, set up to protect the domestic market for Canadian manufacturers from American and European competition. Most of these manufacturers are located in Ontario and Quebec. In effect, western Canadians are coerced into buying manufactured goods ranging from tools and clothing to household necessities at above their international market price, while at the same time selling their products, be they agricultural products such as wheat or hogs, forestry products, oil, gas, potash, coal, etc., in an open international marketplace. Given that most western Canadians live within a short distance of the American border and either visit the United States personally or communicate with neighbours who have recently returned from the U.S., they are constantly reminded of the practical costs of Canadian tariff policy.

Even though Canadian tariffs have been reduced considerably during the past two decades and manufacturing activity in western Canada has increased, western Canadians continue to pay more to maintain Canada's tariffs than they benefit. Canadians tariffs cost western Canada nearly 372 million dollars in 1983 alone, while at the same time benefiting central Canadians by over 474 million dollars.[3] Given tariff reductions over the past several decades and the modest increases in manufacturing throughout western Canada during this same period, it is understandable why Canadian tariff policy has been particularly aggravating to westerners.

# TRANSPORTATION POLICY

National transportation policy constitutes a third set of national policies which western Canadians have found to be blatantly discriminatory. Since [the] time when the federal government utilized western lands to pay for the building of the Canadian Pacific Railway in the late 1800s and permitted the railways to charge discriminatory freight rates, national transportation policy has been particularly aggravating for Alberta, Saskatchewan, and Manitoba. British Columbia, on the other hand, has never been concerned about transportation rates because the province is not landlocked and is favoured by competition between water transportation and rail to obtain optimal cost-benefits.[4]

Whether one picks up a Canadian agricultural magazine of the early 1900s, a contemporary economic analysis of the 1984 Western Grain Transportation Act, or listens to a speech by a western manufacturer, western grievances regarding national transportation policies are an integral part of the discussion. The basic complaint centres around freight rate structures and programs which impose high rates on goods shipped into the three western landlocked provinces and encourages the shipment of nonprocessed goods out of the region. Probably the best example of the impact of transportation policy on western Canadian development is found in the federal government's decision to pay Crow rate benefits to the railways rather than directly to farmers. This policy, which is still in place to this day, encourages the exportation of unprocessed grain and discourages diversification of the agricultural industry.

## THE NATIONAL INTEREST

Whether it be economists analyzing voluntary export quotas on Japanese autos or federal revenue expenditure patterns, or the 1986 auditor general's report focusing on grants handled by the Department of Regional and Industrial Expansion, examples of regionally discriminatory practices by the national government abound.[5] After having examined these and other federal government practices in a 1986 report prepared for the Canada West Foundation entitled "The Western Economy and Canadian Unity," McCormick and Elton conclude that the concept of "national interest" utilized by the national government often excludes the concerns and aspirations of western Canadians. They note: "The term 'national interest' often takes on ominous overtones for western Canadians. When they hear it invoked, it is much like getting a phone call and being asked if you are sitting down: they know that bad news is on the way."[6]

## WESTERN ALIENATION

As a result of a broad range of policies such as those cited above, a long-standing and widespread disaffection with the national government has become embedded in the very heart of western Canada's political culture. This shared attitude, often referred to as western alienation, exists among a broad cross-section of western residents and has persisted regardless of the party in power or the number of western MPs on the government side of the House. Survey research over the past two decades indicates that four of every five western Canadians believe the Canadian political system favours Ontario and Quebec. These sentiments have led approximately one in twenty western Canadians to advocate separation or union with the United States. But approximately four out of five westerners continue to identify strongly with the Canadian political system while simultaneously expressing discontent over real and apparent discriminatory tendencies.

While there have been many attempts to explain western alienation, it is probably best symbolized by the 1914 Prairie Grain Grower's Guide cartoon of the milch cow being fed in the West and milked in Ontario and Quebec. This cartoon is an example of a sentiment that is just as prevalent in the 1980s as it was when it first appeared over sixty years ago.[7]

# CONCLUSION

Western alienation is not based upon the belief that western Canadians receive no benefits from Confederation. Rather it is based upon the belief that benefits are substantially outweighed by the costs imposed by national government policies. It is not that national policies are never beneficial, but rather than even beneficial national policies are often fine-tuned with an eye to central Canada considerations. It is not that the West receives nothing, but rather that the West systematically receives less than its share.

While the milch cow cartoon symbolizes western alienation, the demand for constitutional change such as the creation of the Triple E Senate (i.e., an Elected Senate, with Equal representation, and Effective powers) over the past decade best expresses the western Canadian desire to create a new Canada. For most westerners this new Canada will be a country in which citizens are treated fairly and equitably by their national government, regardless of where they live. This is the Canada into which "The West Wants In."

## NOTES

1. David K. Elton, "Alberta and the Federal Government in Historical Perspective, 1905–1977," in Carlo Caldarola, ed., *Society and Politics in Alberta* (Toronto: Methuen, 1979), 109–10.

2. Ibid.

3. "International Trade: Problems and Prospects," *Western Perspectives* (Calgary: Canada West Foundation, November 1985), 10.

4. T.D. Regehr, "Western Canada and the Burden of National Transportation Policies," in David Jay Bercuson, ed., *Canada and the Burden of Unity* (Toronto: Macmillan, 1977), 115–42.

5. Peter McCormick and David Elton, "The Western Economy and Canadian Unity," *Western Perspectives* (Calgary: Canada West Foundation, 1987), 1.

6. Ibid., 12.

7. For a detailed examination of western alienation, see David Elton and Roger Gibbins, "Western Alienation and Political Culture," in Richard Schultz et al., eds., *The Canadian Political Process,* 3rd ed. (Toronto: Holt, Rinehart and Winston, 1982), 82–97.

# The Myth of the Downtrodden West

## J.M.S. Careless

A recent Toronto *Globe and Mail* article by two western authors contained a crisp synopsis of Canadian history since Confederation: "We take it as a 'given' that ... the Hinterland (West and Maritimes) has suffered economically, socially and culturally under Central Canada's domination of the country for 113 years." The article was on senate reform, but what was most plain about it was the conviction that the West (not to mention the Maritimes) had been thoroughly and steadily held back by a controlling central Canada. Here was a direct expression of western alienation. What had been an attitude of grievance, grown to be a popular tradition of discontent, was a comprehensive view of history. In many parts of Canada this is today the conventional wisdom. But how valid is it? To what degree are current western sentiments justified by the historical record, and to what degree are they a regional distortion of memory and experience—half truths selectively kept in mind by a "hinterland" that thinks it has been exploited and isn't going to take it any longer?

Since the nineteenth century, the West has felt exposed to powerful forces beyond its control—not just huge distances, the vagaries of climate and harvests, and the problem of distant market prices, but the power of outside human interests over the West's promised destiny. Nature and the "natural" laws of the market could be lived with, perhaps to some extent offset. But dependence on eastern-controlled transport and business, and on federal government policies, grew much harder to accept.

People and money from outside first built up the West, laying down the vital rail lines from the 1880s, patterning the settlement of land, investing in towns and business enterprises, and subordinating the West to metropolitan centres half a continent away. The same could be said of other regions in Canada, and of North America in general. But even when the West grew (with startling speed), its undiversified economy and its reliance on long traffic routes to far-off markets left it particularly vulnerable. It was unsheltered, and uncertain, and considerably divided. The Pacific West was clearly different from the plains West, not only in terrain and economy but in outlook. And on the plains, Manitoba was not Saskatchewan, and Alberta was different again. Yet, in their comparative newness, their hopes of progress based on rich internal resources, and their frustrations readily blamed on dark external influences, the young western provinces had a good deal in common. They shared the same historical experience and displayed the same collective response. The West was eager and aggressive, prickly and aggrieved. And its mood could change like a chinook.

Developments from the First World War onward consolidated this outlook. Resentment over the wartime conscription of farm labour, the post-war weight of war-inflated farm debt, and the widespread slowdown in the prairie wheat economy through much of the 1920s all left their marks. In the 1930s the Depression made westerners feel even more helplessly subject to outside forces. The Second World War and the booming 1950s brought dramatic recovery and new advances, but bitter memories of the Depression were all but indelible. And then, in the years approaching the present, came the oil, gas, and potash bonanzas in the prairies, and the coal, gas, logging, and electric-power booms in British Columbia. For almost the first time, the West began to think that its dreams were within its grasp, that it could escape its self-seen role as victim.

Recently this buoyant, increasingly diversifying West was confronted by a fresh outside intervention. Federal power (central Canadian power, in western eyes) sought, it seemed, to seize control of the new western wealth in energy: to draw it off in support of a faltering East and centre. No wonder the West sharply reacted. No wonder western provincial politicians began to raise defensive barriers. No wonder many aroused westerners could ardently agree that the whole history of their region added up to a century of victimization by central Canada.

The reaction is understandable, but not fair. It is grounded in experience, but it sees just one side of history. Western problems have to be judged in the light of the fuller Canadian record: regions are not closed entities, embattled armies of us against them, but interlinked communities in broad national and international frames. At the very least, the historic treatment of the West must be assessed within the wider realm of the Canadian nation. Three of the crucial issues that have affected the West across its history—the tariff, freight rates, and control of natural resources—provide good tests of the West's belief in its past subservience.

Westerners have continually protested that the federal protective tariff, originally created by John A. Macdonald's government, compelled them to buy higher-priced, protected central Canadian goods instead of cheaper alternatives from outside the country, where their own primary products went. Thus they were held subservient. Traditionally they have seen the tariff as imposed to benefit central Canada at the cost of other Canadian regions, diverting part of their incomes to sustain the centre's domination. They have argued that this diversion and imbalance retarded the growth of manufacturing within the West itself, keeping it industrially dependent on the centre.

This whole position expresses one-sided judgements. The original National Policy of protection begun in 1879 was part of a larger package aimed at building the Canadian union, including the West, by promoting a more diversified, higher-level economy with a broad home market—one that would not be absorbed piecemeal by the already highly protectionist United States. The very settlement and development of the West, the construction of costly railways to open it, and the amassing of capital to invest in its growth, were seen by Macdonald's government to depend on the revenues and wealth created by industrial advances in the older, settled eastern regions.

Yet if the would-be nation-builders of the time mainly considered the West a great new property to be developed under central direction— and they did—it's also true that there was virtually no western regional community *until* that process got underway. Of course, there were a few whites and a long-standing, thinly spread community of Indians and Métis in the wilderness West of fur-trade days. And certainly the native peoples were little considered by anyone back East as settlement began to infringe on their ways of life: thus the two western risings of 1869 and 1885. Still, without at all condoning the treatment of Indians and Métis (who in the long run probably suffered as much from local white prejudices as from the patronizing parsimony of distant imperial Ottawa), it is still true that the West as we now know it came into being only under a central, national design—and this included building east–west trade behind a tariff wall. How could the designers think otherwise than in terms of centrally directed purposes, when a western regional society had yet to be created? The imposition of the tariff was not just centralist greed and self-interest, but part of a genuine nation-making effort. The achievement of this design, in fact, was the rapid settling of the West, which then increasingly protested central domination—and the policy which had helped make the modern West possible.

Westerners would still contend that the National Policy did not work out as it should have; that it failed to produce a well-rounded economic unit and left the hinterland thoroughly subjec to central metropolitan interests. The centre developed industrial strength because of the gift of protection, and—secure behind the tariff wall—proceeded to exploit the trade of both a weaker Atlantic region and a subordinate West. Central Canada got the fat of the land (this argument runs) at the expense of the rest.

A good deal else can be said against the historic workings of the Canadian tariff: that it fostered powerful vested interests, especially in Ontario, that it promoted unhealthy alliances between governments and businessmen (who quite liked state support), that it shored up inefficient industries, notably in Quebec. Yet the key question remains: did central Canada obtain and keep industrial mastery because of protection, at the expense of hinterland incomes? Not even economists with computers can really settle the point, or prove what might have been if the tariff had not been established. But an Albertan economist, Kenneth Norrie, has recently argued (to small applause in Alberta) that differences in regional income levels across the country are essentially due not to the tariff but to the inevitable workings of the capitalist market system, under which some get more and others less. Perhaps it might be different under socialism, but that is hardly the demand of the angriest westerners today in Alberta, who inveigh against the "socialist" policies of Ottawa. Besides, there is ample evidence of disadvantaged regions under all sorts of socialist or Communist régimes.

Still, the western assessment goes as follows: in the late nineteenth century, Canada was largely stagnant and depressed, until massive occupation of the West began around the century's end. Then, borne along by the rapid growth of the prairie wheat economy and the big new captive market it offered, the centre and its protected industries at last began to boom, aided as well by mining and logging developments in the Pacific West. In this version, the West saved and strengthened eastern power at its own cost of continued subservience.

But industrialization was advancing strongly in the East long before a significant western market existed. The late nineteenth century, in fact, far from being a time of stagnation, produced industrial expansion in central Canada, remarkably so in Ontario during the 1880s. No doubt the 1879 tariff encouraged that growth, but considerable industrial progress had been made well before the tariff was even introduced; it was a result as well as a cause of the rise of manufacturing interests. There was an already sizable central Canadian population, providing an accessible market and work force, along with a well-developed regional transport system by both rail and water, and close links with the prosperous American heartland. Surely those factors had more to do with advancing central Canadian industrialism than did the tariff.

In the twentieth century the great western wheat boom undoubtedly created a valuable market for central industrialism, but eastern industry was already established. And it was sharing as well in the growing activities of much nearer pulpwood and mining frontiers, and benefiting from its own enlarging supply of cheap hydro.

It is short-sighted, in other words, to view the industrial rise of central Canada from a western perspective alone. The wider record indicates that central economic ascendancy was based on far more than any tariff grip on the West. And later years confirmed as much when the centre continued to expand despite western slowdowns—though in some degree, admittedly, because of north–south trade in the primary products of its resource-rich northern hinterlands.

There remains the claim that the tariff impaired manufacturing in the West. No doubt the record shows the struggles and failures of smaller western enterprises in the face of bigger, richer eastern rivals. But under free trade they would have faced the same competition, or worse, from even bigger American firms. Moreover, under the National Policy, Manitoba still built up decidedly valuable industries: effective units for the regional market, somewhat protected by distance from the East and by the tariff from the Americans. In fact, Manitoba, no less part of the West than its neighbours, has been predominantly favoured by protective rates; above all, in the Winnipeg area.

Western cities in general did well on the east–west flow of trade that was channelled behind the tariff barrier and along the Canadian transcontinental rail lines. Vancouver, as terminus of the CPR, was not only a direct creation of the national rail system, but was assured of regional dominance over the Pacific West by the tariff shield. Without it, markets on the coast and in the interior could have been tapped quite as well by American cities to the south. The Alaska boundary question of the early 1900s, for example, really involved whether Seattle or Vancouver would command trade access by water to the gold-rich Yukon, depending on where the Canada–U.S. border was drawn and which country's tariff wall would thus stand or be breached.

Western centres and their rising industries have gained a lot from a protective tariff, no less than in the East. A more diversified West might want a tariff even more. In that respect, the very push of Alberta to use its new wealth to build a broader-based economy and fatter home markets can only inspire mounting protectionist demands—most likely, in a separate Alberta state itself.

It follows that there is no inherent crime in pursuing a protectionist policy. For all its failings, protectionism historically has been a measure of political exigency, not of social injustice or regional oppression. Everyone looks for protection of his special interests—industrialists and farmers, unionists and university professors, easterners and westerners. One's own needs, of course, are essential and righteous, those of others self-seeking and immoral. But that too is in the historical record. And we are stuck with it.

Because of the West's dependence on long-distance land routes to markets or supplies, and its lack of water routes (like the Great Lakes–St. Lawrence system), westerners have always been crucially concerned with the cost of rail transport and the power of the great eastern-based railways. Even the recent rise of truck and air traffic has changed this in only a limited way, because the bulk and low unit-value of the West's primary products make rail transport still most economic. Nor have pipelines essentially altered the historic pattern. Accordingly, the railway rate structure and the near-monopolies of the big rail corporations behind it have figured large in western complaints.

Rates and railway power were targets of attack from the early years of settlement, through the western farmers' movement of Progressivism in the 1920s, the bleak era of Depression, and down to the present. The eastern-centred traffic octopus, strangling the free peoples of the West, supplied a potent theme of protest. Lower or more preferably arranged freight rates, of course, were sometimes realized through political pressure, but this seemed only to demonstrate the need to fight the central power complex of politicians and business. Yet campaigns for adjustment were more often concerned with advantages for particular western interests or places than with equal justice for all. Certainly the main centres, such as Winnipeg and Vancouver, have enjoyed favourable rates in their time. In any case, westerners again have acted like other Canadians in trying to improve their own special positions in the national traffic system. The system may be focused historically in the more densely occupied centre, but it depends on serving all the country.

The West made one striking gain with the Crow's Nest Pass rates of 1897, an agreement by which the federal government secured low rates for western grain traffic by rail to the Lakehead, in return for subsidizing a costly extension of the CPR through southern British Columbia mountains. This agreement, ended by 1922, was revived largely due to the western Progressives' pressure—and thereby grew the "statutory grain rates" which still today, despite the enormous increase in all kinds of costs, move western wheat at antique price levels. Effectively, the Canadian government (and taxpayers) have provided a western subsidy, huge over the years, which has compensated for many of the higher charges the West has claimed to suffer from tariff and rail subservience. But to draw a balance sheet that covers every factor in the accounting is impossible. No one can deny the worth of the grain-rates arrangement in the national as well as the regional context, but the issue nevertheless demonstrates once more that the record has more than one side.

The same economist mentioned earlier, Kenneth Norrie (a maverick in an Alberta famed for its mavericks), has argued that the West would *not* have done better if it had not been forced by tariff and railway policy to use the Canadian routes. American rail rates, in fact, were higher. This fact upsets the long-held idea of the West's exploitation by the national transport system. Norrie also points out that in recent years some seventy per cent of western shipments from the region moved in the cheapest rate categories, scarcely overburdening producers' incomes; that the prairies receive rates no different from those of the rest of the country for mineral products and manufactures they send out; that the higher charges on their inbound processed goods afford a degree of protection for western industries; and that there is no basis for the view that discriminatory rates are impairing the development of those industries.

All this may not cover every aspect of the cost-of-transport case; notably, differences between the water-accessible Pacific West and the great landlocked interior. In general, however, one still is led to this conclusion: the rail and rate problems of the West owe far more to physical environment than historical mistreatment. The relative remoteness of the whole territory; the costs levied by distance, mountain barriers, and the vast Precambrian shield along its eastern margins; the lack of alternative water routes across its inland sweep—these were far greater hindrances than any human arrangements could be. Without doubting the facts of corporate self-interest, the devious effects of political deals, and the creaky clumsiness of rate regulation and adjustment, we can still conclude that geography is the main factor behind the historic freight-rates issue in the West.

The old but newly heated question of control of natural resources goes back to the very entry of the West into Confederation. At that time, the existing eastern provinces held title over their own unsettled lands and whatever natural wealth those lands might contain. So did British Columbia, since it joined Canada as a province already in being. But the prairies came in as territory transferred from the imperial British government and the Hudson's Bay Company. And while a small Manitoba was immediately erected—the so-called "postage stamp" province—it did not receive control over its own landed resources. Nor did Saskatchewan or Alberta when, thanks to the spread of settlement, they too were set up by federal law as provinces in 1905. The great plains country was treated as a national estate, to be opened, developed, and exploited under central, federal direction.

Almost certainly, there was no other way at the beginning. Quite certainly there was no thought of another way, given the nearly empty West of the day; the new-made Manitoba had only about 12,000 settled inhabitants. Western lands would be laid out, policed, and granted under federal authority. Some land would be used to support schools, some allocated to the Hudson's Bay Company as part of the transfer bargain. And more would go to help fund the railway lines so crucially required to open the West. Thus the CPR was initially granted 25-million acres, along with $25-million, to support the task of construction. The subsequent wealth that company gained by selling off this great land tract might later seem to the West extravagant over-payment out of its own birthright. This was easy enough to feel after the railway was built, and westerners began fuming about its privileged power, but not so easy to feel when a shaky young company was pushing forward in the 1880s in constant danger of financial collapse, its rewards far in the future. Memory is indeed selective.

Under federal management the lands of the West were successfully taken up, in a process greatly stimulated in the early twentieth century by flourishing world demands for resource supplies, including food. Federal resource controls were not seriously challenged in the region until its post-war slowdown in the 1920s, when the Progressives attributed so many western troubles to outside power. Prairie dwellers came to see themselves as downgraded, kept in colonial status by the federal sway over their resources, unequal to the citizens of other provinces. British Columbians could share that sentiment also, since they had transferred large amounts of provincial railway lands to federal jurisdiction back in the 1880s.

At last, in 1929–30, the natural resources of all the western provinces were handed over to them. But the years of controversy, at times agitated and embittered, left sharp memories. And now, these memories have been revived as the question of resource control re-emerges over federal policies affecting the revenues from oil- and gas-producing western lands—a new invasion, westerners feel, of their hard-won birthright. Without examining the present issue, one can see how deep its roots reach into the past. The question is whether the historic record justifies the "victim" attitude of the West. Not, I think, for most of the early years of growth. Given the scope of the task of western settlement and the weakness of actual prairie jurisdictions, central resource control was both justifiable and effective; and federal authority had an aura of successful national leadership right up to the First World War.

Afterwards, it was different. The resources questions emerged amid the involved political manoeuvres of a far less dynamic federal régime. The final settlement looked more like a tardy concession wrung from central expediency than a positive recognition of regional equality. The West had overcome resource control by its own determined stand. Today Ottawa faces such a view once more.

There remains the long-perceived sway of eastern banks and investment houses over western financial life; the roles of eastern-centred media and cultural organizations, held to have neglected or inhibited western cultural developments. Far more critical is the West's sense of its own lack of political power in a federal system that has largely rested on central Canada votes—and never more obviously than today. On this, one still might say that representation based on population has been a powerful historical principle in this country, and it is hard to run democracy except by rule of the majority. Yet, apart from aligning with a political majority, a region with a minority population in a federal system can look to the provincial sphere of powers—and can hope for its own population to increase. For the West, this last looks promising, as economic forces continue to shift Canadian population westward.

Whatever the history behind the West's current alienation, history itself is at work to settle the matter. The West that has grown so far has not escaped geography; but the impact of geography is changing over time, as the whole demographic and economic orientation of North America moves westward. This shift may not make grass grow on Yonge Street—a cheerful western fantasy—but it will change the whole Canadian balance. The centre's dominance, not a sinister plot but a joint product of history and geography, will be modified and offset. The current metropolitan rise of Vancouver, Calgary, and Edmonton, and the new wealth, diversity, and energy of their own western hinterlands, proclaims as much.

What we need, really, is more time to defuse angry issues. We could also use a shrewdly adaptable John A. Macdonald to wangle new political combinations, even a skilfully delaying Mackenzie King, rather than urgent confrontationists in power. If the Canadian genius (of seeming anything but genius) does come through, western alienation could subside without explosions. And history may then confirm that western discontents, while deep in memory, should be seen as no true basis for a belief in steady victimization.

# POSTSCRIPT

**B**oth Elton and Careless address the economic basis of western alienation. Certainly, this is the most important element of the West's frustration, but there are others as well. A certain hostility toward Quebec and the French Canadians has always been a part of western alienation. The West is wary, to say the least, of the federal policy of official bilingualism, and more generally believes that an inordinate amount of time is spent on addressing Quebec's demands.

The West has also been concerned about questions of political representation. It feels that federal institutions, such as the House of Commons, are a prisoner of central Canadian interests, and that the West has no voice—and hence no influence—in Ottawa. As a result, westerners are strong supporters of Senate reform. They believe that the Senate, if fairly constituted, could become a place where the West's interests are represented and properly addressed.

David Elton and Roger Gibbins present a good overview of western alienation in their article "Western Alienation and Political Culture," in Richard Schultz, Orest Kruhlak, and John C. Terry, eds., *The Canadian Political Process*, 3rd ed. (Toronto: Holt, Rinehart and Winston, 1979). Roger Gibbins's *Prairie Politics and Society: Regionalism in Decline* (Toronto: Butterworths, 1980) contains a chapter on western alienation. Interested readers may also wish to consult Larry Pratt and Garth Stevenson's edited collection on the West, entitled *Western Separatism: Myths, Realities and Dangers* (Edmonton: Hurtig, 1981). A book that provides a close-up view of two western provinces, Alberta and Saskatchewan, is John Richards and Larry Pratt's *Prairie Capitalism: Power and Influence in the New West* (Toronto: McClelland and Stewart, 1979). For a look at the Reform Party of Canada, the latest symptom of western alienation, one might examine Murray Dobin, *Preston Manning and the Reform Party* (Toronto: James Lorimer, 1991) and Preston Manning, *The New Canada* (Toronto: Macmillan of Canada, 1992).

In his article "Some Comments on Prairie Economic Alienation," Kenneth Norrie provides a rigorous critique of the economic foundation of western discontent. The article is essential for an understanding of western alienation, and can be found in (among other places) J. Peter Meekison, ed., *Canadian Federalism: Myth or Reality*, 3rd ed. (Toronto: Methuen, 1977).

# ISSUE FOUR

## Can Native Sovereignty Co-exist with Canadian Sovereignty?

**YES** JOHN A. OLTHUIS and ROGER TOWNSHEND, "The Case for Native Sovereignty"

**NO** THOMAS FLANAGAN, "Native Sovereignty: Does Anyone Really Want an Aboriginal Archipelago?"

In Canada, the subject of aboriginal rights has never been high on the political agenda. Most Canadians have a vague awareness of the deplorable living conditions on many Indian reserves, but that is about all. The demands of natives for land, greater autonomy, and even self-government have received little notice. More "immediate" issues such as constitutional reform, Quebec separatism, western alienation, or free trade with the United States have usually pushed native issues off the list of urgent public issues.

However, the dramatic events surrounding the Oka crisis of 1990 did more to change public perceptions of native issues than any other single event. Reacting to municipal plans to expand a local golf course onto traditional native lands, armed Mohawk Warriors began erecting barricades in an effort to stop the work. The protest soon escalated into a full-scale confrontation between the Quebec provincial police and Mohawk Warriors, in which one police officer was killed. Soon a second set of barriers was erected on the Kahnawake reserve near Montreal as a demonstration of support. As the situation appeared to become more violent, Quebec Premier Robert Bourassa called in the Canadian armed forces to restore order to Oka. For the first time in twenty years, Canadian troops were deployed against fellow citizens.

For federal and Quebec officials, the issue was straightforward. The Mohawks, in using arms and barricades to press their case, had broken the law and needed to be brought to justice like any other citizens who had committed illegal acts. Land claims and other grievances would be settled only when arms were surrendered and the lawbreakers brought to justice. But the Mohawks rejected this view. It was not just a matter of land claims that was at stake. It was, the Warriors claimed, a question of sovereignty. The Mohawks occupied sovereign territory that had never been surrendered to any British or Canadian government. Thus the Mohawks had every right, as any other sovereign nation, to take up arms to defend themselves. It was the police and army who were acting illegally.

At the heart of native grievances is the Indian Act, 1867, which set the tone for successive federal government dealings with natives. Under this act, elected Indian band councils, not traditional political institutions, deal with the Department of Indian Affairs and Northern Development. Band councils are granted limited powers, but all financial decisions are ultimately subject to the approval of the minister responsible for Indian Affairs. Thus sovereignty remains undivided and concentrated in the hands of Ottawa. Band councils are like fledgling municipal governments, able to exercise only those powers specifically delegated to them.

Native leaders have long argued that this relationship is humiliating and paternalistic. The real aim of the Indian Act, they argue, has been to use the band councils as an instrument for destroying traditional native institutions and for assimilating and integrating natives into the larger Canadian society. For moderate native leaders, the solution has been to negotiate some greater delegation of powers to the band councils. But for a growing number of native leaders this is not enough. Only when the full sovereignty of Indian nations is recognized will natives be able to overcome their degrading colonial status.

In the wake of the Oka crisis, native issues were suddenly given a more prominent place on the Canadian political agenda. The government of Brian Mulroney appointed a royal commission on aboriginal questions, and gave native leaders an increasingly prominent role in discussions leading up to the constitutional proposals of 1992. The Charlottetown Accord appeared to address many native concerns. The accord included a recognition of the inherent right of aboriginal people to self-government and the commitment to make these aboriginal governments one of three orders of government along with Ottawa and the provinces. Federal and provincial governments would have committed themselves to negotiating self-government agreements with those native bands that wished to do so, while a series of future First Ministers' Conferences were promised to give ongoing consideration to aboriginal constitutional issues.

However, many remained sceptical of the accord. Non-native critics wondered what a third order of government meant. What form would native self-government take? How would it mesh with the notion of a sovereign Canada? At the same time, many natives felt that the accord had not gone far enough. After all, the accord stated that aboriginal laws could not be inconsistent with those Canadian laws that are deemed essential to the preservation of peace, order, and good government. This was hardly a recognition of native sovereignty.

With the defeat of the referendum, many of the questions surrounding the issue of native sovereignty remain unresolved and will likely be the subject of much negotiation during the coming years. In the following essays three specialists in native issues debate the meaning of native sovereignty and its relationship to the concepts of a sovereign Canada. John Olthuis and Roger Townshend, lawyers who have done extensive work on native land claims and aboriginal constitutional issues, set out the case for native sovereignty. Thomas Flanagan of the University of Calgary argues that the demand for native sovereignty as it is posed by native leaders is incompatible with the continued existence of Canada.

# The Case for Native Sovereignty

## John A. Olthuis and Roger Townshend

There is a great divide in perceptions between aboriginal people in Canada and nonaboriginal people. The nonaboriginal Canadian takes as self-evident the legitimacy of the Canadian state and its jurisdiction over Canadian territory. The average aboriginal person, on the other hand, views much of the power exercised by the Canadian state as illegitimate, oppressive, and as infringing on the powers of First Nations. To the extent that nonaboriginal Canadians are aware of this perception among aboriginal people, they are likely bewildered by it and have trouble seeing either a reasonable basis for it or any practical ways in which such a view could be acted on. Yet it is precisely this divergence of views that has caused and will continue to cause confrontations in the political area (such as regarding constitutional amendments) and confrontations on the ground such as at Kanesatake (Oka).

Although nonaboriginal Canadians rarely question the legitimacy of the Canadian state, most thoughtful people would likely be distressed at how flimsy the logical justification for Canadian sovereignty indeed is. There is no question that prior to European contact native nations in North America had stable cultures, economies, and political systems. They unmistakably exercised full sovereignty over their lands, although in somewhat different ways than did European nations. It would be arrogant and ethnocentric to recognize only a European model political organization as a sovereign state. The initial contact of Europeans with native nations generally treated them as allies or as enemies, but in any event, as nations to be treated as equals with European states. How then did this change? International law then and now recognized changes in sovereignty based on conquest, discovery and settlement, or treaty.

There is nothing in Canadian history that could qualify as a conquest in the international law sense. Treaties with First Nations fall into two rough categories. There are "peace and friendship" treaties, which if anything reinforce the concept of the equal nationhood of First Nations. There are also treaties that read as land transactions, which by their silence concerning matters of jurisdiction would seem to provide little help in rooting a claim that they are a source of Canadian sovereignty. Furthermore, there are vast areas of Canada where there are no treaties whatsoever. Thus the invocation of treaties is wholly unsatisfactory as a foundation of Canadian sovereignty. What is left is the doctrine of discovery and settlement. The difficulty with this is that it was intended to apply only to lands that were vacant. Its initial application to a claim of European jurisdiction required the step of considering the aboriginal people as legal nonpersons. In fact, the "discovery" of the Americas sparked lengthy theological and judicial debates in Europe about whether indigenous people indeed were or should be treated as humans. Thus the only justification for Canadian sovereignty (of course, inherited from British sovereignty) that has an air of reality to it requires, as a precondition, a judgment that aboriginal people are not human. This is surely repugnant to thinking Canadians.[1]

Despite the logical flimsiness of its assertion of sovereignty, the British (and later the Canadian state), after an initial period of nation-to-nation dealings, has treated aboriginal people as subjects and indeed as less than equal subjects. After the onset of European settlement, Canadian Indian policy has been aimed at assimilating aboriginal people into Canadian society. This integration was to be achieved on an individual level and preferably to be achieved by entry into the working-class level of society. Efforts of aboriginal people to interact as a group with Canadian society or to integrate at a higher level of Canadian society met with suppression. For example, for many years an aboriginal person who graduated from university automatically ceased to be an "Indian" in the eyes of the federal government. The policy of assimilation came to a head in 1969 with the notorious White Paper that called for the termination of Indian status. This document was resoundingly rejected by aboriginal people and in fact became the catalyst for the Canada-wide political organization of First Nations. This policy of assimilation has been a complete and utter failure. The political resistance of First Nations to assimilation into Canadian society has never been stronger. Most aboriginal people, in a fundamental way, view the Canadian government as a foreign government and not one that is "theirs." This should hardly be shocking since it was only in 1960 that aboriginal people were able to vote in federal elections. Neither have aboriginal communities lost their social, cultural, and economic distinctiveness. The Canadian government has tried long and hard to change this, but it has failed. Its attempts have only created much human misery. The residential school system where Indian children were separated from their families and forbidden to speak their language and often even sexually abused is one of those attempts. Another attempt is the criminalizing of traditional native religious ceremonies. Also, the native traditional economy has in many parts of the country been seriously impaired both by the environmental effects of development activities and directly by legislation restricting hunting rights. Yet the attachment of aboriginal people to the land remains unbroken.[2]

So what options are open? The dismal social conditions in which many aboriginal people in Canada live are the results of failed assimilationist policies of the Canadian government. Aboriginal people firmly believe that the political key to a better future is the recognition of jurisdiction of First Nations. This must be a jurisdiction that goes well beyond a municipal-government type of jurisdiction, and that would allow and encourage the development of new types of structures that would reflect the distinct cultural, political, economic, and spiritual aspects of aboriginal society. This must be a jurisdiction that is provided with sufficient resources to be viable. It would indeed mean a fundamental restructuring of the institutions of the Canadian state, or perhaps more accurately, a rolling back of the jurisdiction of the Canadian state to allow aboriginal institutions to flourish. It is this approach that could allow for a just and peaceful co-existence of First Nations in the Canadian state.

The defeat of the proposed constitutional amendments in 1992 was a missed opportunity to begin to pursue this path. These amendments were rejected by both the nonaboriginal and the aboriginal people. However, it must be realized that they were rejected for very different reasons. The rejection of the Charlottetown Accord by nonaboriginal people seems to have little to do with the aboriginal proposals in the accord. To the extent that these were a factor, nonaboriginal Canadians were probably disposed to view them as giving too much to First Nations. First Nations, on the other hand, rejected the accord because it was too small a step in the direction they wanted to go.

It is puzzling that the idea of native sovereignty should be so threatening to nonaboriginal people. The very nature of the Canadian political system involves a division of powers between federal and provincial governments. It is but an easy step in theory to implement another order of government and provide for an appropriate division of powers. This would not be a challenge to the very essence of Canada since the sharing of jurisdictional powers between different government institutions is already part of the essence of the Canadian state. Canadian sovereignty is also leaking at the other end with increasing globalization and trade agreements. It becomes confusing, then, why Canada should be unwilling to share jurisdiction with First Nations if it is indeed willing to modify its sovereignty with relation to the provinces and also at the international level. Nor would the idea of native sovereignty within a federal state be an uncharted course. In the United States, a country hardly known for being progressive, it is an established legal doctrine that Indian tribes are "domestic dependent nations." The implementation of this concept extends to separate tribal justice and court systems.

Many nonaboriginal Canadians may be troubled by the idea of native sovereignty since they feel that aboriginal people should be able to achieve their social and economic goals by participation as individuals within Canadian society. This misses the entire point of native difference. Most aboriginal cultures have a distinctive and tangible collective nature that goes well beyond the sum of the individuals that constitute them and that would be destroyed by assimilation on an individual basis. The failure of many nonaboriginal Canadians to appreciate this reflects only that liberal individualism is such a pervasive ideology in Canadian society that it is barely recognizable as an ideology at all and often viewed as ultimate truth. (This appears to be the position taken by Thomas Flanagan in the opposing article.) By definition, a group with a culture that differs at significant points from liberal individualism cannot be accommodated within a purely individualistic framework, particularly when any integration with a larger society can only take place on an individual basis. It is true that a society that permits or encourages interaction on a collective basis is not a "liberal democracy" in the sense of the term used by Flanagan. This is the very point. A "liberal democracy" is not an acceptable political structure for most aboriginal people. Fortunately, Canada has never been a "liberal democracy" in a strong sense, as Flanagan seems to admit. For that matter, whether or not "liberal democracy" is a meaningful term is questionable, since the concepts of liberalism and democracy can come into sharp conflict (for example, when a majority wishes to suppress rights of a minority).

Others may view the kind of structural diversity advocated in this article to be extremely impractical. As Flanagan admits, it is not unprecedented—he cites the Ottoman Empire as an example. There are also analogies less unfamiliar to Canadians—the position of Indian tribes in the U.S. system is one. Another example, in a context without an aboriginal element, is that the social and political structure of the Netherlands permits and encourages structural diversity based on philosophical or confessional communities. But apart from whether operating models exist or not, the alternatives to recognizing aboriginal jurisdiction must be looked at realistically. Flanagan's alternative is to do more consistently what the Canadian government has been trying to do for a century. This has failed utterly, and has created much suffering and resentment in the process. What is there to lose in trying something different? Demands for the recognition of aboriginal jurisdiction are not going to go away. If "legitimate" avenues for advancing these demands are shut down, other means may be sought. The continued peace and security of Canada may well depend on accommodating aboriginal jurisdiction.

Respect for the cultural distinctiveness of aboriginal people requires the recognition of institutional forms of First Nations governments with sufficient resources to exercise jurisdiction meaningfully. The sad history of aboriginal treatment by the Canadian state also cries out for redress in the form of recognition of native sovereignty. Nor should this recognition be viewed as completely impractical or as entailing the very destruction of the Canadian state.

## NOTES

1. For more detail on the international law aspects of this, see, for example, O. Dickason, "Concepts of Sovereignty at the Time of First Contact," in Dickason and Green, eds., *The Law of Nations and the New World* (Edmonton: University of Alberta Press, 1989).

2. For more examples of the failure of the policy of assimilation and native resistance to it, see, for example, Diane Engelstad and John Bird, eds., *Nation to Nation: Aboriginal Sovereignty and the Future of Canada* (Concord: House of Anansi Press, 1992).

# Native Sovereignty: Does Anyone Really Want an Aboriginal Archipelago?

*Thomas Flanagan*

"... words are wise men's counters, they do but reckon by them: but they are the money of fools...."

—Thomas Hobbes, *Leviathan* (1651), I, 4

In the spirit of Hobbes, before we can debate native sovereignty, we should be clear on what we are talking about. I have elsewhere defined sovereignty as "the authority to override all other authorities." More specifically, it is

> a bundle of powers associated with the highest authority of government. One is the power to enforce rules of conduct.... Another is the power to make law, [also the power of] raising revenue, maintaining armed forces, minting currency, and providing other services to society. Moreover, in the British tradition sovereignty implies an underlying ownership of all land. Finally, sovereignty always means the power to deal with the sovereigns of other communities as well as the right to exercise domestic rule free from interference by other sovereigns.[1]

That is the abstract meaning of sovereignty in the vocabulary of political science. In this sense, it is a conceptual property of the approximately 190 states that make up the international state system. Most of the entities that possess sovereignty belong to the United Nations or, like Switzerland, could belong if they should decide to apply for membership.

Sovereignty can only pertain to states. It makes no sense to speak of sovereignty unless there is, as in the classical definition of the state, an organized structure of government ruling over a population within defined territorial boundaries. Native societies in what is now Canada did not possess sovereignty before the coming of the Europeans; neither the concept nor the underlying institutions were part of the culture of their hunting-gathering societies. Of course, hunting-gathering societies have political processes that assign rank and dominance within communities and involve conflict between communities, but the political processes of stateless societies are not the same thing as statehood and sovereignty.

As a way of increasing their political leverage in contemporary Canada, native political leaders have adopted the classical language of statehood to describe their communities. What used to be called bands or tribes are now called "nations," and these nations are said to have possessed sovereignty from the beginning and to possess it still.[2] This strategic use of language has served native leaders well in their struggle for greater power within the Canadian polity, but politically effective assertions should not be confused with intellectually persuasive analysis.

When native leaders in Canada now claim to possess sovereignty, they typically mean one of three things, each of which is related to a particular political situation. In what follows, I will argue that all three of these meanings are incompatible with the continued existence of Canada and the maintenance of essential Canadian political traditions. It is not that words alone can destroy Canada; words in themselves do not accomplish anything. But words such as "native sovereignty" are the verbal symbols of political projects that cannot be reconciled with Canadian institutions.

1. Some native leaders, for example those from the Mohawk communities of Kahnawake and Kanesatake in Quebec, speak of sovereignty in the robust sense described above, that is, the international sense. They hold that the Mohawks on their territory constitute a sovereign, independent state not part of Canada or the United States. This sovereign state should be admitted to the United Nations and in other respects become part of the international community. A Mohawk elder told the Royal Commission on Aboriginal Peoples in March 1993: "You have no right to legislate any laws over our people whatsoever. Our lands are not yours to be assumed. You are my tenant, whether you like it or not."[3]

While I respect the honesty of this position, I do not take it seriously as a political proposition. In the ten provinces, Canada has over 600 Indian bands living on more than 2,200 reserves, plus hundreds of thousands of Métis and nonstatus Indians who do not possess reserves. These scattered pieces of land and disparate peoples are not going to be recognized as independent sovereign states, now or ever. They are simply not viable as sovereign states paying their own way and defending their interests in the international community. Nor is there any practical way to weld them into a single sovereign state. Native peoples are deeply divided by language, religion, customs, and history and in no way constitute a single people. They are not seeking emancipation from the tutelage of Indian Affairs in order to lose their identity in some supratribal bureaucracy.

2. The concept of sovereignty, as originally formulated by the philosophers Jean Bodin and Thomas Hobbes, was thought to be a set of powers located in a single seat of authority—perhaps the monarch, perhaps the Parliament, but in any case one sovereign. However, sovereignty can also be divided. Indeed, the classical definition of federalism implies a system of divided sovereignty, in which two levels of government each have shares of sovereign power guaranteed in a constitution that cannot be changed unilaterally by either level of government acting alone. In such a context, it is at least verbally meaningful to speak of giving native peoples a constitutionally entrenched share of sovereign authority.

This is more or less the political theory contained in the Charlottetown Accord. According to that document, "The Constitution should be amended to recognize that the Aboriginal peoples of Canada have the inherent right of self-government within Canada," and aboriginal self-governments should be recognized as "one of the three orders of government in Canada."[4] Although the terms federalism and sovereignty were not used, the most straightforward way to interpret the scheme proposed by the Charlottetown Accord is as an extension of divided sovereignty in a federal system from two to three levels. Although none of the details were worked out, the accord would have endowed aboriginal self-governments with many of the attributes of provinces: an entrenched constitutional basis of authority, participation in constitutional amendment procedures, representation in the Senate, a role in fiscal federalism, broad legislative jurisdiction, and so on.

This proposal cannot be dismissed on a priori grounds. There is no self-evident reason why federalism must be based on only two levels of government. Why not a "third order"? There are in fact many reasons why not, but they are more practical than conceptual.

First, as mentioned above, there are in Canada over half a million status Indians belonging to more than 600 bands on more than 2,200 reserves scattered across all ten provinces. No one has proposed a workable mechanism by which this far-flung archipelago could be knit together into a single political entity, or even a small number of such entities. On the contrary, it was widely assumed in the debate on the Charlottetown Accord that the focus of self-government would be the band, or perhaps small clusters of closely related bands organized into tribal councils. Indeed, one of the widely touted advantages of the third order of government is its alleged flexibility, which would allow different bands or groups of bands to have their own institutions of government, criminal justice systems, schools, and so on.

But surely realism must intervene at some point. We are talking about 600 bands with an average population of less than a thousand, mostly living on small, remote pieces of land without significant job opportunities, natural resources, or economic prospects. There would be virtually no revenue base, let alone the pool of human skills necessary to operate modern public services. How are such small, isolated, and impoverished groups of people supposed to support and operate an untried system of government incorporating a degree of complexity not seen since the medieval Holy Roman Empire?

However, this is only the initial objection. Hard as it would be to harmonize 2,200 reserves into a workable third order of government in a multitiered federal system, the problem is actually much more difficult than that. At any given time, more than half of Canada's status Indians live off reserve. They reside almost everywhere in the rest of Canada, from remote wilderness areas to the city centres of Vancouver, Toronto, and Montreal. Moreover, in addition to status Indians, there are perhaps another half million (the true number is impossible to ascertain) Métis and nonstatus Indians, that is, people of partly Indian ancestry who are not registered under the Indian Act but have some degree of identity as native people. A small number of Métis live in territorial enclaves (the Métis settlements of northern Alberta), but most are mixed in with the general population of Canada. Again, there is every conceivable kind of social situation. There are Métis hunters, trappers, and fishermen in the northern forests; Métis farmers on the Prairies; and Métis business owners, professionals, and workers in Winnipeg and other major cities.

How could one create a third order of government embracing all aboriginal people, as the Charlottetown Accord purported to do, when most of these people do not live in defined territories? Since no one, thank God, was talking of forcibly relocating populations to create separate territories, the only other approach would be to create a racially defined system of government for aboriginal people no matter where they live.

Now there is a historical model for such a system, namely the Ottoman Empire that ruled the Middle East and southeastern Europe from the 15th century until it was dismembered after the First World War. Throughout this immense territory, members of numerous Christian churches (Maronite, Coptic, Chaldean, Greek Orthodox, Armenian Orthodox, etc.) lived alongside the adherents of several Islamic sects (Sunni, Shi'ite, Druze, etc.). There were also important Jewish populations in most parts of the empire. All these ethno-religious communities were allowed a substantial degree of autonomy, including not only religious freedom but also their own systems of private law, so that matters such as marriage, family, and inheritance were regulated within their separate communities.

It was an admirable system in its way, ruling a colourful, polyglot population for five centuries—no mean achievement in itself. But I doubt it is a model Canadians want to imitate, for it was in no sense a democracy. There were no elections or other institutions of representative government. The sultan was theoretically an autocrat, but in fact rule was carried out by the imperial bureaucracy. The empire existed to collect taxes, keep internal order, and wage war against the neighbouring Persian, Russian, and Austro-Hungarian empires.

Like all liberal democracies, Canada is based on an entirely different set of political principles, most notably the twin concepts of the rule of law and equality under the law. The legal equality of all citizens is what makes democracy possible. As John Stuart Mill argued cogently in his *Considerations on Representative Government,* people cannot participate peacefully and cooperatively in one political system unless they feel themselves part of a single community: "Free institutions are next to impossible in a country made up of different nationalities."[5] A territorial definition of the polity is essential to this system of liberal democracy. Political and civil rights must be contingent on residence within a specific territory, not membership in a specific race or ethnic group.

Admittedly, Canada as a liberal democracy is challenged by the linguistic cleavage between English and French as well as the ethnic diversity of our aboriginal and immigrant population. But, at least prior to the Charlottetown Accord, the solutions toward which we groped were always liberal democratic ones based on legal equality within defined territorial jurisdictions. The French fact in Canada was recognized by creating the province of Quebec, which, although it happens to have a French majority, is a province similar in principle to all the others. Similarly, the contemporary Northwest Territories, although it has a native majority, is a territorial, not an ethnic polity. The same will be true of Nunavut if and when it comes into being. It will be a territory within which an Inuit majority will control a liberal democratic system of government; it will not be an Inuit ethnic polity.

The aboriginal self-government provisions of the Charlottetown Accord would have changed this by authorizing an ethnically defined third order of government to sprawl across existing territorial jurisdictions. It was a departure from, not an extension of, our federal system of liberal democracy. It is so incompatible with our system that it probably would not have worked at all. But to the extent that it had any effect, it would have encouraged the segmentation of native people. Wherever there were appreciable numbers of Indians and Métis in our cities, they would have been encouraged to develop their own schools, welfare agencies, justice systems, elective assemblies, and other paraphernalia of government. Instead of being encouraged to take advantage of the opportunities of Canada's urban society and economy, as so many immigrants from the Third World are now doing, native people would have been led to withdraw further into a world of imaginary political power and all too real dependence on transfer payments.

Finally, even if they could have been made to work in their own terms, the aboriginal self-government provisions of the Charlottetown Accord would have set up unacceptable pressures to create segmentary arrangements for other groups. In addition to setting up the third order of government across the country, the accord provided for unique aboriginal participation in national political institutions: aboriginal senators, possibly with a "double majority" veto over legislation on aboriginal matters[6]; aboriginal members of the House of Commons[7]; and aboriginal nominations to the Supreme Court as well as a special advisory role for an Aboriginal Council of Elders.[8] It would not have been long before other groups demanded similar treatment: women's organizations, visible minorities, the disabled, gays and lesbians, and so on. Indeed, demands of this type were heard during the referendum on the accord. Reservation of Senate seats for women was a major issue in certain provinces, notably British Columbia; and Joe Clark promised to revisit the situation of the disabled once the accord was passed. Even if Canada's liberal democracy could have survived the distinct society for Quebec and the third order of government for aboriginals, it could not survive if every identifiable group set out to entrench its political power in the Constitution. It would be the end of equality before the law, and ultimately of liberal democracy itself.

3. A third possible meaning of native sovereignty is the assertion that selected aspects of Canadian law, whether federal or provincial, simply do not apply to Indian bands or other native communities. There have now been many incidents of this type, for example, the assertion by Manitoba and Saskatchewan bands that, regardless of provincial legislation, they can run gambling casinos on their reserves. Now the application of provincial legislation to Indian reserves is a complex and contentious area of the law. The general principle formulated by Douglas Sanders, one of the pre-eminent experts in the field of native law, is this: "Provincial laws apply to Indian reserve lands if they do not directly affect the use of land, do not discriminate against them and are not in conflict with federal Indian legislation."[9] It may well be that the capricious way in which provinces exploit gambling for their own purposes while forbidding private entrepreneurs to enter the field conflicts with the Indian Act, with Section 91(24) of the Constitution Act, 1867, or some other constitutional protection of Indian rights. But this involves interpretation of the Canadian Constitution; it has nothing to do with assertions of native sovereignty. The appropriate remedy, as in fact seems likely to happen in Saskatchewan, is to seek an interpretation of the Constitution by bringing an action before the courts. Wrapping the issue in declarations of sovereignty only obscures the real question.

It is hardly consistent for Indian bands to continue to receive their full range of governmental benefits, including social assistance from provincial authorities, while maintaining that their "sovereignty" allows them to ignore provincial legislation whenever they choose. This self-contradictory position is an obvious nonstarter.

For the sake of clarity, let me repeat that I am not opposing the desire of Indian bands to open casinos on their reserves. Any form of legal entrepreneurship by anyone in Canada should be applauded (though there are serious concerns that in practice the gambling industry may tend to sprout criminal connections that will be as destructive for natives as for anyone else). My point is simply that, whatever the merits of Indians opening casinos on their reserves, it is not a matter of sovereignty.

Up to this point, the tone of my essay has been unavoidably negative, because I was asked to argue the negative side in a debate about native sovereignty. Let me take the opportunity in closing to state my views in a more positive way.

Status Indians in Canada have suffered terribly under the regime of the Indian Act and the Department of Indian Affairs. Bureaucratic socialism has been a failure wherever it has been tried, whether in Eastern Europe or North America. As quickly as possible, Indian bands should receive full ownership of their reserves, with the right to subdivide, mortgage, sell and otherwise dispose of their assets, including buildings, lands, and all natural resources. As much as possible, they should assume the self-government responsibilities of small towns or rural municipalities. What happens afterward should be up to them. This kind of devolution of power is already possible under federal legislation; it has taken place in a few cases, such as the Sechelt band of British Columbia, and is being negotiated by other bands across the country. It does not require an elaborate metaphysics of sovereignty.

However, a large and ever-increasing majority of native people do not live on reserves and never will, except for occasional visits. For this majority, neither self-government nor sovereignty can have any meaning except to the extent that they, as Canadian citizens, participate in the government of Canada. For them, the political illusion of self-government is a cruel deception, leading them out of, rather than into, the mainstream of Canadian life. Their future depends on fuller participation in the Canadian society, economy, and polity. They are, to all intents and purposes, internal immigrants, and for purposes of public policy their problems are fundamentally the same as those of other recent immigrants.

It is now twenty-five years since Pierre Trudeau became Prime Minister of Canada. One of his government's early projects was the famous White Paper on Indian affairs, which articulated an approach similar to the one stated here, namely to encourage the social, economic, and political integration of natives into Canadian society. Sadly (as I see it), native leaders totally rejected the White Paper and set off along the opposite path of emphasizing separate institutions and political power, pursuing the elusive goals of land claims, aboriginal rights, self-government, and sovereignty. As far as I can see, a quarter century of this political approach has produced hardly any beneficial results. There are more native politicians and lawyers than there used to be, but economic and social conditions seem not to have improved at all. We still read every day about unemployment rates of 90 percent on reserves, of Third World standards of housing and health, of endemic alcoholism, drug addiction, violence, and family breakdown.

What the black economist Thomas Sowell has written of the United States is equally true of Canada:

> Political success is not only relatively unrelated to economic advance, those minorities that have pinned their hopes on political action—the Irish and the Negroes, for example—have made some of the slower economic advances. This is in sharp contrast to the Japanese-Americans, whose political powerlessness may have been a blessing in disguise, by preventing the expenditure of much energy in that direction. Perhaps the minority that has depended most on trying to secure justice through political or legal processes has been the American Indian, whose claims for justice are among the most obvious and most readily documented.... In the American context, at least, emphasis on promoting economic advancement has produced far more progress than attempts to redress past wrongs, even when those historic wrongs have been obvious, massive, and indisputable.[10]

In the last analysis, the most harmful thing about the quest for sovereignty is the opportunity cost. The "brightest and best"—the leaders of native communities—are led to devote their talents to a cause that produces nothing except ever-growing levels of discontent and disappointment.

## NOTES

1. Mark O. Dickerson and Thomas Flanagan, *An Introduction to Government and Politics: A Conceptual Approach,* 3rd ed. (Scarborough: Nelson, 1990), pp. 35–36.

2. See Menno Boldt and J. Anthony Long, "Tribal Traditions and European-Western Political Ideologies: The Dilemma of Canada's Native Indians," *Canadian Journal of Political Science* 17 (1984): 537–53; Thomas Flanagan,

"Indian Sovereignty and Nationhood: A Comment on Boldt and Long," ibid., 18 (1985): 367–74; Boldt and Long, "A Reply to Flanagan's Comments," ibid., 19 (1986): 153.

3. Debbie Hum, "Ottawa Has No Right to Impose Its Law on Natives: Mohawk," *The Gazette* (Montreal), March 18, 1993.

4. Charlottetown Accord, Section 41.

5. John Stuart Mill, *Considerations on Representative Government* (Chicago: Henry Regnery, 1962; first published 1861), p. 309.

6. Charlottetown Accord, Section 9.

7. Section 22.

8. Section 20.

9. Douglas Sanders, "The Application of Provincial Laws," in Bradford W. Morse, ed., *Aboriginal Peoples and Law: Indian, Metis and Inuit Rights in Canada* (Ottawa: Carleton University Press, 1985), p. 453.

10. Thomas Sowell, *Race and Economics* (New York: David McKay, 1983), p. 128.

# POSTSCRIPT

The main purpose of the article by Olthuis and Townshend is to demonstrate that native claims to sovereignty have a strong historical and moral basis. Moreover, they argue that there is plenty of room to accommodate broader notions of native sovereignty that would not lead to the destruction of the Canadian state as Flanagan suggests. Nevertheless, even if we accept their argument, there still are a number of nagging practical questions that remain. Would all 573 tribal bands in Canada be given equal sovereign status? Or would sovereignty be granted to some kind of pan-Indian confederation? Would such a body constitute a third level of government as envisaged in the Charlottetown Accord? If sovereignty is recognized, and outstanding land claims resolved, would federal and provincial governments, preoccupied with deficit reduction measures, simply withdraw access to all services currently provided? Would small and dispersed Indian bands be able to fund and staff the social, economic, and governmental programs that self-government would necessitate?

One intriguing response to some of these questions has been put forward by Thomas Courchene and Lisa Powell in a volume entitled *A First Nations Province* (Kingston: Institute of Intergovernmental Affairs, 1992). They suggest that instead of creating a third order of government, a First Nations Province could be created that would represent native aspirations, providing the powers, institutions, and ability to carry out intergovernmental relations in largely the same manner as provinces presently do.

Not everyone sympathetic to native concerns feels that these demands should be pressed in terms of claims to sovereign statehood. For example, Menno Boldt and J. Anthony Long point out that sovereignty is really a Western European concept based on notions of territoriality and hierarchical authority that are foreign to traditional native culture. In their article "Tribal Traditions and European-Western

Political Ideologies: The Dilemma of Canada's Native Indians," *Canadian Journal of Political Science* 17, no. 3 (September 1984): 537–55, Boldt and Long argue that reliance on the concept of sovereignty has led many native leaders to reinterpret their own history in a selective way that actually legitimizes European-Western philosophies and conceptions of authority: "The legal-political struggle for sovereignty could prove to be a Trojan Horse for traditional Indian culture by playing into the hands of the Canadian government's long-standing policy of assimilation" (p. 548).

After having been ignored for so long, a number of excellent books on native issues have appeared in recent years. *Pathways to Self-Determination: Canadian Indians and the Canadian State,* edited by Leroy Little Bear, Menno Boldt, and J. Anthony Long (Toronto: University of Toronto Press, 1984) is a useful set of essays (many written by native leaders) for beginning to explore these issues. *Nation to Nation: Aboriginal Sovereignty and the Future of Canada,* edited by Diane Englestad and John Bird (Concord: House of Anansi Press, 1992) contains a series of thirty essays that deal with the issues surrounding sovereignty, land claims policy, and native/non-native relations. Also useful are the following volumes: J. Frideres, *Native People in Canada: Contemporary Conflicts,* 3rd ed. (Scarborough: Prentice-Hall, 1988) and B. Morse, *Aboriginal Peoples and the Law: Indian, Metis and the Inuit Rights in Canada* (Don Mills: Oxford, 1984).

Because of the key role of the Oka crisis in focusing Canadian attention on the native issue, students will find the following materials useful in exploring some of the issues surrounding these events: Robert Campbell and Leslie Pal, *The Real World of Canadian Politics,* 2nd ed. (Peterborough: Broadview Press, 1991) and Geoffrey York and Loreen Pindera, *People of the Pines: The Warriors and the Legacy of Oka* (Toronto: Little, Brown, 1991).

# PART TWO

## THE CONSTITUTION AND FEDERALISM

*Should individual rights take precedence over collective rights?*

*Is the Canadian Charter of Rights and Freedoms antidemocratic?*

*Should the federal government be strengthened?*

*Was the Charlottetown Accord good for Quebec?*

# ISSUE FIVE

## Should Individual Rights Take Precedence Over Collective Rights?

**YES** PIERRE TRUDEAU, "Values in a Just Society" in Tom Axworthy and Pierre Trudeau, eds., *Towards a Just Society* (Toronto: Penguin, 1990)

**NO** PAUL MARSHALL, "The Importance of Group Rights"

One of the most significant moments in the 1992 referendum campaign on the Charlottetown Accord took place in a working-class district of Montreal, in a Chinese restaurant with the quaint name "Maison Egg Roll." The journal *Cité Libre* had invited one of its founding editors, Pierre Trudeau, to address its invited guests on the subject of the Charlottetown Accord. As guests munched on Moo Goo Guy Pan, Trudeau launched into a withering critique of the accord, which many feel played a pivotal role in the subsequent defeat of the accord in the October referendum. In the weeks that followed, even those people—particularly in western Canada—who had been bitter critics of Trudeau during his years in government now cited his arguments in making their case against the accord.

What was it that Trudeau said that sparked such a responsive chord in Canadians? His argument was in fact a simple one: the Charlottetown Accord must be defeated because it creates a hierarchy of rights, in which each citizen's rights depend on the group to which he or she belongs and the place that group occupies in the "hierarchy of citizens."

In fact, what Trudeau was arguing against—the recognition of the legitimacy of group, or collective rights—has had a long history in Canada. The British North America Act (now the Constitution Act, 1867), gave special protection to the educational rights of certain denominational groups and to the language rights of the francophone minorities.

The distinctive legal traditions of Quebec were recognized and given protection through the composition of the Supreme Court in 1875. Special rights were accorded to the anglophone population of Quebec by entrenching the boundaries of twelve electoral districts with English-speaking majorities at the time of Confederation. (This provision was eliminated only in the 1960s.) When Newfoundland joined Canada in 1949, its denominational school system was given constitutional protection. And even the Constitution Act, 1982, brought in by the Trudeau government retains a recognition of distinct group rights and status. Language rights and the rights of aboriginal peoples were protected in the Canadian Charter of Rights and Freedoms. Section 15(2), the so-called "affirmative action" clause, permits special programs that are of advantage to those groups who have been previously disadvantaged. Even outside the constitutional sphere, Canadian governments have at times accommodated group differences. Quakers and Mennonites have had a long history of being granted an exemption from military service. Tax and educational laws have been modified at times to take into account the special circumstances of groups such as the Hutterites in western Canada who emphasize a collective communal style of life separate from the rest of society. Thus there is a long historical precedence for the kinds of accommodation set out in the Charlottetown Accord.

Despite this historical tradition, the reaction to Trudeau's speech reflects the extent to which the language of individual rights has come to dominate Canadian political discourse. Particularly since the implementation of the Charter of Rights and Freedoms, Canadians have come to see that equality is a fundamental principle of Canadian politics. Equality rights would seem by logical necessity to dictate that no distinctions be made among citizens whether on racial, linguistic, religious, cultural, or socioeconomic background. Thus requests for constitutional protection of certain designated minority groups appear to be nothing more than demands for special group privileges that threaten to undermine the very principle of individual equality.

But is this the case? Do collective rights necessarily threaten to undermine individual rights. In the following excerpts, Pierre Trudeau makes the case for an emphasis on individual rights, arguing that "when each citizen is not equal to all other citizens in the state, we are faced with a dictatorship, which arranges citizens in a hierarchy according to their beliefs." In response, Paul Marshall, a political theorist at the Institute for Christian Studies in Toronto, argues that emphasis on individual rights has been carried too far and that group rights need not necessarily pose a threat to individual rights.

# YES

## Values in a Just Society

*Pierre Trudeau*

... [I]t is no small matter to know whether we are going to live in a society in which personal rights, individual rights, take precedence over collective rights. It is no minor question of secondary importance to know whether we are going to live in a society in which all citizens are equal before the law and before the State itself. And it is no trivial matter to determine if there will be a spirit of brotherhood and of sharing in the society we are going to live in.

The choice we are going to make in the referendum, the choice of which society we want, has an impact on these three questions. And to know what choice to make, we have to look at the texts. I am not trying to say that those people who give preference to a collective society and collective rights over individual rights, do not have the right to state such a preference. I am saying to them that it is not just an emotional decision they are called on to make. We have to look at history—above all we have to look at contemporary history, the history of yesterday and today.

When collective rights take precedence over individual freedoms—as we see in countries where ideology shapes the collectivity, where race, ethnic origin, language, and religion shape the collectivity—we see what can happen to the people who claim to live freely in such societies. When each citizen is not equal to all other citizens in the state, we are faced with a dictatorship, which arranges citizens in a hierarchy according to their beliefs....[*]

The Constitution Act of 1982 was proclaimed on April 17. Essentially, it enshrined the values which, back in 1968, I had defined as those that should be respected in the constitution of a Just Society.

---

[*] Excerpt from Pierre Elliott Trudeau, *A Mess that Deserves a Big "No"* (Toronto: Robert Davies Publishing, 1993), pp. 11–12.

First, the principle of equal economic opportunity was stated in Section 36(1), under which "the government of Canada and the provincial governments undertake to promote equal opportunities for the well-being of all Canadians," and in Section 36(2), which guarantees the principle of equalization payments for the redistribution of revenues from wealthy provinces to the less wealthy ones. Further, Section 6 gives all Canadians the right to take up residence and earn their living anywhere in the country. And, of course, the federal government did not give up the powers it possessed under the old constitution concerning redistribution of wealth through subsidies and fiscal measures as well as through its general spending powers....

Secondly, the principle of equality of French and English in all domains of federal jurisdiction and in New Brunswick was guaranteed by Sections 16 to 20, while Section 23 guaranteed francophones and anglophones the right to education in their own language anywhere in Canada.

But the Canadian Charter of Rights and Freedoms went much further, of course. In the grand tradition of the 1789 Declaration of the Rights of Man and the Citizen and the 1791 Bill of Rights of the United States of America, it implicitly established the primacy of the individual over the state and all government institutions, and in so doing, recognized that all sovereignty resides in the people. (Provincial charters of rights cannot have this effect because they are simply laws and can be abrogated at any time merely through further legislation.) In this respect, the Canadian Charter was a new beginning for the Canadian nation: it sought to strengthen the country's unity by basing the sovereignty of the Canadian people on a set of values common to all, and in particular on the notion of equality among all Canadians.

Clearly, the very adoption of a constitutional charter is in keeping with the purest liberalism, according to which all members of a civil society enjoy certain fundamental, inalienable rights and cannot be deprived of them by any collectivity (state or government) or on behalf of any collectivity (nation, ethnic group, religious group or other). To use Maritain's phrase, they are "human personalities," they are beings of a moral order—that is, free and equal among themselves, each having absolute dignity and infinite value. As such, they transcend the accidents of place and time, and partake in the essence of universal Humanity. They are therefore not coercible by any ancestral tradition, being vassals neither to their race, nor to their religion, nor to their condition of birth, nor to their collective history.

It follows that only the individual is the possessor of rights. A collectivity can exercise only those rights it has received by delegation from its members; it holds them in trust, so to speak, and on certain conditions. Thus, the state, which is the supreme collectivity for a given territory, and the organs of the state, which are the governments, legislatures and courts, are limited in the exercise of their functions by the Charter and the Constitution in which the Charter is enshrined.

Indeed, the Charter specifies that the governments must meet Parliament or the legislatures at least once a year (Section 5); that Parliament and the legislatures must hold elections at least once every five years (Section 4); and that the courts may act only "in accordance with the principles of fundamental justice" (Sections 7 to 14).

## THE ROLE OF THE CHARTER

Thus, the individual is protected from the arbitrary authority of the state. But within a federal or provincial state, individuals may gather together in ethnic, linguistic, religious, professional, political or other collectivities, and delegate to this or that collectivity the task of promoting their collective interests. And since, in a democracy, governments receive their powers from the people by majority vote at elections, what is to prevent a majority from riding roughshod over the rights of a minority?

The answer, of course, is the Charter of Rights and Freedoms and the Constitution. They do this generally, by enshrining the rights of the individual members within minorities; but in certain instances, where the rights of individuals may be indistinct and difficult to define, they also enshrine some collective rights of minorities.

For example, the Canadian Constitution of 1867 provided that in educational matters, Section 93(1) would protect any "*Class* of Persons ... with respect to Denominational Schools," and Section 93(3) would apply to the "Protestant or Roman Catholic Minority."

Similarly, the Charter has clauses to protect certain minority collectivities whose interests could be overlooked in the conduct of the business of the state; this is what Sections 25 and 35 do for the "aboriginal peoples of Canada," and Section 27 for "the preservation and enhancement of the multicultural heritage of Canadians."

Section 93(2) of the 1867 Constitution, on the other hand, addresses individuals as such, in order to protect them: "Protestant and Roman Catholic *Subjects*." Likewise, Section 113 (language before the legislatures and courts) protects "*any* Person."

Except in the two cases I mentioned in the next-to-last paragraph, the Charter always seeks to define rights exclusively as belonging to a person rather than a collectivity: "everyone" (Sections 2, 7, 8, 9, 10, 12, 13), "every citizen of Canada" (Sections 3, 6) "any person charged with an offence" (Section 11), "any party or witness" (Section 14), "every individual" (Section 15), "anyone" (Section 24). It should be noted that this preference holds good even where the official languages are concerned; individuals, not linguistic groups, are ensured of their right to use either language: "everyone" (Section 17), "any person" (Section 19), "any member of the public" (Section 20), "citizens of Canada" (Section 23).

It is clear, then, that the spirit and substance of the Charter is to protect the individual against tyranny—not only that of the state but also any other to which the individual may be subjected by virtue of his belonging to a minority group. Section 15 of the Charter leaves no doubt: all are equal before the law and are entitled to the same protection "without discrimination based on race, national or ethnic origin, colour, religion, sex, age or mental or physical disability."

The reason for this approach is evident. Canada is by nature pluralist—"a mosaic" as Laurier put it—not an American-style melting pot. The Canadian nation is composed of citizens who belong to minorities of many kinds: linguistic, ethnic, racial, religious, regional and so on. Throughout the negotiations leading to the Charter in 1982, our government kept in mind that Canadian history has consisted of a difficult advance toward a national unity that is still fragile and is often threatened by intolerance—the intolerance of the English-speaking majority toward francophones, the intolerance of whites toward the indigenous populations and non-white immigrants, intolerance toward political and religious dissidents such as Communists and Jehovah's Witnesses.

If we had tried to identify each of the minorities in Canada in order to protect all the characteristics that made them different, not only would we have been faced with an impossible task, but we would shortly have been presiding over the balkanization of Canada. The danger inherent in this would have been particularly acute in the case of minorities that are in a position to be identified with a given territory, like the Celts in Nova Scotia, the Acadians in New Brunswick, the French Canadians in Quebec and the Indians and Inuit in the Far North.

This is why Sections 25 and 37 on the aboriginal peoples and Section 27 on multiculturalism avoid any identification of these collectivities with a particular government. Thus, throughout our negotiations with the aboriginal peoples, we refused to talk about "self-determination," and only envisaged the possibility of "self-government" on condition that a heterogeneous population might still live in a given territory.

The case of the collectivity referred to as French Canadians demanded particularly close attention, since the tensions between anglophones and francophones have always been the major source of disunity in Canada. And we were very aware that Quebec nationalist thinking tends both to identify the interests of the French-Canadian collectivity with the province of Quebec and to confuse language with ethnicity, which gives rise to expressions like "the two founding nations of Canada" and "Quebec, the national state of French Canadians." Thus, on May 22, 1963, the Legislative Assembly of Quebec voted unanimously to give itself a mandate to determine "the objectives to be pursued by *French Canada* in the revision of the constitution of Canada, and the best means of obtaining these objectives."

At the time, I was opposed to this approach for several reasons, the most important being that "a state that defined its function essentially in terms of ethnic attributes would inevitably become chauvinistic and intolerant. The state, whether provincial, federal or perhaps later supra-national, must seek the general welfare of all its citizens regardless of sex, colour, race, religious beliefs, or ethnic origin."

Shortly after I wrote this, my friends and I entered federal politics for the precise purpose of proving that French Canadians could be at home in Canada outside Quebec and could exercise their rights in the federal capital and throughout the country. This was also the purpose of the Official Languages Act and of the emergence of what the English-speaking press was soon calling "French power."

The separatists of both Quebec and the West well understood what was happening. Conscious that their ultimate goal presupposed an exclusively English-speaking Canada and an exclusively French-speaking Quebec, they abandoned their minorities in other provinces—French-speaking and English-speaking—and fought tooth and nail against the policy of bilingualism, which in their terms was the work of traitors and double-dealers.

As for the Quebec nationalists, the Quiet Revolution had given them the means to be full-fledged Canadians but also a desire to be not exactly Canadian. Now they were dancing a hesitation waltz, flitting from "special status" to "equality or independence"; from "cultural sovereignty" to "profitable federalism" (profitable or else...).

In answer to our federal law proclaiming English and French to be the official languages everywhere in Canada, Mr. Bourassa saw fit to reply with a provincial law declaring that French alone would be the official language in Quebec—and he observed later that Quebec's self-determination was still an option in his party's platform.

Taking a stand in opposition to the federal policy of bilingualism meant shifting the political debate in Quebec to the only ground on which the separatist party had an advantage over Mr. Bourassa. So, in 1976, a Péquiste government was elected and in due course held a referendum, in which that government asked for a mandate to make Quebec a sovereign country.

Two months after the federalist victory in the referendum, we presented the provinces with a draft charter that would embody a set of values common to all Canadians. Language rights were assigned directly to individuals rather than collectivities. And the reader will understand why, in the lengthy negotiations that followed, we rejected any proposal whose effect would have been to identify a linguistic collectivity (French Canadians) with the government of a province (Quebec).

What we were seeking was the individual himself to have the *right* to demand his choice of French or English in his relationships with the federal government, and the *right* to demand a French or English education for his children from a provincial government. And the individual himself would have access to the courts to enforce these rights.

This is not to say that we were denying the importance of a linguistic community in the defence and advancement of the language spoken by its members. However, it seemed clear to us that these matters would never be settled unless the *individual* language rights of each person were enshrined in the constitution of the country, since the English-speaking community would always outnumber the French-speaking in Canada.

Our approach was indisputably more effective and more respectful of the dignity of Canadians. However, it made things awkward for Quebec nationalist politicians because it made them largely redundant; the moment the survival of "the race" no longer depended on them, their racist preachings became superfluous. So they fought the Charter with much sound and fury and racked their brains for some ploy that would allow Quebec to elude its authority. Years were to pass before they hit upon the "distinct society" formula for interpreting the Charter—and a Canadian prime minister ready to accept it.

But that is another story....

# The Importance of Group Rights

*Paul Marshall*

It is common, especially in the United States, to speak about politics largely in terms of "the government and the individual." In the last few decades this way of thinking of people solely as individuals has more and more affected Canada. Indeed, many Canadians have lost the sense that there is any other way to speak about politics. For such people, individuals are all that exist. For them, all groups are really just collections of individuals, and all supposed group rights ultimately boil down to individual rights. The way to protect the culture of French Canada would be by protecting the language rights of individual French Canadians. If francophones were secure in their individual identity, then their language and culture would naturally survive. Similarly if we would protect native people by protecting the rights of each individual native person, then native culture and traditions would be protected. If everyone in the country were able to exercise their rights, then both their own lives and the life of their communities would flourish.

But despite the fact that this way of viewing the world is so widespread, it thrives only by ignoring or denying certain fundamental realities about the world in general and about Canada in particular. One of the most striking examples of this denial occurred early in Mr. Trudeau's tenure as prime minister. In 1969 his Liberal government introduced a White Paper on the treatment of native peoples. The White Paper sought to treat native rights in the same way as those of other Canadians. Its ostensible purpose was to liberate native peoples. It maintained that their desperate situation was due to the fact that they had been victims of discrimination for many years. It proposed to solve this problem by abolishing all such "discrimination." It would abolish their special legal status with the hoped-for result that they would have no more and no less rights than any other Canadian. It believed that native peoples would then be able to take their equal place in Canadian society and so fulfil their destiny.

The native people's overwhelming and nearly unanimous response was to reject the White Paper. Their rejection was based on the fact that they see themselves not in terms of individual rights, but in terms of community life. Their landholding is not in terms of individual ownership, but in terms of collective use. Their traditional way of decision-making involves reaching consensus rather than counting majorities on one side or another. For the natives, the key right is self-government, the ability to run their own community life. This is something that cannot be dealt with simply in terms of individual rights: it is something that can only pertain to a people as a whole. Native reaction to the White Paper was so intense that it galvanized them into intensive political action and itself became a major factor in the new drive for self-government. This reaction caused Mr. Trudeau and the Liberal government to back away from the White Paper. In so doing he said:

> I'm sure we were very naive in some of the statements we made in the paper. We had perhaps the prejudices of small "l" liberals and white men at that time who thought that equality meant the same law for everybody, and that's why as a result of this we said "well let's let Indians dispose of their lands like every other Canadian. And let's make sure that Indians can get their rights, education, health and so on from the governments like every other Canadian." But we have learnt in the process that perhaps we were a bit too theoretical, we were a bit too abstract.[1]

This example illustrates the point that Canada cannot simply be thought of as a collection of individual persons. Rather, it is comprised of cultures, groups, associations, and institutions. There is cultural and ethnic diversity, a plurality brought about by French, English, and many other languages, varied subcultures, many native bands and nations, diverse schools and educational systems, a wide spectrum of religions and denominations. Over two-thirds of Canadians are members of voluntary associations. There are tens of thousands of such associations including churches, political parties, trade unions, cultural groups, cooperatives, academic associations, and public interest organizations. These are not merely private arrangements. They are central to the public life of the country. Indeed, in some ways they are the public life of the country.

This is not only a Canadian phenomenon. Hardly any country in the world is culturally homogeneous. They nearly all encompass a wide variety of language, ethnic, racial, and religious groups and organizations. These groups are not just private arrangements or purely incidental matters. They are important not only for personal lives, but also for public life. They need to be recognized and accommodated in concrete political arrangements. Sometimes the relations between such groups are violent and vicious, as in the breakup of the former Yugoslavia and the subsequent wars in Croatia and Bosnia-Herzegovina. Sometimes group claims and demands are really a cover for racist, fascist, or communist goals. They can produce bigotry and prejudice, persecution and civil war. People's communal life is a dangerous thing and always needs to be treated carefully.

However, the dangers of group identity should not drive us to futile and repressive attempts to eradicate it from politics, but to deal with it responsibly and justly. And, despite tensions, many countries have found creative and tolerant ways of recognizing groups as well as individuals and have thus allowed their diverse communities to live together in comparative peace and respect. One of the principal ways of doing this is by means of group rights. Essentially what this means is that instead of treating every person as if he or she were the same for legal purposes, we should try to develop rights in such a way that we do justice to communal differences. This can happen either by giving rights to members of some groups that are not held by members of other groups, or else by giving rights not just to the members, but to the group itself as a collectivity. Hence, because of the way native people relate to their land and community, they may need rights to the land and to hunt and fish that others need not have, and they may need to exercise collective self-government as a band or tribe.

These types of rights are often viewed with great suspicion, especially by those with an ideological commitment to an individualistic view of the world. In Canada many critics of the Meech Lake Accord of 1987–90 and of the Charlottetown Accord of 1992 believed, like Pierre Trudeau, that the commitment to group rights contained in these proposals necessarily meant that they were unjust and prejudiced. In more extreme instances there has been a tendency to categorize *any* concern for group rights as a type of incipient fascism that needs to be both rejected and fought.[2]

But both in Canada and throughout the world these types of rights often are means not of exclusion and control, but of mutual respect and harmony. Examples of this can be found all over the world: in Europe and North America as well as in the Third World.[3] For example, the Aaland Islands are a part of Finland, but most of their inhabitants speak only Swedish. The islanders are afraid that since they are a very small minority their language and culture could easily be swamped by the surrounding Finnish speakers. In order to protect the islanders, the government of Finland has passed laws that restrict the ability of nonislanders to buy land or houses in Aaland. Consequently, Swedish speakers are likely to remain a majority in the islands for the foreseeable future, and so their culture is likely to be preserved. Clearly this law makes a distinction between two types of Finns. Some Finns, the islanders, have rights to buy land in Aaland that other Finns do not have. But the purpose and effect of the law is not to maintain a privileged group, but rather to protect a culture that would otherwise be swamped.

The original inhabitants of New Zealand are called Maoris. They often suffered discrimination from the immigrating European population. As more Europeans continued to arrive, the Maoris eventually numbered only about 5 percent of the population. While some of these original inhabitants have assimilated, they still tend to have patterns of life distinct from that of the larger society. Furthermore, since they are not concentrated in any one area of the country, they did not have much weight in the voting system. In a voting system similar to the one in Canada it would be very difficult for a Maori to be elected. In order to combat this problem, New Zealand initiated two separate voter lists: one for Maoris and one for others. Maoris vote for the four seats that have been set aside for them; others vote for the remaining eighty-three seats. In this way Maoris always have seats in Parliament roughly proportional to their numbers in the wider society.

India faces major problems with languages. It has 281 of them, many more if we also count those that are spoken by less than 5,000 people. The government simply cannot provide services in all of these languages. Over the years it has struggled to balance the need to be fair to all the language groups with the need to save costs in a poor country. It has decided to make Hindi (the largest language group) and English the "official languages of the Union" and also to allow each state (province) to choose its own official language or languages. Meanwhile the government commits itself to try to provide basic education in all languages and gives a guarantee to each group that it has the right to "conserve" its language. These seem reasonable and perhaps even the best measures to take in a difficult situation. But we should note that even the best measures necessarily mean that some languages and, of course, those who speak these languages, are being given opportunities denied to others.

In Belgium language rights vary according to which region of the country one is in. Switzerland is similar. The list could go on and on, but the basic point is this: group rights are not some peculiar feature of totalitarian or authoritarian regimes. They are not holdovers from some previous less enlightened age. They are not necessarily expressions of prejudice or bigotry (though, of course, some can be: no part of politics is immune to perversion). They are present in most countries of the world: western as well as eastern, democratic as well as authoritarian. They are widespread and accepted measures to preserve and enhance community life and harmony.

These approaches do not flourish despite international pressure for more uniform human rights. The opposite in fact. The international regime of human rights explicitly recognizes and reinforces many of these approaches.[4] The United Nations itself tries to recognize group rights within its own structure. For example, it gives different status to the different languages of its member countries. Of all the different languages, it selects only some as "official" and some others as "working" languages. The rest do not have official UN status. The organization simply cannot afford to operate in all the languages of the world.

The United Nations recognizes the importance of group rights in its member nations. When it developed its provisions on the treatment of minorities it defined minorities as "non-dominant groups which, while wishing in general for equality of treatment with the majority, wish for a measure of differential treatment in order to preserve basic characteristics which … distinguish them from the majority of the population."

The major international treaties on human rights give formal recognition to this concern. The Genocide Convention forbids not only actions against individuals *within* a threatened group, but also against the *group itself*. It forbids transferring children out of a threatened group (by adoption, for instance) lest the culture itself be gradually undercut. Hence rights of adoption vary depending on which group one belongs to.

More recently the *International Convention on the Elimination of All Forms of Racial Discrimination* defined racial discrimination as "any discrimination, exclusion, restriction or preference based on race, colour, descent, or national or ethnic origin which has the purpose or effect of nullifying or impairing the recognition, enjoyment or exercise, on an equal footing, of human rights and fundamental freedoms in the political, economic, social, cultural or any other field of public life." It is not the simple fact of discrimination that is crucial. It is the purpose and effect of the discrimination. Any measures that impair the enjoyment of human rights are forbidden; any that enhance the enjoyment of human rights are allowed. The *International Convention on the Elimination of All Forms of Racial Discrimination* makes a similar provision. Racial discrimination does not include "special measures taken for the sole purpose of securing adequate advancement of certain racial or ethnic groups requiring … protection."

This widespread international pattern is also followed in Canada. Canada's principal constitutional document before the constitutional changes of 1982 was the British North America Act of 1867.[5] Section 93 of this act stipulated that the provinces could not "prejudicially affect any Right or Privilege with respect to Denominational Schools." This meant that Catholics and Protestants had a constitutionally entrenched right to schools reflecting their beliefs. Similarly, when Newfoundland joined Canada in 1949 it had five denominational school systems: Roman Catholic, United Church, Anglican, Pentecostal, and Salvation

Army. The arrangements for admitting Newfoundland included guaranteed constitutional protection for this system.

Both of these constitutional guarantees were kept in the new provisions of the Constitution Act, 1982. Nor did this act simply maintain group rights because they were impossible to change. It reaffirmed them and in fact introduced new provisions for group rights. Section 15(2) allows governments to develop programs to help particular disadvantaged groups, even though such programs would treat people in different groups in very different ways. The Constitution Act, 1982, also gives particular language rights to the speakers of two languages—French and English (Sections 16 to 23 of the Charter of Rights and Freedoms). These languages have official status; others do not. The reasons for this are that these are the languages of the founding communities, and moreover, they are the most widespread. These are good reasons and I support the policy. But we should not hide from ourselves the fact that we are giving advantages to some language groups rather than to others. Meanwhile, Sections 25, 35, and 37 recognize the rights of aboriginal peoples, and Section 27 calls for interpretations consistent with "multiculturalism." In short, Canada is still finding it necessary to establish rights for groups as well as for individuals.

In commenting on this, the majority of the Ontario Court of Appeal said that "the Constitution of Canada ... has from the beginning provided for group collective rights.... As Professor Hogg ... has expressed it: these provisions amount to 'a small bill of rights.' The provisions of this 'small bill of rights,' now expanded as to ... language rights ... constitute a major difference from a bill of rights such as that of the United States, which is based on individual rights. Collective or group rights, such as those concerning language and those concerning certain denominations to separate schools, are asserted by individuals or groups of individuals *because of* their membership in certain ascertainable groups. Individual rights are asserted equally by everyone *despite* membership in certain ascertainable groups."[6]

A common criticism of these types of observations, one offered by Mr. Trudeau himself, is to agree that collective rights are important and should be protected, but to insist that they should never override individual rights. Only if there is no threat to individual rights should collective concerns and collective rights then be considered. While Mr. Trudeau thinks that both types of rights have a place, he asserts that individual rights must always have priority. He believes that unless this happens the result will be oppressive. One of the principal reasons he argued so strenuously against the Meech Lake Accord and the Charlottetown Accord was that he thought each agreement gave some priority to collective rights over individual rights. His criticism was so effective that it actually became a factor in helping to defeat these constitutional proposals.

In many cases, this criticism is undoubtedly correct. Some funda-mental rights, such as the right to life, should never be subordinated to any collective interest that does not itself involve protecting someone's life. A group cannot demand that human life be sacrificed to its benefit. But for many other individual rights there is no automatic priority. In most cases there is more than one right at stake, and one does not sim-ply override another. Usually courts have to try to balance them in some way. A famous example of this conflict occurred in Canada in the *Love-lace* case several years ago. The Indian Act, the law governing Indian people in Canada, allowed a form of discrimination against women. If an Indian woman married a non-Indian man then she lost her legal sta-tus as an Indian. But this regulation did not apply to Indian men who married non-Indians. Women's groups, including native women's groups, protested this situation. Many native leaders acknowledged that there was a problem, but they objected that white people were once again trying to impose their own view from the outside instead of letting native people work out their own solutions. The result was a conflict of group and individual rights, between the right of native peoples to gov-ern themselves and the rights of native women to have an equal status with native men. As Marc Lalonde put it: "Discrimination against women is a scandal but imposing the cultural standards of white society would be another scandal."[7]

In this instance, it was the individual rights that eventually won out. Nevertheless, this does not support the claim that they should *always* do so. Rather, it shows that the conflict is very real and that there are two important things that are *together* being weighed in the balance. In differ-ent instances either a group interest or an individual one might win out, depending on how important the particular rights are in the particular instance. In cases such as native self-government in general, or native fishing and hunting rights, then the collective rights of native people have won out. Natives can hunt and fish in ways and at times that non-natives cannot. They have rights to self-government that others do not. They have rights to land that others do not. In all these cases a group right has won out over various individual claims to nondiscrimination. Similarly, in the case of denominational schools, the collective rights of Catholics to have schools that reflect their religious beliefs have won out over individual claims to have all schools give equal access to people regardless of their beliefs. In these different issues one or the other type of right may legitimately have priority. There is no automatic procedure where one or the other must always necessarily be successful. It is a case of trying to deal with both of them together. But what this means is that we must always be prepared to recognize group rights and when neces-sary to give them priority over individual rights.

I have argued that Canada must be understood not only in terms of individual people, but also in terms of the groups and communities in which these people live. These groups may need to be protected by recognizing that they have rights as groups. While individual rights can never be ignored or dismissed, at times they may need to be overridden by important group rights. Such recognition is not a violation of human rights, but is an internationally known and respected human rights practice, and one that is also firmly rooted in Canadian history and legal practice. As we consider future constitutional amendments or any other arrangements for our living together in Canada, we cannot assume that all group claims are necessarily valid. But neither can we accept the view that no group right is valid, nor the view that they can never override individual rights. We must be open to either claim, and in the diverse circumstances that our political life produces group rights will often take priority.

## NOTES

1. Quoted in Sally M. Weaver, *Making Canadian Indian Policy: The Hidden Agenda, 1968–1970* (Toronto: University of Toronto Press, 1981), p. 185.

2. See, for example, the widely used work by Paul Sieghart, *The Lawful Rights of Mankind: An Introduction to the International Legal Code of Human Rights* (Oxford: Oxford University Press, 1986), pp. 163ff.

3. Most of the following examples are taken from Vernon Van Dyke's *Human Rights, Ethnicity and Discrimination* (Westport: Greenwood Press, 1985).

4. See the examples given in Natan Lerner, *Group Rights and Discrimination in International Law* (Dordrecht: Martinus Nijhoff, 1991).

5. For Canadian examples, see Michael McDonald, "Should Communities Have Rights? Reflections on Liberal Individualism," pp. 133–61 in A.A. Anna'im, *Human Rights in Cross-Cultural Perspective* (Philadelphia: University of Pennsylvania Press, 1992).

6. *Reference Re An Act to Amend the Education Act*, 53 Ontario Reports 566.

7. Quoted in Michael McDonald, "Indian Status: Colonialism or Sexism?" presented to Collective Rights Symposium, University of Ottawa, March 1985, p. 26.

# P O S T S C R I P T

For most of us raised in a political culture that emphasizes liberal individualism, the assertion of individual rights and freedoms appears to be a central component of what liberal democracy is all about. Nevertheless, Vernon Van Dyke, in "Justice as Fairness: For Groups?" *American Political Science Review* 69 (1973): 607–14, provides evidence supportive of Marshall's argument that the assertion of individual rights can often undermine and even destroy certain linguistic, ethnic, and religious communities.

The concept of group rights as it relates to liberal democratic traditions can be further explored in Michael McDonald, "Collective Rights and Tyranny," *University of Ottawa Review* 56 (1986): 115–23, and Vernon Van Dyke, "Collective Entities and Moral Rights: Problems in Liberal Democratic Thought," *Journal of Politics* 44 (1982): 21–40.

In the past, before the entrenchment of the Charter of Rights and Freedoms, the task of reconciling the competing claims of individual and group rights was largely the responsibility of the federal and provincial legislatures. As a result, governments were able to pursue a pragmatic mixture of policies designed to mitigate the tensions between the two competing demands. With the adoption of the Charter, and the subsequent emphasis on the language of individual rights, the difficulty in resolving the tensions between individual and collective rights has become more complex. This is especially apparent in regard to the issues of native rights and language rights. For two essays that deal with these specific issues, see F.L. Morton, "Group Rights Versus Individual Rights in the Charter: The Special Cases of Natives and the Québécois," in Neil Nevitte and Allan Kornberg, eds., *Minorities and the Canadian State* (Oakville: Mosaic Press, 1985) and K.Z. Patel, "Group Rights in the Canadian Constitution and Aboriginal Claims to Self-Determination," in

Robert Jackson, Doreen Jackson, and Nicolas Baxter-Moore, eds., *Contemporary Canadian Politics: Readings and Notes* (Scarborough: Prentice-Hall, 1987).

# ISSUE SIX

**YES  ROBERT MARTIN,** "The Canadian Charter of Rights and Freedoms Is Antidemocratic and Un-Canadian"

**NO  PHILIP L. BRYDEN,** "The Canadian Charter of Rights and Freedoms Is Antidemocratic and Un-Canadian: An Opposing Point of View"

Do terminally ill patients have the right to a doctor-assisted suicide? Should women have unrestricted access to abortion without fear of criminal penalty? Does freedom of expression include the right to produce and distribute pornography? Are Sunday shopping regulations a violation of freedom of religion? All of these questions raise difficult issues regarding the relationship between individual citizens and their government. In essence they each pose the same question: What civil rights does an individual have and how are they to be protected from the intrusive arm of the state?

In choosing to establish a system of parliamentary government on the "Westminster model," the founders of Canada adopted a British solution to this problem. Parliament would be supreme and would act as the ultimate guarantor of individual rights and freedoms. This solution reflects an implicit trust in both Parliament and the basic democratic values of civil society. It assumes that civil liberties are so deeply engrained in the national political culture that parliamentarians and citizens alike would never seriously consider using the power of government to infringe upon them. Public opinion and tradition would act as a powerful constraint against any violation of the fundamental civil and political liberties that are considered to be an inherent part of a democratic system. With the establishment of a federal system in Canada, courts were given the task of deciding whether federal and provincial legislatures were acting within their respective jurisdictions, not whether their actions violated civil and political liberties. There was no perceived need to give such rights special judicial protection that put them outside the reach of legislators.

Not everyone was happy with this solution. They pointed to a long history of both provincial and federal governments' trampling of the rights of citizens. In the early part of this century, British Columbia passed laws denying Asians the right to vote in provincial elections. During the Second World War the federal government arbitrarily seized the property of Japanese Canadians and placed them in internment camps without due process of law.

These experiences, and others, convinced many Canadians that greater protection of civil rights was needed. The Americans provided an alternative solution: define the rights of citizens in a written constitutional document that is beyond the reach of the legislature. The courts, through the power of judicial review, can then pass judgment on whether the legislation passed by a government infringes on civil liberties. John Diefenbaker began to move Canada in this direction in 1960, when his government passed the Canadian Bill of Rights. But this bill was simply an Act of Parliament and applied only to the federal government. As a result, Canadian courts made only limited use of the Bill of Rights.

With the adoption of the Canadian Charter of Rights and Freedoms as part of a larger constitutional package, the government of Pierre Trudeau brought in a new era in 1982. With the entrenchment of the Charter into the Canadian Constitution, Canadians were not only given an explicit definition of their rights, but the courts were empowered to rule on the constitutionality of government legislation.

There is little doubt that the adoption of the Charter has significantly transformed the operation of the Canadian political system. Since its adoption, the Supreme Court of Canada has been involved in virtually every issue of any great political significance in Canada. As a result, there has been a growing public awareness about the potential "political" role that the Supreme Court now plays in the lives of ordinary Canadians. Increasingly, Canadians define their needs and complaints in the language of rights. More and more, interest groups and minorities are turning to the courts, rather than the usual political processes, to make their grievances heard. Peter Russell has described the dramatic impact of the Charter on Canadian politics as having "judicialized politics and politicized the judiciary."

Has the impact of the Charter been a positive one? Has the Charter lived up to its promise to enhance Canadian democracy through the protection of civil liberties? Robert Martin, a law professor at the

University of Western Ontario, feels that the impact of the Charter has been largely a negative one. In particular, he argues that the Charter has had an antidemocratic effect on the country and has accelerated the Americanization of Canada. In contrast, Philip Bryden, Associate Dean of the Faculty of Law at the University of British Columbia, argues that the Charter plays an essential role in protecting and enhancing the quality of Canadian democracy.

# The Canadian Charter of Rights and Freedoms Is Antidemocratic and Un-Canadian

*Robert Martin*

## INTRODUCTION

On April 17, 1982, the Canadian Charter of Rights and Freedoms became part of our Constitution. Everyone who has written about the Charter agrees its effect has been to change profoundly both our politics and the way we think. Most of the commentators have applauded these changes. I do not.

I believe the Charter has had decidedly negative effects on Canada. It has contributed to an erosion of our democracy and of our own sense of ourselves. It is time for a serious and critical stock-taking.

Let me be clear that I am not suggesting the Charter itself has actually *done* any of this. A central problem with the Charter has been its contribution to our growing inability to distinguish between the concrete and the abstract. The Charter is simply words on a piece of paper. What I will be addressing are the uses to which the Charter has been put by human beings. I will look at the antidemocratic effects of the Charter and then turn to an analysis of its un-Canadian character.

## THE CHARTER IS ANTIDEMOCRATIC

By their nature, constitutions express a fear of democracy, a horror that the people, if given their head, will quickly become a mindless mob. As a result, constitutions, all constitutions, place enforceable limitations on the powers of the state and, more particularly, on the lawmaking authority of the people's representatives.

Prior to 1982 the Canadian Constitution did contain such limitations. Our central constitutional document, the British North America Act of 1867, divided lawmaking authority between Parliament and the provincial legislatures and, thereby, limited that authority. But these limitations were purely functional. The authority to make laws about education, for example, rested with the provinces. Ottawa could not make laws about education, and if it attempted to do so, the attempt could be struck down by the courts. The courts had no authority to tell the provinces how to exercise their authority over education, to tell them what kind of laws they should make about education.

This is what changed in 1982. The federal division of powers remained, but for the first time substantive limitations were placed on lawmaking authority. The judges were given the power to strike down laws that, in their opinion, were inconsistent with the Charter.

It is crucial to understand basic distinctions between legislators and judges. Any Canadian citizen over the age of 18 is eligible to be elected to Parliament or a provincial legislature. Elected members are directly accountable to their constituents. They must face re-election at least once every five years. By way of contrast, to become a senior judge in Canada you must be a lawyer and you must have been one for ten years. You are appointed until age 75 through a closed process that a former chief justice of Canada described as "mysterious," and you are made constitutionally independent, directly accountable to no one.

The defining feature of representative democracy in Canada has been that it is up to the elected members of our legislatures to resolve issues of social, economic, and political policy, subject, of course, to the approval or disapproval of the people expressed at periodic elections. This has changed since the adoption of the Charter. Judges can now overturn deliberate policy decisions made by the elected representatives of the people where those decisions do not accord with the way the judges interpret the Charter. This is undemocratic. Some of our commentators call this "counter-majoritarian," but the phrase is pure obfuscation.

We seem to be experiencing great difficulty today in grasping this simple truth about the antidemocratic nature of judicial review of legislation. One explanation for our difficulty is that we have forgotten that liberalism and democracy are not the same thing. Liberalism is about individual rights, about the ability of individuals to do as they please without interference from the state. Liberalism makes protection of the autonomy of the individual more important than the promotion of the welfare of the collectivity. Democracy is, and always has been, about the interests of the collectivity, about majority rule, about power to the people.

There is an inherent and irreconcilable tension between liberalism and democracy. This tension has always been built into our political system, a system that is ordinarily described as liberal democracy.

The Charter is a liberal document. It sets out fundamental notions about the rights of the individual that have always been at the core of liberalism. More to the point, the Charter has led to a shift in emphasis in

Canadian liberal democracy. The balance has been tilted in favour of liberalism and away from democracy.

Members of the judiciary, led by the Supreme Court of Canada, have shown little restraint in arrogating to themselves a central policy-making role. In 1984 they conferred upon themselves the distinction "guardian of the Constitution." They haven't looked back.

Our judges have not hesitated to substitute their views of acceptable or desirable social policy for those of our legislators. When the judges have not agreed with the policy decisions of our elected representatives they have invalidated the legislation that expresses those decisions. But the judges have been prepared to go further. They have shown themselves willing to write legislation, to even go to the point of imposing financial obligations on the state.

The willingness to interfere with the traditional policy-making functions of legislatures has not been restricted to the courts. Administrative tribunals now sit in judgment on the validity of legislation, and boards of inquiry set up under human rights acts rewrite legislation and create new legal responsibilities for individuals.

We have become more and more inclined to seek to resolve the central questions agitating our society in the courtroom, rather than through the political process. The result of this is to surrender control of the social agenda and of public discourse to lawyers.

In a similar vein, the Charter has given a great boost to interest group politics. Indeed, an active judicial role and interest group politics seem made for each other.

Interest group politics is antidemocratic in two respects. It erodes citizenship, the essential precondition to democratic politics. People are induced to define themselves according to their race or sex or sexual preference or some other ascriptive criterion, rather than as citizens. And, in practice, interest group politics has meant seeking to use the courts as a means of short-circuiting or bypassing democratic processes.

The Charter has thus, in an institutional sense, had an antidemocratic effect. But it has also reinforced ideological currents that are antidemocratic. The most important of these stem from our growing obsession with "rights."

Our fascination with rights has been central to a process through which we seem to have come to prefer the abstract over the concrete. "Rights" appear to be more attractive than real things such as jobs or pensions or physical security or health care. We have been persuaded that if we have "rights" and these "rights" are enshrined in a constitution, then we need not concern ourselves with anything else. It is difficult to describe as "democratic" a public discourse that avoids addressing actual social and economic conditions.

Rights discourse itself encourages antidemocratic tendencies. The inclination of persons to characterize their desires or preferences as "rights" has two unfortunate results. First, there is an inevitable polarization of opposing positions in any debate. And, second, the possibility of further discussion is precluded. If you assert that something is your "right," my only possible response is, "No, it isn't."

Finally, the interest in rights has done much to promote individualistic and, therefore, antisocial ways of thinking. My impression is that many people view their rights as a quiver of jurisprudential arrows, weapons to be used in waging the ceaseless war of each against all.

## THE CHARTER IS UN-CANADIAN

It is difficult to imagine any single event or instrument that has played a more substantial role in Americanizing the way Canadians think than the Charter. The Charter clearly did not begin this process, but it has, since 1982, been central in it.

The basis for my assertion about the Americanizing effects of the Charter is a recognition that, historically and culturally, the Charter is an American document. This truth is seldom adverted to. As a technical drafting matter, the Charter, it is true, was the creation of Canadian lawyers. But the document's roots lie elsewhere. The idea of enshrining the rights of the individual in a constitution and then protecting those rights through judicial intervention is uniquely American. It may well be a good idea, but no one who had the slightest acquaintance with our history could call it a Canadian idea.

"Life, liberty, and the pursuit of happiness" are not simply words in the Declaration of Independence, they are essential notions defining the American experience. Up until 1982 the central Canadian notions were profoundly different. Our social and constitutional watchwords were "peace, order, and good government."

That has changed. I now teach students who are convinced that we did not have a Constitution, that we were not a proper country until we adopted the Charter. We have worked diligently to abolish our own history and to forget what was once our uniqueness. We are now told that the Charter is a basic element in defining what it means to be Canadian. And many Canadians do appear to believe that we can understand ourselves through our approach to the constitutional protection of rights.

The Charter has promoted our Americanization in other ways besides helping persuade us that we don't have a history. We have, as has already been noted, become more individualistic in our thinking and in our politics over the last decade. Again, it would be foolish to see the Charter as the only cause of this, but it is noteworthy that the decade of the Charter has seen an increase in the concrete indicia of social alienation—crime, marital breakdown—as well as in more subtle forms—incivility, hostility, and so on. There was a time when one had a palpable sense on crossing the border of entering a different society. This is no longer true.

The Charter has led us to forget our uniqueness as Canadians and disregard our history. It has had an incalculable effect in Americanizing both the way we think and the way we see ourselves. We have become incomparably more individualistic. Our collective sense of ourselves, our idea of responsibility for each other and the society we share, has been seriously weakened.

Like Americans, we now believe there must be a legal remedy for every social ill. Like Americans, we put me first.

# CONCLUSION

Many Canadians have contrived to forget that most of the things that once made Canada a fine country—physical security, health care for all, reasonably honest and competent government, sound education—came about through the political process, not as gifts from beneficent judges.

The fact is that during the period the Charter has been part of our Constitution, ordinary Canadians have seen a steady erosion of their standard of living. Unemployment is high and rising. Social services, health care, and pensions are threatened. Not only has the Charter not been of any help in preventing this erosion, it has served to distract our attention from what has been going on.

The great beneficiaries of the Charter have been the lawyers. They are consulted on issues of public policy, they pronounce on the morality or desirability of political and social beliefs and institutions, their advice is sought in a vast array of situations. The number of lawyers grows exponentially as does the cost of retaining their services.

The Charter has, to judge by media commentators, become the basis of our secular religion. And the lawyers are the priests. At some time Canadians will decide to take control of their agenda back from the lawyers. That is when we will begin to give serious thought to repealing the Charter.

# The Canadian Charter of Rights and Freedoms Is Antidemocratic and Un-Canadian: An Opposing Point of View

## Philip L. Bryden

Robert Martin's essay launches a two-pronged attack on the Canadian Charter of Rights and Freedoms. The Charter is, according to Professor Martin, both antidemocratic and un-Canadian, and the sooner we Canadians come to our senses and realize that our lawyers have hoodwinked us into believing that the Charter is a good thing, the better off all of us (except maybe the lawyers) will be. My own view is that Professor Martin's essay presents a caricature of both the Charter and modern Canadian democracy, and that when we put the Charter in a more realistic light we will see that the Charter can, and does, make a valuable contribution to Canada's democratic system of government.

The more powerful of Professor Martin's criticisms is his argument that we should get rid of the Charter because it is antidemocratic. Its attraction is that it contains a germ of truth. Like most half-truths, however, it hides more than it reveals.

In its simplest terms, the argument that the Charter is antidemocratic rests on the superficially plausible idea that if nonelected judges are empowered to overturn the decisions of elected politicians, the document that gives them this power must be antidemocratic. The usefulness of the argument lies in its reminder to us that the greatest challenge for a court that has the kind of authority granted by our Charter is to interpret the vague but meaningful generalities on which this authority rests—ideas such as freedom of expression, fundamental justice, and equality—in a way that is consistent with our commitment to democratic government. Where the argument begins to mislead is when its proponents assume that because some judges have had difficulty meeting this challenge in the past, the whole enterprise is doomed to failure.

More specifically, two myths that underpin the notion that the kind of judicial review created by our Charter is inherently antidemocratic need to be exposed. The first myth is that the decisions of our elected legislators and the will of the majority of the electorate are one and the same. Democratic government as it is practised in late-20th-century Canada bears little resemblance to the workings of the Athenian polis or a New England town meeting. That observation is neither a disavowal of our current system of representative democracy nor an assertion that the way we presently govern ourselves stands in no need of improvement. It is, however, a reminder that when sceptics examine the record of judicial review using our Charter and point out some court decisions that deserve criticism, we should be evaluating that judicial performance against the reality of parliamentary government in Canada today and not against some romanticized portrait of government of the people, by the people, and for the people.

The second (and ultimately more damaging) myth is that majority rule is, or ought to be, all that modern democratic government is about, and it is in perpetuating the myth that "there is an inherent and irreconcilable tension between liberalism and democracy" that Professor Martin makes his most serious error. My point is not simply that we need a Charter to protect us from the tyranny of the majority, though I think it is dangerously naive to believe that our fellow citizens are somehow incapable of tyranny. Rather, I want to suggest that democratic government as we should (and to a significant extent have) come to understand it in Canada consists of a complicated web of commitments to each other, only one of which is the commitment to government that in some meaningful way reflects the will of the people.

A belief that important decisions can only be taken after a free and public discussion of the issues, a willingness to abide by a set of rules that govern the way we make authoritative decisions, an acceptance of significant constraints on the use of force—these and many other commitments, some contained in the Charter and others not, are not mere side effects of modern Canadian democracy. They lie at the very heart of democratic government in Canada. And they are part of the reason why the Canadian system of government—notwithstanding all its shortcomings—is respected by people around the world.

This is, I freely acknowledge, a liberal conception of democratic government. Moreover, I recognize that there are other visions of democracy—the kind of Marxist democracy practised by Chairman Mao's Red Guards during the Cultural Revolution, for example—that leave no room for special protection of those who are not able to identify themselves with the will of the majority. For very good reasons, however, Canadians have accepted a liberal notion of democracy, and our commitment to this version of the democratic ideal was firmly in place long before we adopted the Charter.

The real issue is not whether placing some constraints on our legislators is inherently antidemocratic—it isn't. Instead, we ought to ask whether Canadian judges using the Charter can play a useful role in enhancing the quality of our democracy. The answer to this question is not obvious, but I believe that our judges can play such a role, and that by and large our experience during the first few years of the Charter bears this out.

Robert Martin leaves the impression that the Charter has fundamentally undermined the power of our elected representatives to shape the laws that govern our society. If we take a closer look at both the structure of the Charter and the judicial record in interpreting the Charter, however, I find it very difficult to see how that impression can be substantiated.

Because of the types of rights it does (and does not) guarantee, the Charter has little relevance to large and important areas of our political life, notably economic and foreign policy. The judiciary did not bring us free trade with the United States—our political leaders did. And our elected representatives, not our judges, will decide the shape of any new trade pact we may enter into with the United States and Mexico. Our elected representatives decided to commit our troops in the Persian Gulf War, and they, not our courts, will decide what role we play in other trouble spots around the world.

Where the Charter has had some potential to conflict with social policy, our judges have tended to be rather reluctant to accept claims that individual rights should override important governmental interests. Thus our Supreme Court has decided that provincial Sunday closing laws reasonably limit freedom of religion, that Criminal Code prohibitions on hate speech and obscenity are acceptable constraints on freedom of expression, and that mandatory retirement at age 65 reasonably limits our right to equality. We may or may not agree with the wisdom of these and other decisions upholding the right of our politicians to pass laws that place reasonable limits on our constitutionally protected rights and freedoms, but this is certainly not the record of a judiciary that is attempting to undermine democratic government in Canada.

This is not to say that Charter litigation is meaningless because the government always wins. Our courts have made important decisions upholding the rights of refugee claimants, of people accused of crimes, of women, gays and lesbians, and many others. Once again, many of these decisions have been controversial, but I believe they have raised our sensitivity to the concerns of people whose interests are not always well represented through our political process. And in so doing, I would argue, they have enhanced the quality of Canadian democracy.

Professor Martin seems to believe that the Charter has undermined our sense of ourselves as a collectivity and contributed to the rise of a political life that is alternatively characterized by narrow interest group politics or pure selfishness. To the extent that this description of contemporary Canadian politics has an aura of authenticity about it, however, I think it confuses cause and effect. The popularity of the Charter (indeed much of the need for a Charter) arises from the fact that Canadians understand the diversity of their interests and want to incorporate into their democratic system of government a recognition of the vulnerability of some of those interests.

This diversity of interests was not created by the Charter, and getting rid of the Charter is not likely to usher in a return to a mythical golden age of harmony and communitarian spirit. Throughout our history Canadians have recognized and sought to give legal protection to our diversity on regional, linguistic, religious, and other grounds, and I suspect that only someone from Ontario could imagine characterizing this as an erosion of citizenship.

Again, the problem of the fracturing of our sense of ourselves as a political community that Professor Martin identifies is a real one, and it is a challenge for supporters of the kind of political ideals that the Charter represents to realize their goals in a way that does not irreparably undermine other political values that are important to us. What Professor Martin fails to do, in my view, is make a convincing case that it is not possible for us to meet this challenge or that it is not worthwhile for us to try to do so.

Professor Martin's second criticism of the Charter is that it is un-Canadian, by which he seems to mean that the Charter contributes to the "Americanization" of Canadian political life. It would be foolish to deny the influence of the United States Bill of Rights on both the content of the Charter and the political will that animated its adoption. In my view, however, Professor Martin is wrong in his attempt to characterize the Charter as a species of cuckoo in the Canadian political nest that seeks to supplant domestic institutions and traditions with unsavoury ideas from south of the 49th parallel.

In response to Professor Martin I would begin with the rather obvious point that even if some of the important ideas embedded in the Charter were imported into Canada from abroad, so is much of the rest of the apparatus of Canadian government. Canada's parliamentary and common law traditions were imported from England; our federalism was imported (albeit in a substantially altered form) from the United States in 1867; and our civil law traditions were imported from France. In each instance we have made these traditions our own, in some instances by performing major surgery on them in the process.

The Charter itself follows in this tradition of domesticating foreign political ideas and structures. For example, a central element of the American Bill of Rights is the protection of the right to private property. The drafters of the Canadian Charter (wisely in my view) decided that our normal political processes were adequate for the protection of the rights of property owners and that judges should not be given this responsibility under the Charter. In addition, the Charter recognizes certain rights of French and English linguistic minorities, expresses a commitment to our multicultural heritage, and contains approaches to equality and other rights that set it off as a document that is quite distinctive from the American Bill of Rights. The Charter's roots may lie in American soil, but the tree that springs up from those roots is distinctively Canadian.

The more subtle but significant point on which Professor Martin and I disagree is that he seems to use the term "Americanization" as a sort of shorthand for most of what he doesn't like in contemporary Canadian political life. No doubt there are plenty of Canadians who prefer the kind of life we had in the 1970s (or the 1950s for that matter) to the kind of life we have today. What is unclear to me, however, is how unemployment, family breakdown, the consequences of massive public sector debt for our social welfare programs, and the other things that trouble Professor Martin about life in Canada in the 1990s can be laid at the door of the Charter.

In fairness, Professor Martin doesn't ascribe these social ills to the Charter itself, but he says that the Charter has "served to distract our attention from what has been going on." If the Charter has served to distract Canadians from thinking about the problems of high unemployment and threats to the continued viability of our present schemes for delivering social services, universal health care, and pensions, this is certainly news to me. And I dare say it would come as news to those who took part in the recent federal election campaign that revolved around these very issues. Professor Martin is probably correct when he states that the Charter is not going to be of much help in addressing these problems, but nobody ever claimed that it would. More important, we shouldn't assume that because the Charter doesn't address these important problems that the issues the Charter does address are somehow insignificant.

The Charter does not represent the sum total of Canadian political life, any more than the American Bill of Rights represents the sum total of political life in the United States. From a political science standpoint, what the Charter represents is a special way of addressing a limited range of issues that we feel are unlikely to get the kind of attention they deserve in the ordinary process of electoral politics, and a formal commitment to ourselves that the ideals such as freedom, justice, and equality that the Charter enshrines deserve a special place in our democratic political life. I think this was a commitment that it was wise for us to make in 1982, and that Canadians are right to be proud of this new and distinctive feature of our democracy.

# P O S T S C R I P T

Robert Martin is not the only one to express serious reservations about the impact of the Charter on Canadian political life. One of the most caustic critiques of the Charter has been written by Michael Mandel. In his book *The Charter of Rights and the Legalization of Politics in Canada* (Toronto: Wall and Thompson, 1989), Mandel argues that the Charter has led to the "legalization of politics in Canada." Because the scope of interpretation of the Charter is very broad, judges make highly political decisions. They are not just interpreting the law according to some technical, objective criteria, but are actually making the law, usurping the role traditionally reserved only for elected legislators. Because of the high cost of litigation, the legalization of politics, according to Mandel, leads to a conservative, class-based politics that works against socially disadvantaged groups.

Like Martin, Seymour Lipset, a noted American sociologist, argues that the Charter threatens to erase the cultural differences between Americans and Canadians by transforming Canada into a "rights-centred" political culture. See his *Continental Divide* (Routledge, 1990). Christopher Manfredi argues that part of this Americanizing influence is reflected in the frequency with which Canadian judges cite American precedents when making their decisions.

Because of the growing importance of the Charter on Canadian politics, there has been a steady flow of books on this subject in recent years. In addition to the works cited above, students will find the following helpful: Rainer Knopff and F.L. Morton, *Charter Politics* (Scarborough: Nelson, 1992); Patrick Monahan, *Politics and the Constitution: The Charter, Federalism and the Supreme Court* (Toronto: Carswell, 1987); and David Beatty, *Putting the Charter to Work* (Montreal and Kingston: McGill-Queen's University Press, 1987). A book written by a civil rights activist that supports Bryden's arguments is Alan Borovoy's *When Freedoms Collide: The Case for Our Civil Liberties* (Toronto: Lester & Orpen Dennys, 1988).

If we accept Martin's argument that we should be concerned about the impact of the Charter, what can be done? Is Martin's closing suggestion that many Canadians may begin thinking about repealing the Charter a likely outcome? Perhaps a more likely development is that Canadians will begin to take a more careful look at the record of individual judges and to demand more say in their appointment. The potential role of Parliament in reviewing the appointment of Supreme Court judges is examined in Issue Twelve.

# ISSUE SEVEN

## Should the Federal Government Be Strengthened?

**YES** M.W. WESTMACOTT, "Conflicting Constitutional Visions: Is There a Case for a Strong National Government?"

**NO** R.A. YOUNG, "What Is Good About Provincial Governments?"

In 1867 the Fathers of Confederation, charged with the task of creating a new nation, agreed that a federal form of government best suited the needs of Canada. A national government would tend to the national interests, and provincial governments to the regional or local interests. Interestingly, though, the British North America Act, the document that apportioned responsibilities between the two orders of government, revealed a distinct bias. It gave the national government most of the important powers, and also allowed it to override provincial jurisdiction in the name of the national interest. It appeared that Canadian federalism would be highly centralized, dominated by a strong and forceful national government.

Expectations about federalism in Canada, however, turned out to be wrong. At certain times, Ottawa has assumed the predominant position, especially in times of emergencies such as wars and economic downturns. But the major development in the evolution of federalism in Canada has been the emergence of strong provincial governments. In the late 19th century, the provinces first challenged the supremacy of the national government, and since that time Canada has witnessed a steady accretion of provincial power. The result is that Canada has a relatively decentralized federal state.

Many factors contributed to this development. Judicial interpretation of the division of powers often favoured provincial governments, and once-minor provincial duties—in health and welfare, for example—became major responsibilities. Insensitive political institutions at the centre, too, caused influence to gravitate to the regions; too often, Canadians found the doors closed in Ottawa, and had no choice but to solicit help from the provinces. Growing nationalism in Quebec, spurred on by the Quiet Revolution, also played a part. And then there was the nature of Canadian society: it seemed that Canadians wanted provinces to be a salient factor in their lives.

The rise of the provinces has meant a decline in the presence of the federal government. This need not be an undesirable development, but it does imply the relative weakening of a government able to articulate a truly national interest. This fear has led to calls for a strengthening of the national government. It is recommended that national institutions be made more responsive to individual Canadians, and that Ottawa exercise existing powers in a more aggressive fashion. It is even said by some that the federal government should obtain some powers from the provinces.

The suggestion that the federal government be made stronger is, to say the least, not universally supported. In Quebec, governing elites reject it categorically, and instead argue for a greater decentralization of power. In other provinces, too, the idea is received with little or no enthusiasm. Generally speaking, those who find nothing beneficial about a more forceful federal government find there to be good reasons for the existence of strong *provincial* governments. If anything, this group seeks more for provincial governments.

In the readings, M.W. Westmacott, a political scientist at the University of Western Ontario, makes a case—a duly cautious one—for strengthening the federal government. R.A. Young, also a political scientist at the University of Western Ontario, argues that much good comes from influential provincial governments, and that a renewed federal government might threaten these benefits.

# Conflicting Constitutional Visions: Is There a Case for a Strong National Government?

## M.W. Westmacott

E.R. Black[1] argues that there is no universally agreed upon conception of the Canadian federal state. Instead, there has been a continuous debate since Confederation as to the nature and character of Canadian federalism. Black employs several criteria to differentiate the competing visions of Canadian federalism: the manner and extent to which the cultural duality of Canadian society should be recognized in our constitutional structures; the degree of consensus required to amend the written portion of the Canadian Constitution; and the division of tax revenues and constitutional authority between Ottawa and the provinces.

The appropriate distribution of legislative authority between Ottawa and the provinces has been at the centre of constitutional discussions for some time, but no consensus with regard to the appropriate degree of centralization or decentralization within the Canadian political system has been reached. Should national leadership come from Ottawa, or should the national interest be defined through intergovernmental negotiations among eleven first ministers at a federal–provincial conference? The purpose of this article is to argue that within the competing visions of the Canadian federal state there is a national interest that can be defined and articulated by a national government.

## COMPETING CONSTITUTIONAL VISIONS

Peter Russell asserts that for the past twenty-five years Canadians have been engaged in "mega-constitutional politics."[2] He contends that "mega-constitutional politics" is much more than a debate about one particular constitutional amendment because it focuses the attention of the nation on the basic principles that should be enshrined in the Constitution and reflected in our political structures.[3] Mega-constitutional politics, in Russell's words, are "exceptionally emotional and intense."[4] As the constitutional debate evolved over the past two and a half decades, it became increasingly apparent that there is no consensus among Canadians with regard to constitutional priorities. This prompted Russell to argue that Canadians have been unable to define the nature of the Canadian political community. In Russell's words, is Canada "a compact of sovereign provinces? A convenant between two founding peoples? Or simply a community of equal citizens governed by majority rule?"[5]

During a large part of this period, Ottawa's constitutional priorities were (in descending order of importance): the patriation of the Constitution Act, 1867, with an amending formula; the inclusion of a Charter of Rights and Freedoms (including language rights), binding on both levels of government; the reform of national political institutions (the Senate and the Supreme Court of Canada); and finally, the division of constitutional authority between Ottawa and the provinces. These constitutional objectives had a "nation-building" or centralizing thrust, but were in direct conflict with Quebec's constitutional priorities as well as the constitutional objectives of "province-building" premiers such as Peter Lougheed of Alberta.[6] Each vision portrayed a dramatically different role for the national and provincial governments (in particular Quebec). These competing visions of Canada were most dramatically captured in the debate surrounding the enactment of the Constitution Act, 1982.

What were the central principles that characterized each competing vision of the Canadian nation-state? What role was envisaged for each level of government? How should the "national interest" be defined? "Nation-builders," such as Pierre Elliott Trudeau, argued that it was imperative that the authority of the central government not be diminished. Any significant decentralization of power to the provinces should be strongly resisted or at least balanced by a transfer of provincial jurisdiction to Ottawa. Ottawa is seen as the focal point of national decision-making and important regional interests are to be articulated and accommodated through national political institutions (cabinet, House of Commons). In constitutional terms, the national government should retain the overriding constitutional authority to assert the national interest, and there should be no restrictions placed on the federal government's use of the federal spending power. Nation-builders claim that only one government can speak for all Canadians and act in the national interest.

In contrast, a province-centred view of Canada envisages a very different and much more limited role for the national government. "Province-builders" argue that a national interest defined by a national majority as expressed through national political institutions should not be imposed on a provincial majority. Instead, the "national interest" should emerge as a result of intergovernmental negotiations among the eleven first ministers. In constitutional terms, there should be distinct limitations placed on the constitutional authority of the federal government to invade areas of provincial jurisdiction. Furthermore, province-builders advocate a return to a more classical federal state in which the independence and autonomy of each level of government (in particular the provinces) is respected. Advocates of a provincially centred view of Canada also propose a transfer of jurisdiction from Ottawa to provincial governments in areas such as culture, transportation, fisheries, and immigration.

An examination of the debate surrounding the patriation of the Constitution (1976–82) reveals that elements of the two conflicting visions of Canada were incorporated in the provision of the Constitution Act, 1982. Canadians who supported the patriation of the Constitution with a "made in Canada" amending formula strongly believed that this initiative was a significant contribution to Canadian nation-building. However, a detailed examination of the amending formula reveals that important elements of the "province-building" vision of Canada were incorporated into several key provisions of the formula. For example, provincial legislatures could "opt out" of any constitutional amendment that detracted from areas of exclusive provincial jurisdiction even if the constitutionally required degree of consent (two-thirds of the provincial legislatures representing 50 percent of the population of Canada and the Parliament of Canada) was achieved.

The entrenchment of a Charter of Rights and Freedoms constitutionally binding on both levels of government was the most important "nation-building" element of the Constitution Act, 1982. It was anticipated that the Charter would strengthen Canadians' sense of identification with a national political community and with the national government. However, an important "province-centred" provision of the Charter was the inclusion, at the insistence of several provincial premiers, of a "notwithstanding" clause (Section 33). This provision of the Charter enabled the Parliament of Canada or a provincial legislature to explicitly declare that a specific piece of legislation could be exempted from many of the most important sections of the Charter. Critics of the "notwithstanding" clause have argued that it negates the "nation-building" thrust of the Charter. However, the retention of the clause is defended on the grounds that it permits provincial legislatures to determine the extent to which the provisions of the Charter should apply in local communities.

# A STRONGER NATIONAL GOVERNMENT

While there is considerable evidence to suggest that there is a desire on the part of Canadians to work toward a constitutional accommodation that will enhance the unity of the nation, the continued presence of competing constitutional visions will make future accommodation difficult. In retrospect, the intensity of the political debate surrounding the Meech Lake and Charlottetown accords was in its most fundamental sense a debate about conflicting constitutional visions that had developed in Canada since Confederation. This was a debate about how we define the nature of Canadian society and how the Canadian identity should be reflected in the Constitution. For example, should the Canadian nation be defined as a national community of people who define the essential characteristics of their citizenship through the Charter of Rights and Freedoms? Or should the Constitution Act, 1982, recognize the existence of distinctive communities of Canadians who constitute distinct societies with distinct cultures? Should the recognition of the collective rights of particular communities restrict the protection of individual rights guaranteed in the Charter of Rights and Freedoms? How can the concerns of Canadians who believe in a more decentralized federal state be reconciled with an equally strong desire on the part of other Canadians to retain a strong national government? To what extent should parliamentary institutions be reformed to reflect the current Canadian reality—a country that was initially defined by regional and provincial identities but that has become increasingly characterized by transregional/provincial identities?

Critics of the Meech Lake and Charlottetown accords focused their attention almost exclusively on the provisions that decentralized power within the federal system and by implication reduced the capacity of the national government to define and articulate a national interest. Leading opponents of Meech Lake such as former prime minister Trudeau, Premier Clyde Wells of Newfoundland, and Deborah Coyne articulated a convincing "case" for a strong national government. There were several common themes central to their argument:

1. Constitutional reform must focus on the constitutional priorities of all Canadians—a constitutional accommodation that focuses on issues relevant only to one region or province in Canada is not acceptable.

2. The Charter of Rights and Freedoms must be supreme—any attempt to moderate the impact of the Charter by recognizing the existence of distinctive communities of Canadians in the Constitution should be resisted.

3. There should be no significant devolution of powers from Ottawa to provincial legislatures, and there should be no constitutional restriction on the ability of the national government to authorize the expenditure of federal funds in areas of provincial jurisdiction.

4. Any constitutional accommodation must treat all provinces equally—special status for any province is unacceptable.

For the past three decades, advocates of a strong national government have assumed a defensive posture when countering the demands of "province-builders" for a more decentralized federal state. It has become increasingly difficult to defend proposals for constitutional reform that increase or even maintain the constitutional authority of the national government to define and articulate a national interest that transcends the legitimate interests of territorial/linguistic communities. However, there are two significant proposals that have the potential to strengthen the legitimacy of national political institutions while continuing to protect legitimate regional and local interests.

The first of these proposals deals with reforms—such as the Triple E Senate—that would enhance the legitimacy of national political institutions and strengthen the sense of attachment of Canadians to a national political community and to a national government.[7] In the past, regional and provincial interests have been primarily articulated by provincial premiers through their governments. Canadians in various parts of the country have looked to the provinces because national institutions have remained insensitive to their concerns. However, the introduction of reforms such as the Triple E Senate would give voice to regional interests, and enable a national government to define a national interest that would be more responsive to regional and local interests. In theory at least, national policies could emerge that would achieve a broad range of acceptance across the country.

However, reforms designed to strengthen the federal government do not enjoy significant support in the province of Quebec. Premier Bourassa's lukewarm endorsement of the provisions of the Charlottetown Accord for an elected and equal Senate reflected the reluctance of the Quebec electorate to endorse any constitutional reform that had the potential to enhance the legitimacy of the national government. In the future, all proposals for constitutional renewal will be evaluated in Quebec according to the degree to which the jurisdiction of the government of Quebec to protect the distinctiveness of Quebec society has been increased. While there continues to be a debate among federalists within Quebec with regard to the degree of decentralization required to meet this constitutional objective (more than the Charlottetown Accord, but less than the Allaire Report[8]), there is a consensus that there must be a significant transfer of legislative authority from Ottawa to Quebec City.

The second proposal that is designed to reconcile the demands of Quebec for a significant decentralization of power with the apparent desire within English Canada for a strong national government envisages a redistribution of legislative powers between Ottawa and the provinces in an "asymmetrical" fashion.[9] The injection of a significant element of asymmetry into the distribution of legislative powers would permit provincial legislatures to exercise jurisdiction in areas of public policy that in other provinces would be exercised by Ottawa. For example, Quebec—and Quebec alone—might be given authority over broadcasting, unemployment insurance, or regional development, all of which are now under the control of the federal government.

Critics of this proposal have expressed concern about the role of elected Members of Parliament under such a constitutional arrangement. Would it be appropriate for MPs from one region to vote on legislation that would not apply to that region? Supporters of a more asymmetrical distribution of powers note that this happens now, but the concern remains nonetheless. Equally important, asymmetrical federalism clashes with the widely held belief that all provinces are equal and hence should be treated the same way. Asymmetrical federalism, for some critics, amounts to special status for Quebec, which is considered unacceptable. However, it is relevant to note that the Constitution already provides for asymmetrical federalism in certain areas.

# CONCLUSION

In summary, there is a case for strengthening the federal government. A federal state requires a balance between national and regional interests. In Canada, the latter type of interest has been tended to almost continuously, but the former has been neglected. Changes can be made to rectify this situation, to fortify the national government. The result, if we are lucky, may be a situation in which a strong national interest co-exists with a respect for regional and local concerns.

## NOTES

1. E.R. Black, *Divided Loyalties: Canadian Concepts of Federalism* (Montreal: McGill-Queen's University Press, 1975).

2. Peter Russell, *Constitutional Odyssey: Can Canadians Become a Sovereign People?* (Toronto: University of Toronto Press, 1992), p. 75.

3. Ibid., p. 75.

4. Ibid., p. 75.

5. Ibid., p. 191.

6. For more detail concerning the concepts of nation-building and province-building, see R. Simeon and I. Robinson, *State, Society and the Development of Canadian Federalism* (Toronto: University of Toronto Press, 1990), ch. 10.

7. Such reforms constitute an attempt to establish "intrastate federalism" or a federalism in which regional interests are represented and addressed at the national level. See D.V. Smiley and Ronald L. Watts, *Intrastate Federalism in Canada* (Toronto: University of Toronto Press, 1985).

8. The Allaire Report, published by the Liberal Party of Quebec in 1991, effectively recommended that the powers and responsibilities of the Quebec government be increased substantially.

9. For a more detailed discussion of this concept, see David Milne, "Equality or Asymmetry: Why Choose?" in R.L. Watts and D.M. Brown, eds., *Options for a New Canada* (Toronto: University of Toronto Press, 1991), pp. 285–307.

## What Is Good About Provincial Governments?

### R.A. *Young*

If I were a fully committed provincialist, and prone to both rich description and deep normative concerns, and were my editors extremely generous, the essay answering my title question would be very, very long indeed. But none of these conditions obtains.

So I am setting out to defend the provinces, briefly. I defend them mostly because of how well their governments operate, and locate the "good" in this banal criterion rather than in some lofty set of values. I argue for them rather abstractly, as a tier of government in a federal system that happens to be ours. Finally, I am a committed enough *federalist* to reject absolutely the application to the provinces of terms such as "subordinate" or "junior" governments. By definition, a federal state consists of two "orders" of government, which are sovereign in their respective spheres of jurisdiction (as laid out in a written constitution that cannot be changed unilaterally by either order) and co-equal. So let's forget about "levels" of government. Ottawa rules in some spheres over the whole territory of Canada. The provinces rule in others, each over its more limited territory. Collectively, the provinces may exercise more total power than the central government. And that may be a good thing.

## PERIPHERAL ARGUMENTS

One common defence of the provinces' goodness is built on the notion that their governments are somehow closer to the people. This is purely a matter of scale. Canada is big, and Ottawa is far away from most parts of it. Our Members of Parliament represent a lot more of us than do our provincial members. So we can make our voices heard more easily in Fredericton or Toronto or Victoria than in Ottawa. There is something in this argument, but not much. The barrier of geography is minor in the era of planes, faxes, and cellular telephones. And representatives in Ottawa and the provincial capitals are pretty much alike in their busy schedules and their staff/constituent ratio. The same holds for the bureaucracy: in Corner Brook or Mississauga, Ottawa's officials are as "close" as those in St. John's or Queen's Park.

A variant on this argument is more interesting. It is that the sheer existence of alternative politicians and officials who act as receptors of public opinion allows for more participation by citizens. This is particularly important when many areas of jurisdiction, in reality, are shared between the two orders of government, so that effective action in, say, job training requires joint or coordinated programs by the provinces, which are responsible for education, and Ottawa, which is responsible for unemployment insurance. This has two implications. First, with more than one government involved, there are more access points through which citizens and interest groups can make their views known about any policy. Second, citizens have more opportunities to acquire the sense that they have participated in making the rules under which they will be governed. So the provinces by their existence offer opportunities for influence and an avenue for legitimacy. (The counter-arguments to these two virtues—that the result of joint functions and lots of participation is confusion and gradualism, and that participation that is not "meaningful," i.e., effective, produces alienation—need not detain us here.)

Another set of pro-provincial arguments has to do with how people's interests and preferences are voiced to provincial governments and, through them, to the federal system as a whole. One argument that is as common as it is simplistic is that provincial governments are valuable because the distribution of preferences within their territory is more homogeneous than in the country as a whole. (Here, as elsewhere, I take "preferences" to be much the same as "interests," with the former being the subjective reading by individuals of what the latter are.) In this view, Albertans are rather alike, and they are different from Newfoundlanders. Hence, it's good to have an Albertan government that will reflect these preferences, holding taxes down, distributing funds to neighbourhood organizations, keeping environmental regulations lenient, and so on. Provincial governments that accommodate these preferences make governing easier overall, because conflicting sets of preferences do not confront each other in the national arena, on some issues at least.

But part of this argument is foolish. In reality, Canadians everywhere hold preferences that come from a rather limited set. There are lots of Albertans who would prefer higher taxes, Newfoundlanders who think unemployment insurance payments should be cut, Ontarians concerned about resource industries rather than manufacturing, and Quebeckers opposed to abortion. These groups contest in the provincial political systems, and intraprovincial conflict can be intense. So provincial governments, by their existence, do not moderate cleavages between

Canadians. It may well be more difficult to handle linguistic conflict in New Brunswick, for instance, or even in the city of Moncton, than it is to manage this issue in Canada as a whole, or than it would be were the provinces not to exist. The same very likely holds for environmental issues in British Columbia.

So provinces are not more homogeneous and governable than the country as a whole. (Indeed, governing the country may become more difficult when Canadians lapse into easy stereotypes where provinces are seen as having identities, so Prince Edward Islanders are slow farmers, Quebeckers are emotional and Quebec is demanding, Alberta is pro–free enterprise, and so on.) But it is true that the mix of preferences varies across the country, and that somewhat different mixes are found within the various provincial borders. This is the basis of the core argument in favour of provincial governments, soon to be explored.

First, though, it is worth drawing two preliminary implications. Where interests are concentrated within a province, they may prevail in intraprovincial politics, and sway the government on some issue. The full authority of that government then amplifies their voice in the national arena. During the constitutional negotiations of 1991–92, for instance, the First Nations in Ontario got the NDP government on their side, and it pressed hard for aboriginal interests in the talks, insisting that First Nations be admitted to the bargaining process. Similarly, Prairie governments are often thought to throw their whole weight behind the resource industries that are dominant (but not all-powerful) within their economies and polities. Many analysts have worried that this amplification effect heightens conflict in the system. They see this as a defect. Perhaps it is, but it is a defect of federalism itself. And there are offsetting benefits. First, provincial minorities that have lost on some issue can make common cause with people outside the province who share their preferences, and fight in the national arena. Even more important, interests that would lose in a national conflict were Canada a unitary state can find protection in the policies of provincial governments. If Ottawa introduces a measure that hurts wheat farmers or offends pro-lifers, those groups may still prevail provincially to achieve a policy that offsets the damage. Of course, our views on whether this dynamic is a desirable one often depend on how we feel about the policy in question. But, more abstractly, we can think of it as providing an insurance policy that would not be available were we not blessed with sovereign and powerful provincial governments.

# CORE ARGUMENTS

I take democracy to mean a system where people can make informed choices about what they want governments to do, and can act to have those preferences prevail, and can have some protection of their core interests should those with other views win the policy contest. Systems of government I judge by these criteria, and also by whether policies are delivered at a reasonable cost. In these terms, provincial governments are very good indeed. They produce lots of information, and they offer opportunities for participation (as discussed above). Moreover, there are systemic pressures on provincial governments to be responsive, innovative, and efficient.

These pressures can best be appreciated when provincial governments are seen to be competing with each other, like companies in a market. They offer policies to citizens; that is, they supply a set of goods and services, some of which are concrete, such as hospitals and roads and help for the aged and loans for fishing boats, and others of which are less tangible, such as the laws regulating labour relations and gender discrimination and environmental quality. The provinces pay for these operations by levying taxes and borrowing (and through transfer payments from Ottawa in some cases). About all of these policy matters, citizens of a province have preferences.

The pressure to be responsive, innovative, and efficient results from the fact that citizens have options about how to realize their preferences. They can contest in the provincial political arena, by casting a vote for the provincial party whose platform most closely matches their policy preferences, or by organizing to exert pressure on politicians and public servants to deliver what they prefer. But citizens can also contest in the national arena. They can seek countervailing policies, as we have seen, or they can simply pursue different alternatives than their provincial government is providing. Third, citizens can leave the province, moving to another where the mix of policies (and tax levels) is more to their liking.

These last two options put constraints on provincial governments. They tend to make governments supply the policy mix that most nearly reflects the distribution of preferences among their citizens. Otherwise people will "exit," either by moving or by moving their political focus to the other order of government. This responsiveness is a result of intergovernmental competition. And in a federal system this competition takes two forms. There is federal–provincial competition and interprovincial competition. Both are conducive to a policy mix that matches citizens' preferences more closely than would be the case were the country a unitary state rather than a federation (though other factors, such as party competition, also help make the system responsive).

Innovation is another important result. Provincial governments don't often compete consciously to come up with better policies, like firms do, say, in developing better CD players or potato chips. But provincial governments do face many problems in common. And they can be seen as policy laboratories, where different solutions are tried out. Successful policy innovations can then spread. The greatest example here is health insurance, first introduced in Saskatchewan, where the government demonstrated that doctors' resistance could be overcome, that the program was financially viable, and that it was extremely popular. The national medicare program was then propelled by Ottawa, but this probably could not have occurred so fast had the province not blazed the trail. And there are many other examples. In the negotiations that led to the Canada Pension Plan, Quebec officials designed a scheme that was manifestly superior to the one Ottawa had proposed, and all Canadians benefited as a result. Innovations have also spread horizontally. The office of the ombudsperson was first introduced in New Brunswick, and it has been copied in most other provinces. Manitoba first dropped the voting age, British Columbia introduced condominium legislation, Quebec passed laws to protect historic sites, Nova Scotia forced vendors to disclose the cost of the credit they extended, and so on.

Such innovations are vital. This is how governments react to changing socioeconomic conditions and shifting public preferences. Individual provinces may react first because of their different exposure to change and the mix of preferences they contain. What is most interesting is that new policy experiments generate information for other political actors. Governments may use this information to adapt their own policy mix; if they do not, their citizens now have the information to press them to change policies. For instance, it is harder to argue that clearcutting timber near rivers doesn't hurt B.C. fish when Ontario or Nova Scotia has banned the practice. In this way, policies get better.

But we must recognize that interprovincial competition can also be destructive, in the sense that it makes everyone worse off. Say a province innovates by cutting small-business taxes to zero or by relaxing environmental standards to attract industry. Firms are very mobile, and they could threaten to exit from other provinces to take advantage of these policies. The result could be that no province charges taxes on small business, so all have lost revenue, and that environmental standards are lower everywhere—while no firms have moved. (Such a phenomenon can be traced in the gradual disappearance of succession duties, after Ottawa vacated this tax field. The elimination of the tax at the provincial level was spearheaded by the same Saskatchewan government that introduced health insurance: the premier was reported to have said that no one with any money dies in Saskatchewan anyway.)

Many people who support a stronger central government point to such mutually harmful possibilities. I would certainly not deny that such destructive competition can be avoided by centralizing power in Ottawa or by having the central government set the parameters within which competition can occur, perhaps by establishing national standards. But there are other possibilities. One is interprovincial agreement, as is taking place in the national testing of public-school students. Another is that citizens simply resist the competitive devaluation of government services, which is easier when there is information about what standards exist in other jurisdictions and what have been the effects of policy change elsewhere. Arguably, Ottawa could play a more useful role in gathering and promulgating such information than in setting national standards. In any event, against the risks of destructive competition must be weighed the costs of centralized uniformity. These are that the national political outcome—the lowest common denominator—is imposed on groups of people whose preferences it does not match very well. Also one must weigh the benefits of innovation, and in my view these are very large, even if the occasional mistake is made. It is in the provincial policy laboratories that many new and creative policy ideas are conceived.

Of course, some innovations simply don't work. They cause damage. And here again the provincial order of government has its merits. When provinces make mistakes, these are limited mistakes, affecting only a subset of Canadians. When the central government makes policy mistakes, we are all worse off. Moreover, provincial mistakes are more readily apparent as such, because policy outcomes can be compared with those in other jurisdictions that did not experiment. It is much harder to evaluate national policies because there is no base line (except very different foreign countries) to use to determine what would have happened without the policy change. In short, one big government can make big mistakes, and ones that take time to identify as such.

A final result of competition between governments is efficiency in the provision of goods and services. Once more, this is a tendency, not a certainty, but it is a welcome one when resources are scarce, as they are always. By now it should be obvious that citizens who are aware of the level of services in other provinces, and of the taxes levied to pay for them, are more capable of evaluating their own government's performance than would be the case if they were served by only one government. As ever, it is monopoly that produces inefficiency, just as it can produce a lack of responsiveness and innovation. And again, it is the threat of exit and the force of information that make provincial governments hesitate to victimize their citizens through waste, higher taxes, and neglect. Can the same be said of Ottawa?

# A NOTE ON THE CENTRAL GOVERNMENT

The defenders of a strong central government often overlook the virtuous dynamic of interprovincial competition that we have traced here.

Centralists focus on its downside, naturally. They find provincial governments amplifying interests that conflict in the national arena, and impeding their reconciliation. They cite cases of provincial administrations that have been unresponsive to their citizens, or better yet, that have been oppressive, corrupt, or incompetent. They point, in contrast, to the sweeping, creative policies championed by Ottawa, in the face of some provincial resistance—unemployment insurance, medicare, the Canada Assistance Plan, and the Canada–U.S. Free Trade Agreement (and we hear less of the GST, let alone the national debt). Centralists find instances of destructive competition, as when provinces have preferential purchasing policies, so that everything bought by all of them is more expensive, or when policy disagreements among provinces prevent action on urgent problems. They regard federal–provincial competition as a source of needless waste and duplication—"chevauchement" in Quebec—rather than as offering the exit opportunities that induce innovation and efficiency and responsiveness in both governments.

These arguments should be taken seriously. But beware the implication that is so often drawn: Ottawa should do more. Were more functions centralized, or were the provinces starved of resources, Canadians would be deprived of the benefits that flow from a system of strong, competitive provincial governments. If anything, the capacity of the provinces should be increased.

Now this is not at all to say that Ottawa should fizzle away. In the provincialist view, the central government has essential functions. It must be capable of competing with the provinces. It must serve as an umpire in cases of destructive interprovincial competition, if only by using suasion and the force of evidence. It must provide those public goods where there are real economies of scale or where no other government has much incentive to provide them, such as defence, air pollution regulation, monetary policy, national infrastructure, and foreign affairs. It must aggregate regional interests on truly national questions. But provincialists believe that it could do less than it does, and better. Its public service should be the brightest and most competent in the land. It should do much more to gather and diffuse information, to act as a catalyst for better policy. It should provide and build the fundamental commonalities of Canadian citizenship, and assure the mutually sustained safety net that expresses the Canadian community. Provincialists, in short, are looking for a smaller, smarter, better informed, less expansionist, more credible, and appropriately modest central government, one that knows its strengths and its limitations.

## A PRACTICAL EXAMPLE

To this point I have not analyzed particular policy fields or current problems. My defence of the provinces is a general and theoretical one. But as I write, the policy context is both turbulent and constraining. Every Canadian government is struggling to exercise its functions in a globalizing economic environment, with new socioeconomic and political relations emerging in North America, with an expanding domestic agenda pressed by new social movements, with a crushing debt load, and with continuing constitutional uncertainty. Despite all this, or because of it, a tremendous consensus has emerged that our governments must now concentrate on one particular policy bundle, and analyzing how policy should evolve here is worth exploring to illustrate my general, theoretical argument.

The policy bundle is WUTE, which includes Welfare, Unemployment insurance, Training and retraining for workers, and Education at all levels. Scholars and practitioners from all across the ideological spectrum are now focusing on the need to reform WUTE. The existing system is unfair to many caught in the trap of poverty, especially women. It does far too little for older workers displaced from their jobs by technological change and foreign competition. It's got the wrong incentives for many workers (and firms and governments) who anticipate nothing but short-term jobs and a continuing flow of UI benefits. In a liberalized trading environment, the old economic policy instruments of tariffs and subsidies are no longer available: if nations are to remain competitive, governments must help people upgrade their human capital. Social policy and economic policy merge in the WUTE nexus.

But despite the billions of dollars poured into it, the WUTE system seems not to be very effective. It is terribly uncoordinated. The provinces deliver basic education and higher education, with some assistance from Ottawa. Welfare programs, in part, are cost-shared under the Canada Assistance Plan. The central government administers UI, though some active labour-market initiatives that are funded through the program have joint implementation. There is an amazing plethora of job-training programs, mostly with cumbersome administration: some involve three orders of government and private sector partners as well. Most elements of WUTE are delivered in entire isolation from the others. This causes high costs, ineffective results, and terrible frustration among clients who are caught in a bureaucratic maze of offices, obstacles, and disincentives.

Hence the interest already expressed by some provinces for a "single window" for job training, and for much more coordination between welfare, UI, and public education. There has to be an integrated WUTE system. Yet there are two obvious difficulties. First, Ottawa has uncontested constitutional jurisdiction over unemployment insurance while the provinces have the same authority over education. Second, if the central government moved, somehow, to produce a fully coordinated WUTE policy bundle, all the dangers of monopoly would arise and all the advantages of competition would be lost.

The decentralist solution then, in principle, would be to have responsibility for WUTE turned over to the provinces. Were this done, there would be very strong incentives for them to break down barriers between universities, colleges, and worker-training schemes. Welfare and UI could be integrated, no doubt with both being reoriented toward education and getting clients back into the work force. There would be no more sense that waste is tolerable because the money comes from somewhere else. Much more attention could be paid to the interface between WUTE and other provincial programs, such as those in infrastructure and small business. The WUTE system could be tailored to provincial conditions and preferences. And, naturally, a lot of new information about innovative policies would be generated and shared.

This is the ideal, of course. I am not concerned here with the mechanics or the finances. Perhaps UI would be administered regionally in the West and the East, by agencies rather like the lottery corporations. Phase-in periods would be essential for UI, and the federal–provincial fiscal system would need considerable adjustment. But more important is Ottawa's role: What would it do? First, it could provide financing for functions with large national spillovers, such as higher education. This might be delivered through vouchers or income-contingent loan schemes. Second, it would need to ensure mobility, by working with the provinces to establish common standards and portability arrangements. Third, it would gather information and act as a clearing house, supplying the provinces with expertise and serving as a catalyst (like it does in supporting conferences of provincial ministers in education and the environment). Last, it could act directly to base-load the system by delivering a guaranteed annual income at minimal levels, upon which the provinces could elaborate their social assistance and other programs. This would equalize the financial burden somewhat, thus helping the poorer provinces, and it could be coordinated with federal programs of support for children and the elderly. A guaranteed annual income would also embody a fundamental entitlement of Canadian citizenship, right across the whole national community.

## CONCLUSION

My WUTE example may seem utopian. But it is intended simply to illustrate the perspective underlying this whole argument. Provincial governments are competent, and they are in a position to tailor programs to match the needs and preference mixes of their citizens. As this happens, intergovernmental competition emerges as a force for responsiveness, innovation, and efficiency, and all Canadians can be better served. This need not diminish the central government, which should channel and support the competition, while also acting strongly in its appropriate spheres to affirm the basic Canadian community. Ottawa might even gain legitimacy by doing less and doing it well. Certainly the provinces, in my view, are ready and able to do their part.

# POSTSCRIPT

In his essay, Westmacott offers a judicious way of enhancing the place of the national government in Canadian federalism. He recommends that federal institutions be made more responsive to regional concerns, and then suggests that provinces unwilling to accept a stronger federal government—principally Quebec—be effectively granted additional responsibilites. Would this plan work? It certainly is a subtle approach to the issue, but there are some problems. If the past is any guide, provincial governments would act so that federal institutions became more sensitive to them—and not necessarily to individual Canadians. As for asymmetrical federalism, the principle of the equality of the provinces is now so strong that any special status for a province would be challenged under this arrangement.

In his paper, Young makes a key point right at the start: let us refrain from referring to Ottawa and the provinces as *levels* of government. The term "levels" implies a hierarchy of governments, with the federal government on top—and hence more important—and the provinces on the bottom. But the two are constitutionally equal, each sovereign in its areas of jurisdiction.

As for the remainder of Young's paper, it too offers some interesting insights, but it does raise some questions. Young's argument in favour of provincial governments rests partly on his belief that they constitute policy laboratories and centres of innovation. Yet, experience sometimes indicates otherwise. Revenue constraints and the need to remain competitive with other governing units often make it difficult for provinces to introduce new and expensive ideas. Some even contend that a strong national government is better positioned to implement innovative policies. Students interested in this particular issue should read Frederick J. Fletcher and Donald C. Wallace, "Federal–Provincial Relations and the Making of Public Policy in Canada: A Review of Case Studies," in R. Simeon, ed., *Division of Powers and Public Policy* (Toronto: University of Toronto Press, 1985), and Keith G. Banting, *The Welfare State and Canadian Federalism*, 2nd ed. (Kingston and Montreal: McGill-Queen's University Press, 1987).

Our discussion so far assumes that constitutional renewal and rebalancing of federalism is a matter between the two orders of government. But Alan Cairns, a highly respected observer of Canadian federalism, argues that constitution-making now involves the general population as well. The inclusion of the Charter of Rights and Freedoms in the Constitution has given individual Canadians a direct stake in the Constitution. Accordingly, any attempt to change the federal bargain must take into consideration not only the wishes of governments, but also those of the citizenry. It seems that this requirement makes the task of strengthening the federal government an even greater challenge. For more on Cairns's ideas, one should read Alan C. Cairns, *Charter Versus Federalism: The Dilemmas of Constitutional Reform* (Montreal and Kingston: McGill-Queen's University Press, 1992).

This debate concerns itself with a difficult issue. Before students tackle this topic directly, they should first become immersed in the history of Canadian federalism and constitution-making. Two excellent texts on this subject are Richard Simeon and Ian Robinson, *State, Society, and the Development of Canadian Federalism* (Toronto: University of Toronto Press, 1990) and Peter H. Russell, *Constitutional Odyssey: Can Canadians Become a Sovereign People?* 2nd ed. (Toronto: University of Toronto Press, 1993). Both are long, but both reward the diligent student.

Westmacott's argument revolves around national institutions and asymmetrical federalism. D.V. Smiley and Ronald L. Watts address the former matter in their book *Instrastate Federalism in Canada* (Toronto: University of Toronto Press, 1985), and David Milne deals with the latter in Ronald L. Watts and Douglas M. Brown, eds., *Options for a New Canada* (Toronto: University of Toronto Press, 1991). For a more general discussion of the options available to constitution-makers, one might consult the relevant papers in *Options for a New Canada*. Another relevant source in relation to reform of the Constitution is Robin W. Broadway, Thomas J. Courchene, and Douglas Purvis, eds., *Economic Dimensions of Constitutional Change*, 2 vols. (Kingston, Ont.: John Deutsch Centre, 1991).

A further text to consider is R.D. Olling and M.W. Westmacott, eds., *Perspectives on Canadian Federalism* (Scarborough: Prentice-Hall, 1988). Two articles, one by Young, Faucher, and Blais, and another by Breton, relate directly to concerns presented in Young's paper. More generally, the book contains pieces on a wide range of issues concerning federalism.

Finally, students should consider gaining a comparative perspective on Canadian federalism in relation to the United States and other federal states. On this matter, the following publications are useful: Ronald

L. Watts, "The American Constitution in Comparative Perspective: A Comparison of Federalism in the United States and Canada," *Journal of American History* 74, no. 3 (December 1987), and Daniel J. Elazar, *Exploring Federalism* (Tuscaloosa: University of Alabama Press, 1987).

# ISSUE EIGHT

**YES** BENOÎT BOUCHARD, "Good for Quebec," Canada, House of Commons, *Debates*, September 9, 1992

**NO** LUCIEN BOUCHARD, "Bad for Quebec," Canada, House of Commons, *Debates*, September 9, 1992

In the 1993 federal election, the Bloc Québécois, a party that favours a sovereign Quebec, won fifty-four of the seventy-five seats in Quebec. The success of the Bloc underscored the discontent in Quebec, and suggested that Quebeckers felt that only a separatist party could represent their interests at the federal level. More generally, it brought to the fore a question that has bedevilled Canada: What does Quebec want?

A year earlier, in 1992, an attempt had been made to answer this question. The Charlottetown Accord, drafted in the summer of 1992, was a package of proposals to amend the Canadian Constitution. It included, among other things, provisions that attempted to meet the demands of Quebec. The accord, for instance, included most of the elements of the ill-fated Meech Lake Accord—guaranteed representation on the Supreme Court for Quebec, a provincial veto over important constitutional amendments, limits on the ability of the federal government to spend in areas of provincial jurisdiction, and recognition of Quebec as a distinct society.

The Charlottetown Accord also seemingly gave Quebec new powers. In areas such as job training, culture, housing, forestry, and mining, Quebec, along with the other provinces, would have increased responsibilities. Moreover, the agreement included a section that ensured that Quebec's representation in the House of Commons would never fall below 25 percent of the seats—a safeguard against the real possibility of a declining Quebec population in relation to the rest of the country.

For some in Quebec, all this made the Charlottetown Accord acceptable. It was not perfection, but it constituted an honest attempt at renewing federalism in Canada. But for others the accord was completely unacceptable. It diluted, they argued, important aspects of the Meech Lake Accord. The distinct society clause, for example, was now much weaker, and so was the provision that gave Quebec greater control over immigration. As for the transfer of powers, this was a cruel illusion; the accord actually weakened Quebec, and allowed for a stronger and more intrusive federal government. There were other elements that were bothersome, but the point had been made: Charlottetown was clearly not what Quebec wanted.

In October 1992, a national referendum was held to decide the fate of the Charlottetown Accord. Nearly 54 percent of Canadians who voted said no to the accord. In Quebec, the percentage was slightly higher, at 55 percent. Quebeckers, like Canadians elsewhere, had rejected the agreement.

The following readings are selections from the debate in the House of Commons on the Charlottetown Accord. Benoît Bouchard, a former minister from Quebec in the Mulroney government, outlines why the accord was good for Quebec. Lucien Bouchard, leader of the Bloc Québécois, argues the contrary case.

# Good for Quebec

*Benoît Bouchard*

**Hon. Benoît Bouchard (Minister of National Health and Welfare):** Mr. Speaker, next October 26, Canadians throughout Canada will be asked to vote on the agreement [Charlottetown Accord] signed on August 28 by replying to a clear and specific question. They will thus have an opportunity to say whether or not they agree with the vision of the country proposed to them and whether or not they are willing to renew the compromise of 1867 in the context of a modern Canada.

For my part, Mr. Speaker, I not only support this agreement, but I also mean to defend it, both in Quebec and in the rest of Canada. I shall therefore reply "yes" to the question.

The vision of Canada proposed in this agreement remains realistic and open to a recognition of the interests and needs of all those party to it. In a way, it is an effort to reconcile the interests and aspirations of Quebecers, aboriginal peoples and Canadians in the rest of Canada.

Mr. Speaker, I am a member from Quebec representing a riding, that of Roberval, which thoroughly reflects, I believe, the realities of Quebec. If I may, I shall therefore speak first of all to my fellow Quebecers to explain why I feel that this agreement is good for Quebec and why they should support it on October 26.

All of us members from Quebec know how profoundly the failure of Meech hurt Quebecers, how deeply, whether or not we admit it, this was viewed as a rejection of Quebec by the rest of Canada. Since June 1990, Quebecers have been waiting for offers, for proposals reflecting a clear vision of a renewed federalism.

I would like to note in passing the courage of the Canadian Prime Minister who decided to begin again the process of renewal in spite of major difficulties, at a time when so many people were talking about a moratorium. I believe he knew that such a moratorium would only have made Quebecers more impatient and opened the door to the only other possible option, namely independence.

No Prime Minister would preside over the destruction of his own country. This is why, with the constant support of the members of his

139

party, especially those from Quebec, who deserve a lot of credit because they have lived through difficult times, and the steadfast assistance of the Minister responsible for Constitutional Affairs, the Right Hon. Joe Clark, the Prime Minister looked for a compromise, a compromise which we have now found and which proposes a choice based on a federation renewed in those areas it can live up to today, but without precluding the possibility that others might decide to go further tomorrow. Its components are brittle, but they meet the priorities of the various parties.

Reactivating the constitutional debate and broadening its scope to include a "Canada Round" necessarily implied, in Quebec's case, that the original conditions set by the Quebec government for entering into the 1982 Constitutional Accord: distinct society, veto right, control over immigration, control over spending powers and the guarantee of three Quebec judges on the Supreme Court, would have to be met.

The Charlottetown Accord, and I want to make this quite clear, Mr. Speaker, gives Quebec the five elements of Meech Lake in their entirety.

Mr. Speaker, we can put all kinds of interpretations on this. People can have all kinds of reservations, but the fact remains that in the present negotiations, Quebec has recovered every single one of those elements. For me and for many of my colleagues and, I imagine, for many Quebecers, this has always been central to any new agreement. In fact, the Government of Quebec decided to go even further, and that too was fundamental. The Charlottetown Accord gives Quebecers a greater role in our central institutions by adding 18 members and a 25 percent guarantee, meaning that in the future, Quebec will never have less than 25 percent of the seats in the House of Commons. This guarantee provides Quebec with a long-term safeguard that should not be underestimated. As far as spending powers are concerned Quebec has made major advances in 11 different sectors: manpower, culture, immigration, forestry, mining, tourism, housing, recreation, municipal and urban affairs, regional development and telecommunications. However, it seems that for some people that is not enough.

Mr. Speaker, Quebec's society is among the most dynamic and most extraordinary we know. It is a society whose economic, social and cultural policies have made an exceptional contribution to its own development as well as to that of the federation in general. Thanks to the actions of responsible governments and the administrative agreements some people find so appalling, the past 30 years have witnessed outstanding achievements like the Caisse de dépôt and the Quebec Pension Plan.

Furthermore, by guaranteeing control over manpower training, immigration and education, the Charlottetown Accord gives the Quebec government control over the tools it needs to develop a comprehensive human resources policy that is indispensable to Quebec as a distinct society. As a result, Quebec [is] even better equipped to protect its distinct identity than it was in the past. The province will also have new essential powers to develop existing resources.

Of course, this will never convince people who want to see this accord as a step backward for Quebec, as a surrender by the Premier of Quebec. To them, any excuse is a good excuse for perpetuating the myth that the Canadian federation is a straitjacket that has always prevented Quebec from developing its potential and that the Charlottetown Accord will merely consolidate that situation.

Mr. Speaker, every day, Quebecers can see what their quality of life is like within the Canadian federation. I am not interested and they are not interested in the option of leaving Canada without knowing where or why and, above all, without being promised any more than they have already.

I am deeply convinced that Quebecers will prefer our proposals because they offer a vision of a country with a future.

Mr. Speaker, the agreement is far from perfect. As we said before, it is only the result of a compromise and it rests on a basic principle: the existence of a country called Canada. We can either admit this reality of a country called Canada or we can deny it.

We must recognize that this country where we are living today is the result of a wonderful compromise that, for 125 years, despite numerous hardships, frustrations and disagreements, has given us one of the best societies in the world.

Since entering politics I have been amazed by the tremendous potential of this country and its people. I have discovered the realities of Canada outside Quebec. I have discovered Canadians who love their country. I have discovered Canadians who are proud to be Canadian, but not denying their regional roots.

Canada is first and foremost a land of diversity. We cannot exist in this country without a compromise. We should celebrate the fact because Canada was born of compromise. On October 26 Canadians will have to make a decision, if they are still prepared to recognize the diversity and if they are prepared to renew our founding compromise.

Quebecers have faced this choice and they have been disappointed twice in recent memory. In 1980 Quebecers gave Canada a vote of confidence but they did so on the basis of promises which for us have never been fulfilled. Again in 1987 the Quebec National Assembly was the first legislature to ratify the Meech Lake Accord, expressing the desire of Quebecers to rejoin the Canadian Constitution. We all know what happened to Meech Lake.

It is the third time for Quebecers and more than ever before we need to know that the rest of Canada can share this vision upon which a renewed federation can be built. Canada is a remarkable country that will only fulfil its promise to the extent that it can achieve a generous and open understanding between the francophone and anglophone and native components. The future of this country will be built on this understanding culturally, socially and economically.

We are at the frontier of great challenges which will show the world the stuff that we are made of, whether we are a people to succeed in taming a hostile environment and building a modern country or a people who have failed to reconcile their differences and ended in disintegration. We are entering a phase of globalization in which it is vital that we take our place. To get there we have to stop being entangled in endless debates about our future. The time has come to make a decision. It is time to get on with our future. That is the most, most pressing message Canadians are sending us.

On October 26 Canadians will be voting on much more than a dry legal text. They will have to affirm a renewed vision of this country, a vision that includes among other things a fundamental expression of the distinct nature of the French fact in Quebec and the right to self-government for the aboriginal people of Canada, our original founding people. We will have to say yes to the aspirations and contributions of people and regions which were not part of the original compromise, the north part of Canada and the west. All these people, particularly those from western Canada, who play such an important role in maintaining our prosperity and our future, must find their aspirations reflected in this agreement and choose to vote for a renewed Canada.

My last words, Mr. Speaker, will be for my fellow Quebecers. For 125 years, the people of Quebec have emphasized their distinct identity within the Canadian federation as one of their most basic values.

They have been willing to face the risks, the constant frustrations, the often daunting challenges. They have exhausted themselves trying to explain what is so easy to understand: that Quebec is a distinct society, proud of what it is and conscious of its particular role within the federation.

Quebecers have fought against isolation, against constant denunciation; they have made progress at the provincial and federal levels and have marked this country to the point where Canada would not be Canada without Quebec.

Are we going to give up this heritage just because Quebec did not get all it wanted? No, Mr. Speaker!

I think a clear, unequivocal yes would allow us to get on with the future, conscious of our role and our importance. The experience gained will help us build a better Quebec within a renewed Canada.

# NO

## Bad for Quebec

*Lucien Bouchard*

**Hon. Lucien Bouchard (Lac-Saint-Jean):** Mr. Speaker, I want to be very clear. By this I mean that the debate will deal with the Charlottetown agreement. We must therefore immediately get to the heart of the matter. The question is whether or not this agreement is acceptable. To know the answer, we must first clear the way and get rid of the smoke-screens behind which the government and its allies are trying to hide their agreement. They do not want the discussion to deal with the agreement. They want to have a debate on the apocalyptic vision of a choice Canadians would have between chaos, ... or else on being on the side of responsible Canadians, .... Mr. Speaker, we refuse to be confined to such alternatives.

In fact, the debate will not deal with sovereignty. Sovereignty will not be put on trial. We would have liked the debate to deal with sovereignty, Mr. Speaker, as we are well aware that, as long as the question of Quebec sovereignty has not been settled, no decision will have been made about this country. We have to deal with it. Until we have done so, it will always remain in the background and at the centre of our thoughts.

We have always wanted this debate. We have been demanding it for two years. We were able to get legislation passed in Quebec stating that the debate would address necessarily and legally the matter of sovereignty. However, since the federalists, namely this government and its allies including Mr. Bourassa, have decided that the referendum would not deal with sovereignty, the question asked will be on the agreement. Fine, let us reply to the question about the agreement.

There is another thing which should be cleared up. Canadians and Quebecers will not be motivated by fatigue or weariness in this referendum. They will be motivated by the need to decide whether or not the agreement is good for the future of their children.

It is quite strange, Mr. Speaker, that Quebecers and Canadians should be asked to sign with their eyes closed. On this point, I must say that the government and its allies are right. You could only sign such an agreement with your eyes closed.

Recently, Mr. Speaker, Canadians and Quebecers have been told: You are tired, you are fed up with discussions, why not sign now; the agreement is not very good and it is not what you wanted, but why not sign, and then everything will be settled. But such is not the case. Nothing will be settled. The situation will be more unsettled than ever before because the agreement establishes, not a constitutional system, but a system for negotiations. Canada and Quebec as well as all federal departments and provincial governments will be condemned to negotiate for ever.

Hon. members may know that Jean Allaire, who is still a member of the Quebec Liberal Party, the architect of the Allaire Report, the man who engineered the democratic adoption of this report by his own party, the Quebec Liberal Party, is now saying to the newspapers that he has found at least 60 contradictions, instances of weakness or matters for dispute in the agreement. In other words, there is some unfinished business. We are being given a package with all kinds of loose ends. There is still some unfinished business.

This is why the question is worded in such a way, Mr. Speaker. This is why the question speaks about a basis for renewal, that is a basis for further negotiations. That is going to be the basis for further negotiations, for an attempt to deal with the many loose ends that remain. The worst part of all this, Mr. Speaker, is that we are being asked to sign a blank cheque. We are being asked to continue to negotiate a number of essential and fundamental aspects which have not been finalized. They are saying: Later, we will negotiate whatever we please and then we won't have to ask you for permission to sign the agreement we want to sign. People will never agree to a blank cheque where their future is at stake, Mr. Speaker.

What does the question really mean? It means: Citizens of Canada and Quebec, do you trust Mr. Bourassa and Mr. Mulroney to decide what the future of your children will be? We are being asked to trust them to negotiate, without knowing [what] the consequences will be. Mr. Speaker, I refer to a draft, and it is a draft because we don't even have the legal text. When Canadians and Quebecers buy a fridge or a car or sign a lease and when they are asked to sign a document involving sums of $1,000 or $500, for a period of one or two years for minor items, they always want to see the small print first.

Today, we are talking about a contract that will be forever firmly secured by all kinds of nuts and bolts. Today, we have a contract that will be decisive for our own future and that of our children and grandchildren. Today, Quebec's heritage based on nearly 400 years of sacrifice, effort and hard work is about to go down the drain, and they tell us: You won't see the contract before it is signed. It isn't ready. We are in a hurry. We can't afford to wait. Sign right there, on the dotted line, and we will draft the contract later on. Trust us. That is the kind of question we have here.

It is immoral, undemocratic and totally irresponsible to even consider asking people to go through a democratic referendum process to adopt a constitution that has not even been drafted. There is not a single nation in the world that would agree to such a proposal, and certainly not the people of Canada and the people of Quebec.

Let them draft the Constitution and bring us the agreement so we can read it and know exactly what it contains. None of those press releases drafted by press secretaries, after three days of talks in a smoke filled room. No, we want to see the small print. Where is the text of the contract? They say it isn't ready. They said it will be ready after it has been signed. On October 26, the only thing that will be ready will be Quebec's signature and the signature of those who want to sign, if the answer is yes. Then they will start writing the Constitution in reverse, starting at the bottom, just above the signature, like they do in Arabic. People will not buy that, Mr. Speaker. Let these people do their homework, and otherwise we should appoint people who can do a better job.

The agreement is the main thing. And the agreement, Mr. Speaker, is unacceptable. In Quebec … everyone agreed there were two options: sovereignty or a thorough renewal of federalism. So what we have to ask ourselves here is whether this agreement does, in fact, thoroughly renew federalism. In Quebec, the agreement must pass two tests. The first test is this: Do we find all the conditions in Meech in this agreement? The second question is: Are all the additional powers Quebec has been demanding for over 30 years reflected in the agreement? The answer is no in both cases. Any sovereignist and any federalist in Quebec who does not go along with the agreement will tell you this, from what they have read of the text, such as it is. First of all, we must consider the intent of Meech Lake.

The Meech Lake Accord was only a first step. It was about bringing Quebec back to the constitutional table, so that Quebec would have the right, after signing the Constitution, to get down to more pressing business. However, before embarking on this process, Quebec set five conditions, saying: I am not signing and I am not coming back to the negotiating table to discuss the important issues unless five conditions are met. Now you can look for those five conditions, but you won't find them. There are a few, but most of them are not there. Take Quebec's distinct identity. Nobody, but nobody will convince me or anyone else who reads the draft agreement that the wording of the recognition of Quebec's distinct identity is the same one as Meech.

For example ... [just] read the legal opinion published last week in the Quebec press and signed by Quebec's eight greatest experts in constitutional law. Read that legal opinion....

Mr. Speaker, these eight recognized experts from Quebec, people who have published textbooks, who teach in universities, who have taken part in all the legal debates in Quebec in the past ten years, signed a legal opinion saying that this distinct-society clause is meaningless; it is even a setback from the status quo.

The same goes for immigration. The proposed constitution does not contain the immigration clause found in the Meech Lake Accord or the veto right on the process to appoint judges. It is now 7/50 instead of unanimity. Neither is there a veto any more over the admission of new provinces. And we could go on. Very clearly, Meech is not there. So the first condition—never mind all the rest, but the first condition—has not been met. Not just the first condition, but also the division of powers now, because they claim today to do in a single step the two steps that were planned when Meech was begun. Now they claim to settle Quebec's powers until the end of time.

Mr. Speaker, we know the demands that have been made regarding Quebec's powers. It started with Jean Lesage. He has inspired all of Quebec for 30 years. Jean Lesage was a federalist, not a sovereignist. He was not a wicked separatist or heretical. For 30 years, Jean Lesage has inspired Quebec on the basis of being masters in our own house.... For 30 years, we in Quebec have been going on the slogan "masters in our own house." That means more economic powers and complete jurisdiction over culture, language and other fields. We do not find that here. Not a single one of them is here, Mr. Speaker. On the contrary, every apparent gain for Quebec is always subject to administrative negotiations and is never guaranteed in the Constitution and in many cases we find the federal government invading fields where it does not belong.

Take manpower, for example. The federal government is granting itself two new constitutional powers that it did not have before. First is the power to spend on job creation programs, which it did not have before. It will be clearly and finally entrenched in the Constitution. There will be no more negotiations about it. Secondly, there is the power to set national objectives without even spending anything or having cost-shared programs. Those are two additional powers that the federal government is getting in a field where we in Quebec should have made a breakthrough, as everyone involved in the field agrees, especially in the employment forum....

It is the same for culture. For the first time, the federal government grants itself power over Canadian culture in the Constitution. It never had that before. It will get it now.

Then they talk about the six powers, the six related jurisdictions, that the federal government is giving up. The federal government promises to sin no more, not to invade the areas of jurisdiction we already had: recreation, housing, the family, tourism, forestry and mining. We already had those powers in 1867. Georges-Étienne Cartier had negotiated and obtained them and the federal government has been sneaking into them for years. Now it tells us that it won't do that anymore. What a gain, because in the same breath, it tells us that for new programs, it will invade these same fields and any others that exist by using the sacrosanct spending power! I think of the crocodile tears shed today by the Minister for Constitutional Affairs, saying that the federal government abused the spending power. Come on, Mr. Speaker. That is how the federal government has invaded every jurisdiction. That is how it has plunged Canada into bankruptcy: the total debt will soon be $500 billion!

I will speed up, Mr. Speaker, because you are indicating to me that my time is running out. If Quebec were to say yes, we will continue to negotiate, although Quebec will be sorry if it says yes. If Quebec says yes, it will send premiers to Ottawa to negotiate on their knees, with no clout, after having Quebec sign away its hopes and its strength. They will find themselves at the mercy of federal negotiators and federal mandarins. Is that what we want for Quebec's future? I say no.

To top it all is the Senate, where Quebec will count for as much as Prince Edward Island. My region is as big as two Prince Edward Islands. Proportionally to Prince Edward Island, my region would need 12 senators, in other words, 20 per cent of Senate seats would have to go to the Saguenay–Lac-Saint-Jean region. But they are those bad separatists, Mr. Speaker! It would be awful. Yet, this is what is being proposed.

Then, there are the Senate appointments. There will be 9 per cent of us in the Senate to approve the appointments. Do you think that there will be many French-speaking governors of the Bank of Canada, many deputy ministers, many important ambassadors, many CRTC or Canada Council appointees if the decisions are to be made by a Senate with 90 per cent anglophones? I shall conclude quickly, Mr. Speaker.

Then, there is René Lévesque. People always talk about René Lévesque. I thought it was a mistake, because his name is always being brought up by federalists. René Lévesque wanted the Quebec Charter to have precedence over the federal Charter. He wanted Quebec to have exclusive power over linguistic matters. He wanted the existence of the Quebec people to be recognized. He wanted all powers over manpower and employment insurance. He wanted exclusive jurisdiction over marriage and divorce. He wanted the role of Quebec to be recognized internationally in its own areas of jurisdiction. René Lévesque wanted many things. Not one of them can be found in this agreement.

I shall conclude, Mr. Speaker. The people of Quebec will not want to sell their approval cheaply. They do not want to give it away for mere crumbs. The people of Quebec will want to make certain that the vote is not held out of boredom, out of a wish to give up, out of weariness; Quebecers will not want such feelings to be the basis for the future of their country. Quebecers will never again sign any document if they cannot do so with enthusiasm and honour.

# P O S T S C R I P T

In the readings, two positions are presented on Quebec and the Charlottetown Accord. There is, however, at least one additional perspective, represented in the views of former prime minister Pierre Trudeau. Trudeau, like Lucien Bouchard, disliked the accord, but for different reasons. Trudeau had specific criticisms of the accord—he believed, for example, that the distinct society provision might allow the government of Quebec to violate individual rights in the province. But his major concern was a more general one. He thought the accord, with its recognition of Quebec's distinctiveness and its devolution of powers, would cause Quebec to turn away from the rest of Canada. For Trudeau, Quebec's interest lay in becoming more fully incorporated into Canada. The aim was not to create a French Canada in Quebec and an English Canada outside Quebec, but rather a bilingual nation in which French- and English-speaking Canadians could feel comfortable anywhere in the country. The Charlottetown Accord, argued Trudeau, hindered the achievement of this latter goal.

Many Quebeckers reject Trudeau's view, and contend that Quebec needs special recognition and additional powers to ensure its survival. In this respect, Benoît Bouchard and Lucien Bouchard are like-minded. Trudeau responds that Quebec can survive and prosper without special considerations, and that the Lucien Bouchards of the world—Quebec nationalists, in other words—are leading Quebeckers down the wrong road.

Students who wish to investigate further the issue of Quebec and the Charlottetown Accord should read Robert Vipond, "Seeing Canada Through the Referendum: Still a House Divided," *Publius* 23, no. 3 (Summer 1993). The article offers an excellent overview of the accord and the way it was perceived in Quebec (and elsewhere). Peter Russell's *Constitutional Odyssey: Can Canadians Become a Sovereign People?* 2nd ed. (Toronto: University of Toronto Press, 1993) also discusses the

Charlottetown Accord, and includes the accord itself in an appendix. Students might benefit as well from a look at three articles on the accord contained in *PS: Political Science and Politics* 26, no. 1 (March 1993). Finally, the text *How Ottawa Spends, 1993–94* (Ottawa: Carleton University Press, 1993), edited by Susan D. Phillips, contains a chapter on the accord.

With his stunning success in the 1993 federal election, Lucien Bouchard is now a major player. An ardent nationalist dedicated to an independent Quebec is now leader of the official opposition in the House of Commons. Clearly, Lucien Bouchard is a man to watch. For a profile of him, see Jeffrey Simpson, *Faultlines: Struggling for a Canadian Vision* (Toronto: HarperCollins, 1993).

Pierre Trudeau's assessment of the Charlottetown Accord had a significant impact. An essay of his that appeared in the September 28, 1992, issue of *Maclean's* was especially important. His views on the accord can also be found in Trudeau, *"A Mess that Deserves a Big NO"* (Toronto: Robert Davies Publishing, 1992).

Lastly, the issue of Quebec and the Charlottetown Accord needs to be placed in the context of constitutional reform and Quebec nationalism. Stéphane Dion accomplishes this in "Explaining Quebec Nationalism," in R. Kent Weaver, ed., *The Collapse of Canada?* (Washington, D.C.: The Brookings Institution, 1992).

# PART THREE

## INSTITUTIONS

*Is the prime minister too powerful?*

*Do public servants dominate ministers?*

*Should party discipline be relaxed?*

*Should Parliament review Supreme Court nominees?*

# ISSUE NINE

**YES** DENIS SMITH, "Is the Prime Minister Too Powerful?—Yes"

**NO** JOSEPH WEARING, "Is the Prime Minister Too Powerful?—No"

Modern democratic politics is more and more the politics of leaders. We come to identify governments with those who lead them. In the United States, it is the Clinton administration, in Great Britain the Major government, and in Canada the Chrétien government. And there is good reason for this identification. Presidents and prime ministers possess great influence, and at times appear to many as the sole driving force in political life.

This picture of all-powerful leaders is, however, surprising. Democratic governments have been structured to prevent any kind of extreme centralization of power. In the United States, the doctrine of separation of powers, which pits the executive, legislative, and judicial branches against one another, provides a safeguard against one-person rule. In parliamentary systems, such as Canada's, the supremacy of Parliament, among other things, works to limit the influence of leaders. Absolute power corrupts absolutely, so power in democracies is shared.

Yet the perception that politics is essentially the politics of leaders is not without foundation. This is especially so in the United States, where the president at times has power to dominate the cabinet, run roughshod over the Congress, and shape the direction of the U.S. Supreme Court. At times, the three branches of government seem to be at the president's mercy. Moreover, other elements in the political process, including the electoral system and the media, revolve around this figure. Arguably, the best indicator of presidential power is its permanency. A president may fail to reflect the will of the people, but is normally guaranteed a four-year rule.

In Canada, there is concern as well about the emergence of a leader-dominated form of politics. As with the president, the prime minister controls the political executive. Cabinet members, fearful of dismissal, meekly follow the commands of their leader. The House of Commons, to which the executive is responsible, is no match for the prime minister. Party discipline, something that even a president is without, keeps the majority of House members loyal to the prime minister. More generally, the prime minister has attained the status of celebrity, and in a world seemingly obsessed with the goings-on of the rich and the famous this is not an inconsequential development.

The notion of a kind of prime ministerial government is, however, for some an imperfect description of reality. Despite the influence of party discipline, Members of Parliament may act against the prime minister, and there is increasing pressure to give the legislative branch greater influence. As for cabinet, evidence suggests that prime ministers rise and fall on the quality of their cabinet ministers; a prime minister who holds a sword over the heads of ministers is unlikely to attract capable men and women. And then there is the bureaucracy. Its very size and expanse, not to mention its expertise and experience, seemingly makes one-person rule an impossibility.

Finally, one can make the argument that a concentration of power in the person of the prime minister is in fact a *positive* attribute. It allows for decisive action, and avoids the hesitation and equivocation associated with political systems that divide power among the political players. If Canada faces a major problem or challenge, it is well equipped, some argue, to respond quickly and forcibly.

In the following readings, Denis Smith, a political scientist and noted observer of prime ministers, argues that the prime minister is indeed too powerful. Joseph Wearing, an expert on Canadian politics, agrees that power is concentrated in the hands of the prime minister, but finds this to be an acceptable arrangement. The major problem, Wearing says, lies with the institutions responsible for the task of ensuring that prime ministers remain accountable.

# Is the Prime Minister Too Powerful?—Yes

*Denis Smith*

When the Progressive Conservative Party chose Kim Campbell as its new leader in June 1993, the government of Prime Minister Brian Mulroney persisted—as it had for months—at a record low in the public opinion polls. A long and deep recession (aided if not caused by Canada's entry in 1989 into the free trade agreement with the United States); the new Goods and Services Tax; an obscure quest for a new constitutional settlement that finally died in the referendum of October 1992; a servile relationship with the American administrations of Ronald Reagan and George Bush; a series of corruption charges against Conservative MPs; and the prime minister's own abuse of the patronage system to benefit his friends and party colleagues: all contributed to the deep unpopularity of his government. And yet—between general elections whose calling is in the hands of the prime minister—the public had no recourse beyond grousing to the pollsters and radio hotlines, or threatening to vote for a splintered opposition when the time to do so came. For most of his second parliamentary term, Prime Minister Mulroney insisted that the mark of a good leader was that he stuck to his policies in the face of public distaste. He took for granted that he could do so, because a loyal party majority in the House of Commons never challenged his authority.

That familiar record suggests that the Canadian parliamentary system gives great power to prime ministers; and the history of most previous governments since the 1930s suggests the same. The notable exceptions have occurred during a few minority Parliaments (particularly Diefenbaker's in 1962–63 and Trudeau's in 1972–74), when governments were forced to appease the opposition in the House of Commons in order to keep their majorities (or failed to do so). But even some minority Parliaments, such as those of Diefenbaker in 1957–58 or Pearson in 1963–68, have allowed the prime minister wide power because the electorate seemed to desire it.

In a previous article written in 1969, I argued that the Canadian prime minister enjoys the (nearly dictatorial) powers of an American president without the limitations of an independent Congress to hinder him. (The masculine pronoun could apply then, since there had never been a woman prime minister.) What was desirable, I thought, was a series of reforms aimed at reining in the discretionary powers of the prime minister in the name of greater accountability to Parliament and public. Canada claimed, after all, to be a democracy; but it seemed to have drifted uncomfortably close to plebiscitary dictatorship, in which the leader renewed his vast powers occasionally in media-dominated (and manipulated) elections.[1] Is this still the case?

That was the era of the Imperial Presidency, when the American president led a Cold War alliance, fought foreign wars without congressional authority, and commanded substantial secret projects through a variety of information-gathering and dirty-tricks agencies. To suggest that the Canadian prime minister was more powerful in his realm than the American president in his caused a small sensation, and prompted lively debate in the press, classrooms, and eventually in the textbooks.[2] Pierre Trudeau, Lester Pearson, and John Diefenbaker seemed to some observers to be unlikely candidates for so large a claim to power, and several detailed responses pointed out the practical limits (mostly political rather than constitutional) on a prime minister's actions. At last the debate settled into a kind of stand-off, in which both powers and limits were acknowledged–but in an atmosphere, perhaps, of somewhat increased scepticism in the face of prime ministerial claims about their democratic intentions, self-restraint, and innocence.

In the United States, the intervening twenty-five years seem to have emphasized even more the limitations on a president's power. One president, Richard Nixon, was forced to resign from office under threat of a congressional impeachment trial to remove him. That appeared to be a classic display of traditional parliamentary control that turned the old congressional–parliamentary contrast on its head: here was a president removed (in effect) as the result of congressional loss of confidence, while Parliaments in the British pattern seemed unable any longer to exercise such control over their leaders. Following Nixon's resignation, Congress adopted a sweeping series of laws to limit the president's war-making power, to open government records to public scrutiny under "freedom of information," and to exercise limited supervision over foreign spying operations.

The striking exception in this record of limited power came with the accession of Ronald Reagan to the presidency in 1981. The amiable Hollywood actor became known as the "Teflon president" because no criticism (perhaps no thought) seemed able to penetrate his impermeable, smiling surface. Congress was stymied, ignored, lied to, defied, as the administration deregulated at home and engaged in illegal activities abroad. But in the end he, too, was politely restrained by Congress. When leaks revealed the existence of a criminal conspiracy in the White

House and the CIA to sell arms secretly to Iran in exchange for funds to finance a U.S.-sponsored private army in Nicaragua, the Reagan presidency came close to collapse. In the end, congressional fear of another impeachment crisis made it draw back, and Ronald Reagan escaped into retirement mumbling that he could not remember doing or permitting anything illegal. His successor, George Bush, also protected himself from blame by insistent denials. But in general, the period from Nixon's departure to the Gulf War was one of congressional assertion and presidential restraint.

In domestic matters, the president's relationship to Congress was complex. Through a virtual conspiracy of shared interest, the two branches of government combined to create large and uncontrollable budget deficits while allowing national public services to decay under the banner of neoconservatism. The reckoning came by 1992, when all candidates in the presidential elections found it necessary to preach cutbacks and restraint. President Clinton entered office, it appeared, already crippled by the national debt. With the end of the Cold War, America's leadership abroad was also thrown into confusion, and Bill Clinton's own hesitations meant that international leadership no longer gave the president an added aura of authority. The age of the Imperial Presidency was certainly dead; instead, there was frequent talk of inevitable American decline.

In the Canada of the 1970s, 1980s, and early 1990s, the prime minister's dominance in the political system has not been diminished. The contrast between prime ministerial freedom and presidential limitation seems, if anything, more stark. Limited parliamentary reform and access to information legislation were meant to broaden popular influence on the executive. They have given critics of government a marginally stronger base; but on the whole they turn out to be easily ignored or manipulated by those in power.

Despite continuing, widely expressed concern for greater democratic control over policy, Canadian political parties remain deeply subservient to their leaders, and prime ministers set the pattern for that climate of subservience. Dalton Camp, a thoughtful, conservative journalist, reflected recently that "elements of the imperial prime ministership crept in" during the Mulroney era.[3] These were most evident in the expanded coteries of aides, guards, courtiers, and equipment that accompanied the prime minister on his travels outside Ottawa. But that reflected, and underlined, an unusual and widespread deference to the leader's whims. In the summer of 1991, for example, at a particular low point in his popularity, Prime Minister Mulroney gained a sweeping expression of confidence and was able to avoid any hint of censure at a national Progressive Conservative Party meeting in Toronto. Eighteen months later he decided to retire; but that was in anticipation of an electoral defeat rather than out of any urgent threat to his power in party or cabinet. In his last days there was only one maverick challenge to his authority when five Conservative senators voted to defeat a government bill in the Senate; that was so unusual that it looked like a small effort of decency meant to cleanse themselves of the party's reputation for abject servility to the leader.[4]

When Kim Campbell became prime minister in the summer of 1993, she seemed intent on a daring attempt to prove her hypnotic control over party and public. It is common for new party leaders to make efforts—both cosmetic and substantial—to repair the image left by departing leaders. It is something else to expect that a government's entire nine-year record of controversy and unpopularity could be altered, or reversed, by a new leader who herself shared in responsibility for that record as a senior minister—and yet who promised no essential departures from its policies or philosophic assumptions. For the new prime minister, image was everything. The image could be infinitely flexible, even if the substance remained unchanged.

Kim Campbell's assumption seemed to be that the Conservative Party, and the government she led, were simply vehicles for the leader, to make of them what she wished, without past, without record. But her hold on the prime ministership was necessarily tentative, since she governed in the dying months of the parliamentary term. As Campbell entered a general election campaign, it seemed as though she and her advisers had read their opinion polls shrewdly, and that the Canadian public could be jollied and manipulated into believing that the Campbell government was something new and deserving of fresh confidence.

The key to prime ministerial power rests in two features of the Canadian system: the fact that legitimate power is conferred through the ballot box in general elections, and only by that means; and the fact that the role of the prime minister is defined by custom, not by law. A party leader wins a parliamentary majority by organizing for victory in general elections; the machinery of party and media assures the leader's dominance in that effort; and once victorious, the leader carries acclaim and celebrity into office and adds to it control over a vast system of influence and patronage. Taken together, those are recipes for pre-eminent individual power, not for restraint or collegial rule by the cabinet.

As it turned out, Kim Campbell and the Conservative Party disastrously misjudged the mood of the electorate. It punished her unmercifully for an inept campaign and for carrying the burden of the Mulroney record. Superficially, the Liberal victory may appear to reduce the dominance of the party leader because Jean Chrétien campaigned as a team leader rather than as a one-man band, and favours parliamentary reform. But as prime minister, Chrétien faces the traditional temptations to use his wide prerogatives and consolidate his power.

The 1993 election has probably reinforced the dominance of the prime minister, while revealing just how precarious that dominance can be. As the ex-minister John Roberts wrote in the aftermath:

> One lesson from the Canadian election seems clear. The decline of party attachment and the influence of modern communications ... in focusing on party leaders has moved Canada away from party politics to leadership politics. If a party makes a mistake in choosing its leader, the impact on its fortunes is almost irretrievable. The safety net of support for a party on the basis of its programme, traditional voting patterns or past political success has been taken away.[5]

The other leaders need hardly be mentioned, except to note that the party scene in Canada is leader-centred. In 1993, the public heard of, and saw, Campbell, Chrétien, McLaughlin, Bouchard, Manning, Hurtig. Despite the leaders' claims (and perhaps, sometimes, their wishes), the press and television placed their narrow focus on these six as representatives, symbols, incarnations, of their parties—or very nearly as things in themselves needing no broader definition. In the age of television they are celebrities or they are nothing, and the party machines spend their ingenuity and their dollars to make and acclaim that celebrity. In Canadian politics, celebrity turns to power only if it is reflected in the ballot box; but a politician's celebrity is made on the television screens just like that of Peter Mansbridge, Wayne Gretzky, Adrienne Clarkson, and Roberto Alomar. When it is strongly registered in the ballot box, no power can challenge it.

As long as Canada has party pollsters to guide the leaders, its own television networks to display them, and parliamentary elections to legitimize them, nothing much is likely to change the dominance of the prime minister. Most efforts of parliamentary reform will involve minor (though sometimes useful) tinkering. Attempts to make the parties more democratic may, fitfully, place some limits on the leaders' discretion; but the public and the parties have too short memories and too little will to maintain major democratic reforms for long.

Yes: the prime minister is too powerful for the self-respect and autonomy of other citizens. No: there is not much that can be done about it in the short run. But the slow and patient building of a wide range of autonomous social institutions, whenever possible independent of government funding, offers a partial alternative. There are few others.

Nevertheless, there is a paradox at the heart of discussion of the prime minister's power. While the Canadian political system—assisted by the vast Canadian geography, a strong tradition of public deference, and a centralizing technology—has concentrated authority in the prime minister's hands, the power that any Canadian prime minister is able to exercise has been leaching away. The uncontrolled operations of international financial markets, the growing power (beyond all states) of the transnational corporations, the surrenders of sovereignty contained in the Canada–U.S. Free Trade Agreement and NAFTA, the claims to and assertions of power by Quebec and the First Nations, the limits imposed by the constitutional Charter of Rights, and a crippling public debt that has enfeebled political imagination, all undermine the power of the prime minister to achieve distinct national goals. Some of these shifts—but not all—have occurred by prime ministerial choice. Thus, while the system gives the prime minister almost unlimited discretionary power, there are fewer and fewer areas in which it can be exercised. In the end Canada may be left with only the shadow: a celebrity prime minister who is able to do nothing except kiss babies. That could be as dangerous a source of public disenchantment as excessive prime ministerial power.

## NOTES

1. The article, "President and Parliament: The Transformation of Parliamentary Government in Canada," appears in full in Richard Schultz, Orest M. Kruhlak, and John C. Terry, *The Canadian Political Process*, 3rd ed. (Toronto: Holt, Rinehart and Winston, 1979), pp. 302–14. An excerpt, "Prime Minister as President," appears in the first edition of this book, pp. 168–74, with a response by Joseph Wearing, "President or Prime Minister?" pp. 175–83, with comments by the editors.

2. My comments were inspired by the reflections on British prime ministerial power of R.H.S. Crossman in his introduction to the 1964 edition of Walter Bagehot's *The English Constitution*. Crossman's essay stimulated a similar debate in the United Kingdom.

3. On the program "Media," CBC Newsworld, March 20, 1993.

4. The bill proposed various changes to the central administrative structure, including merger of the Canada Council and the Social Sciences and Humanities Research Council. The measure had been conceived in haste and without consultation, offered no financial savings, and was opposed by every witness offering evidence about it to committees of the House and Senate. Conservative members of the House voted loyally for the bill despite the weight of evidence against it.

5. John Roberts, "The Wrong Leader Means Oblivion," *The Independent*, October 28, 1993.

# Is the Prime Minister Too Powerful?—No

## Joseph Wearing

In the early years of Pierre Trudeau's prime ministership, my friend and colleague, Denis Smith, advanced the compelling thesis that in Canada we had created "a presidential system without its congressional advantages."[1] I argued that, on the contrary, in Canada distinctive checks on the power of our head of government had evolved, though in a different manner from either the United States or the United Kingdom. In responding again in the very different politics of the 1990s to the question of whether the Canadian prime minister is too powerful, I would still reply in the negative, in part because the realities of cabinet government continue to impose a certain discipline and restraint on the prime minister, but also because I see the concentration of power and responsibility within the cabinet and especially within the office of the prime minister as one of the great strengths of our system of government. No system of government is perfect (and we Canadians are especially given to indulging in the delights of self-flagellation). So I would argue that we should be more concerned about strengthening the manner in which the prime minister has to answer for her/his government's errors of omission and commission. Finally, in just two areas do I favour any reduction in the prime minister's power, and in a third an actual increase of power.

Ever since the days of Sir John A. Macdonald, the presence of powerful regional ministers was an essential ingredient in a successful federal cabinet. Indeed, the role of the Canadian cabinet in presenting provincial interests in a manner similar to the U.S. Senate was foreseen in the Confederation debates. To the extent that a prime minister lacked such ministers, the cabinet was much weaker and less effective. So this has always been an important restraint on a Canadian prime minister. Even though ministers are now overshadowed by the prime minister during an election campaign and by provincial premiers during federal–provincial negotiations, other changes within the decision-making structures in Ottawa—such as powerful cabinet committees, influential regional caucuses, hugely financed regional development schemes—

have actually enhanced the power of regional ministers, as Herman Bakvis shows in an important, recent study of regional ministers.[2]

Trudeau needed Allan MacEachen and Lloyd Axworthy, Mulroney depended on Don Mazankowski and John Crosbie, Kim Campbell had to have Jean Charest, just as surely as Laurier needed Clifford Sifton and Mackenzie King needed Ernest Lapointe and Jimmy Gardiner. So the prime minister's power is qualified by the need to rely on the leading ministers of his/her cabinet. Sometimes the prime ministerial ego has to be stifled in the course of persuading a reluctant minister to stay in the cabinet. Mackenzie King—more than any other prime minister in our history—knew how important it was for him to have strong men (as only they were then) in his cabinet. He was thus able to reverse the usual process of decline that marks most governments; his were stronger at the end of his period of power than at the beginning of it. There could not be a greater contrast than that between John Diefenbaker and Brian Mulroney in the regard they had for their cabinets. Diefenbaker mistrusted most of his ministers, who in turn abandoned him. His government was defeated as much from within as from without. Mulroney, even when his government was at unprecedented depths of unpopularity, retained his team of ministers—even his arch rival Joe Clark—and retired after nine years as prime minister without ever having suffered an electoral defeat, the first prime minister in Canadian history to have done so.

In no comparable way does an American president depend on his cabinet. Political rivals are not appointed to the cabinet. (More often, a competitor is given the vice-presidential nomination, which effectively emasculates him.) A cabinet secretary does not have an independent power base, as a senator or congressman does, and if one resigns, there is a huge pool from which the president can draw a replacement.

Even though a Canadian prime minister depends on his/her cabinet in a manner that sharply distinguishes our system from the American, there is no question about the Canadian prime minister's absolute centrality to our form of cabinet government. Indeed, what our system does to a much greater degree than the American is to permit *responsibility* to be concentrated on the office of prime minister. The prime minister or premier of a majority government simply cannot avoid being responsible for whatever good or ill his/her government has done. An American president can, with considerable justification, blame an uncooperative Congress for having sabotaged his program. (The Canadian Senate's sporadic flirtation with having a mind of its own is in no way comparable.) Because there are so many checks on presidential power, the American system suffers from periodic bouts of deadlock or "gridlock"—to use George Bush's term. Indeed, over the last sixty years, it has been only under special circumstances, such as the aftermath of

Kennedy's assassination or Reagan's initial popularity, that an American president has been able to count on congressional cooperation. Clinton's struggle to get his first budget approved showed the American system at its worst as the president was forced to concede to any number of special interests just to win the support of his fellow Democrats in Congress. "America's political system continues to reward self-interest and short-termism," observed *The Economist* at the conclusion of the spectacle.[3]

A Canadian prime minister or premier of a majority government can act decisively in what he or she perceives to be the public interest and is judged accordingly and has the time to demonstrate that these policies are right before the electorate is given the opportunity to pass judgment. The GST, the Ontario Social Contract, and free trade are examples. Canadians should not be surprised that we have a universal medicare system while Americans do not, nor that the American gun lobby is able to keep the United States as the most gun-infected of all the industrial nations.

Although the Canadian prime minister has an admirable power to act, the accountability for exercising that power is more impressive in theory than in practice, because political debate in this country is so often lacking in substance. If American politics suffers from "short-termism," Canadian politics suffers from "lack-of-contentism." But the fault lies not so much with the prime ministership as with the ineffectiveness of other parts of the body politic whose job it is to monitor the exercise of prime ministerial power: the parties, Parliament, the electorate, and the media.

One of the most important functions of any political party is recruitment. On the whole, Canadian parties carry out their recruitment in a reasonably democratic manner. Membership in a political party is easy to acquire, and some closely contested nominations have attracted as many as 15,000 members. Several provincial leaders have been chosen by the direct vote of all party members. But what these exercises habitually lack is any sense of choosing among policy alternatives as put forward by the various candidates, alternatives for which they can be later held accountable. (A notable exception to this was the Liberals' choice of Trudeau as leader. His positions on Quebec and the Constitution were well known through his extensive writings. His government's actions, especially the constitutional amendments entrenching a charter of rights, surprised no one who had read what he had written. He had written little, however, on economic issues, and here his government's record was much less impressive.) Recent leadership contests have focused on the candidates' personalities or simply on their "newness." At their worst, these exercises in "recruitment" have sunk to the level of dirty tricks and vote-buying (the Conservatives' leadership contest of

1983 and the Liberals' of 1984 and 1990) or of tribal contests between rival ethnic groups at nomination meetings in the metropolitan centres.

All the parties hold policy conventions—a new experience for the federal Conservatives in 1991—but the results of their deliberations are soon forgotten. With the advent of television campaigns, Canadian party strategists tended to play down the value of the written word and to put all of their effort into television ads and thirty-second news clips. The election manifesto had become a thing of the past, even though British parties continued to publish and sell detailed policy manifestoes and American party platforms retained significance as a kind of blueprint for the policy staff whose candidate went to occupy the White House.[4] The Canadian electorate, by contrast, had to make do with the dribs and drabs of whatever ill-formed policy thoughts the leader chose to hint at during the course of the election campaign. Any post-election accountability for the subsequent exercise of prime ministerial power was virtually nonexistent. Fortunately the 1993 election saw a return of the election manifesto, when the Liberal Party issued "Creating Opportunity" and the Conservatives responded with "Making Government Work for Canada: A Taxpayer's Agenda." In spite of evasions in important areas, both documents at least gave the voter some idea as to the direction in which a Liberal or Conservative government would move—a modest but significant advance in restoring responsibility to the prime minister's office.

Now that the election is over, Parliament ought to be central to the continuing process of responsible government. It is the only elected institution in Ottawa and the most public. It comes from a proud 700-year tradition compared with not much more than a paltry two-and-a-half centuries of the prime ministership. Over the centuries, the mother of our Canadian Parliament emerged as the most effective check on executive power, but its Canadian daughter is a poor shadow of her imposing progenitor. One of its basic problems is that, at less than half the size of the British House of Commons, ours is simply not large enough. Parliament's job is to be a thorn in the side of the crown's ministers, only granting their requests after querying and complaining. Prime ministers both in Britain and Canada have striven to subdue Parliament by means of party discipline and patronage. Canadian prime ministers have had a much easier time, largely because there are so many fewer MPs to contend with. (Even more so Canadian premiers who face legislatures, the largest of which is just 130.) In most Canadian Parliaments, virtually every MP on the government side is a cabinet minister, a parliamentary secretary, a committee chair or vice-chair, or hopes to become one. In Britain, the majority of MPs have to reconcile themselves to being permanently on their party's backbenches. But this means they have less reason to bend to the will of the party whips. No wonder party cross-voting happens so much more frequently in Britain and is reluctantly tolerated by the prime minister, whereas when two Conservative MPs—David Kilgour and Alex Kindy—dared to vote against his government on the GST, Mulroney had them thrown out of the Conservative caucus.

In attempting to provide a check on the executive, the Canadian Parliament is also handicapped by what C.E.S. Franks describes as its pervasive inexperience and amateurism. Once again the contrast with the British Parliament is striking. Half the MPs in a Canadian Parliament do not return after the next election, whereas the typical British MP has been there for over ten years. By contrast, British prime ministers are less secure in their tenure of power than their Canadian counterparts.[5] Conservative prime ministers in Britain are directly accountable to their MPs and can be turfed out by them, as Margaret Thatcher was not the first to discover, and until 1981, the same was true of the Labour Party. (An electoral college in which MPs retain a still significant 30 percent voice is the present mechanism for electing Labour leaders.) A Canadian party leader and thus a prime minister owes her/his job to a transitory party convention that meets just every two or three years. So the problem of prime ministerial power in Canada lies not so much in the extent of the power as in the sporadic nature of the prime minister's responsibility to those who put her/him into power.

Finally, both the electorate and the media have to share some of the blame for the lack of real accountability in Canadian politics. The speed with which the electorate reacts to even the most superficial changes in the presentation of a leader or the party is breathtaking. It used to be the case, for example, that a leaders' debate during the campaign changed very little. The electorate saw the debates for what they are—a continuation of the posturing and jousting that takes place every day in Question Period. But in 1984, John Turner's poor performance in the debates was a turning point in the early days of the campaign. Four years later, Turner's good performance produced a shift to the Liberals, but continuing electoral volatility wiped out those gains before voting day. One might argue that this is an indication of the electorate's sophistication—the weakening of blind party allegiance and the importance given to issues such as free trade. However, an important electoral study by Johnston et al. shows that polls and party advertising had more to do with these fluctuations than any cool, rational assessment of the free trade agreement.[6]

The media have to share some responsibility for this trivialization of politics. A striking example is the manner in which the media went along with the Conservative strategy of providing the new prime minister, Kim Campbell, with "photo ops" during the pre-campaign period in the summer of 1993. Through projecting an *image* that was completely different from Mulroney's, but with virtually no change from his *policies*, this strategy produced an amazing turnaround in the popularity of the Conservative Party's prime minister. From having had the least popular, they had, within the space of just a few months, the most popular in thirty years. But once the election was called the media honeymoon quickly ended and her popularity plummeted again.

In conclusion, it seems to me that the concentration of power in the hands of the prime minister is an admirable feature of our Constitution, but the other half of the equation— responsibility—is weakened by wild gyrations in prime ministerial popularity that have little to do with the way in which that person exercises the powers of the office.

Finally, there are two prime ministerial powers that I believe are excessive and one area where the prime minister has not enough power. The first excess is the very wide discretion for choosing an election date. It is impossible to defend giving the incumbent prime minister such a tactical advantage over her/his opponents. Most European parliamentary democracies—with the notable exception of the United Kingdom— have fixed parliamentary terms combined with some flexibility in providing for the possibility of an early election under special circumstances, which are not left simply to the prime minister to determine. Second, it is also difficult to defend another area of unqualified prime ministerial discretion—the appointment of senators. The full impact of this power is sometimes revealed in a bizarre manner, when senators appointed by a previous prime minister rouse themselves from their accustomed lethargy to fight old battles against opponents who are now in power.

The trimming of these excessive prime ministerial powers would most logically be done through a constitutional amendment, but Canadians have become "constitution shy" following the failures of the Meech Lake and Charlottetown accords. It is worth noting, however, that both powers are the result of constitutional convention, rather than being part of the written Constitution. Indeed, Brian Mulroney for a short time gave up his power to make senatorial appointments in anticipation of a formal constitutional amendment. So changes could be accomplished without any change to the Constitution. But prime ministers have not been noted for their willingness to part with powers that political scientists think they could do without.

The area where the prime minister's power could be strengthened would probably require a constitutional amendment, since it trenches on the federal–provincial division of powers. Because the Constitution gives both federal and provincial legislatures the same access to direct taxes, the eleven governments act independently of each other and with virtually no coordination of their fiscal policies. This has seriously aggravated the problem of the deficit, since each level of government tries to unload the problem or the blame on another level. It is instructive to note that in the area of monetary policy, where power lies clearly at the federal level, Canada's record is exemplary; in the area of fiscal policy, where responsibility is hopelessly tangled, our record is one of the worst. In his study *The Politics of Public Spending in Canada,* Donald Savoie shows that only the prime minister has been strong enough—and then only just—to exert even a modest degree of discipline over the prodigalities of the spending ministers.[7] Giving the federal Parliament—and thus the prime minister—the power and the responsibility for coordinating federal and provincial fiscal policies is probably the only hope for tackling the country's enormous debt problem.

## NOTES

1. The two articles appear in Thomas A. Hockin, ed., *Apex of Power: The Prime Minister and Political Leadership in Canada,* 2nd ed. (Scarborough: Prentice-Hall, 1977), pp. 308–43.

2. Herman Bakvis, *Regional Ministers: Power and Influence in the Canadian Cabinet* (Toronto: University of Toronto Press, 1991), pp. 283–88.

3. August 14, 1993, pp. 15–16. See also August 7, 1993, pp. 25–26.

4. Michael J. Malbin, "The Conventions, Platforms, and Issue Activists," in Austin Ranney, ed., *The American Elections of 1980* (Washington: 1981), pp. 139–40.

5. C.E.S. Franks, *The Parliament of Canada* (Toronto: 1987), pp. 23–25.

6. Richard Johnston, André Blais, Henry E. Brady, and Jean Crête, *Letting the People Decide* (Montreal and Kingston: McGill-Queen's University Press, 1992), especially ch. 8.

7. Toronto: University of Toronto Press, 1990.

# POSTSCRIPT

In his article, Smith employs some very arresting images. The prime minister is a celebrity, a leader with imperial-like ambitions, and an individual with greater power than the president of the United States. The question, however, is whether the images are accurate. Brian Mulroney would have dearly loved to remain prime minister, but he knew his days were numbered. Is this a sign of imperial prime ministership? Moreover, his successor, Kim Campbell, failed to convince the voters of her worth, an outcome that surely conflicts with the notion of an all-powerful prime minister. Smith himself also recognizes, at the end of his paper, the limitations of prime ministerial power. For him, it is a paradox that prime ministers are both strong and weak; but one might deny the paradox and simply observe that prime ministers can be restrained.

For his part, Wearing likes the idea of placing a great deal of influence with the prime minister, but admits that ensuring the responsible use of this power is difficult. However, instead of concluding from this that prime ministers are too dominant, he contends that the institutions authorized to check the prime minister are too reserved. This is a subtle line of argumentation, but it seems that the effect of weak constraints is a strong prime minister. Perhaps Wearing centres on the failings of parties, Parliament, and the media because he fears a focus on prime ministerial power will eventually lead to undesirable limits on the country's national leader. What is to be avoided, it seems, is reducing the prime minister to a president.

Surprisingly, the prime minister and his or her power has not been the subject of much direct analysis. Some books, though, have addressed the matter. Thomas Hockin has collected a series of articles on the issue in the first and second editions of his *Apex of Power* (Scarborough: Prentice-Hall, 1971 and 1977). Also relevant are R. Malcolm Punnett, *The Prime Minister in Canadian Government and Politics* (Toronto: Macmillan of Canada, 1977), William Matheson, *The Prime Minister and the Cabinet*

167

(Toronto: Methuen, 1976), and Leslie A. Pal and David Taras, eds., *Prime Ministers and Premiers: Political Leadership and Public Policy in Canada* (Scarborough: Prentice-Hall, 1988). Patrick Weller's *First Among Equals: Prime Ministers in Westminster Systems* (London: Allen and Unwin, 1985) provides a useful comparative perspective on the question of prime ministers and their power.

An important aspect of the prime ministerial power thesis is the emergence and influence of central agencies. These structures, which include such entities as the Privy Council Office, the Federal–Provincial Relations Office, and most importantly, the Prime Minister's Office, are designed to assist the prime minister in securing objectives. It has been argued that the "superbureaucrats" housed in these organizations supply the prime minister with an invaluable resource. There has been much written on this topic, but the key texts are Richard French's *How Ottawa Decides*, 2nd ed. (Ottawa: James Lorimer, 1984), Colin Campbell and George Szablowski's *Superbureaucrats: Structure and Behaviour in Central Agencies* (Toronto: Macmillan of Canada, 1979), and Colin Campbell's *Governments Under Stress: Executives and Key Bureaucrats in Washington, London and Ottawa* (Toronto: University of Toronto Press, 1983). An up-to-date review of these agencies can be found in Richard A. Loreto, "Prime Minister and Cabinet," in Robert M. Krause and R.H. Wagenberg, eds., *Introductory Readings in Canadian Government* (Toronto: Copp Clark Pitman, 1991).

# ISSUE TEN

## Do Public Servants Dominate Ministers?

**YES** FLORA MACDONALD, "The Minister and the
Mandarins," *Policy Options* 1, no. 3 (September–
October 1980): 29–31

**NO** DON PAGE, "Ministers and Mandarins: Ministers Must
Lead"

"Yes, Minister," a British television series, became widely popular in the
1980s for its satirization of the relationship between government cabinet
ministers and the British civil service. The series traced the career of Jim
Hacker from the lowly post of Minister of Administrative Services to the
office of prime minister. Hacker, always the well-intentioned, if somewhat naive and bumbling minister, constantly struggled to ensure that
his will predominated over the wily machinations of his permanent secretary (the equivalent of a Canadian deputy minister), Sir Humphrey
Appleby. Adept at handling the intricacies of bureaucratic politics, Sir
Humphrey is always able to convince poor Hacker that the civil service
position is the correct one. Sir Humphrey is so cunning in his proffering
of advice that Hacker often ends up thinking that the idea was his in the
first place. Each episode ends with a smiling Sir Humphrey obligingly
stating, "Yes, Minister," happy that the civil service has triumphed. Meanwhile, Jim Hacker sits in silence, wondering if he has been had once
again.

"Yes, Minister" reportedly won a receptive audience in governmental
circles in Ottawa, where more than one minister undoubtedly identified
with the tribulations of the Honourable James Hacker. But behind its
comic exterior, "Yes, Minister" raised an important question: Who controls whom? Are public servants simply a neutral instrument, responding to the requests of their political superiors? Or are they actors in the

political process who use their expertise and experience to direct the decisions of their nominal masters in ways that serve their own interests?

In theory, at least, the answer to this question is an obvious one. The Canadian public service, based on British tradition, is composed of non-partisan professionals who carry out the commands of ministers. The public service is expected to be faithful and responsive to all govern-ments—whatever their political complexion. The public servant is on *tap*, not on *top*. This practice accords with the tenets of democracy and guarantees a corps of officials capable of carrying out the complex administrative tasks of government.

In practice, however, ministers frequently complain that the reality often falls short of the ideal. Jim Hacker has not been alone in wonder-ing if his public servants are consciously frustrating his will. In recent years, former ministers and senior decision-makers have published memoirs citing incidents in which public servants have acted to frustrate the will of elected representatives. Sometimes the problem stems from the political affinities of public servants. There is a fear among some ministers that appointed officials are no longer nonpartisan. But often it is the loyalty of appointed officials to past policies—"civil service pol-icy"—that is at the heart of the problem. In short, the problem is not political affinity, but rather bureaucratic self-interest.

In Canada, few have spoken out so candidly on the subject as Flora MacDonald. MacDonald, in 1979, was named Minister of External Affairs in the short-lived Clark government. In the first selection, she recounts her frustrations in this post. In an account reminiscent of "Yes, Minister," she outlines the various strategies employed by senior officials to secure their own goals.

In the other reading, Don Page responds to MacDonald's accusa-tions. Dr. Page spent sixteen years in the federal public service during which time he was a senior department historian, policy analyst, and speech writer in the Department of External Affairs and International Trade Canada. This reading provides some background to explain why MacDonald found herself in the predicament that she complained about. Page ends his article by outlining the basic requisites for strong ministerial leadership.

# The Minister and the Mandarins

*Flora MacDonald*

As a new Secretary of State for External Affairs, it seemed to me that I ought to establish a foreign policy with the twin objectives that Canada should receive maximum advantage from its foreign relations and that it should play a fully responsible role in the international scene. I was convinced that this required both broad public support for foreign and aid policies and an ability, on my part, to weigh independently the advice I received from public servants.

It is natural that advice from public servants would be based on a continuation of existing policy—policy which, in large part, had had its genesis within the Department. And while it was not necessarily wrong, neither was it necessarily right. A new Minister must be able to assess, for himself or herself, where we have been and where we ought to be going.

This did not mean a wholesale rejection of everything that had gone before or was currently in process; but, given my desire to develop a foreign policy attuned to the turbulent 1980s, I was determined that advice as to how we could achieve that goal should come from more than one quarter. It was, and is, natural that senior bureaucrats would have their own methods of gaining approval for the decisions they both needed and especially wanted. A new Minister, just trying to find his or her way through the labyrinth of bureaucracy, is indeed vulnerable to such practices. A new Minister in a new government which had not paced the corridors of power for some sixteen years is not only vulnerable but, indeed, almost without protection.

To reduce this dependency on bureaucratic advice and to provide a mechanism that would ensure political input into the decision-making process, a cabinet committee system was devised by the Prime Minister which aimed to establish a better equilibrium between Ministers and mandarins. While this mechanism was being set up at the cabinet level, I personally moved on two fronts to ensure that I was the recipient of independent advice I considered would be critical to my own survival as an effective Minister.

First, I determined that my personal staff would play a critical role in the evaluation of all sensitive policy issues. Although few in number, their independent and sometimes irreverent analysis of these issues was invaluable.

Secondly, with the cooperation of some interested persons from outside government circles—experts, primarily but not exclusively from the ranks of academe—I had taken the initial steps in developing what I hoped would be a mildly formalized structure to offer ongoing advice.

Without some such protective mechanisms, the Minister is indeed at the mercy of bureaucratic domination, not because of some devious manipulative plot, but simply because that is the way the system has been allowed to develop. To emphasize the point, and the concerns that flow from it, and because others have documented it so much better than I, I will refer to the memoirs and speeches of several cabinet members who faced a similar situation.

Anthony Wedgwood Benn began a recent lecture, entitled "Manifestos and Mandarins," with the statement: "There are conflicts and tensions within our political system which receive a great deal of public attention. One relationship which has received far less public attention than its importance justifies is the balance of power between Ministers and senior permanent government officials."

He continued:

> It would be a mistake to suppose that the senior ranks of the civil service are active Conservatives (or in Canada, Liberals) posing as impartial administrators. The issue is not their personal political views, nor their preferences for any particular government. The problem arises from the fact that the civil service sees itself as being above the party battle, with a political position of its own to defend.
>
> Civil service policy—and there is no other way to describe it—is an amalgam of views that have been developed over a long period of time. It draws some of its force from a deep commitment to the benefits of continuity, and a fear that adversary politics may lead to sharp reversals by incoming governments of policies devised by their predecessors, which the civil service played a great part in developing.[1]

In a country like Canada with a long history of one party dominance, this tendency is even more entrenched. Benn goes on to list the techniques employed by the doyens of Whitehall when ministerial views differ from their own:

> By briefing Ministers—the document prepared by officials for presentation to incoming Ministers after a general election comes in two versions, one for each major party.

It is a very important document that has attracted no public interest, and is presented to a Minister at the busiest moment of his life—when he enters his department and is at once bombarded by decisions to be made, the significance of which he cannot at that moment appreciate.

The brief may thus be rapidly scanned and put aside for a proper reading when the pressure eases, which it rarely does.

Thus Ministers are continually guided to reach their decisions within that framework. Those Ministers who seek to open up options beyond that framework are usually unable to get their proposals seriously considered.

By the control of information—the flow of necessary information to a Minister on a certain subject can be made selective, in other ways restricted, delayed until it is too late, or stopped altogether.

By the mobilisation of Whitehall—it is also easy for the Civil Service to stop a Minister by mobilising a whole range of internal forces against his policy.

The normal method is for officials to telephone their colleagues in other departments to report what a Minister is proposing to do; thus stimulating a flow of letters from other Ministers (drafted for them by their officials) asking to be consulted, calling for inter-departmental committees to be set up, all in the hope that an unwelcome initiative can be nipped in the bud.[2]

Tony Benn's lecture dealt with the interface between cabinet ministers generally and their senior mandarins. Henry Kissinger in his recent book *The White House Years* deals with the particular problems which confront a Secretary of State:

Cabinet members are soon overwhelmed by the insistent demands of running their departments. On the whole, a period in high office consumes intellectual capital; it does not create it. Most high officials leave office with the perceptions and insights with which they entered; they learn how to make decisions but not what decisions to make. And the less they know at the outset, the more dependent they are on the only source of available knowledge; the permanent officials. Unsure of their own judgement, unaware of alternatives, they have little choice except to follow the advice of the experts.

This is a particular problem for a Secretary of State. He is at the head of an organization staffed by probably the ablest and most professional group of men and women in the public service. They are intelligent, competent, loyal, and hardworking.

But the reverse side of their dedication is the conviction that a lifetime of service and study has given them insights that transcend the untrained and shallow-rooted views of political appointees.

When there is strong leadership, their professionalism makes the foreign service an invaluable and indispensable tool of policy-making. In such circumstances the foreign service becomes a disciplined and finely honed instrument; their occasional acts of self-will generate an important, sometimes an exciting dialogue. But when there is not a strong hand at the helm, clannishness tends to overcome discipline. Desk officers become advocates for the countries they deal with and not spokesmen of national policy; assistant secretaries push almost exclusively the concerns of their areas. Officers will fight for parochial interests with tenacity and a bureaucratic skill sharpened by decades of struggling for survival. They will carry out clear-cut instructions with great loyalty, but the typical foreign service officer is not easily persuaded that an instruction with which he disagrees is really clear-cut.[3]

Finally, Richard Crossman, in his very revealing diaries, has this to say:

Now for my impressions of the ministry and of the civil service. The main conviction I had when I got there was that the civil service would be profoundly resistant to outside pressure. Was that true? I think it was. I found throughout an intense dislike of bringing people in, whether they are politicians or experts.

I should say that in general I have found profound resistance in the civil service to a Minister who brings in outside advisers and experts, and profound resistance to interference by anybody with direct access to the Minister. What they like is sole ministerial responsibility because they are convinced that under this system the amount of outside influence exerted is minimal.[4]

Am I exaggerating when I use these British and American examples of resistance to ministerial attentiveness to outside advice and apply them here in Canada? I do not think so. But I think that that resistance resides almost entirely among those who really have their hands on the levers of power—the senior mandarins. And I sometimes felt they reacted as negatively to the creativity and imaginative proposals of those in the less senior ranks of the foreign service as they did to outside advice. One of my constant frustrations was to find ways in which to penetrate senior management levels so as to tap this well-spring of fresh ideas, creativity and provocative questioning which I know from some experience exists.

I found myself as vulnerable as any new minister in any new government to the techniques Tony Benn attributes to the mandarins in Whitehall. He refers to them as techniques; I often thought of them as entrapment devices. Let me give you some examples:

(a) The unnecessarily numerous crisis corridor decisions I was confronted with—here is the situation; (breathless pause), let us have your instructions.

(b) The unnecessarily long and numerous memos; one of my great triumphs was that, in the wake of the abject plea for mercy, the senior rewrite personnel agreed to reduce their verbiage by half.

(c) The late delivery to me of my submissions to cabinet, sometimes just a couple of hours (or less) before the meeting took place, thus denying me the opportunity for a full and realistic appraisal of the presentation I was supposed to be making to my cabinet colleagues. On a number of occasions my aides resorted to obtaining bootleg copies of such documents on their way through the overly complex bureaucratic approval system.

(d) The one-dimensional opinions put forward in memos. I was expected to accept the unanimous recommendation of the Department, though of course there was always the possibility that I might reject it. Seldom, if ever, was I given the luxury of multiple-choice options on matters of major import.

I mentioned earlier that in order to ensure political input into the decision-making process, the cabinet committee system grouped together ministers whose responsibilities were interrelated. Thus, all those ministers whose duties took them into the international field were members of the cabinet committee on foreign and defence policy, the one body where their initiatives could be coordinated. I was mandated by the Prime Minister to be chairman of that committee.

As such, I had to be rigorously scrupulous not to allow my departmental interests to prejudice my impartiality as chairman of the committee. The system was designed to provide an independent source of information to ministers, and particularly to cabinet committee chairmen, through the cabinet secretariat of the Privy Council Office. Memos for the chairmen, drafted by secretariat officials, analyzed the issues on the committee's agenda and pointed out the strengths and weaknesses of the various departmental positions. Deputy ministers or other officials participated in such cabinet committee meetings only if the agenda item required their attendance.

There was no comparable committee at the deputy minister level. In my view that would have undermined the decision-making role of ministers.

Not that such a committee of deputy ministers wasn't suggested. It was urged on me in a succession of proposals which I consistently rejected. Such a committee headed by a deputy whose mandate was solely that of chief officer in the department of External Affairs would, I felt, hardly be acceptable to National Defence, Industry, Trade and Commerce, Immigration, etc., as the person to coordinate their policies at the bureaucratic level. In addition, such a committee of deputy ministers would usurp or at least conflict with the function of the cabinet secretariat in the PCO. One senior mandarin used these words to describe it when he first heard of the proposal: "A mechanism to facilitate conflict."

I thought it was a dead duck; now I hear it has been activated and given the impressive title of Mirror Committee of Deputies. One wonders how many such mirror committees or deputies a cabinet minister can cope with before he or she ends up surrounded by a wall of mirrors each one reflecting the wisdom of the other into infinity. Even Alice in Wonderland might have difficulty in finding her way through what is likely to become a looking glass jungle, presenting the illusion of ministerial control.

Not only did I discover, after the takeover of the current administration, that senior mandarins had been successful in establishing this committee whose very operation must conflict with that of the cabinet secretariat, but I have also been led to believe that during my tenure copies of the private and confidential analysis done for me as a cabinet committee chairman by the PCO cabinet secretariat found their way to my deputy's desk, without my knowledge or indeed without the knowledge of those who drafted the memoranda.

This would have permitted one senior official to be in a position to have access to privileged information not available to other deputy ministers, nor indeed to cabinet ministers other than the committee chairman. One need hardly speculate on the important role control of information plays in the bureaucratic game.

On a more philosophical level, I am concerned that the proliferation of senior management coordinating committees—coordinating advice not only to senior ministers but now to groups of ministers—will seriously impair the decision-making role of ministers. Such a system effectively filters out the policy options that an entire committee might otherwise consider. Too many bureaucrats, I fear, have the mistaken impression that vigorous debate of policy options by cabinet ministers is an indication that they—the bureaucrats—have somehow failed to properly channel and coordinate views before the cabinet meeting takes place.

Regrettably too few Canadian ministers have followed the example of Richard Crossman, Tony Benn, Harold Macmillan, Henry Kissinger or Dean Acheson in providing a first hand account of the relationship between the minister and the bureaucracy. Regrettably as well, academics in this country have not paid as much attention as they should to the interface between ministers and the senior echelons of their departments. The effective management of that relationship is what distinguishes parliamentary government from bureaucratic management. As Anthony Wedgwood Benn concluded: "In considering these issues, we do not want to find new scapegoats or pile blame upon ministers or civil servants who have let the system grow into what it is. What matters now is that we should examine what has happened to our system of government with fresh eyes and resolve to reintroduce constitutional democracy to Britain" and, I might add, to Canada.

# NOTES

1. Anthony Benn, *Arguments for Democracy* (London: Johnathan Cape, 1981), 50.

2. Ibid., 54.

3. Henry Kissinger, *The White House Years* (Boston: Little, Brown, 1979), 27.

4. Richard Crossman, *The Diaries of a Cabinet Minister. Volume One: Minister of Housing, 1964–66* (London: Hamish Hamilton, 1975), 614.

# Ministers and Mandarins: Ministers Must Lead

*Don Page*

Any student of modern government or contemporary governance will quickly realize that the debate on whether ministers or mandarins make and direct policy will never end for the simple reason that it depends upon who the minister and mandarins are and what policy is being developed and enacted.[1] It thus becomes one of degree as to whether the bureaucracies, created to advise and serve ministers by implementing and administering their programs, have, in the process, substantially lessened the autonomy of ministers. If the minister is determined and assertive, then the mandarins, even with their substantive advantage due to their control of many of the sources of information and expertise, can influence but will not unilaterally be allowed to direct policy to their own ends. As a former minister, Mitchell Sharp, who had previously been a senior mandarin, has observed, while he sought advice from his civil servants and questioned what they gave him, "In the end I made my decisions and they carried them out."[2]

A weak minister, on the other hand, can easily become the willing or unwilling dupe of the mandarins. When ministers abdicate their power and authority, they may become, in the words of one former deputy minister, "toothless tigers who gum the policy proposals of the senior bureaucrats."[3] The strength of a minister depends first upon his or her leadership capabilities and style and secondly on the domestic and international circumstances that make action on policy possible. This is especially true in the setting of long-range goals and the strategies for accomplishing them, but less so in devising the technical tactics of statecraft for dealing with the multitude of issues that are on the government's agenda for any given day. Policy may be the sum of individual tactical decisions that the government makes in response to a given situation, the general strategies for accomplishing certain goals, or the long-range goals that are adopted to accomplish specific ends. A minister will probably be involved in all three levels, but the most crucial are the setting of the long-range goals and the strategies for reaching them rather than the day-by-day decisions that must be taken in order to accomplish those goals. While there is no doubt that the daily tactical decisions can give de facto shape to policy, mandarins should not be allowed to reshape that policy unless there is an absence of the will to control them and make them subservient to the overriding policy objectives of the government. Too often ministers lose control because they are so busy with the next items on the agenda to give much attention to whether past directives are being carried out. This is more of a problem in organizing the work of the minister's office to ensure that such follow-up is being carried on by mandarins who may not be as fully committed to their pursuit as the minister may wish in the light of their more immediate crises and schedules. As Mitchell Sharp reminded Flora MacDonald when she was complaining about the constraints of bureaucratic manipulation, "it was our own fault for letting the system get out of hand."[4]

There is no question that Flora MacDonald had every right to be frustrated with the bureaucratic blocking tactics that she experienced while working as Secretary of State for External Affairs. Her concerns, however, need to be seen in the wider context of what was happening both within the department and the government. In the mid-1970s there had emerged a new agenda for international affairs. The international political and security agenda of the past was now having to accommodate concerns about domestic and international economic and social issues. Environment and energy came to the forefront of international debate. Crime and terrorism took on new international dimensions with hijackings, bombings, and kidnappings. International travel was taking thousands of Canadians into situations that required greater consular protection, new air agreements, the portability of social welfare benefits, and dealing with exposure to international diseases. Business communities were no longer content to deal with market economies; they now expected the government to assist them in opening up trading opportunities with state enterprises abroad. Advances in communication technology opened up the doors to satellite-assisted diplomacy and an international aspect to the information age. Provinces were opening more offices abroad and taking a greater interest in international money markets and trade promotion. Subjects that had previously been considered primarily in the domestic realm suddenly had an international flavour to them, such as science, technology, urban affairs, the seal hunt, etc., with the result that domestic departments created their own international agendas and bureaus and became directly involved in international communications.

In theory, External Affairs was to coordinate all this international activity for the government, but in practice this was not happening because other departments and agencies complained that External's diplomats were too prone to take a soft line in negotiations because they were more interested in finding a way around a problem than in a solution that would uphold Canada's national interests. They also complained that External Affairs did not make a habit of consulting domestic departments about technical information needed to conduct negotiations on these new subjects. Equally frustrating was the fact that External's officers were rotating so often that they were not able to accumulate the necessary expertise to make the right decisions quickly. A review of the situation led to the conclusion that "initiators of activity that affects domestic affairs are also by and large the initiators of policy-decisions affecting external relations." What was even more alarming for External Affairs was the conclusion that, "while it may be theoretically desirable that Canada speak with one voice to other governments on all important matters, that ideal is unattainable. International communication is too easy and too frequent and Canada is not the kind of country that can hope to emulate the national consistency achieved by some countries through centralized state control or by others through centuries of social cohesion."[5]

When Alan Gotlieb became under-secretary in 1977, he was determined to reverse this trend and his means for doing so was in the transformation of External Affairs into a central agency of government, with a role similar to what the Justice Department did for legal affairs and Treasury Board for controlling government expenditures. To do this, External Affairs would have to bring the work of individual departments into harmony with the government's policies and take the leading role in developing national policies. In a short period of time dozens of initiatives were introduced to effect this change in managing Canada's international affairs. The under-secretary began hosting luncheons for deputy ministers and chairing interdepartmental committees that would organize material for cabinet committees. Another level of assistant deputy ministers was established to be responsible for coordinating interdepartmental issues through task forces that they would chair. Foreign service officers were seconded to domestic departments. External Affairs began preparing information sheets and briefings on international events of interest to cabinet ministers of domestic departments. Crucial to making this change effective was the support that Gotlieb had for his endeavours from the Privy Council Office, which had the ability to bring other departments into line.

To make this system for developing and coordinating policy function effectively, External Affairs was structured and operated like a pyramid with all policy recommendations working their way up through the system so that only the final conclusion went from the under-secretary to the minister. The minister at that time was Don Jamieson who was quite content to receive the best advice the bureaucracy could offer and he could sell, as he sought to give Canada's foreign affairs a higher public profile than it had enjoyed under his predecessor. It was, in short, a heyday for bureaucratic managers and manipulators under the guidance of an under-secretary who was determined to see External Affairs rejuvenated as a central agency.

It was into this environment that Flora MacDonald stepped as Secretary of State for External Affairs in 1979. Unlike many of her recent Liberal predecessors, she believed that External Affairs was too given to looking after its own interests rather than that of the government and it was time for Canada to take some new and practical initiatives such as aid to the Caribbean and Central America. Above all, she wanted some fresh initiatives that she believed could come from a review of foreign policy, if input was received from the public and parliamentarians.

At first, Gotlieb welcomed the new minister and sought to establish means for regular communication, but these quickly broke down because Miss MacDonald became so absorbed in not only routine cabinet business but the highly political workings of the inner cabinet that the prime minister had established. She also wanted things done her way, and Gotlieb, who was used to getting the bureaucracy and her predecessor to march to departmental tunes, was not about to give in to an equally stubborn minister who was determined to make actual decisions about policy and not just rubber stamp his advice. To assert her control as minister, she began to seek alternatives to his considered but selective advice by reaching below the under-secretarial level to obtain the views of the desk officers who had been debating various policy options. Gotlieb reluctantly accepted this, if officers kept him informed of what they had told the minister so that he could ensure that a consistent policy line was being developed. Equally troublesome for the under-secretary was the way in which the minister directed or allowed her personal staff to interfere with policy discussions with other departments without having the necessary information to make good decisions. Instances of her staff changing policy recommendations that put them in conflict with international and interdepartmental agreements became legendary and frustrating for all concerned. Before long, the minister and the under-secretary were working at cross purposes, which led to the underhanded tactics that the minister accused the mandarins of deploying against her initiatives and attempts to redirect policy. She would have liked to have had the under-secretary removed from office, but the prime minister rejected her request.

Perhaps in time and with a suitable intermediary, the minister and under-secretary would have found a mutually acceptable means of working together in which the minister would have been able to exert the decision-making and leadership role that she sought in the making of foreign policy. In the end, it was not so much a problem of seeking outside advice, as how she interjected those opinions into an established bureaucratic machinery that she had no time to change. Had she been able to see her foreign and aid policy reviews through to completion we might have seen a different direction to the government's policy for which she would have been the chief spokesperson and champion.

It is also noteworthy that other Conservative ministers faced similar and equally frustrating situations, not because the leading mandarins were beholden to their previous Liberal masters, but because they had come to believe that they, rather than elected officials, knew what was best for the country. A similar situation prevailed when Diefenbaker became prime minister and had to deal with the "Pearsonalities" in the department. In time, the mandarins and the ministers found the means for working well together and there was no question that a determined Howard Green would, as minister, redirect the department onto his own disarmament agenda.[6] The transition in 1984 with Joe Clark as Secretary of State for External Affairs was much quicker as both the minister and the bureaucracy focused their efforts on dealing with "the little White House," as it was dubbed by some, that developed in the Prime Minister's Office.

Liberal ministers have also had their frustrations and vice versa with the mandarins, such as Alan MacEachen, who had his own unique style for conducting or avoiding business that, at times, drove the mandarins to frustrating counter-moves through the prime minister. The first years of the Trudeau government were marked by extreme frustration as neither the mandarins nor the minister could meet the new prime minister's expectations in handling the Biafra–Nigerian Civil War, the review of Canada's role within the North Atlantic Treaty Organization, or the common tasks of speech writing and presenting succinct briefings. Once the department had adjusted its operations and acquired a new undersecretary, Mitchell Sharp was able to exercise significant ministerial leadership in the making and directing of foreign policy.

Ministers before and after MacDonald, notably Paul Martin and Joe Clark, were known for seeking advice from all levels of the department and from outsiders without losing their ability to direct policy. As the following examples will illustrate, MacDonald's frustrations should not lead us to conclude that ministers cannot affect or change policy nor that a deputy minister, like Gotlieb, must necessarily be an immovable obstacle to accomplishing a minister's wishes.

Canadian policy changed when the government announced on December 19, 1977, that because of the South African government's policy of apartheid, Canada would henceforth restrict its trade promotion with South Africa by curtailing grants to Canadian companies wishing to do business in South Africa, enforcing a code of conduct on these companies, closing its Consulate General in Johannesburg, and withdrawing its commercial officers from Cape Town. Hitherto, such initiatives had been repeatedly and strongly resisted by the Export Development Corporation and the Departments of Finance and Industry, Trade and Commerce and those within External Affairs who supported their business-as-usual stance. In the midst of repeated public calls for a change in government policy that would reflect some abhorrence with apartheid, the minister, Don Jamieson, decided that he could no longer defend Canadian trade with South Africa and demanded that the mandarins work toward a change. With strong interdepartmental opposition to overcome, Gotlieb used this as a test case for External Affairs to assert its central agency role in persuading other departments to agree. In the end, it took not only a great deal of bureaucratic manoeuvring to effect even this modest change in policy, but also the minister's strong leadership in the cabinet and the House of Commons before it became a reality. It took the minister's directive before bureaucratic action was taken.

When the Special Joint Committee of the Senate and the House of Commons on Canada's International Relations made 121 recommendations on Canadian foreign policy in 1986, the bureaucracy would have been content to give them only a nod in considering future policy directions had it not been for the obligation of the government to respond to the committee's report within 120 days. Even then, a general statement would have been sufficient for the mandarins who were aware that no additional financial or personnel resources would be available for implementing any changes, had it not been for Clark's insistence that every single recommendation be addressed in the government's response. Right at the outset, he let it be known that he wanted a "positive" response by the government to the committee's report, and to avoid the typical bureaucratic tactic of offering to study them, he singled out eleven recommendations upon which he wanted work to begin immediately, including an international register for the export and import of munitions.

When the first draft of the response was ready in August 1986, the department thought that it had done rather well in concurring with eighty-two of the recommendations, agreeing with twenty-three in principle, finding only six that were problematic, and disagreeing with only ten. For the minister, this was not good enough, and the department was told to get back to the negotiating table with its own bureaus and the nine other departments involved to come up with a more positive response. The response subsequently went through thirteen drafts, into most of which the minister had a personal input. He encouraged, pushed, and cajoled the mandarins into producing what he wanted rather than what they were prepared to advance. He was also willing to provide the necessary ministerial bargaining and clout to bring other ministers alongside when their deputies would not agree. When the final report was tabled on December 4, 1986, the government agreed with and was prepared to take action upon 103 of the committee's recommendations; it partially agreed and was prepared to take limited action on twelve others and only disagreed on six recommendations.[7]

It is noteworthy that in the six disagreements was one of the minister's initial interests. The register had been rejected by the mandarins because in the past it had never been clear that transparency in arms shipments was achievable or would inhibit shipments and it had not received any support from our NATO allies. Despite the rejection, Clark pushed his officials, and together they worked aggressively in the G-7, the European Community, and the Commonwealth to obtain the political support required to get the United Nations to establish a global arms register.

All ministers, including Clark, who maintained an excellent rapport with his bureaucrats, at times felt thwarted by their deputies, but this was more likely because of the slow pace of bureaucracies working within a shared power structure of government more than the opposition of any given mandarin. Thus Clark became annoyed at how long it took to redirect our aid systems to help President Aquino when she first came to office in the Philippines. But on the other hand, the department could swing into action within hours on several diplomatic fronts when, as a result of a story he had read in *The Edmonton Journal*, Clark wanted to protest the Tutsi's killing of the Hutu in Burundi in August 1988.[8]

Ministerial interest is at the forefront of ministerial influence. Memoranda to cabinet set out a full range of policy options and consequences, but by their own admission, few ministers actually read beyond the summary. Thus the leading ministers who have been supported by interdepartmental bureaucratic negotiations are most likely to have their views accepted as government policy. Other cabinet ministers are most interested in factual information that pertains to the policy being advocated, its domestic economic repercussions, and the impact on their political fortunes.

While the mandarins have had in the past a virtual monopoly over the information that goes into the formation of policy, technological changes in communication have reduced the minister's isolation. Equally relevant information may now be available through public broadcasts that have tended to lift the veil of secrecy that traditionally surrounds the conduct of domestic and, even more so, foreign affairs. Furthermore, access to nongovernmental foreign experts and other foreign ministers can prevent the minister from becoming a helpless pawn in the web of information being spun out to a specific policy end that is being crafted by his or her mandarins. The key to a mutually supporting team of mandarins and ministers setting policies and working together to accomplish their objectives is in understanding their respective needs and roles.

Competence for handling the position or managing the administration of the department is assumed in the experience of senior mandarins. There are four other essential things that political masters want from their bureaucratic deputies. First is absolute loyalty to them and their work. A minister must be able to trust a deputy to carry out directions and at all times to act in the minister's best interests. Because of the necessarily close relationship that must prevail between the minister and his or her deputy, the deputy is aware of information and personal attitudes that could easily destroy the minister's position relative to the prime minister, his or her cabinet colleagues, and the public. A trustworthy and discreet deputy is therefore a must.

Second is the right mix of personalities or someone they can get along with. Often, individuals who are perfectly capable of handling the responsibilities of a position fail to do so because of personality differences that breed mistrust or suspicion. This was one of the problems that caused havoc in the MacDonald–Gotlieb relationship.

Third is the ability to move the machinery of government to desired ends. The deputy must be a bureaucratic power broker in the shared-power bureaucracy of government. In the case of changing policy regarding South Africa, it was carried out masterfully.

Fourth is the ability to enhance the minister's political career by offering sound advice that takes account of the prevailing and anticipated political climate. Whatever may be termed the classical separation between ministers and their deputies as elected officials and public servants, any deputy worth his or her salt in the bureaucracy will know and consider the political implications before offering advice. This does not mean that political expediency will necessarily be dominant in the decision-making, but it must be weighed in the process.

In return for this, deputies expect that ministers will offer visionary leadership and their full support when deputies seek to carry out that policy direction. The extent of that support has, however, lessened somewhat of late as witnessed in the Al-Mashat affair when a top mandarin was manoeuvred and pressured into taking the blame for the government's bungling in the handling of this immigration case. When a frustrated mandarin refused to be made the scapegoat and sought to offer a public defence for shifting the blame to others, it became clear that mandarins would no longer be silent when ministers or their staff were equally culpable and ministers could not be counted upon to offer protection from public exposure and malignment for their mandarins.[9]

For some time there has existed among many mandarins a malaise or cynical attitude about their employers as though nothing is to be accomplished by a government except the creation of good feelings and the illusion of action. As a result, the best and the brightest dutifully exercise caution in substantive matters, avoid action, or continually seek another clearance or another authorization to avoid having to take responsibility for their actions. Matters afflicting the current and future well-being of Canadians are too often seen only as nettlesome disruptions that must be calmed, rather than problems that must be solved or responsibilities that must be faced. Those who would dare to cry out for change are isolated as mavericks who don't know how to play the policy game in the genteel and accepted manner that bureaucracies have become accustomed to operating within. This attitude is soul destroying for the creative brains that make up the bureaucracy. It was these creative juices in the bowels of the department that MacDonald so rightly tried to tap. But those creative juices must also be flowing from the top downward.

Government ministries that were once built on visionary leadership have seemingly lost their direction and vigour. Employees, clients, and customers no longer recognize those at the top as being determined and confident in their sense of direction, bold and courageous in their decision-making, and inspiring and uplifting in their vision and management. While there is no question that leadership has become more difficult in the current climate of regulatory controls and shared power, the need for such leadership not only exists but must be enhanced if an organization is to prosper and, maybe, to survive in such challenging times. Without good leadership, a department is like a lifeboat adrift in turbulent seas with no oars, no charts, no compass, and no hope.

Inspired ministerial leadership can transform and renew an organization by energizing and inspiring employees who have lost confidence in their ability to make a meaningful contribution to the enterprise and, through it, to society at large. For many years it was commonly thought in the federal bureaucracy that ministers come and go but the deputies are the ones responsible for not only administration but policy initiatives. But times have changed; deputies are changed as often as ministers and sustained leadership cannot be maintained as it once was. More than ever before, that responsibility must ultimately be on the shoulders of the minister if they are to be effective.

As Burt Nanus explains in his book *Visionary Leadership*: "Effective leaders have agendas; they are totally results oriented. They adopt challenging new visions of what is both possible and desirable, communicate their visions, and persuade others to become so committed to these new directions that they are eager to lend their resources and energies to make them happen. In this way, effective leaders build lasting institutions that change the world."[10]

A visionary minister must play four key roles in giving leadership to the mandarins as a direction setter, spokesperson, change agent, and coach. The minister is ultimately responsible for selecting and articulat-

ing the targets toward which the ministry is to move. As a direction setter, the minister must set a vision that is so compelling that everyone in
the department will want to work toward making it happen. Then the
minister must become the chief advocate and negotiator for accomplishing that vision with both internal and external constituencies. In so
doing, the minister creates the morale and spirit for the organization
that will enable the vision to be realized. Along this course obstacles will
have to be overcome. At the macro-political level, the minister must
assess the current internal and external environment and suggest the
changes that are necessary to accomplish the task. This means setting
the priority for changes and communicating the urgency for change to
others. None of this could be accomplished without a responsive team of
mandarins, and for that reason the minister must mentor, at least the
senior mandarins, in making his or her vision that of the department
and the mandarins who will be empowered for accomplishment. This
involves a commitment to enabling others to succeed, respecting them,
building trust, helping them to learn and grow, and teaching them how
to constantly improve their ability to achieve the vision.

Studies of what motivates people indicate that subordinates want
something to which they can be committed, something that is worth
contributing their best efforts to accomplishing. Mandarins want to
know that they are doing something significant, that it is part of the
larger vision. They want to do something that will significantly make life
better for others, their ministry, and the nation. The absence of this
ministerial coaching has been one of the greatest deficiencies in ministerial leadership at External Affairs and International Trade Canada as
well as generally throughout the government. Mandarins know their
jobs, but they have not bought into the government's vision because it
has been so poorly or rarely communicated by ministers.

Effective ministerial leadership inspires and mobilizes others to
undertake collective action to resolve important public problems effectively and ethically, thereby contributing to the common good. In the
shared-power world of modern government, effective leadership stimu-
lates vision, hope, courage, and commitment.[11] That is the minister's
responsibility if the mandarins are to play their proper role as managers
for accomplishing the government's goals.

### NOTES

1. Joel D. Aberbach, Robert D. Putnam, and Bert A. Rockman, *Bureaucrats and
   Politicians in Western Bureaucracies* (Cambridge: Harvard University Press,
   1981). For a succinct discussion of this issue, see Kim R. Nossal, *The Politics of
   Canadian Foreign Policy* (Scarborough: Prentice-Hall, 1985), pp. 143–54.

2. Mitchell Sharp, "The Role of Mandarins," *Policy Options* (May/June 1981): 43.

3. Douglas Hartle, "Techniques and Processes of Administration," *Canadian Public Administration* (Spring 1976): 32.

4. Sharp, "The Role of Mandarins," p. 44.

5. Allan McGill, "The Role of the Department of External Affairs in the Government of Canada, Part III, What Is the Role and How Is It Performed?" (Ottawa: Department of External Affairs, 1976), pp. 10, 27. This study was issued as Circular Document Admin. No. 41/76 on July 8, 1976, and is available through the library of External Affairs and International Trade Canada in Ottawa.

6. On Diefenbaker's frustrations with the mandarins and how they were handled, see H. Basil Robinson, *Diefenbaker's World: A Populist in Foreign Affairs* (Toronto: University of Toronto Press, 1989) and John Hilliker, "The Politicians and the Pearsonalities: The Diefenbaker Government and the Conduct of Canadian External Relations," *Historical Papers* (Ottawa: Canadian Historical Association, 1984), pp. 151–67.

7. *Canada's International Relations: Response of the Government of Canada to the Report of the Special Joint Committee of the Senate and the House of Commons* (Ottawa: External Affairs Canada, 1986).

8. See "Ottawa's African Policy Ridiculed by Burundi Events," *The Edmonton Journal*, August 24, 1988, p. A2 (a Southam News story by Jonathan Manthorpe) and "Clark Lambastes Burundi Over Tribal Massacre," *The Ottawa Citizen*, September 1, 1988, p. A12 (a Canadian Press wire story).

9. Anthony Wilson-Smith and Bruce Wallace, "Trading Blame: Politicians and Bureaucrats Clash at an Inquiry Into How Iraq's Mashat Got Into Canada," *Maclean's*, June 17, 1991, pp. 16–17.

10. Burt Nanus, *Visionary Leadership: Creating a Compelling Sense of Direction for Your Organization* (San Francisco: Jossey-Bass, 1992), p. 4.

11. John M. Bryson and Barbara C. Crosby, *Leadership for the Common Good: Tackling Public Problems in a Shared-Power World* (San Francisco: Jossey-Bass, 1992), p. 357.

# POSTSCRIPT

Flora MacDonald's article is entitled "The Minister and the Mandarins." The term "mandarin" was first applied to the bureaucratic class of imperial China. In contemporary political science usage, mandarin is generally used to describe a small group of senior officials whose ability to influence public policy is believed to be enormous. Thus the use of the term in her title is intended to reinforce in the reader's mind MacDonald's concern about the expansion of the powers of civil servants.

In examining this debate, an interesting question arises: To what extent is the question of who controls whom a matter of the particular personalities and skills of the individuals involved or a part of a larger phenomenon related to the rise of bureaucratic government? Some social theorists maintain that the power of bureaucrats is really the product of modern forms of bureaucratic organization itself that depend on the skills, technical knowledge, and managerial expertise of its officials. In both public and private organizations, leaders must rely on their bureaucratic officials for advice on what to do and how to implement decisions. Thus the problems that MacDonald complains about would appear to be endemic to all modern bureaucratic organizations. But Page seems to put much more emphasis on the individuals involved and the skills and vision that they bring to their task. In particular, he notes that ministers have at times been ineffective because they have failed to impart to their mandarins a sense of vision, a problem that Page suggests has been prevalent throughout federal government departments in recent years. What factors would explain the malaise that Page finds?

The question of ministerial control becomes more acute when a transition in government is taking place. Incoming ministers fear that public servants are too wedded to the practices and policies of the outgoing administration. The fear is heightened in cases where the previous government has been in office for a prolonged period or is of a significantly different ideological stripe. In such circumstances, it is only natural that newly appointed ministers may feel less than comfortable with their senior officials.

How can an incoming government be assured that the advice the civil service offers is truly objective and that it will not attempt to frustrate achievement of its political agenda? One solution would be to adopt the American approach. With the selection of a new president, the upper echelons of the bureaucracy are replaced. Officials associated with the old administration move out, and those identified with the new move in. This system is intended to create a more responsive administration, but it does raise questions of competency.

The tradition of nonpartisan public service is sufficiently strong in Canada that few governments have tried the American solution to bureaucratic intransigence. One exception was the transition to power of the Conservative Party of Grant Devine in Saskatchewan. In replacing a New Democratic government whose policy preferences were very different from its own, the Devine government believed that the public service might not be receptive to its policy agenda. Thus the Devine government fired a large number of senior and lower-level civil servants while drastically restructuring the public service. Hans Michelmann and Jeffrey Steeves, in "The 1982 Transition in Power in Saskatchewan: The Progressive Conservatives and the Public Service," *Canadian Public Administration* 28, no. 1 (Spring 1985): 1–23, provide an interesting account of these events and evaluate the impact of this "Americanized" approach to the civil service.

Some analysts have attempted to put forward other proposals for maintaining the accountability of the public service while preserving its political neutrality. Thomas d'Aquino, "The Public Service of Canada: The Case for Political Neutrality," *Canadian Public Administration* 2, no. 1 (Spring 1984): 14–23, and Gordon Osbaldeston, "The Public Servant and Politics," *Policy Options* (January 1987): 3–7, both suggest ways in which the position of the minister can be strengthened through the role of senior political advisers. A full-length treatment of these ideas can be found in Gordon Osbaldeston, *Keeping Deputy Ministers Accountable* (Toronto: McGraw-Hill Ryerson, 1990).

As Page notes in his article, the type of relationship that exists between a minister and deputy minister is important. In Canada's parliamentary system this relationship has traditionally been based on the concept of ministerial responsibility. Under this principle, the minister speaks for the department and takes public responsibility for its performance. In return, civil servants are expected to give loyal support to the minister while having their anonymity protected. Despite this tradition, in recent years there have been several occasions when ministers have named and publicly blamed public servants for decisions that they have made. The most notable of these incidents was the Al-Mashat affair. A controversy arose when it was discovered that the Canadian government had admitted a leading Iraqi political figure at a time when Canada was about to participate in a war with that country. When called before a parliamentary committee to explain the decision, the minister responsible, Barbara McDougall, publicly named the specific officials who made the decision and shifted responsibility to them. Does such breach of tradition indicate an erosion of the principle of ministerial responsibility? What implications does it have for the way ministers and civil servants relate to each other in the future? For an interesting discussion of this incident, see S.L. Sutherland, "The Al-Mashat Affair: Administrative Responsibility in Parliamentary Institutions," *Canadian Public Administration* (Winter 1991): 573–603.

# ISSUE ELEVEN

## Should Party Discipline Be Relaxed?

**YES** DAVID KILGOUR, JOHN KIRSNER, and KENNETH McCONNELL, "Discipline versus Democracy: Party Discipline in Canadian Politics"

**NO** ROBERT J. JACKSON and PAUL CONLIN, "The Imperative of Party Discipline in the Canadian Political System"

David Kilgour, a Member of Parliament from Alberta, has had a rocky relationship with the Progressive Conservative Party over the years. Elected to Parliament in 1979 as a member of the Conservative Party, Kilgour quit the party caucus in April 1987 in protest over the Conservative government's policies for the West and its failure to develop adequate ethical guidelines for elected representatives. Kilgour rejoined the Tory caucus in February 1988, but soon became critical of his party's proposed Goods and Services Tax (GST). On April 10, 1990, he voted against the government's bill authorizing the GST, and as a consequence was expelled from the caucus of the Progressive Conservative Party. Kilgour subsequently crossed the floor to sit as a member of the Liberal Party.

David Kilgour's troubles with his party stem from the well-known tradition of party discipline, which requires Members of Parliament to vote according to their party's position. Clearly, the member from Alberta has some difficulty with this tradition, and he is not alone. In 1983, a Gallup poll showed that only 7.9 percent of respondents believed that the first priority should be loyalty to his or her party.

Despite this, political leaders have long felt that the principle of party discipline was vital to the functioning of parliamentary government in Canada. When necessary, as in the case of David Kilgour, party officials have shown that they are willing to take strong measures to enforce party discipline—by withholding support for a candidate at election time, by denying parliamentary appointments, or even by expelling a recalcitrant MP from the party caucus.

The rationale for discipline in political parties is a simple one. Canada has a parliamentary system of government that requires that the party in power maintain the support and confidence of the majority of the members of the legislative branch. Without this support, the government would find it difficult to carry out the mandate on which it is elected and, more important, to remain in power. Party discipline is a means of preventing these occurrences.

For many Canadians, as reflected in the following two readings, the debate over party discipline hinges largely on whether or not Canada should move closer to an American model, where members of Congress are seen as being relatively free to vote according to personal conscience and constituency interest. David Kilgour, John Kirsner, and Kenneth McConnell argue that relaxed party discipline would advance the cause of democracy and provide better representation for individual constituents. Robert Jackson and Paul Conlin counter that the weakening of party discipline would give Canada an American-style system in which special interest groups, not elected officials, would control our legislative representatives.

## Discipline versus Democracy: Party Discipline in Canadian Politics

*David Kilgour, John Kirsner, and Kenneth McConnell*

Representative democracy in Canada is so dominated by political parties that some experts believe the party discipline exerted on most votes in our House of Commons and provincial legislatures is the tightest in the democratic world. Defenders of our model argue that many Canadians prefer it this way because each party's candidates can be assumed at election time to share the party's position on every issue. Others contend our executive democracy, patterned on a system prevailing in Great Britain about three centuries ago, requires iron party discipline if our fused legislative and executive branches of government are to function effectively. Another reason, probably the most important, is that our practice makes life easier for leaders of both government and opposition parties.

Unlike parliamentary systems in places such as Great Britain and Germany, virtually every vote in Canadian legislatures is considered potentially one of nonconfidence in the government. Even a frivolous opposition motion to adjourn for the day, if lost, can be deemed by a cabinet to have been one of nonconfidence. The whips of government parties have for decades used the possibility of an early election to push their members into voting the party line. The opposition attitude is so similar that we had a few years ago the spectacle of both opposition parties in our House of Commons arguing that a free vote on an abortion resolution would "rip out the heart" of our parliamentary system of government. The constituents of both provincial and federal legislators would be the real winners if party discipline is loosened. Private members from both government and opposition benches could then take positions on government bills and other matters based on assisting their constituents instead of their respective party hierarchies.

## PARTY DISCIPLINE IN CANADA

W.S. Gilbert put the present Canadian political reality succinctly: "I always voted at my party's call and I never thought of thinking for myself at all." Canadian Members of Parliament are essentially passive observers in the formulation and administration of most national policy. Indeed, Sean Moore, editor of the Ottawa lobbyist magazine *The Lobby Digest*, told a committee of MPs in early 1993 that they are rarely lobbied by the almost 3,000 reported lobbyists in the capital because "elected officials play a very minor role in governing."

MPs from all parties vote in solid blocs on almost every issue. Government members do so from a fear that a lost vote on a measure will be deemed by their prime minister as a loss of confidence. This stems from the early to mid-19th-century British concept that a government falls if it loses the support of a majority in the Commons on any vote.

Besides the threat of parliamentary dissolution, private members are also subject to rewards and punishments from party leadership, depending on how they vote. A "loyal" MP who votes the party line will be a candidate for promotion (if in the government party, perhaps to cabinet), or other benefits from the party, such as interesting trips or appointment to an interesting House committee. A "disloyal" MP who votes against the party leadership may be prevented from ascending the political ladder and could ultimately be thrown out of the party caucus. In light of this, "caucus solidarity and my constituents be damned" might be the real oath of office for most honourable members in all political parties.

Reg Stackhouse, a former Tory MP for Scarborough West, in a submission to the Task Force on Reform of the House of Commons in 1985, commented on the discipline imposed on private members of the government party:

> Not only is it demanded that [the member] vote with the government on crucial matters such as the Speech from the Throne or the budget, but also that he vote, speak or remain silent according to the dictate of the government. Even though a government may be at no risk of falling, it requires this all but unconditional commitment, and renders the member a seeming robot, at least imaginatively replaceable by a voting machine.

This is the major defect in Canadian parliamentary democracy: most MPs are essentially brute voters who submit to any demand from their respective party whips. In Canada's current political culture, a prime minister or premier could in practice on all confidence votes cast proxy votes on behalf of all government members. The same practice prevails in the opposition parties because they think themselves obliged to vote in uniform party blocs virtually always. If not, some of our media, apparently unaware that parliamentary democracy has evolved elsewhere, including in the matters of the parliamentary system in the United Kingdom, report that the opposition leaders cannot control their caucuses. This status quo has persisted for so long primarily because party leaders and policy mandarins obviously prefer it. Measures going into the House of Commons where one party has a majority usually emerge essentially unscathed. Everything follows a highly predictable script: obedient government members praise it; opposition parties rail against it; and plenty of bad measures become law essentially unamended.

The present regional differences and priorities require much better public expression in Parliament, at least if one central institution of our national government is to reflect adequately all parts of the country. Regional voices are frequently suffocated by rigid party discipline and the entrenched habit of the national caucuses to maintain a close eye on what opinion leaders, particularly columnists in Toronto–Ottawa–Montreal, regard as the national interest on any issue. Therefore, reforming the role of MPs is not only essential for parliamentary legitimacy in postmodern Canada, but is vital to "nationalizing Ottawa."

## ELIMINATING EXCESSES

A report by the late Eugene Forsey and Graham Eglington (*The Question of Confidence in Responsible Government*) lists a large number of measures defeated in the Westminster Parliament. On most, the cabinet of the day simply carried on, presumably either dropping the failed proposal or seeking majority support for a different measure. For tax bills, the list of such defeats begins in 1834. During 1975, for example, a financial bill of the Harold Wilson cabinet dealing with their value-added tax rate was defeated, but the ministry carried on in office, treating it not as a confidence vote.

The Forsey-Eglington Report also emphasizes that in earlier years, government MPs in Canada were permitted to vote against cabinet measures. For example, between 1867 and 1872, their study lists fully eighteen pages of cases in which Conservative MPs voted against measures of John A. Macdonald's government. The sky did not fall; Macdonald's government was able to function effectively; government MPs could keep both their self-respect and their membership in the government caucus.

The study also provides interesting data about voting in our House of Commons during other periods: in 1896, fully sixteen Conservative MPs voted with Laurier's Liberals to adjourn a Conservative measure intended to restore Catholic schools in Manitoba; in 1981, sixteen Conservative MPs, including three who later became ministers, voted against the final resolution patriating our Constitution.

The all-party McGrath Report on parliamentary reform came to the conclusion that the role of the individual member must be enhanced. As James McGrath himself said in 1985, "I wanted to put into place a system where being a member of Parliament would be seen to be an end to itself and not a means to an end." On the question of nonconfidence, McGrath recommended:

- a government should be careful before it designates a vote as one of confidence. It should confine such declarations to measures central to its administration;

- while a defeat on supply is a serious matter, elimination or reduction of an estimate can be accepted;

- in a Parliament with a government in command of a majority, the matter of confidence has really been settled by the electorate;

- government should therefore have the wisdom to permit members to decide many matters in their own personal judgments.

Reg Stackhouse agrees that party discipline must have limits: "Tight party lines need be drawn only when the government's confidence is at stake, i.e., when the government decides the fate of a bill is absolutely essential to its objectives."

One way to reduce party discipline in the interest of greater fairness for every province would be to write into our Constitution, as the West Germans did in their Basic Law, that MPs and senators shall "not [be] bound by orders and instructions and shall be subject only to their conscience." Party discipline diluted this principle in West Germany, but when combined with another feature of their Constitution—that no chancellor can be defeated in their equivalent of our House of Commons unless a majority of members simultaneously agree on a new person to become chancellor—there now appears to be a more independent role for members of the Bundestag than for Canadian Members of Parliament. For example, in the case of the defeat of the minority Clark government in 1979 on its budget, the West German rule would have kept Clark in office unless the Liberals, New Democrats, and Social Credit MPs had agreed simultaneously on a new prime minister who could hold the confidence of a majority of MPs. A similar rule, if adopted by the House of Commons, would inevitably weaken our party discipline significantly because MPs from all parties could vote on the merits of issues, knowing that defeat would bring down only the measure and not the government.

Another approach would be for each new federal or provincial cabinet to specify at the start of their mandate which matters at the heart of their program will be confidence issues. The Mulroney government, for example, might have spelled out in late 1988 that the Canada–U.S. Free Trade Agreement would be a confidence issue. In those situations, party discipline would be justifiable. Otherwise, its backbenchers would be free to vote for their constituents' interests at all times. This restored independence for legislators would lead to better representation for all regions of Canada and much more occupational credibility for Canadian legislators.

A study of the 32nd Legislative Assembly of Ontario (1981–85) indicated that its members voted in uniform party blocs about 95 percent of the time. The same pattern has applied in at least the past four Parliaments in Ottawa. The Canadian pattern indicates that all of the various party leaders could cast a proxy vote on behalf of all their followers without even bothering to have them physically present. It also overlooks that a majority or even a minority government can function effectively without our present stratospheric levels of party solidarity.

# THE AMERICAN WAY

In the United States Congress, where admittedly there is a strict separation of powers between the executive and the legislative branches of government, legislation does get passed with far less party loyalty. The constitutional separation of powers and the weakness of party discipline in congressional voting behaviour greatly facilitate effective regional representation in Washington. Unlike the situation in Canada where a government falls if it loses the support of a majority in the House of Commons on a confidence vote, U.S. presidents and Congress are elected for fixed terms. Neither resigns if a particular measure is voted down in either the Senate or the House of Representatives.

The practices in our two countries are so different that *The Congressional Quarterly* defines party unity votes there as those in which at least 51 percent of members of one party vote against 51 percent of the other party. Under this definition, itself astonishing to Canadian legislators, the *Quarterly* notes that for the years 1975 to 1982 party unity votes occurred in only 44.2 percent of the 4,417 recorded Senate votes and in only 39.8 percent of those in the House of Representatives. This sample, moreover, includes the years 1977 to 1980, the last period before 1993 to 1996 when Democrats controlled the White House and both branches of Congress.

Another feature of the congressional system that fosters effective regional input in national policy-making is territorial bloc voting—something quite unknown in Canada's House of Commons. Representatives from the two political parties of the Mountain states, Sun Belt states, New England states, and others vote en bloc or work together in committees to advance common interests.

A good example of how effective regional representatives can influence the geographic location of federal government procurement, which affects the geographic distribution of the manufacturing sector, is the Southern congressional influence. It played a major role in the postwar concentration of federal military and space expenditures in the

South and in the general economic revival and growth of the Sun Belt. And during 1981–82, the height of the "boll-weevil era," the longtime legislative coalition of Southern Democrats and Republicans was successful more than 85 percent of the time, due to mutual areas of agreement and interest.

The point of this comparison is only to emphasize that, unlike the American Congress, Canadian bloc voting makes bipartisan or tripartisan agreement on anything in our legislatures exceedingly rare. In our current political culture, if a government or opposition MP's loyalty to his or her province clashes with the instruction of the party whip, putting constituents' or regional considerations first in his or her way of voting implies considerable risk to one's prospects for party advancement. Backbench MPs in Canada are thus far less able to represent regional interests effectively than are their counterparts in Washington where the congressional system provides the freedom for effective regional representation when an issue has clear regional implications. This, of course, is not to suggest that Canada should duplicate the American congressional style of government. Rather, it is to point out that the best solution to ongoing problems of representative democracy in Canada might be to adopt attractive features from various systems, including the American one.

## PUTTING CONSTITUENTS FIRST

Canada is a federal state and federalism means that on some issues the will of the popular majority will be frustrated. If the biggest battalions of voters are to prevail over smaller ones under any circumstances, we should drop the charade that we have a federal system of government that respects minorities in times of stress. The notion that the largest group of Canadians, i.e., southern Ontarians and metropolitan Quebeckers, must be accommodated always has resulted in discontent everywhere and accompanying feelings of regional irrelevancy.

In an increasingly interdependent world, many Canadians in our outer eight provinces and the territories at least want new or altered institutions that will represent the interest of both "inner Canadians" (those who live in the Toronto–Ottawa–Montreal corridor) and "outer Canadians" effectively. Unless we move away from the notion that "the national interest" is merely a code-phrase for the most populous region dominating all corners of the country, frictions between inner and outer Canada are likely to worsen.

If party discipline in Canada were relaxed, representation for all areas of Canada would be improved. It would be easier for, say, western MPs to defy their party establishments, if need be, in support of western issues. Coalitions composed of members of all parties could exist for the purpose of working together on issues of common regional or other concern. The present adversarial attitudes and structures of Parliament or legislatures in which opposition parties oppose virtually anything a government proposes might well change in the direction of parties working together for the common good.

Members of Parliament today represent an average of about 87,000 voters. At present, few government and opposition MPs have any real opportunity to put their constituents first in votes in the House of Commons. Real power is concentrated in the hands of the party leaderships. Canadian democracy itself would benefit if we put our present mind-numbing party discipline where it belongs—in the history books.

# NO

# The Imperative of Party Discipline in the Canadian Political System

*Robert J. Jackson and Paul Conlin*

The fact that Canada has been successful as a state leaves some observers perplexed. The Canadian border encases the second-largest geographic land mass in the world under the authority of one Constitution. At the same time, the country is sparsely populated by a narrow ribbon of inhabitants stretched along the 49th parallel. This widely dispersed population is subject to the pull of global economics dominated by its American neighbour to the south. From its genesis, Canada has been a linguistically and culturally heterogeneous society, and is becoming more so with each successive year. Despite the existence of all these centrifugal pressures, what we know today as Canada has existed and thrived for over a century and a quarter.

It is not by historical accident that Canada occupies the position it does today. On the contrary, the fact that Canada exists is the result of deliberate measures taken by Canadian leaders to establish policies and institutions that transcend diversity and bind the country together. Examples include national economic and social policies, a responsible cabinet/parliamentary system of government, and in particular, the establishment of broadly based and national political parties. Institutional structures, such as political parties, can transcend Canadian diversity and provide poles of allegiance against centrifugal influences. In order to fulfil this function effectively, the parties themselves must act as cohesive units and strive for party solidarity. Strong parties, based on a broad consensus, are thus vital to the effective functioning of responsible government and the Canadian state. Party solidarity, the apex of which is party discipline, is the guiding principle of the party system in Canada.[1]

Party discipline refers to the ability of the leader in a democratic state to enforce obedience on his or her followers in the legislature and in the party organization. The argument for relaxing party discipline is that MPs should not be "trained sheep," but should be free to represent the views of their constituents. Members are, after all, elected by their constituents and should be responsible to them. But the issue is not that simple; the Canadian form of government relies on cohesive political parties. In the responsible government model, the party in power is awarded an electoral mandate to enact a legislative program, and its members must support the cabinet and prime minister in order to accomplish this. An MP is not primarily a delegate of his or her constituents. Rather, an MP is elected to serve as a member of a particular party. Within that party, the MP is called upon to deliberate and participate in formulating policies, and then to accept and support the majority decision. The government will not be made more responsive if its members make it more difficult to pass legislation. The prime minister and government must have the means of achieving their objectives.

The Canadian system is premised on the idea that reason and judgment are to be respected in the field of policy-making. Parties must be entrusted to deliberate, decide, and then be judged by the electorate. Otherwise MPs would be elected to deliberate, but constituents, who have not participated in the deliberations, would retain the right to decide. Such a procedure would be ludicrous. MPs do not and should not directly represent their individual constituencies, provinces, or even regions, polling on every issue to see how they should vote. Rather, they are members of a particular party that provides broad perspectives on national issues. They run under the banner of that particular party and seek the privileges offered by it because they are in general agreement with its broad base of national policy directions, directions that can be influenced and adjusted in caucus.

As a British politician pointed out more than a century ago, "Combinations there must be—the only question is, whether they shall be broad parties, based on comprehensive ideas, and guided by men who have a name to stake on the wisdom of their course, or obscure cliques, with some narrow crotchet for a policy, and some paltry yelping shibboleth for a cry." After all, if MPs do not accept the decision arrived at by their executives and party, which groups will they represent? The special pleading of a particular pressure group that has a narrower conception of the national interest?

Party discipline is a feature inherent in the Canadian model of Parliament, and is inextricably linked to the concept of responsible government and the confidence convention. The Constitution Act, 1867, established that Canada would have a responsible cabinet/parliamentary system of government. This is the basis of our current system whereby the cabinet, as selected by the prime minister, is comprised of members of the legislature and must keep the confidence of the House of Commons. The system also presupposes an opposition party or parties that are ready and willing to attack the government in an attempt to alter or reject its legislation. The government must therefore enforce party discipline not only to enact its legislative program, but also for the sake of its own self-preservation.

The United States congressional system of government differs from the parliamentary system in several key areas. Rather than fusing the executive and legislative branches of government, the American system is based on the separation of powers. The president and all of his or her cabinet members are prohibited by the Constitution from simultaneously sitting in the executive and legislative branches. The absence of responsible government and the corresponding absence of confidence convention allows the congressional system to function without party discipline.[2]

Calls for the relaxation of party discipline in Canada are not a recent phenomenon. Like the perennial cure for the common cold, the topic of parliamentary reform provides exaggerated hopes for optimists, then later gives way to despair when it fails. As early as 1923, for example, the MP from Calgary, William Irving, introduced a motion in the House of Commons that would have allowed for the relaxation of party discipline by reducing the number of votes considered to be votes of confidence. The motion was defeated, but to this day "reformers" still look to the United States and see the relaxation of party discipline as the panacea for perceived parliamentary inadequacies. Simplistic prescriptions such as the relaxation of party discipline, while seductive, fail to take into account the complexity of the parliamentary system. It is fallacious to assume that certain selected features of the congressional system can be appended to the parliamentary system without seriously affecting the functioning of the entire system.

Imagine a scenario where party discipline in Canada was significantly relaxed. Issues formerly resolved along party lines, based on consensual lines and accommodation in caucus, would be decided on much narrower grounds. Regionalism and special interests would dominate decision-making in the House of Commons, and political parties would cease to serve their function as institutions that bind the country together. The decision-making model now in place, which requires political parties to produce nationally acceptable compromises, would be replaced by an increase in confrontation. MPs liberated from the yoke of party discipline would be saddled by the demands of lobbyists and others representing narrow special interests and regional interests. This scenario is especially disquieting when taken in conjunction with the fact that there are now five and possibly six parties legitimately competing for seats in the House of Commons, instead of only two or three. The prospect of minority governments has been greatly enhanced following the growth of the Reform Party and the Bloc Québécois. In the context of this development, the importance of party discipline increases exponentially. A lack of party discipline during a minority government would result in a chaotic situation where no prime minister could maintain the confidence of the House.

Many of the arguments against party discipline are founded on misconceptions about the practice. The very term "whip," the name given to the party member charged with the task of enforcing party discipline, conjures up images of a menacing disciplinarian imposing the will of the party on recalcitrant MPs. This is not the case, however. While there are instances where MPs have been coerced or even threatened with sanctions if they do not conform, party discipline is largely self-imposed. Because the majority of MPs enjoy relatively little job security, they do not relish the prospect of facing re-election. Consequently, never in Canadian history has a government been toppled by a breach in party discipline. Furthermore, recent studies indicate that since 1940, no MP from the governing party has ever broken party ranks during a minority government. Nor has any MP ever left the government side with a majority of fewer than nine seats.[3] This indicates that MPs, at least for the sake of their own self-preservation, are willing to tolerate party discipline.

Another misconception is that constituents do not want their MPs to toe the party line. This is a somewhat complex issue owing to the fact that the vote for the executive and legislative representative is fused into the same ballot in parliamentary systems. While it is impossible to determine the exact weight voters give to the individual candidate and the party label, several studies indicate that the determining factor is the party label. One report found that shortly after an election, fewer than two-thirds of respondents could correctly give the name of their recently elected MP.[4] More specifically, from 1940 to 1988, thirty-one MPs ran for re-election in the general election following the parliamentary session in which they revolted against their parliamentary caucus and crossed the floor. Only twelve of them were successful in the election, and three were forced to run under their former party banner. These figures contrast with the argument that the voters will reward an MP for acting independently.

The most recent substantive recommendations for reforming party discipline are embodied in the so-called McGrath Report, released in June 1985. The report had three basic conclusions:

1. there should be attitudinal changes;

2. the parties should relax their discipline; and

3. there should be organizational reform.

The committee reported: "We believe the country would be better served if members had more freedom to play an active role in the debate on public policy, even if it meant disagreeing with their parties from time to time." The report then called for an "attitudinal change" by backbenchers and asked the prime minister to accept more dissension and defeat of government measures without recourse to the threat or use of dissolution of the House.

Unfortunately, this part of the report is romantic nonsense for the following reasons:

1. Calls for an attitudinal change are unlikely to be effective. The only practicable reform is one that changes the organization around members.

2. There never was a Golden Age of Parliament, as the report implies. In the period before parties, when Canadian MPs were "loose fish," MPs were not free of financial and other social ties that constrained their voting behaviour.

3. The question should not be whether MPs are free to vote against their parties, but rather, whose interests or groups are they adopting when they do so? Free voting does not mean that MPs are free of pressures to conform with other groups' positions.[5] Is it better to have MPs' behaviour determined by widely based cohesive political parties or narrower interest groups?

The facts also belie the utopian assumptions of the McGrath Report. Since 1985, there has been no relaxation of party discipline in the House of Commons. The urging cries of "reformers" have had no effect: the reality is that MPs are already free to vote as they wish. The point is that they do not choose to exercise their liberty by taking stands against their parties. They will always be subject to constituents, interest groups, and financial pressures: the only question is whether they will follow the dictates of a broadly based party or those of another group with a narrower conception of the national interest. Those who choose wisely stand solidly with their parties, helping to protect the system of government and providing a counterpoint to the centrifugal influences of our geography and society.

## NOTES

1. Robert J. Jackson and Doreen Jackson, *Politics in Canada*, 2nd ed. (Scarborough: Prentice-Hall, 1990).

2. Robert J. Jackson and Doreen Jackson, *Contemporary Government and Politics: Democracy and Authoritarianism* (Scarborough: Prentice-Hall, 1993).

3. Paul Conlin, "Floor Crossing in the Canadian House of Commons, 1940–1992" (Carleton University: Unpublished B.A. (Hons.) research paper, 1993).

4. William Irvine, "Does the Candidate Make a Difference? The Macro-politics and Micro-politics of Getting Elected," *Canadian Journal of Political Science* 15, no. 4 (December 1982).

5. Robert J. Jackson, "Executive–Legislative Relations in Canada," in Jackson et al., *Contemporary Canadian Politics* (Scarborough: Prentice-Hall, 1987), pp. 111–25.

# P O S T S C R I P T

One's stance on the issue of party discipline depends in part on how one interprets the experience of other countries, particularly the United States. Kilgour, Kirsner, and McConnell like the freedom that the relaxed party discipline of the American system gives members of Congress to represent their constituents, especially their regional concerns. But Jackson and Conlin are sceptical—they fear that an American-style system of lax discipline leaves the door open to the excessive influence of special interests on members' voting decisions.

But is there another model that could be followed? As Kilgour, Kirsner, and McConnell note, in Great Britain, members of the House of Commons may vote against their party without fear of recrimination on issues that are understood by all not to constitute a vote of confidence. Accordingly, a government may be defeated on a particular bill and still survive. It is suggested that such a practice allows MPs some independence in the legislature without putting at risk the life of a government.

Those wishing to understand how Britain has dealt with the issue of party discipline should read John Schwarz, "Exploring a New Role in Policymaking: The British House of Commons in the 1970s," *American Political Science Review* 74, no. 1 (March 1980): 23–37. Schwarz examines the changes made to British parliamentary traditions to permit a greater amount of "cross-voting." He argues that these changes have greatly strengthened the role of the House of Commons in the legislative process.

Not everyone is convinced that the British experience can be readily adapted to Canada. C.E.S. Franks, in *The Parliament of Canada* (Toronto: University of Toronto Press, 1987), notes that there are a number of factors that make the British experience unique. Because of the much larger number of members in the British House of Commons, party discipline is much harder to enforce. A large number of safe seats make MPs less dependent on party patronage for their post-parliamentary livelihood. The cabinet in Britain is much smaller. Long-serving MPs from safe seats, who are not obsessed with promotion to the cabinet, are much less likely to succumb to the brandishments of their leader, as both Margaret Thatcher and John Major have learned to their chagrin. In contrast, there is a much higher turnover among Canadian MPs, who generally do not feel secure enough to challenge a leader they feel is necessary to their own re-election chances.

The applicability of the British experience to Canada is also explored in Peter Dobell, "Some Comments on Party Reform," in Peter Aucoin, ed., *Institutional Reforms for Representative Government* (Toronto: University of Toronto Press, 1985). Dobell is not optimistic about the prospect of Canadian party leaders relinquishing their strong control over party discipline in the near future. However, he does propose some minor modifications that would give some flexibility to individual MPs.

# ISSUE TWELVE

## Should Parliament Review Supreme Court Nominees?

**YES** F.L. MORTON, "Why the Judicial Appointment Process Must Be Reformed"

**NO** H. PATRICK GLENN, "Parliamentary Hearings for Supreme Court of Canada Appointments?"

In Canada, the appointment process for Supreme Court justices is fairly straightforward. Typically, the federal Minister of Justice, with the help of assistants, compiles a list of possible nominees. In this endeavour, the minister usually consults law societies, judges, academics, and other sources of expert opinion, though no formal requirement exists for doing so. The list is then forwarded to the prime minister, who makes a decision. Like the justice minister, the prime minister may seek the advice of various parties, but again this is entirely discretionary. As well, the prime minister is free to choose someone not found on the list.

In carrying out their responsibilities, both the justice minister and the prime minister face some constraints. A Supreme Court justice must be either a lawyer of ten years' standing or have been a judge of a provincial superior court. Also, the Supreme Court Act dictates that three of the nine justices be from Quebec, and convention requires that three come from Ontario, two from the West, and one from Atlantic Canada. Furthermore, questions of gender, race, and ethnicity also enter into the deliberations. Notwithstanding these considerations, it is clear that executive members of the federal government—especially the prime minister—are central to the appointment process.

In recent years, some have begun to question this process, which in turn is a direct result of the enormous impact of the Charter of Rights and Freedoms. Through its interpretation of the Charter, the Supreme

Court has experienced an increase in its influence, and this has produced a call for a more open nomination system. If the justices are to wield significant power, then their selection cannot be left to the prime minister and a handful of experts. Democracy and the concern for an accountable judiciary demand that the public and their elected representatives play a larger role in nomination of justices.

A favourite proposal for changing the present process is the use of parliamentary hearings. In the United States, the president nominates a justice to sit on the U.S. Supreme Court, who then must appear before a Senate committee so that interested parties may gain an appreciation of the nominee's qualifications, past record, and judicial philosophy. The same general procedure is proposed for Canada. The result, many argue, would be a more accountable Supreme Court, and a nation more informed about a most powerful group of men and women.

Others, though, are less convinced of the need for parliamentary hearings. The prospect of public hearings might scare off highly qualified jurists, and the American experience suggests that nominees will offer forthright answers to only the most trivial of questions—what matters will remain a mystery. Perhaps more important, the hearings may impinge upon the independence of the judiciary. For judges to be impartial arbiters of the law, they must be free of political entanglements, but the adoption of hearings might blur the distinction between the law and politics.

In the readings, F.L. Morton, a political scientist who specializes in judicial politics, argues for parliamentary hearings. H. Patrick Glenn, a professor of law at McGill University, contends that Canada should resist the temptation to adopt hearings for Supreme Court appointments.

# Why the Judicial Appointment Process Must Be Reformed

## F.L. Morton

It is time to reform the appointment process for Supreme Court judges. Since the adoption of the Charter of Rights and Freedoms in 1982, the Supreme Court has become a powerful actor in Canadian politics. Yet the appointment of our new constitutional masters remains unchanged, shielded from any public review or comment. Like the selection of a new Pope, Canadians learn who has been chosen as one of their new constitutional priests only after the decision has been made. This closed system was appropriate to the important but secondary role played by judges under Canada's old regime of parliamentary supremacy. It is completely inconsistent with the powerful new role of judges under the Charter. In a properly organized democracy, the exercise of political power must be ultimately accountable. Under the new regime ushered in by the Charter, this is no longer the case. If we are to prevent constitutional supremacy from degenerating into judicial supremacy, we must amend the appointment process to include some form of public review of the candidates.

There can be no questioning the fact that the Charter has fundamentally altered the role of the Supreme Court in Canadian politics. Prior to 1982, the court rarely obstructed the policy choices of Parliament or provincial legislatures. During this era, most of the Supreme Court's decisions dealt with civil (private) law disputes. Legislatures made these laws and courts applied and interpreted them. If a government believed the court had misinterpreted a statute, this mistake could be quickly reversed by legislative amendment. During the 1950s and 1960s, the court averaged less than three constitutional decisions per year, almost all in the field of federalism. Impact studies found that even a negative division of powers decision rarely prevented a determined government from achieving the same policy objective through alternative legislative means.

The adoption of the Canadian Bill of Rights in 1960 did not change the court's low political profile. In keeping with the then strong British influence in Canadian legal culture, the court interpreted the Bill of

Rights in a traditional and deferential manner. In thirty-five decisions over twenty years, the individual rights-claimant won only five cases. In only one case did the Supreme Court declare a federal statute invalid. Writing in the late 1960s, one expert accurately described the Supreme Court as "the quiet court in an unquiet country."[1]

The "Charter Revolution" of the 1980s brought this era to an abrupt end.[2] In the first decade following its adoption, the Supreme Court made over 200 Charter decisions. The court now averages close to twenty-five Charter decisions a year, about 20 percent of its total case load. In these first 200 decisions, the court ruled in favour of the rights-claimant sixty-seven times, in the process striking down portions of twenty-seven federal and fourteen provincial statutes. These statistics, as impressive as they are, still fail to capture the extent of the court's new influence over public policy—of who gets what, when, and how.

The court has virtually rewritten the law of Canadian criminal process, reversing many of its earlier precedents along the way. The court has adopted an exclusionary rule that is at least as rigorous as the American practice.[3] The right to counsel has been interpreted to discourage almost any police questioning of suspects in the absence of counsel[4] and to preclude judicial use of almost any form of self-incrimination at any stage in the investigative process.[5] A recent comparative study concluded that the accused in Canadian criminal cases now enjoy more rights than in the United States.[6] As a consequence of these decisions, the cost of publicly funded legal aid has skyrocketed. In Ontario, legal-aid costs rose from $56 million in 1982 to $213 million in 1992. In Alberta, legal-aid costs grew 42 percent in 1992 alone. As predicted by constitutional expert Eugene Forsey in 1982, the Charter has indeed proven to be a gold mine for lawyers.

The court struck down Canada's abortion law in its 1988 *Morgentaler* ruling, notwithstanding the fact that any reference to abortion—pro or con—had been intentionally excluded from the Charter. In a similar vein, lower courts have added homosexuality to the list of forms of discrimination prohibited by the Charter, again despite clear evidence that this option was explicitly rejected when the Charter was being drafted.[7] The court also struck down the federal Sunday-closing law (which it had upheld under the 1960 Bill of Rights), paving the way for wide-open Sunday shopping in most provinces. In the politically sensitive area of language rights, the court has also been active. It struck down several sections of Quebec's Bill 101, the Charter of the French Language, contributing to Quebec's sense of alienation from English Canada and the failed attempts at constitutional reconciliation in the Meech Lake and Charlottetown accords. The court has aggressively interpreted the official minority language education rights provisions, requiring provinces not just to provide minority-language education services, but in some cases separate facilities and even specially designated "minority-only" seats on school boards. The court's decision in the *Singh* case forced Ottawa to revamp its refugee determination process, at a cost of over $200 million. In addition to such indirect costs of compliance with Charter decisions, the court recently ruled that judges have the authority to order "affirmative remedies" such as the expansion of social benefit programs that unfairly exclude (i.e., discriminate against) a disadvantaged group.[8] While the court stressed such remedies could only be used in rare circumstances, within a month lower courts had ordered a costly extension of spousal benefit plans in the homosexual rights cases mentioned above.

Despite the broad sweep of the Charter's impact on Canadian public policy, no one could reasonably object to these decisions if they were simply dictated by the text of the Charter. In other words, if the Supreme Court has simply been giving effect to the clear or intended meaning of the Charter, any critics would have to direct their ire at the Charter itself and not the judges. But as anyone familiar with Charter decisions knows, the opposite is much more often the case. There have been only one or two cases involving clear-cut violations of the central meaning of Charter rights. The overwhelming number of Charter claims involve activities that fall on the periphery of the meaning of rights, issues over which reasonable citizens can and do disagree. The court's free speech cases, for example, have dealt not with core issues of political speech, but with questions such as whether types of commercial speech—television advertising or on-street soliciting for purposes of prostitution—are constitutionally protected forms of expression. Judicial answers to questions such as these are purely discretionary, and vary from one judge to another, depending on their judicial philosophy and personal judgments. In other words, different judges find different rights.

This was clearly evident in the four different judgments delivered in the Supreme Court's *Morgentaler* abortion decision. Only one justice out of seven—Justice Wilson—declared a constitutional right to abortion. The other four members of the majority coalition found only procedural violations of the Charter, and were further divided on their seriousness. The two dissenters said there was no constitutional violation.

This division of the court was not caused by technical legal disagreements. Rather it reflected two different theories of Charter review, two different conceptions of the proper role of the judge. The fractured *Morgentaler* decision accurately reflected the growing division of the court: more than a third of its Charter decisions now contain dissenting votes. One wing of the court, as exemplified by Justice Wilson, has adopted an activist approach to applying the Charter. These judges are more inclined to read in new and even unintended meaning to the broadly worded principles of the Charter, and are not reluctant to strike down legislative decisions with which they disagree. The other wing of the court, exemplified by Justice McIntyre, attempts to minimize judicial discretion by limiting Charter rights to their "original meaning," as disclosed (when possible) by the intent of the framers, and as a result is usually more deferential to Parliament's policy decisions.

These two different approaches to interpreting the Charter lead to very different results. A study of the Supreme Court's first 100 Charter decisions revealed that Justice Wilson supported individuals' Charter claims in 53 percent of her decisions, while Justice McIntyre upheld Charter claims in only 23 percent. The court average was 35 percent.[9] Wilson and McIntyre wrote the most dissenting opinions, yet never dissented together. Not only did they depart from the majority most frequently, but they did so in opposite directions. In each of her thirteen dissents, Wilson supported the individual's Charter claim, while McIntyre supported the crown in ten of his eleven dissents.

These statistics confirm that the meaning of the Charter, and thus the "existence" of a right, can vary from one judge to another. In most Charter cases, it is the judges who drive the Charter, not vice versa. The policy preferences (conscious or otherwise) of a judge, combined with judicial philosophy, are more likely to determine the outcome than the text of the Charter. Different judges "find" different rights.

Well-intentioned traditionalists have argued that even if all of the above is true, requiring public parliamentary hearings would still do more harm than good, that the cure would be worse than the disease. This analysis is usually premised on recent U.S. experience, most notably the Robert Bork and Clarence Thomas hearings before the Senate Judiciary Committee. These media-circus events featured aggressive interest group lobbying, strong ideological overtones, and character assassination. Most Canadians were repulsed by these transparent "court packing" attempts and thus sympathetic to the argument that this is one American institution that we definitely do not want to import into Canada. If we tease out the different strands of this argument, however, we find that none are conclusive.

The most obvious criticism of confirmation hearings is that they would politicize the process. Special interest groups would leap at the opportunity to influence the choice of the next Supreme Court judge, promoting candidates sympathetic to their objectives and opposing those who are not. This criticism assumes that the current practice is not politicized. In fact, there is growing evidence to the contrary. When Justice Estey retired shortly after the 1988 *Morgentaler* decision, *The Globe and Mail* reported that "activists in the abortion debate and representatives of ethnic communities are lobbying hard.... Many members of the ruling PC Party's right-wing ... are putting pressure on PM Mulroney to appoint a conservative judge." Member of Parliament James Jepson, one of the most outspoken pro-life Tory backbenchers, explained the importance of the new Supreme Court appointment:

> Unfortunately, with the Charter that Trudeau left us, we legislators do not have final power. It rests with the courts.... You have seen the battling in the United States for the [most recent] Supreme Court nominee. Well, it doesn't take a rocket scientist to see we have the same situation here now.[10]

The same kind of pressure is coming from the political left. At a 1991 conference on the Charter and Public Policy, Marilou McPhedran, a leading feminist legal activist in Ontario, challenged several speakers who spoke as if there were no politics in the appointment process. "We're not being completely honest about the present appointment process," she declared. "We've all been involved in judicial appointments."[11] Other sources confirm that feminist organizations such as LEAF and NAC have privately lobbied the government on judicial appointments.[12]

It is hardly surprising that the new role of the court under the Charter has stimulated behind-the-scenes manoeuvring to influence the appointment of ideologically friendly judges. Indeed, it would be more surprising if it had not. It is an axiom of political science that "where power rests, there influence will be brought to bear."[13] The new Supreme Court is no exception. The appointment process has already been politicized. A confirmation hearing would simply bring these politics out into the open.

A related criticism is that the political lobbying that would inevitably accompany confirmation hearings would undermine the rule of law by making the personal preferences of judges more decisive than the content of the law they are supposed to interpret. Once again, this criticism comes too late. As noted above, the approach to interpreting the Charter chosen by the majority of judges has maximized judicial discretion by minimizing the value of the actual text and its intended meaning. This previously heretical view was actually voiced by Justice Estey, *after* he retired from the court, in an interview with *The Globe and Mail:*

> Justice Estey said it worries him that Canadians still do not realize how decisions vary according to the personality of each judge. As the misconception is gradually corrected, he said, people may lose respect and faith in the institution.... People think a court is a court is a court. But it is elastic. It is always sliding.[14]

Another variation on this criticism is that public hearings for judicial nominees will inevitably lead to American-style judicial activism. This view is wrong on two counts. First, American-style activism is already here. The argument that the Section 1 "reasonable limits" provision makes judicial review under the Charter qualitatively distinct from U.S. judicial review—an opinion very much in vogue in judicial circles—is just legalistic myopia. Section 1 simply gives Canadian judges even more discretion than they already had. True, judges can use Section 1 as a vehicle of self-restraint. But they can just as easily use it in an activist fashion, and that is what they have done. Section 1 has become just another path to the same end.

Second, public hearings could also encourage the appointment of more judges who believe in judicial self-restraint. This is what has happened in the United States over the past two decades. As a conservative public reaction set in against the liberal activism of the Warren court of the 1960s, a series of Republican presidential candidates—Nixon, Reagan, and Bush—successfully campaigned on the promise to appoint "strict constructionists" to the Supreme Court. By the late 1980s, these new appointments had made the court much less interventionist and more deferential to the policy decisions of both Congress and state governments. While some would argue the Republican appointments pushed the court too far in the direction of self-restraint, the newly elected Democratic president, Bill Clinton, now has the opportunity to try to redress the balance.

This last aspect of American experience provides the rebuttal for yet another argument against public hearings: that they are inconsistent with the Canadian convention of "ministerial responsibility"—that the justice minister and the prime minister must be "responsible" to the House of Commons for their judicial appointments. Again, this criticism is wrong on two counts. First, the simple fact of holding public parliamentary committee hearings for judicial candidates does not mean that the committee (or the House of Commons) will have a "veto" power, analogous to the U.S. Senate. Presumably this committee, like all parliamentary committees, would be struck in a fashion that reflects the government's majority in the House of Commons. In the final analysis, a government would always have the votes to push through a positive committee recommendation, no matter how badly its nominee had performed.

In this sense, committee hearings would actually strengthen ministerial responsibility, because a government would have something to be responsible for! That is, for the first time, the opposition and the Canadian people would have the opportunity to learn what kind of judge the government was appointing: an activist or an apostle of judicial self-restraint, a conservative or a liberal. What it means is that prior to final appointment, a government's candidate for the Supreme Court will be expected to field responsible questions about his or her judicial philosophy from a multiparty committee. The purpose of the hearings is not to prevent a government from making appointments to the Supreme

Court, but to make it clear—and public—what kind of criteria the government is using.

As U.S. experience indicates, a government's judicial appointments can become an issue at election time. With the adoption of parliamentary committee hearings, an incumbent government could be challenged to defend its appointment record. Whatever else might be said of this, it certainly does not offend any of the tenets of responsible government.

The last criticism is perhaps the most serious and difficult to meet: that public hearings will deter qualified men and women from seeking or accepting appointments to the Supreme Court. There is no denying that many qualified candidates would refuse to submit themselves and their families to the kind of dissection and inspection of their private and professional lives—not to mention slander and innuendo—that both Robert Bork and Clarence Thomas had to endure.

My response is twofold. First, the same thing could be said of democratic politics in general. For generations, many of our most qualified citizens have refused to enter electoral politics because they do not have the stomach or the patience for the public scrutiny that comes with the job. Yet even as we acknowledge the seriousness of this problem, we would not for a minute consider abandoning the free elections, freedom of speech, and independent press that can make political life so uncomfortable. To speak bluntly, having decided to share some of the privileges of elected lawmakers, Canadian judges must also be prepared to share some of the disadvantages that come with the exercise of power.

The second reason is more cheerful: adopting the practice of judicial nomination hearings need not mean adopting the way Americans conduct theirs. Canadians have always prided themselves on conducting politics in a more civil and professional manner than their American neighbours. There is no reason this tradition cannot be extended to judicial nomination hearings. If professional norms and courtesy are observed, there is no reason that Canada cannot reap the advantages of this system while minimizing its potential negatives.

To conclude, those who defend the status quo would have us believe that in preserving a British-style judicial selection process with the new U.S.-style judicial review of constitutional rights, Canadians can have the best of both worlds. In fact, this combination can just as easily produce the worst of both worlds—judicial lawmaking with no accountability. The solution to this problem is public hearings for Supreme Court nominees before a parliamentary committee.

# NOTES

1. R.I. Cheffins, "The Supreme Court of Canada: The Quiet Court in an Unquiet Country," *Osgoode Hall Law Journal* 4 (1966): 259–360.

2. F.L. Morton, "The Charter Revolution and the Court Party," *Osgoode Hall Law Journal* 30, no. 3 (1992): 627–53.

3. *R. v. Collins,* [1987] 1 S.C.R. 265.

4. *R. v. Manninen,* [1987] 1 S.C.R. 1233.

5. *R. v. Hebert,* [1990] 2 S.C.R. 151.

6. R. Harvie and H. Foster, "Different Drummers, Different Drums: The Supreme Court, American Jurisprudence and the Revision of Canadian Criminal Law under the Charter," (1990) 24 *Ottawa Law Review* 39.

7. *Haig (and Birch) v. Canada* (1992), 5 O.R. (3d) 245; and *Leshner v. Ministry of the Attorney-General* (1992), 10 O.R. (3d) 732 (Ont. C.A.).

8. *Schachter v. Canada,* [1992] 2 S.C.R. 679.

9. F.L. Morton, Peter H. Russell, and M.J. Withey, "The Supreme Court's First One Hundred Charter Decisions: A Statistical Analysis," (1992) 30 *Osgoode Hall Law Journal* 1.

10. "Reduced Role for Politicians Urged in Naming of Judges," *The Globe and Mail,* May 16, 1988, p. A1.

11. Morton, "The Charter Revolution and the Court Party," p. 638.

12. Ibid. Also see Sherene Razack, *Canadian Feminism and the Law: The Women's Legal Education and Action Fund and the Pursuit of Equality* (Toronto: Second Story Press, 1991), pp. 36–63.

13. V.O. Key, *Politics, Parties, and Pressure Groups* (Thomas Y. Crowell, 1958), p. 154.

14. *The Globe and Mail,* April 27, 1988, p. A5

## NO

# Parliamentary Hearings
# for Supreme Court of Canada Appointments?

### H. Patrick Glenn

Should there be parliamentary confirmation hearings for Supreme Court of Canada appointments? There has been only limited discussion of the question in Canada, though a number of themes have emerged. Proponents of hearings have said that the Supreme Court, particularly since the enactment of the Canadian Charter of Rights and Freedoms, exercises important political responsibilities, and that a more openly political appointment process is therefore appropriate. The larger role of the Supreme Court is also said to require increased public knowledge of judges and of judicial aspirants. Confirmation hearings are therefore urged as a means of facilitating public awareness and debate. A further argument, more rooted in a particular philosophy of judicial activity, is to the effect that judges are free to decide cases as they wish and that such unlimited discretion requires political surveillance, at least at the stage of appointment.

Since there have never been confirmation hearings of judicial appointments in Canada, few people have tried to explain or justify their absence. Recently, however, in response to arguments in favour of confirmation hearings, it has been said that the existing process has served Canada well ("if it ain't broke, don't fix it"); that changes to the existing process would be difficult to implement and not likely to yield better results; that confirmation hearings would give rise to unseemly and inappropriate attacks on appointees while provoking no meaningful response from them; and that the public ordeal of hearings would deter good candidates from seeking judicial office.

A contemporary observer of this debate would probably come to the conclusion that confirmation hearings should be held. They accord with democratic theory; it is true that the judges of the Supreme Court of Canada, who are accountable to no one for their decisions, render judgments that have major political importance; the arguments against hearings seem both undemocratic and elitist, in seeking to protect important people from public scrutiny. Shouldn't we just get on with it?

There may be more to be said. In particular it seems worthwhile to ask some further questions as to the compatibility of confirmation hearings with existing Canadian institutions, and as to the relations between law and politics.

# CONFIRMATION HEARINGS AND CANADIAN INSTITUTIONS

The creation of confirmation hearings for Supreme Court of Canada appointments is related to the existing political institutions of the House of Commons and the Senate, where the hearings would take place, to the Supreme Court itself, whose composition might be affected, and more generally to the Canadian judiciary, for the model of judicial appointment procedure that would be created. In each case, it will be suggested, confirmation hearings are incompatible with existing Canadian institutions and the philosophy that underlies them.

What is the significance of confirmation hearings for the House of Commons and the Senate? In the U.S. model, hearings of Supreme Court nominees are conducted by a committee of the Senate, in execution of the Senate's mandate to confirm or reject all nominations. The hearings are part of the system of checks and balances written into the U.S. Constitution. The executive, in the person of the president, cannot abuse the appointment process and the Senate holds in effect a veto power over presidential nominees. Moreover, the Senate majority is frequently of a different political allegiance than that of the president. However, neither the Canadian House of Commons nor the Canadian Senate plays the same role as the U.S. Senate. The Canadian parliamentary system is one of responsible government. The government, or the executive, is responsible to the House of Commons in the sense that it can be defeated by it and turned out of office. The result, however, is that the party that obtains the majority of seats will form the government and also control the House. Canada does not have a system of checks and balances. One may agree or disagree on types of government, but ours is unlikely to change in the foreseeable future, at least in this respect. There are, moreover, reasons for systems of responsible government. They have to do with entrusting government to those who have democratically won it, and requiring them to act ethically and responsibly for the public good, or be voted out. Checks and balances are not seen as useful or efficient devices to ensure this outcome. Hearings before a House of Commons committee would therefore not serve the primary purpose of nomination hearings in the United States, that of allowing partisan control to be exercised on governmental nominations.

Some recent constitutional proposals have therefore called for confirmation hearings before a Senate (rather than a House of Commons) committee, but the committee would have been one of a radically reformed Senate. There appear to be no proposals to allow a committee of the present Senate to hold confirmation hearings and vote conclusively on Supreme Court nominations. There are good reasons for the absence of such proposals, given the status of the existing Senate.

There remain the possibilities of hearings before a joint House of Commons/Senate committee, which would then vote conclusively on the nomination, or a simple hearing before a House of Commons committee, with no conclusive vote. No one has suggested how such a joint House of Commons/Senate committee should be composed or the degree of governmental control over it, and this is not a question of simple plumbing or technique. It is a fundamental question of whether an institution other than Parliament itself is to control the government and if so in what circumstances. Adoption of such a committee, with such powers, would constitute a radical change to the system of parliamentary responsible government. The advantages and disadvantages of doing so have yet to be raised in the context of the debate on confirmation hearings.

Should there then be public hearings before a House of Commons committee, with no conclusive vote? This would be in a sense a reversal of the U.S. model, which until the 20th century consisted of a Senate vote with no hearings. Is it publicity alone that is sought? This may depend ultimately on our concept of the relations between law and politics (more on that below).

Parliamentary confirmation hearings therefore do not sit well with our political institutions. What about the Supreme Court itself? Does its mandate require appointments only after hearings and the exercise of some form of political control? Here the importance of the Charter and the intermittent activism of the U.S. Supreme Court have dominated the discussion. What is the nature, however, of the Supreme Court of Canada? In the Western legal tradition it has become a unique type of court, unlike the highest courts of the United Kingdom, the United States, or France. In each of those countries the jurisdiction of the highest court is more specialized than that of the Supreme Court of Canada. In the United States, the Supreme Court is a court essentially for federal and constitutional matters only; its constitutional responsibilities dominate its workload. In the United Kingdom, the House of Lords has no constitutional responsibilities similar to those exercised by the Supreme Court of Canada in application of the Charter. In France, there are three separate high courts, one for constitutional law, one for administrative law, and one for private law.

The Supreme Court of Canada is the only generalist court among these courts. A large part of its docket is given over to criminal appeals, and it continues to hear appeals in all other areas of private and public law. Charter cases occupy only some 25 to 30 percent of its case load. The Supreme Court is very much a court of law in the traditional sense, deciding individual cases involving individual litigants. Its decisions have important precedential value, but this is true of the decisions of all high courts. It is therefore incorrect to treat the Supreme Court as a fundamentally political institution simply because it has begun to decide Charter cases. It certainly does decide Charter cases, and they are important cases. It is not, however, a court dominated by a political workload, a political agenda, and politically motivated judges. This too is related ultimately to our views concerning law and politics. Do we wish to give dominance to the overtly political part of the court's workload? The present structure and jurisdiction of the court does not indicate that this need be done.

Finally, what is the relation of confirmation hearings at the level of the Supreme Court to our entire system of judicial appointments? Would hearings be compatible with the system or constitute a useful model for its reform? Canada originally inherited the British system of appointment of judges, which relies on the professional opinion of a very small number of judges, including the Lord Chancellor, to inform the government's choice of members of the judiciary. As well, judges are chosen from a very small and select group of professionals, those barristers who have become Queen's Counsel. This system of appointment was of course appropriate for the British judiciary, which has historically been very small, with much adjudication being left to lay magistrates (the local notables). The Canadian judiciary, however, has become quite unlike the British judiciary. It is much larger; it is composed almost entirely of professional judges; and its members are generally drawn from a very large, unified legal profession (and not from a very small corps of professional pleaders or barristers). In keeping with these changes to the judiciary, the Canadian system of appointment has changed considerably from the British model. At the provincial level judicial nominating commissions are becoming the rule. These commissions receive applications and nominations for judicial positions, assess qualifications, and make recommendations for appointment (often in the form of short lists) to provincial authorities. At the federal level the process of screening and recommending judicial candidates has become a major activity of the Ministry of Justice, involving consultation with a committee of the Canadian Bar Association that provides formal evaluations of all candidates. The process is neither secretive nor internal to the government. It is simply not conducted in a public forum.

These changes in the process of appointing Canadian judges have been occurring gradually, and the process of change is certainly not complete. One result of change has been a decline in the importance of political patronage in the appointment process. It is reasonable to think that the quality of the bench has also been reinforced, since the procedures allow much more information to be processed about a larger number of judicial candidates than would otherwise be the case. Appointments to the Supreme Court of Canada go through this process, and to this writer's knowledge, there is no criticism of the quality of appointments to the Supreme Court of Canada. It is evident that successive governments have taken the task very seriously and that the visibility of the court has enhanced the likelihood of high-quality appointments.

The underlying political ethic of this appointment process is that of responsible government, i.e., that it is the task of the government to act, as government, in the public interest. The underlying judicial ethic of the process is that of obtaining a judiciary of the highest quality. Quite absent from the process have been the ideas of checks and balances on government action and of democratic approval of the judiciary. Discussion of the existing judicial appointment process in Canada thus provides little or no support for judicial confirmation hearings, given the underlying principles of responsible government and a judiciary of the highest quality. This conclusion in no way prejudices the current movement toward judicial nominating commissions, which have as their task the searching out of the best candidates, as opposed to merely eliminating allegedly bad governmental nominations.

It has not been possible in discussing Canadian institutions to ignore entirely the relations between law and politics. What more must be briefly said on this large subject?

# LAW, POLITICS, AND CONFIRMATION HEARINGS

The relations between law and politics have already been mentioned, in discussing whether confirmation hearings should be held before a House of Commons committee for reasons of publicity alone (with no vote to be taken) and whether judicial appointments and activity should receive some form of democratic approval (notably through election of judges). Since democracy has been a relatively successful form of government, its extension to the judiciary appears to be a good thing. Democracy is a form of politics, however, and its application to law means politicizing the legal process in an explicit manner. Do we want to do this?

One of the most frequently made criticisms of the legal order is that it is ultimately political. Since it is ultimately political we should do away with the legal charade and apply to the legal process the same methods and techniques that are used elsewhere in politics. Law should be the object of public and transparent political debate and be subject to democratic institutions. The notion of the "political" is here very large and appears to extend to most forms of human interaction. Such an attitude underlay the adoption of systems of election of judges in both the former Soviet Union (implementing socialist legality) and the United

States (implementing Jeffersonian democracy). We have now had substantial modern experience with the notion of democratizing the legal process in such a direct way. The problems with this are both theoretical and practical.

Ultimately our view of judicial activity may be driven by our view of law itself. Is there such a thing, for example, as a natural legal order? The aboriginal population of this country tells us there is. It teaches respect for the natural environment. We should continue to act in traditional ways since these ways do least violence to the world. If there is such a natural legal order, it does not require elected judges or a democratic legal process. It requires the legal process that will ensure respect for the natural legal order, and in the aboriginal legal order this meant adherence to the wisdom of people recognized as elders. Nor do religiously inspired legal traditions insist on democratic legitimation; legal authority is derived from religious learning and some form of official recognition of such acquired authority. In the Western, secular world these ancient traditions have had and continue to have great influence. The Western legal tradition is remarkable, however, for its insistence that law is presently *made* by those entrusted with the task. This philosophical attitude emerged with the Renaissance, but the Renaissance did not lead to a radical democratization of the legal process. Something else was also at work.

In contemporary liberal societies people are entitled to different views and different ways of life. Law is used to regulate and conciliate the conflicts that inevitably arise. Since there is no consistently imposed social fabric, law must do more than it does in a society in which common forms of life are accepted by all concerned. In the inevitable turmoil of social relations, the major teaching of the Renaissance was that law had to be separated from politics. Politics would, of course, continue to exist and would give the major forms of direction to society. At the level of daily life, however, where decisions are made that affect the individual, it was felt that the political process was too large, too biased, and too crude to regulate the minutiae of social existence. The person charged with social deviance could not be judged, for example, by those who had made the rules. From the 17th century the notion of an independent judiciary emerged, one that was not subject to the political process and that was given remarkable institutional liberty to pursue justice in the individual case. This is why Canada has professionalized its judiciary. No one wishes to be judged by those controlled by someone else, or by those fearing sanctions for the decision they reach, or by those biased by social position or attitude. In short, most of our present legal institutions have been developed, not because it is felt that law is somehow inevitably different from politics—more scientific, more technical, or more neutral—but because it has been felt that every possible effort should be made to provide institutional protection to individuals—in liberal, democratic states—from the brute forces of politics. The separation of law and politics does not deny the political character of law, but assumes it. It then seeks to control and limit the influence of politics through institutional guarantees of fair process, independent decision-makers, and application of established rules.

The notion of an independent judiciary, one that is not democratically elected and not subject to democratic recall, is thus parallel to and consistent with the political ethic of responsible government. Those entrusted with authority are expected to exercise it in the public interest. There can be no guardians of the guardians, at least in any immediate and direct way. The independence of the judiciary takes the ethic a step further, however, in awarding tenure for life (or its statutory equivalent, the 75th birthday) to those judged best qualified to have it. Since our judiciary is now a large one, there are judicial councils that have been established to discipline judges for nonjudicial conduct, but no political authority can interfere in the judicial decision-making process and no judge need fear official or popular sanction for unpopular decisions. Most of our legal institutions today thus represent efforts to separate law from politics, because their confusion has been recognized by most people at most times to be highly undesirable.

Efforts to democratize and politicize the legal process are visible today because they have been so consistently rejected in the past, and because our existing institutions translate this rejection. It is not that no one thought of parliamentary confirmation hearings before the Charter. It is rather that institutions were created that would, as much as possible, free the legal process from the political one. Judges *are* free to decide as they wish, and this freedom is given to them because you would not want *your* case to be decided on majoritarian political grounds. Creating judicial confirmation hearings would not change a great deal in the unfolding of history. It would be a small, further step in the politicization of law, however, and as such there should be a presumption against such hearings, as indeed there is in this country.

The practical difficulties in democratizing the legal process have been more significant than the theoretical ones, however, in the jurisdictions that have attempted the process. In the former Soviet Union the process of election of judges was party-controlled and the result was the opposite of democratic control. In the United States the election of judges at state levels has been the object of ongoing reforms designed to eliminate party influence and corruption while reinforcing the quality of judges. The democratic control has been largely illusory and voter influence, never strong, has been declining steadily in favour of various forms of judicial nominating commissions. There has, however, been a politicization of the role of the Supreme Court of the United States, and judicial nomination hearings have become a very visible political phenomenon at this level of the judicial process. What should we make of the U.S. experience?

As mentioned above, confirmation hearings are a relatively recent phenomenon in the United States, beginning only in this century, shortly before the First World War. Why did they come about? Why was the presumption against politicization (federal U.S. judges are appointed and not elected) here reversed? It does not appear to have been the role of the U.S. Supreme Court in deciding Bill of Rights cases that caused the change, since this had been going on for a long time prior to the introduction of confirmation hearings. What appears to have brought about the change, according to U.S. writers, was the process by which appointments to the court became to be seen as further means of advancing political goals. Today in the United States there is talk of "transformative appointments," in the sense of appointments that would change the course of decisions of the court, in a broad, political sense. The judges are expected to decide according to a broad, personal political philosophy. Very recently, there has thus been surprise at the emergence of a group of "legal conservatives" on the court, those who refuse to overrule prior decisions with which they disagree because of the need for legal stability. Yet if governments are entitled to use the Supreme Court for political objectives, and its judges are expected to act as majoritarian political appointees, then it is normal that the process of appointment be politicized and even radically so. It is also normal that the process be subject to the full range of political debate and struggle, as unedifying and inefficient as it frequently is. There is no practical means of ensuring only serene and enlightened democratic participation in the nomination process. Most important, there appears to be no means of politicizing the appointment process without also politicizing the court itself.

The Supreme Court has not become a political battleground in Canada. If we are to struggle toward a rule of law rather than a rule of political power, it is undesirable that it become a political battleground. Its present role as a court of law should remind us of why it is there. Let's leave it alone. One day it may have to decide my case, or yours.

# P O S T S C R I P T

In his article, Morton makes a forceful case for parliamentary hearings. If the Supreme Court is now much more powerful than before, then it is only sensible to make it more accountable to the public. Yet, some lingering doubts still remain about the proposal for parliamentary hearings. The American experience suggests that hearings would act to politicize the appointment process and possibly result in the selection of justices of questionable merit. Morton responds that the appointment process in Canada is already politicized, but there seems to be some distance between informal consultation and full-blown public hearings on judicial appointments.

There is also some concern about the impact of hearings on the public perception of judicial decision-making. At present, most citizens believe that justices offer disinterested interpretations of the law. As Morton shows, especially in relation to the Charter, this is not an entirely accurate conception of how judges decide—indeed, for Morton, it is patently false. However, one might argue, as Glenn seems to, that adjudication of conflicts over the law does involve the application of judicial expertise and wisdom, and that the spectacle of hearings might undermine public confidence in the judiciary. If the electorate believes that judges are merely imposing their own preferences on society, then the legitimacy of the judicial branch of government may be placed in jeopardy.

Obviously, Glenn is much happier with the present appointment process, and finds little good to say about public hearings. However, his arguments, like those of Morton's, are not entirely convincing. Essentially, Glenn asks us to trust both those who now appoint justices and those who are asked to sit on the Supreme Court. In an age that is increasingly democratic, such a request is difficult to accept. Surely, one might say, the public can be allowed a more direct role in the appointment of justices without causing any great harm. There are parliamentary hearings on other matters, and this has facilitated public participation in the political process while at the same time respecting the workings of responsible government.

In his book *The Judiciary in Canada: The Third Branch of Government* (Toronto: McGraw-Hill Ryerson, 1987), Peter Russell presents a good discussion of the judicial appointment process in Canada and ways of reforming this process. Students might also consult Peter McCormick and Ian Greene's *Judges and Judging: Inside the Canadian Judicial System* (Toronto: James Lorimer, 1990). As well, Morton has edited an excellent collection of articles on the judicial process entitled *Law, Politics and the Judicial Process*, 2nd ed. (Calgary: University of Calgary Press, 1992).

Clearly, an understanding of judicial interpretation of the Charter of Rights is crucial to the issue of parliamentary hearings. On this issue, one might look at Christopher P. Manfredi, *Judicial Power and the Charter: Canada and the Paradox of Liberal Constitutionalism* (Toronto: McClelland and Stewart, 1993). For an in-depth examination of the Charter and the courts in relation to the issue of abortion, students should read F.L. Morton's *Morgentaler v. Borowski: Abortion, the Charter, and the Courts* (Toronto: McClelland and Stewart, 1992).

On the American appointment process, Henry Abraham's two texts *The Judicial Process: An Introductory Analysis of the Courts of the United States, England, and France*, 6th ed. (New York: Oxford University Press, 1993) and *Justices and Presidents: A Political History of Appointments to the Supreme Court*, 3rd ed. (Toronto: Oxford University Press, 1992), plus David Rohde and Harold Spaeth's *Supreme Court Decision-Making* (San Francisco: W.H. Freeman, 1976) and David M. O'Brien's *Storm Center: The Supreme Court in American Politics*, 2nd ed. (New York: W.W. Norton, 1990), are useful.

Lastly, the American appointment process has recently generated a great deal of controversy. In 1987, President Ronald Reagan nominated Robert Bork for the U.S. Supreme Court, but he was rejected by the Senate after a long and acrimonious set of hearings. Four years later, President George Bush put forward Clarence Thomas, who was subsequently accused during the hearings of having engaged in acts of sexual harassment. Eventually, the Senate accepted the Thomas nomination, but the effects of the hearings still reverberate through American political life. Two good journalistic accounts of these events are Ethan Bronner, *Battle for Justice: How the Bork Nomination Shook America* (New York: W.W. Norton, 1989) and Timothy M. Phelps and Helen Winternitz, *Capitol Games: Clarence Thomas, Anita Hill, and the Story of a Supreme Court Nomination* (New York: Hyperion, 1992).

# PART FOUR

# POLITICAL BEHAVIOUR

*Are political parties in decline?*

*Are polls bad for politics?*

*Should a system of proportional representation be adopted in Canada?*

*Do referendums enrich democracy?*

*Do business groups have privileged access to government?*

*Do the media distort election campaigns?*

# ISSUE THIRTEEN

## Are Political Parties in Decline?

**YES** JOHN MEISEL, "Decline of Party in Canada," in Hugh Thorburn, ed., *Party Politics in Canada*, 6th ed. (Scarborough: Prentice-Hall, 1991) (abridged)

**NO** RONALD G. LANDES, "In Defence of Canadian Political Parties." Revised version of paper presented at the annual meeting of the Canadian Political Science Association, June 1984

In recent years, Canadian political life has witnessed a near rash of new political parties. The Reform Party of Canada, the Bloc Québécois, and the National Party of Canada have all only lately emerged. A country accustomed to three federal parties must now adjust itself to a new reality. It seems that political parties are in strong demand.

Yet, appearances can be deceiving. Some serious observers of Canadian politics claim that parties are actually in decline. Typically, parties have performed functions critical to the operation of democratic governments. They structure the vote, offer alternatives at election time, mobilize participation in politics, and effectively fuse the legislative and executive branches of government through the exercise of party discipline. But increasingly there is evidence that parties are no longer crucial to the political process. Interest groups, television, and polling, among other things, have arisen to compete with parties in the performance of the functions of government. The fact that a similar development is seemingly taking place in the United States also suggests that parties may be past their prime.

Of special interest is the role of parties in providing information on the attitudes and preferences of voters. Thirty years ago, parties represented the best way of finding out what people wanted from government. Party members would become immersed in community life and develop a picture of voter likes and dislikes. Today, however, the parties' hold on this particular function has been greatly weakened—polls do a much better job.

For some, however, the reports of the death of parties, to borrow from Mark Twain, are greatly exaggerated. To be sure, politics is more complicated, and parties now have some serious rivals. Yet, they continue to be essential to the act of governing. Voters still rely on party labels for guidance, the House of Commons is still populated by members of political parties, and party discipline is still central to the operation of parliamentary government. And then there is the development mentioned earlier: new parties such as the Reform Party and the Bloc Québécois are now on the political scene. Growth in the quantity of any entity hardly seems indicative of decay and decline.

In the readings, two political scientists debate the issue of whether political parties are in decline. John Meisel outlines the "decline-of-party" thesis in relation to events over the past quarter of a century, and Ronald G. Landes supplies a rebuttal to this line of thinking.

# YES

## Decline of Party in Canada

*John Meisel*

... Anthony King, in a searching paper analysing the role of parties in liberal democracies, summarizes much of the relevant literature by listing six usually cited functions of parties: (1) structuring the vote; (2) integration and mobilization of the mass public; (3) recruitment of political leaders; (4) organization of government; (5) formation of public policy; and (6) aggregation of interests.[1] He notes that there is a good deal of imprecision in the manner in which political scientists deal with the roles of parties and that the importance of their functions tends to be exaggerated. Nevertheless, he concludes, parties are critical components of the political process and they need to be studied, albeit with greater precision than is often the case.

This article shares King's view and, although it focuses on the relative decline of political parties in Canada, it should not be interpreted as arguing that the parties and the party system are insignificant. Parties clearly still influence critical aspects of politics and, most notably, they influence who occupies the government benches in parliament and who heads the various departments and ministries. The emphasis in this article is on federal politics, although many of the observations also apply to the provincial arena.

Parties still perform the first function listed: they structure the vote in most elections, except at the municipal level. They, to some measure, present options to the electorate about current issues and so can be said to organize mass opinion, although one is often tempted to conclude that they disorganize it. As for the related role of mobilizing the public, a remarkably high proportion of Canadians participate in elections in one way or another, and by no means just by voting. The preparation of electoral lists, staffing the polling booths, and organizing the campaigns on a polling division by polling division basis all takes a great deal of effort, most of which is provided by volunteer activists. This not only enables the electoral process to function, it increases the public's knowledge of political questions and facts. It is well-established that a greater sense of partisan attachment is associated with a greater knowledge of politics.

Nevertheless, an increasing number of Canadians have sought to participate in politics and public life outside the framework of parties—in tenants' or neighbourhood organizations or through voluntary associations, from unions to environmental or anti-nuclear groups. There was an upsurge of such "unconventional" politics in the 1960s in the United States and to a lesser extent in Canada, but there is some uncertainty about the degree to which non-partisan politics has continued to flourish in North America in the 1970s. Although the situation in Canada is a little ambiguous, there is no doubt that the proportion of people in the United States who identify with political parties in the sense that they think of themselves as Democrats or Republicans is steadily declining.

Parties also recruit politicians, although many question whether, in general, politics attracts a sufficiently high calibre of individuals. Data are unavailable on this point but some speculate that other careers appeal to the ablest Canadians and they conclude that we could do with a good deal more talent in the parties. This question raises another, also imperfectly understood puzzle: what characteristics make for a good politician? Indeed, what is a good politician?

By deciding which partisan team forms the government and who is in opposition, parties do organize government in an important way. But there is little doubt that a great many decisions—about what is placed on the public agenda and at what time—are forced on political parties by events, non-political decision makers and very often the preferences of powerful civil servants, whose responsibility to the politicians is increasingly more formal than real. Even the organization of the government—the way in which legislation is drafted and considered by the cabinet and its committees, the extent to which outside interests are consulted, the manner in which policies are administered—is more likely to reflect the wills of a small number of senior civil servants than the decisions of senior party officials, including the ministers. It is indeed questionable whether the government party leader—the prime minister—continues to function as a party person after accession to power or whether the party role and influence are maintained as a successful administration becomes accustomed to power and develops close relationships with senior civil servants.

In short, one must ask whether the parties really play the central role liberal democratic theory ascribes to them in organizing government and in the formation of public policy. And, given the changes in communication and the importance of voluntary associations and interest groups, one wonders about the relative unimportance of parties in the processes which aggregate the interests of various individuals and groups into satisfactory policies....

# LONG-RUN REASONS FOR PARTY DECLINE

## Rise of the Bureaucratic State

Modern political parties evolved from small cliques of power-wielders when the extension of the franchise necessitated the organization of mass electorates. The greater participation of the public in political life led, in conjunction with other factors, to the emergence of the positive state—one which increasingly participated in virtually every aspect of the human experience. But the "ancestors" of our political institutions and the political parties serving them evolved at a time when governments were dealing with a limited range of problems, and when only a small minority of the population was politically active. Under these conditions parties were able to act as suitable links between the small electorate and the even smaller number of political decision makers.

The continuous expansion of governmental activities has created mounting problems for the legislative and representative system. Up until World War I, the Canadian parliament dealt with only a small number of issues, met seldom and required little specialized and technical knowledge to operate. Now the number and complexity of the areas in which the federal government operates are so vast that it is quite impossible for MPs to be abreast of what is going on. At best, each can become reasonably well-informed about one or two areas.

The expansion of government activities and the increasingly complicated nature of government decisions have reduced the capacity of elected officials to deal with many important public issues and necessitated the restructuring of many governmental institutions. Thus MPs and even cabinet ministers are often incapable of fully understanding the problems and options confronting them, and the normal structures of ministries are being supplemented by a large number of quasi-independent administrative, regulatory and judicial boards and commissions not directly responsible to the elected representatives of the public or to party politicians. In short, an important shift has occurred in the focus of power of liberal democracies, from elected politicians to appointed civil servants, whose links to political parties are indirect and increasingly tenuous. This means that parties, supposedly in control of the political process and responsible to the public for its performance, are often little more than impotent observers of processes they cannot control and the results of which they can only rubber stamp.

A good illustration is the case of irregularities in the sale of reactors by Atomic Energy of Canada Ltd., a crown corporation, to Argentina and Korea. There were strong suspicions that bribes had been paid and that the foreign exchange regulations of some countries had been violated. Enormous commissions were also allegedly paid to shadowy foreign agents. One of the reactors was sold at a loss of over $100 million. The Public Accounts Committee of the House of Commons held extensive hearings and questioned closely Mr. J.L. Gray, president of Atomic Energy of Canada at the time of the sales. His stonewalling of the issue, and that by everyone else connected with the matter, was so effective that the House of Commons committee failed to shed light on the sales and finally had to let the case rest.

## Pluralism and the Rise of Interest Group Politics

Before the expansion of governmental activities and the increase in their complexity, the usual pattern of lawmaking was relatively simple. Ministers of the whole cabinet, with or without prompting by their civil servants, decided on the broad outlines of what needed to be done. Civil servants, drawing on expert knowledge and advice, prepared the necessary background papers and draft proposals. These were discussed by the ministers, in the absence of their civil servant advisors, and ultimately presented to parliament for enactment. The basic decisions were essentially those of politicians and their officials. More recently, a more involved process of legislation has evolved, partly because of the need to deal with problems having enormous ramifications, partly in an effort to make government more participatory, and partly in response to the claims of a market-oriented, pluralist society in which political parties depend on the financial support of powerful economic interests or of unions. Before any law or important administrative decision is decided upon, an intense consultation between officials and representatives of various vested interests takes place. There has been a striking increase in lobbying by interest groups who have the resources and capacity to do so. Many important decisions are arrived at through private consultations between civil servants and spokespersons for various vested interests, during which politicians play no role. By the time ministers enter the decision-making process, the die is cast and only minor changes, if any, can be made. The *general* interest, therefore, as aggregated by political parties, tends to receive scant attention and parties are left with little choice but to approve what has already been decided by others. The process of consultation is for the most part totally non-partisan and most ministers engaged in it act as governmental decision makers, far removed from their party personas. For the government party caucus to disown government policies already decided on after considerable negotiations would be politically harmful and is hardly ever heard of. Convincing testimony to the relative impotence of parties is found in Robert Presthus's study of Canadian interest groups, which shows that the latter spend considerably more time and effort lobbying bureaucrats than members of parliament.[2] Furthermore, it is clear that having recourse to pressure group participation in policy making is not a feared or temporary phenomenon. The Canadian government, like many others, has institutionalized the practice by appointing large numbers of advisory committees and other bodies designed to ensure the pressure of interested parties in the policy process....

## Federal–Provincial Diplomacy

Another and increasingly threatening cause of the decline in the importance of parties lies in the changing nature of Canadian federalism. Accommodation between the various regions of the country (and to some extent, between special interests which happen to be in part regionally based) is taking place more and more through two mechanisms which are largely unrelated to party politics. The first of these is the federal–provincial prime ministerial conference, where Ottawa and the provinces hammer out compromises touching virtually every aspect of human experience. Most of these are the result of delicate bargaining on the part of 11 governments which sometimes cannot help but take positions imposed by other negotiators and which therefore cannot be anticipated by legislative caucuses, let alone by party supporters.

The second procedure through which policies are agreed upon by the federal and provincial governments is the regular meeting and consultation among federal and provincial officials. There are now thousands of such encounters annually and hundreds of formally established committees, task forces and work groups in which decisions are made that bind the participating governments. As with prime ministerial meetings, these encounters reach decisions which can be reversed or altered only at great cost—one not likely to be risked by rank-and-file members of political parties.

It can be argued that governments, at the ministerial level, are composed of leading party politicians and that their actions are in a sense those of political parties. This is technically correct, but the infrequent and unfocused expression of party opinion and the almost nonexistent party activity between elections deprive elected officials of any viable contact with their party organisms. There is, in contrast, a striking frequency and intensity of contacts between office-holding politicians and civil servants and spokesmen for vested interests. It is no exaggeration to argue that although ministers, and through them, the officials who serve under them, formally reflect party interests, they do not do so in any meaningful way. Between elections, except for occasional and exceedingly rare party gatherings, the cabinet *is* the party, insofar as the government side of the equation is concerned. Thus, such major policy changes as the introduction of wage controls in the 1970s and Trudeau's 1983 resolve to play a mediating role between the superpowers were introduced without any party involvement of any sort.

# The Rise of Electronic Media

Until the advent of radio and particularly of television, politicians were the most effective means through which the public learned about political events. In many communities across the country the political meeting was not only an important means of communication but also prime entertainment. Political issues were personalized by politicians who, in addition to adding colour to the consideration of matters of public policy, lent the political process a gladiatorial dimension that heightened its public appeal.

Television has, to a great extent, changed all that. The average Canadian spends several hours a day watching all manner of programmes among which political material plays a relatively minor role. The entertainment value of face-to-face politics has declined since there are so many other exciting things to watch. And the public perception of the political process and of political issues that remains is derived from television treatment of the news and of political personalities. Public taste and public opinion on almost everything is being shaped by television programmes and television advertising. Politics and politicians are filtered by a medium in which the primary concern is often not enlightenment, knowledge or consciousness-raising but maximal audiences and profits. This has meant that even major political events like the choosing of national party leaders are dominated by the requirements of television. The organization and scheduling of meetings are arranged so that the most appealing events are broadcast during prime time, and all other aspects, even the quality of discussion and the time spent on critical issues, are made subservient to the demands of the electronic media.

Television has to some extent wrested the limelight from party politicians; but, on the other hand, it provides a matchless opportunity for the public to witness the party game. Its coverage of the most colourful political events—leadership conventions, elections, and so-called debates between party leaders—furnishes unprecedented opportunities for parties to be seen in action. The problem is, of course, that the exposure is chosen by the media largely for entertainment value, rather than as a continuous in-depth exploration of the dominant political issues and partisan strategies. The focus tends to be on the people who report and comment on political news rather than on the political actors themselves. One result of this tendency is that public opinion on political matters is shaped as much by media intermediaries as it is by the protagonists representing the various parties. Furthermore, the key role of television is changing the character of political leadership. It is now virtually impossible for anyone who is not "telegenic" to be chosen as party chief. His or her presence and style on television can make or break a politician; yet these are only some (and not the most important) attributes of an effective political and governmental figure.

## Investigative Journalism

Although television has come to occupy a key position in the manner in which the public perceives political and party life, it has not eclipsed the more traditional ways of reporting and analysing news and of entertaining the public. Newspapers and periodicals still receive considerable attention, particularly among the politically most active members of the public. Partly, no doubt, in response to the competition provided by TV and partly because of the intense rivalry among some of the major printed media, newspapers and magazines have recently resorted to numerous ploys designed to attract attention and a wider audience. Among these, investigative journalism—a return of sorts to the old muckraking days—has been particularly important. Many of the major papers and some of the periodicals have sought to discover governmental lapses and to reveal wrongdoing on the part of local, provincial and federal authorities. These efforts at exposing flaws and shortcomings, errors, dishonesty and inefficiency perpetrated by governments have often led to the establishment of judicial and quasi-judicial inquiries and to the corroboration of the sins unearthed by the sleuthing journalists. The watch-dog function of the print and electronic media is important to the present argument because it can be seen as an encroachment upon, or at least a complement to, the role of opposition parties. They, of course, are the agents par excellence, according to conventional theory, for keeping governments on their toes and for publicizing their misdeeds.

Although opposition politicians and investigative journalists no doubt derive mutual benefit from one another's activities, the recent increase in the role of the media as agents unearthing governmental malfeasance, regardless of how beneficial it may be, detracts from one of the most essential roles of opposition parties—that of criticizing the government. This is not to say the activities of the journalists inhibit or hamper opposition politicians; on the contrary, the latter exploit them; but the relative importance of government debate is reduced when much of the combat occurs outside the party arena—on the printed page or the television screen. One of the questions presented by the new or, perhaps, revived emphasis in the media on tracking down governmental errors of commission or omission is, in fact, whether the often vigorous reportorial initiative of the media does not reflect a decline in the energy and resourcefulness of opposition parties. Like many of the arguments presented above, this is a question requiring systematic research.

Whatever the reasons, a considerable challenge of, and check on, governments today originate outside the realm of political parties and tend to reduce the effectiveness of the party system. The media may be able to report governmental failings, but they cannot provide alternative governments—one of the functions of opposition parties. By sharing with others the task of exposing and criticizing official actions (and by often being outdone by them) opposition parties lose some of their credibility as alternatives to the current power-holders.

## Opinion Polling

Increasingly widespread use of opinion polls by the small groups of officials and cronies working with the party leader has diminished the need to rely on the knowledge of public attitudes by local militants and elected politicians. The vast, sensitive network of contacts, reciprocal favours, and exchanges of information which characterized the relationship between party leaders and their followers has to some extent been attenuated by the use of scientific sampling, sophisticated interviewing techniques and subtle statistical analyses. While the results are in some respects more reliable, there is also a decided loss: the interplay between public opinion and the leadership exercised by politically informed and concerned activists is substantially reduced. There is likely less debate and argument, since local party people are no longer encouraged to take the pulse of their "parishioners" and to mediate between the grass roots and the leadership. Public opinion, as defined by pollsters, guides political decisions more and political decision makers are less involved in forming public opinion. Two consequences, at least, are relevant for our purposes: the character of political leadership and of political styles has changed and the party organization is no longer needed as an essential information network.

## The Domination of Economic Interests

There is little agreement among scholars about the exact role of economic factors in the sociopolitical realm. Are the forces and relations of production basic causes of all other aspects of social organization or can social organization be manipulated through political means? Whatever one's judgment, one does not need to be an economic determinist to acknowledge that governments have frequently found it difficult to resist certain kinds of economic pressures or to work against certain economic realities. This vulnerability is enhanced by the greatly increased number and power of multinational corporations. These vast, globe-girdling enterprises are rarely dependent on their operations in any one political jurisdiction and are adept at playing one interest against another. The behaviour of the oil companies before, during and after the oil crisis of the 1970s is a case in point. Even those who doubt that Canadian industry and business can withstand governmental pressure cannot ignore the fact that the multinationals, recognizing no loyalties other than to their balance sheets, can obviate, ignore, influence and even dominate Canadian governments. A striking example came to light in the autumn of

1977 when Inco, a Canadian-based multinational, which has benefited from lavish tax and other concessions, announced that it would lay off 3000 employees in Canada. Against arguments to the effect that the company was at the same time using funds provided by Canadian taxpayers to expand productive capacity overseas, a senior vice-president indicated that "fears of government takeover and other economic recriminations in Indonesia and Guatemala forced Inco … to cut back production in Canada where massive layoffs could be made with little prospect of serious political interference."[3] This episode provides an illuminating vignette illustrating the impotence of the Canadian government[4] and of Canadian political parties in the face of economic pressure from industry. This subservience of the political realm to the economic is related to the prevailing value system and dominant ideologies: when parties and governments buckle under economic pressure, they do so because they do not believe in interfering with private enterprise.…

# NOTES ON THE DECLINE OF PARTY IN THE 1990s

The appearance of the sixth edition of *Party Politics in Canada* provides an opportunity to reassess briefly the above arguments about the decline of party, first formulated over 10 years ago, and to take note of some recent developments.…

Some tendencies identified earlier continue to affect the role of parties more or less as before, while others are becoming more intrusive and complex. The lavish pluralism and the accompanying vigorous political involvement of interest groups, and the impact of the electronic media are fixed elements of Canada's political life, just as they were in the 1970s. The bureaucratic state, on the other hand, is becoming even more noticeable and is undergoing further transformations that affect political parties. Among the features of this development is the increasing politicization of the public service. This is manifested particularly in two domains: (1) the blurring of the line between the world of nonpartisan officials and the performance of civil servants of partisan roles; and (2) the activities by government departments of acts which have unmistakable political (i.e., partisan) consequences.…

The two developments just described further enhance the encroachment of the bureaucratic state on the sphere of the parties, noted in my original article.

As for investigative journalism, the media are becoming increasingly aggressive about prying into the private lives of people in public life. While this practice, like so many others, is more muted in Canada than in the United States, it is nevertheless clearly noticeable. One result is that people contemplating a political career must be prepared to have their past and present life, and that of their family, scrutinized in minute detail. Health records, past academic performance, youthful peccadillos, friendships, family life, holiday activities, entertainment preferences and all else are now fair game in North American journalism. This may serve a useful purpose in keeping undesirable individuals from being elected but it also deters potentially excellent politicians from seeking public office. People of talent, capable of making a valuable contribution to our political parties, may not wish to expose themselves to the fish-bowl world of the new journalism even if they do have a blameless past. Although it is too soon to reach firm conclusions here, it is likely that as a consequence, the overall quality of politicians is declining, and may decline further as the result of the intrusion of the media into matters they formerly avoided. This deprives political parties of the opportunity of drawing on the most promising pool of talent and so weakens their competitive position in relation to other institutions in society.

A new dimension has emerged in the manner in which economic interests encroach on the domain of political parties. During the concluding phase of the 1988 general election, so-called "third-party advertising" flooded the media in an effort to influence voters' attitudes to the free-trade issue and, hence, to the return to power of the Conservatives. The term "third-party" in this context no longer refers to minor political parties but to normally non-political interests who became involved in the campaign. Unions, and a coalition of nationalist groups, advertised to oppose the trade agreement between Canada and the United States, and, consequently, the Conservative government. The business community, on the other hand, bought media time and space to support the government's espousal of the trade pact. The latter groups substantially outspent the anti-free trade groups, and many observers concluded that the outcome of the election was materially affected by the massive infusion of these resources into the campaign. The funds involved in this advertising were not, under the then existing laws, subject to any of the restrictions on electoral expenses or requirements for disclosure applying to the parties and candidates.

While the involvement of non-political groups in an election does not necessarily encroach on the role of the parties, it nevertheless means that various vested interests engage in electioneering. They therefore compete with the parties for the attention of the public and do influence public opinion. The political information they convey may not reflect the priorities or even the perspectives of the parties and may, therefore, deflect the latter from the courses they had sought to pursue. Electoral choices may, as a result of third-party advertising, be influenced by nonparty agencies grinding their own axes....

# THREE NEW DEVELOPMENTS

In addition to the changes noted so far, some of which either weakened or removed factors contributing to party decline, there are three new developments that deserve notice as Canada enters the 1990s.

First, that senior public service appointments were made by two prime ministers without any involvement of their respective parties illustrates an important development in our political system that has implications for the role of parties. This development can be characterized as the "imperial prime ministership." The term is an adaptation of a phrase used in the United States to describe the immense rise in power of the president. This new style and might of the prime minister manifests itself at two levels: the actual power exercised and the ceremonial features of the office.

The aggrandisement of the prime minister evolved slowly but took an immense leap forward with the advent of television and the consequent personalization and nationalization of politics, the stress on short news clips and the popularity of leadership debates. But the process was also aided by the management style and the personalities of Trudeau and Mulroney.

Trudeau outshone his ministers in many respects and provided strong leadership in areas he considered important and congenial. Under him, decision making became firmly located in cabinet committees, and, particularly, the Committee on Priorities and Planning over which he presided. The Treasury Board and the powerful coordinating ministers of state (such as that responsible for social development) vetted policies proposed by ministers and often second-guessed the work previously done by government departments. The Privy Council Office (PCO) and the Prime Minister's Office (PMO), both under the prime minister, were immensely influential and towered over the other departments, partly as the result of direct influence and partly because of the informal network of their senior personnel embracing, *inter alia*, the other central agencies and ministries of state. As a result, the power of the ministers slipped to that of the central agencies and, particularly, to those closest to the PCO, the PMO and, through them, to the prime minister. The remarkable growth in the size and budget of the PMO during the Trudeau years represents the degree to which the prime minister's power had increased. Another quantum leap occurred under Mulroney.

Insofar as the ceremonial aspects are concerned, Trudeau had a more patrician manner than his immediate predecessors. Whether because of his personal preferences or because of the changing times, the prime ministership under him became more aloof and august. A small, possibly insignificant but, nevertheless, telling example is that it was during his occupancy of 24 Sussex Drive that the practice was established of providing Canadian prime ministers with bullet-proof limousines.

Mulroney's chosen instrument for the domination of the decision-making process was the PMO which came to be dreaded by ministers and government departments alike. Its involvement in every facet of decision making has become legendary and is among the most characteristic features of Mulroney's governing style.

Mulroney also acquired the habit of making statements about policies falling under the immediate jurisdiction of his ministers. This was nowhere so evident as in the field of foreign policy where he, on many occasions, not only upstaged but also contradicted Joe Clark, the Secretary of State for External Affairs. Mulroney also enlarged the sphere of his office at the expense of the Governor-General. This was particularly evident during the first Canadian visit by President Reagan. It would have been normal and customary for the American Head of State to be greeted by his Canadian counterpart, the Governor-General. But, although there is a vice regal official residence in Quebec City, the site of the first Reagan-Mulroney summit, Jeanne Sauvé was nowhere to be seen. The prime minister on the other hand, constantly occupied centre stage.

Brian Mulroney not only enlarged the scope of the prime minister's role but also added considerably to the trappings associated with it. On his numerous trips, he has been unfailingly accompanied by a massive phalanx of aids, including his own photographer, and preceded by a troop of advance people who ensure that the prime minister will be treated in a manner befitting an august personage and that he would be displayed in the most flattering setting and manner. At international gatherings it was not unusual that the hotel suites and floors graced by the prime minister and his staff rivalled in size and splendour those occupied by the heads of delegations of the United States and other world powers obsessed by a mania for security and an affinity for ostentation. Prior to the Trudeau era, the Canadian pattern was similar to that prevailing in the Scandinavian countries, where even first ministers behave, and are treated, like any other citizen. Particularly under Mulroney, the prime minister's style and ceremonial manner have become quite ostentatious and substantially more exalted than that of ordinary mortals, including other ministers.

An exalted prime ministership has important consequences for the role of parties. In a sense, the prime minister is, of course, every millimeter a party person and everything he or she does can be seen as a party act. But much depends on the degree to which the prime minister's decisions are reached with the involvement of the party, and to what degree they reflect contributions of non-party forces, such as various interests, personal cronies or hired gun consultants. The network of daily contacts and influences enmeshing a prime minister may include so many non-party forces that the party's role in the decision-making process becomes narrowly circumscribed.

Second, one significant non-party force is reflected in the rise in number and influence of highly specialized advisors, particularly in the field of opinion formation and manipulation. The grand strategy of parties, their conduct during elections, their contacting the public and their conducting so-called media events are now influenced by specialists who are not associated with a party but who act as consultants for a fee. A relationship of deep and complete trust must obviously develop between the party leaders and the special advisors, many of whom actually tend to sympathize with the cause of their clients, but the consultants are nevertheless independent of the party.

One of the consequences of this process is that the ideas and preferences of party members, as embodied in the leadership of the party organization, tend to be played down in favour of the expert's advice. The latter is held to be more reliable and electorally rewarding. The fact that the public relations advisors and other spin doctors have access to secret daily polls conducted during a campaign further diminish party positions and party views. Decisions, not only on *how* the party's case is to be presented but also on *what* is put forward, are made on short notice on the basis of the latest shifts revealed by opinion polls. Thus, the stance espoused by parties during a campaign is to some extent the result of the close interaction between party strategists and the powerful experts on public opinion and its management. As elsewhere, expert opinion tends to triumph over that of people considered to be amateurs.

Third, a new set of circumstances rooted in the political environment also diminishes the influence of parties. It is not only parties and the political game which are being modified but also the overall environment in which they operate. Relevant in this context are two features that did not exist or were not evident 11 years ago. They are the adoption in the 1982 constitution of the Charter of Rights and Freedoms, and changes in the nature of the Canadian community.

The Charter, as has been widely observed, has considerably enhanced the powers of the courts and has consequently contributed to the relative reduction in the importance of political, as distinct from judicial, decision making.[5] Political parties, like other political institutions, therefore cede some of their previous sphere of influence to that exercised by judges.

The impact of changes in the Canadian community is more complex and still only very imperfectly understood. During the last third or quarter of the twentieth century, new ways emerged in the manner in which many Canadians defined themselves and their role in the larger community. Previously, the salient reference points followed by most Canadians in thinking about themselves and the place they occupied in their community were religion, ethnic origin and the geographical setting they called home. A Canadian would, consequently, think of himself or herself as, say, a Catholic, a French Canadian and an inhabitant of Montreal. More recently, a new set of categories became important to many of us, which often diminished the old attachments and either replaced or augmented them with new ones. Some of these new ways of thinking are reflected in parts of the Charter.

The most salient of these new links are those of sex and a different conception of ethnicity. Feminism has made many Canadians aware of the manner in which society has been largely blind to a critical distinction in humankind, and of the manner in which society's structure and the allocation of its values discriminate in favour of one sex at the expense of the other. A growing number of people consider the redress of this neglect to be among the most critical issues on the public agenda.

Religion has been largely (although not completely) privatized and removed from public discourse. Ethnicity used to, at one level, centre on one's attachment to the French or British families. Those Canadians whose ancestry was not among what the terms of reference of the Royal Commission on Bilingualism and Biculturalism called "the founding peoples," thought of themselves as belonging linguistically to one of the two dominant groups. Ethnicity was generally considered to be a private matter more or less unrelated to the public agenda. With Canada's growing multicultural population, this has changed, and many "new" Canadians or their descendants now see themselves not only as Canadians speaking one of the official languages, but also as members of an ethnic group whose interests are of relevance to the public agenda.

Native peoples, who have traditionally been considered a very special problem with only certain vestigial limited rights, came to be recognized as falling into a number of communities whose identity and rights deserve specific recognition not only in public policy but also in constitutional guarantees.

Before the redefinition of how Canadians identified themselves, the structures, programmes, and activities of political parties had been designed to respond to the linguistic and territorial context of Canadians by focusing on regions and constituencies. The new identities evoked by considerations such as sex, multiculturalism and native rights have so far had a very limited impact on the ways in which parties attempt to respond to the emerging needs of Canadians. If the abortion issue—one of the most important "women's issues"—is taken as an example, it appears that parties are experiencing great difficulty in accommodating themselves to the new identities and the resulting cleavages in society and in playing an effective role in finding solutions to the problems posed for the country by the changing composition and definition of its constituent communities.

It is largely non-party organizations that have addressed the challenges of the "new Canada" and have become deeply involved in the resolution of resulting tensions. Parties have so far failed in becoming the principal players in the emerging politics affecting the new claims of groups and interests which had for so long lain dormant. In this way, too, their influence can be seen as having declined relative to other political players. It is too soon to say whether this situation is likely to endure or whether parties will manage to adjust to the new circumstances and recover some of the lost ground.

This brief review and extension of the analysis of the changing role of parties developed 11 years ago may not convince all readers that the influence of parties is diminishing, but it is most likely to persuade them that the contribution parties make to our political world and the manner in which they go about it is changing, and that these alterations have far-reaching consequences.

## NOTES

1. Anthony King, "Political Parties in Western Democracies," *Polity*, Vol. II, No. 2 (Winter 1969), pp. 111–41.

2. Robert Presthus, *Elite Accommodation in Canadian Politics* (Toronto: Macmillan, 1974).

3. Roger Croft, "Safer to Fire Canadians Inco Admits," *The Toronto Star,* 29 October 1977, p. A3.

4. There is little difference between the federal and provincial spheres here: *The Globe and Mail,* 28 October 1977, p. 3, ran a story entitled "Davis Cautions Critics of Inco Layoffs," with a sub-head reading "Cites threat to investment climate." Similarly, even more reform-minded regimes have floundered in the face of industrial pressure.

5. Michael Mandel, *The Charter of Rights and the Legalization of Politics in Canada* (Toronto: Wall and Thompson, 1989).

# NO

## In Defence of Canadian Political Parties

### Ronald G. Landes

To an ordinary democratic citizen the question "Do Parties Matter?" might seem a typical pseudoproblem of scholars. Everybody knows that parties matter, otherwise nobody would leave
home on election day and cast his vote. Even the enlightened
politicians have hardly any doubts that parties matter.... How
did scholars come to ask such a stupid question—so contrary to
democratic common sense?[1]

For many critics of the Canadian party system, the idea that parties matter and an ensuing defence of representative democracy's most vital element would, in and of themselves, be indefensible. Perhaps reflective of
a general historical dislike of factions and later of parties, the Canadian
public seems never to have fully appreciated the significant role of parties in the democratic political arena. For example, only in quite recent
history have parties even been officially recognized both in Parliament
and in law.[2]

The antipathy toward parties in Canada is both a historical and contemporary phenomenon. For example, in the early 19th century in
Nova Scotia, Joseph Howe, who would later help to create both responsible government and party government in pre- and post-Confederation
Canada, was initially an "anti-party man," declaring himself as belonging
only to the "party of Nova Scotia."[3] In the 1930s, a royal commission on
the future of Newfoundland recommended, among other things, that
the "country should be given a rest from party politics for a period of
years."[4] More recently in the 1970s, during the national unity crisis following the 1976 separatist election victory in Quebec, the then editor of
*Maclean's* magazine, Peter C. Newman, went so far as to suggest the possible elimination of parties altogether. Needless to say, such a suggestion
was not warmly received by either Prime Minister Pierre Elliott Trudeau
or the other party leaders. However, Newman's views are reflective of
generally negative assessments by academics and journalists during the
past several decades. Such analyses have increasingly concluded that the

party system and, in many cases, representative democracy itself have both failed in the Canadian context.[5]

However, such criticisms of the Canadian party system have increasingly "rung untrue." Thus, as a way of assessing these judgments, we will evaluate how effectively Canadian parties are performing the basic functions of parties in democratic polities.

# PARTY FUNCTIONS

Within the context of a competitive party system, the political parties are multifunctional institutions: they "can be put to almost any political or governmental purpose."[6] A typical list of party functions is that developed by Anthony King, which included six major categories: structuring the vote, integration and mobilization of the mass public, the recruitment of political leaders, the organization of government, the formation of public policy, and the aggregation of interests.[7] For the purposes of this paper, we will use a modified three-fold classification of party functions: electoral, governing, and opposition functions.[8]

Electoral functions of parties include structuring the vote, partisan identification, constituency-level political recruitment, and party finance. Governing functions would consist of mobilization and integration, policy development, and national leadership recruitment. The opposition function refers to the competitive battle for power, primarily during elections, but between elections as well.

In the following section of the paper, we will comment on each of these three major party functions, as a way of assessing the strengths and weaknesses of the Canadian party system. Rather than presenting a detailed critique of existing research, we have concentrated on those areas and themes that seem to belie the conclusion that the party system has failed.

# CANADIAN PARTIES: A FUNCTIONAL ASSESSMENT

The electoral functions of the party organizations are central, of course, to their acquisition of power in a democratic polity. In this regard the parties structure the vote by defining the range of alternatives from which the electors must choose, at both the constituency and national levels. The importance of this task can be seen in that the local candidate has relatively little impact on the electoral decision of most voters. Citizens vote increasingly for or against a party, usually defined by their attitudes toward the party's national leader and policies. The addition of party labels to the federal ballot in 1972 would seem to suggest an increase in this party role. Moreover, while other registered parties competed, the federal party system in the 1980s in Canada was more solidified in terms of support for the major parties than it had been for twenty-five years. The growth and participation of new parties in the 1993 federal election, especially the Reform Party and the Bloc Québécois, simply shows that more parties are structuring the vote than in the immediate past—not that the parties are somehow failing in this function.

An important aspect of giving structure to the vote is the pattern of party identification. A series of studies have found that partisan identifications are weaker, more flexible, and less consistent in Canada than in many other democratic systems. Moreover, partisan identifications seem to change frequently, often as fast as a person's electoral choice. As a result, the conclusion has often been made that the parties are not as successful in structuring the vote in Canada as they appear to be in other countries.

While we would not disagree with the specific findings on the fluctuations of partisan identifications at the individual level, we do dissent from some of the implications derived from such a basis. What is often overlooked is that individual changes in partisanship have not led necessarily to significant oscillations in the larger federal party system. The federal party system (1968–1992) in the aggregate has been stable (e.g., fewer challenges from both new and old minor parties), at the same time that individual partisan preferences have become more volatile. For example, while at the individual level there were obviously massive shifts in partisan preferences in Quebec between 1980 and 1984, at the system level it was still an electoral contest between the two old-line parties. That macro-level fact is more significant than voter volatility at the micro-level in most elections. However, as the 1993 federal election results demonstrate, occasionally voter volatility does not simply switch between the existing parties, but instead switches from them to new parties, such as the Bloc Québécois and the Reform Party. When such a change occurs, then voter volatility does produce at least temporary instability in the party system.

From our system-level perspective, we would assert that the aggregate pattern of partisan preferences is considerably more significant than the volatility of party attachments of individuals. A good example of this difference in perspective can be seen in how we interpret changes in partisan identifications and voting patterns over time. In their national election study, Harold Clarke and his colleagues found that 20 percent of the electorate had switched parties between 1972 and 1974.[9] That is a significant finding, but one that tends to receive a lot more attention than the corresponding result that 69 percent had not altered their vote in the same period. What two-thirds of the electorate does not do is a more significant finding than what one-fifth does in terms of the ability of the parties to structure the vote.

A related aspect of the parties' electoral function is the recruitment of candidates to stand for office in each of the constituencies. In this area the parties seem to be much more vibrant than they have been in the past. Over the past few elections (1984, 1988, 1993), some contested nominations have seen the size of the constituency organizations increase from several hundred to several thousand or more. In ridings from Alberta to Nova Scotia, as many as four to five thousand people voted in some of the contested nominations within the major parties. While such extensive participation is still relatively rare, constituency-level nomination meetings in recent elections have involved more people than at any other time. With the increase in the size of the House of Commons, the parties are also recruiting more people than ever before. In 1988 about 1,600 people were nominated for office, with an increase in 1993 to about 2,000 party representatives (plus fifty-two independents and ninety-nine individuals with no affiliation indicated). Moreover, there has been a trend toward better organization and earlier nominations (before the official election call) at the constituency level in recent campaigns. Parties that recruit more people, with more citizens involved, with better organizations and earlier meetings than ever before can hardly be classified as withering institutions.

The last electoral function to concern us is the topic of party finances. While the area remains, even after the 1974 Election Expenses Act, one that could still be improved, the ability of the parties to raise money, in both election and nonelection years, is a good indication of how well they are performing as organizations. The annual reports of the parties reveal that it cost, in a nonelection year in the early 1980s, about $4 million to maintain the activities of the organization, a figure that has approximately doubled in the last decade. In 1989 and 1990 the twelve registered federal parties received a total of $37 million and $43 million, respectively. In 1992 the Conservatives garnered $11.5 million in contributions, the Liberals $7.6 million, and the Reform Party $6.2 million. Moreover, during this same time period, the number of individuals contributing to party finance has significantly increased for all three national parties. In an election year, the parties have been able to raise millions of dollars (in 1988, $50 million), in addition to their support from the public treasury. At the constituency level, the parties are wealthier and in better financial shape than ever before.

In their electoral functions of structuring the vote, as objects of attachment, as recruitment agencies at the constituency level, and as fundraisers, the political parties are performing well. Parties, historically, developed as mechanisms for acquiring power through the election process; they remain effective organizations, in that regard, in Canada.

The second basic set of party tasks are various governing functions. Parties provide not only the personnel to fill the state offices, but also the means for ensuring the fusion of executive and legislative powers in the Canadian parliamentary system, that is, the principle of party discipline. Walter Bagehot's famous description of the mid-19th-century British cabinet as "the hyphen which joins—the buckle which fastens—the executive to the legislative part of the state" is obsolete since the advent of parties. It is the party that lays the foundation for the fusion of executive and legislative powers, and only after the party does so can an institution such as the cabinet implement the fusion of powers on a day-to-day basis. In the modern era, cabinet government is predicated on party government; Walter Bagehot's buckle has a party label. Failure to realize this relationship has often led to a denigration of the significant role parties play in the governing process.

While the implementation of a fairly rigid pattern of party discipline (i.e., few free votes or breaks in party unity) has made the legislature subservient to the executive (the usual focus of the critics), it has, nonetheless, also allowed for forceful executive action. One example might suffice: it is highly unlikely that we would have a patriated and revised Constitution, with an amending formula and a Charter of Rights and Freedoms, without the imposition of party unity in the House of Commons. However, this benefit of party discipline seems to be downplayed, if not outright ignored, by the critics.[10] As well, the mass public has little appreciation of the contributions that the principle of party discipline makes to the governing process.[11]

As mobilizers and integrators, the parties are not as successful as in the previous areas that have been discussed. If voting is used as an indicator of mobilization, then the Canadian party system is less effective than many other democratic countries. Although the turnout in federal elections since 1945 has averaged about 75 percent, Canada ranks only nineteenth out of twenty-four democratic countries on this measure of participation.[12] Except during election campaigns or a party leadership contest, the parties, internally, mobilize few activists. As organizations, the parties are not well suited to inspire much participation in nonelectoral situations.

Critics often point to the inability of the parties as integrators in relation to both regionalism and English–French relations. Particularly with respect to seats in the House of Commons, the parties are regionally based. While the plurality electoral system certainly magnifies the regional composition of the party caucuses, it should not be forgotten that the basic reason parties fail to win seats in a region is that they do not win enough votes in those areas (i.e., they lack sufficient popular support). Moreover, parties can modify their appeal to particular regions by selecting a new leader or adopting new or revised policies.

Regional loyalties can shift (and they often do) in response or reaction to party strategies. In 1993, the major regional shift in party loyalties was not between the existing parties, but instead it was from the existing parties to two new regional protest parties: the Bloc Québécois based solely in Quebec and the Reform Party based in Western Canada.

While particular parties, such as the Tories in Quebec from 1921 to 1984, may not be effective integrators in relation to the English–French split, the dominant federal party in that same period (i.e., the Liberals) was effective. The alternation of English and French leaders, the adoption of specific policies such as bilingualism, and the defence of Quebec's interest in the larger federal system made the Liberal Party the normal governing party in Canada. The selection of Brian Mulroney as Conservative leader in 1983 illustrates that finally, perhaps, this lesson has been grasped by the normal opposition party as well. Overall, as integrative institutions, the parties are not as effective as they might be, although they are likely better than their critics sometimes perceive. For example, the federal parties played a significant role in shaping the constitutional drama and the final product between 1980 and 1982.[13] Although the Meech Lake and Charlottetown accords both failed to be adopted, they both demonstrated a desire and willingness by the major parties to serve as vehicles of national integration.

Since one of the national political leaders will end up as the prime minister, we have classified the process of national party leadership as a governing function. Several aspects of current leadership selection are worthy of mention. First, the size of such national meetings has been increasing, so that more party workers are involved now than ever before. Second, the campaigns receive national media coverage and seem to be widely followed by the mass public. Third, more and more people are involved at the constituency level in the process of delegate selection. Fourth, unlike earlier periods, a leader can no longer necessarily ordain his or her successor (e.g., Trudeau) or even necessarily keep his own position, even with a huge lead in the polls (e.g., Joe Clark). The leadership-review processes adopted by our national parties run counter to Robert Michels's "iron law of oligarchy" thesis. The parties are now more internally democratic than they have ever been in the past, a statement that is particularly true at the provincial party level.

The final governing function of policy development, a main target of the critics, is one where the parties are sorely lacking. A long list of current as well as historical assessments[14] confirms the perception that a political party in a democratic system "is not a thinking organization."[15] The parties, especially the Liberals and Conservatives, fail as organizations that seek to originate, develop, and implement specific measures of public policy. More often than not they act like Downsian creatures:

they propose policy as means of winning elections, they do not win elections in order to implement specific promises.[16]

The failure of the parties in the policy function is a direct result of the dominance of their electoral functions over all others. Policy is sublimated to the quest for power. Organizationally, the parties are not structured to be effective policy actors. However, I am not sure that this conclusion is as devastating as most critics make it out to be. As the historical assessments by Smith, Siegfried, and Bryce indicate, the parties in Canada have never been particularly adept as policy mechanisms. How can we say that they are doing less well today as policy developers, when they have probably never carried out such a function in the political process?

The final function of political opposition, while not solely given to the parties, is primarily a result of a competitive party system, both inside and outside of Parliament. The obvious competition for power among the political parties in the election period is carried on between elections in the House of Commons. From our perspective, the power of the opposition parties has increased in recent years, partly as a result of internal parliamentary reforms (e.g., opposition days) and partly as a consequence of their increasing willingness to challenge the government (e.g., the various bell-ringing episodes). The opposition in the Commons was surprisingly effective, for example, during the long periods of constitutional reform, so much so as to force the government to change important segments of the revised Constitution. While the government can certainly carry the day when it has the political will to do so, increasingly the opposition has challenged such a pattern, even in majority government situations.

In considering these various party functions, we have maintained that the Canadian party system is performing better in most areas than the critics would have us believe. The parties, as they were designed to be, are most effective as electoral organizations. As policy generators they are mostly ineffective, and as integrators they fare only modestly well. This report card on party strengths and weaknesses clearly gives them a passing mark overall, even with their low grades in the policy and integration functions. Certainly the parties are doing well enough to undercut any interpretation that sees them as failing, withering, or dying. As organizations, the parties are, on the whole, organizationally sound, financially solvent, and pragmatically vibrant elements of the Canadian pattern of representative democracy.

# NOTES

1. Klaus von Beyme, "Do Parties Matter? The Impact of Parties on the Key Decisions in the Political System," *Government and Opposition* (Winter 1984), Volume 19, Number 1, p. 5.

2. John C. Courtney, "Recognition of Canadian Political Parties in Parliament and in Law," *Canadian Journal of Political Science* (March 1978), Volume 11, Number 1, pp. 33–60.

3. J. Murray Beck (ed.), *Joseph Howe: Voice of Nova Scotia.* Toronto: McClelland and Stewart, 1964, p. 36.

4. Susan McCorquodale, "Newfoundland," in Martin Robin (ed.), *Canadian Provincial Politics: The Party Systems of the Ten Provinces,* 2nd ed. Scarborough, Ont.: Prentice-Hall Canada, 1978, p. 138.

5. John Meisel, "The Decline of Party in Canada," pp. 119–35 in Hugh G. Thornburn (ed.), *Party Politics in Canada,* 6th ed. Scarborough, Ont.: Prentice-Hall Canada, 1991; Dimitrios Roussopoulos, "The System is Outmoded—Says the New Left," *Toronto Daily Star* (April 6, 1970), reprinted in Paul W. Fox (ed.), *Politics: Canada,* 5th ed. Toronto: McGraw-Hill Ryerson, 1982, pp. 320–22; Vaughan Lyon, "Parties—Inevitable or Obsolete?" Paper presented at the 1981 annual meeting of the Canadian Political Science Association, Halifax, Nova Scotia.

6. Kay Lawson (ed.), *Political Parties and Linkage: A Comparative Perspective.* New Haven: Yale University Press, 1980, p. 3.

7. Anthony King, "Political Parties in Western Democracies," *Polity* (Winter 1969), Volume 2, Number 2, p. 120.

8. Ronald G. Landes, *The Canadian Polity: A Comparative Introduction,* 3rd ed. Scarborough, Ont.: Prentice-Hall Canada, 1991, pp. 261–62, 308.

9. Harold G. Clarke, Jane Jenson, Lawrence LeDuc, and Jon H. Pammett (eds.), *Political Choice in Canada.* Toronto: McGraw-Hill Ryerson, 1980, abridged edition, pp. 237–42.

10. For an example, see Mel Hurtig, *A New and Better Canada: Principles and Policies of a New Canadian Political Party.* Toronto: Stoddart, 1993.

11. Ronald G. Landes, "Public Perceptions of the Canadian Parliament," pp. 206–10 in Landes (ed.), *Canadian Politics: A Comparative Reader.* Scarborough, Ont.: Prentice-Hall Canada, 1985.

12. David Glass, Peverill Squire, and Raymond Wolfinger, "Voter Turnout: An International Comparison," *Public Opinion* (December/January 1984), Volume 6, Number 6, p. 50.

13. Robert Sheppard and Michael Valpy, *The National Deal: The Fight for a Canadian Constitution.* Toronto: Fleet Books, 1982. See also Nathan Nurgitz and

Hugh Segal, *No Small Measure: The Progressive Conservatives and the Constitution.* Ottawa: Deneau Publishers, 1983.

14. Goldwin Smith, *Canada and the Canadian Question.* Toronto: Hunter, Rose and Company, 1891; André Siegfried, *The Race Question in Canada.* London: Eveleigh Nash, 1907; James Bryce, *Canada: An Actual Democracy.* Toronto: Macmillan of Canada, 1921.

15. Richard Rose, *Do Parties Make a Difference?* Chatham, N.J.: Chatham House, 1980, p. 44.

16. Anthony Downs, *An Economic Theory of Democracy,* New York: Harper and Row, 1957.

# P O S T S C R I P T

**M**eisel's article raises some disturbing questions. Parties and elected representatives are typically thought to be at the centre of the democratic process, yet Meisel suggests that nonelected elements (especially bureaucrats) are now assuming greater importance. If so, does this mean that democratic polities are now witnessing the triumph of the unelected over the elected? Meisel writes that responsibility for mobilizing and aggregating the citizenry is increasingly in the hands of pressure groups and the like. Again, if so, does this mean that parties are no longer the essential link between the people and their governments? For a final point, Meisel says that the selection of leaders, typically the purview of parties, now reflects the demands of television. If so, does this mean that physical appearance has become all-important?

Meisel also says that the most recent developments in Canadian politics serve only to speed the decline of parties. The increasing power of the prime minister, the reliance on nonparty advisers, and the judicializing of political life further undermine the place of political parties. On reading Meisel, one must believe that parties are doomed—they are to be the dinosaurs of Canadian politics.

If Meisel is troubling, Landes is reassuring. The latter suggests that the "decline-of-party" thesis is nothing new. There have always been criticisms of parties and predictions of collapse, yet parties have survived and prospered. Landes also claims that parties are actually improving their performance in areas such as candidate recruitment, finance, and selection of leaders. As for the observation that parties have little role in policy formation, Landes responds that parties have never taken an interest in this area of governing—power, not policy, has been the chief concern of political parties.

It has been argued that parties are not in decline, but rather are undergoing a *transition* in which they take on new responsibilities and shed old ones. An element of the transition thesis, though, seems to be the notion of decline, for its proponents suggest that parties are engaged in a new life-and-death struggle with other forces in the political process. The transition thesis is explored in Alain-G. Gagnon and A. Brian Tanguay, eds., *Canadian Parties in Transition* (Scarborough: Nelson, 1989).

Another variation on the notion of parties in decline centres on the *dysfunctions* of parties. Here, the argument is not that parties are being replaced by other elements, but rather that the behaviour of parties damages the political process; however, one effect of the latter is to diminish the reputation of parties, which in turn contributes to their decline. The relevant reading for this topic is John Meisel, "The Dysfunctions of Canadian Parties: An Exploratory Mapping," in Hugh Thorburn, ed., *Party Politics in Canada*, 6th ed. (Scarborough: Prentice-Hall, 1991). Finally, A. Brian Tanguay has written an informative article on the issue of party decline entitled "Reflections on Political Marketing and Party 'Decline' in Canada ... or, A Funny Thing Happened on the Way to the 1988 Election." It can be found in Alain-G. Gagnon and A. Brian Tanguay, eds., *Democracy with Justice* (Ottawa: Carleton University Press, 1991).

For additional readings on parties in Canada, students should consult George Perlin, ed., *Party Democracy in Canada: The Politics of National Party Conventions* (Scarborough: Prentice-Hall, 1985), Hugh Thorburn, ed., *Party Politics in Canada*, 6th ed. (Scarborough: Prentice-Hall, 1991), and Joseph Wearing, *Strained Relations: Canada's Parties and Voters* (Toronto: McClelland and Stewart, 1988).

# ISSUE FOURTEEN

## Are Polls Bad for Politics?

YES  JEFFREY SIMPSON, "Pollstruck," *Policy Options* 8, no. 2 (March 1987): 3–7

NO  MICHAEL ADAMS, "Pro Polling," *Policy Options* 8, no. 6 (July 1987): 28–30

During the past two decades, polls have come to play an integral role in the political process. Because of their claim to scientific accuracy and validity, polls have a great appeal to politicians, campaign strategists, and bewildered voters. Increasingly, public opinion polls appear to determine the nature and strategy of electoral campaigns. They guide governments in the selection of policy priorities and shape the way politicians present their policies to the electorate. It has even been suggested that pollsters, next to the party leaders, are the most important players in Canadian politics.

While few doubt the significance of polls, there is a wide divergence of opinion as to their impact on politics. Some view polls as instigators of "horse-race" elections in which voters lose sight of the issues and become transfixed by the performance of parties in the polls. Polls have transformed elections into personality contests that trivialize substantive debate over policy issues. Still others are concerned that polling itself is a technically flawed process that is taken at face value by a gullible public. A subtle change in wording a question, or the nature of the sample chosen, can significantly alter the outcome of the poll.

The most important concern of critics, however, is the impact of polls on the behaviour of politicians. Elected representatives can become virtual slaves to polls, avoiding actions that may conflict with the "scientific" advice of their pollsters. As a result, the government too often does what the pollsters say the nation wants, not what it needs.

Not surprisingly, the supporters of polls paint a much different picture. To them, polls greatly enhance the quality of democracies. Polls help governments to govern more effectively by allowing politicians to understand public opinion and formulate sound policies that have strong public support. Most important, polls give the average voter a direct say in the political process. Gone are the days when politics was a game played by only a few privileged insiders. By giving everyone a voice, polls have made politics truly democratic.

In the following readings written in the late 1980s, Jeffrey Simpson, one of Canada's most respected political journalists, debates the impact of polls on democratic politics with a professional pollster, Michael Adams. One thing to emerge from the debate is that polling is a good deal more complex than merely counting heads. The question is whether such a sophisticated and subtle tool can be used effectively to enhance the quality of democratic politics.

# YES

---

# Pollstruck

---

*Jeffrey Simpson*

There is no agreement among political practitioners when polls first arrived on the Canadian political scene. The Quebec Liberal Party under Jean Lesage in 1960 may have been the first party to use them systematically. In federal politics, the Liberals were undeniably first, bringing in Lou Harris from New York, in the wake of the 1960 Kennedy triumph, to assist them in plotting strategy and keeping abreast of public opinion. The Conservatives, predictably, were not far behind, so that by the late 1960s both major national parties had incorporated polling information into their planning.

In the 1970s, first the Liberals, then the Conservatives, threw off imported American pollsters and turned to Canadians: Martin Goldfarb of Goldfarb Consultants for the Liberals; Allan Gregg of Decima Research for the Conservatives.

By the mid-1980s, imitation had proven again the highest form of flattery. Other firms—Environics, CROP, SORECOM, Angus Reid and Associates, to name a few—had joined the field, adding to the original core of so-called "market research" firms: Gallup, Canada Facts, Market Facts and others. In a decade the number of polling firms doubled and doubled again until polling joined biotechnology, robotics and freshly squeezed papaya juice as secrets for competing in the forbidding world of tomorrow.

In one important sense, this explosion brought undeniable benefits to journalists, academics and the alert public. For far too long, those interested in politics had been unwilling victims of the tyranny of the Gallup Poll. Gallup was for years the only publicly reported poll of consequence. Its numbers, and its numbers alone, were the yardstick by which political progress or decline was measured, political careers broken. Gallup's reliability didn't matter all that much; it was all we had, a little ritual as comfortable as the *Saturday Evening Post*, Hockey Night in Canada and the older, better version of *Maclean's* magazine.

The tyranny of Gallup was unhealthy, for the company and for the consumers of its products. The proliferation of firms at least provided competing assessments of public opinion, and the discerning could observe over time which organizations seemed the most sophisticated. The gospel according to Gallup suddenly became one among many.

The parties have not paid much attention to Gallup for some years, certainly not since they bought their own polling expertise. Both parties consider Gallup an anachronism, a dinosaur among polling firms, stubborn, erratic and hopelessly crude. Yet they are aware that by tradition and circumstance, Gallup's monthly numbers of the state of political feeling are important, not because the numbers themselves are accurate, but because, in their indiscriminate way, the media believe them to be. And so we have the first example of my themes in this article: the degree to which political perception animates reality, and the linked fates of pollsters, politicians and the media.

Political polling has now reached a stage of considerable sophistication. Just a few years ago, it was considered a breakthrough to assess accurately the motivations, rather than simply the voting intentions, of a group of people. Now, parties can reach out and discover on a street-by-street basis, yes even a house-by-house basis, what might motivate voters. It is still terribly expensive to do this, but the Conservatives, with their lead in cash and sophistication over the Liberals, can manage it in important areas.

Computers allow, as nothing else ever has, the exploitation of micropolitics, the direct link between party or leader and voter. To put this simply, a computer can dial your number, for which it has been programmed, ask you questions, discern your responses, then spit out a letter signed by the leader or the candidate explaining the party's position on whatever issue concerns you. This is just one of many techniques for monitoring ever more closely the state of public opinion.

Some people are dreadfully frightened by this increasing sophistication because it speaks of Big Brother and the diminution of human will in politics. Others, including naturally the pollsters, see their work as rendering more representative the democratic system. They believe the more sophisticated the measurement of public opinion, the more sensitive rulers will be towards the governed.

Yet two funny things happened on the way to the pollsters' heaven.

First, without being mathematical about this, the rise in the pollsters' influence has been roughly matched by the decline in respect for those who govern by them, namely the politicians.

Second, most of the pollsters, if asked to assess their influence, modestly disclaim any and point to policies their masters introduced "against the numbers"; that is, against what polling data suggested was the most prudent political course. And, lo and behold, upon examination it turns out that these policies "against the numbers"—bilingualism, patriation of the constitution, the abolition of capital punishment, the reduction of the federal deficit—are precisely the ones for which politicians win grudging, but lasting, political respect, whereas many of the policies "with the numbers" merely lead politicians in circles like hunting dogs, noses down to public opinion.

It has been my lot to listen to or read many speeches by pollsters, most of which disclaim with unbecoming modesty any undue influence on those they advise. Yet none of them finds it curious, to say nothing of revealing, that the decisions for which the politicians they advise will be remembered are invariably those in which the politicians ignored, or at least tempered, the pollsters' advice.

Another observation frequently advanced by pollsters is that their craft, with all its scientific splendours, represents the purest form of democracy short of plebiscitary democracy. Polls, argue those who take them, are a modern-day equivalent to the Athenian polis. True, citizens are not speaking out in front of their fellow-citizens, but their voices are nonetheless being recorded and heard.

Michael Adams, president of the Environics Research Group Limited, put the point this way in a speech last year: *In many government departments, the most powerful forces are interest or advocacy groups working for a specific cause. The public has difficulty making its voice heard. But if polls are taken into consideration, the popular will is less likely to be drowned out by powerful organized interests.*

"The popular will." Note the phrase. Defining the popular will, measuring it, circumscribing it, giving effect to it—these have been among the themes of political philosophy down through the ages. Now pollsters pretend that through the magic of their methods and the insights of their analysis, they can define more precisely than ever before this notion of the "popular will."

I do not dispute the sophistication of much of the pollsters' methodology and analysis. But I worry about the claims made for their work, some of which are exaggerated and dangerous. Polls offer a snapshot. It is true that a series of polls tracing public opinion over time can deliver a historical perspective on public opinion. But, by and large, a sense of history and polling data rest uncomfortably together, because polling results tend to encourage both takers and consumers into quick judgments.

I believe that if there is any effect polls generally produce it is to reinforce timidity in those who use them. Change is often deeply upsetting to individuals, communities or nations. Living with the *status quo* is something we all do, for we have no choice. We made our accommodations, our compromises, our adjustments to deal with reality as it comes. It is exceptionally difficult for most of us, caught up as we are with managing our own affairs, to think deeply about alternative ways of organizing our lives and that of our community or country. It is therefore not surprising that polling results often reveal at best a deep ambivalence about change, at worst a blind aversion to it. We know the devils we live with, and we feel more comfortable with them than the ones we know little about.

The message from polls, not surprisingly, is often that political change, especially fundamental change, will be deeply upsetting, or at least very difficult. The risks involved are therefore likely to be great for any politician who preaches change. And if the politician consults the polls, he or she will often be scared off from preaching for or trying to effect fundamental changes.

The current government, which uses polls as extensively as any government we have seen in Canada, offers an interesting illustration of this point. The party's polls after the 1984 election revealed an overwhelming desire for change. But when the pollsters probed for what kind of change the country wanted, they ran up against that deep ambivalence I mentioned. Certainly people seemed to want a change in the style of government. The country was fed up with the bruising confrontations of the Trudeau period, especially the last Trudeau government. We seemed to want federal–provincial harmony, a more responsive federal government, a Prime Minister who would not lecture us.

But the pollsters could not uncover any groundswell in the country for a change in the substance of policy. Rather, there seemed to be yellow lights of caution showing up everywhere.

People thought deficit reduction was a good idea, unless it deprived them of certain services or caused their taxes to increase.

They thought better relations with the United States was a good idea, but not if we became too cosy with our American neighbors.

Giving the private sector a wider scope for unfettered action seemed popular, until people were asked if they wanted environmental de-regulation, lower corporate taxes or the dismantling of major crown assets, in which case the yellow lights shone brightly.

So the federal Conservatives, acutely sensitive of their historical status as the country's minority party, governed by the polls. They delivered a change in the style of government, but they moved cautiously to change the substance. It is now the most ironic criticism of the federal Conservatives that they lack a sense of vision, of where they wish to take the country, although these alleged failures were really a reflection of the country's ambivalence about change, an ambivalence recorded by the polls.

By paying close attention to the polls, politicians invariably consign themselves to leadership by incremental change because they come to fear the public reaction to change. If anything, polls have a conservative, deadening effect on public policy. The pollsters argue, not without reason, that their work can help the making of intelligent public policy because it prevents parties from tempting fate. But their work, it seems to me, also inhibits creative leadership by supplying politicians with a fair reading of what citizens want, as opposed to the politicians' judgment of what the nation needs.

It may seem the height of arrogance—and it certainly runs against the grain of the pollsters' argument about their craft representing the advantages of plebiscitary democracy—to argue that not giving people what they want constitutes good public policy. After all, we live in a democratic society, the philosophical underpinning of which is that the people are always right and that the "popular will," as expressed at election time through the ballot box and between elections in public debate, must prevail.

But if my hunch is correct that polling tends to underline the ambivalence or opposition to change, then politicians come to fear public opinion, or at least to worry excessively about it. There is little incentive for the politician who follows the polls to educate the public about his intentions, to speak unsettling truths, to challenge existing assumptions; in short, to get out in front of public opinion and to lead and, of course, to risk the consequences if he cannot get his vision accepted.

By giving politicians an increasingly sophisticated reading of public opinion, pollsters have actually made many politicians the prisoners of that opinion. The consequence is the kind of timidity I mentioned earlier, coupled with an increasing desire to fudge issues so as not to arouse hostility to the prospect of change.

Expediency in politics long pre-dated polls, as even a cursory glance at Canadian political history reveals, but polls have now made expediency that much easier by providing politicians with the clearest picture they have ever had of what the public wants or, to put it more crudely, for what price voters can be influenced.

Canada's party system arose out of the nature of our country, especially the need to tie together diverse regions and linguistic groups into a political whole. Non-ideological parties at the national level seemed best able to fulfill those pre-eminent tasks. Certainly John A. Macdonald and Mackenzie King didn't have polls to tell them that political success lay in pragmatic, brokerage politics. They knew it from their lives' experience in politics.

These days, polls can certainly be used to confirm the wisdom of Macdonald and King: namely that the country still prefers pragmatic, brokerage politics. Within our largest province, the Ontario Conservative party, in later years known as the Big Blue Machine, governed as if polls were the Holy Grail. Certainly the Ontario Conservatives achieved a quite remarkable degree of political success. It's intriguing to note, however, that the Liberals who replaced them put a good deal less stock in polls.

The Prime Minister took the Big Blue Machine as a role model for his own political success. As the pollster for both has told friends, he,

Allan Gregg, has never, ever worked for someone who hangs on the polls as much as the current Prime Minister. Forget, therefore, as self-serving, defensive twaddle that stuff about Mr. Mulroney paying little attention to the polls. Yet it's pretty clear that two years and a bit of poll-watching by Mr. Mulroney have not produced resoundingly effective or attractive government.

Polls certainly give politicians who wish to use them for this purpose an enhanced capacity to govern through pragmatic, brokerage politics because they can provide such a multiplicity of snapshots, even down to a given neighborhood. Yet I'm not sure whether all this proliferation of information is necessarily useful. It can be confusing, and it probably reinforces the impression of the inherent conservatism of people and groups. Even if the data show one group willing to move, they likely show another unwilling to be budged. Hegel might have been able to make a synthesis from the pushes and pulls of competing groups; politicians are somewhat less insightful, or arrogant, as the case might be.

Within government, polls have accelerated a centralization of power in the Prime Minister's office. That process has been underway for some time and there are many reasons for it that go far beyond the influence of polling. But polling data, usually carefully guarded by the Prime Minister, a few of his advisers and a handful of Cabinet ministers, have weakened the influence of strong regional ministers. No longer can they speak with authority about the state of public opinion in their province or region, when the Prime Minister and his advisers have access to polling data that might contradict what the regional minister is saying.

As Keith Davey correctly boasted in his memoirs, why would he have ever wanted to be a mere Cabinet minister? He had much more influence than most ministers, in part because he had the polls in his hip pocket. He and one or two other non-elected advisers commissioned the polls, listened to Martin Goldfarb's analysis of them, then presented a summary of the findings to those who needed to know. If information is power, as the saying goes, then those with the polling information have it all over those who don't in modern governments.

Yet it is intriguing to see now on the political stage two leaders who disdain polls and seldom, if ever, use them. Premier David Peterson of Ontario drove his senior advisers to distraction before and during the last campaign by his refusal to countenance extensive polling. Circumstances partly dictated moderation; the provincial Liberals had very little money. Partly Mr. Peterson's own sense of what was politically wise and saleable gave him the self-confidence to reject polls.

In British Columbia, some of the Ottawa imports from the Conservative party wanted to transplant their methodology from federal and Ontario Conservative politics. In other words, they wanted to poll, poll and again for the Socreds under William Vander Zalm. The new leader, however smiled them down. He didn't want their polls, and he didn't need them. However, these are the exceptions. The pollsters are now our modern-day Richelieus, fixtures at the leaders' right hands.

Thus far, I have dealt with a few of the consequences as I see them of polls on public policy and government. I now want to turn to the media and polls, and to offer a few observations on how both relate to politicians.

In one sense, polls have greatly assisted the capacity of journalists (and social scientists for that matter) to understand the body politic. They have offered a degree of precision not previously available about public attitudes, voting intentions and political culture. But they have also brought in their train many unfortunate, and in some cases dangerous, tendencies.

Polls are like nuclear weapons, not in their destructive power, but in the fact that neither can be abolished. We might hope for, even work for, nuclear disarmament, but no one can disinvent the capacity to make a nuclear bomb. And since the possession of one bomb confers on its creator an unbridgeable advantage over those who have none, everyone with the capacity to have one will insist upon it except those willing to rely on a larger ally for protection. So, too, with polls.

No party will now forsake them totally. Nor can they be outlawed. Several jurisdictions have tried but gave up when they realized human ingenuity and curiosity could not be denied.

So the trick with polls, as with nuclear weapons, is learning to live with them, to understand their perils and possibilities, to treat them with prudence, and to beware of all those, but especially the creators, who insist with a beguiling insouciance upon the undeniable benefits for our world of these new technologies. And when I write of learning about the trick, I am referring directly to those charged with reporting and analysing the polls; namely the media.

I am deeply worried about the way the media treat polls. Just as love is often wasted on the young, so polls are often wasted on the media. The substantial increase in the pollsters has been matched only by the explosion in the number of journalists reporting them. Many journalists, including those who write about political matters, are unschooled in Canadian history, in polling methodology, in an understanding of any part of the country but their own. Yet the beguiling simplicity and easy accessibility of polling data embolden all journalists to become instant pundits, or worse still, experts. They can pontificate on the meaning of this, the likely outcome of that, the significance of everything, on the basis of a few stark numbers.

Polls, as I argued earlier, are nothing more than snapshots. At the very least, therefore, the significance of a given poll can only be attributed to where it stands in a continuum of polls on the same subject. Parties know this, which is why during an election campaign, they run so-called "tracking polls" to monitor daily public opinion. Yet in the rush to judgment, many journalists forget all about the continuum and concentrate only on the snapshot.

Similarly, every pollster, no matter how self-confident, must ascribe to his work a margin of error. These margins can change the meaning of any poll, yet they are systematically ignored after the first reporting.

Let's say the most recent poll shows the Liberals with 37 per cent of the vote, the Conservatives with 33, and the NDP with 28. Now if the margin of error is four per cent, that could mean the Liberals are anywhere between 33 and 41 per cent, the Conservatives between 29 and 37 per cent, the NDP between 24 and 32 per cent. In other words, it's possible the order might be Liberal-Conservative-NDP, or Conservative-Liberal-NDP, or even Liberal-NDP-Conservative. But if you watch closely what happens in the reporting of the polls, you will find that, while the organization that commissioned the poll will perhaps describe the margin of error, all the other organizations which scalp the poll will forget about the qualifications. All you'll hear are the so-called "headline" numbers which, as I said, may be grossly misleading. These numbers then take on a spurious, but nonetheless real, life of their own. They become accepted wisdom, and they are thrown willy-nilly in the faces of politicians for reaction.

Whether they are accurate or not, misleading or otherwise, the polls are the yardstick by which too many journalists measure political success. And this, in turn, contributes to the horse-race kind of reporting that so colors elections and what transpires between them.

Polls also contribute to the blurring of reporting and analysis which characterizes much of what is written in today's media. Since any journalist figures he can read a poll properly and derive therefrom instant insight, a fragile barrier of humility that should stand in the way of premature analysis falls down. The ever present temptation to punditry, a temptation from which I was never immune myself even before becoming a pundit on a full-time basis, seems irresistible. I could point you to dozens of examples of so-called "back-grounders," "news analyses," "features," and sometimes even "reports" that took as their theses a proposition purportedly illustrated by a poll.

Sometimes, the media don't even bother with the margins of error. My own newspaper, which I love dearly, ran a front-page, line-story poll which purported to show that Jean Chrétien was more popular than John Turner. The poll was conducted by Gallup. Yet we did not provide readers with the following information: Who commissioned the poll. How many people were sampled. The precise question asked. The margin of error. The dates when the poll was taken. Comparative data from other polls on the same, or related, questions. Despite these flagrant gaps, we led readers to a certain set of conclusions. We didn't even allow sophisticated readers the chance to judge for themselves whether we had stretched the evidence, because we offered no evidence.

Tucked away in preliminary news stories is another salient point, the probability of error. This is usually reported to be one time in twenty. Or to put things another way, polls usually claim "to be accurate to a margin of four (or three, or two) per cent, 19 times out of 20." I cannot prove this, except by seat-of-the-pants experience, but I would put that number somewhat higher.

In the last two election campaigns, for example, Gallup's final poll before voting day was spot-on in 1984 and a mere 10 points wide of the mark in 1980. That's a .500 batting average: great in baseball, rather less than "19 times out of 20." Angus Reid, the new boy on the polling block from Winnipeg, published a poll on the eve of the last election in his home province. It predicted a nine-point NDP lead. The popular vote ended in a tie.

I could go on ticking off weaknesses in the reporting of polls, but I'll stop with the following observation. Pollsters, for all their purported scientific rigor, are distinctly fallible. Their work should be treated as such and the interpretation of that work by an exceedingly fallible media should make all consumers of polling information doubly dubious.

I plead, then, for more rigor by journalists in handling polling, for more modesty in the claims made by pollsters for their material, for greater skepticism on the part of consumers of polling data, for a more widespread understanding of the limits and liabilities of polling.

We—the media and the politicians—would do well to pay less attention to polls, and to remember their weaknesses when we pay them any heed.

I'm afraid, however, that despite a few encouraging signs the drift is entirely the other way. Not only are there more pollsters, but they seem to be competing ever more fiercely, saying the most awful, backhanded things about each other.

Pollsters who work for political parties freely sell their services to newspapers and magazines, leaving themselves open to the perception of a conflict of interest. Each poll is now amplified with diminishing regard to prudence.

No wonder politicians, however they treat polls in the organization and management of their government, cannot escape the public impact of polls. Polling numbers take on a life of their own; and perception becomes reality. Once the media rush to judgment following a given poll or series of polls, the politicians instinctively feel they must shift their behavior accordingly. They can soldier on in the face of adverse perceptions built upon questionable interpretations of fallible polling data, but invariably the temptation arises to cut and run, or at least to trim and tack.

Learning to live with polls, their uses and limitations, is one of the great challenges of contemporary public policy. Neither the practitioners of the arts of politics nor those who chronicle the politicians are meeting that challenge. Both groups give inordinate, unjustified weight to polling results, seldom pausing to ask whether these results are reliable guides to current attitudes, let alone future intentions. The pollsters have run far ahead of the politicians, the media and certainly the population at large in selling their wares and getting us to accept them. It's time common sense, prudence and wisdom, the antithesis of snap judgments, caught up and brought the pollsters' influence back into line.

# Pro Polling

*Michael Adams*

In his article on polling entitled "Pollstruck" (*Policy Options*, Vol. 8, No. 2), *Globe and Mail* columnist Jeffrey Simpson exhorts politicians and the media *to pay less attention to polls, and to remember their weaknesses when they pay them any heed.* Mr. Simpson feels that there is a growing trend for Canadian political leaders to become prisoners of public opinion and for journalists in this country to report polling data uncritically.

He notes that *the rise in pollsters' influence has been roughly matched by the decline in respect for those who govern them, namely the politicians,* and goes on to state that *the decisions for which the politicians they advise will be remembered are invariably those in which the politicians ignored, or at least tempered, the pollsters' advice.*

Mr. Simpson contrasts the timidity and lack of a sense of vision characteristic of the pollstruck Mulroney government with the current popularity of Premiers David Peterson of Ontario and William Vander Zalm of British Columbia, both of whom "have the self-confidence to reject polls." Polls, he concludes, *have a conservative, deadening effect on public policy and contribute to the blurring of reporting and analysis which characterizes much of what is written in today's media.*

I disagree with a number of these points. However, Jeffrey Simpson's article is the first thoughtful critique of polling to have appeared in this country in a very long time and raises important questions.

Public opinion polls may ultimately be judged one of the most significant inventions of 20th century social science. However, and here I am in solid agreement with Mr. Simpson, some of the practices of politicians, journalists, and the polling fraternity itself, may be diluting the value and diminishing the necessary public acceptance of this unique tool.

I think it is important for politicians to use polls to help them to understand and to lead public opinion, rather than to attempt to follow blindly "last night's numbers."

I think it is also important for journalists to do a better job in evaluating what poll data they will present—just as they check the credibility of other news sources—and to educate the public on how to use and interpret polling data. It is time for Canadian journalists to question pollsters and their clients when they release or leak poll data *before* they publish or broadcast. And we should see more critical investigative journalism on polls, especially if there are conflicting findings on a particular topic or issue. We have had some very unfortunate examples of suspicious polls released during recent party leadership campaigns and unless journalists and pollsters govern themselves better there will be more abuses in the future.

Within the Canadian marketing and opinion research industry where the professional standards already exists, there must be greater emphasis on the enforcement of those standards, if the industry is to maintain its credibility with the media and the public.

Likewise journalists should take steps to make sure that standards for the reporting of poll data are more closely adhered to, in order to reverse the trend towards biased media polls, or the biased interpretation of government and other public polls to support an editorial position.

Certainly, the response to the pollsters' surveys by one or two thousand Canadians has become as powerful a social fact as the unemployment or interest rates. This is because the world of politics and public affairs is driven as much by perception as by reality itself. Indeed during election campaigns perceptions are the paramount reality. And, what is perhaps more important, pollsters help shape the public policy agenda by the very act of framing survey questions.

There is disagreement as to whether the act of polling merely reflects the state of public opinion in a country, or does in fact have an influence on that opinion. I think it does both.

During an election, private polling by the political parties determines almost everything: the campaign theme and platform; the leadership image to be projected; the timing and location of announcements; the leader's tour; the paid advertising campaign; even the role of the leader's spouse.

The platform devised to win the election becomes the conscience, if not always the mandate of the government. Public policy priorities become oriented to this reality.

The published polls conducted for the media also influence the atmosphere during an election campaign. These polls affect media coverage, the morale of party workers and fundraising. The precise extent to which published polls contribute to a bandwagon effect for the "perceived winner" is not known. Nor, for that matter, is the effect of a collapse in support on the "perceived loser."

Voters tell us they are not influenced by the polls, but I think they sometimes are, as in the 1984 federal campaign where there was a bandwagon for the Conservatives in Quebec, strategic voting for the NDP as the only effective opposition in the west, and a sympathy vote for Mr. Turner in the riding of Quadra.

Does this mean that the publication of poll results should be banned during election campaigns, as was the case in British Columbia until 1983, or that poll results should be banned during the week before election day, as is the case in France?

In my view both proposals are impractical and philosophically repugnant. If the publishing of polls were made illegal during campaigns, presumably political parties would still be allowed to conduct their own private polls. This would only increase the likelihood of leaked polls or rumours of polls designed to mislead the public, the kind of thing that happens often during Canadian election campaigns.

Without properly-run media polls, journalists and voters would have no way of assessing the claims of the parties and their pollsters. Besides, why should politicians have information that the public cannot have?

If polls were banned during campaigns, then the most significant poll would presumably be the one conducted just before the election is called. In the 1984 general election, Canadians would have gone to the polls on September 4th thinking John Turner's Liberals had a ten point lead over the Mulroney Conservatives. Would that misperception have served the public interest? I think not.

Of course, if polls were abolished across the board, this problem would be solved; but is such a ban conceivable in a free society with such a deeply rooted tradition of free speech and a free press? To any reasonable person the cure would be surely be worse than any imagined disease.

Finally, I see nothing wrong with the public taking polling information into account when casting their ballot. Why should any region, group or individual not have the right to jump on a bandwagon or vote for the more realistic alternative to the expected winner?

I would be prepared to support the federal government's proposal, as set out in the June, 1986 White Paper on election law reform, which would not ban the publication of polls during campaigns, but rather require the disclosure of the methodological details of published polls. A better informed public can only strengthen our democracy.

As Mr. Simpson points out, polling has a profound effect on our democratic process quite aside from its impact on elections in this so-called era of "government by poll."

Polls are used to help senior government officials assign priorities to public policy issues and to choose the most effective strategies to communicate government policies and programs. The pollsters' objective in this research is to go well beyond the opinion sampling published in the media. Good public policy polling reveals the level of awareness, knowledge and interest respondents have in a subject. In the best research, pollsters attempt to uncover the basic values, attitudes and beliefs that drive public opinion on the transitory issues of the day.

Regularly conducted in-depth attitudinal surveys make it possible to track perceptions of public policy issues and to monitor underlying sociocultural trends over time. Tracking research reveals the relative volatility or stability of opinion as it monitors the effects of events and new information of public perceptions.

At their best, pollsters help government officials give Canadians policies and programs that are more responsive to the public and therefore ultimately more effective. Many people like Jeffrey Simpson believe, however, that we have reached a point where our leaders' ability to lead is circumscribed by the proliferation of public opinion surveys, that the polls act as psychological manacles on the men and women we have selected to make the tough choices demanded by the present environment, and that the polls are creating a generation of "weak-kneed" representatives who will not move without the oracle's blessing.

Nobody can deny that governments pay a lot of attention to opinion polls. The Parti Québécois' move away from a sovereignty position before the last provincial election exemplifies a recent policy shift dictated by the public mood. This mood was expressed very clearly in polls.

Nevertheless, there is little reason to believe that polls have nearly as significant a role in sterilizing politics as this argument would suggest. Ideas and policies are still the currency of Canadian political life. Politicians often act in response to their principles, even when polls tell them that this will be risky or unpopular. Areas in which moral considerations have often outweighed tactical ones include capital punishment and immigration policy. An overwhelming majority of the Canadian population favours capital punishment and opposes more immigration; yet many politicians refuse to respond to the pressure of public opinion.

Former Prime Minister Pierre Trudeau brought his own agenda to the office. No one can accuse him of being run by polls. Yet he stayed in power for sixteen years with a skillful mix of principle, personality and pragmatic polling. In the United States and Britain, Ronald Reagan and Margaret Thatcher use polls extensively, not to help them follow, but rather to understand and to lead public opinion. No successful politician can afford to follow the polls slavishly. A politician must still have ideas of his or her own.

Historically, the most successful politicians have taken office with a clear point of view, if not always an agenda. These leaders understood the prevailing values and attitudes of their era and employed the best technology at their disposal to understand those values and to communicate their goals and policies.

Prime Minister Mulroney's problem is not that he pays too much attention to the polls, as is popularly believed, but rather that he pays too little attention to their findings. Here I am not referring to the opinion polls on issues like capital punishment (which he opposes), but the polls on the basic values and attitudes of Canadians today. The decline in public respect for politicians has nothing to do with the rise of the pollsters as Mr. Simpson suggests, but rather with the deep sense of betrayal felt by Canadians who had trusted a party which had promised to bring to public office a higher moral tone and a consistent set of principles and policies.

Mr. Simpson applauds leaders who have the courage to ignore the polls and he says politicians will be remembered for the decisions that contradicted the pollster's advice. Surely he does not wish our leaders systematically to ignore or oppose public opinion. Just because an idea is popular does not make it bad public policy. Nor, of course, is it necessarily good public policy, but surely in a democracy the leaders ought at least to take public opinion into consideration when making important decisions.

Another reason to doubt the deadening effect of polls on public policy is that even when governments do want to be responsive to polls, survey results are not always much help. Polls are excellent vehicles for understanding people's basic concerns, fears and aspirations, but when you get down to the details of designing a new program, many of the issues are so esoteric or technical that the public has no opinion about them.

A further reason for doubting the sweeping claims about polls is that governments have always behaved as if they wanted to get re-elected. Just because they still do today does not mean that they would behave differently if polls did not exist.

Historically, the logic of political competition between parties in liberal democracies has usually been enough to ensure that politicians do what they can to stay in power. Public opinion polls have only allowed them to pursue this goal more efficiently—in government and during election campaigns.

It is not always such a bad thing, anyway, when governments listen to what the polls say. Sometimes it is the only way that the opinions of the average voter can have much impact on policy. In many government departments, the most powerful outside forces are interest or advocacy groups working for a specific cause. The public has difficulty in making its voice heard. But if polls are taken into consideration, the popular will is less likely to be drowned out by powerful organized interests.

Polling, in my view, is an important component of modern government everywhere and good polling almost invariably serves the public interest.

In the communist countries of Eastern Europe and even in the Soviet Union polling by governments is increasing, as is the publication of polling data. In the West, polling, like universal suffrage before it, is the natural extension of democratic principles made possible by the combination of advanced technology and an informed citizenry. In the East, polling may be the precursor of more democratic freedoms.

I do not share Jeffrey Simpson's nostalgia for the good old days of Canadian politics and journalism when exclusive elites, old-boys' networks and self-interest groups ran this country. For me, there is nothing wrong with leaders understanding their followers and with journalists understanding their readers. I think such understanding will help them do a better job.

# POSTSCRIPT

Readers, having the benefit of hindsight, will find it interesting to test some of Simpson's observations. He mentions specifically David Peterson and Bill Vander Zalm as examples of politicians who had sufficient confidence in their own judgment of the public to ignore public opinion polls. Did their judgment necessarily serve them well in determining the fate of their subsequent political careers?

As the above discussion reveals, several issues of concern emerge in the debate over polls. What impact do polls have on the way politicians make policy decisions? Do polls unduly influence the way people vote? Do the media report the results of polls in a responsible and fair way? Do polls turn leaders into followers?

One intriguing issue raised, and rejected by Adams, is whether the publication of polls should be banned during election campaigns. Certain types of advertising are already prohibited or strictly regulated during elections. If polls can distort the electoral process, then why not ban them during the election campaign or at least during the final weeks? There has been a precedent for this in some European countries. Would voters be any less well informed or unprepared to vote if such polls were unavailable?

This issue was recently examined by the Royal Commission on Electoral Reform and Party Financing. While rejecting the outright banning of polls, the commission did recommend the prohibition of publication of opinion polls from midnight the day preceding election day until the close of all polls on election day. The aim here is to avoid publication of last-minute polls that do not give politicians an opportunity to reply, and to prohibit the publication of exit polls, which the commission deemed to be generally less scientific and that may unfavourably influence voters in parts of the country, especially in different time zones, who have not yet voted. See the Royal Commission on Electoral Reform and Party

Financing, *Reforming Electoral Democracy* (Ottawa: Minister of Supply and Services, 1991).

Paul Fox examined this issue in "The Danger of Private Polling," *Parliamentary Affairs* 8, no. 4 (Winter 1985). He concludes that the banning of public opinion polls actually misses the point. He is much more concerned about the private polls commissioned by parties, government, and interest groups and the detrimental use that might be made of this information (for example, sponsors of private polls may release only those results that either support their own cause or discredit alternative policies). In particular, Fox questions why governments should use public funds to acquire knowledge about voters that can be used essentially for partisan benefit.

Despite the growing role that polls play, especially during elections, there has been surprisingly little explicit scholarly attention paid to the subject. Clair Hoy has written a journalistic exposé of the politics of polling in a book entitled, *Margin of Error: Pollsters and the Manipulation of Canadian Politics* (Toronto: Key Porter, 1989). A more scholarly and objective treatment of the subject, although briefer, can be found in Hugh Whelan, "The Rewards and Perils of Polling," in Paul Fox, ed., *Politics: Canada*, 5th ed. (Toronto: McGraw-Hill, 1982). For two profiles of prominent pollsters and a discussion of their impact, see Jeffrey Simpson, "The Most Influential Citizen in Canada," *Saturday Night* 99, no. 7 (July 1984) and Robert Fulford, "This Brain for Hire," *Saturday Night* 100, no. 12 (December 1985).

# ISSUE FIFTEEN

## Should a System of Proportional Representation Be Adopted in Canada?

YES John Hiemstra, "Getting What You Vote For"

NO Paul Barker, "Voting for Trouble"

In the federal elections of 1979 and 1980, the Liberal Party of Canada won almost no seats in the West and the Progressive Conservatives (PCs) very few in Quebec. These results were profoundly disturbing. Canada was a country with deep regional divisions, and parties were expected to bridge these differences by securing support in all parts of the country. Political parties would serve to integrate the nation by providing a forum in which representatives from the various regions could discuss and resolve their differences. But now the two major parties reflected the very problem they were supposed to solve. Like Canada, their defining quality appeared to be their regional nature. Moreover, this quality was not recently acquired—the 1979 and 1980 elections only highlighted an enduring fault.

Despite this most serious failing, there was still hope for parties. The election results of 1979 and 1980 showed that the Liberals had received votes in the West, and that the PCs had accomplished the same in Quebec. In other words, both were in fact national parties. The real problem lay with the electoral system. The system, called "first-past-the-post" (FPTP), divided the country into numerous constituencies or ridings, and then declared the winner in each riding to be the one who received the most votes. In the West, the Liberals had attracted many votes, but rarely enough to win seats; in Quebec, the PCs suffered a similar fate.

Obviously, then, the solution was to introduce a new electoral system, and the one that made the most sense was proportional representation (PR). Though PR comes in many variations, it basically allocates seats in proportion to the number of votes received. If a party obtained one-quarter of the votes, it would be awarded roughly one-quarter of the seats in the House of Commons. In the 1979 and 1980 elections, PR would have given seats in the West to the Liberals and seats in Quebec to the PCs—and made national parties out of both. In the early 1980s, many proposals for PR did indeed come forward, and the governing Liberal Party promised to examine  the matter closely.

Reform of the electoral system, however, did not take place. In the next two federal elections in 1984 and 1988, the PCs managed to receive seats in all regions, and formed governments that were truly national in composition. The need for reform thus appeared less urgent. As well, the problems with PR assumed some prominence, of which the most serious was its propensity to produce minority governments. PR seemed to offer the prospect of weak and unstable rule at the federal level.

The lack of change in the electoral system, though, has not elimi-nated interest in the issue. In some eyes, the ability of a party to receive national support under FPTP is weak, and eventually the circumstances that led to discussion of PR earlier—regionalized parties—will reappear. The results of the 1993 federal election, which witnessed the emergence of parties with legislative support centred in either Quebec or the West, suggests that this may already be happening. Also, another perceived effect of FPTP, namely its tendency to allot the majority of the seats to parties without a majority of the votes, has caused some vigorous ques-tioning of Canada's electoral system. In recent years, the majority gov-ernment of Brian Mulroney managed to pass important pieces of legislation even though it received less than one-half of the popular vote. For many, this is inconsistent with the workings of democratic gov-ernment.

In the following articles, John Hiemstra and Paul Barker debate the merits of introducing a system of proportional representation in Canada.

# YES

## Getting What You Vote For

*John Hiemstra*

A commonly accepted principle of democracy is that governments should make decisions according to majority rule. While a majority of the Progressive Conservative Members of Parliament (MPs) passed the Goods and Services Tax in 1992, these MPs represented only 43 percent of the Canadian voters. This is only one of many problems caused by Canada's "first-past-the-post" (FPTP) electoral system. The FPTP system fails to provide a just and equitable reflection of Canadians' political opinions in the House of Commons. Using FPTP to constitute the House deepens divisions within Canada, weakens the accountability of Members of Parliament to electors, and undermines representative democracy.

This essay[1] argues that the FPTP method for electing MPs to the House of Commons should be replaced with list-system proportional representation (PR).[2] Both the FPTP and PR electoral systems have had mixed records in other countries, sometimes producing excellent and sometimes poor results. For Canada's distinct needs, however, PR is the best electoral system. PR would make every vote count, enhance national unity, give an accurate reflection of the political opinions of Canadians in the House, and strengthen the sense of obligation of MPs to the voters. This essay draws on national and provincial examples to make this case, since both levels use the FPTP electoral system.

## A MODEST REFORM

Canada's FPTP electoral system is used to decide who will be our representatives in the House of Commons. The country is divided into 295 single-member districts that correspond to the 295 seats in the House of Commons. The winner in each district is decided by the "first-past-the-post" or plurality electoral formula. Simply put, the candidate in a riding who wins more votes than the other candidates—even if less than 50 percent—is declared the winner and takes a seat as MP in the House of Commons.

Adopting the widely used PR system would require only modest reforms to our current system. While it may be difficult to secure parliamentary support for these reforms, they can be done by a simple Act of Parliament. The number of federal MPs per province is determined by several factors, of which population is the most important. Under FPTP, the provinces are carved into electoral districts with one MP elected in each district. For example, under the current formula, New Brunswick is entitled to ten seats in the House of Commons. To change this to list-system PR, the provinces would not be divided into districts, but each province would remain a single district with multiple members. Thus, New Brunswick would be one district that sends ten representatives to the House.

Voting in a federal election under PR would be straightforward. In the New Brunswick district, for example, voters would receive a ballot featuring lists of ten candidates for each political party contesting the election. Voters would place an "x" above the list they support. The ten seats in New Brunswick would be divided among the parties based on the percentage of the popular vote that each party won. If the federal Liberal Party won 30 percent of the popular vote, it would receive 30 percent or three seats. The three candidates on top of the Liberal list would be declared elected. If the Tories won 40 percent of the vote, they would get four of New Brunswick's seats in the House of Commons. Thus PR ensures that the MPs returned to the House from each provincial district would closely mirror the preferences of Canadian voters.

# MAKING EVERY VOTE COUNT

As a democratic state, all Canadians should have a just and equitable say in the composition of the House of Commons, since it deliberates on and approves the laws that govern us all. Sadly, Canada's FPTP electoral system repeatedly fails to deliver just and equitable representation by allowing the "winner to take all."

The FPTP system often fails to do justice by not giving each vote its "due." In the 1984 federal election, for example, less than 50 percent of the voters supported the Conservatives, yet that party won 75 percent of the seats. That means one-quarter of the Canadian voters did not get their "due" because they were represented by an MP from a party they did not vote for.

The injustice done by FPTP is illustrated even better in two recent provincial elections. In the 1993 Prince Edward Island election, Catherine Callbeck's Liberal Party won 97 percent of the seats (thirty-one of thirty-two) with only 55 percent of the vote. This left 40 percent of the voters who voted Tory with one MLA and the 5 percent who voted for the New Democratic Party with none. More dramatically, in the 1987

New Brunswick election, Frank McKenna's Liberal Party won 100 percent of the seats with 60 percent of the popular vote. This left the other 40 percent of the voters unrepresented by the party they supported.

The other serious defect in the FPTP electoral system is its inequity; that is, it often makes your vote count for less than others. For example, in the 1993 federal election, it took an average of 32,321 votes to elect a Liberal MP, while it took over a million votes on average to elect a Tory MP.[3] Clearly, a Liberal vote in this election was worth far less than a Tory vote.

FPTP is a "winner takes all" system that almost always overrewards the winning party. In contrast, PR is widely recognized as a just and equitable system that accurately translates the percentage of the vote each party wins into a proportionate percentage of seats in the House of Commons. PR greatly reduces the injustice and inequity that are so common in the FPTP system. In short, PR gives you what you vote for, which is reason enough to adopt it in Canada.

# PROPORTIONAL REPRESENTATION AND GOVERNMENT STABILITY

PR is usually acknowledged as the fairest electoral system. Yet many critics still reject PR for Canada because they fear it would make the government unstable. They argue that FPTP produces stable majority governments out of minority electoral returns, while PR would produce unstable minority governments. This implies that Canadians must make an unacceptable choice between the value of stability and the values of justice and equity. Fortunately, the facts show that we do not have to make this decision.

Canada has had stable[4] government since well before Confederation. Yet there does not seem to be any connection between this stability and the FPTP electoral system's ability to produce majority governments. Between 1962 and 1992, Canada's FPTP system produced six minority and six majority governments, which is not exactly a stellar record.[5] In spite of these minority governments, Canada's governments have generally been stable and productive. Commenting on the Liberal minority governments in the years 1963–68 and 1972–74, Van Loon and Whittington observe that with some adjustments "a minority can be made to work very successfully."[6]

It is true that minority governments have tended to fall quicker than majority governments in Canada. However, this is due less to the inherent instability of minority governments and more to the incentive FPTP gives to some parties to collapse minority governments. The large parties know that a small shift in the vote toward their party will often be translated by the FPTP system into a majority government for them.

If Canada adopted PR, minority and coalition governments would be more common. But we have already seen that the frequent minority governments under FPTP were not the direct cause of government instability in the past. Nor is it the case that coalition governments are automatically weak or unstable. In PR systems, political parties normally win a steady percentage of the vote in each election. This neutralizes the incentive FPTP gives to parties to collapse minority or coalition governments. Since forcing an election under PR will not dramatically alter party strengths, parties are encouraged to work for just policy compromises within Parliament. Thus coalition governments will be able to "get things done" for Canada. The resulting improvement is that coalitions get things done while involving a majority of the MPs who truly represent a majority of Canadians. PR gets rid of artificial majority governments that make decisions on issues such as free trade and the Gulf War with support from less than half of the voters.

Critics also suggest that PR causes unstable governments by promoting too many small parties. Under FPTP, however, Canada has already produced many small parties, a direct contradiction of "Duverger's law," which asserts that FPTP tends to produce a two-party system. This diversity of smaller parties should not be denied, since it reflects the views of Canadians. The system of PR proposed in this article would give fair representation to small parties, while requiring them to cross a threshold— a minimum number of votes needed in a district to win a seat—before getting their first seat in the House. In all provinces but Ontario and Quebec, small parties would need to win at least 3 percent of the vote to qualify for a seat.[7]

# PROPORTIONAL REPRESENTATION CAN INCREASE NATIONAL UNITY

The spectre of national instability is also raised against PR because it would magnify divisions between regions and between English and French cultures. While the FPTP electoral system has treated this diversity unfairly, some claim that at least FPTP has kept our country stable and united. The facts show, however, that quirks in FPTP actually serve to worsen these divisions in Canada.

One tendency of FPTP is to "reward" small, regionally concentrated parties. For example, the federal Social Credit Party regularly won more seats in Quebec than its popular vote justified. In 1968, Social Credit won 4.4 percent of the popular vote but took 20 percent of the Quebec seats. PR would give small parties their electoral due, without allowing them an unfair number of seats.

A particularly troublesome feature of FPTP's tendency to reward regionally concentrated parties is that some regional parties have promoted separatism or a sectional view of Canada. FPTP has multiplied their negative impact by rewarding them with far more seats than their electoral support warrants. In the 1993 federal election, for example, the separatist Bloc Québécois won 72 percent of the seats in Quebec with the support of only 49.2 percent of the Quebec voters.[8] This also occurred in several Quebec provincial elections where the FPTP system allowed the separatist Parti Québécois to win majority governments with only a minority of the provincial vote.[9]

Another bias of the FPTP electoral system is that it hurts small parties with supporters dispersed across the country. For example, the NDP is a national party with a democratic socialist vision that has some support in all regions of the country. Yet, under the FPTP system it always receives less seats in the House of Commons than its support would justify. For every 2 percent of the popular vote won by the NDP in the last four federal elections prior to 1993, it received about 1 percent of the House of Commons seats. In the 1993 federal election, the NDP won 7 percent of the national vote but took only 3 percent of the seats. Unfortunately, FPTP hurts small parties with regionally dispersed supports even when they promote a unifying national vision. FPTP therefore hurts small parties with regionally dispersed support even if they promote a unifying national vision.

FPTP is also predisposed to overreward large parties in regions where they have strong support while underrewarding them where their support is weak. Thus Canada often lacks truly national parties in the House of Commons. When large parties win the majority of the seats in one region but none in another region, divisions in Canada are perpetuated and worsened. For example, in the 1980 federal election, the Liberal Party formed the government, but did not win a single seat in British Columbia, Alberta, or Saskatchewan, although it won over 20 percent of the vote in these provinces. Meanwhile, the Liberals won seventy-four of seventy-five seats, or 99 percent of the seats, in Quebec with 68 percent of the popular vote. This flaw leads voters to develop a regionally skewed perception of the parties' support. It also handicaps the governing and opposition parties' ability to include regional viewpoints in their caucus discussions. In fact, FPTP gives parties an incentive to favour regions where they might receive large electoral payoffs, while ignoring other regions.

The weaknesses of FPTP, Alan Cairns concludes, make Canada's electoral system "divisive and detrimental to national unity."[10] PR is a better way to handle Canada's regional divisions since it gives seats to national parties in direct proportion to the percentage of popular vote they win in the election. Since every vote counts in PR, parties have a strong incentive to take a national viewpoint on issues and to search for votes in all regions. PR encourages the growth of parties that will integrate the regions of Canada. PR also gives party caucuses MPs from each region of Canada, thus allowing parties to understand more fully regional needs. At the same time, PR permits small parties to form in response to genuine regional needs, but without overrewarding them.

Canadians know that FPTP produces artificial majorities and tends to suppress controversial divisions, yet why do we continue to support democratic politics? Why does Canada remain stable even though FPTP produces minority governments and encourages destabilizing regional parties? Much of the answer lies in Canada's strong, democratic and tolerant political culture. Adopting PR would not suddenly change this political culture. Nor would PR transform Canada into an unstable regime such as pre–Second World War "Weimar Germany" or present-day Italy.[11] Canada's strong, democratic political culture has kept, and will continue to keep, our system stable. Canada with PR would more likely resemble the Netherlands, which has used PR for seven decades and remains eminently stable and unified in spite of its serious divisions.

# PROPORTIONAL REPRESENTATION IS EASY TO USE

It is often claimed that FPTP is the simplest and thus the best electoral system. FPTP is certainly simple. The candidate who wins more votes than the other candidates—even if it is less than 50 percent of the total popular vote—wins the riding. The calculations are straightforward. FPTP, however, also requires the drawing and redrawing of its district boundaries every time the population grows or shifts. This complex and time-consuming process encourages corrupt practices such as malapportionment and gerrymandering.[12] In the last few years alone, Alberta, Saskatchewan, and British Columbia have all faced major court challenges over the fairness of their electoral boundaries.

List-system PR is just as easy to understand and use as FPTP.[13] My experience teaching electoral systems in university classes suggests that it actually takes longer to explain how FPTP works and why it produces so many anomalous results. As stated above, using list-system PR is simple. The ballot for each provincial district contains as many lists of candidates as there are parties contesting the election. You vote by marking your preferred list. The percentage of the vote that each party wins is counted, and the same percentage of candidates off the top of each party's list are declared elected. Since PR would treat provinces as districts, it would be immune to the corrupt practices of malapportioning or gerrymandering of riding boundaries.

# FIRST-PAST-THE-POST PRODUCES FALSE MAJORITIES

Another claim for the FPTP electoral system is that it allows voters to select a government at the same time as they elect their representatives. Indeed, forming a cabinet is largely routine in Canada's parliamentary system, where the party winning the most seats usually forms the government. But it is an illusion to suggest that voters purposefully or automatically select a government. In fact, the majority of Canadians have not been involved in selecting most of Canada's governments. In the last seventy-two years, only two of our national governments have been formed by a party that won a majority of the popular vote in an election (1940 and 1958).

FPTP actually allows a minority of voters to select the majority of the seats, and thus to select the government. This problem with FPTP is closely related to Canada's multiparty system. In the 1988 federal election, when three parties each won 20 percent or more of the votes, FPTP translated the Conservative Party's 43 percent of the vote into 57 percent of the seats. Even more striking, when three strong parties ran in the 1990 Ontario election, Bob Rae's New Democratic Party formed the provincial government with the support of only 38 percent of the voters. In the 1993 federal election, when five major parties contested the election, FPTP translated the Liberal Party's 41 percent of the popular vote into 60 percent of the seats in the House of Commons.

The FPTP electoral system frequently magnifies a small shift in the vote to determine who will form the next government. In the 1979 election, Joe Clark's Conservatives were supported by 36 percent of Canadians and took 48 percent of the seats to form a minority government. The Liberals gathered 40 percent of the vote and took 40 percent of the seats. In the 1980 election, the Liberals increased their share of the vote by only 4 percent, but won a clear majority government with 52 percent of the seats. And in the following election of 1984, a shift of 17 percent of the vote to the Mulroney-led Tories allowed them to increase their seats by 38 percent, from 37 percent to 75 percent of the seats.

This type of chancy outcome in the formation of governments under FPTP is illustrated even more pointedly in two provincial elections in British Columbia. The NDP failed to form the government in 1986 when their 42.6 percent of the vote translated into 31.9 percent of the seats. In the 1991 election, however, NDP popular support dropped to 41 percent of the vote, yet they took 68 percent of the seats and formed the new government. Sometimes, FPTP allows a party to win more seats and form the government with fewer votes than the main opposition party. In the 1979 election, for example, the Conservatives formed the government when they won 36 percent of the vote and 136 seats while the Liberals won 40 percent of the vote and only 114 seats.

Selecting a government through the FPTP electoral system has the further side effect of distorting the public's perception of the parties' strengths. That is, a month after the 1988 federal election nobody remembered that the Tories won 57 percent of the seats with only 43 percent of the vote. The public is constantly reminded of the percentage of seats a party obtained, but not the percentage of the vote it won. Yet Mulroney used his minority electoral support to pass the highly unpopular Goods and Services Tax as well as the controversial free trade agreement with the United States. Governments should only make dramatic policy changes if they are selected and supported by the majority of Canadians.

It is a mistake to think that the problems of FPTP can be solved by abolishing Canada's multiparty system rather than reforming the FPTP system. We must accept that Canadians have deeply held political views and choose different parties to express these views. The democratic answer is to amend our electoral system so that it responds to the beliefs and actions of Canadians, and not to make the system fit what the critics want the people to believe and do. The real challenge is to allow the deeply held political views of Canadians to be properly, safely, and fairly expressed in politics. People with different ethnic, religious, or ideological views often arrive at, or endorse, a particular policy for their own distinct reasons. A PR system will give no viewpoint a hegemonic grip on the system while forcing all parties to discuss their real differences as a means of arriving at mutually acceptable policies.

Since PR would make the House of Commons accurately reflect the opinions and views of Canadians, it would be better to shift the duty of forming governments away from "chance" and to our MPs. This would give the majority of voters a stronger say in the creation of government. It would place the task of forming governments in the hands of our MPs who currently hold the power of dissolving governments. This conforms with and develops Canada's parliamentary theory.

# FIRST-PAST-THE-POST WEAKENS REPRESENTATIVE DEMOCRACY

Indeed, voters would have a greater say over all aspects of their MPs' actions if MPs were obliged to represent their supporting voters. The FPTP electoral system, however, is weakening representative democracy in Canada. Representative democracy was created in response to the increasing number of citizens entitled to be involved in politics, but who lacked the time or energy to study political issues and devise fitting solutions. Most Canadians expect their representatives to actively engage in policy-making for them. Even so, FPTP fails to give representatives a clear mandate from the voters and does not allow voters to hold MPs responsible for their actions.

Instead, FPTP encourages Canadians to weaken or even bypass representative democracy. The weakening of the relationship between voters and representatives occurs because FPTP requires politicians and parties to compromise too early in the process. Before an election, politicians are forced to develop lowest-common-denominator policies that will appeal to a plurality of voters in each riding. For example, some voters believe the state should strongly intervene to protect the environment while others believe market forces will correct environmental problems. In response to this spectrum of opinions, political parties develop a compromised platform that homogenizes the environmental views of Canadians. This is done to attract the widest range of voters necessary to win in an FPTP electoral system.

Early compromises on policy produce pragmatic, look-alike parties. Election campaigns increasingly focus on party leaders and image and downplay principles, policy platforms,[14] and the teams of politicians behind the leaders. Pragmatic parties make principled discussion rare in the House of Commons and foreclose the opportunity for compromise between principled party platforms. Consequently, voters seldom know what their MPs and parties stand for and find it difficult to hold them accountable. At the same time, MPs do not receive clear mandates from voters. In these and other respects, FPTP weakens the relationship between voters and representatives.

The much vaunted "close contact" between a representative and a voter in the FPTP electoral system is largely illusory. Certainly, if a voter has trouble with Revenue Canada, his or her MP will help. But should you want your MP to represent your principles in a debate on major taxation legislation, he or she will refuse for fear of offending other voters who are needed to win the next election. FPTP encourages MPs and political parties to reflect the direct concerns of their geographic districts while ignoring the deeply held principles of the voters. MPs seem to feel very little moral obligation to act for their voters on matters of principle except when necessary for re-election.

Increasingly, voters are turning away from these indistinct parties and turning to interest groups for better representation. Political parties are responding to this challenge to their representative role by merely becoming brokers for the interest groups. Other voters are pushing reforms such as recall, referenda, and initiatives. Recall, however, weakens the MP's ability to act, while initiatives and referenda totally bypass the elected representative. Thus the dynamic set in motion by FPTP actually encourages voters to bypass their representatives, a process that is undermining the very essence of representative democracy.

# INCREASING THE REPRESENTATIVES' OBLIGATION TO VOTERS

In contrast to FPTP, a PR electoral system would strengthen Canada's political system by encouraging a new dynamic. PR would continue to rely on political parties and party discipline, but would force parties to define how they are distinct from the others in order to attract votes. Parties would be encouraged to develop clearer principles and to define their policy platforms. This would allow political parties to become vehicles for voters to give mandates to MPs and to hold them accountable between elections. MPs would clearly be obliged to act in accordance with the principles and policies that they agreed to with their supporters. This would include serving the individual voters according to these principles, if the parties want to maintain electoral support. MPs with a sense of obligation to voters would be a clear advance over FPTP, which limits voters to rubber stamping or jettisoning representatives at election time.

While PR would encourage a sense of obligation between representatives and their supporters, it would not guarantee this outcome. However, evidence from other countries shows that PR has been superior to FPTP in bringing in minority parties. It has also increased the parliamentary representation of women, ethnic groups, and cultural minorities.[15] Significantly, PR has done so without extensive affirmative action programs. PR has also allowed parties to increase the overall quality of individual MPs on their lists. PR also allows citizens to be free to join the political party of their choice and to decide whether their party's MPs will serve as trustees who independently deliberate on issues, delegates who mechanically reflect their views, "mirrors" that reflect their gender, age, ethnic or other characteristics, or defenders of their party's interests and positions.[16] If "party bosses" dominate under PR, it will be the fault of those who create parties that tolerate them.

PR allows parties and governments to be as good or as flawed as the people they represent. It leaves the public free to decide which groups or principles or approaches they want represented, by creating parties to reflect these concerns. PR ultimately leaves the voters to decide which parties they want to be represented by in the House of Commons. For example, if 7 percent of Canadians support the Green Party's approach to environmental issues, PR will give that party 7 percent of the seats, no more and no less.

# CONCLUSION

Democratic principles are the foundation upon which political life in Canada rests. FPTP and PR are structures through which Canadians can exercise their democratic choices. But structures are not neutral. They reflect values that the people in a society want the system to advance and thus encourage citizens to act in a certain way. The dominant value of the FPTP system is stability—which it is supposed to achieve by translating a minority of votes into a majority government. In spite of the FPTP electoral system, however, Canada has frequently produced minority governments. FPTP also produces electoral outcomes that aggravate and intensify Canada's regional and nationalist divisions. Too many outcomes of the FPTP electoral system have been chancy, unfair, and inequitable. Also, FPTP has encouraged the growth of pragmatic and brokerage parties that weaken the incentives of MPs to represent their voters. In spite of these problems, Canada remains a stable, democratic political system.

Since Canada is stable in spite of FPTP, it has ample room to add the values of justice and equity to stability by adopting a PR electoral system. PR makes every vote count and produces results that are proportionate to what voters desire. Canada's distinctive needs would also be best served by PR. It would increase Canada's stability by improving regional representation in major parties, while reducing the unjustified strength of small, divisive parties that happen to have regionally concentrated support.

The biggest asset of PR, however, is that it enhances representative democracy by encouraging MPs and parties to develop a clearer profile on principles and policies. Voters will have a better idea of the mandate they are giving to MPs and thus be able to hold MPs accountable for their principles, policies, and political actions. A PR electoral system should be adopted in Canada, since it is the fairest and most effective way to involve Canadians in their representative democracy.

## NOTES

1. I would like to thank Harold Jansen, Tom Bateman, David Long, Karen Jansen, and Paul Barker for reading and suggesting corrections to this essay. Any errors are, of course, my responsibility.

2. List-system PR is one of many types of PR. If PR is used for the House, the Senate should use single-member districts and be elected with the FPTP system, since its function is to include geographically defined concerns of the regions in the national policy-making process.

3. "How rep by pop wins converts," *The Globe and Mail,* 27 October 1993.

4. The term "stable" can mean many different things, depending in part on the world-view assumptions of the person using the term.

5.  FPTP not only fails to produce regular majority governments, but frequently fails to produce the strong oppositions needed to effectively run a parliamentary system. See Alan C. Cairns, *Constitution, Government, and Society in Canada*, in Douglas E. Williams, ed. (Toronto: McClelland and Stewart, 1988), pp. 111–40.

6.  Richard J. Van Loon and Michael S. Whittington, *The Canadian Political System: Environment, Structure, and Process*, 4th ed. (Toronto: McGraw-Hill Ryerson, 1987), p. 600.

7.  To qualify for a seat in any provincial riding, a party will need to win roughly the same number of votes (where x = total national votes divided by 295 national seats). But the percentage of the vote needed in each multimember provincial riding would vary from 1 percent in Ontario to 25 percent in Prince Edward Island. If higher "thresholds" were deemed desirable in Ontario and Quebec, these provinces could be divided into three districts, each with about twenty-five to thirty-three seats.

8.  "How Canada Voted," *The Edmonton Journal*, 27 October 1993.

9.  In 1976, the Parti Québécois formed the provincial government with 71 of 110 seats but only 40 percent of the popular vote. In 1981, it won 80 of 122 seats with 49.3 percent of the vote.

10. Cairns, p. 119.

11. Even though Italy's political culture has serious problems with corruption, in 1993 Italians still voted to maintain 40 percent of its PR system. And Enid Lakeman reports that if Weimar Germany had used FPTP, the Nazis would likely have won all the seats; cited in Michael Lind, "A Radical Plan to Change American Politics," *The Atlantic Monthly* 270, no. 2 (August 1992), pp. 73–83.

12. Malapportionment is the practice of skewing the number of voters in each riding so that the electoral outcome favours one of the political parties. Gerrymandering involves reshaping districts to alter their partisan composition so the electoral outcome favours one party.

13. Other types of PR, such as the Single Transferable Vote, are more complicated, but as *The Economist* states, "the Irish can work it, so why not others?" "Electoral Reform," May 1, 1993, p. 21.

14. The Liberal Party platform, "The Red Book," was notable in the 1993 federal election precisely because it was an exception to the practice.

15. Arend Lijphart and Bernard Grofman, eds., *Choosing an Electoral System: Issues and Alternatives* (New York: Praeger, 1984), p. 7.

16. Several conflicting definitions of representation confuse this debate; see Hanna Fenichel Pitkin, *The Concept of Representation* (Los Angeles: University of California Press, 1967).

## NO

## Voting for Trouble

*Paul Barker*

At first glance, proportional representation (PR) is an attractive proposal for reforming Canada's electoral system. It promises to make the House of Commons more representative of the population and in so doing enhance the legitimacy of public authorities. It also speaks to our concern for fairness and equity through its impartial treatment of both parties and voters. Perhaps most important, PR replaces an electoral system that aggravates regional tensions in this country with one that lessens them.

On close inspection, though, the shortcomings of PR become evident. PR creates new problems, the most important of which is weak and unstable government. It also underestimates the advantages of the present way we elect members, and falls well short of delivering on its own promises. Finally, it exaggerates the importance of the electoral system. On certain matters of significance, proponents of PR believe—mistakenly—that adjusting electoral rules will make a major difference.

## BACKGROUND

Democracies all have their own set of rules for structuring the electoral process. In Canada, the rules stipulate the existence of geographically based constituencies or ridings in which parties present their candidates for election. Persons residing in these constituencies consider the candidates and make a choice. The candidate with the greatest number of votes—which may not be a majority of the votes—wins the constituency and the right to represent the riding in the House of Commons. Usually, the party that prevails in the greatest number of constituencies forms the government.

Canada's electoral process thus has two major features. First is the single-member constituency. One and only one member may be elected. Some electoral systems allow for multimember constituencies, but not

Canada's. The second feature is that the winner need only secure a plurality of the votes, which means that he or she only has to finish first. A majority of the votes, a requirement of some systems, is not necessary. These two features combine to create an electoral system that is commonly called first-past-the-post (FPTP).

Though FPTP is used by all governments in Canada, it has been heavily criticized, so much so that some have advocated its replacement by PR. The indictment against FPTP is long and detailed.[1] It supposedly misrepresents the wishes of the people because of its failure to translate accurately the popular vote into legislative seats. It also plays favourites, rewarding parties that finish first in the popular vote and punishing third parties with diffuse support. It treats voters differently—in some ridings, it takes a relative few to elect a member of a particular party, in others it takes a great many. FPTP facilitates as well the formation of majority governments even when the government party fails to convince one-half of the electorate to vote for it.

Lastly, FPTP makes it difficult, if not impossible, for governments and parties at the national level to receive representation in all parts of the country. In Canada's electoral history, many national governments have failed to achieve legislative representation in crucial areas of the nation. Sometimes Quebec goes unrepresented, other times it is the West. In a country with strong regional and language differences, the absence of truly national parties is of some concern. Political parties are meant to integrate this country, to pull all Canadians together, but they can hardly accomplish this without seats in the major regions.

The purported failings of FPTP have spawned a large number of proposals for reforms, one of which is list-system proportional representation.[2] Under this particular version of PR, each province would constitute a single riding with multiple members. So, for example, Ontario would be one constituency with 100 members. For each province, parties would place before voters a list of candidates corresponding to the number of seats available. Voters would then vote for one of the lists, and the resulting distribution of votes would determine what percentage of the candidates on a party's list would be elected. For instance, in a province with 100 seats, a party that secured 50 percent of the vote would see its first fifty members on the list elected.

PR is supposed to deal with the failings of FPTP. It provides for a more accurate matching of votes and seats, it affects all parties and voters fairly, and it offers the prospect of a national government with backing in all regions of the country. Canada, say proponents of PR, can only benefit. The reality, however, is quite different. There are many arguments against PR, and the following pages outline them. These arguments demonstrate that adoption of PR is not in Canada's interest.

# WEAK AND UNSTABLE GOVERNMENT

A major argument against PR is that it would produce weak and unstable governments. For a government to rule effectively, it must have the support of the legislature, but PR—unlike FPTP—would make this impossible. The result in most cases would be minority governments. Under these circumstances, the party in power could never be assured of passage of its policies, and accordingly would find it difficult to respond to the issues of the day.

Weak government would also entail unstable government. The prospect facing every minority government is defeat. Each time it submits a bill for consideration by the legislature, there exists the chance the government will fall. That is how our system works. The survival of any government under PR would be a day-to-day affair.

In some cases, a party facing a minority government situation might ally itself with another to form a coalition government. A coalition would provide the seats necessary for majority support in the House of Commons. But this solution would only transfer the problem from the legislature to the government. Now, the lack of support would be found within the government itself. The haggling and the disagreements would be centred in the cabinet, and the same forces that frustrate minority government in the legislature would emerge in the executive.

Proponents of PR are sensitive to these criticisms. They respond that FPTP is no guarantee of majority governments, and point to the minority governments that have been elected at the national level in the last three decades. What they do not mention, however, is that these minority governments lasted at most one or two years—FPTP acts to correct its mistakes. The short life of minority governments also directs our attention to a point already made, namely the instability of minority governments.[3]

When this general line of defence fails, advocates of PR suggest that minority governments have no real effect on stability. Canada has had many minority governments throughout its history, they say, and yet it has remained a stable democracy. It is also argued that coalition governments might actually be beneficial. The present complexity of public policy supposedly requires more than one voice. For example, the increasing impact of the international economic order demands the participation of all major parties.[4]

These claims, too, are without support. Take the second point first. Imagine a coalition government at the bargaining table with other countries discussing international trade policies. It would be difficult enough trying to represent Canada's interest without having Canada's own representatives fighting among themselves and being unable to agree on what to do. As for the claim that minority governments have no impact on stability, it is true that they have not undermined the democratic nature of government in Canada. But stability is more than the preservation of democracy. It also suggests governments with the time and support to make sound, coherent public policies. But minority governments have neither time nor support. They are here today and gone tomorrow.

## DECLINE OF RESPONSIBLE GOVERNMENT

The system of government we have in Canada is called responsible government. If PR were to be implemented, responsible government would be undermined. Responsible government means that the government in the form of cabinet must maintain the confidence of the legislative branch—it requires a majority in the House of Commons. But repeated government defeats in the legislature, which PR almost guarantees, would force a reform of this practice. If not, Canada would experience frequent elections. Somehow the government in a PR system would have to become less dependent or even separate from the legislature. Even PR proponents admit this eventually.[5]

Responsible government also means that the government is expected to look after the welfare of the country.[6] Under responsible government, a party is charged with the task of tending to the public interest. It formulates policies, administers programs, makes laws, submits budgets—the list is almost endless. All of this requires strong and confident government, something that PR denies. Another element of responsible government would thus have to be abandoned.

Responsible government is at the heart of the governing process in Canada. It *is* our system of government. In trying to make it more representative, PR weakens responsible government. If Canadians truly want a different system of government, then this should be addressed head-on. It should not occur as a by-product of electoral reform.

## SEVERS TIES BETWEEN CONSTITUENT AND MP

A valuable part of FPTP is the relationship between constituent and representative. The people's representative—the Member of Parliament (MP)—represents the views of constituents in the legislature, and tries to deal with any specific problems in the riding. An MP also reports the viewpoints of his or her constituents to the major policy-makers in cabinet. In exchange for these services, the constituent supports the MP and, frankly, provides the raison d'être for most elected representatives. Without the constituent, the MP has little to do.

PR would cripple this relationship. No longer would one MP be responsible for the concerns of a specific constituency. Instead, there would be one large constituency and a multitude of MPs. The intimacy and direct nature of the relationship between voter and MP thus would be lost. At present, if a person has a problem receiving, say, a pension benefit, that person can contact his or her MP and expect some action. With PR, the very size of the constituency might prove daunting to the voter, and there would be some uncertainty over whom to call. Should the first person on the Liberals' list be contacted, or the second one, or perhaps the first one on the Conservatives' list? There is also the possibility that no one would respond to the call. If everyone is responsible for the constituents, which is the case with PR, then no one is really responsible. The potential for "passing the buck" becomes real.

The cutting of the ties between voter and MP is not only damaging to the voter. MPs would be hard-pressed to become familiar with their constituencies. Campaigning would also be difficult. Further, MPs would find themselves beholden to party leaders with the power to put them on the party list. MPs would spend more time courting party bosses than talking to voters.

PR proponents disagree with these points. They show, correctly, that the way we vote and our general orientation to the political system is determined largely by party labels.[7] When we come to vote, we tend not to look at the name on the ballot, but rather to the party affiliations. Moreover, the only thing an MP can really do is address minor concerns. Due to the operation of party discipline, individual MPs have little way to affect party policy. They must adhere to the party line.

All of this is true, but it does not follow that the relationship between voter and MP is without value. Parties and leaders are the most significant short-term factors affecting our voting behaviour, but studies also show that MPs still matter.[8] It is also true that MPs (unless they are ministers) can at best deal with small matters, but for many voters that is all they really care about. Free trade, the GST, and the Constitution are important, but getting one's child tax benefit or student grant also counts.

One final point needs to be made, namely the symbolic value of individual MPs. MPs may not have much of a voice in the inner sanctums of government. Nevertheless, it is still comforting to know there is at least one person in government whose job it is to look after your interests. In a country as large as Canada, there is the very real possibility of losing touch with the political system.

# FPTP DOES NOT PRECLUDE NATIONAL PARTIES

One of the most damning charges made against FPTP is its alleged bias against the emergence of parties with representation across the country.

The regional divisions present in Canada and splits between English- and French-speaking Canadians demand parties that can integrate the country, and this in turn requires parties with nation-wide representation. But the electoral system supposedly works against this. In 1980, the Liberals won 24 percent of the vote in Saskatchewan, 21 percent in Alberta, and 22 percent in British Columbia, but won no seats in any of these provinces; for their part, the Conservatives won nearly 15 percent of the vote in Quebec, and only one seat. The major parties had support—the votes clearly showed this—but FPTP denied them legislative representation. The electoral system, it seems, works against the unity of the country.

And this is not all. The absence of national parties supposedly feeds perceptions that Canada is indeed rife with division—the Liberals represent the East, the Conservatives the West, or the Liberals are to be found in Quebec and the Conservatives in Ontario. Also, the failure of parties to secure representation in certain areas gives them little incentive to do so. Parties are much like investors. They only invest in areas that provide a good return, and investing in areas that produce little hope of seats is a bad investment. Parties are doomed to be regional entities, forever incapable of integrating the country.

It is this alleged effect of the electoral system that has precipitated many attacks against FPTP. Canadian politics is concerned, some would say obsessed, with unity. Anything that works against unity receives much critical attention.

The problem with this charge is its obvious falsity. In 1984, a Conservative government won seats in all provinces. To be sure, for the previous two decades the Tories had almost no representation in Quebec, a product in part of the electoral system. But in 1984, it won fifty-eight of the seventy-five seats. And it still managed to hold on to its support in traditional areas of strength. The same thing happened in 1988. The Conservatives achieved support in all major regions. Canada had a genuinely national government. As for the most recent federal election in 1993, the victorious Liberal Party, though admittedly weak in some parts of the country, also gained representation in all provinces.

What happened? One response is that nothing happened. The elections of 1984 and 1988 were aberrations, and the outcome of the 1993 race suggests a movement back to regionally based parties. The next election, it is argued, will show something different. This is, however, an answer of convenience.

A better answer is that the critics of FPTP misunderstood the interaction between FPTP and party behaviour. Parties were indeed investors, but the bad investments were the areas already under control. What was the sense of putting additional resources into areas in which a party already had support? Alternatively, the unrepresented areas constituted a benefit of some magnitude. The risk of no return was there, but unlike the controlled areas, there was a promise of a windfall.[9]

A more straightforward version of this argument is that the FPTP system presented a challenge to parties. If you could win all the regions, power was almost guaranteed. FPTP made this difficult, but this very difficulty caused parties to make the kind of effort necessary for success. The FPTP system, seen this way, is a kind of test that only committed parties can pass.[10]

Whatever the reason, the fact is that the 1980s and the early 1990s have seen three elections return governments with country-wide support in the House of Commons. As we shall see, this has not meant an end to regional conflict, but it has dampened the enthusiasm for electoral reform.[11] This lack of support is evidenced most vividly in the fact that a recent federal royal commission on elections found no reason to consider PR seriously.[12]

# LIMITED IMPACT OF ELECTORAL SYSTEMS

Underlying the push for PR is an unexamined assumption: electoral systems have an important impact. On some matters, they do. In this paper, it has been argued that a shift to PR would exert a negative effect on some aspects of Canadian politics. It would weaken the ability of governments to govern, challenge the practices of responsible government, and break the link between voter and MP. But on other issues, some might say the truly important ones, electoral systems have no real impact. Arguably, the two issues central to discussion of electoral systems in Canada are *representation* and *regional conflict*. Changes in electoral systems, as we will now see, would have little effect on either.

Let us take representation first. PR supposedly provides for government whose makeup mirrors the wishes of the electorate. But does it? It would certainly do so in the legislature, but government in Canada is executive-dominated. What counts, ultimately, is representation in the cabinet. Would the composition of the legislative branch be reflected in the cabinet? Not necessarily. Assume in a federal election with 295 ridings that the Conservatives win 130 seats, the Liberals 120, and the NDP 45. One possible scenario would be for the Liberals and the NDP to enter into some kind of implicit coalition government. Would this arrangement mirror representation in the House of Commons? No. What about all those who voted PC? Furthermore, the NDP, given that it allowed the Liberals to form a government, would wield a great deal of power even though it had only paltry representation in the House of Commons. It must be recognized, then, "that achievement of fairness in the allocation of seats is no guarantee of fairness in the allocation of power."[13]

The negligible impact of the electoral system on representativeness can be seen in another way. Critics of FPTP note that it punishes the NDP. The NDP has been the classic third party with diffuse support. From this fact, many jump to the conclusion that the NDP is without representation or has little effect on public affairs. But most students of Canadian politics know this to be untrue. The ideas of the NDP, and its predecessor the CCF, have had a profound impact on political life, especially in the area of social policy. This influence has just not been exercised through NDP members in legislative assemblies. As Wiseman says, "The NDP may not get its 'fair share' of the seats, but it has its 'fair share' (and perhaps more) of influence in fashioning the public policy arena."[14]

The minor effect of electoral systems also emerges when we examine the way FPTP exacerbates regional divisions. PR promises to diminish this problem by facilitating representation of all regions in governing parties. The belief is that a national government with nation-wide representation would contribute to national unity. In 1984 and 1988, Canada achieved the former, albeit not through PR. But the point is that we had a government capable of integrating the country. But did it? The tussles over Meech Lake, free trade, and regional development policy suggest not. And this should not be surprising. The deep divisions within Canada are unlikely to be papered over by a shift in the electoral map.[15] The differences that divide Canadians are much more deeply rooted.

# FRAGMENTED POLITICAL SYSTEM

PR would enrich, its supporters say, the quality of representative democracy in Canada. FPTP leads to bland or "lowest-common-denominator" policies because of the need to appeal to as many voters as possible. The fact that there can be only one winner forces parties to act in this manner. Consequently, many views in society go unrepresented and voters are faced with little choice. Alternatively, PR would permit a full flowering of parties representing varied perspectives and outlooks. The diversity found in a society would be reflected in its legislative bodies.

This line of argument is premised on the belief that PR would lead to more representative government. As shown in the previous section, this is a dubious proposition. But let us assume for the sake of argument that it is true, or that Canadians would be content with a representative House of Commons. Would the resulting diversity in the political system be beneficial?

Admittedly, this is a difficult question to decide. Faithful representation of different societal beliefs is an important goal in a democracy. But so is order. Indeed, the key function of government is the establishment of order, and this is accomplished by the integration of competing views.

Giving voice to many divergent positions may make integration a feat of Herculean proportions. There might be a party for the environmentalists, for women, for the West, for separatists, for industry, and so on. The political system could fragment into many parts, and it is not clear that it could be put back together.

This brings us back to a point already made. PR fosters instability. In its zeal to achieve representation, PR neglects the need for a stable governing authority.

# CONCLUSION

To the unwary, PR is appealing. It lists the perceived inequities and failings of FPTP, and puts in its place a system that leads to unity, fairness, and representativeness in politics. But in truth, PR does none of these latter things. It does not provide for representative government, and is helpless against the forces that divide this country. As for its impact on the actual machinery and operation of government, it reduces the influence of our public decision-makers and eliminates the one direct tie each of us has with government. Canada would be unwise in adopting PR.

## NOTES

1. For the classic critique of FPTP in relation to Canada, see Alan C. Cairns, "The Electoral System and the Party System in Canada, 1921–1965," in J. Paul Johnston and Harvey E. Pasis, eds., *Representation and Electoral Systems: Canadian Perspectives* (Scarborough: Prentice-Hall, 1990).

2. For a discussion of the various reform proposals, including part-list PR, see William P. Irvine, "A Review and Evaluation of Electoral Reform Proposals," in *Institutional Reforms for Representative Government, Volume 38*, prepared for the Royal Commission on the Economic Union and Development Prospects for Canada (Toronto: University of Toronto Press, 1985).

3. For those who doubt the more general point about the relationship between minority governments and PR, the following article is recommended: A. Blais and R.K. Carty, "The Impact of Electoral Formulae on the Creation of Majority Governments," *Electoral Studies* 6 (1987). The two authors show a definite correlation between minority governments and PR.

4. William P. Irvine, "'Additional Member' Electoral Systems," in Arend Lijphart and Bernard Grofman, eds., *Choosing an Electoral System: Issues and Alternatives* (New York: Praeger, 1984), p. 71.

5. Tom Kent, *Getting Ready for 1999: Ideas for Canada's Politics and Government* (Halifax: Institute for Research on Public Policy), pp. 44–45.

6. C.E.S. Franks, *The Parliament of Canada* (Toronto: University of Toronto Press, 1987), p. 11.

7. William P. Irvine, "Does the Candidate Make a Difference? The Macro-Politics and Micro-Politics of Getting Elected," *Canadian Journal of Political Science* 15, no. 4 (December 1982).

8. Harold D. Clarke et al., *Absent Mandate: Interpreting Change in Canadian Elections*, 2nd ed. (Toronto: Gage, 1991), p. 115.

9. J.A.A. Lovink, "On Analyzing the Impact of the Electoral System on the Party System," in Johnston and Pasis, eds., *Representation and Electoral Systems*, p. 342.

10. John C. Courtney, "Reflections on Reforming the Canadian Electoral System," in ibid., pp. 377-78.

11. F. Leslie Seidle, "The Canadian Electoral System and Prospects for Its Reform," in Alain-G. Gagnon and A. Brian Tanguay, eds., *Canadian Parties in Transition: Discourse, Organization, and Representation* (Scarborough, Nelson, 1989), pp. 252, 265.

12. Royal Commission on Electoral Reform and Party Financing, *Final Report, Volume 1* (Ottawa: Minister of Supply and Services, 1991), pp. 18–21.

13. R.J. Johnston, "Seats, Votes, Redistricting, and the Allocation of Power in Electoral Systems," in Lijphart and Grofman, eds., *Choosing an Electoral System*, p. 69.

14. Nelson Wiseman, "Cairns Revisited—The Electoral and Party System in Canada," in Paul W. Fox and Graham White, eds., *Politics: Canada*, 7th ed. (Toronto: McGraw-Hill Ryerson, 1991), p. 270.

15. Ibid., p. 273.

# POSTSCRIPT

The two articles on PR present some compelling arguments, but they also leave some questions unanswered. Hiemstra believes, correctly, that PR would allow for the emergence of a wide range of parties and give the voter greater choice. He applauds this development, but it seems that this very diversity would make Canada almost ungovernable. Would not a true expression of the differences separating Canadians prove fatal to Canadian unity? As well, he makes much of representation in the House of Commons, but says little of the executive branch, where the true power lies and where accurate replication of the popular vote is not guaranteed under PR. His argument here appears to presume an American-style government in which the legislative branch has real policy-making power; at a minimum, his argument requires an important change in the operation of parliamentary government in Canada. Finally, Hiemstra ignores or understates the importance of a number of concerns about coalition governments. Would coalition governments not be held hostage by small parties crucial to the survival of the coalition? Would coalition governments not be difficult to form? Would the formation of coalitions not require the kind of backroom dealing now so detested in Canadian politics?

For his part, Barker seems unnecessarily harsh on minority governments. At times, they have worked well. Could the past not repeat itself? Barker also notes that FPTP can produce parties with nation-wide support in the House of Commons—but only with great difficulty. Is it not safer to proceed with a system such as PR that makes fully national parties more probable? The emergence of two highly regionalized parties in the 1993 federal election certainly suggests so. As for his claim that national parties have no impact on regional conflict, it seems rather premature. More study is required. Finally, Barker may exaggerate the close relations between MP and constituent. To test his claim here, ask yourself whether you know your MP's name. If yes, then Barker may have a point; if not, then students should lean toward Hiemstra.

The debate between Hiemstra and Barker revolves around one type of PR. However, other proposed reforms of the electoral system have been forwarded. A particularly popular one is a combination of FPTP and PR. Some MPs would be elected under FPTP, others under PR. The House of Commons would thus have two types—or classes, some say—of MPs. Another reform is called the single transferable vote, which is a version of PR in which voters would have a greater voice in determining who would be elected from party lists. It is, however, complex in structure, an attribute that characterizes many versions of PR.

Students wishing to pursue the subject of electoral reform might begin with Leslie Seidle's "The Canadian Electoral System and Proposals for Its Reform," which can be found in Alain-G. Gagnon and A. Brian Tanguay, eds., *Canadian Parties in Transition: Discourse, Organization, and Representation* (Scarborough: Nelson, 1989). Another source to consider is J. Paul Johnston and Harvey E. Pasis, eds., *Representation and Electoral Systems: Canadian Perspectives* (Scarborough: Prentice-Hall, 1990). It contains nearly all the best articles on electoral reform in Canada, including the seminal article by Alan C. Cairns and the reaction by J.A.A. Lovink. Any examination of electoral reform must eventually address the work of William Irvine. His *Does Canada Need a New Electoral System?* (Kingston: Institute of Intergovernmental Relations, 1979) is an exhaustive study of electoral reform. Many of his other articles, all worthy of consideration, are cited in Barker's paper. For a look at the attitudes of Canadians toward the electoral system, one might consult André Blais and Elisabeth Gidengil's *Making Representative Democracy Work: The Views of Canadians*, volume 17 of the Research Studies, Royal Commission on Electoral Reform and Party Financing (Ottawa: Minister of Supply and Services, 1991). Lastly, the experience of other countries with FPTP and PR should be of interest to students. On this topic, the following should be consulted: Arend Lijphart and Bernard Grofman, eds., *Choosing an Electoral System: Issues and Alternatives* (New York: Praeger, 1984), and Vernon Bogdanor and David Butler, eds., *Democracy and Elections: Electoral Systems and Their Political Consequences* (Cambridge: Cambridge University Press, 1983).

# ISSUE SIXTEEN

## Do Referendums Enrich Democracy?

**YES** PATRICK BOYER, "Our Democratic Reformation," from *Direct Democracy in Canada: The History and Future of Referendums* (Toronto: Dundurn Press, 1992)

**NO** MARK CHARLTON, "The Limits of Direct Democracy"

In recent years the number of Canadians feeling a sense of frustration and disillusionment with Canada's political system has steadily increased. This discontent is rooted in the perception that Canada's political institutions are less responsive and less representative of the public's true interests. The emergence of new political parties and the increased attention given to special interest groups have become alternative vehicles for political expression.

As more Canadians become disenchanted with Canada's system of representative government, they argue that simply voting for public officials is no longer enough. Canadians need to have the opportunity to participate directly in making their own laws. As a result, there has been a renewed interest in the instruments of direct democracy, especially the use of referendums, initiatives, and recall.

This wave of populist sentiment is reflected in a number of recent developments. The Reform Party of Canada has made direct democracy an important part of its party platform. It argues that citizens should be able to make use of citizen initiatives and referendums to give clear instruction to Parliament regarding the laws that should be passed. In addition, the Reform Party endorses the use of a recall procedure, which would enable voters to unseat Members of Parliament who appear to be acting against their wishes. For Reformers, the October 1992 referendum on the Charlottetown Accord was a healthy lesson in direct democracy that should become more commonplace in Canada.

There has also been increased interest in direct democracy at the provincial level. In a special 1991 plebiscite, 83 percent of British Columbians answered yes when asked whether citizens should have the right to propose legislation for popular approval through referendums. And in the same year, Saskatchewan voters were asked to address several questions on the use of referendums to ratify constitutional amendments, public financing of abortion, and a balanced budget. Approximately 80 percent of the voters felt that there should be a law requiring a referendum to approve any constitutional amendments before they are implemented.

What is direct democracy? The concept of direct democracy is rooted in the notion that all citizens should have the opportunity to participate personally and directly in collective decision-making about how they should be governed. Direct democracy may take a number of different forms. In a *referendum*, a policy question or a proposed law is submitted directly to the electorate for approval or rejection, rather than being dealt with exclusively through the legislature. Referendums may be merely *consultative*, in which case they are intended to serve as a guide to politicians in their decision-making on an issue. In Canada, these are generally referred to as *plebiscites*. Or, referendums may be *binding*, in which case, politicians are required to enact the legislation that has been approved, whether or not the government agrees with the outcome.

Another common variation of direct democracy is the *initiative*, which is common in many American states. This method allows citizens to propose new laws that are then submitted to voters for approval. Each proposal requires a petition with a certain number of signatures before it can be added to the ballot. The procedure in effect shifts the whole referendum process into the hands of citizens, bypassing elected officials altogether.

A third technique of direct democracy is the *recall*, which allows citizens to remove a public official from office by filing a petition that demands a vote on the official's continued tenure in office. This technique enables voters to discipline elected officials who are not performing adequately.

The current wave of populist sentiment reflects an antiparty, anticabinet feeling that is impatient with the compromises and delays inherent in the parliamentary system of representative government. Our political institutions are rapidly losing their legitimacy, it is argued, because Canadians no longer sense that they truly represent our needs. Only by moving swiftly to give more direct say in decision-making to citizens will a profound crisis of legitimacy be avoided and confidence in government be restored. The Citizens' Forum on Canada's Future, chaired by Keith Spicer, found that what Canadians wanted most was a "more responsive and open political system, whose leaders—they think—are not merely accountable at election time but should be disciplined swiftly if they transgress greatly" (Canada, *Citizens' Forum on Canada's Future: Report to the People and the Government of Canada,* 1991, p. 135).

One of the most prolific advocates of direct democracy in Canada has been Patrick Boyer, the Conservative Member of Parliament for Etobicoke-Lakeshore from 1984 to 1993. Boyer has published three books on the role of referendums in Canada. He believes that the current interest in direct democracy is a healthy sign of a populist revolution that promises to revitalize and strengthen Canadian democracy. In contrast, Mark Charlton argues that, despite their promises, referendums pose a number of serious problems that could undermine our system of representative government and further shift power away from elected officials to unelected and unaccountable special interest groups.

# YES

## Our Democratic Reformation

*Patrick Boyer*

Canada is in the midst of an important and exciting democratic transformation of which direct democracy, through referendums and plebiscites, actually constitutes but a small part. The broader process, so necessary for Canadians, is a new politics based on constructive engagement of the people with the process and decisions which affect them and their communities.

## PART OF A DEMOCRATIC TRANSFORMATION

Any conscious Canadian can hardly doubt that today something is amiss in our country. In the face of so many blessings and opportunities, political discontent permeates our society. Many in public office feel the frustrations as sharply as Canadian citizens in general, and in some ways more acutely. Even those who live beyond our borders look at Canada's current debates and preoccupations and scratch their heads in wonderment about our "problems." The reality that something is clearly wrong with the current functioning of our political system has sunk in, and our procedures for defining and resolving public issues are obviously out of sync with the outlook and imperatives of most Canadians. A responsible citizen cannot observe all this without asking how the political system needs to be reformed, and in some important aspects, completely transformed.

I doubt that many of us believe in a single magic solution. I do believe, however, that making Canada a more thorough-going democracy is a fundamental part of the opportunity now presented by the transformation already under way in the political sub-strata of our country. The occasional, careful use of referendums and plebiscites ought to be part of that democratic transformation.

If the story of the past five or ten years in Canadian government and politics had been one of moving from success to success, I certainly would not be looking for alternatives. Certainly there have been valuable accomplishments. Yet the stark reality of failure and frustration on the part of politicians and the public alike has lead me to recognize how a constructive role for referendums and plebiscites can exist in concert with our existing political procedures. That has been the reason for this book [*Direct Democracy in Canada*], to show how such a role for the people themselves is already part of our Canadian way of doing things, and that it need not be feared but rather seized hold of and improved upon. We used to have serious problems in conducting elections in Canada (people killed in election riots, intimidation of voters, drunkenness, bribery, fraudulent voters' lists, personation, excessive spending, and general corruption). Some saw the shortcomings of such wholesale buying of elections and set about—not to abolish elections—but to reform election law. It is that reformer's instinct, not the abolitionist's, that should inspire us now.

# DIRECT VOTING CAN ENHANCE EXISTING PROCEDURES

The idea is not to displace our existing parliamentary procedures or the role of elected representatives, but to enhance them through the additional use, from time to time, of direct voting by all Canadian citizens on the fundamental questions concerning our country's future. The process envisaged here would complement, not compete with, parliamentary democracy.

A second point concerns the appropriateness of such direct voting in our parliamentary system. Some critics of referendums and plebiscites allege that procedures for full citizen participation are incompatible with our system of government.

However, Canada and other countries have had considerable experience with these devices of direct democracy. Our Canada-wide plebiscites would have been even more numerous had Prime Minister Robert Borden got his way in 1914 for a plebiscite on Senate reform, or Wilfrid Laurier in 1917 on conscription, or even Pierre Trudeau in the early 1980s on the constitution. The provincial plebiscites and referendums include many that are recent—October 1991 in Saskatchewan, October 1991 in British Columbia, and May 1992 in the Northwest Territories. In the last round of municipal elections, more plebiscites were added to the list of several thousand direct votes at the local level.

In addition to the Canadian experience, other parliamentary democracies of the Westminster model have combined direct democracy with representative democracy. In Great Britain, for instance, a country-wide plebiscite in 1975 asked citizens to vote directly on whether they wanted their country to continue its membership in the European Common Market. On two other occasions in the 1970s, referendums were held in Britain relating to devolution (a mild form of "sovereignty-association") for Scotland and Northern Ireland.

An even better example is provided by Australia, since that country is so similar to Canada. We both have a federal system of government, and are constitutional monarchies operating with a parliamentary system of government. In 1900 the Australians decided that any constitutional amendment would have to be ratified by the people. They added a provision to their constitution expressly requiring popular ratification. As a result, on 32 occasions during this century, when someone came up with a new idea to change the constitution, the proposal was submitted to Australian citizens to express their verdict at the ballot box. On eight occasions a majority of the people were persuaded that the proposal was good and voted to ratify it; on all the other occasions they defeated the proposal. That is exactly how a democracy should work. If you cannot persuade a majority of the people to make a change in the constitution of the country, you have no business—legally or morally—changing it.

## GOVERNING WITHOUT CONSENT LEADS TO DISENCHANTMENT

A democracy is governed ultimately by consent of the governed rather than by their coercion. Governing against the value system of a society or politicians attempting to cobble together new arrangements without bringing the people along with them only spells long-term difficulties for a country. The current level of disenchantment with Canadian government and politics has much to do with the series of major and transforming policies implemented in our country over the past two decades which did not involve the democratic exercise of public persuasion and consensus-building.

The idea I am advancing is about "the politics of engagement"—where the Canadian people themselves are engaged in both the risk and the consequences of deciding issues. This applies not only in government, but in industry and education, in environmental issues from east coast fisheries to west coast logging, and in personal, family, and community life as well.

## A TRANSITION FROM SPECTATORS TO PARTICIPANTS

The referendum process changes Canadians from passive spectators into active participants. Many people have lamented that in contemporary Canada individuals are quick to assert their rights, but slow to take up their responsibilities. They want to see equal emphasis placed on the duty of citizens.

In reality, however, most Canadians are preoccupied with many demands on their time. Lack of interest in constitutional proposals, for example, may not only be attributable to many Canadians' bleak sense of *déjà vu* on this topic. Most of us have more immediate preoccupations of an economic and social nature which produces the phenomenon of "intelligent ignorance." A busy Canadian might understandably choose to ignore constitutional proposals, perceiving the time and effort to learn about them to be of academic interest only and of no apparent use. Why study for an exam if nobody is going to ask you the question? Yet if there is going to be an exam—if you are going to be handed a ballot paper and asked to mark your choice on a major Canadian issue—a new imperative suddenly enters the picture. A valid reason now exists for paying attention.

How this process works in practice was shown in Prince Edward Island. For years, even before Confederation, politicians, engineers, and promoters had spoken about tunnels, bridges, causeways, and ferry boats between the mainland and the island. In the election campaign of 1962, national Liberal party leader Lester Pearson promised a causeway. Yet only in 1988 did Premier Joe Ghiz actually put the question directly to the Islanders in a plebiscite, asking whether they favoured a fixed-link connection to the mainland. I saw how, for the first time ever, Islanders could focus on their future and define what the island meant to them, because each of them had to vote on the issue. That process, and the deadline for a decision, forced a concentrated debate involving economic benefits, tourism impacts, environmental concerns, and "the Island way of life." The passive spectators had become active participants and were forced to define themselves and the future of their island—not a bad exercise to go through.

Similarly, the "politics of engagement" has worked its beneficial transforming effects on Canadians in many direct votes. Quebecers approaching the May 20, 1980 referendum on sovereignty-association, for example, were forced to face the difficult question of whether they wanted an independent Quebec or a Quebec in a greater Canada. The debate was intense, because the issue raised by the separatists was fundamental and emotional, and there was no escaping the fact that the process would be cathartic. Yet at the end of the campaign, the issue had been fully and fairly examined from all sides, and each Quebecer could express his or her personal verdict at the ballot box.

If we call ourselves a democracy, we must not be afraid to use democratic procedures. The many examples of plebiscites and referendums in Canada—from prohibition to conscription, from fluoridation of the water supply to settling questions about time zones, or from produce marketing to abortion—have been important both for the issue involved and the process by which the matter was handled. Balloting on constitutional and territorial questions has been part of our heritage—from Newfoundland in 1948, to Quebec in 1980, to the Northwest Territories in 1982 and again in 1992. As Nelson Mandela told members of Canada's Parliament in June 18, 1990, just four months after his release from thirty years of imprisonment in South Africa, "We must use democratic means in our search for a democratic result."

# IS A PLEBISCITE REALLY DIVISIVE?

One fear sometimes expressed by those reluctant to hold a plebiscite on a transcending issue is that the process is divisive. Such individuals usually point to the 1942 plebiscite on conscription and contend that it divided Quebec from the rest of Canada. A deeper understanding of Canadian history suggests the opposite.

It is worth recapitulating some points about the alleged divisiveness of that 1942 vote and the 1898 plebiscite on prohibition. When Prime Minister Laurier saw the narrowness of the prohibition result on a national basis and the strength of support in much of Canada but opposition in Quebec, he wisely recognized that no single Canada-wide policy was possible and left the matter to provincial jurisdictions and municipalities. He saved the country from disunity and the awful fraud of prohibition combined with unwilling compliance and organized crime which most non-Quebec provinces came to experience as they voted themselves (in theory and in law, but not in practice) dry. Moreover, as Canadians saw the plebiscite results, they understood Laurier's position, even if they may not have agreed with it. When Prime Minister King saw the national results of the 1942 plebiscite, he wisely chose to buy time for as long as he could prior to implementing conscription for overseas military service, given that Quebecers had voted strongly against it, and he wanted to avoid an even more calamitous conscription crisis than that which had destroyed part of the Canadian soul in World War I. The government was able to successfully prosecute the war effort *and* delay bringing in conscription for overseas service for two years. Moreover, the whole country understood the reasons for this temporizing approach, even though many (including a few of King's Cabinet ministers) did not agree with it, because the plebiscite results spoke clearly of the deep divisions within Canadian society. When the 1992 referendum results became known, it appeared the country had divisions alright, but they were reflected generally across the entire country.

Did the plebiscites *create* these divisions, or merely *record* them? Does a surgeon create a tumour, or simply reveal it, in the course of an exploratory operation? Plebiscites are like mirrors; they show us collectively, at the same time, the nature of our society in a way that cannot be replicated by opinion pollsters, duplicated by media pundits, imagined by policy élites, or imitated by the political establishment. It is not the creation of division that is feared, I suspect, but the fact that those perched precariously atop the political superstructure of our country may discover, through a direct vote, the divisions and differences they prefer to pretend do not exist.

Yet those "reality checks" with the electorate may reveal more unity among the people than those whose practice it is to exploit the differences may themselves wish to discover. Or, if the situation is really as bad as they contend, why should we keep avoiding it and second-guessing it. Why not have the true nature of Canadian attitudes on a particular topic shown so that we can pass through that to a new stage of evolution or reconciliation, instead of continually trying to cobble together some makeshift and inappropriate "solution" that never treats the underlying and unresolved problem?

It became the catechism of those who believe in timid democracy, according to the dogmas of "peace, order, and good government," that one should not risk uncertainty of outcome in matters of governance. Like a chartered banker evaluating the loan risks for a new business enterprise, some Canadians have sought security by not taking the risk at all—and their excuse for refusing to lend trust to the people and credibility to democracy was that the enterprise of direct voting may be divisive. Of course it is divisive; that is its purpose: to divide us up into those who favour a particular course of action and those who oppose it, so we can all take our bearings and proceed as wisdom and political judgment suggest the best course of action.

## LEADERSHIP IN A DEMOCRACY

A statement often advanced by those reluctant to entrust the people with a ballot question is that often heard from MPs and Cabinet ministers: "I was sent here to lead!" The assertion is that a few individuals in the Cabinet or the legislature can take a decision and make it stick (with the coercive powers of the state, if need be), and that this is leadership.

Obviously, those who are in a cabinet and in a legislature have a duty and a responsibility to make decisions and provide leadership on important public issues. Yet to submit a transcending issue to the people for their resolution, or to involve them as citizen-partners in the process of resolving the issue, can hardly be described as an abdication of leadership. It takes a bolder act of leadership to define an issue that is ripe for resolution, to distil its essence, to articulate that clearly in public, and to ask the people to express their wishes. I would be more impressed by the arguments concerning leadership if those in government and in our legislatures could point to an unblemished record of having squarely faced and dealt with all the difficult issues on our public agenda. We all know the record is quite mixed, and the concept of leadership hardly serves as a strong platform from which to contend that the people ought not be involved in arriving at policy decisions.

A further consideration about decision-making and leadership is that we are describing a matter of degree, a question of relativity. Easily 98 percent of the issues that come before a government or Parliament can be dealt with in the routine fashion, by the men and women who are paid to inform themselves about these issues and resolve them in the public interest. Yet occasionally there are transcending issues that require a major and broad appraisal, because the way in which the question is decided could dramatically alter the future direction of public policy or the country itself.

Former Prime Minister Arthur Meighen, writing about this subject in 1937, said that when a rare question came before Parliament that would "affect a positive principle of the constitution or government of the country," a clear public mandate should be obtained. Meighen believed this so strongly that he even suggested the Senate could delay or postpone approving such a measure until a public vote had taken place to clarify popular support.

# THE CONSTITUTIONAL FICTION OF ELECTORAL MANDATES

It is time to be more realistic about the constitutional fiction of a government "mandate" received in a general election campaign. To a very great degree, modern Canadian elections are about people and personalities as much as they are about policy. Numerous policy issues and proposals are mixed into the course of a single general election, and from that process it is impossible to extract a specific mandate for a particular course of action. Our constitutional doctrine about a government having a mandate actually means only that it has majority support in the House of Commons. However, this has been too generously interpreted in Canada as meaning that the government has a blank cheque to govern as it sees fit, provided it can keep its majority in the Commons.

This constitutional fiction is handy for the routine daily operation of Parliament and the Government of Canada, but it should never be stretched so far as to provide justification for transforming measures that were never debated or contemplated in the preceding election campaign. The danger in repeatedly doing so can be accurately measured in the current levels of political discontent and disillusionment across our country.

Another fiction is that parliamentarians understand the issues but the people do not. Some of my colleagues in Parliament, a great many senior civil servants, some academics, a few journalists, and a number of my constituents allege that the Canadian people cannot be trusted to deal with important public issues because they are not adequately informed about the implications. This is a bit like "the pot calling the kettle black." As pointed out by Dr. Jim Henderson, an Ontario MPP who is a critic of the shortcomings of our Canadian legislative assemblies, it is true that the private member technically has the potential to influence decisions. Yet a network of traditions has developed in most legislatures that pull in the contrary direction; members almost always vote as their parties instruct them. Thus Henderson also observed, "Once a newly elected member has learned this lesson, some of them easily and understandably lose interest in always knowing what a particular vote is all about." Often MPs vote on legislation without being adequately informed about all of its implications. In some cases, members do not even know what bill they are voting on but simply see their party voting for, or against, the measure and act accordingly when their turn comes. Gordon Aiken, MP for Parry Sound–Muskoka from 1957 to 1972, wrote a book about his experiences in Parliament, calling it *The Backbencher.* For a long time during its writing, he intended to entitle the book *Trained Seals.*

# THE COST OF DIRECT DEMOCRACY

Those who seek arguments to camouflage their real reasons for opposing greater public participation through direct voting sometimes trot out the cost. I believe in being careful with money, too, but there is a difference between knowing the price of something and understanding its value.

Are plebiscites costly? The price-tag on the 1992 plebiscites in the Northwest Territories was $893,900. The 1991 direct votes in British Columbia cost $567,455, and in Saskatchewan approximately $175,000. Quebec's 1980 referendum on sovereignty-association totalled $18,261,160. The 1993 "fixed link" plebiscite in PEI cost approximately $200,000. The Chief Electoral Officer of Canada reported that the 1992 referendum cost $142 million. By far the largest component of this cost (about $85.5 million) related to the expense of preparing and revising the voters' list. That expenditure alone is a good argument for maintaining a permanent Canadian voters' list, which would also permit shorter general election campaigns.

The financial cost must also be evaluated in terms of other expenditures made on public participation, which are seen in some quarters as an alternative to direct voting. These are numerous and expensive, such as the Citizens' Forum on National Unity (the Spicer Commission) ($22 million); the travelling parliamentary committees on constitutional questions, such as the Charest Committee, the Beaudoin-Edwards Committee, the Dobbie-Beaudoin Committee ($7.2 million); and the other halfway houses to democracy, such as the six regional conferences on the constitution ($9 million).

The quest for consultation is not the same as the genuine dialogue engendered throughout all society by a national plebiscite or referendum. The direct voting process involves everybody, not just the privileged few who can appear during the working day at hotel rooms or committee room hearings to discuss their ideas or proposals with MPs or royal commissioners. No matter how expensive the committees, how extensive their itineraries, how numerous their members, how long their sitting days, how voluminous their traffic of written briefs and submissions, they hear from only a small fraction of our population of 27,000,000. Committee meetings have a place in our system, but they are not the only instrument available. The wise practice of statecraft ensures the best and most timely use of the available instruments and appropriate methods in a secure democracy; a direct vote involves every voter.

# ULTIMATELY A DECISION COMES TO A CHOICE BETWEEN TWO WORDS: YES OR NO

Another concern or criticism expressed about direct democracy is that the question on a ballot has to be overly simplified and therefore could not possibly do justice to the complexity of the issue. With respect to most economic and social questions, I readily accept that it may be difficult, if not impossible, to distil a single ballot question. With respect to the 1992 referendum on the Charlottetown Accord, the question was simple, but it referred in turn to a host of complex matters all lumped together.

Twenty-eight proposals were contained in the Mulroney government's package of constitutional changes tabled in Parliament on September 24, 1991, which ultimately led to the Charlottetown Accord. Clearly it is not possible to list all the proposals individually on a single ballot. Nor is it possible to list each for a separate choice by every voter, since the package is an integrated one. In a plebiscite there must be the possibility for a single choice, yes or no. Between aboriginal self-government, distinct society status for Quebec, an elected Senate, removal of economic trade barriers within the country, entrenchment of property rights, and other measures, there could be reasonable differences of opinion. Yet each Canadian would, after considering these points, have to choose whether he or she favoured the total package or rejected it. This is no different than a member of Parliament voting either "yea" or "nay" on a resolution to adopt the same proposals. On a matter as important as constitution-making, we have seen the difference between the collective wisdom of millions of informed Canadians in contrast to just the votes of 295 MPs and 100 or so members in each provincial legislature.

All public issues are complex and intricate, yet, ultimately, the decision comes down to a choice between two words. My argument is simply that for truly major decisions, a better choice can be made collectively by a large group of informed people than by a smaller group. I respect the collective wisdom of informed people from diverse walks of life.

## A SPECIAL DEVICE TO BE USED ON RARE OCCASIONS

I repeatedly emphasize that not every issue has to be "put to the people." As an elected representative with a deep-seated belief in the indispensable role of Parliament, I could hardly suggest otherwise. The main work of enacting laws, resolving issues, and debating public concerns must continue in our elected and deliberative legislative bodies. These are the places where the necessary compromises for a country with diverse economic activities and a pluralistic society can and should be worked out. Representative assemblies discuss, refer, study, delay, amend, and give and take. Direct voting in a referendum or plebiscite is for a different purpose; it should never be trivialized or overused. Issues that go directly to the people are generally of a different order than those which routinely come before Parliament.

Perhaps every decade or once in the life of each Parliament, one or two topics of overriding national importance should be subjected to the fullest expression of popular opinion. Certainly major constitutional amendments should be submitted for ratification by a referendum, and it seems clear following the experience of October 26, 1992, they henceforth will be. Who would dare amend the constitution now without proving that a measure had majority popular support? Direct voting can also be especially appropriate when a government of the day lacks a "mandate" for a fundamental policy change that could significantly alter the nature or operation of our country. This approach of using the instrument of direct democracy for special purposes would not threaten or displace our institutions of representative democracy (the legislatures), but could complement them and enhance their role.

## BLENDING REPRESENTATIVE AND DIRECT DEMOCRACY—HOW SEMI-DIRECT DEMOCRACY REALLY WORKS

Most contemporary, democratic nation states not only incorporate the apparatus of representative legislative assemblies into their constitutions, but also balance this by maintaining some provision for direct democracy. In Canada, the uses of direct democracy have been somewhat limited, and one of the main reasons has been the political establishment's fear that direct voting undercuts Parliament.

Our system of government depends, ultimately, upon the consent of the people being governed. Canada is not a dictatorship where tyrannical force is used to obtain public acquiescence in the measures and dictates of our leadership. Ours is a democracy where there simply must be public consensus about where we are going and general agreement on how to get there. Without consent, the whole elaborate superstructure—the legislatures, the courts, the financial system, the commercial marketplace, and the acceptance of laws and norms of behaviour—will corrode until it collapses.

How are we to achieve consent, this indispensable glue of a democratic society? Elections every four or five years? Opinion polls? First ministers' meetings? One method, that of diffusing among the electorate a greater sense of personal responsibility for the actions of government, as British political scientist Vernon Bogdanor has noted, results in decisions of government acquiring greater authority and legitimacy because they are based upon a wider degree of support.

Because the major issues facing Canada now are just as much political and psychological as they are economic or technical, the all-important educative role of referendums and the consent created by a participatory approach are both vital. The environmental and social behaviour challenges currently facing our country cannot simply be resolved by a mechanical application of legal rules or precepts of the social sciences; they depend crucially upon the mobilization of popular consent.

"This consent requires that there be in the political system some focus for the public interest," says Bogdanor, adding that this interest would come about through "a feeling that the policies of a government reflect more than merely the interests of its supporters," and that such a community of interest "cannot be assumed, but must be constructed through intelligent political action."

Of course, many of the social and economic issues of concern to most Canadians are not simple, and these complex decisions could not be readily solved through a single direct vote of the people. Direct voting must be used intelligently. This book gives a number of examples of both wise and unwise uses. Where referendums and plebiscites can be appropriately used, they serve the fundamental role of creating consent for the actions of government. If they do no generate consent *for* proposals, they may still produce a consensus *about* those proposals, as we tended to see across Canada on October 26, 1992.

Referendums, plebiscites, and initiatives are voting procedures whereby citizens—in concert with their elected representatives in Parliament, provincial legislatures, and municipal councils—may play a role in making public decisions and enacting laws. Because the traditional law-making procedures remain part of the process, a more accurate expression to describe this form of government is probably "semi-direct democracy," which is the term customarily used by Swiss constitutional lawyers to reflect that country's democratic process. The use of this term, notes Peter Studer, editor of the Zurich newspaper *Tages-Anzeiger*, is appropriate because the Swiss system is bound by a unique combination of representative and direct components. Although it may be too cumbersome an expression to gain popular usage, semi-direct democracy is an accurate description of the actual practices in most modern democracies.

These instruments of direct or semi-direct democracy, which are sometimes coupled with the concept of recall, may be seen to constitute a challenge in some respects to the traditional pattern of representative government. Although they are variants of the political and legislative processes, the limited extent to which people resort to them indicates, in part, a favourable verdict on the effectiveness of Canada's traditional lawmaking and political procedures. They can also be seen as an important adjunct to existing procedures for the betterment of all concerned.

That betterment is the extent of what is being advocated.... The approach suggested here is not an either–or proposition where we must choose *only* representative legislatures or *only* direct voting, but rather an intelligent blending of the two, so that on truly significant issues the people can complement or supplement the process normally engaged in by the representatives they have elected.

# DIRECT DEMOCRACY CAN HELP IN OUR SELF-DEFINITION AS CANADIANS

Our Canadian identity can be strengthened through the use of direct voting, because we are forced, in very specific terms, to speak out and debate with one another about the kind of country we want. The process can actually help to define what it is to be Canadian, to provide some "vigorous goading of the national intelligence," and to supplement the "weary mixture-as-before" approach whose patient acceptance by Canadians was identified by Robertson Davies, the Canadian novelist of international renown, as preventing "the required awakening to the numinous in our personal and national life."

Instead of passively letting elected representatives in Parliament make all the decisions, or relying on editorial writers and CBC commentators to do our thinking, it is stimulating and productive to have everyone come to terms with his or her own view on a public issue. It happened in Prince Edward Island in 1988, as the heritage and future of the island were debated in relation to the fixed-link crossing. It happened in Quebec in 1980 when the referendum forced Quebecers to consider their individual futures in a province as either a separate entity or within a greater Canada. It happened in 1982 in the Northwest

Territories as northerners came to grips with the division of the NWT into two territories. It happened across Canada in 1992 as a range of diverse proposals going to the heart of who we are as Canadians gave a refreshing opportunity for each person to participate.

While the debates can be emotional and the confrontations difficult, that is what democracy—and real life—is all about. A cathartic exercise, while draining, is ultimately positive and creative. Certainly general elections can be emotional, divisive, and partisan events, yet no one suggests abolishing them. Our attitude towards wisely exercised referendums and plebiscites should be the same. The result is worth the sometimes messy process.

Statecraft must be carefully exercised in respect to how and when referendums and plebiscites are used. The campaign process and voting procedures must be fair so that the people's verdict is not open to controversy or doubt. Impartial administration of the referendum is essential, and the government must be sincere in consulting the people. The questions submitted on the ballot must be as neutral and clearly worded as possible. The nature of the issue must be within the jurisdiction of the government holding the direct vote. The timing of a referendum or plebiscite is a crucial consideration. Information about the pros and cons of the issues, as well as about the voting process itself, must be fully communicated to voters. Rules for the financing of the campaigns are important. When all of these conditions are judiciously followed, the result is a more vigorous democracy.

# THE POLITICS OF ENGAGEMENT

The Canadian experience with direct democracy, which like any tapestry threaded together after-the-fact from various strands of historical events, shows a wide array of colours. Some are most pleasing to the eye, others less so. Yet, together they form a whole and should be judged in their entirety and in their context. One thing this tapestry shows is that direct democracy in Canada has been about the politics of engagement.

The politics of engagement means that, in public policy and decision-making in government, all analysis and action proceeds on the understanding that genuine democracy involves a partnership. The partnership is between those who wield power—whether they be parents, bosses, judges, public servants, union leaders, bankers, police, Cabinet ministers, military officers, or elected representatives—and those who live with the consequences of how that power is exercised. The central value in this partnership is to achieve the greatest good for the greatest number, and that good can best be identified by the active involvement of all concerned. It is not a selfish exercise of power or a self-aggrandizing process, but an altruistic one. The lessons of history are harsh, and this century has contributed many horrific examples of self-aggrandizing powermongers—Hitler, Stalin, Pol Pot, Idi Amin, the bosses of organized crime and corrupt unions, merciless "captains of industry," corrupt leaders of "religious" organizations. The lesson is clear: human nature requires power to be diffused, not concentrated.

If the object is to diffuse power, what better way than by ensuring it is shared with those whose existence gives the power-holders their meaning in the first place. The way to bring about this sharing is the politics of engagement. One of the many methods of engaging the people in the risk of decision-making and the obligation to live with the joint decision is of course direct democracy.

Resort to the methods of direct democracy in Canada has, in a number of cases, been a fairly good answer to the age-old question: *where* should power rest and *how much* should rest there? As author Ron Graham observed in his book about promise and illusion in Canadian politics, these "two great questions of political ideology, political history, and political organization" are at the root of every political culture.

Canada's democratic process, under increasing criticism for not providing sufficient voice to the public at large, can be broadened and strengthened through greater use of referendums and plebiscites, not in a frivolous way, but as an effective means of helping Canadians achieve an energizing degree of self-government. The power of voter initiatives to bring forward major issues is another element in the future of direct democracy in Canada.

The illusion has been that the strength of a country lies in its leaders. The reality is that it resides in its people. Too much history has been written from the perspective of kings and emperors and presidents and prime ministers. The ideal that forms the core of our democracy is more than trust in the people by those who are in government; trust by the people in our system of government and in its elected representatives is the nobler vision; mutual trust is the ideal for a democracy. Pierre Trudeau was groping for this idea when he said of Canada: "The land is strong." Had he pushed further, he would have realized the truth: "Canadians are strong." The truly important next step is to recreate a healthy relationship between the leaders and the people, since each depend upon the other.

Many Canadians now *are* questioning the gap between rhetoric and reality in our country's government operations, particularly between our political leadership and the people. Critical thinking is more widespread in our society than ever before. While the language of our classical parliamentary arrangements continues to be used, a great many Canadians—I would now say a substantial majority—understand that the meaning has changed. What we now await is for the system itself to be transformed—into one based upon trust of the people.

It seems unbecoming, in a democratic country, to appear too reluctant to incorporate in the conduct of public business a procedure for public participation or to only threaten that such a direct vote might be held "as a last resort." A balanced and moderate approach requires being open to the positive role of direct voting in dealing with vital questions, including those of a non-constitutional nature. A really bold stroke would extend the laws now available at the municipal level to the provincial and Canadian levels of government as well, so that citizens have the legal power to initiate direct votes on questions of national and public importance. These are all variations on the theme of empowerment through "the politics of engagement."

At the end of the day, we are either democrats, or we are not. We either trust the people, or we do not. In the long course of Canadian history, I believe that most often, when given information about a subject, the chance to deliberate on it, and then to express a collective verdict, the people have made the right decision. Who would disagree with most of the decisions reached by voters in the plebiscites and referendums described in the preceding pages...? Who would still contend that on balance the process was more harmful than helpful to the public interest?

In this age when the public agenda is too often set by a small political élite, a coterie of senior public servants, opinion pollsters, media gurus, special interest groups, and paid lobbyists, extra efforts must be made to rescue the public agenda. When the political classes can operate within a cosy and intellectually incestuous relationship, an occasional "reality check" with the citizens of the country is not a bad idea.

When everyone bathes in the same bath water, it is important every now and then to run a little fresh water into the tub. I don't think this new flow will cause anyone to drown. Rather, as we saw on October 26, 1992, the exhilarating experience of a Canada-wide plebiscite can be invigorating and cleansing for the Canadian body politic.

# The Limits of Direct Democracy

*Mark Charlton*

In the current climate of cynicism and disillusionment with Canadian political institutions, reform-minded citizens argue that Canada needs a more participatory form of democracy that gives citizens the right to vote directly on critical issues. For many populist supporters of direct democracy, the use of referendums, citizen initiatives, and recall are seen as important steps toward the implementation of a more genuine form of democracy in Canada, giving Canadians renewed hope and confidence in their political system.

Despite these noble aspirations, the concept of direct democracy is not without serious shortcomings. Referendums and initiatives, especially if combined with other techniques such as recall, could ultimately prove to be disruptive, expensive, and damaging to the structure of government decision-making without measurably increasing the quality of democracy in Canada. In fact, the experience of American states shows that direct democracy may simply represent a shift of power from one elite to another, without really giving effective voice to the aspirations of the "common" voter. Canadians should be aware of these shortcomings and potential dangers before pressing forward with this latest "democratic reformation." In order to make this case, we will critically examine the major claims that are generally made in support of referendums and initiatives.

## REFERENDUMS ENHANCE CITIZEN PARTICIPATION

Proponents of direct democracy claim that it "empowers" the voter. As Patrick Boyer puts it, the referendum process "changes Canadians from passive spectators into active participants." Whereas citizens may ignore issues because they feel the outcomes are already decided by others, referendums stimulate citizens to take up their responsibilities, become informed on the issues that they must vote on, and voice their opinions. In short, referendums overcome voter apathy.

On the surface, this claim is logical and straightforward. Citizens are cynical about the political process because they feel voiceless and alienated. Citizens feel a greater sense of efficacy when they have a voice. As they feel more confident of influencing the political system, they become more active participants in the political process.

Unfortunately, the empirical evidence does not provide clear support for such claims. Certainly, in the case of Canada's national referendum in 1992, voter turnout and interest were high. However, this may have been a reflection of the uniqueness of the event and the sense of its historical importance. In countries such as Switzerland and the United States where direct democracy is a common feature, voter turnout is actually lower than in most other Western liberal democracies. In Switzerland more than 350 national referendums have been held since 1848. But compared with other Western European democracies, voter turnout is very low, dropping to 35 percent for referendums and initiatives in recent years. Many Swiss voters choose not to vote because of a widespread feeling of helplessness and lack of political efficacy.[1]

This phenomenon has also been found in some American states where legislative proposals appear on virtually every election ballot. In examining the level of voter turnout in these states, David Magleby found that there is no strong correlation to the use of direct legislation. When voters were asked what brought them out to vote, only 2 percent named a specific proposition as the main reason.[2] In cases where referendums and elections are held separately, there are generally lower turnouts for the referendums. Thomas Cronin, a leading American authority on direct democracy, reports that in states where initiatives appear on the regular election ballot, as many as 15 percent of voters do not even bother to vote for the propositions.[3] Such empirical evidence suggests that referendums are not any more likely to transform a spectator into a participant than the normal election process itself.

# REFERENDUMS ALLOW THE COMMON PERSON TO BE HEARD

A second claim made for direct democracy is that the "average" voter has a stronger voice in government. This argument in part reflects a populist discontent with the "professionalization" of elections in which the citizen's role as participant seems to be usurped by professional party organizers, public relations firms, media pundits, and "expert" pollsters. In the process of creating "sound bites" and "photo ops," the needs and aspirations voiced by the alienated and marginalized voter are drowned out. In bypassing these intermediaries, direct democracy affords the common citizen the opportunity to be heard without distortion and reinterpretation by professional politicos.

A careful examination of the experience of direct democracy in other constituencies does not support this argument. In fact, the empirical evidence suggests that those taking advantage of the opportunities of direct democracy are generally unrepresentative of the general population. Studies in Switzerland show that most voters in referendum are between the ages of 40 and 60, male, well educated and affluent.[4]

The American experience also provides an instructive lesson. In California, it is common for every election ballot to contain citizen-initiated proposals. An issue is placed on the ballot only after it receives a required number of signatures. In many cases, the proposal may be binding on the legislature if passed, thus letting voters write the legislation themselves. Surely, this system would seem to give the greatest opportunity for the marginalized to have their voices heard.

However, a closer look at the evidence is hardly reassuring. Political scientists have found that in the beginning civic groups and volunteer organizations took the lead role in gathering signatures for the petition process. But, increasingly, this task has been turned over to professional firms who pay petitioners for each signature gathered. In many cases those who sign the petitions have little understanding of what they are signing.[5] Over time the petition process has come to be dominated by special interest groups who can afford the expensive petition-gathering process.

Special interest groups have come to dominate the entire referendum campaign process. Since the American Supreme Court struck down efforts to restrict campaign spending by interest groups, such groups may spend as much as they want on their campaigns, limited only by their ability to raise funds. Referendums have become big business, with professional public relations firms, media consultants, direct mail specialists, and pollsters dominating every phase of the referendum process.

Interest groups now dominate the California referendum process because they use citizen-initiated referendums to advance their own special interests that were previously rejected or ignored by the state legislature. Thus direct democracy can be a powerful instrument in the hands of special interests to circumvent the legislative process.

Like the Swiss experience, direct democracy in America does not seem any more successful in drawing those with lower educational levels and from a socioeconomic status into the political process. As David Magleby has found, those who benefit the most from referendums are those "who can understand and use the process."[6] In particular, he found that the "less educated, poorer, and non-white citizens" failed to benefit because they lacked organizational and financial resources to have their voices effectively heard in referendum campaigns.[7] Those who dominate the whole direct democracy process, whether it be in initiating legislative proposals, campaigning for support, or actually voting, are no more representative of the population at large than is the case in other traditional forms of political participation.

Patrick Boyer believes that "special interest democracy represents one of the most important challenges to Parliament and the Canadian people."[8] This is because "their recommendations and criticisms are seldom filtered through a broader consideration for the good of Canada as a whole."[9] Thus Boyer defends the use of referendums because "any direct link that reconnects citizens and their elected representatives is valuable in part because it goes over the heads of those who speak on behalf of partial and vested interests."[10]

But, as the extensive involvement of interest groups in the 1992 federal referendum on the Charlottetown Accord demonstrated, such groups are unlikely to pass up the opportunity to have their voices heard. After the recent Canadian court decision to strike down federal restrictions on interest group spending during election campaigns, Canadians should not be so naive as to believe that California-style referendums, dominated by powerful, big-spending interest groups, would not come to Canada. Thus, rather than empowering the average citizen, and giving voice to the marginal and alienated in society, referendums may simply mean the transfer of power and influence from one group of elites to another.

## REFERENDUMS PROVIDE A BETTER FORUM FOR DEBATING NATIONAL ISSUES THAN DO ELECTIONS

Supporters of direct democracy generally argue that the referendum process, with full debate and consideration of an issue, provides the best forum for considering issues of national importance. They criticize their opponents for taking a condescending view of voters, feeling perhaps that contemporary national issues are far too complex for the average voter to understand. Populists such as Boyer argue that referendums fulfil an educative function, prodding voters out of their apathy and forcing them "to define themselves." Thus a national referendum is a civics lesson writ large, which can drive citizens to new levels of understanding by forcing them to concentrate on the "real" issues. Referendums are assumed to fulfil this function because they are qualitatively different from elections, which Boyer laments are "about people and personalities as much as they are about policy."

Nevertheless, there are serious doubts whether referendums do enable the citizenry to come to some new level of national enlightenment. In cases where referendums are used frequently, citizens are often overwhelmed by the plethora of issues. In many American states it is not uncommon for voters to be faced with a dozen or more referendum questions on the ballot. In the November 1990 mid-term elections in the state of California, there were twenty questions on the voters' ballots. The electoral guide explaining the questions for the voters took up 144 pages! Needless to say, even a well-educated voter can soon feel a sense of overload in facing such a daunting list of questions. Even when voters have had only one question before them, as in the 1992 national referendum, pollsters found that a majority of voters still complained that they did not know enough about the issue just days before voting. Thomas Cronin notes that the notion that direct democracy serves an educative function "was plainly overstated from the start."[11] In his studies of American voters, Cronin found that most voters do not make up their minds until  the very end of the campaign, and that "as many as a quarter of those polled at the time of voting state that they could have used more information."[12]

The issue, however, is not so much whether voters are competent or overloaded, but whether referendums provide a better forum for resolving national issues than election campaigns. Populists, such as Boyer, rightly note that voters are tired of slick media campaigns and staged political events that give little opportunity for genuine debate and discussion. But this assumes that referendums would be unencumbered by partisanship, preoccupation with the personality of the party leaders, sound bites, targeted direct mailing, and the media's traditional obsession with horse-race-style reporting.

Nevertheless, there is little reason to suggest that referendum campaigns do not take on all of the modern accoutrements of election campaigns. Here the 1992 federal referendum campaign provides some troubling evidence. Although the campaign was unique in the way that political leaders from competing parties came together to support a common position, the actual conduct and reporting of the campaign was very similar to that of an election campaign. Political leaders staked out their positions, putting their political reputations on the line and feeling compelled to "win the vote." This ran against the expectations of many voters, who complained frequently that the politicians were telling them how to vote rather than simply giving them neutral information to decide. The media reported the referendum much like any election campaign, focusing on the latest developments in the polls and which leader had performed the best in a particular debate. Even the strongest proponent of direct democracy, the Reform Party, could not resist the temptation to launch an election-style, personality-oriented campaign against the "Mulroney deal," in an attempt to capitalize on voter animosity toward the prime minister. Certainly this does not suggest, as Patrick Boyer would have us believe, that referendum campaigns are any freer of people and personality issues than traditional election campaigns.

# ULTIMATELY ALL POLITICAL DECISIONS ARE A SIMPLE CHOICE BETWEEN YES OR NO

Critics of direct democracy frequently argue that complex political issues cannot be easily boiled down to a simple yes or no answer on a referendum ballot. However, Boyer is not worried about this criticism. Instead, he argues that even a complex issue such as the Charlottetown Accord, which included twenty-eight proposals, always ultimately comes down to a simple yes or no. Some final decision had to be made about whether or not to reject the whole constitutional package. This, Boyer suggests, is no different than what a Member of Parliament would have to do in voting to approve a resolution adopting the same proposal.

Despite this claim, there is a significant difference in the way Members of Parliament vote on complex bills and the way voters are forced to make a choice in a referendum. During the committee stage on legislation, Members of Parliament have the opportunity to voice objections to the bill and to propose amendments. Once bills are sent back to the House of Commons floor, new amendments may again be proposed and voted on. Even with party discipline, MPs can still amend or modify a legislative proposal and bargain for changes that will make either a yes or no vote more palatable for them. Voters in referendums do not have the luxury of suggesting changes or alternative wording. Their only real choice is to say yes or no, not "maybe if you make this amendment."

Direct democracy makes it easy to veto proposals, but difficult to propose positive alternatives. Thus the influence granted to voters through the instruments of direct democracy is largely negative. Voters who want changes other than those summarized in a simple yes or no are not heard. As Butler and Ranney have argued, "there is no opportunity for continuing discussion of other alternatives, no way to search for the compromise that will draw the widest acceptance."[13] Rather than leading to creative solutions that reflect a broad political consensus, referendums lead to easy decisions that appeal to the lowest common denominator.

# REFERENDUMS ARE NOT DIVISIVE

A common concern about referendums is that they cause division and confrontation rather than leading to consensus and accord on an issue. Butler and Ranney contend that "referendums by their very nature set up confrontations rather than encourage compromises."[14] Concern about the divisive impact of referendums is especially relevant in Canada's case, where regional and linguistic cleavages have always made national unity a fragile thing at best.

In his essay, Patrick Boyer assures us that referendums will not unleash greater disintegrative tendencies in Canada. But his examination of the historical cases seems to undercut his own view. He notes, for example, that Prime Minister Wilfrid Laurier responded to the referendum on prohibition by deciding simply not to adopt a single Canada-wide policy and leaving the decision to the provinces and municipalities. He also notes that Prime Minister Mackenzie King chose to delay the implementation of conscription for as long as possible because Quebeckers had voted so strongly against it. Thus both referendums actually threatened to produce a greater level of conflict and division, which was avoided only by delaying implementation of the results of each referendum. This undercuts the more general, populist argument that referendums are more effective vehicles for national decision-making because they avoid unnecessary delays.

However, Boyer seems to argue it both ways in his essay. On the one hand, he argues that referendums do not create divisions, they merely reflect them. On the other hand, he notes later that, "of course, it is divisive; that is its purpose: to divide us up into those who favour a particular course of action and those who oppose it." His arguments, however, ignore certain key points. As Butler and Ranney note, referendums "divide the populace into victors and vanquished."[15] Losers in a passionate referendum campaign feel a sense of betrayal and alienation. One has only to remember Ovide Mercredi's bitter statement on the evening of the October 1992 referendum that natives had once more been rejected by Canada to realize how deep these wounds can run. This is especially dangerous in Canada where a majority of voters in one region of the country can be within a particular linguistic or ethnic group (francophones, for example, or natives). The entire region may vote on the losing side of a referendum that vitally affects its interests. Such defeats can easily enter into the political mythology as yet another injustice forced on a dissenting group within society. Although Quebec voted against the Charlottetown Accord along with most of the rest of Canada, many Quebec nationalists nevertheless interpret the defeat as another demonstration of English Canada's rejection.

A complicating factor here is that simple yes–no votes can in no way measure the level of intensity behind the votes. A small majority of voters who are largely indifferent to the issue, or who have little understanding of it, may vote in a measure. At the same time a large minority of voters may have an intensely passionate commitment to their position. This is a sure recipe for producing an alienated and bitter minority who feels even more betrayed by the democratic process.

Defenders of referendums have proposed ways of avoiding this. For example, David MacDonald has recommended that a formula similar to the amending formula in the Constitution Act, 1982, could be used. Thus, for any national referendum proposal to pass, it would need the endorsement of at least seven of the ten provinces making up at least 50 percent of the population. But recent constitutional experience has amply demonstrated that this formula has not worked well in permitting compromise on sensitive constitutional issues. It is unlikely to work any better in diminishing regional conflict over other sensitive national issues.

Part of the drive behind populist sentiment is an impatience with the delays and frustrations involved in the parliamentary system's reliance on compromise and brokerage. Referendums offer the opportunity of resolving in a relatively short time span a controversial and sensitive issue that may have nagged at the country for years. By forcing people to stake out positions and resolving the issue in a final vote, Boyer argues in his essay that referendums can have a cathartic effect on the body politic. His position overlooks the fact that referendums rarely ever represent the last word on the issue. Ireland has gone through three referendums on the abortion issue, and there is still heated controversy over making some abortions legal.

## MAJORITIES WILL ALWAYS MAKE THE RIGHT CHOICE

The populist sentiment that undergirds the pro-referendum movement reflects an impatience with the bargaining, compromises, and logrolling that often appear to be a central part of representative government. Referendums are a way of short-circuiting that painstakingly slow process by directly asserting the will of the majority, without the mediation and reinterpretation of too many intermediaries.

However, there are real dangers in identifying democracy simply with the will of the majority. The whole history of liberal democracy has been an effort to come to some balance between the principle of majoritarianism and the rights of individuals and groups outside of the majority. One hazard of referendums is that they might easily be used as an instrument of one group to attack and undermine the rights and interests of other smaller groups. In the United States, citizen-initiated proposals have been used for just such purposes. In some southwestern states where the Spanish-speaking population has been growing rapidly, propositions have been put forward promoting the establishment of English-only laws. Similar efforts have been made to strike down legislation that prohibits discrimination against gays. These uses of direct democracy have led some minority groups to feel increasingly under assault at the ballot box and have exacerbated tensions between various segments of society.

# REFERENDUMS WILL NOT UNDERMINE REPRESENTATIVE GOVERNMENT

The populist argument for direct democracy reflects a pervasive frustration with the system of representative government found in our parliamentary system. Populists argue that their legislators are so heavily influenced by party policy and discipline that they can hardly be said to truly "represent" those that elected them to office. Direct democracy is thus seen as a way of making elected officials more directly accountable to the wishes of the voter.[16]

Is there a fundamental contradiction between direct democracy and representative government? Patrick Boyer thinks not. He argues that the two can be combined in a form of "semi-direct democracy" that actually strengthens the confidence and trust that we place in our representative system. Despite these reassuring words, there are three areas—accountability, leadership, and consensus-building—in which direct democracy does threaten to undermine representative government.

(1) *Diminished accountability.* Representative government provides a clear means of identifying those who are responsible for public policies. A group of individuals are chosen by the electors and given a mandate to carry out the functions of government. We expect that at election time we will be given an opportunity to hold these members of government responsible for policies that they have produced.

In cases where referendums and initiatives are used on a regular basis, some studies suggest that "voters increasingly will bypass the legislative process, especially on issues that generate intense feelings."[17] But this poses a problem in identifying who actually is responsible for the policies that are passed. As Neil Johnson notes, the "striking thing about consultation and the right to vote on this or that is that the person consulted or voting bears no responsibility for the decision and what follows."[18] If the voter has no real duties in carrying out the decision, is not held accountable for the results, and may not even be affected by the consequences, have we really moved toward a more responsible form of democracy?

It is easy for voters to make decisions that satisfy some short-term interest while not having to take any responsibility for the consequences. Elected officials realize that each time they make a public decision, they will be held accountable for its results at the next election. This is not true for those making decisions in a referendum. Voters in Victoria, British Columbia, rejected a referendum proposal to build new sewage treatment facilities that would end the dumping of raw sewage into the ocean, a practice that has irritated not only environmentalists, but also the thousands of Americans living south of Vancouver Island. While voters may have avoided the immediate problem of additional tax increases needed to finance the project, they have merely shifted the responsibility to future taxpayers who may also have to pay for the ongoing environmental damage. Businesses, facing a threatened tourist boycott by Washingtonians, will be left to cope with the economic costs of lost revenue.

(2) *Weaker leadership.* When voters themselves do not bear direct responsibility for their decisions, elected officials become more reluctant to make difficult decisions. Politicians may become apprehensive about making decisions that may be unpopular or deemed illegitimate if not referred directly to the public for a vote. As Thomas Cronin states, referendums, especially on a national level, could "reduce some aspects of political leadership and policymaking in a large and diverse nation to a Gallup-poll approach to public policy."[19] David MacDonald notes that the danger referendums pose to representative government is especially potent if they are held at the same time as elections. The result, he argues, is that "a certain symbolic threshold would be crossed, and elected representatives would have limited legitimacy to manage critical issues of the day without direct endorsement from a majority of voters. Under such circumstances, governments would have insufficient discretion to establish priorities, to make choices, to affirm the value of minority interests, and to respond to changing political and economic events—in short to do what governments are supposed to do."[20] A wider use of referendums is unlikely to give disillusioned voters the stronger leadership they desire.

(3) *Lack of consensus-building.* A vital function of representative government is to reconcile the various competing interests among citizens. Governments are most effective when they can develop a broad consensus regarding the major problems they are facing. However, Joseph Zimmerman concludes that "popular decision making in the form of the direct initiative and the referendum is incapable of developing such a consensus."[21] The Royal Commission on Electoral Reform and Party Financing, in reviewing the evidence on referendums, also concluded that while they provide "citizens with more opportunities to express their policy preferences or to pass judgment on their elected representatives outside of general elections, they are less well suited to accommodating and representing the many different interests of citizens."[22] The commission felt this was a critical weakness in referendums since "effective reconciliation of these interests is crucial for any democratic government."[23]

# CONCLUSION

Historical experience with direct democracy has several telling lessons for us. Referendums have not been very effective in addressing the grievances of disillusioned citizens. They cannot ensure that voters do not feel alienated. They do not guarantee that powerful interests will not continue to dominate contemporary political life. They cannot provide a basis for creative and balanced consensus-building. They do not accurately reflect the intensity of feelings on an issue. When voters realize that direct democracy cannot possibly deliver on all that it promises, they may feel more alienated and disillusioned from the political process than ever before.

Direct democracy is not the path toward democratic renewal in this country. In his study of direct democracy in America, Thomas Cronin concludes that nation-wide use of referendums is undesirable. Instead, he notes "those who are dissatisfied with Congress should find ways to make it more responsive, accountable, and effective rather than inventing ways to bypass or supplement it with these potentially dangerous devices."[24] The recent Royal Commission on Electoral Reform and Party Financing sounds a similar note, arguing that attention on the referendum issue actually detracts from the real issue—the need to strengthen the institutions of representative government. Many of the current concerns about the unresponsiveness of Canadian political institutions are really rooted in deeper concerns about the functioning of the present electoral system and the credibility of political parties. As the royal commission argues: "Strengthening representative government will ensure that individual citizens are provided with political institutions that reconcile conflicting views and interests."[25] This is clearly the direction that we need to take in order to achieve true democratic reform.

## NOTES

1. Oswald Sigg, *Switzerland's Political Institutions* (Zurich: Pro Helvetia Division Documentation-Information-Press, 1987), p. 25.

2. David B. Magleby, *Direct Legislation: Voting on Ballot Propositions in the United States* (Baltimore: Johns Hopkins University Press, 1984), p. 127.

3. Thomas Cronin, *Direct Democracy: The Politics of Initiative, Referendum, and Recall* (Cambridge: Harvard University Press, 1989), p. 67.

4. Sigg, *Switzerland's Political Institutions*, p. 25.

5. Magleby, *Direct Legislation*, p. 62.

6. Ibid., pp. 183–84.

7. Ibid.

8. Patrick Boyer, *Direct Democracy in Canada: The History and Future of Referendums* (Toronto: Dundurn Press, 1992), p. 242.

9. Ibid.

10. Ibid.

11. Cronin, *Direct Democracy.*

12. Ibid.

13. David Butler and Austin Ranney, eds., *Referendums: A Comparative Study of Practice and Theory* (Washington, D.C.: American Enterprise Institute for Public Policy Research, 1987), p. 226.

14. Ibid.

15. Ibid.

16. It should not be surprising that those who argue for direct democracy are generally strong advocates for relaxing party discipline in the House of Commons as well.

17. Joseph Zimmerman, *Participatory Democracy: Populism Revived* (New York: Praeger, 1986), p. 170.

18. Neil Johnson, "Types of Referendum," in Austin Ranney, ed., *The Referendum Device* (Washington, D.C.: American Enterprise Institute for Public Policy Research, 1981), p. 32.

19. Cronin, *Direct Democracy*, p. 194.

20. David MacDonald, "Referendums and Federal General Elections in Canada," in Michael Cassidy, ed., *Democratic Rights and Electoral Reform in Canada, Volume 10*, Royal Commission on Electoral Reform and Party Financing (Ottawa: Minister of Supply and Services, 1991), p. 331.

21. Zimmerman, *Participatory Democracy*, p. 172.

22. Royal Commission on Electoral Reform and Party Financing, *Reforming Electoral Democracy: Final Report, Volume 2* (Ottawa: Minister of Supply and Services, 1991), p. 229.

23. Ibid.

24. Cronin, *Direct Democracy*, p. 195.

25. Royal Commission on Electoral Reform and Party Financing, *Reforming Electoral Democracy*, p. 229.

# POSTSCRIPT

The current wave of populist interest in direct democracy is not new to Canada. In the 1920s and 1930s there was a similar wave of populist, antiparty sentiment. Taking their cue from the progressive movements in the United States, Canadian agrarian movements organized themselves to challenge the two major parties, the Liberals and the Conservatives. Both parties, the populists charged, catered too much to the interests of economic elites in eastern Canada while ignoring the needs of farmers and workers. Because of party discipline, elected representatives were unable to represent the interests of their constituents. In the period following the First World War, these populist groups gained strength. The Progressive Party, after winning sixty-five federal seats in 1921, displaced the Conservatives as the second-largest party in Parliament. In Alberta, the United Farmers of Alberta (UFA) and the Social Credit Party came to power in 1919 and 1935 respectively, both selling themselves as parties committed to implementing a plebiscitarian democracy. However, once in power, both parties eventually backtracked on their commitment to govern by direct democracy and functioned much like any other parliamentary government. Despite their changed views, both parties also governed for long periods of time, using the traditional instruments of representative government.

A good place to begin examining the issue of direct democracy in detail is in the writings of Patrick Boyer himself. His book *The People's Mandate: Referendums and a More Democratic Canada* (Toronto: Dundurn Press, 1992) provides a good overview of the issues relevant to the debate on direct democracy. Boyer's *Direct Democracy in Canada: The History and Future of Referendums* (Toronto: Dundurn Press, 1992) presents extensive historical information on the role of direct democracy in Canada.

In the above articles, both Boyer and Charlton make allusions to the experiences of other countries with direct democracy. The most authoritative and comprehensive source on the American experience is Thomas

E. Cronin's, *Direct Democracy: The Politics of Initiative, Referendum, and Recall* (Cambridge: Harvard University Press, 1989). A useful set of essays that compares the experiences of a number of countries can be found in David Butler and Austin Ranney, eds., *Referendums: A Comparative Study of Practice and Theory* (Washington, D.C.: American Enterprise Institute for Public Policy Research, 1987). David Pond, "Direct Democracy: The Wave of the Future?" *Canadian Parliamentary Review,* 15, no. 1 (Winter 1991–92), 11–14 provides a useful review of the lessons that Canadians may draw from the American and Swiss experiences.

An issue not directly addressed in the above debate is whether referendums should be held at the same time as election campaigns. Lawrence Leduc, in a paper presented to the Royal Commission on Electoral Reform and Party Financing entitled "A New Proposal for Reviving the Spirit of Canadian Democracy," argues that since elections fail to give governments a clear mandate to implement policy, citizen-initiated proposals should play a role in Canadian elections. Not everyone agrees. David MacDonald, in an essay entitled "Referendums and Federal General Elections in Canada," in Michael Cassidy, ed., *Democratic Rights and Electoral Reform in Canada,* volume 10 of the Research Studies, Royal Commission on Electoral Reform and Party Financing (Ottawa: Minister of Supply and Services, 1991), argues that holding the two at the same time would likely exacerbate some of the problems of referendums. He concludes that "referendums held on election day would strip elections of some of their meaning and value ... [and] would not lead to the kind of unfettered, immediate kind of decision making by citizens that is promised by the advocates of populism" (p. 335).

# ISSUE SEVENTEEN

## Do Business Groups Have Privileged Access to Government?

**YES** WILLIAM D. COLEMAN, "One Step Ahead: Business in the Policy Process in Canada"

**NO** W.T. STANBURY, "Assessing the Political Power of Business Interests"

"The flaw in the pluralist heaven is that the heavenly chorus sings with a strong upper-class accent." These words, written by E.E. Schattschneider in his book *The Semi-Sovereign People*, are meant to describe the inordinate amount of influence business groups have on government in America. The theory of pluralist politics, which contends that most groups have roughly equal access to government, fails to hold up in American politics.

In Canada, there is also evidence that politics favours business interests. As in the United States, many in Canada assume that the political process has a place for those who make an effort, but experience suggests otherwise. Business groups typically find it easier to gain access to political leaders, and to establish one-to-one relationships with bureaucratic agencies. The effect is to shut out other interests. It appears that business does have privileged access to government.

The prominence of business groups, some say, follows directly from the nature of society. We live in a capitalist society that leaves major decisions to private businesses. Government's role is to correct for failures in the private sphere. In this environment, governments are naturally beholden to business for tax revenues, jobs, and overall political stability. Pluralism assumes a society of classless producers, but the reality is a class society in which some are more powerful than others.

The implications of a pluralist heaven with an upper-class accent are disturbing. For one, it is unlikely that policies will receive the kind of thorough consideration promised by pluralist politics. Furthermore, a persistent business influence makes it difficult to achieve the type of society that distributes resources in an equitable manner—the rich get richer, and the poor get poorer. Democracy also comes under considerable strain, for the notion of "one person, one vote" is difficult to sustain. Money and class position become the determining factors in politics.

The claim that business is favoured in government circles has not, however, been universally accepted in Canada. It is granted that pluralism strictly defined is nowhere to be seen. Nevertheless, some argue—persuasively—that business groups face competition in the political arena from the likes of labour, environmental, and consumer groups. Moreover, the dynamics of the governing process—the competition between parties, the need to appeal to the general electorate, and the impact of a culture that espouses democracy—also create problems for business concerns. Finally, there are policies that clearly go against business interests. It is not easy to find a business leader happy with government.

In the readings, two of Canada's most respected observers of relations between business and government address the issue of whether business enjoys privileged access to government. William D. Coleman contends that business groups do have privileged access to government, and W.T. Stanbury argues that they do not.

# One Step Ahead: Business in the Policy Process in Canada[1]

## William D. Coleman

Business groups *do* have privileged access to government. Before outlining an argument in favour of this position, let us define our terms. By *business*, we are referring to companies, public corporations, partnerships, or individually owned firms that aim to generate a surplus for their owners from the sale of goods, capital, or services. Business *groups*, then, may refer to these individual firms, the interest associations those firms belong to, and the professional lobbyists they hire. When we say business groups have *privileged* access, we refer to the fact that first the political demands of business receive closer and more sympathetic attention than those of other social groups, and second that the resources available to business to make those demands and to apply pressure to have them acted upon are superior to those of other groups. Having outlined our terms, let us examine why business groups have privileged access.

We live and work in a society that brings together a capitalist, market economy and a liberal democratic political system. Many political philosophers feared that the combination of these two social structures would have some highly unfortunate results. De Tocqueville wondered whether it would lead to a kind of tyranny of the masses. Marx predicted that the contradictions inherent in the combination would end in the revolutionary overthrow of the economic and political systems by an outraged working class. But the combination has worked better than most expected because a compromise emerged involving an understanding between business and political authorities. Those who own the instruments of production, the business class, consent to political institutions (liberal democracy) that allow other social groups to make claims for a redistribution of wealth. Those who do not own the instruments of production consent that these be privately owned. Based on this compromise, there develops a strong boundary between what is public and what is private. State authorities come to enforce this boundary, and normally are reluctant to infringe on the rights of private ownership and private property. As leaders in a democracy where the majority of citizens are not business owners or managers, however, they can be pushed to redistribute some of the wealth accumulated by business to other social groups.

When we reflect a little further on this arrangement, we see that it means that ultimate responsibility for the health and growth of the economy rests with business, and not the state. Business firms decide what goods are to be produced. They also determine how to invest capital—whether it should be on research and development, on new equipment, on an expanded factory, or on personal luxury goods. From these decisions flow others: what professional and technical training will lead to the best jobs, where people will live and work, what kinds of standards are needed for particular goods, which natural resources will be the most valuable, where roads, railways, and airports should be built, and so on. Because business leaders are making important decisions that affect the common good, Charles Lindblom writes that business persons are, in fact, *public officials.*[2]

The privileged access of business arises out of these special characteristics of business as a social group. There are four different dimensions of this privileged access: business groups are listened to more attentively than other groups; business groups possess more resources than other social groups; the expert, technical knowledge of business is more needed for the making of public policy; and business interests are more easily mobilized than those of other interests. Let us look at each of these dimensions in turn.

## BUSINESS GROUPS ARE LISTENED TO MORE ATTENTIVELY THAN OTHER GROUPS

Let us take a hypothetical example. Suppose a provincial government was faced with a decision on whether to permit the building of a hydroelectric dam in a remote forest area. Two groups opposed the plan. The Sierra Club, a prominent environmental organization, argued that the dam would lead to the flooding of a valuable wilderness area, disrupting the migration patterns of birds and killing an unknown number of other wild animals. A band of First Nations people, with several villages in the area, objected that the dam would require the relocation of one of the villages, would disrupt hunting practices, and would lead to the death of many fish, a traditional food staple.

On the other side, a coalition of business groups supported the plan. They argued that building the dam would create close to 1,000 jobs over a period of five years in an area where unemployment was high. For this part of their plan, they were able to convince some construction workers' labour unions to back their efforts. The business coalition added that the new dam would increase the supply of power in a more remote area of the province, sparking the relocation of a mineral processing plant from the United States. Finally, when integrated into the province's hydroelectric grid, the dam would increase the overall supply of power, lowering its cost over the longer term. Lower-priced power would enable an unknown number of plants in the province to expand their operations, thereby creating still more new jobs.

Place yourself in the position of senior public officials and politicians reflecting upon this decision. If you accede to the environmentalists and the First Nations band, you are responding to *special* interests. Those who cherish the wilderness and those who live in particular harmony with it will benefit. If you agree with the business coalition and its trade union supporters, you cannot help but think that you are responding to a more *general* interest. Not only will business firms benefit from approval of the dam, but also an unknown number of workers and other citizens. As stewards of the public interest, you know as well that the new jobs and growth in the economy that result from the decision will increase the government's tax revenues. With these new revenues, you will be able to enrich programs for other citizens, whether by building new hospitals or by adding special resource teachers in the schools. In short, the situation is one where what appears to be in the interests of business also seems to be in society's general interest.

So when we say that business groups are listened to more attentively than others, we are referring to the fact that the demands of business leaders, given their overall responsibility for the economy, take on the appearance of being in the general interests of society. By comparison, those opposing business often appear to be arguing on the basis of a narrow or special interest. This distinction between an apparent general interest and apparent special interests is a social construction. In itself, it serves as an indicator of business groups' political power. In noting this phenomenon, we do not wish to say that business will always win out in these decisions. They will lose some decisions, but fewer than they win. And always, business will be listened to very carefully.

This structural power of business is somewhat impervious to party politics. In fact, the amount of private power possessed by business in a capitalist economy may, at times, overwhelm partisan political forces. We have some good recent examples of this power in Canada. Why should a social democratic NDP government in Ontario, which hardly muttered the word "deficit" when sitting on the opposition benches, assimilate the business community's alarm about the deficit when it comes to power? Why should the social democratic Parti Québécois government forget about its party program calling for widespread nationalization of business when it came to power in 1976? Both of these parties had a strong base of support among the less advantaged groups in society and a very weak base in the business community. Did they just forget their roots and become opportunists as the cynical press (owned by big business) would imply? Such a conclusion is too facile. Rather, as governments, they found themselves called upon to act in the "general" interest, and the "general" interest in our society appears to coincide with the interests of business more often than not.

## BUSINESS GROUPS HAVE MORE RESOURCES FOR CONTACTING AND MAINTAINING RELATIONSHIPS WITH GOVERNMENT THAN OTHER GROUPS

Let us begin with another example. The Canadian Dairy Commission is a federal government agency that makes decisions on the pricing of milk in Canada's dairy supply-management system. Before making a decision, the commission solicits the advice of a consultative committee upon which sit representatives of dairy producers, dairy processors (the companies that manufacture the milk into yogurt and ice cream), the after-processors (the companies that use dairy products such as cheese to make frozen pizzas), and consumers. Each of the first three groups, all arguably sectors of business,[3] have interest associations, with permanent, full-time staffs, that sit on the committee. There is only one association representing consumers in Canada, the Consumers' Association of Canada, and it finds it difficult to hire enough staff to cover all the policy areas it is concerned with. In practically every area where it is active, it finds another set of well-resourced business associations across the table. In the end, the Consumers' Association hired someone part-time to cover the dairy policy area. In many other policy areas, it simply does not act at all.

More generally, business interests in Canada have over 600 associations active on the national level. Several hundred more work at the provincial and local levels. Systematically, if we compare their resources with the other "special" interests they compete with in a given policy arena such as consumers, environmentalists, women's groups, and the poor, business groups almost always come out on top. For example, the Consumers' Association of Canada employed twenty persons in 1993–94. The Grocery Products Manufacturers, Association of Canada, only one of its competitors in only one policy area, dairy, employed thirty. The Canadian Bankers' Association, the Canadian Manufacturers' Association, the Canadian Chamber of Commerce—each of these employs over 100 persons.

If we add to these interest groups the professional lobbying firms in Ottawa and the provincial capitals and the government relations divisions that many large corporations have in-house, the advantages of business are magnified. What is more, we know that business corporations contribute about one-half of the funds used by the two major political parties, the Progressive Conservatives and the Liberals. When coupled to the predisposition of the state to look upon business demands as being in the general interest of society, these impressive resources magnify the privileged access of business to government.

There is one other resource that can, at times, be important: business and political leaders often come from, and live in, the same elite social circles. Studies by political sociologists such as John Porter and Wallace Clement show that economic and political elites have a tendency to be educated at a restricted set of private schools, to attend particular universities, to belong to special private clubs, to have summer homes in the same areas, and even to have their families intermarry. These kinds of social ties by no means guarantee that political leaders will favour requests by business over others. But they do mean that political leaders at times have a better understanding and set of personal relationships with business leaders than they do with other social groups. This understanding also works in business leaders' favour.

## BUSINESS GROUPS HAVE KNOWLEDGE AND EXPERTISE NEEDED BY THE STATE

Let us return again to our example of the Canadian Dairy Commission. As noted, the commission has the mandate to decide upon the price of milk paid to farmers by processors. This decision is a complex one as it needs to take account of the cost of production to the farmer, consumer demand for milk products, processors' costs, and so on. Much of the information needed to make an informed decision rests not with the commission itself, but with business. In making its decision, the commission needs to obtain from business a host of economic data and to have those data interpreted and explained. In short, the commission cannot do its job without the expertise and advice of business.

The pricing decision on milk is but one example of economic regulation. There are many, many others: definitions of core capital for banks, rules for chemicals in waste water from pulp mills, the content of advertisements for pharmaceuticals, the cost of stumpage to logging companies. In addition to regulatory policy, there are many other policy areas that require close consultation with business: international trade, vocational training, and agricultural finance to name but a few.

In short, managing a complex market-based economy in the context of a highly populated, relatively wealthy society requires ongoing, close collaboration between business and the state. Many of the public policies developed and maintained by the state require information and expertise that only business can provide. After all, as we have seen, it is business in our economic system that has the responsibility for managing the economy. The knowledge and expertise gained in fulfilling that responsibility are essential to the state if it is to carry out many of its duties. In this respect, then, business groups again have privileged access.

# BUSINESS INTERESTS ARE MORE EASILY MOBILIZED THAN THOSE OF OTHER SOCIAL GROUPS

To illustrate this point in our argument, we will compare a business interest association and a labour union in terms of their relationships with the state.[4] In making this comparison, we might be able to substitute an environmental group, a women's group, or a group representing the socially disadvantaged for the labour union.

First, communications between the state and the business association will normally be *more private* than those involving the labour union. The power of business lies in its control of the instruments of production, a factor outside the business association. Labour does not control the instruments of production. It gains power by mobilizing its members, by using its greater numbers as an electoral threat, or by proposing that its members thus mobilized might stop production through a strike. By definition, labour's approaches to the state become *more public*. As such, labour's relationships are likely to take on a more threatening air from the point of view of state officials.

Second, interchanges between the state and business will usually appear to be *technical* in character. As we have seen, business and the state share in the management of the economy. Discussions between the two often centre around the best way or the best approach for maximizing economic growth (thus business profits and government revenues) while not harming unduly other individuals or groups in society. Problems to be resolved are thus practical, demanding rather specialized discussions and knowledge.

The task is different for labour. In making their case, they will often be challenging the primacy of economic growth as a policy objective, or even more significantly, calling into question business firms, use of the instruments of production. Perhaps, they might even ask whether business firms should have such control. In addition, let us remember that labour to be successful must mobilize its members. Thus, in making their plea to the state, union leaders must be mindful not only of the policy content of their demands, but also of using language that nurtures and sustains that mobilization. For these reasons, interchanges between labour and the state will appear *ideological* rather than technical. State officials will tend to dismiss ideological arguments as not being "practical" or as "unhelpful."

Third, for reasons that we have noted, communications of business associations with the state will appear more *universal* or *general*. When one asks the question, "Who will benefit in society from a healthy, growing economy?" the answer is "almost everyone." Business demands, if acted upon, have the virtue of seeming to provide the greatest good to the greatest number. In contrast, if a labour union is demanding a law favouring closed shops, or rules to prevent the hiring of strike-breakers, or tighter rules for safety in the workplace, they appear as more *self-serving*, as demanding something for themselves at the expense of the rest of society. In short, because labour's approaches to government will appear more political, more ideological, and more self-serving than those of business, the task of mobilizing broader public support for their positions becomes that much more difficult.

The problems for labour do not end here. The political strength of trade unions depends significantly on how well they can mobilize their members. Their success in the policy process rests on how well they can marry that mobilization to a knowledge base that makes them credible in policy discussions. Mobilizing members and developing that knowledge base require a permanent staff and some kind of bureaucracy. As this union bureaucracy develops, it takes on a professional character that is rather different from the ethos and interests of the workers it organizes. It often becomes distant from these workers, leading to their alienation and demobilization. If the demobilization becomes well entrenched, the labour union loses its base for political influence and power.

Business does not face these problems to the same extent. Business power does not lay primarily in its political mobilization, but in its control of the instruments of production. Defining what the interests of business are might still be difficult; they often must address complex policy questions where answers are far from obvious. But the discussion is a technical, problem-solving one. It does not require at the same time the mobilization of hundreds or thousands of individuals to press the point once answers are found. Business association leaders are not faced with doing these two complicated, somewhat contradictory tasks at the same time. Theirs is a bureaucracy for defining interests and resolving technical problems only. Because their demands will often take on a more universal or general character than those of their opponents, political mobilization is less essential to their being accepted by the state.

Perhaps the final straw that breaks the proverbial camel's back is what Mancur Olson has termed the "logic of collective action."[5] In a somewhat complex argument that we cannot summarize here, Olson points out that it is much easier to organize small groups rather than large groups. In a small group, given members can see readily that their adhesion and contributions will lead to the provision of a desired collective good. Hence, there is a ready, self-interested reason for joining.

In contrast, in a large group, a single individual's contribution will not make a perceptible difference to the group as a whole. Thus if the

Consumers' Association of Canada has 20,000 members and you do not renew your membership, the group will barely notice. If one of the fourteen companies manufacturing potato chips that belong to the Canadian Potato Chip/Snack Foods Association fails to renew, the consequences are much different. Everyone notices. Hence, to be successful, large groups must either coerce members to join or provide some selective benefits such as a useful magazine or lower prices for books or a decorative calendar to get them to adhere. Even here there are political costs. Members join a small group because they can see direct relationships between its collective goals and their own self-interests. In large groups, if members join for the decorative calendar and not because they see a relationship between group goals and their self-interest, then it will be more difficult to mobilize them politically. Furthermore, they can always act as *free-riders*. Since it will not be noticed if they do not join, as potential members of large groups they can sit on the sidelines and still enjoy any benefits that come from the groups' actions.

This logic of collective action is important because in practically every circumstance the business group will be smaller than those opposing it. There are more consumers of dairy products than there are dairy plants, more purchasers of loans than there are banks, more persons concerned about the smell of pulp mills than there are pulp and paper companies, more workers making automobiles than there are automobile corporations. Accordingly, based on Olson's logic of collective action, it will almost always be easier to organize the business interests around an issue than those opposing business.

In conclusion, arising out of their structural power over the economy, business groups will rarely be just "one of the crowd" when dealing with bureaucratic officials and politicians. Their crucial place in a capitalist economy often makes their concerns appear to be all of society's concerns. It provides them with exceptional resources for competing in the political arena. And it creates among political authorities a particular dependence on their expertise and advice. This convergence between business interests and the perceived "common good" also makes it easier to organize groups. All of these factors ensure privileged access to government for business groups.

## NOTES

1. I would like to thank Tony Porter, Department of Political Science, McMaster University, for his comments on an early draft of this chapter.

2. Charles E. Lindblom, *Politics and Markets* (New York: Basic Books, 1977), p. 172.

3. Some might argue that dairy farmers are not part of the business community. This question is a difficult one. The past thirty years in Canada have seen the gradual elimination of many small dairy farms. Under supply-management, dairy farming has become much more like running a business, with quota to produce milk selling on exchanges for thousands of dollars. For these purposes, we will include dairy farming as part of the business community.

4. This part of our argument draws its inspiration from Claus Offe and Helmut Wiesenthal, "Two Logics of Collective Action: Theoretical Notes on Social Class and Organizational Form," *Political Power and Social Theory* 1 (1980): 67–115.

5. Mancur Olson, *The Logic of Collective Action* (Boston: Harvard University Press, 1965).

# Assessing the Political Power of Business Interests[1]

### W.T. Stanbury

# 1. INTRODUCTION

I have chosen a different title for this paper because I believe that by better framing the issue a more useful analysis will follow. The number of
confusions in Professor Coleman's paper are so great that a detailed critique would exceed the length of his paper. For example, consumers
(not firms) decide what goods are to be produced in a market economy—that's why every introductory economics textbook speaks of "consumer sovereignty." The fact that thousands of businesses go broke each
year is evidence that consumers determine which businesses succeed
and which fail. Second, and more generally, many of the bases for the
"privileged access" of business also apply to organized labour groups.
They certainly have the financial and organizational resources to gain
access and to bring political pressure to bear on policy-makers.[2] While
there is no simple statistical series to prove the point, there are several
indicators to suggest that more Canadian firms are spending more effort
in trying to influence public policy. For example, a recent survey of the
firms in the *Financial Post 500* obtained 216 usable responses of these
firms, of which seventy-two had a "distinct government relations unit"
(Baetz, in press). Litvak's (1988: 57) survey of 275 firms in the "Canadian Business 500" for the period 1985–86 found that seventy-three had
a senior "external affairs" executive listed as a corporate officer. In addition, the number and volume of activity of government relations consulting firms have grown rapidly over the past decade. Further, as data
generated by the federal Lobbyist's Registration Act make clear, a number of law firms are also acting as professional lobbyists. Business firms
are the most important clients of both types of assistance in lobbying
(see Stanbury, 1993a: 32–39).

The organization of this paper is as follows. Section 2 seeks to clarify
the concepts of economic and political power. Section 3 suggests some
ways in which the effectiveness of *any* interest group in influencing public policy may be ascertained. Section 4 outlines the objectives and

means by which business interests seek to influence public policy. Section 5 examines the characteristics of business firms as interest groups—including their advantages and disadvantages in this role. Finally, Section 6 addresses the question, "How much power do business interests have in Canada?"

# 2. TERMINOLOGY/KEY CONCEPTS

In everyday speech, in the newspapers, and frequently in this book, reference is made to "the business community," to "business interests," or to the power/weakness of "business." Such terms imply that business in Canada is a homogeneous or even monolithic entity. This is not true, of course, but it is often convenient to speak in terms of large aggregations such as business, labour, and government. When we look more closely we often find that the intragroup differences in interests are as great as the intergroup differences. Government may even receive conflicting advice from different firms in the same industry on an industry-specific issue.

While there are many types of power, in general terms power is the capacity of individuals or organizations to intentionally alter the behaviour of others, or to resist others' efforts to do the same thing. The exercise of power may involve changing attitudes, values, or beliefs, but most importantly, it involves changing behaviour, involuntarily if necessary.

## Economic Power

Economic power is the ability to command scarce economic resources on a large scale relative to others so that the decision-maker is able to exercise considerable discretion. If there is absolutely no discretion, even when the scale of resources is large, the actor has little power. He (or she) is, in the extreme, merely a cipher in transmitting coercive market signals to the levers of the firm. Economic power also consists of having sufficient wealth to be able to not have to maximize profits (shareholders' wealth). The possession of substantial wealth permits individuals/firms to use part of that wealth to pursue noneconomic goals.[3]

## Political Power

In general terms, political power is simply the exercise of power in a *political* context such as elections, the exercise of discretion by a government decision-maker, and efforts to influence present or future public policy.

The most formal type of political power is the ability to control levers of the state with their capacity to exercise legitimate coercion. The scope of governing instruments is enormous and the constraints on the cabinet of a majority government are relatively few, particularly in the first two years or so after a general election. More generally, political power is the ability to mobilize the resources of the state to advance the values, beliefs, or pecuniary interest of those able to exercise that power.

The exercise of power in the political/policy-making arena is dynamic. The amount of power a particular organization or group can exert very much depends upon the particular context. The context includes the nature of the specific issue(s), the timing of the group's actions, the temporal context (e.g., stage in the electoral cycle), and the amount of effort exerted by the group.[4] A normally quite powerful group may be quite ineffective in "getting its way" on issue I at time $t_n$, for example, immediately after certain of its leaders have been the subject of highly negative stories in the national media. The converse is also true—sometimes mice do roar (or put elephants to flight).

Power is at all times *relative*. What matters is the degree of asymmetry in the power possessed by various groups (in a particular context).

> Pressure groups can help to shape changes in public policy when there is a shift in the dynamic balance of power among various interest groups. In other words, changes in public policy are most likely to occur in disequilibrium situations when the working balance among various contending groups and/or between interest groups and the government is upset (Egri and Stanbury, 1989: 280).

A particular business group may appear to be powerful in some absolute sense (e.g., by reason of having large amounts of economic resources), but if its opponents in a particular situation jointly have slightly more power, its opponents are likely to prevail at that time. However, "staying power" can be important, because, for institutionalized interests—such as most large firms and trade associations—participation in public policy-making is like a baseball game with an indefinite number of innings. Opponents may score some runs—even hit the odd grand slam home run—but the team with capacity to come back, regularly score runs, and "hang in there" is more likely to achieve a higher cumulative score. That's where economic resources (which can be converted into political resources, albeit in a nonproportional fashion), organizational strength, and sheer persistence[5] can be most effective.

# 3. MEASURING THE EFFECTIVENESS OF INTEREST GROUPS

Measuring the effectiveness of any interest group is one of the most difficult aspects of understanding interest group behaviour for several reasons: public policy-making is a complex process, many factors shape policy outcomes, and there is often a long lag between actions by interest groups and outcomes. To properly assess the extent of influence on public policy that business interests have, we need to consider the possible manifestations of policy influence—or lack of it. These can be grouped into two categories. First, there are manifestations of power in terms of influencing policy *outcomes*. These appear to include the following:

- The ability of a group to veto policy actions that otherwise had wide support.

- The ability to initiate and have implemented on a regular basis policy actions that are strongly opposed by other major players.

- The ability of a group to alter (or even reverse) a well-established policy when it is seen to work to the disadvantage of that group—despite the fact that the policy is satisfactory to everyone else.

- The ability to shift one's political support to another party and thereby move the party from opposition to government (or the reverse). In short, I refer to the ability to determine the outcome of elections. This requires extraordinary power.

The influence of an interest group can also be seen in relation to the *process* of policy-making. (In general, groups that are better "woven into" the process tend to have more influence on policy outcomes over time.) Process manifestations of a group's power include the following:

- A group has easy access/multiple points of access to the policy-making process relative to other interests.

- The group has an institutional position (or positions) in the policy-making process, i.e., it has a reserved seat at the table around which the "movers and shakers" participate in the development of policy.

- A group's views always receive respectful attention; they are weighed carefully if not always followed.

- The group has the ability to create (or change) the fundamental assumptions or "givens" (including "facts") under which a policy is being made.

- The group benefits from forbearance by politicians and bureaucrats (e.g., to avoid the wrath of a group, the alternatives seriously considered in policy-making may be sharply limited).

# 4. OBJECTIVES AND MEANS OF INFLUENCING PUBLIC POLICY

## Objectives of Corporations' Political Power

In a world in which the scope of government activity and influence over the private sector is great, it is not surprising that large business enterprises (and groups of small ones) should seek to influence the political agenda. Governments can confer great benefits on individual firms, on specific industries, and on the private sector in general.[6] They can also impose complex and costly burdens (taxes, regulation, quotas, etc.).

One of the principal objectives of efforts by big business to assert political influence is to create a general climate favourable to its endeavours so that it may grow and prosper.[7] Political power can also be used to obtain specific regulatory, tax, or procurement decisions that are advantageous to a specific firm or to an entire industry. For example, when the domestic automobile industry was unable to meet competition from Japan, it sought (in conjunction with the union) help from government in the form of capital subsidies and quotas on imports. As a result, Canadian car buyers were forced to bail out an inefficient industry.

Corporations appreciate that effectiveness in the political arena is often based on the role they are able to play in the complex process of making public policy. Therefore they seek to strengthen their role in the policy-making *process* as a means of increasing the likelihood of obtaining favourable decisions in the future.

## The Means Through Which Political Power Is Exercised

Most people think of lobbying as the principal means by which any group seeks to influence public policy, and that term is used to cover a wide range of efforts designed to shape existing or proposed public policies (see Stanbury, 1993a).

Large corporations can capitalize on their superior economic resources by using them to make strategic use of the legal system (e.g., to mount challenges to the constitutionality of new legislation), and to acquire sophisticated polling information so as to better understand (and anticipate) how politicians are likely to see certain issues. They also have the money to make large contributions to political parties in the expectation that their generosity will not go unrewarded in the fullness of time, although only the naive believe that such contributions can be tied directly to benefits from government, e.g., a lucrative contract, an advantageous regulatory decision, etc. (see Stanbury, 1993b).

Corporations may seek to influence policy-making by means of media and public relations campaigns.[8] Large corporations, as do other interest groups, find it useful to engage in extensive informal contacts with senior bureaucrats and politicians as another means of exercising the arts of persuasion. They will also form alliances with other groups to advance (or defeat) particular issues. In an effort to compete in the marketplace of ideas, some large corporations have begun to support certain public policy research organizations, e.g., the Fraser Institute.

# 5. BUSINESS FIRMS AS INTEREST GROUPS
## "Tower of Babble"?

Many public servants and politicians might be excused from describing the "voice of business" as a "tower of babble," for there are many business associations advancing viewpoints that, at times, clash sharply. When he was president of the Toronto Board of Trade in 1976, A.R. Murrich observed that "business in our society is a kaleidoscope, as diverse in its problems and aspirations as the country itself."

Business firms often have conflicting interests largely because all firms face direct or indirect competition from domestic or foreign rivals, i.e., *intra-industry rivalry*. In dealing with government, firms often seek to reinforce their competitive advantage over rivals (or obtain one) by gaining discriminatory benefits, i.e, those that improve their position relative to their rivals. For example, a pulp and paper company whose mills are new (and less polluting) may urge stringent enforcement of across-the-board pollution regulations in order to force its rivals with older, higher effluent mills to incur higher costs in the form of expenditures on abatement or new, less polluting production equipment (see Stanbury, 1993c).

Different industries tend to be concentrated in certain provinces or regions in Canada, e.g., a large fraction of Canada's exports of forest products come from British Columbia. Governments within each province or region tend to support its major industries. The effects of this tendency are exaggerated by the important role of the provinces in Canadian federalism. This *interregional rivalry* is a major source of conflict within the business community in Canada.

Conflicts also originate between those industries favouring free trade and those favouring protectionism. Manufacturing is highly concentrated geographically, with Ontario and Quebec accounting for over three-quarters of Canadian manufacturing. Canadian manufacturers have traditionally favoured protectionist policies. On the other hand, the industries concentrated in western Canada, such as forestry (British Columbia), petroleum (Alberta), and agriculture (Saskatchewan), are export oriented. These industries have traditionally favoured a policy of freer trade for Canada, recognizing that liberalization is a reciprocal proposition.

Canadian firms that sell a substantial fraction of their output abroad are naturally concerned about the terms of access to foreign markets and the exchange rate. Firms that focus on the domestic market are likely to be more concerned about competition from imports and macro-economic policies that stimulate demand.

There are attitudinal differences between Canadian-owned and for-eign-controlled firms operating in Canada. These include differences in attitudes toward wage, salary, and benefit costs; legislation regarding competition policy; and Canadian economic nationalism. Again, these differences may contribute to conflicts within the business community over government policies and priorities.

## Common Interests

While these conflicting interests are often important, it is useful to iden-tify and consider those interests that all or nearly all members of the business community share. These include the following:

- Political stability—in the sense that governments change in response to democratic elections, that the decision-making "framework" and important public policies are not changed capriciously but through well-defined processes.

- Legal and preferably constitutional protections for the rights of pri-vate property. (While governments must pay compensation when they formally expropriate private property, property rights are *not* protected in the 1982 Constitution.)

- Macro-economic stability, i.e, monetary and fiscal policies that act in a contra-cyclical fashion to reduce the amplitude of economic cycles.

- Well-defined and practicable "framework" legislation, e.g., corpora-tion, bankruptcy, intellectual property, labour, competition, and contract legislation.

- The process for making public policy should be quite well defined, accessible, and reasonably predictable or at least measures should be included to ensure that the changes are subject to reasonable notice. Further, the policy actions produced by the process should be based on rational argument and subject to appeal to the courts where they are believed to be unconstitutional.

- The public service should be efficient and effective with individuals selected/promoted on the basis of merit, not political favours.

- The government should be concerned that the total net burden of its interventions on business (taxes, regulations, subsidies, etc.) is no greater than those of Canada's trading partners and competitors.

- There should be an independent judiciary to settle both private interest disputes (e.g., over contracts or torts) and challenges to the constitutionality of the actions of the executive and the legislature.

- Because Canada is so dependent on foreign trade, many firms have a strong interest in having the federal government make a vigorous effort to negotiate and maintain easy access to foreign markets, making this trade as free of discriminatory regulatory constraints as possible.

## Advantages and Disadvantages of Business Firms as Interest Groups

A business firm or a trade association is one of many interest groups seeking to influence public policy (see Stanbury, 1993a: ch. 5). But business firms (particularly large ones) have certain *advantages* as an interest group relative to other interest groups. First, the firm is already organized for other purposes so that the "free-rider" (collective action) problem has already been solved. (This is also the case for trade unions.) Second, the firm's "agency problem" is tiny compared to those of interest groups with a broadly based membership (see Stanbury, in press). Third, business executives (and labour leaders) are familiar with strategic thinking, which is very useful in the political arena. Fourth, business firms have a strong functional role in society that provides them with legitimacy. Fifth, business firms are seen to play an important role in the society in maintaining a high standard of living. Sixth, large firms (and large unions) have extensive economic resources that can be used in their efforts to influence public policy. They can hire expertise in business–government relations and pay the cost of major efforts to influence public policy. Seventh, expenditures by firms on lobbying and other efforts to influence public policy are tax-deductible expenses.[9]

At the same time, business firms have a number of *disadvantages* in their efforts to influence public policy relative to other interest groups. First, pecuniary private interests are widely perceived to be morally inferior; business firms are deemed to be exclusively focused on increasing profits. Second, it is widely believed that business interests are antithetical to "the public interest," a highly evocative, but ill-defined concept (see Stanbury, 1993a: ch. 13). Third, as noted above, there are plenty of internal cleavages within the "business community." Fourth, market/institutional failures (e.g., pollution) are often blamed on firms. They are seen to be attributable to the greed of managers rather than problems in institutional design. Fifth, capitalism has an "unacceptable face" and its excesses often lead to more general government intervention. Sixth, many top executives have little training in dealing with government (and other interest groups). (Many are acquiring the necessary skills or hiring consultants who have them.)

## Limitations on the Political Power of the Largest Corporations

It is often argued that the largest corporations—say the 100 largest privately owned firms—have a disproportionate influence on public policy in Canada. Certainly, they account for a very substantial fraction of total revenues, assets, and profits of business enterprises. However, several factors or forces constrain the political power of large corporations: political resources are not equivalent to political power; other social interests have political resources (countervailing power); the opposition of the general public, particularly the emphasis on social pluralism; and constraints within the business system such as problems of coordination and internal conflicts over public policy.

The political power of large corporations is constrained by the competition (countervailing power) of other interests such as labour, consumers, environmentalists, nationalists. Canada is a pluralist society in the sense that a number of different interests are contending for a place in the sun and competing to influence government policy. This does not mean, however, that reality is close to the pluralist ideal.

Business managers' behaviour is constrained by the market for corporate control. The capital market (through hostile takeovers) can extract its revenge on inefficient managers including those who have pursued political objectives at the expense of profits for shareholders.

Competition among political parties, notably from the left ("contagion from the left"), represents an important limitation on the political power of corporations. Populist values, the belief in the tenets of popular democracy, and the distrust of "vested interests" by at least some fraction of the electorate all limit the exercise of political power by large corporations.

Abuses and scandals involving corporations, with their attendant media exposure, also act as a constraint. Nothing promotes reform like well-publicized excesses. The news media believe that the reporting of scandals and illegal behaviour by established organizations and individuals is highly popular with their readers/viewers.

The lack of unanimity within the business community or even among the top fifty corporations on important matters of public policy limits the actual impact of the potential political power of big business. The absolute size of the corporate elite militates against a conspiracy among a few thousand people—even if one-quarter went to Upper Canada College! (This is not to say that such individuals do not have a loose community of interest.)

# 6. HOW MUCH POWER?

## Perceived Influence of Business on Government

It is not hard to find conflicting views regarding the ability of business interests to influence the behaviour of government in Canada. Most business people writing or speaking on the subject stress how little influence they have and point to a host of government actions inimical to business interests that were inspired by the desire to garner votes or placate other lobby groups, such as environmentalists, consumers, or particular regional interests. In general, business portrays itself as ineffectual in influencing government. On the other hand, writers from a Marxist perspective (e.g., Clement, 1983), or those who stress the process of elite accommodation in Canada, see business interests as highly influential in their dealings with government (see Professor Coleman's paper above).

Public opinion polls provide an indication of how Canadians perceive the power of the business community. For example, a national Gallup poll conducted in April 1989 indicated that 34 percent believed that the business community is "too powerful" in terms of its "power and influence in Canadian society," while 34 percent believed that it had "just the right amount" of power and influence. Only 21 percent thought the business community "is not powerful enough."

Some additional insights into the perceived influence of business can be seen in other polling data (*Maclean's*, January 7, 1991, p. 32), which indicate that business is being looked to most frequently by an increasing fraction of Canadians to look after their economic interests. In the mid-1980s, 31 to 33 percent of those polled said they mostly looked to business to look after their economic interests. This increased to 50 percent in 1989 and then fell slightly to 45 percent in late 1990. The increased reliance on business was accompanied by a sharply reduced reliance on government—from 49 percent in 1984 to 25 percent in 1989 and 27 percent in 1990.

In general, an individual's ability to influence others is increased if they are perceived favourably by those they seek to influence. In 1990, business leaders were more frequently perceived as "principled" (51 percent) than were politicians (40 percent), but both had fallen in public esteem since 1980 (*The Globe and Mail*, October 1, 1990, p. B3). Both politicians and business leaders were seen as far more concerned with money than people in 1990, and in both cases the percentage had increased since 1980. The perception that business leaders are more concerned about money than people is not surprising given their role and responsibilities. It is surprising to find that Canadians perceive their politicians to be almost as concerned about money (versus people) (81 percent in 1990) as business leaders (91 percent). Further, in 1990 Canadians rated business leaders as "competent" far more frequently (59 percent) than politicians (32 percent). In both cases, however, perceived competence had declined sharply from 1980, particularly for politicians.

In June 1989, 45 percent of the public stated that government is usually more concerned about business than about the public's interests. In September 1989, some 75 percent of respondents agreed that governments pay more attention to the interests of big business than to those of the common person. Further, "big business particularly is increasingly regarded not as a creator but as a harvester of wealth" (Gregg and Posner, 1990: 54).

Most Canadians agree with the statement, "people who run corporations don't really care about people like me." Most assume that business people "cannot be expected to put their country's interests before their own or their company's." And those least likely to trust business people are also least likely to trust politicians. "By 1990 a significant segment was disillusioned with both the nation's economic and political leadership—and the numbers are growing" (Gregg and Posner, 1990:58). Decima's polling data indicate that the public trust/confidence in most institutions in Canada declined during the 1980s (see Gregg and Posner, 1990: 59).[10]

## Counter Examples

Professor Coleman's paper is likely to leave readers with the idea that business interests dominate Canada's political life and that they seldom fail to obtain the changes in public policy they seek (or prevent those of other groups that they find distasteful). Yet he has provided very few good examples to illustrate the benefits of what he ways is the "privileged access" of business. What matters is not access, but *outcomes* (although access may help to achieve desired outcomes). Readers might reflect upon some recent developments in the political/policy-making arena that seem inconsistent with the idea that business interests virtually always "get their way." Consider:

1. There has been an explosion of litigation engendered by the Charter of Rights and Freedoms (1982), which has expanded the scope of both individual and group rights (see Knopff and Morton, 1992). A major part of the litigation has been funded (at least in part) by federal government grants to various "new social movement" groups (e.g., women, handicapped, ethnocultural, visible minorities). In general, the effect of their legal victories is to expand the role of the state, which, in turn, often imposes cost-increasing obligations on business firms.

2. There has been at the federal and provincial levels, a "green tsunami" of new/more stringent environmental protection legislation (regulations). And there is more coming if the promises in the December 1990 federal *Green Plan* and provincial governments are kept. Initially, the costs of these new/more stringent regulations are borne by business firms. For example, the cost of the three sets of *federal* pulp and paper industry regulations made in May 1992 is estimated to be $4.85 billion. The new regulations made in the past few years by British Columbia, Alberta, Ontario, and Quebec to reduce

the volume of organochlorines will cost at least as much (Stanbury, 1993c). These—and may other environmental initiatives—demonstrate that environmental interest groups (partly funded by government) can "out muscle" business interests.

3. With the help of trade unions, and a variety of "social activist" groups, the NDP formed majority governments in Ontario (1990), British Columbia (1991), and Saskatchewan (1991). While those governments in Ontario and Saskatchewan have had to trim their traditional sails to cope with very serious deficit/debt problems, their coming to power hardly represents the fondest wishes of business interests.

4. It is now virtually taken for granted by Canada's political/policy elite that native Indians should have the "right of self-government" (although no one can say what that means in operational terms).[11] This massive, contingent economic liability for all Canadians will fall heavily on businesses in the resource industries. For example, the NDP government in British Columbia appears to be seriously contemplating expropriating, without compensation, the timber harvesting rights on crown lands held by private firms so as to be able to meet the land claims of Indian bands (as well as to create environmental preserves).[12]

5. In June 1987 the minority Liberal government in Ontario enacted what was then widely regarded as the most far-reaching pay equity legislation in North America. Women's groups, labour unions, and some academics supported the legislation. They prevailed over business interests (see Egri and Stanbury, 1989). In 1993, the NDP government enacted stringent employment equity legislation—despite the loud objections of parts of the business community.[13]

6. In 1975, the Conservative government of Bill Davis in Ontario imposed sweeping rent controls. Competitive promises by the NDP and Liberal parties during a hard-fought election campaign forced the Tories' hand (Stanbury and Thain, 1986). Although controls were imposed in other provinces in conjunction with federal wage and price controls in late 1975, Ontario's controls—modified and extended by Tory, Liberal, and NDP governments—remain in force today. Rent controls represent a state-imposed levy on the wealth of landlords in order to benefit hundreds of thousands of tenants (see Stanbury and Todd, 1990).

It would not be hard to extend the list of *notable* examples (see Stanbury and Lermer, 1983; Stanbury, 1992a; Globerman et al., 1993).

## Competition in the Marketplace of Ideas

Professor Coleman is clearly unhappy with what he believes is the ability of business interests in Canada to impose their values/political agenda on the nation. As noted above, he greatly exaggerates the power of business in this regard. As importantly, he misconstrues the likely source of business interests' successes in the political arena. Business does not "impose" its values/agenda. Rather, it must *compete* in the marketplace of ideas and values (see Reich, 1988). It must offer a superior "product" if it is to be successful in gaining support for its ideas/values, for there is no shortage of alternatives—as Professor Coleman's paper itself demonstrates. Contrary perhaps to Professor Coleman's desire, the majority of Canadians simply *prefer* the set of "outputs" produced by a market economy—tempered by considerable government intervention—to the alternatives offered by the left: more government intervention and less economic freedom and opportunity to achieve individual destinies. The common interests of the business community—outlined in section 5 above—appear also to be shared by a large fraction of the population.

Business leaders in Canada in the 1990s do not command from the heights. Rather, they negotiate with all manner of entities in their firm's environment: government, labour unions, a variety of (often government-funded) interest groups—ranging from environmental groups to natives to NIMBY groups. They have to take into account an increasing number of "stakeholders," not simply the owners of the common stock (or major creditors). Most of all, corporate leaders have to anticipate and react to the initiatives of competitors (often on the other side of the world) and the forces of technological, economic, and political change. They might accept the idea that they have fairly easy access in the sense of meeting with politicians and senior public servants to discuss their problems. They would be bewildered by the idea that they can routinely produce the *results* they desire in the political/policy-making arena.

Business interests—like other interests—must persuade. In a democracy, governments are moved by persuasion, not by force or the threat of force. Governments have a monopoly on the legitimate use of coercion in a democracy. Their size and scope and the limited protections for private property mean that governments can dominate any and all business entities if they wish to do so.

The ultimate constraint on government's arbitrary exercise of power over a business lies in the mobility of capital (not a strike by capitalists as Coleman implies). For an enterprise with large amounts of *physical* capital, a government can effectively expropriate a large part of its value by excessive regulation (or primitive taxation). Because the plant and equipment can't flee, it is *captive* to the government in whose jurisdiction it lies. The owners suffer large capital losses in financial terms. The results of this and other types of opportunistic behaviour by governments take two principal forms: (1) over the longer term, financial capital seeks a more hospitable environment[14]; (2) the opportunity cost of capital rises to reflect the evidence of government opportunism. This effect tends to persist even after government "swears off" such tactics.[15]

Politicians intent upon seeking or retaining power can be amoral. They may not be constrained by any philosophical commitment to individual freedom or small government or other specific issues favoured by large enterprises. They must balance competing interests in order to retain power. That is why no single group or even broad interest dominates in a democratic society.

# NOTES

1. This paper was written while I was the Frederick H. Paulus Distinguished Professor of Public Policy, 1993/94 at Willamette University, Salem, Oregon. I am indebted to the Atkinson Graduate School of Management for its highly supportive working environment. Parts of this paper have been adapted from Stanbury (1988), (1992b), and (1993a).

2. For example, in the 1988 federal election, the Canadian Labour Congress gave the NDP almost $1.1 million (seven times the largest corporate donation to the Conservative or Liberal parties) and other labour bodies donated $0.6 million in kind to the NDP. In addition, hundreds of union officials—paid by their employer—worked in the campaigns of individual NDP candidates. See Stanbury (1993b).

3. Economists find it hard to believe the firms would ever fail to maximize profits—even when they have market power and so have at least some discretion that may be used to pursue goals other than maximizing the shareholders' wealth. There is, however, a growing literature focusing on the "agency problem." One of its most prominent forms occurs when top management pursues its interests at the expense of shareholders' wealth due to asymmetric conformation and the costs of monitoring and enforcing the will of the owners.

4. The nominal power of a group might be likened to the rated horsepower of a car engine. The actual power being generated at a particular moment depends on the amount of fuel being supplied as well as the rated capacity (potential) of the engine.

5. There are many examples of interest groups that achieved their goal only after repeated bursts of effort. For example, the major pharmaceutical companies in Canada (almost entirely foreign owned) began working to get rid of the provision shortly after the Patent Act was amended to require the

compulsory licensing of new drugs in 1969. Several "big pushes" to change the law over the years failed until 1991 and 1992 when the Mulroney government—against the determined opposition of both Liberals and the NDP—legislated the changes sought by the big drug companies.

6. These include new or amended legislation or subordinate legislation, favourable interpretation of existing policy, and the provision of information to help corporations adapt easily to government policies.

7. The head of the Business Council on National Issues—arguably the most important voice of "big business" in Canada—put it to me this way:: "Our objective is to shape the climate in which business operates rather than to determine the weather over the next few days."

8. For example, private automobile insurers in Ontario began an advocacy advertising campaign for a limited form of no-fault insurance in March 1987 to try to forestall a government-run no-fault insurance scheme. They were only partly successful as the government promised to regulate auto insurance premiums.

9. Government direct financial support for other types of interest groups is extensive in Canada. See, for example, Stanbury (1993a, ch. 5).

10. A recent poll provides further insights into the public's perception of politics, politicians, and business executives—see *Maclean's,* January 4, 1993, pp. 18–22.

11. The best illustration of this is the language of the Charlottetown Accord. Although it was rejected in the national referendum in the fall of 1992, opinion polls indicate that there is considerable support for native self-government.

12. See the Schwindt Report on the taking of resource interests submitted to the B.C. government in 1992, and the Council of Forest Industries briefs to the provincial government in 1992 and 1993.

13. See "Business Split on Equity Bill," *The Globe and Mail,* August 18, 1993, pp. B1, B2.

14. Of course, short-term money can move almost immediately.

15. An excellent example occurred in Ontario. In 1975 when it imposed rent controls, the Conservative government promised (on a stack of Bibles) that rental buildings completed *after* the date controls were announced would be exempt. However, rent controls were *extended* to cover the previously exempt new buildings in 1986. The effect was to further reduce the value of rental buildings to reflect the obviously riskier political environment. See Stanbury and Todd (1990)

# REFERENCES

Baetz, Mark C. (in press), "Rethinking the Government Relations Unit," *Canadian Journal of Administrative Studies*, forthcoming.

Clement, Wallace (1983), *Class, Power and Property: Essays on Canadian Society* (Toronto: Methuen).

Egri, C.P. and W.T. Stanbury (1989), "How Pay Equity Legislation Came to Ontario," *Canadian Public Administration* 32, no. 2: 274–303.

Globerman, Steven, W.T. Stanbury, and Ilan B. Vertinsky (1993), "Analysis of Fair Wage Policies: British Columbia and Other Jurisdictions" (Vancouver: University of British Columbia, Faculty of Commerce and Business Administration, Working Paper, October, mimeo).

Gregg, Allan and Michael Posner (1990), *The Big Picture* (Toronto: Macfarlane Walter and Ross).

Knopff, Rainer and F.L. Morton (1992), *Charter Politics* (Scarborough: Nelson).

Litvak, I.A. (1988), "External Issues, Public Affairs and Corporate Boards," *Business Quarterly* 52, no. 4: 55–61.

Reich, Robert B., ed. (1988), *The Power of Public Ideas* (Cambridge, Mass.: Ballinger Publishing).

Stanbury, W.T. (1988), "Corporate Power and Political Influence," in R.S. Khemani, D.M. Shapiro, and W.T. Stanbury, eds., *Mergers, Corporate Concentration and Power in Canada* (Montreal: The Institute for Research on Public Policy), pp. 393–452.

Stanbury, W.T. (1992a), "Notes on Environmental Issues and Interest Groups" (Vancouver: University of British Columbia, Faculty of Commerce and Business Administration, May, mimeo).

Stanbury, W.T. (1992b), "Interest Group Behaviour and Policy Making in Canada," in Jerry Dermer, ed., *The Canadian Profile: People, Institutions, Infrastructure* (Toronto: Captus Press).

Stanbury, W.T. (1993a), *Business–Government Relations in Canada: Influencing Public Policy* (Scarborough: Nelson).

Stanbury, W.T. (1993b), *Money in Politics: Financing Federal Parties and Candidates in Canada* (Toronto: Dundurn Press).

Stanbury, W.T. (1993c), *Regulating Water Pollution by the Pulp and Paper Industry in Canada* (study under review by the Government and Competitiveness Project, School of Policy Studies, Queen's University, August).

Stanbury, W.T. (in press), "A Skeptic's Guide to the Claims of So-Called Public Interest Groups," *Canadian Public Administration* (forthcoming Winter 1993/94).

Stanbury, W.T. and George Lermer (1983), "Regulation and the Redistribution of Income and Wealth," *Canadian Public Administration* 26, no. 3: 378–401.

Stanbury, W.T. and Peter Thain (1986), *The Origins of Rent Regulation in Ontario* (Toronto: Ontario Commission of Inquiry into Residential Tenancies).

Stanbury, W.T. and J.D. Todd (1990), *Rent Regulation: The Ontario Experience* (Vancouver: The Canadian Real Estate Research Bureau).

# P O S T S C R I P T

**D**oes the heavenly chorus in the pluralist heaven sing with a strong upper-class accent? As Coleman shows, there are good reasons to think so, yet some doubt still exists. Coleman believes that business interests are perceived positively by society, which in turn makes it easier for them to gain access to government. But as Stanbury argues, business is often seen as morally inferior and acting in a manner that does little to advance the public interest. Coleman also contends that business interests find it much easier to organize themselves than do other interests. This may be true, but the relative ease with which business comes together does not necessarily mean that other groups—environmental, consumer, labour, and the like—go unorganized. Finally, there appear to be many developments in political life that clearly go against business interests. Defeat is not unknown to the captains of industry.

If there is some doubt about the influence of business groups, can one conclude that the heavenly chorus has many different accents? William Stanbury thinks one can, but his arguments raise some questions. Are the constraints on business sufficient to reduce it to merely one interest among many? Surely the fact that Canada is a capitalist country gives business a decided advantage. Stanbury also suggests that access to government need not translate into real power, but he himself concedes that access does have an effect on what government does. More generally, Stanbury appears at times to conceive government as a free-standing entity able to make decisions in any manner it sees fit; but in fact the state in a capitalist society, as Coleman argues, is dependent on—and thus vulnerable to—representatives of business.

Both Coleman and Stanbury have written extensively on the matter of relations between business and government. For further insights into Coleman's thinking on business and government, one should consult his texts *Business and Politics: A Study of Collective Action* (Montreal: McGill-Queen's University Press, 1988) and *The State, Business and Indus-*

*trial Change in Canada* (Toronto: University of Toronto Press, 1989) (co-authored with M.M. Atkinson). As for Stanbury, his ideas are fleshed out in W.T. Stanbury, *Business–Government Relations in Canada: Influencing Public Policy* (Scarborough: Nelson, 1993). Another work worth considering is Stephen Brooks and Andrew Stritch, *Business and Government in Canada* (Scarborough: Prentice-Hall, 1991). The book offers a good introduction to its subject matter.

Any student concerned with the study of business and government must become familiar with the operation of interest groups and organized interests. In his book *Group Politics and Public Policy*, 2nd ed. (Toronto: Oxford University Press, 1992), A. Paul Pross offers a comprehensive analysis of interest groups in Canada. The set of readings edited by William D. Coleman and Grace Skogstad entitled *Policy Communities and Public Policy in Canada: A Structural Approach* (Toronto: Copp Clark Pitman, 1990) is also helpful in this regard.

# ISSUE EIGHTEEN

## Do the Media Distort Election Campaigns?

**YES** DAVID TARAS, "Bad Habits and Broken Promises: The Media and Election Campaigns"

**NO** MICHAEL NOLAN, "Don't Shoot the Messenger: The Media and Election Campaigns"

In the federal election campaign of 1993, Canadian voters learned that Kim Campbell could dance, that Jean Chrétien struggled with the English language, and that Audrey McLaughlin liked to talk to her friends on the telephone. These perspectives on three of the major party leaders were brought to us by way of the national media. Canada faced a number of serious problems, many of which might have been addressed during the campaign, yet television, newspapers, and other elements in the media seemingly slighted any serious discussion of the issues. Dancing appeared more important than people without jobs.

In the minds of many, the media actively distort and trivialize election campaigns. The aforementioned coverage of the party leaders was typical, and one need only look at any facet of the electoral process for further evidence of the negative impact of the media. Take, for example, the leader's tour, an important part of any campaign. The media might report on the philosophies and beliefs of the various leaders and their parties, and thus serve to inform the electorate. But instead, it is argued, we get pictures and stories that emphasize style over substance. We know all about the personal lives of the candidates, but little about what they would do as prime minister.

Others aspects of election campaigns also supposedly suffer at the hands of the media. Increasingly, political parties employ ads that have only a very tenuous relationship with the truth. It might be expected that the media would alert voters to this fact, but they rarely do. As well, the media rely obsessively on polls. What matters, it seems, is who is in the lead. The issues become unimportant, an unwanted intrusion into the excitement of the race.

Though most agree that the media are not without fault, there are some who argue that the charges against the media are exaggerated or misdirected. Election campaigns do focus on personalities and steer away from the issues, but this is largely a product of party strategies. Political parties, not the media, package the leaders, and ensure that the tough questions receive little attention. Similarly, parties create the ads, and expecting the media to offer a critique of the latter seems somewhat paternalistic. Why not let the voters—the targets—assess the ads? Finally, it is contended that the media do actually provide useful information to voters, and they have recently adopted practices that increase the chances that voters will receive a clear view of party beliefs.

In the readings, David Taras, a leading student of media and politics, argues that the media have a distorting effect on electoral campaigns. Michael Nolan, a professor of journalism, agrees that election campaigns have some less than ennobling features, but lays most of the blame with political parties.

# Bad Habits and Broken Promises: The Media and Election Campaigns

*David Taras*

In the last generation, politicians, political parties, and the House of Commons have fallen drastically in public esteem.[1] Politicians tend no longer to be believed, and many of our national institutions are under challenge and attack. Cynicism among Canadians runs deep, as do feelings of anger and disappointment. There is a sense that a trust has been broken.

Most Canadians learn what they know about politics from watching television. Television has been for quite some time the basic organizing principle of politics. It is the window through which leaders communicate with citizens and citizens view their leaders. Yet the television lens is a distorted one, and in that distortion may lie some of the reasons that Canadians have developed such a profound distaste, such a deep disillusionment, with the political process. For most citizens, elections are the time when the political system is most on display.

To a large degree journalists know what has gone wrong with election reporting. They know that their daily reporting from the leader's tour is often shallow and sensational, dwelling on gaffes and blunders and hot visuals rather than on the substance and consequences of policy proposals. They know that they focus on the "horse race," who's ahead and who's behind, because it's easy to do; far easier than attempting to capture or sustain a debate about the issues that confront the electorate. And they know that they promote and report poll results in ways that are often hyped and misleading. They also know that political ads, which can strike with devastating effectiveness, sometimes play to people's fears and prejudices and may be based on falsehoods. But these ads are seldom analyzed or questioned by the networks who show them. Yet journalists feel trapped. It's difficult to depart from the old ways and old routines and to kick bad habits.

This article will review some of the problems that have plagued election coverage in Canada and recommend ways in which the seriousness of the process and its integrity might be enhanced.

# FEAR AND LOATHING ON THE LEADER'S TOUR

The leader's tour has become the site for ritual combat between the politicians and the reporters who cover them. The parties know that the election will be won by the party that sets the agenda—that can get its message and priorities, its vision of reality, across to voters. The key, then, is to package campaign events to fit the needs and requirements of television. Leaders will try to "win" each day of coverage by giving reporters the lofty-sounding phrases, humorous quips, or insulting rebukes of their opponents that fit into the ten- to twenty-second sound bites that are required for TV stories. Campaign appearances are choreographed so that journalists are given exciting and compelling pictures that are designed to be irresistible to television, pictures that contain the candidate's message. Michael Deaver, the impresario behind Ronald Reagan's election campaigns, described how the tactical game is played: "The media, while they won't admit it, are not in the news business; they're in entertainment. We tried to create the most entertaining, visually attractive scene to fill the box, so that the networks would have to use it."[2]

The 1993 Canadian election was filled with images of the party leaders at boisterous campaign rallies, main-streeting with voters, and speaking in front of colourful backdrops. One of the most enduring images was of Preston Manning catching a pass and taking the ball in for a touchdown during a touch-football game. Earlier in the same report he was shown talking to reporters in front of a pioneer log cabin. In the weeks leading up to the election, voters were treated to Kim Campbell taking a subway ride in Toronto, doing the twist on the dance floor, and playing with a lobster's tail at a Nova Scotia barbecue. Jean Chrétien was shown water-skiing and kayaking. During the campaign Chrétien emphasized his patriotic message by speaking in front of a backdrop of twelve Canadian flags. Campaign events that were once genuine opportunities for leaders to meet and speak directly to voters are now designed to look and, in effect, to be a TV advertisement.

Reporters are well aware that there are dangers that come with the bait that is dangled in front of them each day. They are wary of swallowing the candidate's message whole and of falling into the traps that are set for them. Moreover, the media have their own agenda. They filter the events of the campaign through their own routines and requirements: the perceived need to show confrontation and controversy, a focus on the personalities and foibles of the leaders, and a fixation with reporting the excitement of the horse-race, the drama of who's ahead and who's behind. Reporters also have a justifiable fear of "flackery," of appearing to be a mouthpiece for the politicians. There is now a well-developed cult of machismo that expects reporters to treat all claims made by political leaders with scepticism, and to be tough in questioning politicians and in pointing out their weaknesses. Instead of reporting the pretty pictures and cotton-candy comments that the campaign has neatly laid out for them, TV journalists are just as likely to be telling their viewers about campaign strategies, behind-the-scenes politics, and the ways in which the events being reported have been staged for television.

Both sides are caught in a vicious circle. The politicians try to fit their messages into the media's frame, and journalists are critical of politicians, and deny them air time and access, precisely because their messages seem so contrived and false. The continual complaint of politicians is that their messages are either abbreviated into such short sound bites or so twisted out of context by reporters that they cannot reach voters effectively through network news coverage. During the 1988 federal election the average amount of time in which leaders were heard on CBC's *"The National"* was approximately twenty seconds per broadcast. This was extended to thirty seconds in the last week of the campaign after complaints were received from the political parties.[3] While an analysis has not yet been done for the 1993 election, it appears that there was little difference from the 1988 campaign.

In American presidential races the average length of a sound bite has been reduced from 42 seconds during the 1968 presidential election to 7.3 seconds in the first five months of the 1992 campaign. Reporters' comments "ate up" 72 percent of all election-news air time during the 1992 campaign.[4]

The deadlock appeared to have been broken, however, during the last American election as presidential contenders decided to bypass regular network news programs and appear on outlets that would give them greater access to voters. The format explosion that had rocked the American media in the late 1980s and early 1990s gave candidates a host of new vehicles for campaigning. Candidates held forth on everything from drive-time radio hotline shows to pop culture venues such as MTV, from the TV talk show circuit with its cast of irascible characters Donahue, Arsenio Hall, Geraldo Rivera, and Larry King to early morning programs such as "Good Morning America." *Rolling Stone* magazine went so far as to describe these programs and channels as the "New News."[5] These formats differ from the "Old News" in that they offer long interviews, easy access, and direct unmediated communication between candidates and voters. They are also, of course, quirky and driven even more than network news by the freakish and sensational.

In Canada, political leaders have not been able to break out of the old cycle. There are fewer outlets in Canada that allow political leaders to circumvent the routine pathways of election campaigning and therefore the elaborate and predictable ritual dance that must be performed with a critical press. While there are a myriad of radio hotline shows, early morning news programs, new specialty channels such as Much Music and CBC Newsworld, the audiences for these programs and channels tend to be quite small. Nonetheless, following the American trend, Kim Campbell made an appearance on Radio-Canada's counterculture show "L'enfer, c'est nous autres" and Jean Chrétien was interviewed in-between rock videos on Much Music.

The most disturbing aspect of coverage for the parties, however, is the extent to which performance rather than ideas and mood rather than policies have become frameworks for analyzing the campaign. According to Matthew Mendelsohn's study of TV coverage of the 1988 election, for reporters "strategy equals motivation: why a leader does something is based solely on strategy."[6] Leaders are almost never depicted as having firm principles, or as acting on the basis of strong ideologies or beliefs. The assumption is that policies are just conveniences that politicians grab on to and then dispose of at the right moments.

Moreover, leaders are judged by their performances rather than by the content of their policy proposals or their visions of the future. Mendelsohn has described how during the 1988 election leaders were continually evaluated based on whether or not they performed well or were seen as "strong," "relaxed," "confident," or "pleased," as opposed to appearing "weak," "nervous," "troubled," or "beleaguered."[7] This is especially the case with respect to leaders' debates. The debates are described almost as if they are prize fights with reporters looking for the "knockout punch," who got in the most blows, and who would remain standing at the end. Winning and losing depend on performance rather than on having the most sensible prescriptions or the most innovative ideas.

While the debates are one of the few opportunities that leaders have for unmediated access to the voters and to challenge each other directly, television still manages to distort the picture. TV reporters and producers inevitably choose a single twenty- or thirty-second exchange out of a two- or three-hour debate to be replayed as the highlight of the debate on newscasts. The leaders and their handlers know that it is the sharp confrontations and biting one-liners that will make the TV news clips, and that those clips will be shown again and again throughout the remainder of the election. Not surprisingly, all of the leaders come well armed with hard-hitting or humorous quips and zingers in anticipation that their one-liner will be part of the "demon or enduring" clip that, in effect, wins them the debate.

During the 1984 debate, Brian Mulroney's stinging rebuke of John Turner on the issue of patronage appointments, in which he lectured Turner, "Well, you had an option, sir," became the symbol and in some ways the defining moment of the election. In 1988, Turner won the battle of the TV clips when he tore into Mulroney on the issue of free trade, claiming that Mulroney had "sold us out to the Americans."

The "winning" clip from the 1993 election appears to have been Lucien Bouchard's confrontation with Kim Campbell over the size of the deficit for 1993. Bouchard battered and hectored Campbell about why she was unwilling to reveal the deficit number. The clip showing Campbell's steadfast refusal to answer Bouchard was repeated on network news programs throughout the remainder of the campaign. It became, one can argue, a symbol of a leader who seemed aloof, out of touch, and indifferent.

The question is how to reform the process that has both politicians and the media becoming in Tom Oliphant's words, "the serial killers of democracy."[8] One suggestion is that the networks broadcast the leaders' "stump speeches" in their entirety and that these be analyzed and dissected for their meaning and accuracy. Another idea is that there be many more opportunities for unmediated interaction between candidates and voters; a series of town hall meetings, for instance, where party leaders would field questions from ordinary citizens. Moreover, this should be done on the main channels and not be relegated to the back alleys of cable—to CBC Newsworld and the Parliamentary Channel—where audiences remain small.

The town hall meetings that were broadcast by the CBC's "Prime Time News" during the 1993 election did not feature party leaders, except for Preston Manning and Mel Hurtig who appeared in the last town hall meeting of the campaign, and the audiences seemed to consist of some very "unordinary" Canadians, people who seem to have been chosen because they had extremely hostile attitudes toward politicians. Indeed, the CBC seemed through the town halls to be legitimizing voter cynicism and the denigration of the political process.

Journalists should be urged to step out of their traditional frames of analysis to discuss the political philosophies that distinguish the political parties and the consequences of some of the specific policies that are being proposed much more than is presently the case. This might force politicians to discuss proposals in a detailed way, to do their homework, and to address issues that they would like to avoid. The CBC's "Prime Time News" did an in-depth analysis of Jean Chrétien's policies only after the Liberals had been elected.

There is also a place for dealing with character issues that goes beyond evaluating the superficial aspects of performance or searching for the smoking gun of scandal. Doris Kearns has proposed a checklist of questions that political reporters should ask when they are on the campaign trail.[9] Some of these are:

- How does a candidate cope with setbacks, aggravations, frustrations?

- Does a leader evoke emotion in the crowds that she or he is addressing?

- How is the leader with people? Does a politician reach out and touch or does she or he shrink from physical contact?

- How much mental and physical energy does the leader display?

- How truthful is a candidate's picture of reality?

Jay Rosen has argued that the primary mission of journalists should be to make politics "go well."[10] Elections with the help of more conscientious reporting can produce in Rosen's view "a discussion in which the polity learns more about itself, its current problems, its real divisions, its place in time, its prospects for the future."[11] Canadians have to ask whether that vision is now being fulfilled.

# ADVENTURES IN ADVERTISINGLAND

One way the political parties have of reaching voters directly is through TV ads or spots. Parties spend most of their total election campaign expenditures on TV advertising. The 1988 national election study found that "the impact of advertising on the bottom line—the vote—may be indirect but it is not obviously trivial."[12] This is a convoluted way of saying that advertising made a difference. TV spots are powerful weapons because they allow parties to define themselves, and perhaps more important, to define their opponents without interference from journalists. Their power also lies in the fact that they strive for a feeling and not a position. They appeal to basic instincts and fears. The best ads touch raw nerves and produce hot-button emotional responses.

In a previous work, I described TV advertising as the "nuclear weapons" of the political system because they have the capacity to lay waste any possibility for meaningful debate.[13] They are an open door for false claims, incomplete facts, half-truths, and innuendoes. And as advertising techniques have become more sophisticated and the ads more symbolic, more allegorical, falsehoods are less blatant and more difficult to detect.

Studies indicate that negative ads, called "attack" or "black" spots, can be especially effective if they are rooted in voters' existing beliefs. While voters are likely to tell pollsters that they don't like negative advertising, studies indicate that voters have greater recall of negative material and that they process it more deeply.

Perhaps the most startling ad of the 1980s was the famous Willie Horton ad that appeared during the 1988 U.S. presidential election. The spot, which was paid for by a private pro-Republican group, showed pictures of Willie Horton, a black man who had been convicted of murder, and described how he had committed rape and assault after being let out on a weekend pass from a Massachusetts prison. The intention was to paint Massachusetts Governor Michael Dukakis as weak on crime and to remind voters that George Bush supported the death penalty while Dukakis didn't. The ad hit with devastating effect. Focus-group testing revealed that the ad tapped racially based prejudices, with many respondents even embellishing the grisly events described in the ad. According to Kathleen Hall Jamieson, Dean of the Annenberg School of Communication at the University of Pennsylvania, "Willie Horton came to incarnate liberalism's failures and voters' fears."[14]

Through the power of sheer repetition Dukakis's "record" on crime was driven home to voters. What the ad had neglected to point out was that the Horton incident was an extraordinarily rare occurrence and that the crime rate had actually fallen during Michael Dukakis's tenure as governor of Massachusetts.

A new innovation during the 1992 U.S. presidential race was Ross Perot's thirty-minute "infomercial," a free-wheeling lecture on the problems of the American economy replete with charts and graphs. The ad attracted a surprisingly large audience. Perot's version of America's economic troubles was, however, filled with a welter of exaggerations and inaccuracies, such as his much heralded claim that 70 percent of the microchips used in the United States were imported. The problem, according to Tom Rosenstiel of *The Los Angeles Times*, is that thirty-minute commercials are much more difficult to police or counter than thirty-second commercials.[15]

The low point in the history of election advertising in Canada was probably reached during the 1990 Ontario provincial election when the NDP ran an ad that looked as if it contained genuine TV news reports. An actor pretending to be a news anchor reported, "Drinking water has sent hundreds to hospital but the Liberal government says it cannot pass legislation." Another actor playing a TV news reporter told viewers "He accepted a Caribbean vacation and a food processor; the Liberal minister reacted angrily." None of the stories "reported" in the ad were true, but the fact that they had appeared in a newscast format gave them resonance and credibility.

The use of attack or black ads always runs the risk that the ads will cause a backlash that puts into question the judgment and credibility of those who made and sponsored them. During the 1993 election the Conservatives ran an ad that used photographs focusing on Jean Chrétien's partially paralyzed mouth. The ad, which caused an immediate uproar, was quickly pulled off the air. Tory strategists have pointed out, however, that the ad appeared to be working.

What has added to the problem in Canadian federal elections is that the playing field is tilted in favour of established parties and especially the party that is in power. The amount of time allocated to each party for both paid and free-time TV broadcasts is arrived at through a formula based on how the parties performed in the previous election. During the 1993 election each broadcaster was required to sell 390 minutes of advertising to the political parties based on the following breakdown:

Conservatives: 116 minutes
Liberals: 78 minutes
NDP: 55 minutes
Reform: 17 minutes
Christian Heritage: 16 minutes
Green: 15 minutes
Bloc Québécois: 5 minutes
National: 5 minutes

Under these rules, the Tories and the Liberals were able both to swamp the air waves with images of Kim Campbell and Jean Chrétien and to target specific groups of swing voters by buying time on shows that attracted audiences with certain demographic characteristics. Newer parties such as the Reform Party and the Bloc Québécois were not allocated enough minutes to allow them to get their basic messages out.

One can argue that the success of Reform and the Bloc is evidence that TV ads are not as influential as some analysts believe. Of course, the ineptness of the Conservatives' ad campaign may have had something to do with the success that these parties achieved, and they may have done even better had they had greater access to the air waves.

Over the years there have been a number of attempts to reform campaign advertising. In Canada, the Royal Commission on Electoral Reform and Party Financing (the Lortie Commission) has suggested that parties be limited to buying 100 minutes of advertising on each broadcaster, and that free-time ads be organized into magazine-style programs so that voters could compare party messages.

In the United States, newspapers, led by *The Los Angeles Times*, began in the late 1980s to feature "truth boxes" that evaluated the accuracy of claims made in campaign spots. These efforts proved quite haphazard during the 1992 presidential election as newspapers such as *The Washington Post* and *The New York Times* sometimes missed ads altogether or discussed the strategies behind the ads rather than their truthfulness.

Some analysts believe that steps need to be taken to regulate the content of the ads. One view is that candidates should be forced to appear in the ads themselves. This would eliminate endorsements by celebrities, the use of figures like Willie Horton, or symbolic or allegorical ads that attempt to stir emotions. Another proposal would limit candidates to speaking about the merits of their own platforms, positions, and proposals rather than engaging in pit-bull attacks against their opponents.

The current morality is perhaps best exemplified by the philosophy of Roger Ailes, one of the leading political strategists and consultants in the United States, who offers the following advice: "Hit the opponent at his weakest point, at the most opportune time, with the least loss to one-self. If you don't have anything bad to say about the opponent, why don't you just let him have the job."[16]

# THE POLLING MONSTER

Polling has become the addictive drug of election reporting. Close to fif-teen polls were reported during the 1993 Canadian federal election, almost one every three days of the campaign. During the 1992 U.S. pres-idential race, over 200 polls were reported between July and election day. As Tom Rosenstiel has observed: "Polls had become the press's big-gest bias, not liberalism or malice or recklessness. Polls were the lens by which the press viewed everything."[17]

As polls dominate news coverage, this inevitably washes over into the campaign, structuring the behaviour and strategies of both parties and voters. Matthew Mendelsohn has documented the extent to which polls fuelled television's obsession with reporting the horse race, making it the singular frame of analysis during the 1988 federal election. Accord-ing to Mendelsohn, "A good poll changes the tone of the coverage, posi-tive or negative, but the frames continue to retain momentum and standing."[18] He quotes, for example, Peter Mansbridge's lead on CBC's "The National" on October 29: "Liberal euphoria. A new poll says they're tied with the Conservatives. Taking off the gloves—Mulroney says he's coming out to fight. What a difference a poll makes. The whole complexion of the election campaign has changed...."[19]

The effects of this kind of coverage are difficult to calculate. Some analysts believe that there is a "bandwagon" effect. The party that is lead-ing in the polls can receive an enormous lift; more money from corpora-tions and interest groups for whom it is important to back a winner, and for the same reason, a larger and more eager force of campaign workers. But most important, the image of being a winner breeds its own success. The leader and the campaign are seen as having momentum, as hitting the right notes. Studies also suggest that journalists are not as tough on politicians that are riding a crest of popularity.[20] Alan McGirr, the Reform Party's communications director, has described the effect that poll results had on the coverage given to the Reform Party during the 1993 campaign: "There is absolutely no denying that the media took their cue on how to cover this thing from polls they saw at the start....

When our numbers came up, they joined the bus, I have to confess it—we needed the polls."[21]

For those who are behind in the polls the calculus is different. The stampede moves in the opposite direction. Poor poll results are a knife at the heart of the campaign. A losing image can stick like tar as leaders are continually badgered by reporters about why they are doing so poorly, what they are doing wrong, why the campaign isn't working. This can quickly become a self-fulfilling prophecy as panic sets in and campaigns resort to desperate strategies to repair the damage. In the last two weeks of the 1993 election, poll results ate away at Kim Campbell's campaign, forcing her into ever more fitful attempts to head off the stampede of voters to other parties.

A 1988 national election study described the resonating effect that the reporting of polls had in that election: "The impact of polls was not small; net of all other factors in the estimation, a unit shift in the Liberals' poll standing induced roughly a 0.4 point further shift. This is just the first-round impact. Unlike other factors, polls are reflexive; earlier shifts induce later ones, as their impact is registered in subsequent polls and further transmitted back as expectations and preferences."[22] During the 1993 election, media reports continually reminded voters about the importance of "strategic" voting, the notion that one should not necessarily vote for the party that one preferred but in a way that would make one's vote count in the larger picture. Studies have not yet been done on the effects that the media's "cues" about strategic voting have had on voting behaviour.

The most disturbing aspect of the media's handling of polls is that they are often reported in a misleading way. Often TV reports or newspaper headlines will trumpet the fact that a particular party or leader is ahead in a poll without any information about the discrepancies that can result from the margin of error. If the Liberals are described, for instance, as having 35 percent support while the Reform Party has 31 percent, and if the poll has a margin of error of 4 percent (based on the size of the sample), then Liberal support is actually anywhere from 31 to 39 percent and that for Reform between 27 and 35 percent. If the poll was conducted again, the same sample could show Reform as being in the lead or both parties running neck and neck. News organizations are often too interested in declaring winners and losers, and in sensational results, to bother explaining these critical nuances.

Surveys are such sensitive instruments that even small changes in the wording or sequence of questions can produce dramatically different results. One pollster recently noted that when the name Hillary Clinton was used, the American First Lady scored 15 percent higher in popularity than when respondents were asked about Hillary Rodham Clinton. It has also not been unknown for pollsters to "stack" the results by leading respondents through a series of sensitizing or softening-up questions that subtly suggest a particular choice or course of action, i.e., the "correct" answer.

Some media organizations remain oblivious to the problems associated with polls because publishing or reporting polls is a tremendous boon in terms of publicity and prestige. Polls create headline-grabbing stories and they give the impression that journalists are on top of events. News organizations that sponsor polls gain increased stature and credibility as they are catapulted to the centre of a news story and become players in the election game. Moreover, the polling firms for whom elections are a publicity "Olympics," a once in four years opportunity for massive public exposure, are often willing to offer their services to news organizations at cut-rate prices. This makes using polls even more irresistible.

Some analysts believe that there should be a ban on reporting survey results in the last week or ten days of an election campaign. The argument is that such action would force the media and voters to concentrate on party messages and policies rather than on which party is ahead in the horse race. It would break the passivity that infects many voters. To paraphrase one political veteran, "voters will have to go to the game because they won't be able to tune in the score."[23] Others contend, however, that this would be a form of censorship that deprives voters of one of the most important rights in a democracy—access to the opinions of their fellow citizens. Voters will make better judgments, moreover, if they have all of the available information at their disposal.

One might ask whether voters are being deprived of information in another way. Are basic messages about party policies and the choices that the country is facing being drowned out by a media-created cacophony? If, as Rosen has argued, the role of journalists is to make politics "go well," then don't citizens have the right to expect both a greater professionalism in explaining how polls work and what they mean, and some self-restraint to ensure that surveys do not become, in and of themselves, the decisive weapons in the political battlefield? Much depends on whether journalists are willing to kick bad habits and use polls differently.

Polls could go beyond the horse race to probe more deeply the attitudes to important public policy issues. News organizations could provide temperature readings about changing opinions on health care, free trade, the educational system, or about how and in what ways people would like to see the deficit cut. These findings could be used to ask questions of the leaders on the campaign trail and to ensure that vital concerns are not lost amid mud-slinging attacks and election hoopla. They could be used, in short, to make politics "go well."

# CONCLUSIONS

This article argues that horse race journalism, advertising spots, and the media's handling of polls are areas in which reforms are necessary. A main concern is that politicians and news organizations through their constant emphasis on image and hype and gaffes are actually displaying a contempt for voters. They don't seem to believe that citizens have the capacity to deal with the issues that affect their lives in a serious and sophisticated way. Horse race journalism and the politics of "photo ops," however, are usually seen by citizens for what they are, and this ultimately brings the entire political system into disrepute. Politicians feel abused by the media's brutal editing of their messages into brief sound bites, journalists feel manipulated because party messages are so contrived and campaign events are staged for the cameras, and the public is short-changed because it doesn't receive a realistic picture of the kind of world and the kinds of choices that governments are facing. There is in all of this the gravest of broken promises, the failure of the system itself.

While powerful vested interests are likely to ensure that the election music will go on playing pretty much as it has been, dramatic changes in tone are needed to restore and heal the political process.

## NOTES

1. Royal Commission on Electoral Reform and Party Financing, *Reforming Electoral Democracy*, vol. 1 (Ottawa: Minister of Supply and Services Canada, 1991) pp. 223–28.

2. Quoted in Timothy Russert, "For '92, the Networks Have to Do Better," *The New York Times*, March 4, 1990, p. 23.

3. *Reforming Electoral Democracy*, vol. 1, pp. 377–78.

4. Paul Taylor, "Political Coverage in the 1990s: Teaching the Old News New Tricks," in *The New News v. The Old News: The Press and Politics in the 1990s* (New York: The Twentieth Century Fund, 1992), p. 41.

5. Ibid., p. 38.

6. Matthew Mendelsohn, "Television's Frames in the 1988 Canadian Election," *Canadian Journal of Communication* 18, no. 2 (Spring 1993): 154.

7. Ibid., p. 160.

8. Quoted in Taylor, "Political Coverage in the 1990s," p. 55.

9. Ibid., p. 58.

10. Jay Rosen, "Politics, Vision and the Press: Toward a Public Agenda for Journalism," in *The New News v. The Old News: The Press and Politics in the 1990s*, p. 10.

11. Ibid.

12. Richard Johnston, André Blais, Henry Brady, and Jean Crete, *Letting the People Decide: Dynamics of a Canadian Election* (Montreal and Kingston: McGill-Queen's University Press, 1992), p. 243.

13. David Taras, *The Newsmakers: The Media's Influence on Canadian Politics* (Scarborough: Nelson, 1990).

14. Kathleen Hall Jamieson, *Dirty Politics: Deception, Distraction and Democracy* (New York: Oxford, 1992), p. 42.

15. Tom Rosenstiel, *Strange Bedfellows: How Television and the Presidential Candidates Changed American Politics, 1992* (New York: Hyperion, 1993), p. 295.

16. Quoted in Paul Taylor, *See How They Run: Electing the President in an Age of Mediaocracy* (New York: Alfred A. Knopf, 1990), p. 194.

17. Rosenstiel, *Strange Bedfellows,* p. 329.

18. Mendelsohn, "Television's Frames in the 1988 Canadian Election," p. 154.

19. Ibid.

20. David Paletz and Robert Entman, *Media Power Politics* (New York: The Free Press, 1981), pp. 69–70.

21. Quoted in Kirk Makin, "How Chrétien Rose in the Media Market, "*The Globe and Mail,* November 4, 1993, p. A1.

22. Johnston et al., *Letting the People Decide,* p. 222.

23. Taras, *The Newsmakers,* p. 193.

# NO

# Don't Shoot The Messenger: The Media And Election Campaigns

*Michael Nolan*

In the interplay between federal politicians and the mass media, an underlying tension has existed at election time. Since effective communication with the electorate is a prerequisite for the attainment of power, politicians look for and require favourable media exposure. The political parties through their hired media specialists seek to control the election campaign environment.

The electronic media are placed at the disposal of the political parties as in the case of paid and free broadcast time. At another media level, party strategists seek to manage journalists who report the principal campaign developments for newspapers, radio, and television.

In short, the mass media by themselves do not distort the electoral process. Both paid and free-time political broadcasts serve as facilitators for the parties in the transmission of their policies and campaign messages. Print and broadcast journalists are placed in reactive positions and made to adhere to campaign formats and structures that do not always allow for the practice of effective and meaningful reportage.

The Final Report of the Royal Commission on Electoral Reform and Party Financing in 1991 noted: "It is important to distinguish between the broadcast media, which have been regulated almost since their inception, and the print media, which have not (though they are subject to some legal restrictions of general application, such as the laws of libel and slander). This discussion will focus on the broadcast media given television's major role in campaign strategies; the print media will receive only passing comment.

It is also essential to distinguish between those forms of campaign communication that allow the parties relatively direct access to voters and those that are filtered through journalists and commentators."[1] Paid-time and free-time broadcasts are the "unmediated" forms of campaign communication, because they give parties direct access to the electorate largely free of intervention by journalists. A second channel of campaign communication that the royal commission report described as "partially mediated" involves such campaign events as televised debates among party leaders and radio and TV talk shows. A third "mediated" channel of communication includes news coverage and public affairs shows where the broadcast media dictate the format.[2]

# UNMEDIATED FORMATS: PAID AND FREE PARTY BROADCASTS

Throughout the 1960s and early 1970s election campaigns became skilfully managed; political parties devoted much of their campaign efforts to communicating their messages through paid and free-time party broadcasts. While they naturally sought to give themselves every advantage in such advertising, the political circumstances and general attitude of voters in the country could neutralize the capacity for distortion in the political broadcasts. Typical was the Liberal Party's attempt to conduct the 1972 election campaign based on a political slogan, "The Land is Strong."

The slogan, devised by George Elliott, a MacLaren Advertising executive, was central to the Liberal Party's paid advertising; still "The Land is Strong" was largely ineffectual, because the disquieting state of the economy and voter concern over unemployment prevented its intended impact. In the end, the Liberals led by Pierre Trudeau, who four years earlier had basked in "Trudeaumania," nearly went down to defeat.

Nicholas Cotter, a corporate relations staff member of a Toronto industrial firm, offered the following comment in *The Globe and Mail* on the advertisement: "It is probable that given a more confident economy, the Liberal slogan of The Land is Strong would have been a powerful one. But the timing and manner in which it was exposed to the electorate seemed to represent a grotesque mismatch with the prevailing public mood."[3]

Two years later, Richard Gwyn concluded that the paid and free-time broadcasts in the 1974 federal election were "empty" but did not mislead: "The ads and free-time broadcasts (each party pays the production costs for programs watched by about 1.5 million people on the full CBC-TV network) are pure propaganda. Yet they contain no mistruths or gross distortions."[4]

However, Dennis Braithwaite lamented the fact that paid political broadcasts did lead to distortion in an article entitled "Parties' TV Ads Distort the Campaign." Significantly, he placed the blame squarely on the shoulders of the party strategists and not the television medium itself: "Just as television itself is debased in our society by being placed almost exclusively at the service of admen instead of used as a means of communicating art, entertainment and information to an intellectually-starved public, so we find the medium at election time employed in corrupting the democratic process."[5]

Although heavy emphasis was given to the electronic media by all political parties in 1974, newspapers still could play an important role in party advertising. For example, the Conservative Party announced plans for "a massive advertising blitz" involving newspapers, radio, and television in the two weeks preceding the vote on July 8.[6] Among all three media, newspapers perhaps have the least capacity for distortion. Campaign specialists have viewed the newspaper as having an essentially informational role as opposed to the capability of the electronic media for persuading and capturing the uncommitted voter.[7]

From the early 1970s to the present, all political parties have continued to refine their "unmediated" electioneering practices. A recent innovation has been the controversial negative advertising or "attack" ads. Regardless of any potential for distortion and no matter how distasteful the advertisements may be perceived, parties appear to be entitled to have available to them such campaign weapons. The open nature of the democratic electoral process and the freedom provided to the parties in paid and free-time broadcasts allow them maximum latitude to reach voters directly on their own terms.

A Republican consultant, Michael Murphy, told a Campaigns and Election Training program conference in Toronto in November 1990 that negative election campaigning is part of both the Canadian and American political cultures. In his report of the conference, Graham Fraser noted Murphy's concern about the simplicity of the message in negative advertising and his placing of responsibility for such techniques on the voters: "If the voters wanted more complex messages they would get them."[8]

Clearly there appears to be no discounting the considerable impact of negative advertising. Walter I. Romanow and Walter C. Soderlund, in their book *Media Canada: An Introductory Analysis,* have written: "Negative information appears to be far more powerful than positive information in crystallizing [*sic*] decisions for the electorate."[9] In a "post-election mea culpa" following the 1988 Canadian federal election, Jeffrey Simpson, the *Globe and Mail* political columnist, offered this comment on the Conservative advertisements against John Turner, the Liberal leader, late in the campaign: "That they were intellectually offensive and utterly contrived did not diminish their political impact in undermining the credibility of the Liberal Party and its leader."[10] Clearly this form of political advertising appears to be deliberately designed to accentuate a political opponent's leadership vulnerabilities; such campaign practices must be seen in the context of the competitive nature of electoral politics where parties are allowed to exploit the television medium. Here the parties—not the media—are responsible for any distortion of the election process.

# PARTIALLY MEDIATED EVENTS: INTERVIEW SHOWS AND LEADERS' DEBATES

The capacity for media distortion appears marginal in partially mediated events such as radio and television talk shows and televised leaders' debates during election campaigns. Political leaders can carefully select the talk shows on which they wish to appear and can largely avoid mediation of their efforts; such programs also enable politicians to target those voters they hope to win over.

Similarly, political party strategists who wish to see their candidate have every advantage are intimately involved in the discussion of the formats to be followed in TV debates among party leaders. In general, these forms of communication enable the political parties to have considerable scope in controlling the campaign environment. The chances of media deception or distortion seem to be reduced given the nature of the events, which are designed to facilitate the politicians.

The radio talk show format developed in the 1960s. As with other forms of electronic communication, federal politicians adopted a cautious, wait-and-see attitude before choosing to participate. However, in the 1972 federal campaign, their hesitant attitude gave way to the advantages to be gained from open-line programs: free broadcast time and news coverage. In his examination of the 1972 federal election, Walter Stewart has explained that the politician "has yet to be born who will refuse the chance to send his own golden voice along the airwaves at someone else's expense."[11]

By 1972, politicians had overcome their earlier conservative attitude toward the electronic media. As far back as May 1929, R.B. Bennett, then the opposition leader, refused to take part in a series of broadcasts between elections on the "Nation's Business" program over the Canadian National Railways radio stations. According to E. Austin Weir, Bennett, the Conservative leader, became convinced the programs were "Liberal propaganda."[12]

Similarly, all political parties turned down an invitation from the Canadian Broadcasting Corporation to participate in free-time televised broadcasts in the 1953 federal election at a time when the CBC network linked Ottawa, Toronto, and Montreal.[13] The politicians seemed uneasy about adjusting to the requirements of television, just as they had been cautious of radio; a much higher level of intimacy with voters was required in a television performance and a more conversational style of rhetoric.

Forty years after the introduction of television to Canada in 1952, and having enjoyed the security of familiarity with the radio talk show format, politicians were willing participants in televised talk shows. The political season surrounding both the 42nd presidential election campaign in 1992 in the United States and Canada's 35th general election in 1993 ushered in a new campaign age.

Rather than distorting the electoral process, the television talk show format, the newest campaign vehicle, afforded the politician every opportunity to discuss the issues closest to the people and to expose leadership capabilities in the most personalized way. The politician appeared to audiences as more populist than partisan, and was able to transcend political journalists and thereby remove a major adversary.

For example, H. Ross Perot made great use of this format early in 1992 when he declared an interest in seeking the U.S. presidency on the CNN phone-in show "Larry King Live"; Perot became an almost instant celebrity. Perot's successful campaign innovation later appeared to motivate Democrat Bill Clinton into an appearance on the Arsenio Hall show where he could display his versatility and saxophone artistry. Clinton offered viewers his personalized version of "Heartbreak Hotel," a song made popular by singer Elvis Presley whose electric performances in the 1950s shattered that quiescent decade.

Similarly, Jean Chrétien, the Canadian federal Liberal leader, and future prime minister, experimented with the televised talk show early in 1992 on CTV's "Shirley," a program hosted by Shirley Solomon. The intimacy and length of such programs, which often are free of serious cross-examination of the politician, enable political leaders to have a much broader field of action than that afforded through either paid "spot" advertising or the terse news sound "bite" when journalists act as mediators. The failure to provide a sufficient amount of hard and relevant political information, rather than any grave distortion of the truth or the electoral process, would appear to be the main constraint surrounding this particular campaign technique.

The televised leaders' debate is a campaign event that draws enormous media attention and can be perceived as a major campaign highlight. In Canada, there have been five election debates among federal party leaders: during the elections of 1968, 1979, 1984, 1988, and most recently 1993. While it is true that the journalistic focus on sound bites, knock-out lines, and winners and losers may trivialize and personalize the debates, there is no discounting the vital role that such partially mediated events play in the electoral process.

In initiating televised political debates, the television networks in Canada have extended themselves to ensure that distortion of the electoral process would be kept to a minimum. The question of fairness to all political parties and the public has been a matter of the highest priority for the media. The Canadian Broadcasting Corporation underlined the attention paid to the questions of "equity" as well as "flexibility" in its submission to the Royal Commission on Electoral Reform and Party

Financing: "Particular attention has been paid to the need for both apparent and real equity, as well as to the fact that circumstances dictate a need for flexibility, for a dynamic approach designed to recognize the public's right to assess both the parties' platforms and their leaders' abilities to explain and defend those platforms in a scrupulously fair context."[14]

Political TV debates are really the only campaign events that give voters visual opportunity to compare and measure the choices before them. Wilbur Schramm noted how the Kennedy–Nixon TV debates in the fall of 1960 got around the problem of "selective exposure"; Schramm explained that "no longer would it be possible for Republicans to hear Republican arguments only while Democrats stuck to Democratic arguments."[15]

At a public hearing of the Royal Commission on Electoral Reform and Party Financing, Peter Desbarats, Dean of the Graduate School of Journalism at the University of Western Ontario, argued that "the institution of the leaders' debate should be enshrined in electoral law." He explained to the commissioners: "Only in the televised debates, do voters have an opportunity to see their leaders unedited and to make judgments based on their own assessment of a leader's personality, intelligence, debating ability and so forth."[16]

# MEDIATED EVENTS: NEWS COVERAGE AND PUBLIC AFFAIRS SHOWS

During the six federal election campaigns between 1974 and 1993, the political parties shifted their campaign strategies toward nightly TV newscasts; journalists acted as filters of the political leaders' performances on the campaign trail. Party strategists have recognized that Canadians rely heavily on television news for their daily political information. Therefore, getting media exposure on TV news is considered crucial in devising a party's campaign strategy.

Not surprisingly, campaign specialists aware of the requirements of television have become exceedingly adept at providing journalists accompanying the party leaders with the necessary TV visuals and appropriate sound material of the political leaders' words. Journalists have been managed and forced to operate within the constraints imposed by party strategists. Paid political advertising appeared to give way to, in the words of columnist Douglas Fisher, "the pseudo-events of the leadership trail."[17]

The Kent Report of the Royal Commission on Newspapers in 1981 lamented the media's neglect of regional issues, the tendency for journalists to focus on elections as a "horse race," and the absurdity of "pack journalism." Yet the report also noted that newspapers have provided "a wealth of detail about candidates and issues in election campaigns. Without this background information, many election reports on radio and TV would hardly make sense."[18]

Since the Kent Commission's findings, the electronic media have continued to attempt to refine their election coverage. The CTV network reported to the Canadian Radio-television and Telecommunications Commission following the 1988 federal election: "The combined domestic news gathering resources and facilities of CTV and its affiliated stations were applied to provide comprehensive coverage of the Federal General Election. CTV provided the national perspective and the affiliates focused primarily on the local and regional aspects." The network underlined the focus on issues: "CTV reporters crisscrossed the nation during the campaign in pursuit of the platforms and positions of the three main parties and of the emerging issues which would dominate the decisions of the electorate."[19]

Given the competitive aspect of electoral politics and the parties' emphasis on leadership, journalists have virtually no choice but to report the progress of the party leaders' campaigns. In some ways, a political campaign resembles a horse race. This style of uniform journalism tends to revolve around the reporting of public opinion polls and on a comparison and frequent assessment of the party leaders' campaigns. There is clear indication that the media recognize the heavy responsibility involved in this form of journalism necessitated by the polling techniques employed in modern-day elections.

The CBC submission to the Royal Commission on Electoral Reform and Party Financing noted: "As practising journalists, we are more than well aware of the pitfalls of easy interpretation and reliance on the superficialities of poll results." For this latter reason, the CBC introduced a reporting innovation during the 1988 federal election; the Corporation "regularly presented on 'The National' a graphic tracking of all the polls that had been reported thus far in the campaign." The intent was "to put the latest poll results into perspective" and also "to provide a context in which those results might be judged."[20]

# CONCLUSION

Whether the channels of campaign information are unmediated, partially mediated, or mediated, the broadcast media are either placed in the service of, or must respond to, the political parties and their agents who largely establish the structure and set the tone of the election campaign. Parties recognize that public opinion is media induced and try to exert control over the information provided to voters. The mass media are essentially the campaign messengers. They can hardly be held responsible for distortion of the electoral process.

# NOTES

1. Canada, *Final Report, Royal Commission on Electoral Reform and Party Financing, Reforming Electoral Democracy,* vol. 1 (Ottawa: Supply and Services, 1991), p. 375.

2. Ibid.

3. *The Globe and Mail,* February 6, 1973.

4. *The Toronto Star,* June 25, 1974.

5. *The Toronto Star,* June 18, 1974.

6. *The Globe and Mail,* June 5, 1974.

7. Interview between the author and George Elliott, February 11, 1974.

8. *The Globe and Mail,* November 12, 1990.

9. Walter I. Romanow and Walter C. Soderlund, *Media Canada: An Introductory Analysis* (Mississauga: 1992), p. 319.

10. *The Globe and Mail,* November 26, 1988.

11. Walter Stewart, *Divide and Con: Canadian Politics at Work* (Toronto: 1973), p. 109.

12. E. Austin Weir, *The Struggle for National Broadcasting in Canada* (Toronto: 1965), p. 32.

13. Interview between the author and Finlay Payne, December 14, 1974. See also Khayyam Z. Paltiel and Larry G. Kjosa, "The Structure and Dimensions of Election Broadcasting in Canada," *Jahrbuch des Öffentlichen Rechts der Gegenwart,* Neue Folge/Band 19, Tübingen, pp. 368, 356.

14. Submission to the Royal Commission on Electoral Reform and Party Financing by the Canadian Broadcasting Corporation, Ottawa, May 1990, p. 12.

15. Wilbur Schramm, *Men, Messages and Media: A Look at Human Communication* (New York: 1973), p. 279.

16. *Hearings of the Royal Commission on Electoral Reform and Party Financing,* Public Hearing, London, Ontario, May 10, 1990 (International Reporting Inc.), pp. 6918, 6915.

17. *The London Free Press,* June 26, 1974.

18. Canada, *Report of the Royal Commission on Newspapers* (Ottawa: Supply and Services, 1981), p. 143.

19. *A Report to the Canadian Radio-television and Telecommunications Commission by CTV Television Network Ltd. Regarding Coverage of the 1988 Federal General Election,* 4–5, 6. This report was provided to the author by staff of the Royal Commission on Electoral Reform and Party Financing.

20. Submission to the Royal Commission on Electoral Reform and Party Financing by the Canadian Broadcasting Corporation, Ottawa, May 1990, p. 5.

# P O S T S C R I P T

There is no question that the media play an important role in elections. Given that the electoral process is central to any democracy, it is imperative to determine whether this role is a positive one. For his part, Taras suggests that the media come up short, but doubt can be thrown on some of his assertions. Taras clearly dislikes the leaders' debates, where the quick repartee and amusing quip triumph over a learned discussion of the issues, and favours instead the broadcast of full speeches. It seems, however, that television viewers are unlikely to sit still for any speech, and one could argue (as Nolan does) that debates allow voters to acquire a clear and unadulterated picture of the candidates.

Taras also believes that the media uncritically accept party claims, but as he himself shows, important changes have been made to reduce this problem. Moreover, a charge made against the media is that they are *too* critical—the media are "damned if they do and damned if they don't." Finally, Taras seems to believe that an informed electorate requires a rational, almost scholarly, presentation of the facts. Yet, debates, talk shows, roadside interviews—the trappings of elections—can be revealing.

In his piece, Nolan offers a much more optimistic view of the media and elections, but his claims, too, raise some questions. Nolan asserts that the media are merely delivering party messages, and can hardly be blamed for trivializing the campaign process. But as Taras argues, parties are responding to the demands of the media—especially television—for stories filled with drama, conflict, and confrontation. The media want entertainment, not information, and all must dance to their tune. More generally, Nolan's depiction of the media as victims of party practices requires further examination. Is it credible to argue that the media giants are helpless before a handful of political parties?

For an introduction to the media and politics, students should consult David Taras's *The Newsmakers: The Media's Influence on Canadian Poli-*

*tics* (Scarborough: Nelson, 1990). Though Taras is critical of the media, his book offers a thorough review of its subject matter. Taras has also authored an interesting article on how the media dealt with the Meech Lake Accord, which appears in Roger Gibbins et al., eds., *Meech Lake and Canada: Perspectives from the West* (Edmonton: Academic Printing and Publishing, 1988). As well, he has edited, with Helen Holmes, a text on the media entitled *Seeing Ourselves: Media Power and Policy in Canada* (Toronto: Harcourt Brace Jovanovich, 1992).

There are other relevant publications that address the relationship between politics and the media. These include Edwin R. Black, *Politics and the News* (Toronto: Butterworths, 1982), Arthur Siegel, *Politics and the Media in Canada* (Toronto: McGraw-Hill Ryerson, 1983), Walter C. Soderlund, "Mass Media in Canadian Politics: A Survey of Contemporary Issues," in Robert M. Krause and R.H. Wagenburg, eds., *Introductory Readings in Canadian Government and Politics* (Toronto: Copp Clark Pitman 1991), and Frederick J. Fletcher and Daphne Gottlieb Taras, "Images and Issues: The Mass Media and Politics in Canada," in Michael S. Whittington and Glen Williams, eds., *Canadian Politics in the 1990s*, 3rd ed. (Scarborough: Nelson, 1990). The Royal Commission on Electoral Reform and Party Financing also released some research studies on this topic.

In his paper, Taras refers to texts that deal with the American media and their impact on elections in the United States. Canadian students interested in gaining a comparative perspective on the media and elections might benefit from a look at these works.

# PART FIVE

## PUBLIC POLICY

*Is employment equity fair and necessary?*

*Is censorship of pornography consistent with liberalism?*

*Should capital punishment be restored?*

*Should universal medicare be preserved?*

*Does Canada need an entrenched social charter?*

*Does continental free trade benefit Canada?*

# ISSUE NINETEEN

**YES** CAROL AGÓCS, "Employment Equity: Is It Needed? Is It Fair?"

**NO** JACK ROBERTS, "Employment Equity—Unfair"

Consider the following qualities of employment in Canada. Aboriginal peoples with university degrees earn on average about one-third less than nonaboriginals with comparable levels of education. Women are largely absent in the professions and managerial jobs, yet can be found with little trouble in the clerical and secretarial positions. Visible minorities experience relatively high unemployment rates, and disabled persons are much more likely to remain outside the labour force than others.

For many, these rather uncomfortable truths provide clear evidence of discrimination. Certain social groups in Canada are the victims of practices that deny them equal employment opportunities. If justice is to be served, it is argued, then this situation must be remedied through the introduction of employment equity.

Employment equity is a policy that seeks to eliminate barriers to employment *and* to improve the representation of designated groups in the workplace. Employment equity can include the abolition of unreasonable employment requirements and the provision of services (such as child care) that facilitate the carrying out of job responsibilities. It can also involve explicit preferential treatment for those traditionally under-represented in the various occupations. For example, quotas or numerical targets might be set to ensure that women, aboriginals, and other disadvantaged groups are both hired and promoted. Employment equity may be voluntarily adopted by private companies, but effective action in this area typically requires the intervention of government.

In the opinion of its supporters, employment equity is a positive step. It not only provides for greater equality, but also has the potential to increase the productivity of organizations and to ensure the supply of skilled employees. A country that fails to capitalize on the abilities and talents of women, minorities, and the disabled cheats ony itself.

Others, though, are less enamoured of employment equity. They contend that differences in employment situations may reflect forces other than discrimination. Age, education, and culture are just a few of the factors that might explain income differences, employment rates, and representation in upper-level jobs. If this is true, then any preferential treatment for certain designated groups constitutes a form of discrimination against those not included in employment equity programs— employment equity fosters discrimination instead of eliminating it.

Critics of employment equity also contest other alleged benefits of employment equity. It has, they say, a detrimental effect on productivity, for it prevents the selection of the most qualified person. As well, it stigmatizes groups designated under employment equity programs; they will be seen as beneficiaries of an unfair policy and unworthy of their position. Perhaps most seriously, the perceived inequities of employment equity programs may create serious societal divisions in Canada.

In our readings, Carol Agócs, a professor of organizational behaviour at the University of Western Ontario, argues in favour of employment equity. Jack Roberts, a professor of law at the University of Western Ontario, argues against it.

# Employment Equity: Is It Needed? Is It Fair?

*Carol Agócs*

Employment equity is the Canadian policy framework that endeavours to bring about equality in the workplace for aboriginal peoples, persons with disabilities, racial minorities, and women—four populations that still experience the effects of historical and continuing discrimination and disadvantage in employment in Canada. By identifying and eliminating discrimination and the disadvantages these groups experience, employment equity seeks to improve their access to employment, their participation in a broader range of jobs throughout the occupational hierarchy, and their opportunity to contribute and be rewarded equally in the workplace.

As it is implemented in the workplace, employment equity is a long-term process of organizational change that involves critical assessment and updating of traditional policies and practices across the whole range of human resource management decisions that affect access to jobs, job assignment, training, compensation, promotion, and terms and conditions of employment. In addition, employment equity entails creating a workplace culture or climate in which women, persons with disabilities, members of racial minorities, and aboriginal peoples are accepted and respected as equal participants.

## CANADA'S EMPLOYMENT EQUITY LEGISLATION AND REGULATIONS

In Canada in 1993, the instruments of employment equity policy include the Employment Equity Act (1986), which applies to approximately 350 employers and 617,000 employees in the federally regulated sector. In addition, the Federal Contractors Program (1986) covers employers that employ 100 people or more and sell goods or services worth $200,000 or more to the federal government. About 1,350 employers, including most universities, and a million employees are covered under the Federal Contractors Program (Employment and Immigration Canada, 1992: 2–3).

In Ontario, employment equity legislation currently applies to police services, and additional legislation covering most employers has been introduced and is expected to be in force beginning in 1994. The city of Toronto has for many years had employment equity requirements for contractors that sell it goods or services, and for its own workforce. The federal and some provincial governments also have employment equity requirements for the public service and, in some cases, the broader public sector. Some employers in the private and broader public sectors have undertaken voluntary employment equity initiatives.

Employment equity regulations and legislation in Canada, generally speaking, require employers to use voluntary employee self-identification to collect and report data on the representation of women, persons with disabilities, aboriginal persons, and racial minorities in their work force. Employers that fail to report such data may be fined, but there are no requirements or sanctions in force as of 1993 that impose quotas or other specific actions on private sector employers, except for a few instances in which courts or tribunals have imposed such measures as remedies when employers were found to have discriminated. This is one of the many differences between Canada's employment equity policy and affirmative action as it has been implemented in the United States.

The draft Ontario legislation and regulation (Government of Ontario, 1992) propose a three-step process: (1) a work-force survey based on voluntary employee self-identification; (2) a review by the employer of employment policies and practices to identify unnecessary or unfair barriers to the hiring, promotion, and retention of members of the employment equity groups; and (3) an employment equity plan in which the employer sets out qualitative measures and numerical goals for hiring and promotion for a three-year period. The qualitative measures would eliminate discrimination, disadvantage, and barriers identified in the review. The goals and timetables are set by the employer in cooperation with bargaining agents and employees, taking into account the level of underrepresentation of each employment equity group, the availability of qualified members of each group in relevant labour markets, and available opportunities to hire or promote.

Employers have a lead time of twelve to thirty-six months to implement these requirements. Employers face fines if they fail to make reasonable efforts to attain their goals and implement their plans. No specific numerical quotas, qualitative measures or other actions are imposed upon employers who comply with the law. Clearly, under Ontario's draft legislation, employers are free to determine how best to achieve employment equity within their own organizations.

Prior to 1986 when federal employment equity policy was established, employers very rarely initiated voluntary employment equity programs, although they were permitted under federal and provincial legislation. Furthermore, dealing with discrimination in employment through the individual human rights complaint process has not

addressed the issue of systemic discrimination, which creates and perpetuates inequality for entire groups through traditional and unexamined
approaches to decision-making in the workplace. (How this occurs will
be discussed later in this article.)

Employment equity policy, established by legislation, regulation, or
court order, and appropriately implemented and enforced, is needed if
the principle of equality in the workplace is to become a reality in Canada. Three national political parties have acknowledged this, since the
Employment Equity Act and the Federal Contractors Program were
enacted by a Conservative government with support for still stronger
measures from the Liberal and New Democratic parties, while in
Ontario, various employment equity initiatives have occurred under
Conservative, Liberal, and NDP governments. Yet there is still a large
gap between the spirit of employment equity legislation and policy on
the one hand, and the level of employer activity toward equity and the
results attained, on the other (Agócs, Burr, and Somerset, 1992: ch. 1).

## WHY IS EMPLOYMENT EQUITY NEEDED?

Why should there be effective legislation, policy, and enforcement
directed toward the goal of equality in the workplace for women, racial
minorities, persons with disabilities, and aboriginal peoples? There are
four reasons that have been widely acknowledged.

First, at present and over the decade to come, the majority of new
entrants to the work force in Canada are and will be women, racial
minorities, persons with disabilities, and aboriginal peoples (Johnston,
1991; Harvey and Blakely, 1993). Demographic trends, including rates
of labour force participation, the aging of the population, birthrates,
and immigration make this a reality. As members of these groups make
up an ever growing proportion of the work force it becomes more costly
to maintain barriers that impede their access to employment, and that
detract from the productivity they would contribute if they were permitted full use of the education and abilities they have to offer. Furthermore, in an economy that is increasingly based on services to a diverse
population of consumers and clients, within a global and highly competitive environment, the experience and knowledge that women, minorities, and people with disabilities bring to the workplace will be more and
more in demand. Employment equity helps to create a workplace in
which all can participate and contribute, and be equitably rewarded.

Second, democratic principles and expectations regarding social justice are important forces for change. Political parties, business firms,
governments, the media, and community service agencies and organizations have all found it necessary to become more responsive to public
demands that the behaviour of institutions reflect principles of democ-

racy, social justice, and equality. Advocates for the equality of women, racial minorities, aboriginal peoples, and people with disabilities are influencing the policies and practices of public and private sector organizations, just as advocates for the environment and for health have raised awareness and brought about changes in people's behaviour and attitudes, and in government policy.

Third, the legal framework for employment equity is becoming more clearly defined and more explicit as to what employers are required to do in order to ensure equity in the workplace. The Charter of Rights and Freedoms as well as legislation and policy at the federal and provincial levels, and the developing body of case law, are moving Canada ahead of the United States and other countries in requiring employers to take action to ensure that discrimination and harassment on the basis of gender, race, and disability do not create disadvantage in the workplace.

Finally, and most important, there is strong evidence that organizational structures and cultures continue to demonstrate the impacts of discrimination on the basis of gender, race, and disability, and as a result they put women, persons with disabilities, racial minorities, and aboriginal peoples in a position of relative disadvantage in comparison with the traditional working population of able-bodied white males. The evidence shows that the four employment equity groups are disadvantaged in some or all of the following ways: higher unemployment, less access to full-time jobs that offer opportunities for advancement, less job security, representation in a narrower range of jobs, shorter career ladders, poorer pay and benefits, absence from or poor representation in senior management, and harassment on the basis of gender, race, or disability. Research evidence and experience in the workplace also show that racist and sexist organizational practices can be changed and replaced with practices that are fair to all groups, if decision-makers choose to commit themselves to change and to accepting diversity in their organizations.

# THREE MYTHS ABOUT EMPLOYMENT EQUITY

Critics of the idea and practice of employment equity often claim that the changes it seeks to bring about are not needed because, they argue, there is no problem of discrimination or inequality in the workplace. Denial of the reality of discrimination and disadvantage is reinforced by myths about inequality in employment that have gained currency in the media and in popular discourse. These misconceptions need to be challenged by facts about how inequality stemming from discrimination and disadvantage continues to affect the employment equity groups. Since it is not possible in this brief overview to review and reference the extensive literature on discrimination and disadvantage in employment, the reader is encouraged to seek out and consider other sources that examine these issues in depth. In the following paragraphs we briefly consider three commonly heard myths about inequality in the workplace.

## MYTH #1: There's really no problem of inequality. Systemic discrimination based on gender and race is a thing of the past.

An editorial in *The Globe and Mail* (March 21, 1992) illustrates how myth-making about complex issues such as discrimination and inequality can occur. The editorial claims that a 1992 Economic Council of Canada report (deSilva, 1992) tells "the" story of the relationship between race and income in Canada: there is allegedly no evidence of racial discrimination in employment. The editorial concludes with the question, "If there are no significant economic disparities attributable to race or racism, should we be pursuing policies, such as employment equity legislation, which exist to rectify race-based economic disparities?"

The editor's assumption that racism is not an issue does not accurately represent the findings of the ECC study, which itself draws conclusions that are not supported by its own data. The ECC's findings actually show that there is discrimination against some racial minorities, as well as against women.

The ECC study found that immigrants from the Caribbean and East Asia whose education and work experience occurred in Canada are paid significantly less than all other immigrants, and less than the Canadian-born population (deSilva, 1992: Table 4-2). Canadian-educated immigrants from the Caribbean were found to earn 27 percent less than other immigrants, and Canadian-educated immigrants from East Asia showed earnings of 21 percent less, when educational levels and other characteristics were controlled (deSilva, 1992: 33). Although he affirmed the existence of gender discrimination on the basis of his data, deSilva concluded that there was no racial discrimination, and *The Globe and Mail* editor endorsed this unwarranted conclusion as definitive.

A number of other recent studies (e.g., Boyd, 1992; Reitz, 1990) have also found evidence of racial discrimination in employment. Furthermore, the methodological limitations of the ECC study do not support the generalization that there is no racial discrimination in employment in Canada. For example, the ECC study did not examine data for the black population, but only for persons born in the Caribbean or "other Africa" (outside of southern or northern Africa), and the sample used for the study contained very small numbers of specific birthplace groups other than the Caribbean and East Asian categories— too small to support conclusions about the significance of discrimination in Canada (Reitz, 1993). Also, the ECC study did not report a separate analysis of gender effects.

In an analysis of the same 1986 census data, Reitz (1993) found that when education, work experience, language knowledge, government employment, province of residence, urban residence, and weeks and hours worked are taken into account, black males born in Canada have a disadvantage of about 10 percent in earnings. In her multivariate analysis of 1986 census data, in which age, metropolitan residence, and education were statistically controlled, Boyd (1992) found that immigrant women who are members of racial minorities suffer significant income disadvantage compared to men, or to women—both Canadian and foreign born—who are not racial minorities.

There are various ways of studying a complex issue such as discrimination in employment, and it is essential to critically evaluate the claims made as well as the assumptions and methodology on which they are based. Careful research is imperative as a foundation for making weighty policy decisions that affect the working lives of millions of Canadians. When the available research evidence is examined, it is clear that income is influenced by gender and race, and that racial and gender discrimination are realities in Canada. Denying that discrimination in employment exists will not make it go away.

## MYTH #2: There is still some inequality, but it is rapidly disappearing as a natural consequence of changes in our society and economy. Time will fix the problem.

The lead editorial in *The Globe and Mail* on January 1, 1993, dismissed Statistics Canada's finding of a systematic pay disadvantage of women relative to men, saying, "it's hard to imagine a future in which the wage difference will not continue to narrow." As evidence, it cites the fact that for full-time, full-year workers aged 15 to 24, women's average earnings were 86 percent of men's. Now, in an age group of women whose labour force participation rate equals men's, whose educational attainment on average exceeds their male peers, and who are too young to have left the labour force for long periods to care for children, a 14 percent disadvantage doesn't look like equality for women. Despite *The Globe and Mail*'s reassurance, it would seem to require considerable imagination to envision a future in which gender equality in pay is a reality even for the youngest generation of workers. Certainly there is little evidence that time alone is correcting the problem of gender inequality in employment.

In a 1987 survey about senior management in ninety-nine Ontario companies covered by the Federal Contractors Program, I found little reason to be optimistic about a major influx of women into positions of corporate power any time soon. Of the 635 senior managers identified in the study, 8 percent were women. But even these women were not equal participants with their male peers in senior management, since they were concentrated in the functional areas that were rated as having the least power and influence on corporate decisions—staff functions such as human resource management. Most of the companies had policies of promoting from within, and women made up a very small proportion of the middle managers in the traditional specialties from which top managers were recruited. These data again offer no evidence that time alone will correct the problem of women's absence from decision-making roles in organizations.

## MYTH # 3: There is still some inequality in our society based on gender, race, and disability, but we now have laws that are fixing the problem.

The visibility of so-called "handicapped parking," automatic doors, curb cuts and ramps for wheelchairs, along with a few highly publicized voluntary attempts at "affirmative action" hiring of women and minorities by employers, have met with loud complaints about unfairness to white able-bodied males. Although such visible initiatives are modest in scope and still involve far more talk than action, they have been met with resistance, and with the complacent assumption that current laws and policies are making discrimination and disadvantage a thing of the past.

Many Canadians appear to assume that most employers are subject to affirmative action or employment equity legislation, and that employers must implement what are referred to as "quotas" that require them to ignore qualifications and hire on the basis of gender or race. These assumptions are false and reflect a misunderstanding of how employment equity is actually implemented, or possibly an inaccurate generalization from an example of inappropriate implementation of the concept. Many critics of employment equity also make the mistake of confusing it with U.S. affirmative action policies. Canada's legal and policy framework is very different from that in the United States, and there are many practical differences between employment equity and affirmative action; hence American examples don't have much relevance to the Canadian context.

It is true that under Canada's Constitution, and under the human rights codes of many provinces, employers are permitted in some circumstances to voluntarily give preferential treatment of various kinds to members of historically disadvantaged groups. But most Canadian employers are not required to implement specific affirmative action or employment equity measures, nor are they held accountable for results. Employers covered by the Employment Equity Act face sanctions only for failure to report work-force statistics to the federal government; there are no penalties for lack of action toward employment equity. Perhaps it is not surprising, then, that the work-force statistics submitted by employers covered by the act between 1987 and 1992 have not shown significant improvements in the representation and distribution of the employment equity groups.

In 1993, the only Canadian employers who are *required* to implement hiring targets or guidelines are police services in Ontario, and those few Canadian employers that have been found by the courts or by human rights tribunals to have discriminated. Yet there seems to be a widespread misconception that there is wholesale implementation of preferential or quota-based hiring in Canada.

The three myths we have discussed are contradicted by a large body of research evidence, and by the experience of many members of the employment equity groups. To paraphrase Mark Twain, the deaths of gender and racial inequality, and of discrimination on the basis of sex, disability, and race, have been greatly exaggerated. Furthermore, allegations that employment equity is unfair to white able-bodied males, who have traditionally enjoyed privileged access to employment, advancement, and rewards in the workplace, are highly exaggerated and often false. In general, such claims lack credible research support.

Systemic inequality in the workplace on the basis of race, gender, disability, and aboriginal ancestry is still very much with us, as is shown by evidence from a variety of sources including academic research; survey findings and statistical data collected by federal and provincial government departments including Statistics Canada, Employment and Immigration Canada, and various royal commissions and special committees and task forces; records of testimony before the courts and human rights tribunals; and studies conducted by employers and by groups working for the equality of women, people with disabilities, aboriginal peoples, and racial minorities. The literature dealing with patterns of inequality and discrimination is much more extensive for the United States than for Canada, and for women than for groups disadvantaged on the basis of race, disability, or aboriginal ancestry. There is scanty but powerful evidence pertaining to the double disadvantage experienced by women who are also disabled, or members of racial minorities, or aboriginal; this issue has been too often neglected by researchers.

# IS EMPLOYMENT EQUITY FAIR?

In order to assess the fairness of employment equity legislation, regulation, policy, and implementation, one must understand their goal or purpose, and have accurate information about what employment equity actually is—in contrast to myths and misconceptions about what it is. Employment equity is not one specific kind of measure, such as preferential hiring of members of employment equity groups, although in some cases, and for defined periods of time, some forms of preferential treatment may be part of an employment equity strategy. Employment equity certainly does not mean that employers are expected to hire individuals just because they are women, minorities, or persons with disabilities, or to hire people who are not able to perform the duties of a particular job. But it does mean hiring without making unfounded and unexamined assumptions about which types of people are able to perform in particular jobs, and it means making an effort to recruit people who may not fit the profile of the traditional employee in a job. It also means providing conditions that will help the new employees to be successful, and that will help the organization to adapt successfully to its changing work force.

Employment equity is a complex change process involving many kinds of actions directed toward identifying and removing the various kinds of barriers encountered by women, persons with disabilities, aboriginal peoples, and racial minorities in the labour market and workplace. Employment equity is therefore a problem-solving process that is based upon data and information about the experience of employment equity group members. Based on this knowledge, a diagnosis of a workplace is developed in order to identify and remove barriers and respond appropriately to diversity.

A careful diagnosis that identifies patterns of inequality and disadvantage on the basis of gender, race, disability, and/or aboriginal ancestry suggests the presence of job barriers—formal and informal employment policies and practices that have discriminatory impacts on the designated groups, whether or not such impacts are intended. The complex of barriers and constraints that continue to limit the access and full participation in the workplace of historically disadvantaged groups has been called systemic discrimination. The purpose of employment equity is to identify and remove these barriers.

Although employment equity is not just a "numbers game," numerical representation is often the first issue that comes up in discussions of inequality and employment equity remedies. Numerical representation is not simply a question of whether women, racial minorities, aboriginal peoples, and people with disabilities are present in an organization. It also includes their concentration in job ghettos, their absence from decision-making positions due to glass ceilings that impede their career advancement, and their lack of access to jobs on career ladders. These groups may be underrepresented relative to the availability of qualified members of these groups in the labour market because of high turnover resulting from sexual or racial harassment, part-time employment or job insecurity, lack of equal opportunity for training or promotion, inequitable pay, failure of the employer to accommodate special needs related to disabilities, or other forms of discrimination.

The culture of the organization clearly influences the numerical representation, distribution, and retention of members of the employment equity groups. The culture of a workplace encompasses its fundamental values, its dominant beliefs and assumptions about people and work, prevailing stereotypes about gender, race, and disability, norms of social behaviour, informal networks through which interaction and communication take place, attitudes toward change, and behaviours surrounding organizational power and politics, cooperation, and conflict. Decisions about people in organizations—their access to employment, job assignment, career development, and daily treatment on the job—tend to reinforce and reflect the values and norms of historically dominant social groups that continue to occupy positions of power and privilege in the organization: typically white able-bodied males. For example, have you noticed how often the board members and top managers whose photos appear in corporate annual reports all look alike? Workplaces that are equitable for everyone can exist if organizations make a serious and sustained effort to change traditional cultures in which white able-bodied males are privileged and women, minorities, aboriginal peoples, and persons with disabilities are treated as if they don't really belong.

Employment systems encompass the entire spectrum of organizational rules—policies, practices, and procedures—that affect access to jobs and advancement opportunities for individuals and groups. Employment systems include procedures for recruitment and selection, job assignment, compensation, terms and conditions of employment, scheduling of work, performance appraisal, access to training and development, promotion, transfer, layoff, and termination. There is extensive research evidence from U.S., British, and Canadian settings of discriminatory impacts that employment systems may have in relation to women, racial minorities, and people with disabilities. For example, there have been many studies of how discrimination can occur as a result of recruitment practices, selection criteria that are not job-related, selection interviews, compensation decisions, performance appraisal, promotion, and job assignment (for examples, see Arvey and Faley, 1988; Henry and Ginzberg, 1992; Collinson, Knights, and Collinson, 1990).

Removing discriminatory barriers in employment systems requires a critical examination of how human resource decisions are usually made. For example, are new employees recruited only from traditional sources, so that they are clones of the existing work force? Are criteria for selection and job assignment clearly linked to performance on the job, rather than just criteria that are customary or convenient? Do co-workers and supervisors receive training on how to identify, prevent, and deal with harassment on the basis of gender, race and ethnicity, and disability? Are managers accountable to ensure that performance appraisal, training and development, and promotion practices are free of bias, and that vigorous efforts are made to recruit and retain members of underrepresented groups? Do the leaders and the formal policies and practices of the organization support the principles of equity in the daily life of the workplace as well as in decision-making? Improvements in the representation of disadvantaged groups can occur over time, without unfairness to any group, if barriers in workplace culture and systems are identified and removed, and if decision-makers are sincerely committed to employment equity goals.

## FAIRNESS TO ALL: DEALING WITH INEQUALITY IN THE OCCUPATIONAL STRUCTURE

Analyses of data on occupational distribution and income, including multivariate analyses that control for the influence of education, urban residence, and other explanatory variables, show that aboriginal and racial minority populations are consistently disadvantaged in comparison to British, French, and European ethnic groups in Canada (Agócs and Boyd, 1993; Reitz, 1990; McDonald, 1991). The expectation that occupational inequality on the basis of racial minority status would diminish or disappear as disadvantaged groups acquired educational credentials and became culturally assimilated into Canadian society has proved illusory.

By the late 1970s, the persistence and importance of structural constraints was widely acknowledged in stratification research in Canada, as well as in Britain and the United States. This research shows that inequality arises primarily from persisting structural constraints that act as barriers to the access and advancement of individuals in the occupational structure. These structural constraints include racial and gender discrimination, which is not only expressed in biased acts toward individuals, but is built into customary patterns of behaviour in a world of work that was designed by, and in the interests of, a white able-bodied male population. Individuals who are not male, white, and able-bodied—and who are now the majority of the Canadian work force—are often disadvantaged by their gender, race or ethnicity, or disability in gaining access to employment, and to the rewards, quality of life, and opportunities for advancement that are attached to occupational status.

A structural perspective redirects the attention of researchers and policy-makers away from the individual worker as the unit of analysis and the object of policy intervention, toward fundamental change in the workplace, beginning with the removal of the structural barriers in organizational systems and culture that serve to maintain occupational inequality on the basis of gender, race, aboriginal ancestry, and disability.

Employment equity is an organizational change strategy that can lead to equality by providing remedies for workplace disadvantage that is due to structural barriers. It is a fair policy that reflects and responds to the current reality of the changing Canadian workplace.

## REFERENCES

Agócs, Carol and Monica Boyd, "The Canadian Ethnic Mosaic Recast for the 1990s," in James Curtis, Edward Grabb, and Neil Guppy, eds., *Social Inequality in Canada*, 2nd ed. Scarborough: Prentice-Hall, 1993, pp. 330–52.

Agócs, Carol, Catherine Burr, and Felicity Somerset, *Employment Equity: Cooperative Strategies for Organizational Change.* Scarborough: Prentice-Hall Canada, 1992.

Arvey, Richard and Robert Faley, *Fairness in Selecting Employees.* Don Mills: Addison-Wesley, 1988.

Boyd, Monica, "Gender, Visible Minority and Immigrant Earnings Inequality: Reassessing an Employment Equity Premise," in Vic Satzewich, ed., *Deconstructing a Nation: Immigration, Multiculturalism and Racism in the 1990s Canada.* Toronto: Garamond Press, 1992.

Collinson, David, David Knights, and Margaret Collinson, *Managing to Discriminate.* London: Routledge, 1990.

deSilva, Arnold, "Earnings of Immigrants: A Comparative Analysis." Ottawa: Supply and Services Canada, 1992.

Employment and Immigration Canada, *Annual Report: Employment Equity Act, 1992.* Ottawa: Supply and Services Canada, 1992.

Government of Ontario, 35th legislature, 2nd session, "Bill 79, An Act to provide for Employment Equity...," 1st reading June 25, 1992; with draft regulation released June 16, 1993.

Harvey, Edward and John Blakely, "Employment Equity in Canada," *Policy Options* (March 1993): 3–8.

Henry, Frances and Effie Ginzberg, "Racial Discrimination in Employment," in James Curtis, Edward Grabb, and Neil Guppy, eds., *Social Inequality in Canada*, 2nd ed. Scarborough: Prentice-Hall, 1993, pp. 353–60.

Johnston, William, "Global Work Force 2000: The New World Labor Market," *Harvard Business Review* 69, no. 2 (1991): 115–27.

Leonard, Jonathan, "Anti-Discrimination or Reverse Discrimination: The Impact of Changing Demographics, Title VII, and Affirmative Action on Productivity," *Journal of Human Resources* 19, no. 2 (1984): 145–74.

Leonard, Jonathan, "Employment and Occupational Advance Under Affirmative Action," *Review of Economics and Statistics* 66, no. 3 (1984): 377–85.

McDonald, Ryan, "Canada's Off-Reserve Aboriginal Population," *Canadian Social Trends* (Winter 1991): 2–7.

Reitz, Jeffrey, "Ethnic Concentrations in Labour Markets and Their Implications for Ethnic Inequality," in Raymond Breton, Wsevolod Isajiw, Warren Kalbach, and Jeffrey Reitz, eds., *Ethnic Identity and Equality: Varieties of Experience in a Canadian City.* Toronto: University of Toronto Press, 1990, pp. 135–95.

Reitz, Jeffrey, "Statistics on Racial Discrimination in Canada," *Policy Options* (March 1993): 32–36.

# Employment Equity—Unfair

*Jack Roberts*

# INTRODUCTION

Why not employment equity? Why shouldn't the state legislate an employment equity program designed to force every workplace, university, and other institution to "look like Canada," proportionally representing our populace in all its diversity? Because employment equity would be unfair to our society and every person in it. That's why.

From a societal point of view:

(1) The idea that employment equity will promote a nondiscriminatory result by requiring proportional representation of our populace is a myth;

(2) Employment equity will corrode our competitiveness by replacing the ideal of advancement on merit with a "victim culture" that encourages trying to get ahead by marketing our miseries and maladies;

(3) Employment equity will promote a wasteful proliferation of organized "victim groups" lobbying in the legislatures and the media for official government preferences in, for example, admission to higher education, employment, and promotion;

(4) The success of many of these "victim groups" in obtaining official preferences for their members will polarize and fragment our society;

(5) This fragmentation will promote the segregation of our society and its institutions.

From an individual point of view:

(1) Employment equity will officially disadvantage every member of the amorphous majority, i.e., everyone who cannot succeed in convincing the government to grant them official preferences based upon some "victim" characteristic they share with others, regardless of whether they are children of privilege or poverty;

(2) Conversely, employment equity will officially advantage every member of successful "victim groups," regardless of whether they are children of privilege or poverty;

(3) Employment equity is subject to gross manipulation, in that people are classified into one group or another on the basis of information that they personally volunteer;

(4) Employment equity is condescending, in the sense that it suggests that members of official victim groups are incapable of succeeding without being given official preferences;

(5) For the same reason, employment equity casts into doubt the merits of the accomplishments of members of official victim groups—did they get there only because of their ethnic origin, race, gender, etc.;

(6) Employment equity is not a temporary expedient to be suffered by members of the amorphous majority for a short period of time; it will disadvantage them throughout their lifetimes.

# THE SOCIETAL REASONS FOR REJECTING EMPLOYMENT EQUITY

## (1) The Myth of Proportional Representation

Not too long ago, U.S. President Bill Clinton was trumpeting how he intended to make his cabinet "look like America." There is an undeniable resonance to such rhetoric. It just sounds right: If discrimination never existed, wouldn't our entire population be proportionally represented at all levels of government, industry, and the professions? So why not deliberately create that nondiscriminatory result?

We should not "buy into" this myth. In a country such as Canada, where waves of immigration have created rapidly shifting distributions of population, it is entirely misleading to suggest that a regime of nondiscrimination would ever have created this kind of proportional representation. Immigrants to Canada are selected, *inter alia*, on the basis of having skills and/or investment capital that Canada needs. As a result, many skilled trades, businesses, and professions are heavily laden with relatively recent immigrants. Other occupational categories, where sufficient numbers of Canadian residents have always been available, are not. Unless you take the position that immigration to Canada should not be based upon the needs of the country, a dubious proposition if there ever was one, you can hardly label the result a form of discrimination that needs to be corrected through employment equity.

Add to this the different cultural attributes that immigrants to Canada may bring with them. Some cultural groups may value education more than others, and as a result large numbers of their children may move more rapidly than others into higher education and professional careers. Other cultural groups may not share the modern North American attitude toward careers for women. Most of the first generation of women among these groups may never seek to enter the work force. In neither case would the disproportionate overrepresentation or underrepresentation of the cultural group in the work force represent the outcome of domestic discrimination.

But perhaps most fundamentally, the plain truth is that employment equity never was designed to promote proportional representation of everybody in the populace. You will never see employment equity investigators surveying student populations and work forces to find out, for example, if Roman Catholics, Anglicans, Presbyterians, and/or Jews are proportionally represented at every level. Employment equity is limited to promoting proportional representation of victim groups that, by dint of lobbying efforts or otherwise, manage to make it onto the government's employment equity list. Employment equity is indifferent to the degree of inclusion or exclusion of any other group. They are all rolled into one—an amorphous majority whose members must be held back while the members of the victim groups on the government's list are preferred.

## (2) and (3) The "Victim Culture" and Organized Victim Groups

As can be seen, employment equity places a high premium upon getting on the government's list of victim groups. Get on the list and you have struck gold: you will be preferred, *inter alia,* in admission to higher education, employment, and promotion. Don't get on the list and you will fall into the amorphous majority who must "ride in the back of the bus" and accept being officially disadvantaged at every stage of their careers.

Welcome to the "victim culture," where everyone, it seems, wants to organize a victim group and try to get ahead by marketing their miseries and maladies. When you think about it for a minute, there are lots of reasons why many of us may not have been given a fair shake in employment or promotion—reasons that have nothing to do with the traditional categories of race, ethnic origin, or gender. Perhaps we were regarded as too young or too old (ageism); too bald (follicly challenged); too hairy (hirsutism); too overweight (weightism); too short or too tall (heightism); not good looking enough (lookism); too quiet or shy (vocalism); not athletic enough (athleticism); or having only experience instead of formal credentials (credentialism).

I mention the above categories because if you have been watching any of the U.S. talk shows on television lately, you would have seen representatives of victim groups organized around one or more of these characteristics lobbying to be added to the U.S. government's victim group list under its affirmative action program.[1] Certainly, you would have seen representatives of another organized victim group, gays and lesbians, parading and lobbying, *inter alia,* to reach this objective.

They are simply following the pattern established by other successful victim groups. Twenty-five years ago, when affirmative action preferences were first mandated by Congress, only blacks and women were on the list. As other groups learned the ropes of victim politics and launched successful lobbies, they too were added. These groups included Native Americans, Hispanics, and most recently, people with disabilities. Fewer and fewer Americans remain in the disadvantaged category of amorphous majority.

Some might say that Americans should encourage this trend. Sooner or later no one would be left in the category of amorphous majority. Everyone—and hence no one—would get preference. Maybe the whole affirmative action program would self-destruct.

Wishful thinking, perhaps, and it begs the real question. That question is, why would we in Canada want to create a "victim culture" like that? Why would we want to destroy the ideal of meritocracy, the ideal of advancement on merit, and replace it with a system where he or she who cries the loudest is the one who succeeds? In a world where international competitiveness will make or break the future of a small trading country like Canada, why would we want to deliver such a crippling blow to Canada's overall potential for economic efficiency?

## (4) and (5) Polarization, Fragmentation, and Segregation

The practice of victim politics depends upon creating divisions between people. To succeed, the "victim group" must hive itself off from the amorphous majority and argue that its members are disproportionately underrepresented at the more senior levels of education, government, industry, and the professions because they were oppressed and discriminated against, either overtly or systemically, by the amorphous majority. In the United States, this lobbying effort is usually made by (1) marshalling as many anecdotes as possible of how certain members of the amorphous majority abused, undervalued, overlooked, or held back members of the victim group because of their common "victim" characteristic; and (2) pointing to statistical evidence demonstrating that persons sharing this common "victim" characteristic are underrepresented in the desired areas.

While such evidence does not add up to proof, in any legal sense, that a cultural norm embraced by the amorphous majority promoted oppression of the victim group and actually caused the alleged under-representation, the pressure created upon the government through the use of this evidence in an effective lobbying campaign may induce the government to add the victim group to its official affirmative action list. From that point onward, the government will require universities, employers, and other institutions to prefer all members of the victim group at the expense of all members of the amorphous majority, regardless of whether those individuals who are so penalized ever actually committed or benefited from the acts of oppression alleged by the victim group.

It is not difficult to imagine the resentment soon felt by individuals in the amorphous majority who are turned upon in this way. This resentment may be expressed in an emotional "backlash" directed against all members of the victim group. In other words, the victim group and the amorphous majority soon became polarized into opposing camps.

Further fragmentation soon follows. Once again, the United States provides the best example. Because more than one victim group has been officially recognized in the U.S. government's affirmative action program, deep divisions have developed among them. In the world of official victimhood, the question soon becomes, who will be first among equals? If a single job or promotion opens up at a workplace where all official victim groups are underrepresented, from which group will the incumbent be selected? If a university has limited funds available to finance a single additional course in minority studies, which minority victim group will get it? Official victim groups are excellent at reasoning why they should be first among equals in the contest for such scarce spoils. The result? Fragmentation: group against group, all against the amorphous majority.

Next comes segregation, with everybody choosing to "stick to their own kind." If you think I'm exaggerating, take a tour of the campus of any major American university. You won't see black, white, Hispanic, Native American, or Asian students happily intermingling. The students "stick to their own kind." Each minority group exerts considerable social pressure upon its members to ensure that they do not stray into social relationships with others. To the dismay of university administrators, their students have divided themselves into competing collectives and adopted an "us against them" mentality.

And why not? Each group or collective has learned only too well the lessons of victim politics. It has been said that at one university, the Asian students even capitalized upon the fact that the affirmative action classification system of the university depended upon information personally volunteered by the students. They threatened to register as "white" in the next academic year if their demands for an Asian studies program were not met. This would have thrown the affirmative action statistics of the university way out of line, possibly prompting a government inquiry. The university capitulated. The Asian students got what they wanted. Other minorities were not amused.

Collective destinies promote collective identities. Some victim groups have gone so far in this direction as to advocate a deconstruction of democracy as we know it. Rather than proportional representation by geographic area and a legislature based upon one representative, one vote, they advocate proportional representation by victim group, with each victim group either having a veto or more than one vote per representative upon issues they identify as their own.

You may recall the insistence of certain victim groups that they be represented at the table in the last round of negotiations for constitutional reform. You may also recall that traces of their unique philosophy of democracy actually made it into the proposals for an elected Senate. Quebec senators were to be given either veto power or more than one vote per senator upon issues affecting Quebec. It was thought that this would accommodate the Quebec government's concerns about centralization of power in Ottawa, a prospect that had long been anathema to the francophone majority in Quebec. (It is observed in passing that the francophone majority in Quebec is regarded by many as having pioneered the use of victim politics in Canada.)

These are scary proposals. Grouping people by geographic area is relatively benign. Geographic borders within Canada are not exclusive. An Ontarian can become an Albertan simply by moving there, and vice versa. This fluidity prevents the development of strong bloc identities. Not so when you group people according to their official "victim" status. Victim groups are exclusive. If you don't possess the "victim" characteristic that defines the group, you are "out." Strong collective identities are the inevitable result.

Do we really want to condition Canadians to segregate and think collectively in this way? Strong bloc identities promote strong bloc prejudices. The sins of one invariably are laid at the feet of his or her entire bloc. Consider the recent campaign of one victim group that claimed that it wanted to "stop male violence against women." The entire collective of the male sex was sought to be held responsible for the crimes of very few men. Do we really want to unleash the human curses of mistrust, resentment, fear, and hatred between well-defined collectives? Do we really want group mistrusting group, group fearing group, group hating group? This is not my vision for the future of our society in Canada. I hope it is not yours.

# EMPLOYMENT EQUITY'S UNFAIRNESS TOWARD INDIVIDUALS

## (1) and (2) The "Head-Count" Orientation of Employment Equity

No race, gender, or ethnic group has a monopoly upon the poor. The same may be said for the rich. While the relative proportions of rich and poor may vary from group to group, it cannot be denied that rich and poor populate every victim group on the government's employment equity list as well as the amorphous majority.

The targets, goals, and quotas of employment equity completely ignore this fact. The only thing that matters is the head-count. What employment equity demands is that an institution or employer prefer persons sharing a particular "victim" characteristic until proportional representation is reached. Whether those who are so preferred are children of privilege or poverty is a matter of complete indifference.

This presents a "double whammy" to the children of poverty in the amorphous majority. Having already begun life at a serious deficit relative to those more fortunate, they now have heaped upon them the further disadvantage of being on the receiving end of official discrimination at every stage of their careers. You can imagine how galling it must be for those who have fought their way up from poverty to be told that they must be held back while a child of privilege from an official victim group is preferred.

If you can't imagine this, let me give you an example from my own experience. In the early 1970s I was a young lawyer in Washington, D.C. Two of my friends, Myles and Art, decided that they would like to go to law school (at the time, Myles was a defence analyst at the Pentagon; Art was a White House aide). Myles had had to fight his way up through the inner-city schools in New York city. Art was a child of privilege. When he was growing up, he lived in mansions. He attended private schools. His father was a successful politician from the southwest. Nevertheless, Myles had the superior academic record and law school admission test score. Myles was rejected by every law school to which he applied. They all accepted Art. He also received warm letters of welcome and multiple offers of scholarships. Today, Myles is still at the Pentagon; Art is a successful lawyer in the southwest. They are no longer friends.

You see, Myles was Jewish. Art was Hispanic. Despite their long history of suffering prejudice and discrimination, Jews never made it out of the amorphous majority and onto the government's affirmative action list. Hispanics did. Under pressure from the government to meet targets for numbers of Hispanics in their student bodies, the law schools were only too anxious to recruit Art. It didn't matter that his prior academic record and law school admission test score fell far below the floors established for applicants from the amorphous majority. It didn't matter that Art was a child of privilege who had never suffered an ounce of discrimination in his life. All that mattered was the head-count of Hispanics.

It seems ironic, doesn't it, that such an inequity between Myles and Art should be worked by a process that Canadians call employment equity? We shouldn't be surprised, though. Employment equity was never designed to be fair as applied between individuals. Its only objective has always been to work for equity on behalf of its official victim groups, in the sense of requiring their proportional representation. It has narrowed the broad concept of equity down to a "numbers game" that is devoid of any sensitivity to other criteria of fairness.

## (3) Gross Manipulation of Volunteered Information

In a free and open society, where until recently human rights laws forbade employers and other institutions to ask about an applicant's race or ethnic origin, gathering employment equity statistics can be a touchy subject. Forcing Canadians to carry racial or ethnic identity cards is out of the question. Even requiring Canadians to fill out employment equity questionnaires is unthinkable. Many Ontarians who received such questionnaires from the provincial government last year reacted with considerable hostility and refused to provide the requested information. As a result, just as in the United States, the government must rely upon information that is voluntarily provided in administering its employment equity program.

Relying upon volunteered information involves considerable potential for gross manipulation of the employment equity program. You will recall the threat of the Asian students at one U.S. university to register as white if they did not get their way. But gross manipulations also occur in other ways.

Not too long ago the press ran a story about two brothers in Philadelphia. They were white. When they applied to join the fire department, they received the highest test scores; however, they were rejected in favour of minority applicants who had not done as well. The next time they applied, the brothers had learned an important lesson. They identified themselves as African American. They were immediately hired. It wasn't until the brothers applied for promotion some time later that grumbling among their colleagues prompted the fire department to require some proof that they were, indeed, African American. When they couldn't come up with any, they were fired.

It is difficult to say how often applicants for admission to university, jobs, or promotions commit such flagrant manipulations, but the temptation at least to embellish the minority aspects of your pedigree must be great. Friends of mine in New York had this happen with their daughter. The daughter, whose academic record was not strong, had been rejected by every university to which she had applied. Then, recalling that her grandmother came from Portugal, she reapplied, stating that she was of Hispanic origin. There were acceptances all around.

These instances raise considerable doubt about the reliability of the statistics that must be used in administering an employment equity program. How many members of the amorphous majority might be "passing" as members of official victim groups? How many members of official victim groups might have chosen to be counted as members of the amorphous majority because of a desire to be seen as advancing solely upon their own merits? How are those people counted who choose not to submit completed employment equity questionnaires? When the voluntary nature of the information-gathering process makes employment equity subject to this much manipulation and, hence, potential for unfairness, why implement it at all?

## (4) and (5) Condescension and Doubt

These objections to employment equity probably require little in the way of expansion. Employment equity programs are condescending to members of official victim groups because they imply that without the special preferences of employment equity, they cannot succeed. For the same reason, employment equity programs cast into doubt the achievements of members of official victim groups. The unasked question always lurking in the background is, did they make it on their own or was it because of their official victim status?

## (6) No Temporary Expedient

If there is one thing that the past experience of the United States can tell you, it is that employment equity is not a temporary expedient to be eliminated in, say, ten years, when proportional representation of all victim groups is achieved. It is not a "quick fix." Twenty-five years after the implementation of affirmative action, the United States still has not even come close to achieving the goal of proportional representation.

More than a full generation after the fact, it seems clear that the billions of dollars spent in implementing, policing, and enforcing affirmative action programs would have been better invested in improving the living conditions and educational opportunities of, for example, African American children in the urban ghettos of the United States. In other words, the investment should have started at the beginning of youth. The goals, targets, and quotas of affirmative action only begin to apply at the end, when the child reaches university age.

By then, the damage is already done. Very few buck the odds presented by a harsh environment and make it through to high-school graduation. What good are affirmative action goals, targets, and quotas to the rest? They are already ineligible. They are beyond the downward reach of the affirmative action program.

Many U.S. commentators, both African American and white, have noted that because of this, affirmative action mainly helped those who really didn't need it—those African Americans from middle- and upper-class families who would have gone on to university and successful careers anyway. For the most part, the rest remained stuck where they were a quarter-century ago—in the lower rungs of society.

Even the enforcement objective of affirmative action was changed to reflect this phenomenon. No longer was the enforcement objective to reach proportional representation of victim groups in student bodies and work forces, measured on the basis of their proportion of the population, but rather proportional representation was measured on the basis of their proportion of the pool of minimally qualified applicants. It is highly unlikely that, in the present scheme of things, proportional representation on the basis of population ever will occur. Until then, affirmative action will continue as a permanent part of the American landscape.

## CONCLUSION

No one disputes that in Canada many people in positions of power may still treat others differently solely on the basis of their race, gender, ethnic origin, or some of the other possible victim characteristics that I set forth earlier in this paper. Because of this, the best qualified people may have been passed over for, *inter alia*, employment or promotion. That is unfair. Something must be done about it.

The only dispute is about that "something." In my submission, employment equity programs are not the way to go. I have set out in this paper extensive reasons for opposing their implementation. Perhaps it is beyond the scope of this paper to explore possible alternatives. It is important, however, to stress that such alternatives exist. One such alternative is to review personnel procedures to ensure that reliance upon tools such as interviews, where subtle prejudices may influence the evaluation, are minimized. Another is streamlined enforcement of anti-discrimination laws. Still another is to do what the United States didn't do—invest the dollars that would have gone into employment equity into specialized programs designed to minimize the social and educational deficits now suffered by children of poverty. Another is to educate and foster changing attitudes in the workplace to accommodate the needs of different people, for example, the provision of flexible working hours and day care. There obviously are many more alternatives, none of them that involves dividing the people of Canada up into collectives and officially advancing one collective at the expense of another.

### NOTES

1. "Affirmation action" is the U.S. term for "employment equity." Actually, employment equity is a broader—and hence more accurate—term, since even in Ontario the government's so-called "equity" initiatives are designed to reach beyond employment to embrace, *inter alia*, university admission.

# POSTSCRIPT

Agócs and Roberts both present credible arguments for their respective positions. Nevertheless, some nagging doubts remain. Let us take the case for employment equity first. Employment equity programs focus on groups, but surely there are members in these designated groups who are not victims of discrimination. (Recall Roberts's story about Art and Myles.) If this is the case, then why not centre on individual instances of discrimination? A related concern with employment equity is its argument about the impact of discrimination. Canadians of Japanese and Jewish descent have in the past been the target of many discriminatory practices, but they have managed to thrive economically in Canadian society. Such evidence leads one to doubt whether the difficulties women, aboriginals, visible minorities, and the disabled experience in the workplace are the fault of unfair employment practices. Lastly, even if discrimination prevails, it is questionable whether reverse discrimination in the form of preferential treatment is a prudent course of action. Two wrongs do not necessarily make a right.

To say that the position for employment equity is less than fully convincing is not to say that the contrary position is sound. At times, critics of employment equity come perilously close to denying the existence of discrimination in the workplace, yet study after study documents its existence. In their book *Employment Equity: Cooperative Strategies for Organizational Change* (Scarborough: Prentice-Hall, 1992), Carol Agócs, Catherine Burr, and Felicity Somerset present the results of a survey of Canadian corporate recruiters and hiring managers in which nearly all the respondents admit to discriminating against potential employees on the grounds of handicap, age, sex, and colour. Critics may also be blamed for presenting a narrow conception of employment equity, one that concentrates on quotas and the establishment of proportional representation in the labour force. In reality, employment equity represents a wide range of actions, many of which endeavour only to eliminate

417

barriers and ensure that all have an equal opportunity to secure employment.

For students wishing to acquire an initial understanding of employment equity, the aforementioned text by Agócs, Burr, and Somerset is a good starting point. Though the authors are unabashed supporters of employment equity, they provide a disinterested overview of the meaning of employment equity and existing governmental programs in this area of public policy. Another important reference is Rosalie Abella, *Report of the Commission on Equality and Employment* (Ottawa: Minister of Supply and Services, 1984). This report offers strong arguments for employment equity, and was instrumental in drawing the attention of government decision-makers to the issue of discrimination in the workplace. Not surprisingly, the report elicited some critical commentaries, two of which are Walter Block and Michael A. Walker, *On Employment Equity: A Critique of the Abella Royal Commission Report* (Vancouver: The Fraser Institute, 1985) and Conrad Winn, "Affirmative Action and Visible Minorities: Eight Premises in Quest of Evidence," *Canadian Public Policy* 11, no. 4 (December 1985). Block and Walker also provide a more extended critique of employment equity in their book *Discrimination, Affirmative Action, and Equal Opportunity: An Economic and Social Perspective* (Vancouver: Fraser Institute, 1982). As well, students may wish to refer to debates on employment equity in Ronald Hinch, ed., *Crosscurrents: Debates in Canadian Society* (Scarborough: Nelson, 1992).

Employment equity programs in Canada have been influenced greatly by developments in the United States. In the 1960s, the American government introduced programs aimed at reducing discrimination in the workplace against black Americans. These programs, which have expanded to include other groups, come under the name of affirmative action. A set of articles entitled *The Annals of the American Academy of Political and Social Science: Affirmative Action Revisited* (Newbury Park: Sage Publications, 1992), edited by Harold Orlans and June O'Neill, offers a good discussion of affirmative action in the United States.

Employment equity and affirmative action have engendered a good deal of philosophical debate about whether these initiatives are consistent with various notions of justice. Two books that address this matter are Michael Rosenfeld, *Affirmative Action and Justice* (New Haven: Yale University Press, 1991) and Kathanne W. Greene, *Affirmative Action and Principles of Justice* (New York: Greenwood Press, 1989).

Finally, students interested in employment equity would be well advised to examine the issue of employment equity in Ontario. At the time of this writing, the NDP government of Ontario is attempting to introduce the most ambitious employment equity program in Canada. Whether the proposed legislation eventually becomes law or succumbs to opposition forces, it deserves careful study.

# ISSUE TWENTY

## Is Censorship of Pornography Consistent with Liberalism?

**YES** LEO GROARKE, "Pornography: From Liberalism to Censorship," *Queen's Quarterly* 90, no. 4 (Winter 1983): 1108–120

**NO** WILLIAM WATSON, "Pornography and Liberalism," *Policy Options* (June 1985): 18–21

Canadians exhibit a decidedly ambivalent attitude toward the subject of pornography. Polls have consistently shown an emerging consensus that pornography is an important public issue needing governmental regulation. At the same time, Canadians have been buying more pornographic material than ever before, making pornography a major multimillion dollar business.

The advent of pornography as a public policy issue appears to have almost as much to do with the revolution in communications technologies as it does with changing social mores. Sexually explicit materials have been available in one form or another for centuries, but generally only to a limited few. The new communications technologies of the late 20th century have now made pornography more affordable and accessible to greater numbers than ever before. Seedy X-rated theatres and back-alley porn vendors are virtually a thing of the past. Pornography has become a genuinely mass-market item, to be promoted and marketed like any other consumer item. Next to the candy racks at the local convenience store can be found X-rated videos and magazines that leave little to the imagination.

Opposition to the dissemination of sexually explicit materials has generally come from those arguing within a conservative tradition. To conservatives, such materials represent an assault on the moral fabric of society and accordingly should be strictly regulated under the Criminal Code.

Traditionally, the counter-argument to the conservative position has been presented by liberals. From their perspective, the fundamental value is the freedom of individuals to seek self-fulfilment without direct interference or regulation by the state, or the majority. According to this view, derived in large part from the writings of John Stuart Mill, government intervention is warranted only when the actions of an individual cause harm to a third party. In this case, liberals such as William Watson argue that there is no scientific support for the belief that widespread availability of pornography leads to violent behaviour. Liberals thus oppose treating pornography as either a moral or criminal issue. Instead, they view pornography as a rights issue, and say that it should be protected from regulation like any other form of free speech. The onus is clearly on those wanting to regulate the pornography to prove that some harm has been committed.

Although the liberal position has had an important impact on the writing of obscenity laws in North America, it has come under renewed attack in recent years. This stems from the fear that there has been a proliferation of increasingly violent and degrading forms of pornography that legitimizes the commission of sexual crimes against women. Even liberals are now asking whether contemporary pornography has become so violent and malevolent in nature that some degree of censorship is necessary. But can such censorship be carried out without undermining the fundamental liberal commitment to freedom of expression?

In the following essays, two liberal thinkers debate the relationship of pornography and censorship to liberal principles. Leo Groarke, a philosophy professor at Wilfrid Laurier University, builds the case that some censorship of violent pornography can be justified within the context of Mill's traditional defence of liberalism. William Watson, an economist at McGill University, responds by arguing that even the most violent forms of pornography should not be exempted from the protection of freedom of speech. For him, censorship of any type poses a far greater danger to society.

# Pornography: From Liberalism to Censorship

*Leo Groarke*

In his now classic essay *On Liberty* John Stuart Mill defends a liberal conception of the state. One aspect of the essay is its suggestion that individuals should, in principle, be free to form opinions and express them at their will. Mill nevertheless concedes that there are limits to such freedom,[1] though he is not as clear about these limits as one might wish. In the present essay I shall pursue the question of such limits in light of contemporary discussions of pornography, censorship and the freedom of the press.[2] There is, I believe, a case to be made for censorship in this regard, and I shall ask whether such censorship can be made compatible with a liberal account of the relationship between individuals and the state. Other commentators (Cohen, McCormack et al.) have assumed that Mill's account of liberalism excludes any form of censorship,[3] but I shall argue that this is not the case. It is true that Mill does not endorse censorship, but he does not consider the extreme kind of pornography I will discuss and it is difficult to say how he would have reacted to it.[4] Whatever position he would adopt, I will argue that his liberalism does leave room for a particular form of censorship, and that commentators like Lorenne Clarke are mistaken when they conclude that liberalism is unable to meet "pornography's Challenge to Liberal ideology."[5]

Given that there is a form of censorship which is compatible with Mill's liberalism, it is natural to compare it to censorship as it operates in Canada. To this end, the later sections of this article will consider the present laws on obscenity, and the way the Ontario Censor Board reaches its decisions. In both cases I will argue that pornography is dealt with in a way that is *not* compatible with a liberal point of view. I shall finish with some suggestions as to how this could be changed, and will argue that they would allow for a more just and more acceptable form of censorship than is the case at present.

Before we turn to a philosophical discussion of Mill's views and censorship, we may note some cases which have fueled the contemporary debate on the censorship issue. It is in light of these cases that I shall ask

421

whether a no censorship attitude to pornography is an acceptable part of the liberal point of view. I begin with such examples because too many commentators reject censorship on philosophical grounds without realizing, in practical terms, the consequences of such a policy.[6] As one commentator wrote after viewing materials confiscated in Toronto (material that would currently be available if there was no censorship), "We can't discuss pornography in the abstract, we're fools if we try."[7] In order to gain some understanding of the consequences of a no censorship policy, I propose to consider the kind of pornography which is available today, and that which would have been available had no censorship been in place. I will eventually argue that censorship is justified in most (though not all) these cases, and that such censorship can be justified in terms of a liberal point of view.

The most recent incident which has sparked debate about pornography in Canada is the recent decision by the pay TV channel First Choice to contract with Playboy Productions to produce "soft-core" pornography for its subscribers. The news of the agreement was greeted with much criticism and a public outcry. Communications Minister Francis Fox lambasted First Choice, demonstrations were held in ten cities and the CRTC warned the networks that they should adopt a voluntary code of ethics. It stated that it would take strong action against any programs featuring "gratuitous" violence against women, violence which is characteristic of some of the programs aired by Playboy on their pay TV channel in the United States. In response, First Choice and its defenders argued that freedom of expression was at stake and that those who objected to the programs did not have to buy a subscription to them.[8]

The uproar over pay TV was only the latest incident in a growing anti-pornography movement in the United States and Canada. Sparked by a feminist reaction to violence against women, the movement has grown to encompass a very broad concern with the way women are portrayed in the media. Some illustrative examples of the images and themes which have led to this concern are noted by Laura Lederer in her introduction to the recent anthology *Take Back the Night: Women on Pornography*. She discusses the research into pornography undertaken by the California group Women Against Violence in Pornography and the Media. In one three-month period they viewed twenty-six pornographic films in San Francisco to gain some understanding of their content. Twenty-one of the films which were viewed contained rape scenes, sixteen featured bondage and torture, two were films of child molestation, and two included the killing of women for sexual stimulation. In their examination of pornographic magazines they found images and themes like the following:

A *Penthouse* spread entitled "The Joy of Pain," illustrated with a large needle piercing a woman's painted fingernail and finger.

An article in *Oui* magazine (published by *Playboy*) entitled "Jane Birkin in Bondage," in which Jane "explains the solution to all disciplinary problems." It is illustrated with several colour photos of Jane Birkin handcuffed, gagged, whipped, and beaten.

*Hustler* magazine's "Chester the Molester." Until 1978 Chester was a regular feature of *Hustler*. Each month he molested a different young girl, using techniques like lying, kidnapping, and assault.

A magazine called *Bondage*, in which women are tied up and scissors, hot irons, torches, and knives are held to their breasts and vaginas.

A magazine called *Brutal Trio*, in which three men successively kidnap a woman, a twelve-year-old girl, and a grandmother, and beat them senseless, kicking them in the face, head and body. After they have passed out, they are raped and beaten again.[9]

These examples are from American magazines, but many of them are available in Canada, and some of the legal questions which have arisen have resulted from restrictions on the importation of pornographic material from the United States....

The most disturbing aspect of such examples is the increasing trend toward violence in pornography. As Thelma McCormack notes:

A new hard-edged sado-masochistic pornography has appeared in which women are mutilated and abused with chains, whips, and fists. The women in this pornography are presented as seeking and enjoying their own punishment, while violence heightens the erotic excitement of both partners....[10]

Many commentators argue that these prevailing trends make untenable a "hands off" attitude to pornography, though McCormack and others still argue against any form of censorship. It is in view of this disagreement that we may turn to the liberal point of view.

In order to see that liberalism is compatible with censorship, it is important to begin with a careful analysis of liberalism. It should, for a start, be noted that liberalism does not mean complete freedom for the individual. On the contrary, it holds that an individual's freedom must be accompanied by a respect for others' rights and freedoms, and this respect is essential to the survival of the liberal state. It is this mutual respect which holds the state together, and accounts for its ability to allow for individuals differences which might otherwise rend the state asunder. Without it, such a state inevitably degenerates into a battle between different individuals with competing interests and alternative points of view.

Given the respect for others which is crucial to the liberal state, the importance of *On Liberty* lies in its demarcation of the appropriate range of individual freedom (and, thereby, the appropriate limits on the intervention in an individual's affairs). As Mill puts it in the principle which forms the basis of his views, "the only purpose for which power can be rightfully exercised over any member of a civilized community, against his will, is to prevent harm to others."[11] It is harm to others which constitutes a rejection of their freedom and their rights, and it is for this reason that the state may intervene to prevent such harm. It follows that an individual may act as he wishes as long as "self-regarding" actions are in question, though not when he performs "other-regarding" actions which have consequences for others. Mill himself provides an ample discussion of his principle, and it is enough for us to note that he is concerned to use it to defend an individual's right to adopt his own political and religious point of view.

Before we consider how one may extend Mill's principle to provide a basis for censorship, we should note that it provides no *prima facie* grounds for censorship. It does allow us to take action against pornography which involves coercion or actual harm to others, but this leaves the bulk of pornographic materials untouched. Films like *Snuff* [in which a female production assistant is apparently murdered in real life] and articles which incorporate actual child abuse are available, but most pornographic material is based on staged, rather than actual incidents.[12] Moreover, films like *Snuff* could be simulated and this restriction would, for this reason, have little effect on the material that was available. At most, it would (if it could be enforced)[13] place minimal restrictions on how pornographic materials were produced, though this might have no discernible effect on the finished product.

Another way one might attempt to go from Mill's principle to censorship is by arguing that there is a casual link between pornography, violence and sex-related crimes. Given this link, one could argue that the kind of pornography already mentioned does harm others and can legitimately be banned. There are problems with this argument, however, for psychological research on pornography is at present inconclusive.[14] Moreover, it is arguable that Mill would endorse this appeal to his principle, for he apparently holds that state intervention must be restricted to actions which cause *direct* harm to others. In his discussion of drunkenness, for example, he argues that it often leads to harm, but that this does not provide sufficient grounds for action against it.

> If a man, through intemperance or extravagance, becomes unable to pay his debts, or, having undertaken the moral responsibility of a family, becomes from the same cause incapable of

supporting or educating them, he is deservedly reprobated and might be justly punished; but it is for the breach of duty to his family or creditor, not for the extravagance.[15]

In a similar way, it might be argued that the "extravagance" involved in the viewing of violence in pornography should not be punishable in itself. Rather, it might be said that one whose indulgence in such extravagance leads him to violent acts should be punished (for his acts do harm others), but not for the extravagance itself. Given this interpretation of *On Liberty*, Mill would have to hold that pornography should not be censored, and that there is no cause for social intervention until an individual becomes involved in acts which encompass (direct) harm to others. As Clark notes in "Pornography's Challenge to Liberal Ideology," the stipulation that direct harm to others is the only justification for social intervention does not allow for censorship.

Despite the apparent fact that there is no direct route from Mill's liberalism to censorship, there is a way in which his principle can be extended for use in this regard. To see how this extension can be accomplished, we should note that Mill's account of harm is in many ways unclear. As Joel Feinberg notes in this regard:

Hardly anyone would deny the state the right to make criminal such directly injurious conduct as willful homicide, assault and battery, and robbery. Mill often wrote as if the prevention of private harm is the *sole* valid ground for state coercion, but this must not have been his considered intention. He would not have wiped from the book such crimes as tax evasion, smuggling, and contempt of court, which need not injure any specific individuals, except insofar as they weaken public institutions in whose health we all have a stake.[16]

On this account of Mill's intentions, he holds that the liberal state can legitimately take action to prevent harm to public welfare. Yet we have already seen that its survival (and its cohesion) requires a mutual respect for others, and we can conclude that it can legitimately take action to insure such respect. Mill wishes to insure it by state intervention into acts which cause harm to others, but we may add the stipulation that the freedom of the press is not to be allowed in cases where it seeks to undermine the very principle that harm to others is not acceptable. It is in this way that we may construct a restriction on the freedom of the press which is analogous to Mill's restriction on individual freedoms. Mill himself does not suggest this restriction, but he does not consider the possibility that the press will be used to suggest that harm to others is acceptable. He seems to assume that the press will not be used in such a fashion, but experience shows us otherwise.

One way to construe this justification of censorship is in terms of Mill's remarks about the dispositions that lead to harmful other-regarding actions. These dispositions are, he holds, properly speaking immoral and "fit subjects" for disapproval.[17] As he puts it in a passage which sounds as though it were directed at present-day pornography:

> Cruelty of disposition; malice and ill-nature; ... insincerity, irascibility on insufficient cause, and resentment disproportioned to the provocation; the love of domineering over others; the desire to engross more than one's fair share of advantages ..., the pride which derives gratification from the abasement of others; the egotism which thinks self and its concerns more important than everything else ...—these are moral vices and constitute a bad and odious moral character ....[18]

These other-regarding vices are particularly unacceptable in a liberal state because they militate against the respect for others which is essential to its survival. Given the importance of such respect, and Mill's views, we can see the proposed censorship as an attempt to discourage dispositions that cause harm to others, where harm is understood as physical harm or the denial of one's legitimate rights and freedoms.

Given this general account of censorship, we may turn to its specific consequences for contemporary pornography.[19] It suggests that pornography is not acceptable, and may be censored, when it encourages, glorifies or makes light of activities that cause harm to others, where harm is understood in terms of physical harm and/or the denial of one's appropriate rights and freedoms. Such activities are not permissible, and neither is the suggestion that they are desirable as a means to sexual satisfaction. It immediately follows that pornography which features coercion, rape, torture, bondage, and child molestation is unacceptable whether it is based on actual or staged incidents.[20] It suggests that a respect for others (in particular, women and children) is secondary to the goal of sexual excitement, and that should not be tolerated in a state which depends on mutual respect for its survival. Magazines like *Brutal Trio* and *Bondage* must therefore be censored, and so must games like "Custer's Revenge," for they portray rape and other kinds of harm as light-hearted activities to be pursued for one's enjoyment.[21]

One aspect of such censorship which needs to be noted is its consequences for the way in which pornographic materials must be judged. It should, in particular, be noted that an acceptable or unacceptable film, book, etc., must not be judged in terms of content, but by a consideration of the attitude it expresses towards its content. Sexual explicitness is not, for example sufficient grounds for censorship, and pornography is unacceptable only when it condones an element of harm or coercion. Even a film which contains a rape scene is not *ipso facto* obscene or unacceptable, and the crucial factor is the attitude it expresses towards the rape. A magazine which glorifies rape as a route to sexual satisfaction must be censored, while an anti-rape film like *Scream from Silence* (a film which graphically portrays a rape) does not warrant censorship. In a similar way, documentaries and other films may or may not contain obscene material depending on the attitude they express towards their sexual subject matter.

In view of the important role that attitude plays in making certain kinds of pornography unacceptable, it will no doubt be pointed out that there may be borderline cases which are difficult to judge. This is perhaps inevitable, but it can still be said that the proposed account allows for a relatively clear distinction between what is and is not acceptable. Hence any particular case can be decided by asking whether the material in question (1) depicts (verbally or pictorially) sexual acts which involve physical harm or the violation of an individual's rights, and whether (2) such acts are presented in a way that encourages, condones or makes light of the acts in question. Condition (1) is straightforward as it stands, and though (2) leaves room for some interpretation, it should not make decisions impossible. There is, for example, no difficulty in concluding that most of the material we have already examined is not allowable.[22] Moreover, we shall see that the proposed account of censorship leaves much less room for doubt than the kind of censorship which is currently in place...

Given this liberal account of censorship, we may end the present discussion by examining censorship as it operates in Canada. This is not the place for a detailed discussion of the law, but we may note its general nature. The legal basis for the censorship of pornography is provided by the various sections of the Criminal Code that deal with obscenity. Section 159(1)(a) stipulates that:

> Everyone commits an offence who makes, prints, publishes, distributes, circulates, or has in his possession for the purpose of publication, distribution or circulation any obscene written matter, picture, model, phonograph record, or other thing whatsoever....

Section 159(8) defines an obscene publication as:

> any publication a dominant characteristic of which is the undue exploitation of sex, or sex and any one or more of the following subjects, namely, crime, horror, cruelty and violence, shall be deemed to be obscene.

In their interpretation of these sections of the Criminal Code, Canadian courts have consistently held that the "undue exploitation" of sex is to be judged on the basis of community standards of tolerance. Hence a judge who is to decide whether material is or is not obscene is to make his or her decision on the basis of an assessment of what is in keeping with present community standards.

It is in view of the courts' appeal to community standards (and the 1975 Supreme Court decision that the censorship of films was within provincial jurisdiction)[23] that the Ontario Censor Board has used similar criteria to accept and reject films proposed for public viewing in the province: "Concerns and values of the community as a whole are researched to determine guidelines, which, with reasonable flexibility, are applied to all films for public exhibition."[24] The role of the Censor Board is now being challenged under the provisions of the new Charter of Rights, but it continues to regulate the films shown for public viewing in Ontario. Moreover, even if it were dissolved, the ultimate test as to whether a film was obscene would still rely on an assessment of community standards, though this assessment would then be undertaken by the federal courts rather than by the Censor Board. Given the common appeal to community standards, we may end by noting the problems with such an appeal, and the way in which these problems can be handled by the liberal account of censorship which has already been developed.

One of the recurring problems which has confronted those who deal with censorship has been their inability to construct a definition of obscenity and pornography capable of demarcating what is acceptable and unacceptable in this regard. One of the common attitudes was expressed by an American Supreme Court Judge who declared that "I can't define pornography, but I know it when I see it." Such an attitude will not do, for it can only lead to inconsistency as different individuals decide that they "know" different things to be obscene. It might initially be thought that an appeal to community standards might eliminate this problem, but their vague and elusive nature has meant little progress in this area. As the Standing Committee on Justice and Legal Affairs notes:

> Our test for obscenity has been called the "community stan-
> dards" test. It has led to a great deal of controversy and inconsis-
> tency in the obscenity case law in Canada.... The determination
> of "community standards" by the experts appearing in obscenity
> trials is ... left largely to their hunches, impressions and subjec-
> tive judgments.[25]

Further controversy has arisen over whether community standards should be understood to be Canada-wide standards or those of the particular locality where the offence occurs. It is in view of such problems that obscenity laws have provided "much confusion and dismay in the minds of the public, retailers, distributors, police officers, Crown prosecutors, defence lawyers, judges and juries."[26]

In contrast to the vagueness inherent in an appeal to community standards, the proposed account of censorship can provide a more precise definition of obscenity which is easily applied. Hence it suggests that the Criminal Code should define an obscene publication as "any publication which depicts (verbally or pictorially) sexual acts which involve harm to some individual in such a way as to encourage, condone, or make light of the acts in question," while harm should be defined as "physical harm or the violation of an individual's legal rights and freedoms." Given an account of obscenity along these lines, the present confusion on the issue could quickly be resolved, and all concerned would be in a better position to judge what is and is not "obscene" from a legal point of view.

More important than the practical problems with the legal definition of obscenity is its complete lack of any persuasive moral justification, and the illegitimate restrictions it can place on individual freedom. Hence community standards cannot determine what is obscene (or indecent or immoral) from a moral point of view, and it follows that they should not be imposed on particular individuals. If the majority of Canadians were Shakers, for example, it would not follow that any acts which violated their Puritan ethics were immoral and constituted the "undue exploitation" of sex which the Criminal Code equates with obscenity. Conversely, if the Canadian public were to fasten on rape, bondage, torture, and child molestation as methods of sexual gratification, it would not follow that one should accept them as morally acceptable and as featuring no undue exploitation of sex and violence. In the one case, any sexual act could be judged to be obscene, while in the other no act would satisfy the present legal definition. Given that there is no reason to believe the majority adopt the appropriate view of sexual morality, it is wrong to force their views on other individuals. Within reason, the majority does have a right not to be subjected to public displays they find offensive, but they overstep this right when they dictate what an individual must do or not do in private. Provided an individual's actions do not harm others (and do not encourage harm to others) he should be allowed to live in accordance with his own sexual morality. It is, in the final analysis, for this reason that a liberal form of censorship is preferable to that which is in place.

## NOTES

1. He says, for example, that one is not free to incite a mob to violence. (*On Liberty,* [New York: Penguin, 1974], p. 119.) His restrictions on public actions that offend public morals might also be taken to imply some restrictions on freedom of expression.

2. I use the expression "freedom of the press" in a broad sense to cover any public presentation of one's views. Hence "press" in this sense includes film, radio, television, and other forums for public presentation.

3. See Marshall Cohen, "The Case Against Censorship," in Burr and Goldinger, eds., *Philosophy and Contemporary Issues*, 2nd ed. (New York: Macmillan, 1976); and Thelma McCormack, "Passionate Protests: Feminists and Censorship," *Canadian Forum*, March 1980. Note also Laura Lederer's comment that "the liberal approach ... presents pornography as just one more aspect of our ever expanding sexuality." (Laura Lederer, ed., *Take Back the Night: Women on Pornography* [New York: William Morrow, 1980], p. 19. A similar view of liberalism is taken for granted in the essays in David Holbrook, ed., *The Case Against Pornography* (La Salle, IL: Open Court, 1973).

4. If Mill's views in "The Subjection of Women" are any indication, it is hard to see how he could accept the cases I will consider (see John Stuart Mill and Harriet Taylor Mill, *Essays on Sex Equality* [ed. Rossi] [Chicago: Univ. of Chicago Press, 1970]).

5. See Lorenne Clark, "Pornography's Challenge to Liberal Ideology," *Canadian Forum*, March 1980.

6. See, for example, F.E. Sparshott's article "Art and Censorship: A Critical Survey of the Issues," in *Philosophy and Contemporary Issues*. Note also that the kinds of incidents discussed by periodicals like the *Index on Censorship* are not concerned with the kind of pornography I will discuss.

7. Anne Cameron, "Hard Core Horror," *Broadside*, February 1983, 5.

8. For a general account of the controversy, see *Maclean's* 31 January and 7 February 1983.

9. *Take Back the Night*, pp. 18–19.

10. "Passionate Protests: Feminists and Censorship," 9.

11. *On Liberty*, p. 68.

12. Whether staged or actual incidents are in question, particularly serious questions arise when children are involved in the production of pornography. In the present paper, however, I will not pursue questions of this sort (though they have recently arisen in view of films like *Pretty Baby* and *The Tin Drum*).

13. One must wonder how effectively such enforcement could be carried out given that it would be practically impossible to inspect the production of the material in question (particularly that produced elsewhere). It might be noted in this connection that there has been some controversy over whether the film *Snuff* records an actual incident. The fact that there is room for doubt in such instances indicates how difficult such judgement is.

14. For some indication of recent research findings, see the articles by Irene Diamond, Diana E. Russell, and Pauline Bart and Margaret Joza in Section IV of *Take Back the Night*. Earlier research does seem vitiated by flaws in its

methodology (in particular, a failure to distinguish between violent and non-violent pornography).

**15.** *On Liberty*, p. 148.

**16.** Feinberg, *Social Philosophy*, (New York: Prentice-Hall, 1973), pp. 25–26.

**17.** *On Liberty*, pp. 144–45.

**18.** Ibid.

**19.** This general account of censorship could also be used to argue for censorship in others areas—e.g., in regard to the publication of racist political views. There are, however, other considerations that would have to be taken into account before deciding whether such censorship was desirable. The kinds of issues which arise are those which were raised in response to the decision of the Illinois Supreme Court that constitutional guarantees of freedom gave the members of the American [National] Socialist Party the right to march in Nazi uniforms through Skokie, Illinois, a predominantly Jewish community.

**20.** In view of such restrictions, it might be said that some individuals consent or wish to partake in sado-masochistic activities, and that this is their right. The proposed restrictions are not, however, restrictions on actions, but restrictions on the publication of material which encourages such actions. Whether or not the actions themselves should be illegal is a question I shall not take up here.

**21.** Another case of pornographic humor which might be mentioned is an article entitled "How To Rape A Retarded Girl," which appeared in the *National Lampoon* some years ago. The gist of the article was that it was alright to rape a retarded girl because even if she told someone, one could simply reply that she was crazy.

**22.** If there are borderline cases, it is probably better to err on the side of being too restrictive rather than too lenient. The change that one will in this way censor something that is of tremendous social value seems to me unlikely.

**23.** *McNeil v. N.S. Bd. of Censors*, [1975] 2 S.C.R. 662, 25.

**24.** From the 1981 Report of the Theatres Branch of the Ministry of Consumer and Commercial Relations.

**25.** "Report on Pornography," *House of Commons Journal*, Vol. 123, No. 86, p. 532.

**26.** Ibid.

# Pornography and Liberalism

*William Watson*

In recent years the strategy of many people who take a generally permissive view of pornography has changed from the classic liberal position, which holds (with some qualifications) that people should be free to read or view whatever they wish, to one based on the rival notion that the community should proscribe the publication of any materials that offend against its standards.

The occasion for this change in strategy is increased concern, emanating originally from the women's movement, about crimes against women and children, as well as what is widely thought to be an increase in the availability of pornography in which sexual gratification is achieved through violence.

Quite apart from being illiberal, this adoption of the "community standards" strategy is unwise—even, it should be emphasized, if it does not currently restrict the access of most people to sexual materials that interest them. The reason, obviously, is that community standards can change. It was barely 50 years ago, after all, that *Ulysses* and *Lady Chatterley's Lover* were forbidden reading in most otherwise civilized jurisdictions.

It is not far-fetched to suppose that the wave of moral conservatism apparently gathering in the western world will wash away many of the legal protections to self-expression that have been built up over the last fifty years. If so, would-be civil libertarians who have given in on the "community standards" question will then find the game has been lost even before it is begun.

Of course, most people who wish to control violent pornography are not unmindful of this difficulty and therefore argue that censorship of such materials in fact is consistent with classical liberalism (see especially Leo Groarke's "Pornography: From Liberalism to Censorship," in Winter 1983 *Queen's Quarterly*).

In what follows, I argue that this simply is not true. On the other hand, while a truly liberal view of pornography would allow for publication of virtually any material, it would also place much stricter controls than we now have on how and to whom such materials are distributed.

I do not wish to argue about what position John Stuart Mill would take on the question of violent pornography were he alive today. To my (amateur's) knowledge, he did not pronounce on the subject. What is more interesting—and germane—is to try to see whether an application of the principles of liberty which Mill enunciated so persuasively can justify censorship of outrageous materials in an age in which the outrageous has become mundane. In my view, this is not possible.

The essence of Mill's argument on liberty is familiar. As he has it: *The only part of the conduct of anyone, for which he is amenable to society, is that which concerns others. In the part which merely concerns himself, his independence is, of right, absolute. Over himself, over his own body and mind, the individual is sovereign.*

In other words, unless a man's actions do harm to others, he should be free to do precisely as he pleases. What is perhaps more important for present purposes, however, is that Mill has a quite narrow notion of the types of action that can be construed as causing harm to other people. He says: *When I say himself, I mean directly, and in the first instance: for whatever affects himself, may affect others* through *himself,* and: *The acts of an individual may be hurtful to others, or wanting in due consideration for their welfare without going the length of violating any of their constituted rights. The offender may then be justly punished by opinion, though not by law.*

Finally, Mill specifies that when he refers to harm to others he means: *perceptible hurt to an assignable individual except himself.*

Thus, in discussing habitual drunkenness, Mill argued that it was not the "extravagance"—i.e., the drunkenness—that should be punished, but the acts of direct harm to family, friends, and creditors that may be committed by drunkards (or, for that matter, by anyone). But while legal sanctions clearly should be applied to such acts, there is no reason to suppress the distribution of alcoholic beverages. (Whether it should be legal to sell alcohol to people who are already inebriated is another matter.)

The possibility of a parallel with pornography is obvious. In developing this parallel further, it may be useful to consider a specific case. In late 1984, *Penthouse* magazine published a series of photographs depicting naked and partially naked women who had been bound and gagged and were being submitted to various other indignities. The relevant question for present purposes is how these photographs cause direct harm in any sense that satisfies Mill's quite narrow definition of such harm.

A first possibility is that the women in the pictures were in fact juveniles, as certainly is the case with many of the materials currently available. Classic liberalism obviously has no difficulty with outlawing both photo sessions involving juveniles and the distribution of any pictures that result, since the juveniles are not legally competent to authorize distribution. Nor does it have difficulty with laws proscribing the freedom of guardians to sign away their wards' rights: the state clearly has an obligation to protect the legally incompetent.

A second possibility is that the photos in question record actual crimes—in other words, that the women in the pictures did not submit to indignity voluntarily. In this case, the sessions themselves obviously were illegal and could have been stopped. On the other hand, the fact that whatever violence took place had been arranged for the benefit of photographers presumably would not merit additional punishment. The presence of cameras on the scene is relevant only in so far as it demonstrates rather careful premeditation.

Needless to say, the victims of "arranged" crimes usually will object to having the visual record of their victimization distributed, and this is an objection society presumably will wish to honour. (A conundrum arises, however, if someone—a news photographer, say—were able to film the criminals filming their crime. Should publication of *these* pictures be permitted?)

Moreover, allowing people to profit from crime in this way creates a clear "moral hazard" encouraging the commission of crime. "Snuff films," in which what is portrayed is an actual murder, depend for their profitability on the sad fact that people apparently will pay large amounts of money to see such materials. In this case, it is reasonable to expect that allowing distribution of such films would lead more or less directly to more deaths.

Of course, in the vast majority of cases the various crimes portrayed have been simulated. This raises a third possibility—and the one most likely to have been true in the *Penthouse* episode—namely that the models treated in such an undignified way were of age and in fact were well paid for their time and trouble. Was direct harm done to them? I would say not.

While it may be regretted that the economics of the smut business are such that people will be tempted to take up posing for such materials as a career, it would be highly inappropriate for the state to intervene legally to require them not to. Were this a better world, they might not have to earn a living this way; but it is not yet a better world. (For the contrary view that pornographers do social good, see Al Goldstein's comments in *Harper's*, November 1984.)

Of course, none of this addresses the major concern of those who wish to outlaw violent pornography, which is that pornography can bring harm to third parties if those who view it are encouraged to commit violent crimes.

A first difficulty with this argument is that the psychological evidence apparently is not yet conclusive. Moreover, given the significant methodological limitations of most social sciences, it seems unlikely that there ever will be widespread agreement on the effects of pornography on crime.

No doubt many people who commit violent, sex-related crimes also have a taste for violent pornography. By the same token, it may well be that most people who have committed acts of political violence in Canada in the last 30 years have read *The Communist Manifesto*, though this obviously is no reason to ban it.

There is also the well-known alternative hypothesis that violent pornography may serve as a substitute for, rather than a spur to, actual violence. In any case, the link between the pornographer and the victim of sexual violence is a tenuous one. Freedom of speech, as is widely recognized, does not include the freedom either to incite riot or to shout "Fire!" in a crowded theatre. Mill's own example was that: *An opinion that corn-dealers are starvers of the poor ...ought to be unmolested when simply circulated through the press, but may justly incur punishment when delivered orally to an excited mob assembled before the house of the corn-dealer.*

While the need for some constraints on free speech is obvious, in the liberal view of things these constraints are kept extremely narrow. In most western societies the latitude given to self-expression is quite considerable. All sorts of loose talk about revolution and the overthrow of established order, if, when, and but, is widely permitted. It is only when people advocate specific violent actions at specific times and specific places that notice is taken—and this is as it should be.

If pornographic materials do present an imminent danger to the public safety or, in a credible way, explicitly advocate violence against given groups or individuals, then there is ample reason to suppress them. But by any dispassionate standard the private viewing of pornography is a far cry from incitement to riot. The great mass of such materials, however distasteful to majority opinion, have a more limited purpose, namely, the immediate and usually private sexual gratification of an individual or group of individuals.

It is far-fetched to suppose that the people who produce such films seriously intend to convey the message that bondage, violent rape, and chainsaw massacres are or should be approved forms of social behaviour. Indeed, in many cases the titillation presumably arises from the fact that the act portrayed is illegal and the observer therefore unlikely ever to engage in it.

The most enduring message most people will come away with from such materials is not that violence against women and children is approved conduct, but that it is truly amazing what some people will do for money—or kicks. We can both regret and condemn the fact that fellow citizens apparently require such forms of stimulation to achieve sexual gratification, and we can offer them sympathy and psychiatric help, but I fail to see how the private production and viewing of violent pornography constitute direct harm to others in any sense Mill would have understood.

To be sure, it may not occur to some misbegotten soul that murder can be committed with a chainsaw until he sees a movie in which it is. But to place the blame for any chainsaw murders this unfortunate may commit on the director or producer of the movie that gave him the idea would be a dramatic departure from the usual principle that people must be held responsible for their own actions. Similarly, it would be a major reconstruction of the laws of negligence to require that movie producers and directors assure that their movies are shown only to the mentally competent.

Except in very special circumstances, the law must proceed on the assumption that people are free agents.

An even more ingenious defence of the idea that restricting access to violent pornography is consistent with liberalism has been devised recently by Leo Groarke (in the *Queen's Quarterly* article cited above). Mainly because the empirical evidence is so shaky, Groarke rejects the idea that the alleged causal link between violent pornography and violent crimes justifies censorship. Instead, he argues that the direct harm pornography does consists in the fact that the person who has viewed pornographic violence is less likely to respect his or her fellow citizens and their rights.

Since Mill argues that mutual respect is a pre-condition for civil society, such materials may well threaten the foundations of established order—which would constitute harm by virtually anyone's standards.

An obvious problem here is that it is not just *sexual* violence that can cause the loss of respect for others which may predispose us to remove or devalue their rights. The depiction both of "ordinary" violence and "ordinary" erotica can also do the job.

Many members of the modern women's movement presumably would wish to ban any depiction of sexual relations meant primarily to titillate or arouse, on the grounds that when men, in particular, receive sexual gratification from watching strangers commit sexual acts, the lesson this teaches is that women are to be viewed primarily as sex objects.

Unfortunately, people are likely to make up their minds about what materials are corrosive of the social order mainly by asking themselves what materials they themselves would not care to view. Thus Groarke's regime of censorship, provided it were responsible to some government or other, could easily devolve to a system in which the majority of the population simply outlawed those materials it did not approve. This might well be a workable regime of censorship; it would hardly be a liberal one.

But the idea that society should use criminal sanctions to enforce mutual respect among its citizens raises more fundamental difficulties.

"Respect" comprises both a state of mind and the actions that follow from being in that state of mind. Mill would have had no difficulty with state sanctions against *acts* of disrespect—spitting on someone, say, or defaming or harassing them, or advocating that they be denied their civil rights. I doubt, however, that he would have been comfortable with the notion of society trying to enforce various states of mind.

Unless our disrespect for fellow citizens leads us to take disrespectful action against them—action which is sanctionable—it is hard to see what interest society can have in changing our view. Presumably we would be better people if we did not harbour such feelings, but the notion that the state should make us better people has more to do with 20th-century welfare-ism than 19th-century liberalism.

Of course, the most fundamental difficulty of all is that unless we take some sort of action as a result of our state of mind, it may not be possible for others to know what that state of mind is. But the proposition that the act of viewing pornography is itself an act of disrespect which should be proscribed stretches the notion of direct harm well beyond its breaking point.

A woman may well be upset to know that a man has arranged with his pornographer to view depictions of disrespectful acts committed against members of her sex but—to date, at least—the courts have not found that provoking other people's moral outrage is a damageable action. Were they to adopt this doctrine, of course, the implications for many other questions of private morality would be far-reaching.

This raises the whole question of consistency, for consistent application of the principles that have been adduced to justify the suppression of violent pornography would require equally vigorous intervention in many other areas. Consistency may be the hobgoblin of little minds; it is also the cornerstone of most systems of justice, including our own.

One obvious inconsistency in censoring violent pornography is that it creates two classes of crimes, those whose depiction in words or on film is permitted and those whose depiction is itself outlawed. If violent pornography is to be disallowed on the grounds that it is disruptive of the social order, then presumably it would be best to disallow *all* depiction of violence, for the idea that violence is an acceptable means for resolving disputes poses a serious danger to civilized society. This obviously would require significant changes in the current regime of censorship.

Alternatively, it might be argued that the problem with pornography is that it provides a *sympathetic* depiction of illegal acts. Thus films that depict illegal acts but ultimately demonstrate that crime does not pay—in other words, the standard fare of the U.S. television networks—should be permitted, while those that simply glorify crime should not be. However appealing this construction may seem at first blush, it clearly represents a reversion to the highly illiberal doctrine of "redeeming social value."

In Mill's world, people are allowed to do what they please not because it improves either themselves or their neighbours, but simply because it does please them.

From a practical point of view, as well, this approach is seriously flawed: pornographers are likely to see it mainly as a challenge to their ingenuity in packaging the truly scabrous between large dollops of the anodyne. The doctrine of redeeming social value would also create difficulties for "ordinary" erotica, much of which provides a sympathetic display of acts which, even when performed by consenting adults, remain illegal in many jurisdictions. If it is to be illegal to encourage people to commit crimes, in many places it also will have to be illegal to view most of the more exotic voluntary sexual practices.

If the principle that encouraging citizens to think disrespectful thoughts about one another should be prohibited is to be widely adopted—as it should be if it is a good principle—then other significant changes in current social behaviour will have to take place.

In particular, consistency before the law will require a much more careful vetting of social and political discourse.

*Sister Mary Ignatius,* the play in which a lapsed nun lampoons the idiosyncrasies of the Catholic religion, has proved an enriching experience for many ex-Catholics, but in the view of a large number of practising Catholics seems mainly to promote disrespect for Catholicism.

Similarly, research into heredity in humans conceivably could produce results that would encourage some citizens to argue that members of various racial groups should be denied their civil rights. Should the research itself be outlawed, as some might argue, or rather advocacy of the denial of civil rights?

Finally, should we now not merely prevent the Nazi Party and the Ku Klux Klan from harassing the groups they would victimize—and the unsuspecting citizens they would proselytize—but also simply outlaw these organizations, so that they will no longer be able to purvey their racism even to the like-minded?

Perhaps legal sanctions *are* called for in these and similar situations. On the other hand, I would argue that it is more in the liberal tradition to limit these and like aberrations by trusting in the good sense of an intellectually self-reliant citizenry and, of course, by arguing against specious doctrines whenever they are proposed.

When the balance is taken on this question it should be remembered that agencies that are given power to censor political views will not always confine their interventions to the transparently crankish. The McCarthy period is only 30 years past. On balance in Canada, constitutional and other safeguards against political persecution probably are stronger than they were in those days. I would hesitate to conclude that all dangers in this regard have passed, however. One of the sadder aspects of the human condition is the continual rediscovery of just how intolerant a species we can be.

To suggest that, with rare exceptions, society should not censor any form of pornography is not to argue that all is right with the way pornography is currently treated. In fact, liberals probably should be just as exercised about the current regime—though obviously for different reasons—as most feminists are.

Pornography does do direct harm in Mill's sense of the term when people who do not wish to see it are exposed to it involuntarily. Displays of nudity and explicit sexuality in storefronts, on magazine racks, and on billboards and cinema marquees are not entitled to the protection of liberals. Where passersby can be offended, "externalities" exist and Mill's conditions for non-intervention do not hold.

Censorship of the public airwaves is easily justifiable on these grounds—though with the advent of pay-TV, "broadcasting" of what are essentially private television signals has become possible. Similar reasoning suggests that much more should be done to restrict the access of minors to pornographic materials.

It would be unwise and perhaps even inappropriate to duplicate the full panoply of regulations and laws that currently govern the distribution of alcohol in most provinces, but tighter control over the distribution of pornography clearly is called for. At some stage, of course, zoning laws and display codes may be used mainly to harass those who wish to exercise their right of access to pornography, but a walk through the downtown section of any major city, especially if it includes a stop at a newsstand, will persuade most people that harassment of this sort is not yet a serious problem.

I have argued that, except in very special cases, even violent pornography should not be exempted from the standard liberal presumption that people should be free to read and view whatever they choose. Since people who take the contrary view are unlikely to pursue the logical implications of their policy position to its often radical conclusions, it seems to me to represent an attempt to impose an essentially arbitrary set of preferences on society.

Those people who do follow their reasoning to its logical conclusions and therefore propose new state interventions in many areas of public discourse have, I think, quite simply got the balance of costs and benefits wrong.

I therefore conclude that at bottom such people are appealing to the "community standards" view of censorship, a view which in the long run is inimical to liberalism. To use Mill's phrase, we are back to a situation in which *there is ... no recognized principle by which the propriety or impropriety of government interference (can) be tested.* Whatever a majority of voters agrees to wins.

This is an unfortunate—and illiberal—development. The purpose of liberalism is not to make us better than we are but to enable us— imperfect as we are—to live in society with one another. To this end, much more should be done to prevent involuntary exposure to offensive materials. But the attempt to eliminate even radical forms of vice is misguided and, carried to its logical extremes, may well be harmful, for, as Mill has it, "unless ... reasons are good for an extreme case they are not good for any case."

# P O S T S C R I P T

In recent years, the debate over pornography has been increasingly influenced by feminist forms of analysis. In contrast to liberals and conservatives, feminists see pornography as essentially an equality issue. To many feminists, pornography is dangerous because it is an instrument of patriarchal society in its promotion of a sexual class system that perpetuates women's inferior status and role in society. Pornography objectifies women and perpetuates stereotypes of their different and inferior position in society. However, feminists do not go as far as conservatives in seeking to regulate all forms of sexually explicit material. Instead, many argue that a distinction needs to be made between erotica, which celebrates consensual sexuality, and pornography, which degrades and subjugates women. Only the latter merits strict regulation and censorship.

But how does one draw a distinction between erotica and pornography? When former Conservative Minister of Justice Ray Hnatyshyn brought in new and tougher legislation to regulate pornography (Bill C-54), many feminists expressed alarm that he had gone too far. Jane Rhodes of the Art Gallery of Ontario's Reference Library estimated that 55 percent of the AGO's collection could be banned under the proposed legislation. In an article entitled "Silencing Ourselves?: Pornography, Censorship and Feminism" in *Resources for Feminist Research* 17, no. 3 (September 1988): 133–35, Rhodes explores the dilemma that censorship poses for the feminist position. She argues that censorship of the type expressed in Bill C-54 could deprive the women's movement of the means to criticize the reasons underlying the demand for pornography. As Rhodes contends, the issue is "not whether pornography encourages violence against women but whether censorship could actually silence the women's movement."

A sampling of diverse feminist views on pornography can be found in Laura Lederer, ed., *Take Back the Night: Women on Pornography* (Toronto: Bantam Books, 1984). *The Report of the Special Committee on*

*Pornography and Prostitution* (Ottawa: 1985) presents a useful discussion of the various ideological approaches to pornography and their implications for public policy.

Although successive Canadian governments have promised to introduce stronger measures to regulate pornography, attempts to do so have been largely frustrated. On five different occasions in recent decades, federal governments have introduced new legislation to regulate pornography, and each time they failed to have their legislation passed. Robert Campbell and Leslie Pal present a useful overview of these failed efforts in *The Real Worlds of Canadian Politics* (Peterborough: Broadview Press, 1989), with special attention to the two ill-fated bills presented by the Conservative government of Brian Mulroney during its first term in office. The Conservative government did make a final attempt to address the issue of pornography by introducing new legislation in the final months preceding the 1993 election. The bill focused specifically on child pornography, calling for increased prison sentences for those either producing or possessing visual materials depicting sexual activity by anyone under 18 years of age. When the bill successfully passed in the House of Commons and the Senate, many greeted it as a step forward. However, by focusing only on pornography involving children, many feel that the issue of how the government should deal with pornography that is degrading to women has still not been resolved.

# ISSUE TWENTY-ONE

## Should Capital Punishment Be Restored?

YES GEOFF WILSON, "The Case For Capital Punishment,"
House of Commons, *Debates*, June 22, 1987, pp. 7421–
423

NO ED BROADBENT, "The Case Against Capital
Punishment," House of Commons, *Debates*, April 27,
1987, pp. 5219–222

On December 11, 1962, Ronald Turpin and Arthur Lucas were hanged at the Don Jail in Toronto. There is little about their lives that most historians would care to remember—except for one particular detail. Turpin and Lucas were the last to be executed under the death penalty in Canada. During the next four years, the government of the day used its powers under the Royal Prerogative of Mercy to commute all death sentences passed by the courts. In 1967, a bill was passed calling for an experimental moratorium on executions for five years. After an extension of the moratorium, Parliament finally took action in 1976 to remove the death penalty from the Criminal Code altogether.

Almost immediately, however, individuals and groups supporting the death penalty began a campaign for its restoration. The initial strategy was for individual Members of Parliament to introduce private members' bills seeking to restore the death sentence to the Criminal Code. Under the Conservative government of Joe Clark, which came to power in 1979, no fewer than eighteen such private members' bills were introduced. But the defeat of the Clark government and the re-election of Pierre Trudeau, who opposed restoration, deferred any hopes for the restoration of the death penalty.

The election of the Mulroney government in 1984 precipitated a more concerted effort on the part of the retentionists. The prime minister had promised during the election that the issue would be debated and put to a free vote in the House of Commons. But it quickly became evident that the issue was not an important priority for the new government. Resenting the delays of their own government, in 1985 Conservative MPs introduced no fewer than nine private members' bills that dealt with capital punishment, but few were even debated.

Despite these setbacks, pressure continued to mount on the government to take some action on the issue. Police associations and other public lobby groups became increasingly vocal in their efforts to put capital punishment on the parliamentary agenda. Facing increased pressure from his own caucus, in 1987 Mulroney finally promised to introduce a government-sponsored bill.

But now the government faced a dilemma. Mulroney himself was an abolitionist who had committed himself to opposing any restoration of the death penalty. However, polls showed that enough Conservative MPs favoured restoration to pass such a bill. Would the prime minister be forced to sign legislation that he opposed as a matter of conscience? One way out would be for the House of Commons to pass the bill and permit the Liberal-dominated Senate to defeat it; but this was hardly a precedent that Mulroney wished to endorse.

The government's compromise strategy was to introduce a government bill that asserted only that Parliament supported in principle the reinstatement of capital punishment. This meant that if the bill actually passed, then the government would have to introduce a second measure to amend the Criminal Code. Thus a positive vote on the initial measure would not mean an immediate restoration of the death penalty.

Preparation for the debate began almost immediately. Retentionists, who had already been active for years, escalated their public campaign. Abolitionists, who had been relatively inactive, quickly organized a Coalition Against the Return of the Death Penalty, and initiated a mailing campaign to MPs with cards proclaiming, "Don't Kill for Me."

Debate on the bill finally began in the House of Commons on April 27, 1987. Although the bill technically dealt with setting in motion a procedure to consider amendment of the Criminal Code, most participants in the debate focused on the general arguments regarding the justification of capital punishment. Geoff Wilson, at that time a Conservative MP, typified the position of the retentionists in arguing that "no system of justice is complete unless it contains the ultimate penalty for the ultimate crime." Ed Broadbent, then leader of the New Democratic Party, spoke against the reinstatement of capital punishment.

In examining this debate, a number of complex issues are raised regarding the proper role of the state in a democratic society. We may agree that, in order to maintain a basic level of order in society, it is proper for the state to punish those who break the law, but there is still widespread disagreement over what that punishment should be and in what cases it should be applied. Even in a country like the United States, which has retained the death penalty, individual states vary widely in their approach to the issue. Some states do not use the death penalty, while others use it quite frequently. States also vary in how they define when capital punishment is an appropriate sentence and how the death sentence should be administered.

In seeking to understand these widely divergent viewpoints, it us useful to ask several questions: How does a person's view of human nature and the sociological causes of crime shape their response to this issue? What role should sociological evidence regarding such issues as the deterrent value of capital punishment or the racial bias of sentencing play in this debate? How are the needs for society to protect itself from violent offenders balanced against the rights of the offenders, irregardless of the crime they have committed? Does the state ever have the right to take a human life?

## The Case For Capital Punishment

*Geoff Wilson*

**Mr. Geoff Wilson (Swift Current–Maple Creek):** Mr. Speaker, I speak today against the amendment and in favour of the principle of reinstatement of capital punishment. Many of my constituents have written requesting information both pro and con concerning this topic. It is interesting to note that there is a considerable amount of abolitionist material put out by a number of well-organized and well-funded groups. On the other hand, pro capital punishment material is difficult to find. The reason for that, I believe, is that, as in many other issues, there is a silent majority out there which is unorganized. As my constituent, Mrs. Ruth Lee Knight points out:

> Many who oppose the return of the death penalty are the same people who have lobbied so successfully over the years for the rights of offenders and they are well organized in their efforts.

> Many operate on Government funds and our concern is that, because of their resources, the Canadian public will be presented with only one side of the issue as they have in the past.

In considering this matter I propose to deal with a number of the arguments against capital punishment in order to better explain my position. We are first told it is cheaper to keep murderers in prison than to execute them. Some have suggested that execution would save costs of prolonged incarceration while others say the threat of the death penalty would lead to endless appeals and legal manoeuvres which could cost even more. I would prefer to reject both approaches. I believe there is a matter of principle here about the value of human life and the validity and integrity of our justice system. I believe the question is one which is beyond monetary considerations.

The second argument put forward is that capital punishment is barbaric. Some abolitionist material tells very graphically of lingering death at the end of a rope, the faulty electric chair and of agony in the gas chamber. But no matter the method, it is clearly the death itself which opponents of capital punishment consider barbaric.

One does not have to like the death penalty in order to support it, any more than one has to like radiation or radical surgery or chemotherapy in order to treat cancer. We are faced with letting the cancer spread or trying to cure it using the methods available today, methods which one day may be viewed as barbaric. In the context of capital punishment, the disease, of course, is injustice. We may not like the death penalty, but it must be available to punish the most heinous crimes of murder, cases in which any other form of punishment would be inadequate and, therefore, unjust.

In this context I cannot help but think of the 11 individuals who have killed six or more times over the past 20 years in this country, those who would assassinate their political enemies on our soil or those who would place bombs in airplanes, thus intentionally taking hundreds of lives. If we create a society in which injustice is not tolerated, then incidents of murder, surely the most flagrant injustice of all, will diminish.

A third point put forward by those opposing the death penalty is that no other civilized country has it. Obviously, the laws of each country will differ according to conditions and traditions, but the fact is there are only 28 countries in the world which do not have capital punishment at all. These countries have less than 10 percent of world population. The death penalty in fact is available in Ireland, Belgium, China, Japan, the United States and in 123 other countries for ordinary crimes and in another 18 countries, including Canada, under conditions of military law.

A fourth argument is that capital punishment cheapens the value of human life. Surely, for example, if the penalty for rape were lowered, it would signal a lessened regard for the victim's suffering and humiliation. It would cheapen their horrible experience and expose them to an increased danger of recurrence.

What does lowering the penalty for murder do? It displays a lessened regard for life, the victim's life. It is by exacting the highest penalty for the wanton and inexcusable taking of human life that the state reaffirms the highest value of life. I say that those who support the death penalty are no less human, no less compassionate, no less concerned and no less Christian than those who oppose it.

Another argument is that the death penalty somehow discriminates against the poor and disadvantaged. With the greatest respect, I do not believe this is so at all. We have in Canada a system of justice wherein all Canadians are entitled to counsel and to the full protection of the law. It is a system which is second to none.

A number of opponents of capital punishment put forward the Biblical admonition, "Thou shalt not kill." Others translate that as "Thou shalt not murder." In this debate it seems, and I say this with the utmost respect, that the problem with a number of the Biblical points of view is that the passages taken from scripture are often pulled out of context. I have received many letters and representations from constituents and others quoting scripture, some offered in support of abolition and just as many offered in support of reinstatement. Many of the great philosophers including Kant, Locke, Hobbes, Rousseau, Montesquieu and Mill, agreed that natural law properly authorized a sovereign to take life in order to vindicate justice. Indeed, the Constitution of the United States, which is widely admired as a model, condemns cruel and inhuman punishment, but does not condemn capital punishment.

I think it is important at this stage to point out that the rights and duties of the state are different from those of the individual. Jack McIntosh, a Member of Parliament for Swift Current–Maple Creek in the 1966 debate, said:

> We have one duty as individuals and because we are Members of Parliament we have another duty so far as the state and its laws are concerned for we are members of that state. If such an interpretation is not correct, then in my view there is no Christian justification for pride in being a member of the Armed Services and no Christian justification for asking anyone to join the Armed Services.

> As an individual you cannot kill, but if you are a member of the Armed Forces of the Government, you must repel an aggressor.

Another popular argument is that the death penalty is nothing more than state sanctioned murder. To say that the state should not under any circumstances have the right to kill is simply nonsense. The state has a duty to protect its citizens from threats and violence, externally and internally. Every November 11 we honour the hundreds of thousands of Canadian men and women who served in three wars and who gave so much that we might enjoy the freedoms of today. Some of them killed the enemy in order that we might be free to assemble and debate in this House. Their actions, far from cheapening the value of life, strengthened it. Those who killed did so as instruments and representatives of the state. Their actions were justifiable because they were done as part of, and on behalf of the Armed Forces of Canada in time of war. They did not murder, they killed, and there is a difference.

There is a duty on the state to protect its citizens against the enemy in peacetime as well as in war, whether through defence expenditures to provide a deterrent against would-be aggressors, or through the kind of justice system which provides the appropriate penalties to punish those who offend against society by breaking its laws.

The murderer who says "You are no better than I am," seeks to bring law abiding society down to his level. This is a false argument. Clearly the state has rights the individual citizen does not. In a democracy, these rights are given to the state by the electorate. The execution of a lawfully

condemned killer is no more an act of murder than is legal imprisonment an act of kidnapping. If an individual forces his neighbour to pay
money under threat of punishment, that is extortion. If the state does it,
that is taxation. The rights and responsibilities surrendered by the individual are what gives the state its power to govern. This contract constitutes the very foundation of civilization itself.

Some say the death penalty creates an atmosphere which breeds violence. It appears that not everyone wants the responsibilities, especially
the difficult ones which come with law enforcement.

Back in the early 1960s a woman was assaulted and murdered on a
New York street. Bystanders looked the other way. The neighbours who
heard her cries for help did nothing. They did not even call the police.
In such a climate, surely, the criminal must inevitably grow bolder. In the
words of Ed Koch, the Mayor of New York City:

> The death of anyone—even a convicted murderer—diminishes
> us all. But we are diminished even more by a justice system that
> fails to function. It is an illusion to let ourselves believe that
> doing away with capital punishment removes the murderer's
> deed from our conscience. The rights of society are paramount.
>
> When we protect guilty lives we give up innocent lives in
> exchange. When opponents of capital punishment say to the
> state: I will not let you kill in my name, they are also saying to
> murderers: You can kill in your own name as long as I have an
> excuse for not getting involved.
>
> It is hard to imagine anything worse than being murdered
> while neighbours do nothing. But something worse exists.
> When those same neighbours shrink back from justly punishing
> the murderer—the victim dies twice.

Abolitionists also suggest that capital punishment brings out the
negative side of humanity—bloodthirstiness, vengeance and so on. With
respect, this says to me that our society is indicating more concern for
the murderer than for the victim. I question this dismissal of the victim
with a shrug saying that he or she cannot be brought back to life and
therefore let us help the murderer, let us rehabilitate him.

Protection of the criminal appears to become the primary objective
of punishment. The rights of the victim have been forgotten. Surely, our
society must first provide resources for the victims of crime. The state
must get its priorities in order. It is wrong, it is indefensible, it is irresponsible to endanger the lives of law-abiding Canadians by sparing a
homicidal sex offender with a previous record of murder.

If we have priorities in Canada I would place the rehabilitation of
murderers way down the list. A much more positive approach would
involve the reform of our corrections and parole system, a system under

which over the past 10 years 95 inmates released under mandatory supervision committed homicide, a system wherein 37 inmates on parole committed murder.

In this context I welcome the remarks made earlier in the debate by my colleague, the Hon. Member for Ottawa West (Mr. Daubney), whose Justice Committee will be looking at the parole system. I urge him to tighten up bail procedures and all forms of early release for violent offenders.

Again, I quote Mrs. Lee Knight who said:

> But if common sense prevails the innocent will have a better chance. If a "life" sentence becomes "Actual Life" and-or if the death penalty is reinstated so judges have some scope of sentencing to choose from, then your life may be spared, your daughter has a better chance of living, your friends and relatives could feel safer. A lot of good it will do to society if you are murdered before you've had a long enough life to establish the Utopia you concentrate on so single mindedly.

Opponents of the death penalty say that an innocent person might be executed by mistake. Our system of criminal justice has evolved over hundreds of years. It is a system which provides every safeguard to an accused, one under which I would consider execution of an innocent person to be virtually an impossibility. Indeed, Adam Bedau, one of the most resolute opponents of capital punishment in the United States, said:

> It is false sentimentality to argue that the death penalty should be abolished because of the abstract possibility that an innocent person might be executed.

But the main point is this. If government functioned only where the possibility of error did not exist, then government would not function at all. I am prepared to accept that risk, especially when I weigh it against the sure knowledge that some murderers murder again.

The other side of this innocent person argument is the repeat killer situation. While we know of no cases in this country where an innocent person has been executed, we know for certain that there are numerous cases wherein convicted murderers have, upon release or while on parole, murdered again. Human life deserves special protection. One of the best ways to guarantee that protection is to ensure that convicted murderers do not murder again. It can be argued that only the death penalty will accomplish this end.

Another point put forward by abolitionists is that capital punishment is not a deterrent. Obviously, many statistics have been put forward by both sides, and they are viewed as conclusive or insufficient, depending on the viewpoint of the presenter or the viewer. How could one ever measure the numbers of those in our society who have contemplated taking someone else's life for whatever reason? Some hopefully discard the idea as a result of realizing its repugnancy. Nevertheless, there must still be some in our society who are deterred by the consequences of imprisonment. I suggest there are still others who do that dreadful act but who, were they to face the ultimate penalty of death, might not.

Common sense tells me that there is an incremental group who are deterred. We are not here talking about a crime of passion done on the sudden, under provocation, or where the person is mentally imbalanced or is swayed by alcohol or drugs. Those are circumstances, of course, which result in a lesser offence. We are talking about a considered, deliberate, conscious act. I believe the penalties prescribed in the Criminal Code, concerning, say, impaired driving or theft, do act as deterrents. I likewise believe that the penalty of execution is a deterrent for some.

Statistics can be paraded out *ad nauseam.* But the deterrence issue boils down to a personal belief. Either you believe in your heart or in your guts that capital punishment is a deterrent or you do not. My sense tells me that it is, that it has to be deterrent to some would-be murderers.

If we could assume that everyone committing murder were of unsound mind and lacked the required intent, then our decision would be easy. But despite all the rules of law providing defences, the mitigating circumstances of alcohol, drugs, provocation and so on, there are still those who, after every safeguard provided by our system of justice, are found guilty beyond any reasonable doubt, by a jury, of intentionally taking the life of another person. Some of those murderers may be worthy of mercy with a provision of imprisonment. But I submit that there are some acts of murder, some acts toward civilized society that must carry with them the maximum penalty. These may be situations of mass murder, hijacking, terrorism, air piracy, or hired killing. These must be situations of cold-blooded, premeditated murder proven beyond any reasonable doubt in the absence of any extenuating circumstances. Where there are no redeeming circumstances at all, I believe the state should make provision for the death penalty.

Surely, the circumstances of a Clifford Olson, who murdered 11 young people, the Air India bombers who cost over 300 lives, or the Hindawi human bomb case in England, had it been successful, are crimes so dastardly and so inhuman as to be deserving of the ultimate penalty. I believe that no system of justice is complete unless it contains the ultimate penalty for the ultimate crime. The failure to provide capital punishment for premeditated murder causes sentencing for all other crimes to be reduced. This in turn leads to diminished respect for the law, a lack of respect which must be evident to all Canadians.

In conclusion, this is clearly an issue on which there are significant numbers of thoughtful and deeply moral people who disagree fundamentally with each other, who disagree as to the means to achieve a less violent society, a society in which law-abiding Canadians can feel secure. At my nomination in 1983, and in the campaign of 1984, I pledged to support the reinstatement of capital punishment and the reform of the parole system. After hearing and earnestly considering the submissions, the expressions of deeply-held belief put to me by constituents and others on both sides of the issue, I remain convinced that our society provides the accused murderer with every safeguard that he has denied his victim. Should that accused be proven guilty beyond reasonable doubt, then I believe the state should provide the death penalty as a sentencing option.

## The Case Against Capital Punishment

*Ed Broadbent*

**Hon. Edward Broadbent (Oshawa):** Mr. Speaker, there is not a subject matter more important for Members of Parliament to debate and deliberate upon than the one that is now before us. As all members on both sides of this issue know, what is at stake here is whether this country will reintroduce into law the right of the state, calmly and deliberately, to take a human life.

It is the importance of this issue that leads me immediately to say to Members of all Parties that I intend to address my comments on this profoundly important matter, not to those who argue with me that capital punishment is wrong, but to those who are either undecided or, up to this moment, believe that it is appropriate for capital punishment to be reintroduced into our laws.

I have concerns about the origin of the resolution, the way it has been brought forward, and I have some concerns about the details of it. But I put those concerns aside to deal with the fundamental question that is at the root of the motion. As the right to experience life, Mr. Speaker, is the most basic of values, so too is the destruction of life, its denial to another, the most horrible of crimes. Whether that destruction is of a child or an elderly person, an invalid or an athlete, a scholar or a cab driver, a man or woman in the home, or whomever, whether that destruction is one of a random mass murder or an act that is premeditated and specific, the result, Mr. Speaker, is the same. The victim's life is snuffed out; it is finished, there is no more. The ultimate impingement on another human being has been carried out.

I am sure everyone in the House agrees that murder is horrible, that we must do all we can to prevent it, and that those who murder must in some sense be punished. However, these are not the central matters before us.

What is central is the obligation of those who want capital punishment to justify that course of action. What is central is their obligation, those who believe that killing our neighbour is morally wrong, to show

453

that the same act of terminal violence when carried out by the state in the name of law is morally right.

Those who want us to approve of the motion, which in its essence, if established, would bring about the restoration of the death penalty, have the obligation to prove their case. If they want to take life, they must provide us with arguments which lead us to conclude that when sanctioned by the state the taking of a life is right.

People who are in favour of capital punishment have a moral duty to prove that killing by the State is justified and to argue their case. That is in fact the major moral concern of this debate, since a debate on the death penalty is about the right of the State to kill.

People who are in favour of capital punishment will have to provide moral arguments to justify the right of the State to kill a human being. In my opinion, killing is justifiable only in two situations. One is self-defence. If a man, woman or child is attacked by another person, he or she has a right to kill the attacker, if necessary, to protect his or her life. The second is when a country or a state declares war or invades another country to forcibly impose its laws on it, thereby making use of violence and death. I think it is right and morally acceptable for the people of that country to defend themselves against the attacker.

The principle involved in these two examples is identical, Mr. Speaker. An individual has the right to protect his life when it is seriously threatened. A State or a community also has that right.

When the only defence against a violent attack on life is the use of violence, then that violence is morally justifiable. Individuals or states have the moral right to survive and to defend that survival when it is being assailed.

However, the question before us is of a different order entirely. It is whether the state is justified in killing a human being, not in active defence, but cruelly, deliberately, in a premeditated way, long after some crime has been committed. Those Members of Parliament who favour this premeditated destruction of human life by the state must make the case for it. It is their responsibility and theirs alone. They cannot shift the moral burden of justifying this kind of violence to those who elected them. They cannot claim they are merely following the wishes of the population.

In this context I say to the government spokesperson who initiated the debate that surely much more is required than simply stating a commitment to one side or the other. Surely the Conservative Member who spoke today had an obligation not simply to restate his position but to give to the people of Canada and to the Members of the House of Commons his moral reason for reaching the conclusion he did. He did not, and to that extent he let down the seriousness of this occasion.

Mr. Speaker, some Members of the House are saying that most Canadian men and women, or rather that most of their constituents want capital punishment to be reinstated. You have heard that argument. Several Hon. Members have adopted a position based on the results of public polls which indicate that most Canadians or most of their constituents are in favour of capital punishment. For such an argument to be valid, one would have to recognize that a democratic government should be satisfied simply with counting votes. It is a bad conception of democracy generally and especially representative democracy.

Mr. Speaker, history's major democrats, from Pericles in ancient Greece to John Stuart Mill, the first democrat of the modern era, have always claimed that discussion based on reason and facts is an essential element of democracy. Within a small community, it is possible for all men and women who are affected by a specific situation to legislate. It was possible at the time of the ancient Greek cities, except for women and slaves, who did not have the right to participate.

Within small communities, people could take part in public debates and listen to conflicting opinions. However, it is impossible to hold such a rational discussion in view of the huge population of modern states. The state is not simply a city or a small community. A modern state is a country. That is why we have representative democracy, not direct democracy. In the case of representative democracy, elected representatives must take into account certain basic principles, listen to the opinions of men and women taking part in the debate and look for evidence at home and abroad.

The great majority of our constituents simply do not have time to weight the pros and cons and analyze the arguments made. They are busy earning their daily bread. That is their preoccupation.

Unlike us in the House of Commons, they do not have an opportunity to analyze the arguments and listen to each of us give his opinion before making a final decision.

As elected Members of Parliament we must accept the consequences of our decisions, not only with respect to capital punishment but also with respect to any other issue.

The principle I uphold does not apply to the death penalty debate but, as I said before, to all our activities as members.

It is such a basic principle in our system that I was very surprised to hear members say that all we need to do is consult our constituents and add up the numbers, or to conduct a public opinion poll throughout the country.

Democracy is not a poll-taking process. Otherwise we could install a computer in every household and there would be no need for Members of Parliament.

In my opinion such an approach is both erroneous and anti-democratic. Mr. Speaker, such a process amounts to denying that decisions must be made after rational discussions, after hours of persuasion and in-depth examination of the question.

This is why I come to the conclusion that every member, whether for or against capital punishment, has one essential democratic duty, and that is to make his or her own decision. And for the reasons I have indicated, it is the responsibility of those members who want to give the state the right to kill to explain their logic, that is their responsibility.

I submit that none of the reasons given to support capital punishment is sustainable. I want now to deal with those arguments.

First, there is the contention that punishment must suit the crime and, say some, this means that only by killing a murderer can the punishment fit the offence. The Leader of the Official Opposition (Mr. Turner) has already dealt with this argument and I can agree totally with what he has said. The logic of the position of those who take this stand can be persuasive only after the most superficial consideration. If someone destroys my car or deliberately breaks my leg, no one would argue that the state should then destroy his car or break his leg. We immediately see, Mr. Speaker, that such a response would not constitute justice. In fact, most advocates of capital punishment would agree with us in these matters in discussing those subjects. They do not advocate breaking the leg of a man who has deliberately done that to another. Many of them would correctly see such punishment for what it would be, namely, vengeance, not justice. It is too bad that these same people do not see that capital punishment is a response to murder of exactly the same logical order.

I want now to turn to the deterrence argument, which most people who have discussed this matter, who have thought about it, consider to be the most serious argument to be dealt with before reaching a decision.

Perhaps at this point I might parenthetically observe and recommend to my colleagues one of the greatest essays, I think, in modern literature, by Albert Camus, a great freedom fighter in the French underground during World War II, a Nobel prize winner for literature, a man of utter and complete integrity who wrote beautifully and intelligently. I commend his superb essay "Reflections on the Guillotine" to all those who have either not made up their minds or who are, at this point, on the side of capital punishment. He dealt with not only the deterrence question that I now come to, but with many other profoundly related matters to the whole issue of capital punishment in modern society.

The principal argument that could persuade those of us who are on the other side to come over to support capital punishment has to be that of deterrence. If we could be persuaded that lives could be saved by having capital punishment, if it could be seen that individual or mass murders could be avoided by taking the life of an individual with the instruments of state power acting as a deterrent, then many of us could be persuaded to support this motion. But, Mr. Speaker, I appeal to those who have not made up their mind on this issue, or who have made up their mind and are on the other side, to look at the evidence on this question because the evidence is clear in the following sense. If you are going to make any social analysis, any explanation in terms of social change in society and you want to relate that to the notion of deterrence about capital punishment, then the onus of proof is for you to show us that capital punishment acts as a deterrent. It is very clear that no such persuasive argument can be made. I have a few very specific points on this.

In the distant past, as has already been noted in the debate, capital punishment was used for a whole variety of crimes and it was gradually abolished. In some countries, including our own, we abolished it for everything. During the evolution of history in the last 100 years with the abolition of capital punishment for many crimes, we have actually seen the incidence of many of those crimes going down radically and not up. In country after country where there is a variety of experiences with capital punishment and non-capital punishment, again there can be no linear connection between the establishment of capital punishment on the one hand and a decline in the rate of murder on the other.

Just on the weekend we heard the horrible news of a mass murder in the state of Florida. It was a terrible incident. Florida is one of the states that recently brought back capital punishment. Is anyone going to seriously argue that capital punishment would have acted as a deterrent for the kind of man or woman who would indulge in that kind of mass murder? Of course not.

In Canada we last voted on this issue in 1976. According to the most recent figures from Statistics Canada, the homicide rate is now at the lowest level in 13 years. Clearly, renewing capital punishment is not going to improve that situation. The abolition of capital punishment did not lead to an increase in the murder rate.

Another point not widely discussed but which has been understood by classic Greek writers—it was understood by Dostoyevsky, it was certainly understood by Sigmund Freud and modern psychologists—is that for a certain kind of mentality the existence of capital punishment is in fact a lure to crime. There is a kind of sickness in some people, a fascination with the extremes of punishment. So the very existence of capital punishment, I say to those who are supporting it, can be conducive to an increase in a certain kind of criminal violent activity.

Even the more thoughtful of those who defend capital punishment have recently conceded that the evidence cannot be mounted to show that capital punishment is a deterrent. Mr. Don Cassidy, Executive

Director of the Canadian Association of Police Chiefs, is quoted as saying recently "It cannot be proven statistically." If it is the case that the fundamental argument for the reintroduction of capital punishment, the reintroduction of state violence because that is what it is, cannot be proven statistically, then I would ask what we are doing here. Surely, out of all respect for human life and out of what ought to be our commitment to justice, we ought to reach the appropriate conclusion and say that capital punishment ought not to be restored in Canada.

Many opponents of capital punishment at home and abroad have pointed out that, in the final analysis, those defending capital punishment ultimately fall back and rest their case on vengeance. I was disturbed to hear not long ago a Member of the House of Commons lending support to the idea of vengeance. Vengeance is simply a basic impulse, and I believe that all of us have this impulse from time to time. However, we must not confuse an aggressive impulse, emotively produced, with justice. Such primordial aggressive, emotional, violent aspects of human nature exist, and I believe will always exist, but as human beings living in a society we must guard against these, not indulge them. Surely as lawmakers, we in particular must bear this in mind.

Consider the responses of some people most immediately affected by murder recently. If anyone can be thought to be entitled to act on the impulse of vengeance, it would surely be a member of the family of, or one who is close to a victim of murder. I personally found most moving and touching some of the responses of those victims in our own country to horrible acts of murder inflicted on dear ones and family members.

The daughter of Gerald Ruygrok of Ottawa was brutally murdered at a halfway house, a daughter fondly and deeply regarded by her father. Did he respond with an act of vengeance? Did he say that we must have an eye for an eye? No. He said: "We should use reason rather than instinct." He opposes the reintroduction of capital punishment.

Esther Aucoin is the widow of New Brunswick patrolman Manny Aucoin who was shot on duty not long ago. Did she respond with vengeance? Not at all. She requested that a letter be read at her husband's funeral making it clear that she opposed the reintroduction of capital punishment.

A third example of this is Leslie Parrott of Toronto. Her daughter Alison was murdered in Toronto last year and the killer, the one who committed a brutal, terminal, horrible act, is still at large. Leslie Parrott has written to all Members of Parliament, I believe. I received a letter as did other Hon. Members not long ago. She does not respond with vengeance, seeking an eye for an eye. She knows that she will not be compensated for the loss of her daughter by the loss of the life of the person who killed her daughter and who has not yet even been apprehended. I would like to read a short paragraph from her letter:

> Alison's murder has given me a very personal and agonizing experience of the horror of violence and killing. It has more than ever convinced me that we as a society cannot ever and must not ever condone killing, whether by state or individual, in any shape or form.

She too is opposed to capital punishment.

One can make other arguments about this horrible instrument that is open to the state to use. Not only in Canada but in virtually every other country there is the possibility that an innocent person may be executed. It is also very important that, as we know from studies done at home and abroad, it is the person of a minority or the poor in society that is most likely to be convicted when charged with murder. The rich, the affluent and the powerful are frequently able to hire better lawyers. They are least likely to be convicted. In this act of justice which involves a human life above all others, surely we ought not risk the destruction of another human being, particularly if this destruction is much more likely to occur in the poorest elements of society. I say, a number of other arguments could be elaborated upon, and no doubt they will be. I attempted to deal with the central argument and the question of [deterrence]. I have argued that the evidence is not there and therefore one should not support capital punishment for that reason.

Before concluding, I would like to make two points. First, all of us in the House on both sides of the issue see murder for the horrible act that it is, and we should all be redoubling our efforts to try to understand those causes that can be removed, as some of them can be, and to accept the probable reality that because human beings are the violent creatures we are from time to time, there will likely and definitely be murders to deal with in the history of society. However, we should do what we can to ensure that those who commit murder are appropriately punished. As I said, that is not the central issue of this debate. The issue is whether or not there is a moral argument that would justify bringing back capital punishment.

I would like to conclude by saying that capital punishment simply adds to the degree of brutalization that is going on in society. In coldly taking the life of a murderer, the state would simply compound the moral unacceptability of the original violent act. We need less, not more violence in Canada. We need justice, not vengeance. We should encourage life, not death. We should oppose the restoration of capital punishment.

# POSTSCRIPT

Although the government had promised to permit full debate of the capital punishment issue before it was put to a free vote, after only nine hours of debate the government decided to invoke closure and thereby end discussion. Only twenty MPs had spoken on the issue, and fifteen of these opposed the bill. On June 30, 1987, when the vote was called on the motion, it was clear that many MPs had shifted to the abolitionist side. The motion to move toward reinstatement of capital punishment lost, with 148 voting against and 127 in favour.

In the debate on this issue, Geoff Wilson defends capital punishment by first summarizing, and then refuting, each of the major arguments of the abolitionists. Ed Broadbent uses the same debating strategy by outlining the major arguments of the retentionists and attempting to demonstrate their fallacies. An important element in this debate is the question of whether capital punishment is, in fact, a deterrent to murder. It is interesting to note that both speakers avoid using statistics to bolster their arguments on this point. Wilson suggests that the issue of deterrence is a matter of "personal belief," while Broadbent argues that the "onus of proof" is on the retentionists to show that capital punishment is demonstrably a deterrent.

Since Canada and numerous other countries have gone through periods both with and without the death penalty, one might assume that social scientists could determine, with relative ease, what impact the presence or absence of the penalty has on the incidence of murder. However, the empirical study of the deterrent effect of capital punishment is a complex and controversial field. While some have argued that there is some evidence of a deterrent effect, others question the data on which such conclusions are drawn. A good summary of these issues can be found in C.H.S. Jayewardene, *After Abolition of the Death Penalty* (Ottawa: Crimcare Inc., 1989). In addition to a discussion of the implications of social science research on the impact of the death penalty,

Jayewardene presents a very useful overview of the politics of the restoration issue in Canada, including the role of interest groups and public opinion.

Proponents of restoration frequently point to the most dramatic cases to buttress their argument. Are not the crimes of a mass murderer such as Clifford Olson so terrible that only the death penalty is a sufficient punishment? Abolitionists counter that the question of innocence and guilt is generally not as clear-cut as the Olson case suggests, and point to Donald Marshall as an example. In 1971 Marshall, son of a native chief in Nova Scotia, was accused of murdering another teenager and eventually sentenced to life imprisonment. Marshall's family, convinced of his innocence, tried without success to have his conviction overturned. It took eleven years before the Nova Scotia Supreme Court finally declared Marshall innocent of all charges and released him from prison. Subsequent inquiries have shown that antinative attitudes on the part of the police and judges had contributed to the miscarriage of justice in the Marshall case.

Opponents of capital punishment argue that such cases are not at all rare and constitute a powerful argument against imposition of the death penalty. In *Miscarriages of Justice in Potentially Capital Cases* (New York: American Civil Liberties Union, 1985), Hugo Bedau and Michael Radelet argue that in the United States at least 343 persons have been wrongfully convicted of potentially capital offences since the turn of the century. During this same period at least twenty-five cases of mistaken execution have taken place. Michael Harris documents the Marshall case in *Justice Delayed: The Law Versus Donald Marshall* (Toronto: Totem, 1987). A comprehensive overview of the issues in the capital punishment debate and current practices worldwide can be found in *When the State Kills ... The Death Penalty v. Human Rights* (London: Amnesty International, 1989).

# ISSUE TWENTY-TWO

## Should Universal Medicare Be Preserved?

**YES** TAYLOR ALEXANDER, "Universal Medicare: Can We Afford to Lose It?"

**NO** DOUGLAS J. MCCREADY, "Social Justice: Universality and Health Care in Canada"

Canada has a publicly funded universal health-care system. The term *universal* refers to the fact that under medicare—the name given to the system—*all* Canadians may receive medically necessary care. In some countries, government-run health services offer care only to select groups such as the aged and the poor, but not in Canada. Everyone here is eligible.

Medicare is an extremely popular program, and for good reason. Before medicare, when families were directly responsible for their own care, the cost of paying for health services placed some in dire financial straits and caused others to forsake care altogether. Medicare is also popular because it reflects a widely held belief that each member of society has a right to health care, and that health care is too important to be left to the vagaries of the private market.

Despite the popularity of universal medicare, the program is not without its problems. In the eyes of governments, medicare is an incredibly expensive program. At present, federal and provincial governments share in the financing of medicare, and each level has taken action to reduce its spending on health care. Nevertheless, medicare remains a very costly endeavour for governments.

For others, the failings of medicare lie in its operation. Too often patients must wait some time before receiving care, and in some cases—albeit isolated ones—patients have reportedly died while waiting. It is also said that medicare slows the development of new technology in health care, largely because governments fear its cost implications. Consequently, the quality of care suffers, as patients go without the best possible care. Finally, medicare in general suffers allegedly from *insufficient* funding; the problem is not too much spending, but rather too little.

One possible solution to these problems is to end the universal character of medicare. A program targeted only at certain groups would, it seems, lessen the pressure on government health budgets. It might also have a beneficial effect on the problems of waiting lists and quality of care, for governments would then be better positioned to finance a program that offers high-quality care to all eligible persons in a timely fashion. Those left uncovered, too, might benefit. They may find that arrangements in the private sector offer superior care to that now available under medicare. The end of universality thus offers the possibility of everyone being better off.

In the readings, Taylor Alexander, a health policy consultant, argues that universal medicare should be preserved. Douglas McCready, an economist at Wilfrid Laurier University, contends that there are serious costs associated with the pursuit of the principle of universality.

## YES

# Universal Medicare: Can We Afford to Lose It?

*Taylor Alexander*

# INTRODUCTION

The U.S. struggle to achieve universal health care should be a sobering reminder for Canada. It's also a good time to stop and compare history notes. We had a system much like theirs once. Thankfully, we got rid of it, and replaced it with our world-acclaimed universal medicare system, Canada's most popular social program. In fact, we Canadians are more satisfied with our health-care system than any other citizens in the world, while Americans are the least satisfied with theirs. Yet, some Canadians now want us to import the pre-reform U.S. system, just when many Americans dream about a system like ours.

As of this writing, Americans are so unhappy with their system that fully 89 percent of people polled felt their system needed "fundamental change or complete rebuilding."[1] It's not hard to understand why. About 37 million Americans have no health insurance at all, and another 22 million are underinsured. For example, five million U.S. women aged 15 to 44 have insurance plans that exclude such essentials as care for childbirth. To make matters worse, those Americans who do have insurance are losing it at the rate of almost one person per second, or about two million people each month. Also, imagine the difficulty U.S. governments and patients have dealing with a maze of at least *1,500* private health insurers, many of whom cancel coverage when their clients get seriously ill.[2] What the United States has is a profit-driven, two-tier system: one tier for the rich and one for the poor. Patients get the care they can afford, if they can afford it at all. In other words, it's survival of the fittest. We rejected that unfair approach time and again, but as shown later, we're now about to lose our hard-won universal system, astonishingly, at our own hands!

# LET'S NOT FREE TRADE OUR PRINCIPLES AWAY TOO

To Canadians, the U.S. system sounds nightmarish, yet we could easily have ended up in a similar mess almost four decades ago had we not won a series of tremendous social and political struggles to avoid these problems. Instead of a dog-eat-dog system, we built our system on compassionate principles that reflected a very different vision of health care and of our society. First and foremost among these principles is universality, which means that 100 percent of our population is covered by public health insurance. In Canada, health care is a right of citizenship, not something you buy and sell. Why is universality so important? Because it puts into practice the lofty idea that all Canadians are equal, no matter what our income, education, gender, age, religion, or culture may be. As increases occur in unemployment, gender issues, the elderly, cultural diversity, and so on, the principle of universality is more relevant than ever. Universality is especially important to the disadvantaged, especially the poor, because they suffer much higher rates of illness and even death than well-off Canadians. Universality ensures that the less fortunate have ready access to care without having to jump over humiliating hurdles such as income tests.

The principle of universality first became reality in the federal 1957 Hospital Insurance and Diagnostic Services Act, which launched Canada into universal hospital insurance. For the first time, Canadians would not have to worry about whether they could afford hospital care. However, this solved only part of the problem, because nonhospital medical care was still provided by doctors on a private, fee-for-service basis for those who could afford it. To remove the worry that many Canadians couldn't afford to go to their doctors when they needed to, Canada then passed the 1966 Medical Care Act, which set out the now-famous five principles of medicare: universality, portability, accessibility, comprehensiveness, and public administration.

These principles were reaffirmed and updated in the 1984 Canada Health Act after widespread user charges threatened to undermine universal medicare. The act also banned user charges, allowing the federal government to penalize, dollar for dollar, any province that allowed doctors or hospitals to charge patients fees. User charges are a serious threat to universality because studies show they deter low-income people from getting the care they need. Our medicare principles have stood the test of time and, together, ensure the fairness and efficiency that distinguish our system internationally. The most recent version of the principles are stated in the Canada Health Act, and are paraphrased as follows:

1. *Public administration*: ensures that we have a single-payer, publicly run and accountable, nonprofit system;

2. *Comprehensiveness:* ensures that all hospital, medical, and certain other services provided by dentists and other health-care workers are insured;

3. *Universality:* ensures that 100 percent of the population is covered according to the same terms and conditions (formerly 95 percent were covered under the 1966 Medical Care Act);

4. *Portability:* ensures that if you move to another province, you are still covered by your home province for up to three months until you can be registered in the new province; it also ensures that if you need care while out of the country, you will be covered at least at the level it would have cost your home province to provide the care in Canada;

5. *Accessibility:* ensures that services are reasonably accessible no matter where you live, whether in an urban, rural, or remote area; it also ensures that doctors and dentists who provide services under the plan are reasonably paid.[3]

# IT DOESN'T GET MUCH BETTER THAN THIS

What do these five principles give us? Our universal system is more efficient, cheaper, and fairer than the U.S. system, while still providing high standards of care. In short, we have a win–win system that benefits patients, providers, and government alike. Getting sick is difficult enough without having to cut through a tangle of red tape, worry whether your insurance will be cancelled, or feel like a second-class citizen if your income is low. Providing care is difficult enough without wondering whether you're ever going to be paid for the valuable work you've just done.

Universality means that in Canada, if you can't work, don't have a paid job, lose your job, work part-time, or are self-employed, you still get the same health care as anyone else. Nowhere in Canada is anyone denied health care because of low income, and nowhere must the poor identify themselves as poor in order to qualify for care. Contrary to some opinions, Canada does not have socialized medicine. Canadians can freely choose whichever doctor they want, and can change doctors if they are not happy with their care. There is no complicated paperwork to fill out in the doctor's office. No hospital emergency department will try to find out whether you're insured before treating you, or even send you to another hospital that treats noninsured patients, as happens in the United States. Canadians can move freely from province to province without worrying whether they'll have health care. In the most populated areas of the country, quality health care is readily available, and in many remote regions special transportation services take patients to treatment centres elsewhere for appropriate care.

Doctors are guaranteed payment, which is a big advantage; prior to medicare, they had many problems with late or nonpayment of fees, just like any other business. Another real plus for doctors, hospitals, and patients is having to deal with only one payer—the government. For example, before medicare, there were more than 200 private medical-care insurers in Ontario alone.[4] Because of medicare, the average Ontario doctor, for example, consistently earns four to five times more than the average wage-earner, usually giving doctors higher net incomes than many other leading professions.[5]

Hospitals used to have special wards for charity cases in the pre-hospital insurance days, but now have no way of knowing a patient's income level. Like doctors, hospitals also used to worry whether patients could pay their bills, either out of their own pockets or through private insurance plans. This insecurity made planning very difficult, since hospitals were never sure how much money they would have from year to year. Since 1957, however, hospitals too have been guaranteed payment, and even when many repeatedly went over budget, provincial governments usually bailed them out, although less so in recent years.

# WHERE DOES UNIVERSALITY FIT IN?

As mentioned earlier, the cornerstone of our health-care system is *universality*, arguably the most important of all the five principles of medicare. It is not surprising that universality has long been the most elusive goal of U.S. health-care reformers, and the main target of President Clinton's new health-care package. Their numerous insurance plans create many serious problems. One of the worst is that many Americans probably don't even fully understand their policies because about *50 percent* of all U.S. adults, approximately *90 million* people, lack sufficient language and mathematical skills either to write a business letter or to understand a bus schedule.[6] Just imagine their difficulty in trying either to understand all the complicated financial and legal information in their existing policies, or to choose a new plan that better fits their needs and pocketbooks. Our universal medicare completely avoids this problem, but if we hadn't changed our system, many Canadians would face a similar barrier—today, 20 to 24 percent of our own citizens are functionally illiterate. This rate jumps to more than 50 percent among welfare recipients in Ontario, for example.[7] In other words, the most vulnerable people in Canada would have the hardest time getting proper coverage.

Another serious problem we have solved is the mind-boggling amount of paperwork the U.S. plans generate for patients, doctors, hospitals, and governments. This inefficiency is the main reason why the U.S. system would save about *$4.2 trillion* dollars between 1992 and 2002 if Americans had a Canadian-style system.[8] During his 1993 address to Congress on health-care reform, President Clinton rightly called their system "the costliest and most wasteful system on the face of the earth."[9] With 14 percent of their GDP going to health care, compared to only about 10 percent in Canada, the United States is the highest per capita spender on health in the world.

Let's not forget that before we had universality, our private insurance plans were causing similar problems and excluding high-risk groups such as the elderly and the previously ill. Such inefficiency and unfairness were among the driving forces behind our push toward universal health insurance. Those Canadians who would like to return to a two-tier health system have just not realized the implications. First, some experts estimate that we would have to income-test up to *eleven million* Canadians to see if they qualified for government-subsidized health care.[10] Second, there is no practical way we could develop an integrated computer system that could stay up to date to track all these people as they moved, changed or lost jobs, started receiving employer health benefits, and so on. Perhaps even worse, there would be an enormous amount of highly confidential, personal information circulating throughout countless computer terminals in such a system.

# ON THE FAST TRACK BACKWARD

Universal medicare is quickly slipping through our fingers, and we must get a firm grip on it before it's gone. But, how did we get into this crisis? The answer lies in a fatal change the Mulroney Conservatives made to federal health policy, a change that is now bleeding medicare dry. By way of background, health is a provincial responsibility. The federal government, however, has the power to get involved in health and other social programs because of its unlimited spending powers under the Constitution. Over many years, different federal governments had the determination, and the public support, to use these spending powers, usually in the form of cash, to create our social safety net.

However, federal governments didn't just give their cash away to the provinces to spend as they pleased. Instead, they wisely attached strings to it in the form of national standards, such as the five medicare principles, that all provinces had to meet. Without these standards, there would have been no uniform programs across the country, resulting in a patchwork of services. This is a key point. Cash is an all-important federal lever, because the federal government can threaten to withhold it as a way of pressuring the provinces to meet national standards set out in the legislation. Without the federal government's cash weapon, the Canada Health Act, for example, would be a toothless tiger.

In order to develop universal medicare, the federal government paid about 50 percent of the costs, *in cash*, until 1977. At that time, it switched over to a combination of cash and tax points under legislation known as the Established Programs Financing Act or EPF. Later, when the Mulroney Conservatives came to power, they made changes to EPF that will steadily choke off all federal cash for medicare by about 2010. Not only will these changes undermine medicare, they will leave the federal government with no way of ensuring that the provinces comply with the Canada Health Act. In the early 1990s, the Conservatives brought in legislation that allowed the federal government to withhold cash earmarked for nonhealth areas from any provinces that violated the Canada Health Act. In reality, it is doubtful whether this legislation will prevent provinces from introducing user fees and other barriers to universal health care.

Federal cash cutbacks are already hitting the provinces hard. For example, by as soon as 1996 they will have lost about $30 billion in federal health cash,[11] and will lose about another $35 billion by the year 2000.[12] There is no way that universal medicare can survive these slash-and-burn federal attacks. Federal cash is already drying up, and the provinces are increasingly having to pick up the shortfall. When all federal cash is finally gone, the provinces will have to fund health completely. Naturally, provincial governments are becoming desperate, and have been looking at ways to cut costs including: bringing in user fees; closing hospital beds and cutting staff; increasing waiting periods for patient care; dropping some insured health services and drugs; and turning over the running of provincial health plans to private companies. Some of these steps have already taken place. Sadly, the poorer provinces will suffer the most. Provincial cost-cutting strategies will snowball as finances get tighter, and before long universality will be gone.

## FINDING THE MONEY TO PROTECT UNIVERSALITY

Many Canadians believe that ending universality will help to provide a quick fix for our recession and bloated national debt. More and more, we hear that Canada can't afford "free" universal medicare anymore, and many accept these statements as obvious truths. However, such Canadians neither understand health-care funding, nor the real financial problems with medicare. These quick fixers usually blame patients for "abusing" the system—ignoring the fact that doctors primarily decide the type of care required—and propose user fees as the magic solution. Neither is effective nor fair. First of all, universal medicare is not "free" because about 75 percent of the approximately $70 billion we now spend on health comes out of our own pockets through the tax system.[13] That's nearly $53 billion we all pay for health care; hardly free!

Second, since the beginning of medicare, Canada has been one of the most successful countries in the world in controlling health-care costs. It is the United States that has spiralling health costs. Our single-payer, tax-based system is about five times cheaper to run than the American system, which in 1985, for example, spent about $50 billion more on physician and hospital costs than it would have spent with a system like ours.[14] Also, we don't have to worry about costly premium hikes from private health insurance companies. Although we are the second highest spender on health among the OECD countries, our spending is not much above the average of the major countries in that group.

Third, how many Canadians realize that, each year, the federal government intentionally gives up enormous sums that could be used for health? For example, each year the federal government loses more revenues through its tax breaks for well-off Canadians than it spends in cash for medicare; nearly $17.5 billion in 1989.[15] Also, because it doesn't put enough pressure on big businesses to pay their taxes, in 1987 alone the federal government lost about $10 billion in tax revenue, nearly 80 percent of the federal cash contribution for health that year.[16] We *can* afford universal health care, if we get our priorities right.

Fourth, despite the excellence of our health-care system, as in the United States there is a considerable amount of waste here, too. The United States has estimated that about 20 percent of its total patient-care costs, about *$130 billion* worth, involve unnecessary treatment-related services.[17] Our systems use similar science, technology, and drugs, so it's not unreasonable to think that Canada's percentage of waste may be in the same vicinity. But how can so much waste be possible? The answer can partly be found in the comments of one Canadian doctor: "The scientific evidence that much of what we [doctors] do is wasteful and/or useless is in our medical journals but is largely ignored."[18]

Another reason is that many technologies have never been properly tested by governments to see whether they actually work and are safe. For example, there are about 490,000 medical devices for sale in Canada. The government primarily relies on the manufacturers themselves to assure us that they have tested their products for safety and effectiveness. As a result, the government ends up testing only about 5 percent of the 20,000 new medical devices put on sale in Canada each year. It has been estimated that up to 70 to 80 percent of medical technology has never been evaluated for its effectiveness.[19] If medical devices malfunction, serious health problems can result, driving up costs.

Fifth, as gate-keepers to the health-care system, doctors are largely responsible for how our health-care dollars are spent. It is doctors who primarily admit patients to hospitals, prescribe drugs, perform hospital surgery, refer patients for special tests, and so on. Obviously, with so much power to influence health-care spending, doctors should keep one eye on costs at all times. Yet, some doctors admit similar types of patients to hospital more often than their colleagues; some prescribe more drugs than their colleagues; and some order more tests than their colleagues. Medical training is part of the problem because most medical schools don't teach doctors how to ensure that their decisions and actions are cost-effective.[20]

Another part of the problem is related to the fact that doctors currently don't have any standard-treatment guidelines to follow, a matter of concern to national medical and other health-related groups. Instead, doctors largely rely on their own independent judgments concerning which treatments, drugs, and tests are necessary. The absence of guidelines causes two problems. First, treatment rates for the same illnesses vary widely by province, age, gender, and sometimes even culture. A few examples will help illustrate this point.

Why do Canadian females have their tonsils removed about twice as often as males? Why are Newfoundland's female tonsillectomy rates about three times higher than Quebec's? Why do Canadian females have two to three times more gall bladder operations than males? Why are Alberta's rates for Caesarean-section surgery nearly 2.5 times higher than Prince Edward Island's?[21] Why is Canada's Caesarean-section surgery rate three times higher than in the Netherlands? Canadian estimates show that overall, one-third of all surgical procedures are not necessary,[22] and the costs involved are enormous. Why do many elderly in-patients in high-cost, acute-care hospitals commonly have to wait for several months, and sometimes more than a year after their treatment has finished, before they are discharged? Why are provincial governments increasingly convinced that entire acute-care hospitals can be closed without adversely affecting the quality of health care in some communities, both large and small?

Another part of this problem relates to the way we pay doctors on a fee-for-service basis. Most doctors are in private business and don't work on salary. Fee-for-service medicine means that the more patients doctors treat, the higher their income, all paid by the public purse. Is this a wise use of scarce health-care dollars? We have already discussed the problem of widely different treatment practices across Canada. Clearly, the present fee-for-service method does not encourage efficient use of resources. Arguably, it also unfairly puts doctors in a difficult, potential conflict between their clinical judgment and their pocketbooks. One way out of this dilemma is to pay doctors according to salary scales negotiated between their professional associations and the provincial governments. Although most doctors have fiercely resisted salaried payment in the past, provincial health plans may have no alternative as federal health cash dries up.

Aggravating the fee-for-service problem is the fact that for many years Canada has graduated too many doctors for the size of our population. Since doctor oversupply adds unnecessary health costs, many provinces are now taking steps to reduce the number of medical school graduates in order to contain excess costs.

A sixth problem area involves drug overprescriptions. The large drug companies in Canada spend about *half a billion* dollars each year marketing their products, mostly to doctors. To put this figure in perspective, it's twice as much as the companies spend on research each year.[23] The elderly are a rapidly growing segment of Canadian society, and a rapidly growing market for drug manufacturers. However, because drug costs are high, and many elderly live on fixed incomes, most provinces provide them with subsidized drug plans. We should not be surprised, then, that one expert on Ontario's $1 billion drug plan said that the elderly are being "drugged silly."[24] This problem has a domino effect on costs, because elderly drug reactions are responsible for up to 20 percent of all visits to hospital emergency rooms, generating yet another unnecessary high cost.[25]

Nor should we be surprised that a study of the Saskatchewan drug plan described the pharmaceutical industry as a "public health hazard" because of the amount of overprescribing occurring there.[26] To add insult to injury, the Mulroney Conservatives increased the brand-name drug companies' patent protection from about seven years to twenty years. This means that lower-cost generic drugs are greatly delayed from coming onto the market. As a result, governments, health benefit plans, and consumers will pay much higher drug prices for a longer time. Let's not underestimate the importance of drug prices to our medicare system. Even the federal Minister of Health and Welfare at the time publicly feared that unless controlled, high prices for patent drugs could destroy the health-care system.

# CONCLUSIONS

Universality has proven its worth more than often enough. It's time to stop casting longing glances at the United States, and it's time to stop bickering about whether we can afford universality. We can. Universality is not bankrupting Canada. Canadians have chosen decisively and repeatedly that we don't want a dog-eat-dog society divided into "haves" and "have-nots," especially when it comes to health care. Universality is again being scapegoated by groups who misunderstand how the health-care system works, who favour the private market, and who have misguided solutions to Canada's economic woes. Killing universality is no quick fix to our problems.

Canada's health-care system is in crisis, but that crisis has nothing to do with universality. Instead, it has everything to do with actions of the previous federal government, and only the federal government has the power to end it. Rather than quietly vanishing from the national health-care scene, the federal government should take a strong leadership role to preserve Canadians' health, especially now as poverty rates increase. Effective solutions are available if there is the will to change. First, we urgently need to reinstate federal cash to protect universality. Second, we must start reducing the waste that makes our system more expensive than it need be. If we succeed, we can pass on our most popular social program, intact and improved, to future generations.

## NOTES

1. See Malcolm G. Taylor, "Another Look at Canada's Health Care System," *Policy Options* (May 1992): 32–35.

2. Canadian Labour Congress, *Health Care in the U.S.*, July 12, 1993, p. 2.

3. For a more formal description of these criteria, see Health and Welfare Canada, *Canada Health Act Annual Report, 1991–1992* (Ottawa: Minister of Supply and Services, cat. no. H1-4/1992), p. 9.

4. National Council of Welfare, *Medicare: The Public Good and Private Practice*, a report by the National Council of Welfare (Ottawa: Minister of Supply and Services, May 1982, cat. no. H68-5/1982E), p. 9.

5. John K. Iglehart, "Canada's Health Care System (First of Three Parts)," *New England Journal of Medicine* 315, no. 3 (July 17, 1986): 202–8.

6. "Illiteracy's Tragic Toll," Editorial, *USA Today*, September 10, 1993.

7. See Burt Perrin, "Literacy and Health: Making the Connection," *Health Promotion* (Summer 1989): 2–5.

8. Taylor, "Another Look at Canada's Health Care System."

9. President Bill Clinton, Address to Congress on Reform of the American Health Care System, CNN television, September 22, 1993.

10. Taylor, "Another Look at Canada's Health Care System."

11. Alistair Thomson, *Federal Support for Health Care: A Background Paper*, in New Democratic Party of Canada, *Beyond Medicare: Equal Opportunity for Health* (Ottawa: New Democratic Party of Canada, June 1992), p. 31.

12. New Democratic Party of Canada, *Beyond Medicare: Equal Opportunity for Health*, p. 32.

13. National Council of Welfare, *Funding Health and Higher Education: Danger Looming* (Ottawa: Minister of Supply and Services, cat. no. H-68-30/1991E), p. 1.

14. Robert G. Evans, Jonathan Lomas, Morris L. Barer, Roberta Labelle, Catherine Fooks, Gregory Stoddart, Geoffrey M. Anderson, David Feeny, Amiram Gafni, George Torrance, and William G. Tholl, "Controlling Health Expenditures—The Canadian Reality," *New England Journal of Medicine* 320, no. 9 (March 2, 1989): 571–77.

15. The Caledon Institute of Social Policy, *Memorandum: To the Next Prime Minister of Canada* (Ottawa: The Caledon Institute of Social Policy, September 1993), p. 2.

16. New Democratic Party of Canada, *Beyond Medicare: Equal Opportunity for Health*, p. 38.

17. "Wasted Health Care Dollars, Part 1 of a Three-Part Series," *Consumer Reports*, July 1992, p. 436.

18. Gary Gibson, "Doctors Must Choose the Way to Go," *The Globe and Mail*, June 18, 1993.

19. *The Ottawa Citizen*, Monday, May 13, 1991, p. A2.

20. Gibson, "Doctors Must Choose the Way to Go."

21. Institute for Health Care Facilities of the Future, *A View of the Horizon: A View of Regional Trends*, report written by Katherine Tregunna (Ottawa: Institute for Health Care Facilities of the Future, 1990), pp. 230–31.

22. *The Ottawa Citizen*, Monday, May 13, 1991, p. A2.

23. "Costs of Prescription Plan Skyrocketing in Ontario," *The Globe and Mail*, Tuesday, March 10, 1992.

24. Ibid.

25. "Cuts to Drug Funding Worry Seniors," *The Ottawa Citizen*, Friday, August 21, 1992, p. B1.

26. Anne Crichton and David Hsu, *Canada's Health Care System: Its Funding and Organization* (Ottawa: Canadian Hospital Association, 1990), p. 142.

# NO

# Social Justice: Universality and Health Care in Canada[1]

*Douglas J. McCready*

If we are to answer the question, *"Why universality in health care?"* the thinker must go beyond logic to examine the definitional base on which universality or lack of universality is built. It is a common conception of universality that it implies equality or social justice. Universality implies that everyone is covered in the same plan and receives exactly the same subsidy toward his or her health insurance (in this case) from government.

It is the hypothesis here that universality does not now exist, and that if it were to exist it would be economically inefficient. In fact, attempts in Canada to achieve universality have led to significant costs that have been borne by society, and have contributed to a system in which excellence cannot exist.

How should the goods of society be distributed? What should we do with the poor? How much should a medical doctor or a soldier or a tradesman be paid? What is the good society? What is our essential relationship to our fellow human beings, and what obligations do we have for one another? Is it just for there to be poor people living virtually next door to people who have more money than they could possibly spend? Is it fair that hard-working people go unrewarded while others smiled upon by fortune are constantly rewarded in return for no work? Should the rich be taxed to help the poor? Should people be paid or should students be graded according to their effort or according to their results?

It is hard to divorce oneself from one's discipline and the precepts that attach to that discipline. Thus I am interested in questions of incentives and resource allocation, for if economics is anything, it is a study of resource allocation, and if the incentives in allocating resources are not studied, a horribly flawed analysis would result. I also point out that an economist is interested in achieving the most per dollar cost, even if that refers to services such as health care rather than to the traditional widgets.[2]

Unless one has an economy left at the end of the day, no amount of compassion will have any impact. Indeed, the best way to get services to people is to do it efficiently and effectively without creating incentives for an underground economy or riots or even movement out of the country (one former Ontario cabinet minister is now a permanent resident in the United States, finding he could pay so much less in taxes that he could afford the over $2,000 per year health insurance premium and still be better off). There are some people who would like to think that Canada does not have to worry about the deficit and debt that we face, but as expressed by the former health minister of New Zealand, that was the biggest single factor in New Zealand going, in 1984, from a universal system to "a three-tiered system with strict budget limits and open competition between private and public health organizations. User fees are the rule and universality is but a fond memory."[3]

The writings of John Rawls may be helpful to us in exploring the problems associated with universality and health care in Canada. His concept that inequality might benefit society will be useful to our examination of the value of universality.

## SOCIAL JUSTICE: WHAT IS IT?

There are two words for justice in the Greek language, and neither translates well into English. The first is *isotes*, which means equality, but according to Greek scholars it also means justice. Then there is *dikaiosune*, which probably meant righteousness. Notwithstanding its attractiveness, justice has been viewed critically. For example, according to Friederich Von Hayek, a noted philosopher and economist:

> The appeal to social justice has ... become the most widely used and most effective argument ... for government action.... [To] assure the same material position to people who differ greatly in strength, intelligence, skill, knowledge and perseverance as well as in their physical and social environment, government would clearly have to treat them very differently to compensate for their disadvantages and deficiencies it could not directly alter.... [To] achieve particular results for the individuals [government] must be given essentially arbitrary powers to make the individuals do what seems necessary to achieve the required result. Full equality for most cannot but mean equal submission of the great masses under the command of some elite who manages their affairs. While an equality of rights under a limited government is possible and an essential condition of individual freedom, a claim for equality of material position can be met only by a government with totalitarian powers.[4]

Let us turn to Rawls for instruction from a social philosopher. Rawls's attempt to define social justice depend on five axioms, which I set out here:

1. Members of society make decisions on the basis of enlightened self-interest.

2. Members of society are capable of discovering their own preferences and of evaluating with reasonable success the consequences of their and others' actions.

3. Members of society have roughly similar needs and interests that make self-interested cooperation among them rational.

4. People in our society are sufficiently equal in power and ability to guarantee that in normal circumstances none is able to dominate the others.

5. People in our society are not envious, which is to say "the bare knowledge or perception of the difference between their condition and that of others is not, within limits and in itself, a source of dissatisfaction."

Rawls examines a bargaining problem and discovers that, with these precepts, equality is preferred but inequality is possible when there is the possibility of achieving what has been called an *inequality surplus*. That is to say, an *inequality surplus* that is distributed to society will cause people to permit inequalities to exist.[5]

An example makes this much clearer. Let us consider a shoe shop. Suppose that in order to produce shoes, six roles have been defined (tanning leather, cutting leather, sewing, finishing, packaging, shipping). Suppose that there is no difference in pay scales between the six functions. Sixty workers occupy the six roles (not necessarily ten to each role), and the net amount of income of the shoe manufacturer before wages is $600,000. Each worker will thus be paid $10,000.

In this factory, there are no incentives to make the production more efficient—people work at a leisurely pace. Suppose, however, that if the tanners and the sewers were to increase the pace with which they do their jobs, output would rise substantially because these two functions cause bottlenecks in the production process (people have to await the tanned leather and the stitched shoes before they can do their tasks). If those two types of workers could be enticed to work faster, the bottlenecks would disappear and the factory would be able to increase the output of shoes by 50 percent. Now remember, according to Rawls, that the workers in these two tasks are assigned without prejudice, and consequently all workers could have been assigned to these jobs; the fact that some are and some are not is not subject to envy or any other such problem. As an incentive for those workers to speed up production, it is necessary to pay $20,000 per worker. Suppose that there are fourteen tanners and sixteen sewers, leaving another thirty workers unaffected. Now because the output of shoes has increased by 50 percent, the amount to be distributed has increased from $600,000 to $900,000. The thirty workers who have received an increase in their wages will take an additional $300,000, and there would thus be no surplus to distribute to the other workers in this shoe factory. Suppose, however, it took only $18,000 to increase the productivity of the thirty sewers and tanners, which would leave $60,000 to be distributed among the remaining thirty workers; their wages could rise by $2,000 each, and they might accept that solution even though an inequality now exists.

Now, suppose that in order to sell the additional output, the net income available for wages had increased only to $840,000. There would have been no *inequality surplus* to distribute, so thirty of the workers would have been no better off and would not have voted for the improvement, while the other thirty would be assumed to be better off and thus would have voted for the improvement. In majority voting, such an improvement would not have been accepted. It is only when there is an *inequality surplus* that there would be acceptance of the change.

The conclusion of Rawls's problem is that equality will be preferred in most instances. It is only when there is clearly some benefit to people through the distribution of an *inequality surplus* that it is possible to accept other than an equal distribution of the spoils of work: "Since I do not care how much more my fellow workers gain so long as I too benefit, I will allow such inequalities to work to everyone's benefit."

Many of us could find fault with this analysis. For instance, the assumption that envy is not present could be questioned. There are likely reasons why envy would arise. In later versions of the theory, and particularly in *A Theory of Justice,* Rawls complicates some of the assumptions to meet some of the objections to his theory. It is clear, however, that Rawls builds on the principles of maximization of societal good through the maximization of game theory. It starts from the principle that each individual has self-interest and acts upon it. It is an assumption that economists, for the most part, are entirely happy with. In other words, most economists will argue that if productivity can be enhanced enough by inequality, and if everybody can be compensated, then that is an optimal move.

# HEALTH CARE IN CANADA

In this section I wish to address the issue of what the costs might be of obtaining a socially just (read equal) distribution of societal resources.

Of course, I have to judge what that distribution "should" be in terms of what we have said about views of social justice.

Rawls argues for inequality on a limited scale when it enhances economic efficiency. However, he does argue for equal access to opportunity, if not to resources. Rawls perhaps best defined when a deviation from equality (universality) is acceptable—when it benefits everybody through the distribution of an *inequality surplus*. However, I do not want us to forget Von Hayek, who warned that in order to achieve equality a government must have such arbitrary powers as to make it dictatorial, with the resultant loss of individual freedoms. Surely it is in this debate as seen by both Rawls and Von Hayek that we get to the heart of the issue as to what are the costs of achieving equality. *Universality* usually refers to equality of access at a minimum. Rawls refers to the inherent problem of equality—people need incentives to produce at more than some minimum level. Von Hayek puts it in political terms that most of us can understand—terms that refer to the loss of personal freedom.

I must, at this point, remind the reader that there are only three ways one can allocate resources:

- The first is the preferred method advocated by economists—the use of a price system.

- The second is the system known well by those who have dealt with the British health system (myself included) and has a typically British name—queuing (or lining up).

- The third system is sometimes called a command system; however, I prefer to call it "allocation by government fiat" rather than the more pejorative term sometimes used, "communism."

It is implicit in a health-care system that when resources are not allocated by a price system, some other system of allocation must be used. Both queuing and government fiat are the only two other ways in which resources can be allocated—and there are costs associated with each.

In Canada, there is anger and fear about the fact that 37 million Americans (more than the total Canadian population) are not covered by any form of health insurance. Mind, I have been told by some Americans that many of those 37 million actually choose to be without insurance because of religious belief or the desire to self-insure (how believable?).

I am also aware that in the fractured health-care system available in the United States—in which some employers pay health insurance and others do not, and where there are variations in the amount of coverage provided—there is an impediment to mobility of population, and that in itself is a reason Americans must be looking at alternatives to their present health system. Finally, the U.S. system costs more (13.4 percent of GNP versus 10 percent in Canada, 8.5 percent in Germany, and 6.6

percent in Great Britain.[6] Surely the drain of funds devoted to health care means less resources for other goods and services.

I accept that the Canadian system is more socially just. However, I want to examine costs associated with achieving what some deem to be social justice. In my conclusions, I return to the policy issue of universality.

The Canadian health-care system, which started under federal law passed in 1966 (previously hospitalization had been introduced nationally in 1957), but only taken up by most of the provinces five years later, is one in which basic care (physician visit, hospitalization, X-ray, and lab test) is paid for by the government. In 1961 Saskatchewan had introduced medicare provincially,[7] with a provincial doctors' strike taking place for most of that summer.[8] As part of the agreement to end the strike, the doctors were told very clearly that there would be no interference with their ability to practise medicine—that government was only going to handle the purse strings. As will be seen, that is not the case today.

To the individual, the cost of Canadian health care appears to be zero. Initially, the federal government paid out of its tax revenues 50 percent of a province's costs. Since 1977, the federal government has controlled its expenditure by transferring tax points to the province plus a cash grant based on transfers in 1977 roughly adjusted for inflation and population growth. Since 1984, the cash grant has been conditional on the province not having any user fees or extra-billing. There have been a number of modifications in EPF financing because of the paucity of federal funds and also because EPF represents a large proportion of the federal budget—nearly 20 percent.[9]

One can get medical care so long as one is a resident of a province and has a medical card. If visiting another province or moving there, up to three months of present coverage is available until coverage in the new province can be arranged. At least 95 percent of residents in a province must be registered in order for a province to qualify for federal funds.

Ontario *had* a compulsory health premium for all employers to pay (collect from employees or pay themselves or some combination) if they had five or more employees, although they did not have to pay it out of their own pocket as they could charge the premiums as a deduction from pay (needless to say, most large employers paid somewhere between 50 and 100 percent of the premium). The system was changed in 1988 to an employment tax, based on payroll charged to all employers, and all residents in the province can now get a health card whether employed or not. Here is one cost of this universality: in raising funds, it does not take into account the ability of the individual firm to compete with firms that do not have to pay such a tax in other jurisdictions, and thus fails to account for the jobs that are lost because of some businesses being forced to shut down or move.

A further cost relates to the classic "moral hazard" problem of people not being rewarded for taking care of themselves and thus not taking as good care as they might otherwise, resulting in higher costs just because of the form of financing.[10] Moral hazard has to be crucial in any debate about universality. A nonuniversal system would contain incentives to reduce the use of health care, but not necessarily health status, while a universal system encourages use of health care even if that leads to no improvement in health status.[11]

Still another cost relates to the available services and the practice of medicine. Some procedures are covered and some are not, and until recently that was subject to negotiation between the Ontario Medical Association (OMA) and the government, or whatever province and its medical association.[12] Doctors in Ontario *have* been able to bill for as many procedures as they wish to perform.[13] In recent years, in an attempt to control costs, doctors were limited to 100 procedures per day and more recently to a maximum billing of $400,000 per annum with a reduced reimbursement from $400,000 to $500,000 and no reimbursement beyond that level.[14] There have been doctors who have reached their caps (often the brighter and harder-working doctors), and some of them have migrated from the province.

When the provinces became responsible for the funding in 1977, Ontario negotiated a zero fee schedule increase with the OMA for two years, which caused many doctors to opt out of medicare. Opting out was a situation in which the doctor would collect the fee from the patient and the government would reimburse the patient. Opting out permitted extra-billing as well; here the doctor could charge the patient an extra fee (it was usually about $1 over the OHIP fee and based on 100 percent of the OMA fee schedule, so that in about three weeks the patient received back what he or she had paid the doctor less about $1, depending on the procedure).[15] In 1984, when the federal government passed legislation that told the provinces it would deduct any extra-billing charges from the cash grant, Ontario decided to legislate away extra-billing.[16] The latter decision, enacted in 1986, maintained the integrity of the federal grant, but cost the province greatly in the form of higher fees to compensate doctors for the loss of extra-billing.

I want to refer back to my earlier reference to the three ways of allocating resources. In its efforts to control costs, Ontario has also decreased the amount it spends on capital equipment and procedures. Initially rationing took the form of telling hospitals they could not have the latest equipment.[17] Dialysis units, for instance, are limited in number and size by the government, and the government screens every new capital expenditure that is proposed by each hospital. If one needs a heart bypass, the waiting list is six to nine months, and some people do die waiting. If one requires dialysis, a hospital committee will look at the need and determine whether (a) there is room in the dialysis program, and (b) whether the person would make a good candidate (and here ethics rears its ugly head, for if one is over the age of 65 and has another ailment such as a heart problem, there is virtually no chance that the application for dialysis will be approved).[18] In the area where I live (Kitchener–Waterloo) there are sixty-five spaces in the dialysis program and they were all full the last time I checked, so a new patient in need of dialysis would have to go elsewhere until a spot became available. Radiation therapy for cancer has a waiting list of up to six months depending on where you can sign on—it is assumed that you will have to travel to one of the hospitals that provides radiation treatment, and stories abound about the personal hardship this places on individuals.[19] Hip transplants have a waiting list of three years. I think I have made my point. Cost savings are achieved through queuing, which is itself often the result of rationing or government fiat.

A list of provincial cost-constraint packages makes even the most timid individual aware of the need for further thought about our universal health-care system.[20] Physicians can still perform "delisted" items, but will charge directly (and it is not always clear that honesty need be followed; billing for an alternative procedure instead would perhaps permit the patient to have the procedure paid for by OHIP). In addition, it appears that once a service is delisted, it becomes far more difficult to get, let alone more costly. Thus doctors no longer control the medical services one gets.

One of the problems associated with the current system is that there is no statement to the patient of what services have been billed. The patient cannot see whether the doctor has honestly billed for services, or what drain the consumer has been on the system.

Casual empiricism tells me that Canadians now use the U.S. health-care system as a back-up. To all intents and purposes, we do not have a universal health-care system anyway. I will cite three real examples. A man who had a severe blockage leading to the heart and was unable to work had a place in Florida and went there to wait out his minimum six months before surgery. While in Florida, he had a heart seizure and received his bypass immediately, returned to Canada, and to work. Because the heart seizure occurred while outside the country and was deemed emergency treatment rather than normal, privately purchased travel health insurance paid for the operation. In the second instance, Paul Tsongas, whom many remember from the U.S. Democratic primaries last year, was quoted as saying that the type of treatment he needed for his cancer would not have been available to him in Canada, even though the research that discovered the procedure was conducted here.

Finally, I will mention a university professor who developed a malignant tumour on the stem of her brain; she was told it was inoperable in Canada. Through a literature search and personal contacts, she was able to go off to Pittsburgh; after three operations she returned to the classroom and has been cancer-free for five years.

I can cite other examples, but I don't wish to appear alarmist. It is my intention to return to the theme of the costs of achieving social justice (equality or universality). A survey of Canadians will tell you that they believe overwhelmingly in the social justice of their health-care system. While 67 percent in a recent poll would approve of some form of user fee of up to $5 per day in hospital and $2 per physician visit, there is currently equal opportunity to access the resources of physicians and hospitals at zero cost. Note that I did not say equality, but equal opportunity.

One of the first papers I ever delivered to an academic audience in 1975 had to do with a study I had conducted of usage of health care by different income groups.[21] One thing that became very clear in that study was that the well-off used the system more often and more expensively than poorer people at a statistically significant level when controlled for age, gender, and other sociodemographic characteristics. The biggest difference occurred geographically in that people in "undoctored" areas had statistically significant smaller costs and less contact and were *not* statistically different in health status from those who made use of the system. It appears that poorer people view it as foolish to visit a physician if all the physician will do is prescribe something they cannot afford anyway. There is also a socioeconomic barrier in that doctors tend to come from a relatively higher socioeconomic status and some poorer people find it more difficult to relate to physicians due to language or other constraints.

The costs of the universal health-care system that we have in Canada are immense. These costs include the following factors:

- services are not available;
- services are available only with a long time delay;
- choice is reduced by the reduction in services available;
- medical doctors are no longer free to practise medicine as they deem fit;
- experts leave the constrained system; and
- innovation and research is reduced.

## OTHER OBSERVATIONS

I would like to address one further issue prior to closing. That has to do with the U.S. health-care system, which is the epitome of a nonuniversal system. In the United States I am always amazed at the disparity between the excellent and the awful. The infant mortality rate in the United States is higher than in most countries in the world—more like Third World countries because some mothers get no prenatal care at all. Canada restrains costs by not permitting the latest in technology and by not permitting hospitals to develop beyond what the government determines is appropriate. In other words, there is little choice and a less than excellent system, although I think it is probably correct to say it is *above average*. In the United States, one has access to world-renowned care if one is rich or has the right insurance, but abysmal or no care if one is poor.[22] Think of it in this way: Canadians have Chevrolet care while U.S. residents have either Cadillac care or public transit care.

The Canadian health-care system gives more equity in access and even in distribution, but there is a tremendous cost involved, and I would not recommend the current Canadian system precisely because the costs associated with it are too high. Universality encourages medio-crity. It encourages us to put into the hands of government allocation and ethical decisions that rightly belong to us as individuals. The basic theme of this paper has been that a Rawlsian inequality surplus is superior to pure equality, and yet the point must be made that to go too far toward inequality also leads to problems. Thus, while I have found the U.S. system wanting, I have also found the universality of the Canadian system means that we cannot collect the benefits of the inequality surplus.

It does not appear that a socially just system can also operate efficiently. Indeed, I have not begun to address the incentives here regarding research. In a system in which there is no profit motive, research is clearly lessened. There is no possibility of getting treatment in a Cadillac manner—we just have to take our trusty Chevy. I argue that if the system were not universal, there would be more opportunities for innovation, research, and a better health-care system. I am not advocating that anyone be left untended on the street, but I am advocating differences in the type of care system that we have. However, it is not necessary for us to adopt the U.S. system in order to have a nonuniversal system that operates efficiently and yet maintains some semblance of equity of access to health care. Thus it is necessary for us to look at alternatives.

I am reminded of when I lived in Alberta during the 1960s. I was newly married, we had a new baby in the household, and I was a poor graduate student. The government paid our health insurance premiums, and no doctor could tell that we were different than the next patient whose employer paid the premiums. That was less expensive and far more efficient and no one suffered from lack of care or poor care as has happened in the United States in the last few years.[23]

An alternative suggestion would be a "smart card," which would carry a photo. The card would be activated at every medical encounter so the cost of the encounter would be entered onto the card and a hard copy given to the patient. The user charges would accumulate on the card until a ceiling amount was reached, and the charges would then be a taxable benefit under the Income Tax Act. The user charges could then be related to ability to pay and would eliminate the disincentive for early treatment that a cash user charge would involve. This would not be universal and certainly would not be lacking in compassion for the poor. It would act as a disincentive for doctors to create more supplier-induced demand. It would act to catch people who contact a third or fourth doctor on a given day.[24]

The German Sickness Funds involve a certain amount of managed competition, which has been advocated in part by the Clinton health care proposals for the United States. The German system is universal in that everyone is eligible to receive insurance in one of the sickness funds. Some funds are employer sponsored and paid through that source, some are regional, but whichever, the poor can have their premiums subsidized by government and all the provider of care knows is that the individual is a member of one of the funds.

It should be clear that I advocate a caring system in which everyone can get care, but also a system in which government does not determine who can get what and when. A universal single-payer system is one that really does not achieve economic efficiency without costs. Thus movement to a compassionate nonuniversal system is important if Canada is going to survive the financial problems of dealing with deficit and debt and yet retain world-class health care.[25] This paper has pointed to the problems engendered by universality and has given some alternatives that would ensure our health-care system is both compassionate and accessible while also encouraging innovation, research, and excellence.

## NOTES

1. This work draws upon previous research, including a talk to doctoral students of Walden University and a paper for the American Economics Association. I would like to thank Wilfrid Laurier University for financial assistance with research costs. The paper has benefited from the contributions of one of the editors of this volume. I have also benefited from the comments of David J. Reinhardt, M.D., and Pastor Marshall Eizenga in preparation of this paper. However, the faults that remain are mine alone.

2. I have had training and an interest right up to the doctoral level in political science and teach in the social work faculty so I may have a somewhat broader view than many economists.

3. "Former New Zealand Health Minister Offers Blunt ..." p. 669. Michael Bassett, Minister of Health in New Zealand from 1984 to 1987, says "the signs of decay here are all too familiar" to him.

4. Robert C. Solomon and Mark C. Murphy, eds., *What is Justice?: Classic and Contemporary Readings* New York: Oxford University Press, 1990.

5. Robert Paul Wolff, *Understanding Rawls: A Reconstruction and Critique of a Theory of Justice* (Princeton, N.J.: Princeton University Press, 1977), pp. 27–29.

6. Organization for Economic Cooperation and Development. Reported in *The New York Times*, May 16, 1993.

7. Saskatchewan was also the first with hospitalization in 1948.

8. It just so happened that as a teenager I had my first summer job in Saskatchewan in a resort area where most of the doctors were staying, so I became very interested in that strike.

9. In 1986, the EPF formula was modified to limit the rate of growth of federal transfers to 2 percent less than the average nominal GNP growth in the preceding three years. In 1989, this was further modified to be 3 percent less than GNP growth in the same three years. In February 1990, the per capita EPF transfers for 1990–91 and 1991–92 fiscal years were frozen at 1989–90 levels. The 1991 budget extended the freeze on the per capita EPF entitlements. Then, on February 1, 1991, the Government Expenditure Restraint Act sought to eliminate the cash portion of federal transfer payments within fifteen years. These measures were designed to reduce the federal deficit, but what they have done is to put pressure on the provinces to find ways in which to control health costs. To ensure that the removal of cash transfers from EPF financing does not result in removal of medicare as a program, the federal government introduced Bill C-20, which would extend the federal power to withhold funds from other transfer programs if the province did not meet the five conditions of medicare as established in 1966. This debate about the ability of the government to control its expenditures is very much a debate about universality and the financial ability of governments to maintain a universal system.

10. "Moral hazard" is a term used in the economics literature to indicate that when someone has insurance, that insurance drives up the risk that the insurance is insuring against. Let me use an example from another field— workers' compensation. Since employers are not penalized for lack of safety (to the extent of the costs of putting safety equipment in place), the employer may decide not to put into place safety equipment to the extent possible. Further, the employee is not penalized for taking risks on the job and thus there will be some people who will do things because the insurance is there which they would have been careful not to do otherwise. The result is a higher worker's compensation bill than would have been the case in the absence of the insurance. In the case of health insurance, if people were penalized through premiums geared to risk (obesity, smoking, unprotected sex with multiple partners), some of these activities would not be engaged in and there would be a lower health bill as a consequence. Even supplements such as vitamins are expensive but would be much more readily used if health insurance (at a seemingly zero price) were not available.

11. There is also a point to be made here about health care not being healthy. If more health care makes you sick (iatrogenic disease) then health care in itself is not desirable. What would be ideal is for people to use only that portion of health care that enhances their health status.

12. Among the procedures being removed from the list of paid services this year are the following:

| | |
|---|---|
| Electrolysis | Tattoo removal |
| Sex reassignment surgery | Sterilization |
| Reversal of sterilization | In vitro fertilization |
| Reduction mammoplasty | Augmentation mammoplasty |
| Panniculectomy | Repair of torn earlobes |
| Blepharoplasty | Septorhinoplasty |
| Umbilectomy | Newborn circumcision |
| Male mastectomy (benign) | Penile prosthesis for impotence |
| Gastric bypass for morbid obesity | Sclerotherapy |
| Dermabrasion | Psychoanalysis |

13. In the spring of 1993, graduates of the medical schools were told that they would be able to locate in certain designated parts of the province of Ontario only, and if they chose to locate in other areas they would be paid only 25 percent of the fees that they billed. While the government backed down on this proposal, it demonstrates the direction that the government is taking with respect to freedom to practise medicine and using the purse strings to control that freedom.

14. Beyond that, under the social contract in Ontario, doctors from October 1993 to March 1994 are having their billings reduced by 10 percent each month. Starting in 1994, doctors are expected to reduce their own billings by 5 percent or there will be a clawback of billings of a larger amount by the government. This results in fewer services being available to consumers and a decrease in the freedom of physicians and surgeons to practise medicine in the way in which they were taught.

15. There was a chance to study the option of user fees when Saskatchewan introduced user fees of $1.50 per physician visit and $2.00 for home, emergency, and outpatient visits, and per diem fees for hospitalization. These fees were small enough not to preclude care, but were designed to reduce unnecessary care. Beck and Horne found in their work that there was a reduction of 5.6 percent in quantity of physician services when there was a 33 percent increase in the price of physician care, with the bulk of the decrease in use occurring among the poor.

16. The province was losing $50 million in cash grants from the federal government per year. The doctors went on strike, and to get them to agree to start work again the province negotiated a fee increase. In the year following the

doctors' strike, billings to the province increased by $3 billion. Not only did the higher fee go to all doctors whether they had extra-billed or not, but the number of contacts with physicians rose by 11 percent since many doctors would no longer renew prescriptions over the phone but insisted on a visit for which they billed OHIP. How is that for a cost-benefit ratio—spend $3 billion to get $50 million?

17. Take, for example, magnetic resonance imaging (CMRI) machines, which provide sophisticated X-rays of the body. There are more MRI machines in the city of Seattle than in all of Canada. The result is that queuing has become endemic. If one needs an MRI, on an emergency basis, it can be arranged within three to six weeks, but the normal wait is nine months and I have heard of longer waits as emergencies bump those who are already on the list down even lower.

18. Here it is clear that rationing by government ends up causing the queue to lengthen as people vie for scarce equipment.

19. Recent information coming from the K-W Academy of Medicine is that some surgeons are undertaking unnecessary surgery to remove cancerous tissue since the less invasive radiation is not available.

20. "Some hospitals will be closed down entirely. Hospital budgets have been limited to meagre increases resulting in hospital bed closures, staff lay-offs including nurses and middle managers, programs being cancelled, construction, renovations and capital expenditures being postponed, and equipment purchase plans being curtailed. In many provinces, some acute care hospital beds are being converted to long term care beds, outpatient services are being curtailed and emergency services are being rationalized. In most provinces, mergers between hospitals have occurred or are being actively considered as a way to reduce administrative costs and improve operating efficiency. Day surgery and outpatient care is being substituted for inpatient stays. Many provinces have announced limits to and reductions in out-of-country benefits and de-insured some services so that they are no longer covered under Medicare. In one or another province of Canada, basic vision assessment was de-insured; routine dental extractions performed in hospitals were de-insured; fluoride treatment of children up to age 4 was de-insured; removal of impacted wisdom teeth was de-insured; a charge for insulin was instituted; age of eligibility for coverage under Dentacare was increased; optometrist services were de-insured for all persons between 18 and 40; existing fee levels for chiropractic, podiatry, and osteopathic services were frozen or reduced; air and ground ambulance fees raised; 'better-off' elderly were no longer covered by provinces' drug benefit plans; ... list can be tediously extended but alas with such a barrage of announcements, any list is bound to be incomplete and outdated." Manga, "Health Economics and the Current Health Care Cost Crisis," pp. 189–90.

21. "Social Class and Health Care Benefits Among Consumers in Ontario: A Pilot Study of Source Problems in Research," jointly written with Conrad J.

Winn, Eastern Economics Association Annual Meeting 1975. The paper was also submitted to the Ontario Economic Council as a report, and a portion of the paper was published as "A Note on Regional Differences in Health Care Usage in Ontario," *Growth and Change* (October 1978).

22. The very poor have Medicaid but doctors often refuse Medicaid patients. In an area like Los Angeles, many Medicaid patients turn up at hospitals without having had any prenatal care at all. All U.S. residents can get hospital care whether they are on Medicaid or not, it is just that not all hospitals will provide such care, or if they do it is often not under the best circumstances. An excellent video produced by the Public Broadcasting Network in the United States comparing the Canadian problems and the U.S. problems with providing health care is entitled "Borderline Medicine" and produced in 1991. It is well worth seeing and is available to universities.

23. It is clear that many hospitals and health-care practitioners in the United States will not accept Medicaid because of the red tape and longer payment times involved.

24. New Brunswick Premier Frank McKenna has introduced the card, which will permit this in his province. In announcing the new system on September 28, 1993, Premier McKenna said, "We may find out for example, through this technology a patient has been to four doctors in a single day or that there is over drugging that's chronic with respect to a patient." That is not to say that patients' initiatives are what is costing the health-care system great amounts of money, but if it is we don't currently have that information. The smart card would also permit the identification of doctors who refer patients excessively to other doctors.

25. Anyone who questions the problems of the deficit and debt should look at the recent literature regarding the International Monetary Fund (IMF) and the problems associated with having to ask the IMF to prop up the currency. New Zealand had a smaller debt as a proportion of GNP than does Canada today when the IMF entered the picture. In some countries in which the IMF has been asked to intervene to prop up the currency, the IMF has insisted as a condition of such guarantees that the health system be made 100 percent private. I cannot guarantee that the IMF will ever be asked to come into Canada, but it seems at least a possibility; we ought to consider our situation with some degree of concern and decide for ourselves how to control the increase in government deficit and debt before such an event.

## REFERENCES

Alves, Joseph J., "The Impediments to Health Care Reform in Ontario: The Problems and Politics of Physician Resource Management," Unpublished Master of Arts Research Paper completed and defended April 1993, Wilfrid Laurier University.

Beck, R.G. and J.M. Horne, "Utilization of Publicly Insured Health Servies in Saskatchewan Before, During and After Copayment," *Medical Care* Vol. XVIII, No. 8.

Bobadilla, José-Luis and Helen Saxenian, "Designing an Essential National Health Package," *Finance and Development* 30, no. 3 (September 1993): 10–13.

Gladwell, Malcolm, "Failing Health," *Saturday Night*, October 1993, pp. 26–30, 66, 69.

Hamilton, Vivian and Barton H. Hamilton, "Does Universal Health Insurance Equalize Access to Care? A Canadian—U.S. Comparison," Unpublished Working Paper 16/93, McGill University.

Hecht, Robert and Philip Musgrove, "Rethinking the Government's Role in Health," *Finance and Development* 30, no. 3 (September 1993): 6–9.

Hoye, Robert E., "Viewing the Canadian Health Care System as a Model for the United States," *Journal of the Royal Society of Health* 3, no. 2 (April 1991): 61–63.

Jamieson, Dean, "Investing in Health," *Finance and Development* 30, no. 3 (September 1993): 2–5.

Manga, Pran, "Health Economics and the Current Health Care Cost Crisis: Contributions and Controversies," *Health and Canadian Society* 1, no. 1, 177–203.

McCready, Douglas J. and Conrad J. Winn, "A Note on Regional Differences in Health Care Usage in Ontario," *Growth and Change* (October 1978).

Mhatra, Sharmila L. and Raisa B. Deber, "From Equal Access to Health Care to Equitable Access to Health: A Review of Canadian Provincial Health Commissions and Reports," *International Journal of Health Services* 22, no. 4 (1992): 645–68.

Ontario Conference of Catholic Bishops, *100 Years of Catholic Social Teaching* (Toronto: Ontario Conference of Catholic Bishops, 1991).

O'Reilly, Michael, "Former New Zealand Health Minister Offers Blunt Warning to Canadian Doctors, Politicians," *Canadian Medical Association Journal* 149, no. 5 (September 1993): 669–72.

Reagan, Michael D., *Curing the Crisis: Options for America's Health Care* (Boulder, Colorado: Westview Press, 1992).

Tan, Jee-Ping and Kenneth Hill, "The Foundation for Better Health," *Finance and Development* 30, no. 3 (September 1993): 14–16.

# POSTSCRIPT

Taylor Alexander offers a persuasive and spirited defence of universal medicare. Alexander's comparison of Canadian and American health systems is especially effective, and the fact that the United States is desperately trying to implement some kind of universal plan also speaks well of medicare. Nevertheless, the paper is not entirely convincing. Taylor admits the problem of cost, but then suggests that this can be solved—through increased federal funding to the provinces and reforms to the operation of medicare. But how can a federal government burdened with a large deficit—$45 billion at last count—begin transferring large amounts of money to the provinces? As for the reforms, some of them amount to major adjustments to the way medicine is practised in Canada and hence are unlikely to be accepted. Increasingly, it appears that cost is not really a problem, but rather a basic feature of health care in modern times. If government is to provide universal care, it must accept the fact that health care is expensive; if it cannot, then perhaps it should rethink its present position on the provision of health care in Canada.

In his paper, McCready outlines some problems with medicare, and suggests that these represent grounds for eliminating universality. He knows that this will result in some people receiving better care than others, but he is ready for this eventuality. Using the ideas of John Rawls, he argues that the end of universality might generate what he calls an "inequality surplus," which can be used to make things better even for those located on the lower level of a two-tier health system. But is this plausible? The United States has a two-tier system, and one would be very hard-pressed to argue that the less well-off receive better health care than the average person in Canada. Admittedly, McCready rejects the American system, and obviously has something different in mind when talking about a reformed Canadian system without universality.

However, it is difficult *not* to imagine that the end of universality would start Canada down the road to an American-style health system.

There has been a great deal written on health care in Canada. For an overview of medicare and its present challenges, one might start with two papers by Robert G. Evans, "Canada: The Real Issues," *Journal of Health Policy, Politics and Law* 17, no. 4 (Winter 1992) and "Hang Together, or Hang Separately: The Viability of a Universal Health Care System in an Aging Society," *Canadian Public Policy* XIII, 2 (June 1987). Once these articles have been read, students might consider one or more of the following detailed discussions of medicare: Malcolm C. Brown, *Health Economics and Policy: Problems and Prescriptions* (Toronto: McClelland and Stewart, 1991); Raisa B. Deber and Gail G. Thompson, eds., *Restructuring Canada's Health Services System: How Do We Get There From Here?* (Toronto: University of Toronto Press, 1992); and Robert G. Evans, *Strained Mercy: The Economics of Canadian Health Care* (Toronto: Butterworths, 1984).

A complete understanding of any policy issue requires an appreciation of the relevant history, and medicare is no exception. For a complete account of the development of medicare, see Malcolm Taylor's *Health Insurance and Canadian Public Policy: The Seven Decisions that Created the Canadian Health Insurance System and Their Outcomes*, 2nd ed. (Kingston and Montreal: McGill-Queen's University Press, 1987).

Scholars are not the only ones interested in medicare. In recent years, provincial governments have established review mechanisms in an attempt to deal more effectively with medicare. Sharmila L. Mhatra and Raisa B. Deber summarize the findings of these reviews in "From Equal Access to Health Care to Equitable Access to Health: A Review of Canadian Provincial Health Commissions and Reports," *International Journal of Health Services* 22, no. 4 (1992).

As both Alexander and McCready show, any examination of medicare inevitably involves comparisons with health care in the United States. Uwe E. Reinhardt offers a useful discussion of the American health-care system in his article "The United States: Breakthroughs and Waste," *Journal of Health Policy, Politics and Law* 17, no. 4 (Winter 1992). A more in-depth treatment of the subject can be found in Michael D. Reagan's book *Curing the Crisis: Options for America's Health Care* (Boulder: Westview Press, 1992).

Finally, those concerned with medicare and universality might benefit from examining a previous debate between McCready and Malcolm Taylor. See Douglas J. McCready, "Don't Copy Canada's Health Care System," *Policy Options* 12, no. 8 (October 1991); and Malcolm G. Taylor, "Another Look at Canada's Health Care System," *Policy Options* 13, no. 4 (May 1992). (The second reference contains a short reply by McCready.)

# ISSUE TWENTY-THREE

## Does Canada Need an Entrenched Social Charter?

**YES**  R. Brian Howe, "The Case for a Canadian Social Charter"

**NO**  Janet Ajzenstat, "A Social Charter, Eh? Thanks, but No Thanks"

It has been suggested that the history of Western democracy has been the gradual definition and development of the concept of citizenship, especially in regard to the rights and entitlements that one derives by virtue of membership in a political community. In the 18th and 19th centuries, the focus was primarily on the securing of civil and political rights. These rights—freedom of speech and thought, liberty of the person, religious freedom, the right to vote and hold office, to name only a few—were seen as essential components of liberal democracy. The argument for civil and political rights was rooted in a fundamental distrust of government, which led to the belief that only a constitutionally entrenched bill of rights could afford individuals adequate protection from interference by the state.

In the 20th century, some of these rights continue to be given broader definition, as witnessed in recent reforms to the Electoral Act that permit some prisoners to vote in federal elections for the first time. However, in this century much more attention has been given to the need to secure social and economic rights as well. Social rights generally refer to the right to some basic standard of economic welfare and security. The expansion of the concept of social rights would seem to be a natural companion to the rapid expansion of the welfare state in the decades following the Second World War. The rise of the welfare state was based on a commitment by political leaders that the state should guarantee the means for a decent life for all citizens, irrespective of their financial ability or status in society.

But whereas political and civil rights have been given constitutional protection, as in the Canadian Charter of Rights and Freedoms, social rights have traditionally relied on an informal understanding between political leaders and citizens. A social contract, as Richard Lipsey points out, "is an unwritten set of understandings between the state and the people about the rights and obligations of each for the other." In the postwar period, the development of the welfare state was largely based on just such an informal commitment on the part of successive governments to pursue social justice through measures that redistributed income and wealth.

However, by the 1980s this informal social contract began to break down under the weight of dramatic economic changes. The postwar economic boom that had made the growth of the welfare state possible had come to an end. The rise of neoconservative governments, in the United States, Great Britain, and Canada, placed new emphasis on the downsizing of government and the privileging of market forces.

For many Canadians, the implicit social charter that has undergirded the growth of the welfare state in Canada appears to be under assault on two levels. The past decade has seen a gradual decentralization of federal powers in the areas of taxation, spending, and administrative powers to the provinces. Recent constitutional reform proposals, particularly the Charlottetown Accord, pointed in the direction of an even more dramatic devolution of federal powers, which appears to threaten the future viability of social programs that many have come to see as an essential component of the Canadian political identity.

Second, with the growing emphasis on the globalization of market forces and the need for national reforms to ensure global competitiveness, many fear that the erosion of national economic boundaries will lead to pressures to lower social security and labour market rights for the sake of global competitiveness. This downward pressure could ultimately lead to a lowering of social standards, and possibly the abolishment of the social programs that many feel are a part of the Canadian national identity.

In this context, it is not surprising that a growing number of theorists have argued for stronger constitutional protection of social and economic rights by entrenching a formal Social Charter into the Constitution, thereby giving them the same legal protection as political and civil rights. But whereas political and civil rights in the Charter of Rights and Freedoms are intended to defend the individual from the state, a Social Charter would have as its goal a guarantee by the state to provide protection for the individual against the vagaries of the marketplace. And if the Social Charter was made justiciable, that is, enforceable through the courts, citizens would be able to use the courts to force governments to provide some minimally adequate standard of living uniformly across Canada. In doing so, the Social Charter would help to unify Canada, by preserving and strengthening its social identity in the face of both globalizing economic pressures and decentralizing political pressures.

Should economic and social rights be given the same status and protection as political and civil rights? Is a Social Charter important to the protection of Canada's national identity? In the following essay, Brian Howe, a political scientist at the University College of Cape Breton, argues the case for the entrenchment of a Social Charter in Canada. Janet Ajzenstat, a political theorist at McMaster University, examines the disadvantages of entrenching a Social Charter.

# The Case for a Canadian Social Charter

*R. Brian Howe*

The purpose of this paper is to make the case for a Canadian Social Charter that constitutionalizes social and economic rights similar to the way the Charter of Rights and Freedoms constitutionalizes political and legal rights. Thanks to the architects of the Charlottetown Accord, the concept of a Social Charter has now become part of the constitutional reform agenda for Canada. It is likely to remain so, long after memories of the death of the Charlottetown Accord have faded, because its rationale is so compelling. A Social Charter is desirable for two general reasons. One is its protective function: the basic social rights of Canadians such as health care will be better protected with a Social Charter than without one. The other is its symbolic national unity function: like the Charter of Rights, the Social Charter will be symbolic of shared Canadian values and common citizenship. Before elaborating on these arguments, I will look at the initiative for a Social Charter in the early 1990s and subsequent criticisms of the concept. I will conclude with possible modifications of the version found in the Charlottetown Accord.

## INITIATIVE FOR A SOCIAL CHARTER

The concept of a Social Charter arrived on the constitutional reform agenda as part of the 1992 Charlottetown Accord proposal. It was contained in a section of the Accord called Canada's Social and Economic Union, which spelled out a number of fundamental social policy goals requiring governmental action in the areas of health care, social services, education, collective bargaining, the environment, standards of living, and full employment.[1] To ensure compliance, the accord indicated that some form of governmental/administrative mechanism would be established—its specific nature to be determined by a future First Ministers' Conference—for monitoring how governments fulfil their commitment to the objectives of the Social Charter. But the Social Charter would not be justiciable, that is, it would not be enforceable through the regular courts.

Much of this conception of a Social Charter was based on the Ontario NDP government's proposal for a Social Charter contained in its discussion paper *A Canadian Social Charter*. The discussion paper was released in September 1991 as momentum was gathering for constitutional reform.[2] Ontario's proposal in turn was influenced by a broad range of factors: a tradition of postwar writings on the need for constitutional social rights as well as political rights, including those of Frank Scott and Pierre Trudeau; a large body of international human rights literature and the various declarations and covenants of the United Nations; and the important example of the European Social Charter, adopted by the Council of Europe in 1961, which showed the viability of a Social Charter. In the early 1990s, as new items were placed on the constitutional reform agenda, Ontario was able to raise the issue of a Social Charter with its discussion paper and put it on the agenda. From September 1991 to February 1992, after gaining substantial support for the concept, Ontario was able to have its proposal incorporated into the February 1992 report of the Special Joint Committee on a Renewed Canada (the Beaudoin-Dobbie Committee), in a section called the Social Covenant, and passed along virtually unchanged in August 1992 to the architects of the Charlottetown Accord.[3]

The justification for a Social Charter was provided in Ontario's discussion paper. The rationale given was twofold. First, a Social Charter was desirable for the symbolic reason that it would recognize and affirm the fundamental social values of Canadians as a nation and that it would define a central part of the Canadian identity. Like the Charter of Rights, the Social Charter would be a symbolic force for national unity and shared Canadian citizenship. Second and more important, a Social Charter was desirable for the practical reason that it would better protect the social rights of Canadians. It would work to maintain national standards for Canadians in social policies and programs and to ensure that competitive economic pressures would not become used as an excuse by governments for weakening or abandoning social policy goals. In short, according to Ontario, "the social charter will guarantee that basic national values and principles are maintained, and the commitment of governments to abide by these values, and to finance the programs to implement them, are enforced."[4] Given the leading role of the federal government in financing social programs and maintaining national standards, primary attention would be on ensuring social policy commitments by the federal government.

To illustrate the need for a Social Charter, Ontario pointed to the recent failure of the federal government to honour its commitment under the Canada Assistance Plan to share the cost of social assistance with the provinces (in the amount of 50 percent of the province's eligible expenditures). As noted by Ontario, in 1990, as part of its expenditure control plan, the federal government had made the decision to limit the growth in size of payments to the financially stronger provinces not receiving equalization payments. This was enacted as the Government Expenditures Restraint Act in 1991, allowing the federal government to no longer fund 50 percent of the affected provinces' spending on social assistance. In response, British Columbia, one of the affected provinces (the others were Alberta and Ontario), took the federal government to court. British Columbia argued (with Alberta and Ontario as interveners) that the federal government lacked the legal authority to limit its obligations under the Canada Assistance Plan and that the agreement gave rise to a legitimate expectation that the federal government would not legislate reductions in its fiscal obligations without provincial consent. In 1991, in Reference re Canada Assistance Plan, the Supreme Court of Canada ruled that the federal government had the legitimate authority to act as it did and to limit its obligations under the cost-sharing agreement.[5] Moreover, the Supreme Court ruled that the federal government did not act illegally in altering the agreement without provincial consent. This action was in keeping with the legitimate exercise of the federal spending power.

According to Ontario, such federal action and such a court decision underlined the need for a constitutional Social Charter, one that could shield Canadians from political irresponsibility and insensitivity to basic social rights. What the Charter of Rights can do in the area of political rights a Social Charter can do in the area of social rights. A point not mentioned by Ontario, however, is that shielding may be necessary from any level of government—the federal government does not have a monopoly on irresponsibility and insensitivity.

## CRITICISMS AND RESPONSES

Ontario's initiative did not go without criticism. According to critics, the idea of a Social Charter is misguided. John Richards, for example, argues that a strong Social Charter implies more government expenditure, larger deficits (as citizens will resist paying higher taxes), and less efficient delivery of public services (as governments no longer need to be as accountable).[6] Hugh Mellon suggests that a rights-based approach to social policy makes policy-making much more difficult because it raises public expectations (expectations once raised are difficult to meet) and encourages unreasonable public demands, unhelpful in a world of ideological disagreement, taxpayer unrest, and government debts.[7] These are pragmatic counter-arguments. But counter-arguments made by William Robson and Janet Ajzenstat are ones against the Social Charter in principle. Robson argues that the Social Charter is highly undemocratic, transferring power from electorates and politicians to judicial or quasi-judicial bodies that are unaccountable.[8] Further, he says that the Social Charter puts in constitutional stone the social welfare state, representing an absolutist, inflexible, and unconstrained vision of the political world. Similarly, Ajzenstat argues that the Social Charter is undemocratic, putting to an end free and open debate about the welfare state.[9] She suggests that welfarism and the positive state will be put on a pedestal, constitutionalizing the ideological demands of the left.

Similar responses may be given to Robson and Ajzenstat as to earlier critics of the concept of a Charter of Rights and of a Bill of Rights.[10] In all of these criticisms, it is claimed that a constitutional structure for protecting basic rights is a contradiction of democratic principle—political power passes from citizens and their elected representatives to unelected officials. But to throw the term "democracy" against the Social Charter (as against the Charter of Rights) is to assume that the current system of parliamentary majoritarian democracy works well to achieve equality and to protect the rights of minorities and disadvantaged groups. A history of elite-driven democracy and periodic governmental insensitivity to basic rights shows such an assumption to be flawed—so flawed that simple parliamentary democracy is no longer tenable among a Canadian citizenry conscious of rights and cynical of politicians. As the Charter of Rights is designed to provide constitutional protection of basic political and legal rights (in large part), the Social Charter is designed to provide protection of basic social and economic rights (in the form of public policy goals). In both cases, although the kinds of rights may be different, constitutional protection is necessary because majorities, politicians, and governments cannot be relied upon to provide effective protection of the rights of minority citizens or the weaker/ disadvantaged members of Canadian society. Good will and sensitivity are not always in plentiful supply. That Canada has had a relatively good historical record of protecting rights is no reason to gloss over historical shortcomings—such as the mistreatment of native peoples and Asian minorities—and not to seek more effective constitutional protection of rights.

Social and economic rights may be no more important than political and legal rights, but they also are no less important. As stated by Henry Shue, basic social and political rights are interdependent.[11] The effective exercise of one requires as a condition the effective exercise of the other. The right to freedom of expression is not fully effective without adequate health care, but also the right to education is not fully effective without freedom of expression. Thus social rights in the Social Charter are as fundamental as political rights in the Charter of Rights, and are equally deserving of constitutional entrenchment. Social rights are far from secure in Canada given recent developments that threaten to undermine social programs and policies. Lars Osberg and Shelley

Phipps point to threatening developments over the past two decades such as increased polarization of the distribution of wages, increased unemployment, and increased financial pressures on lower-income families, especially female-headed, single-parent families.[12] They also point to the implications of future constitutional change (as provided for in the Charlottetown Accord) that would enhance the mobility of goods, services, capital, and labour within a Canadian common market, thereby putting social programs more at risk under the impact of market forces. One can also point to similar implications and risks of a future North American Free Trade Agreement. Put together, these developments pose a threat to social programs and underline the need for a Social Charter to insulate social rights from market forces and from irresponsible or insensitive governments.

If democracy is conceived as simple majoritarian parliamentary democracy, a Social Charter is indeed contradictory—as is a Charter of Rights. But if democracy is conceived more broadly to include the effective exercise of basic political and social rights, there is much less of a problem. While some political power may pass from electorates and politicians to administrative officials (in an administrative Social Charter) or the courts (in a justiciable Social Charter), the Social Charter serves as a constraint or check on the power of market forces, majorities, and governments. As in the case of the Charter of Rights, the capacity of legislatures or governments to deny or override rights is constrained by the countervailing force of the Social Charter. Just as the Charter of Rights and its sophisticated jurisprudence provides a rationally based system of protection of political rights, the Social Charter is designed to provide similar protection in the area of social rights. The Social Charter is designed not to undermine democracy, but to enhance democracy. Moreover, it has broad public/democratic approval. Just as the Charter of Rights had substantial majority public backing in an earlier round of constitutional reform, the concept of a Social Charter has gained broad public support and even the support of business groups.[13] Surely it is not undemocratic if a majority of Canadians want fundamental social policy goals in a Social Charter to take priority over other governmental goals.

A Social Charter is beneficial not only for Canadian democracy, but also as a symbolic force for national unity. Like the Charter of Rights, it can help provide a sense of common citizenship. It is true, as William Matheson and others have argued, that the symbolic value of the Charter of Rights has been overestimated.[14] The use of the "notwithstanding" clause has been controversial, and the Charter has not been successful in incorporating French Canada and First Nations into a shared sense of Canadian citizenship. Can the Social Charter really be of much symbolic help? It is important to note that the Charter of Rights has had important symbolic effects in most—though not all—of Canada. Most Canadians are united in the high regard they have of the Charter. Controversy over Quebec's use of the "notwithstanding" clause reflects this high regard. A Social Charter can only add to the symbolism of Canadians bound together by the high value they place on basic rights. But cleavages between French and English and between native and non-natives run deep. Charters of constitutional rights in themselves certainly will not bridge these cleavages. They can, however, make a contribution to building a symbolic sense of common citizenship that otherwise would be lacking.

This leaves the pragmatic counter-arguments. Will the Social Charter mean more government spending, larger deficits, and less efficient delivery of public services? Will the Social Charter put Canada at an economic disadvantage in face of global competition? The Social Charter attempts to ensure the basics in a relatively wealthy country. As emphasized by Lars Osberg, it is concerned with minimum adequate standards and with outcomes, not with means.[15] Governments are free to experiment with different cost-effective means and delivery systems as long as the overall policy objective of adequate health care, for example, is achieved. Competitive economic and political pressures may encourage such experimentation, but not at the price of basic needs. A Social Charter may imply a higher level of social spending, but this does not preclude measures to improve the efficiency of programs and it does not mean inordinately big government. Furthermore, it is highly questionable to assume a simple trade-off between strong social programs and policies, on the one hand, and economic growth and international competitiveness, on the other. Among Western industrialized nations over the past decade, European countries with a Social Charter and with relatively high levels of social spending, also had relatively high levels of economic growth and labour productivity.[16] During the same period, the Social Charterless United States (and Canada to a lesser extent) had relatively low rates of economic growth. Healthy social programs and healthy economic growth *can* go together.

Will the Social Charter make social policy-making more difficult because of raised public expectations and rights-minded thinking? As with the Charter of Rights, the Social Charter indeed will likely raise the level of rights consciousness in Canada. It also will likely increase the public expectation of access to adequate health care, food, shelter, and education. This in turn will make policy-making more difficult in the sense that decision-makers will now be constrained by political obligations in the Social Charter. But from the point of view of basic human needs, is this not desirable? In possible trade-offs between fundamental social policy goals and other governmental goals, decision-makers indeed will have less room to manoeuvre, given the forces of rights consciousness, public expectations, and the Social Charter. But this is to the good. No doubt many other difficulties and pragmatic considerations can be raised. But surely if these were not enough to discourage members of the European community—with many more obstacles— from implementing a Social Charter, they should not be enough to discourage Canada.

## ALWAYS ROOM FOR IMPROVEMENT

The demise of the Charlottetown Accord provides the opportunity for rethinking and refining parts of the Social Charter contained in the Accord from which improvements may be made in a future constitutional reform. I suggest that refinements may be beneficial with respect to both social policy objectives and means of enforcement.

The Social Charter policy objectives spelled out in the Charlottetown Accord are comprehensive, ranging from health care and education to full employment and a reasonable standard of living. These are similar to ones found in the European Social Charter. However, there is an important difference. Unlike the Charlottetown Social Charter, the European Social Charter requires governments to pursue policies against discrimination in such basic areas as employment and accommodation. Why not follow the European lead and incorporate social rights against discrimination into a new Social Charter along with other rights? Few Canadians would disagree that rights to equal opportunity and equal treatment are of fundamental importance. While the Charter of Rights does not provide for these rights, they do receive recognition and protection in human rights legislation, now regarded by the Supreme Court of Canada as fundamental and quasi-constitutional law. But a major problem with human rights legislation is a lack of national standards. Most responsibility for the control of discrimination is with provincial governments. Over time, as human rights legislation has been established in the different provinces, considerable variation has occurred with respect to the scope of antidiscrimination protections, the structure of enforcement, and the funding of human rights programs.[17] Standards simply are lacking. I suggest that provision for the social policy goal of antidiscrimination protection in a new Social Charter would be useful in securing national standards.

Enforcement is another area of possible improvement. In the Charlottetown Social Charter, a governmental and administrative system of enforcement would have been used, similar to that used in the European Social Charter. Social rights would not have been justiciable through the courts. Rather, some form of intergovernmental agency or commission (call it a Social Charter Commission) would have been responsible for receiving reports, monitoring compliance, and making recommendations for improvement when governments did not fulfil their Social Charter obligations. According to Martha Jackman, a justiciable Social Charter is much more preferable.[18] She argues that a justiciable Social Charter would be more effective because it would elevate the status of social rights to that of political rights, and courts ultimately would provide for a better system of protection. The problem with a Social Charter Commission, in her view, is that a two-tier system would be created whereby social rights would be accorded second-class status and protection. Not only would the system be subject to bureaucratic inefficiency and political interference, but an administrative Social Charter simply would not be able to command the respect and commitment necessary as a basis for vigorous enforcement. The courts command much greater respect than does administrative authority and are quite capable of protecting social rights as well as political rights. Court rulings backed by the force of the law provide a much better means of enforcement than administrative recommendation backed by the force of public opinion.

This argument for a justiciable Social Charter warrants serious consideration. The usual argument against such a Social Charter is that it would transfer social policy-making power from elected politicians to unelected judges who lack competence to deal with complex social and economic policy issues. But as Jackman and others have pointed out, the courts in some measure have always engaged in social policy-making when interpreting constitutional documents and social and economic legislation. There is no reason to assume that courts (with experience and with administrative support) cannot take on a larger role than they already possess. A role for the courts and the availability of a judicial remedy to violations of a Social Charter would greatly strengthen the system of enforcement. The European experience is instructive as the introduction of a judicial remedy is being considered there, together with other reforms, in face of mounting criticism that enforcement needs to be more effective.[19] A justiciable Social Charter does not mean a system of complete judicial responsibility. Some form of judicial and governmental/administrative cooperation would be necessary. As in the case of antidiscrimination legislation, where enforcement is based on the administrative work of a Human Rights Commission, backed up by human rights tribunals, the enforcement of a Social Charter would require a large role for a Social Charter Commission or similar body, backed up by the authority of the courts. Certainly, there are many difficulties in such an arrangement. A system involving a role for the courts may mean lengthier and more costly enforcement with uncertain outcomes. But courts would have the advantage of providing for an effective legally binding remedy otherwise absent. The idea is well worth looking at.

## NOTES

1. *Consensus Report on the Constitution,* Charlottetown, August 28, 1992, Final Text.

2. Government of Ontario, *A Canadian Social Charter: Making Our Shared Values Stronger* (Toronto: Ministry of Intergovernmental Affairs, September 1991).

3. Special Joint Committee of the Senate and the House of Commons on a Renewed Canada, *Report* (Ottawa: Queen's Printer, February 1992).

4. Government of Ontario, *A Canadian Social Charter,* p. 13.

5. For the decision, see 83 *Dominion Law Reports* (4th) (1991).

6. John Richards, "A Social Charter: Two Cheers but Not Three," in Havi Echenberg et al., *A Social Charter for Canada?* (Toronto: C.D. Howe Institute, 1992). But Richards is in favour of a modest administrative Social Charter.

7. Hugh Mellon, "Proposals for a Social Charter: Misguided if Noble," *Policy Options* 14, no. 3 (April 1993).

8. William B.P. Robson, "Examining the Case for a Social Charter: A Constrained Comment," in Echenberg et al., *A Social Charter for Canada?*

9. Janet Ajzenstat, "Against Entrenching a Social Charter," *Brock Review* 2, no. 2 (Fall 1993).

10. For a discussion of arguments in the Charter of Rights movement, see Peter Russell, "The Political Purposes of the Canadian Charter of Rights and Freedoms," *Canadian Bar Review* 61 (1983).

11. Henry Shue, *Basic Rights* (Princeton: Princeton University Press, 1980).

12. Lars Osberg and Shelley Phipps, "A Social Charter for Canada," in Echenberg et al., *A Social Charter for Canada?*

13. Strong public support of the Charlottetown Accord debates is found in a CTV/*Toronto Star* poll, *The Toronto Star,* October 15, 1991. For business support, see "Social Charter Gathers Support," *The Globe and Mail,* February 1, 1992, pp. A1, A2.

14. William Matheson, "Some Comments on a Triple E Social Charter for Canada," *Brock Review* 2, no. 2 (Fall 1993).

15. Lars Osberg, "Democracy, Affordability, and the Social Charter," in Echenberg et al., *A Social Charter for Canada?*

16. A recent account of this is given by Linda McQuaig, *The Wealthy Banker's Wife* (Toronto: Penguin, 1993), chs. 3, 4.

17. For discussions of the variation, see Walter Tarnopolsky and William Pentland, *Discrimination and the Law in Canada* (Toronto: Richard De Boo, 1985), Ken Norman, "Problems in Human Rights Legislation and Administration," in Sheilah Martin and Kathleen Mahoney, eds., *Equality and Judicial Neutral-*

*ity* (Toronto: Carswell, 1987) and R. Brian Howe, "Human Rights in Hard Times," *Canadian Public Administration* 35, no. 4 (1992).

18. Martha Jackman, "Reflections on a Social Charter," *Inroads* 1, no. 1 (Fall 1992).

19. For recent discussion of the European Social Charter, see Victor Canales, "A New Boost for the Council of Europe's Social Charter," *Forum* (Council of Europe, September 1991) and John Myles, "Constitutionalizing Social Rights," in Echenberg et al., *A Social Charter for Canada?*, pp. 56–63.

# A Social Charter, Eh? Thanks, but No Thanks

*Janet Ajzenstat*

As we learn from Brian Howe's article, advocates of the Social Charter are not satisfied with the Charlottetown Accord's toothless formula. In the next round of constitution-making they will demand something closer to Premier Bob Rae's original dream of justiciable social and economic rights. A justiciable Social Charter would put the power of the courts behind the Charlottetown objectives: comprehensive health care, "adequate" social services and benefits, high-quality primary and secondary education, reasonable access to post-secondary education, collective bargaining rights, full employment, environmental protection, and a "reasonable standard of living" for all Canadians.[1]

What's wrong with entrenching these aims in the form of constitutional rights? Surely everyone believes that good health care and high educational standards are goals to strive for. Who doesn't want to see full employment, an adequate standard of living for all, a green Canada? As Professor Howe points out, the Social Charter's objectives are humane. But it is also true, as he admits, that many Canadians have doubts about the idea that governments should be the chief providers of these goods, to the exclusion of the private sector. I suggest that even more are of the opinion that the Social Charter is something we can't afford at present. They may accept the welfare state in principle, but they don't want to see taxes rise.

The Social Charter will undoubtedly result in more government regulation and higher taxes. It is designed to ensure that governments maintain and extend present levels of spending. The great hope of the Social Charter's advocates is that it will protect the welfare state from government cutbacks.[2]

In my opinion the fact that the Social Charter does not command universal support is the principal reason why it must be rejected. Entrenching economic and social rights will put an end to free and democratic debate about economic and social policies in the electoral and legislative arenas. It will inscribe the objectives of the political left in the

Canadian Constitution, making it virtually impossible for our elected representatives to respond to democratic demands. On the basic issues outlined in the Social Charter, they will not be legislators, but mere administrators of predetermined programs. The alternation of political parties in office, a change of heart on the part of the electorate, will make no difference in the constitutional commitment to welfarism.

Professor Howe knows that the Social Charter will limit the powers of political decision-makers in the area of economic and social policy. But he believes the limitation on democracy is acceptable because he has satisfied himself that the objectives of the Social Charter are good. My argument is that preventing our democratically elected representatives from defining the good in the area of social and economic policy can never be acceptable. If we introduce the Social Charter we lose the right that is the essence of democracy in a country such as Canada, to live under laws freely determined by our elected representatives.

Howe draws our attention to the distinction between positive (economic and social) rights and negative (legal and political) rights. Positive rights describe services that governments must provide; they require legislation to flesh them out. Negative rights, in contrast, limit government; they mark out an area of freedom where there should be no law, and governments should not trespass. Consider the classic negative rights described in the Fundamental Freedoms and Legal Rights sections of the Canadian Charter of Rights and Freedoms. Section 2 of the Canadian Charter prohibits governments from passing laws that trespass on citizens' right of free speech, freedom of religion, and freedom of assembly. Section 15(1) prohibits governments from passing laws that discriminate against minorities.

I think it is perhaps the finest thing about liberal democracy that it guarantees negative rights, limiting the power of democratic majorities to pass laws regulating free speech and treating citizens unequally. But it is a very different thing to write protection for economic and social benefits into the Constitution. In that case what is being limited is the ability of democratic majorities to determine economic and social policy: how taxes are raised, and how the taxpayers' money is spent.

Howe doesn't deny that legal and political rights are good. His position is that economic and political ones are just as important. He contends, in fact, that the kinds of arguments that lead us to entrench political and legal rights should persuade us to entrench economic and social rights. What he means comes to light in his claim that political and legal rights are not secure if governments are free to cut back on social and economic benefits. The suggestion is that poor and badly educated people cannot easily make their voice heard in politics and are not in a position to contest legal rights in court. In short, Howe is saying that positive rights are good in themselves and are also good because they are the condition of negative rights.

The idea that Canada needs laws providing disadvantaged citizens with publicly funded benefits because extremes of poverty deprive people of freedom is very common on the political left. I am not denying that the argument has a great deal of appeal. It has persuaded many Canadians in the past to support the parties of the political left and centre-left. But note that Howe is not arguing for welfare legislation, but for constitutionally entrenched welfare rights. The difference is crucial. Let me explain.

For more than a century democratic debate in liberal democracies, that is, debate between the political right and the political left, has been concerned with exactly this question: Should governments ensure a degree of material equality?

Political parties and groups on the left favour legislation to regulate the economy, temper the effects of capitalism, and provide the disadvantaged with tax-funded benefits. I don't think anyone could deny that what inspires the women and men of the left is a truly compassionate desire to enable all citizens to enjoy secure, dignified lives.

Parties and groups on the political right argue that governments should spend less, tax less, and in general leave people alone as much as possible to get on with their lives. They may well agree that poor living conditions deprive people of freedom. But they contend that the left's proposals will not save the situation. Taxing the rich and regulating business kills the capitalist goose that lays the golden egg of prosperity. Everyone's standard of living falls, and the poor especially suffer. Everyone's freedom is compromised.

I could continue. The right argues that welfare programs empower demeaning bureaucracies, and sap the dignity of those on the receiving end; true freedom is not compatible with dependence on government any more than it is compatible with poverty. The left maintains that the greatest affront to human dignity comes when women and men are exploited by powerful elites whose chief concern is to enrich themselves and the members of their political class.

What usually happens in liberal democracies is that the left and right work out a compromise. Welfare programs ensure benefits for the disadvantaged, but the idea of absolute material equality for all is shunned. Business is regulated, but not regulated out of existence. The exact nature of the compromise is always open to change, as the will of the electorate changes.

It is this ability to juggle economic and social claims to suit the electorate that is threatened by the Social Charter. Howe's argument that social and economic benefits should be entrenched in the form of rights would "guarantee" the left's political program regardless of decisions reached by the voters.

The Social Charter's right to full employment will require governments to play a much larger role in managing the economy. The guarantee of "adequate social benefits" will push governments to legislate new services and fund new social agencies. Hospitals, physicians, existing agencies, universities, and in time numerous other bodies will be able to demand more money in their new role as providers of constitutional rights.

Under a justiciable Social Charter the final determination about services and spending will lie with the courts. Judges, not the legislatures, will determine who gets what, when, and how much. The Supreme Court of Canada will have the last word on whether a government's budget satisfies the "reasonable standards of living" provision. If the court decides that more services and increased spending are necessary, governments will have to comply. Even governments that are anxious to reduce taxes will be forced to keep spending. It might be argued that a government truly determined to cut back could always resort to constitutional amendment, and write the Social Charter out of existence. But once those rights are entrenched, once precedents are set in the courts, and agencies and coalitions of interests begin to turn to the courts routinely on the basis of the judicial decisions, getting rid of the Social Charter is going to be next to impossible.[3]

Let me repeat: Howe is not asking for welfare legislation. He's asking for welfare rights. To ask for welfare legislation is compatible with participating in the debate among parties and interests that characterizes a free society. To ask for welfare rights is to suggest that the debate between right and left should come to an end, and that the left should be declared winner in perpetuity. Entrenching the Social Charter will put an end to ideology in dramatic fashion.

I am not arguing that the objectives of the Social Charter are unworthy, or that social justice is not a condition of legal justice. The case against the Social Charter is nothing more than a plea to leave these issues to be determined in the democratic arena. There's no reason at present why Canadians can't pass laws providing a degree of material equality for all and more security for the disadvantaged, or establish programs for better education and environmental protection. My argument is simply that these objectives should not be written in constitutional stone.

In fact, those who are committed to the idea that social justice demands the regulatory and welfare state should be the first to reject the Social Charter. Entrenching the policy objectives of the Social Charter argues a lack of faith in the justice of the left's cause. It suggests that free and open debate on it won't show its value. It is certainly a bid to take away from future generations the power to determine the issue for themselves. There is considerable evidence today that Canadians of all ideological orientations are dissatisfied with the opportunities for political participation in this country. The complaint of the Reform Party, the National Action Committee on the Status of Women, and the New Democratic Party has been that Canadians are not able to influence lawmaking and lawmakers; Canada isn't democratic enough. Should we now entrench measures that will render it still more difficult for Canadians to determine issues in the electoral and legislative arenas?

A liberal democracy can only thrive where there is open debate on political alternatives. It is essential that the electorate should be able to choose freely between parties supporting the welfare state and parties recommending retrenchment and the transfer of responsibilities to the private sphere. It is intolerable to suggest that the people's elected representatives should be bound in the straitjacket of a constitution that sets out one particular ideological program.

There is one more point to be considered. My argument throughout this paper has been based on the assumption that liberal democracies distinguish between constitutional law ("constitutional stone") and ordinary legislation, the kind of law that emerges from the political process. But in Canada today this distinction is in danger of being forgotten. One reason why it seems less salient is that for more than a decade governments and political interests have taken an intensely political approach to the process of constitution-making.

The various interests and governments that were engaged in drafting the Meech and Charlottetown accords were attempting to promote the particular interests of their political followers and clients by means of constitutional reform. They did not distinguish between constitutional reform and social reform, or between the constitutional process and the political process. They expected to carve up "constitutional stone" with as much ease as politicians carving up the proceeds of a patronage deal.

The result has been just what one would expect: the old idea that the Constitution is above politics, and that constitutionally entrenched rights are well protected from the political process and the whims of particular interests, is breaking down. It has been easier for the advocates of the Social Charter to advance their ideological argument in this climate of confusion. They are, in fact, the foremost group of all those who have attempted to use the rhetoric of constitutional reform for particular ideological advantage.

It would take a longer argument than I can make in a short article to suggest that Canada was better off when the distinction between constitutional law and ordinary, garden-variety law was still honoured. I will mention only one point: if the distinction fails, even the negative rights such as free speech, freedom of assembly, and equality will be subordinated to the push and shove of the political process and the will of the majority.

The best recipe for a just political society, the best we have found so far, is the liberal democratic one that Canada has been working toward for more than 126 years. It couples opportunity for democratic debate on economic and social issues with constitutional protection for the fundamental freedoms and equality rights.

## NOTES

1. The Charlottetown Accord, Draft Legal Text, October 9, 1992, Section 36.

2. Joel Bakan and David Schneiderman, "Introduction," in Bakan and Schneiderman, eds., *Social Justice and the Constitution: Perspectives on a Social Union for Canada* (Ottawa: Carleton University Press, 1992), p. 5.

3. For the argument that even the negative formulation of the rights in the Canadian Charter of Rights and Freedoms enables special interest groups to petition in the courts for funding and benefits, see Rainer Knopff and F.L. Morton, *Charter Politics* (Scarborough: Nelson, 1992). If a justiciable Social Charter becomes a reality we can expect to see feminist organizations, antipoverty coalitions, minority language associations, aboriginal associations, and others using the courts to advance political demands more often than at present, and with more success.

# P O S T S C R I P T

**A** good starting point for further study of this issue is the Ontario NDP government's paper, which has been the stimulus for much of the subsequent debate on the concept of the Social Charter in Canada. See Government of Ontario, *A Canadian Social Charter: Making Our Shared Values Stronger* (Toronto: Ministry of Intergovernmental Affairs, September 1991).

A very useful collection of essays on the concept of the Social Charter and its application to Canada can be found in Havi Echenberg et al., *A Social Charter for Canada? Perspectives on the Constitutional Entrenchment of Social Rights* (Toronto: C.D. Howe Institute, 1992). In this volume, Lars Osberg and Shelley Phipps set out a defence of the concept of the Social Charter and its relevance to Canada in their essay "A Social Charter for Canada." Students will find a useful critique in John Richards, "A Social Charter: Two Cheers but Not Three," in the same volume. Richards particularly criticizes the notion that the entrenchment of social rights is a natural extension of the meaning of citizenship. And the final essay in this volume, Lars Osberg's "Democracy, Affordability, and the Social Charter: A Reply," provides some useful rebuttals to the line of argument pursued in Professor Ajzenstat's essay.

Brian Howe has elaborated upon his ideas in an article co-authored with Franca Mandarino, "Rethinking the Social Charter," *Policy Options,* 14, no. 3 (April 1993): 16, 18–19. Another useful critique of the Social Charter proposal by Hugh Mellon, entitled "Proposals for a Social Charter: Misguided if Noble," can be found in the same issue of *Policy Options,* pp. 17, 19–21.

Even if you accept Brian Howe's basic arguments for a Social Charter, the path of constitutionalizing social rights within Canada could still be fraught with difficulties. John Myles, who is sympathetic to the concept, nevertheless points out that the courts have frequently been "biased in favor of corporations and others with the resources to finance costly legal proceedings." ("Constitutionalizing Social Rights," in Echenberg et al., *A Social Charter for Canada?*, p. 62). Although in general Canadians compare their social programs favourably with those of the United States, Canada in fact has a relatively weak and underdeveloped welfare state by most European standards. By constitutionalizing social rights on the basis of this weaker present model, Myles argues that we face the possibility that we "would trap the country in the past ... making it more, rather than less, difficult to address the new social problems that confront the country" (p. 62).

# ISSUE TWENTY-FOUR

## Does Continental Free Trade Benefit Canada?

**YES** IAN WOOTON, "The Case for a More Liberal Trade Regime"

**NO** ANDREW STRITCH, "The Costs of Free Trade"


For Canada, the subject of free trade with the United States is, as one historian says, "the issue that will not go away." At various points in Canada's history, the matter of free trade with America has loomed on the political horizon. It figured prominently in the creation and early development of Canada, and has caused governments to fall that dared to advocate it. The past has also recorded free trade agreements between the two nations and seen a gradual reduction in barriers that inhibit the circulation of goods and services between Canada and the United States.

Now, free trade is once again an issue. In 1987, Canada and the United States agreed to an ambitious and far-reaching trade agreement. The Canada–U.S. Free Trade Agreement (FTA) eliminated tariffs—the most common obstacle to free trade—and sought to reduce the impact of nontariff barriers. Five years later, Canada, the United States, and Mexico signed the North American Free Trade Agreement (NAFTA), which effectively extended the FTA to include Mexico.

In some quarters, these recent trade developments—amounting to continental free trade—are believed to be beneficial. They offer Canada preferential access to the huge American market; now Canada, unlike competitors in Europe, Japan, and elsewhere, will no longer face difficulties in gaining access to customers in the United States. The trade agreements also make Canada's access to American markets more secure. The majority of Canada's exports are to the United States, so any arrangement that solidifies relations between the two is viewed positively. As well, free trade with both the United States and Mexico will facilitate, some argue, a restructuring of Canadian industry, the result of which will be an industry dominated by strong, vibrant corporations ready to do battle with international competitors.

Finally, continental free trade may cause the adoption of what free trade supporters consider the best arrangement, namely a trade situation in which *all* nations agree to lower or abolish their trade barriers. The fear of the world breaking into separate trading blocs, each closed to the other, might precipitate the emergence of free trade on a global basis.

In other quarters, the advantages of continental free trade are far less obvious. Canadian industry, some claim, is simply not ready to tussle with foreign competitors—it will suffer serious losses. As well, businesses and jobs may relocate in parts of the United States and Mexico where wages are low and fringe benefits marginal. At present, many corporations set up in Canada because it allows them to forgo payment of tariffs; but the elimination of trade barriers would cause them to rethink their initial decision. Perhaps most important, free trade connects Canada more so than ever before with the United States, and hence threatens the very survival of Canada.

In the readings, Ian Wooton, a trade specialist at the University of Western Ontario, outlines the benefits of continental free trade for Canada. Andrew Stritch, a political scientist who has written on government–business relations, discusses the costs of continental free trade.

# The Case for a More Liberal Trade Regime

*Ian Wooton*

For more than forty years Canada has been a strong advocate of and an active participant in the multilateral trade negotiations conducted by the GATT (General Agreement on Tariffs and Trade). The major goal of these discussions has been the gradual lowering (and eventual elimination) of the barriers that countries have put in place to restrict imports of goods from other nations. Driving all of the GATT's activities is the principle of non-discrimination; that is, groups of countries cannot cut any special deals between themselves, and must instead make the same trade concessions to all countries. Yet, despite its apparent enthusiasm for the GATT process, Canada has recently seemed to have turned its back on its ideals and has instead negotiated trade deals with its close neighbours, the United States and Mexico.

In this article I shall address the question of why continued trade liberalization is a good objective for Canada, relative both to the status quo of the current state of global trade and compared to a reverse policy of increased protectionism. I shall further discuss whether a North American trade agreement is a substitute, or a complement, for global trade liberalization, and whether Canada has indeed abandoned the multilateral process in its quest for continental free trade. I shall argue that simultaneously pursuing the goals of continental free trade and multilateral trade liberalization is not inconsistent, and reflects a pragmatic approach to capturing the greatest benefits from trade. In particular, I claim that while multilateral free trade should be the goal of Canadian trade policy, continental free trade is an imperfect substitute that captures a large part of the gains and may provide the political impetus to achieving the main goal.

My approach will focus on the economic issues underlying these free trade initiatives, rather than examining the details of specific trade agreements.

# THE BENEFITS OF TRADE

Why pursue a policy of free trade? At one time it was argued that international trade was necessary as a means of obtaining essential natural resources and as a way to create markets for a country's products. Thus much of Canada's early history involved the opening up of trade routes to supply Britain's factories with raw materials and sell their industrial products to settlers. But this argument does not seem so persuasive today. Synthetic alternatives to natural materials have been developed and new production processes have been invented, such that the reliance on many raw materials has been reduced. But perhaps more important, the economies of many countries (including those of North America) have themselves become developed and industrialized, and are no longer dependent on other countries (such as Europe) for imports of high-technology goods. Nowadays, to a large degree, it would be possible for most countries to replace imports with domestically produced goods. Given that domestic production means jobs for our workers, why would we consider buying the goods from other countries?

The continuing justification for trade is captured in the term *comparative advantage*. Countries have only a limited capacity to produce: there is only so much cultivatable land, physical plant, and labour force available in a country, and it is quite impossible to satisfy the insatiable appetite of the population for consumption. As a result, decisions have to be made as to what goods should be produced. What this requires is some way of determining how best to allocate the nation's scarce resources so as to maximize the well-being of the people. While it has been argued that virtually any country can produce any good, this does not imply that the costs of production are necessarily the same across countries. Thus countries with an abundance of well-skilled workers will have lower production costs in high-technology manufacturing than a nation with low education levels, while a country with a climate that permits year-round outdoor cultivation will have lower costs in agricultural production than a country with a shorter growing season or one that can only grow the plants in heated greenhouses. International trade allows a country to specialize in what it does best, that is, in producing the goods in which it has a relative cost advantage, selling them to countries that cannot produce them as efficiently, and buying from them the goods that it finds relatively expensive to produce for itself. As a result, a country, as a whole, enjoys better consumption opportunities through international trade than it would have in isolation.

A problem for many countries is that the pattern of comparative advantage is not static, but is constantly changing as nations grow and industrialize, sources of natural resources are exhausted or newly discovered, and new products and services are invented. This means that a country's established comparative advantage may be eroded over time, international demand for its products will wither, and even domestic consumers will switch to competing imports from the countries who now have the comparative advantage. Given the historical importance of the industry and its entrenched importance in many cities, there is often very strong pressure put on the government by firms and unions alike to protect the industry's products from this new international competition. If the government gives in, and they very often have done so, it imposes a *tariff*, a tax on imports of the competing good, which gives the domestic industry a price advantage in the home market and encourages domestic production. While the tariff props up the production of the protected good, it does so at the expense of the consumer, who has to pay higher prices, and of the firms in industries that have a comparative advantage but are being discouraged by the distortionary effects of the tariff. In general, attempting to halt the drift in comparative advantage by using tariffs to protect the ailing industries involves heavier costs for a larger proportion of the population than the benefits that it bestows.

It is often claimed by proponents of protectionism that firms in small countries, such as Canada, just cannot compete against those of the United States, Europe, and the huge global multinationals. Hence, they recommend the building of high-tariff walls around the domestic market in order to keep out foreign goods and ensure continued demand for domestically produced goods.[1] But this is a prescription for disaster. Not only do consumers lose out, facing higher prices and reduced choice, but the industrial policy will almost certainly fail as well. Firms that are protected from international competition have no incentive to become efficient or technologically innovative. Instead, they will enjoy the monopoly power that protection endows; they will not need to invest in research and development of their products, and will rapidly lose their ability to compete on international markets.

Removing protection will lead to an expansion in international trade and allow the necessary adjustments in a country's industrial structure to take place. The resources that a nation once devoted to producing the goods, whose prices have been undercut by imports, will be reallocated to some other (perhaps export-oriented) industry. This will necessitate changes for firms and their workers that may involve having to relocate, retool, or retrain. Thus not everyone in the economy will necessarily gain from trade; but the gains are generally sufficiently large to permit compensation of the losers. That is, the benefits to consumers from lower prices and to workers and manufacturers in export industries are expected to be large enough to compensate firms and workers in the declining, import-competing industries. In order to soften the impact of the changes, tariff reductions are normally made over a number of years, to give firms and workers the chance to adjust.

Countries that are very large, exerting a dominant influence on international markets, also benefit from international trade, but may not want free trade. They can exert their monopoly power and increase their gains from trade by using tariffs. However, even these benefits from tariffs are eroded (and often reversed) if other countries retaliate and impose import tariffs of their own. A relatively small economy, such as Canada, does not have much market power and so tariffs, whether imposed by itself or by other countries, are harmful. Indeed, the best *independent* action for a small country, enabling it to reap its greatest gains from trade, is a *unilateral* move to free trade, involving the elimination of all its tariffs and other trade barriers.

But an even better outcome for these countries would be realized if they could persuade their trading partners to reciprocate and remove their trade barriers as well. Thus, while Canada would gain from eliminating its trade impediments immediately, it would benefit more from negotiations with other countries that resulted in *multilateral* trade liberalization. This has been Canada's strategy for almost fifty years, being an active participant in the GATT since the founding of that institution in Geneva in 1947. The decades preceding the foundation of the GATT saw escalating levels of international trade protection. The GATT negotiations have been conducted in a series of rounds, which have resulted in agreements on the mutual lowering of trade barriers and have been extremely successful, leading to dramatic reductions in tariff levels.

But multilateralism has not always been central to Canadian trade policy, which often concentrated upon a special trading relationship with the United States. Prior to Confederation, the provinces had a free trade agreement with the United States (the Elgin-Marcy Treaty, from 1854 to 1866). After the highly protectionist National Policy of 1879, Canada repeatedly approached the United States in attempts to negotiate *bilateral* trade treaties, but with little success, largely due to Canadian fears of the loss of sovereignty that an alliance with the United States might entail. Once the GATT was established, Canada focused its primary attention on multilateral tariff reductions. But trade relations with the United States remained important and, despite the GATT process, never were truly ignored. Indeed, in 1967 Canada and the United States concluded a deal on free trade in automobiles (the Autopact). This has been an extremely important agreement for Canada, as the auto sector now accounts for the largest trade flows (both imports and exports) for the country.

In the 1980s, what appeared to be a major redirection of Canadian trade policy took place when, once again, Canada approached the United States with the intent of negotiating a bilateral trade agreement. The result was the Canada–U.S. Free Trade Agreement (FTA), which was implemented in 1989. Subsequently, these two countries have agreed with Mexico on a continental trade agreement, the North American Free Trade Agreement (NAFTA). While trade with the rest of the world has not been neglected, Canada and the United States both being active participants in the Uruguay Round of the GATT, this apparent return to bilateralism has created some anxiety both at home and abroad as to its implications for the multilateral trading system.

Before going any further, I would like to examine the economic implications of trade agreements made by small groups of countries. The basic question that should be addressed is whether such agreements (such as the FTA) move the participating countries (and the world as a whole) *toward* free trade, or are essentially protectionist. This will allow us to answer the main question of this paper, whether continental free trade will benefit Canada.

# REGIONAL INTEGRATION

A regional integration agreement (RIA) is one in which the participating countries give their partners improved access to their domestic markets through preferential reductions in their trade barriers.[2] Thus the core of such a free trade agreement is the reciprocal elimination of tariffs on trade between the participating countries. This is effectively a very discriminatory act, in that the tariff barriers remain on imports from all other countries. Indeed, free trade agreements violate the spirit of the GATT (and have to be accommodated by a special GATT exemption under Article 24). An RIA does involve a move toward free trade, in that tariffs on the trade between the partner countries are eliminated, encouraging countries to import goods from their partners, rather than producing them less efficiently themselves. This beneficial effect is known as *trade creation.*

But an RIA may encourage too much trade between the partners, at the expense of excluded countries, potentially harming the importing country. This is *trade diversion*, where a country switches its source of imports from an outside country to one that is part of the RIA because, although the partner's selling price is higher than that of the other country, the partner's goods enter duty free while the others face the tariff. Trade diversion disadvantages the outside country and may or may not harm individual members of the RIA. It certainly involves a distortion of trade patterns from what would have been arrived at under multilateral liberalization. How much trade diversion actually occurs when an RIA is formed, and how much harm is done, cannot be resolved in the abstract and is essentially an empirical matter.

Given that RIA formation has ambiguous welfare consequences arising from trade creation and trade diversion effects, evaluation of its benefits (or otherwise) for a particular group of countries has to be done on a case-by-case basis. What, then, might be said about free trade between Canada and its continental neighbours?

# CONTINENTAL FREE TRADE AND CANADA

Long before the FTA was signed, the United States was Canada's most important trading partner, accounting today for more than 60 percent of its export volume. This is due to the enormous size of the U.S. market and the diversity of its production, as well as the country's proximity. Trade creation is likely, as the tariff walls, which were often erected to protect Canadian industry from U.S. competition, are dismantled. Indeed, there is some evidence that bilateral trade volumes between the two countries are expanding as a result of the FTA. The problem of inducing a great deal of damaging trade diversion is probably rather limited as, even in the absence of preferential treatment for imports from the United States, most of Canada's imports already came from that country.[3] As a result, the bad effects of trade diversion are likely to be swamped by the gains from trade creation. In this respect, an RIA would be a genuine move toward free trade.

Extending the RIA to the whole continent by incorporating Mexico into the NAFTA may have less clear-cut implications. Mexico itself should almost certainly benefit from the liberalization of trade with its dominant trading partner, for the same reasons as were argued for Canada and the United States in the FTA. But the benefits to Canada of expanding the FTA to the NAFTA are less clear. The existing bilateral volumes of trade between Canada and Mexico are very small but would be expected to increase. The possibility of trade diversion exists, but this is tempered by the fact that most of Canada's trade (with the United States) is already (or soon will be) duty free. Undoubtedly Canada will start to import some goods from Mexico that it previously produced for itself. This is at the heart of the principle of comparative advantage, that countries specialize in producing what they can make best. Thus, as the trade barriers come down with Mexico, Canadian industry will turn away from some of the low-skill manufacturing jobs and focus on expanding the industries to which it is best suited.

It has already been argued that it is in the best interests of small countries, such as Canada and Mexico, to unilaterally eliminate trade barriers. So why should they pursue an RIA, given the potential problems of trade diversion that such agreements might generate? The answer lies in the *preferred* and *secure* access to the partners' markets that an RIA guarantees.

First, consider the issue of preferred access. Concurrent with the home country's removing tariffs on imports from its partners, the partners are also lowering their trade barriers on imports from the home country. This means that the consumer prices of the home country's exports fall in its partners' markets, because the import taxes that they previously faced have been eliminated, and so demands for these goods rise. The home country's firms also benefit from the price advantage they get from trade diversion. The competing products from the rest of the world still face the partners' tariffs, and consequently the home country's exports become relatively cheaper and hence more attractive to consumers. Thus for countries like Canada and Mexico, the preferred access that they receive through an RIA with their major trading partner, the United States, may be more valuable than the rewards of unilateral free trade.[4]

Now, consider the issue of security of access. The GATT negotiations have been dragging on for years, and there are genuine, and widely held, fears that no resolution will be found this time. In addition, a country as large as the United States need not want free trade. In some industries it would prefer to influence international prices, and thereby protect its domestic firms and workers. These two elements, and the perception that other countries were trading "unfairly," led the United States to become more active in trade policy in the 1980s, using domestic (nontariff) policies to police and control imports.

Canada, as the United States, largest trading partner, felt especially vulnerable and wanted some way of guaranteeing continued access to the U.S. market, what may be called a "safe-haven" agreement, such that, should the industrialized countries become more aggressive in their trade policies, Canada would still be assured of access to the U.S. markets. Neither the FTA nor NAFTA truly provides this, but they do at least have a dispute-settlement procedure that ensures that U.S. trade policy cannot be hijacked for purely political or capricious reasons, which is an (at least perceived) improvement on what was afforded Canada prior to the FTA.

What is much less clear is why a large country, such as the United States, would want to be part of an RIA. Its optimal tariffs are not zero and so a move to partial free trade need not be in its interests. If the RIA is with small countries, their tariff concessions are likely to have a negligible impact and the possibility of significant trade diversion assumes greater weight. Indeed, the arguments used in the United States in favour of the FTA and the NAFTA have been largely political—maintaining cordial relations with the country that shares the longest undefended border in the world (for Canada) and helping to ensure the continuation of political stability through economic growth (for Mexico).

# CONTINENTAL VERSUS MULTILATERAL FREE TRADE

But there may be other incentives for a continental RIA: as a counterbalance to the growing influence of other regional trading *blocs*, and as a spur to the stalled multilateral negotiations. North America has not been alone in its attempts to form RIAs. There are examples of regional integration in virtually every part of the world (for example, the Latin American Free Trade Association; the East African Common Market; the European Free Trade Association; and the Association of South East Asian Nations). By far the most successful, and powerful, RIA has been the European Community (EC). This is a *common market*, where the level of integration between the countries goes beyond merely internal free trade and includes common trade policy, free internal factor migration, and centralized policy-making, particularly for agriculture. The EC has grown from an initial six countries in the late 1950s to currently twelve, with several other countries trying to gain admission. As countries have joined the EC, their trade has expanded with their European partners, some of it being diverted from trade with other countries.[5] Indeed, Canada's trade with the United Kingdom dropped dramatically when the United Kingdom joined the EC and had to eliminate its preferential tariffs on imports from Commonwealth countries.

A continental RIA would give North American producers preferred access to a huge continental market, similar to that given by the Europeans to their own firms. This permits industries to take full advantage of any economies of large-scale production and would counter the discrimination they face on foreign markets. This is much the same argument that was heard in favour of protectionism, this time on a regional scale. Thus RIAs may become the new mode of protectionism, based on geographic regions rather than individual countries. Grave concerns have been expressed that regions will focus their attention on trade within their blocs, and will neglect the multilateral system, perhaps leading to its eventual demise.

But the fear of the world trading system collapsing into such fortress-like blocs may provide the much-needed impetus to the multilateral negotiations, as the best way to undermine the trade diversionary effects of the RIAs is to remove the trade barriers between the blocs. Thus the creation of a North American trading bloc may increase the incentives for other countries, fearful of being excluded from North American markets, to pursue the multilateral negotiations of the GATT, in order to reduce the external trade barriers. It may also give the North American countries more negotiating power than they individually possess, both in terms of the sheer economic might of the bloc (greater than that of the EC) and also the legitimacy that it may accrue from representing a group of nations rather than a single country.[6] Thus an optimist might view the NAFTA, which is an explicitly discriminatory trading institution, to be a catalyst for a more liberal global trading system.

# CONCLUSION

I have argued in favour of continued trade liberalization by Canada as a necessary component of national growth and industrial expansion. Faced with the uncertain future of the multilateral trading system, as reflected in the difficulties associated with the latest round of GATT negotiations, the appropriate response for Canada is not protectionism, but a search for other trading opportunities. The free trade agreement with the United States provides Canada with many of the gains from a multilateral agreement. Indeed, the establishment of a continental trading bloc in North America may provide the spur toward a resolution of the global trade discussions.

## NOTES

1. Protectionism is often referred to in more euphemistic terms as "managed trade" or "levelling the playing field."

2. There are many different terms that can be used for these preferential trading agreements. As they tend to be formed by countries that are geographically close together, I have chosen to use the designation, *regional integration agreement*, which is also the name adopted by the GATT.

3. A trade agreement with some other group of countries, say, in Europe or the Pacific Rim, might therefore cause much more trade diversion.

4. Canada already has relatively low tariffs, thanks to the GATT, and (to re-emphasize) continues to participate in the multilateral, tariff-cutting rounds. Mexico has pursued membership in the GATT and has also made great unilateral strides in reforming its trade regime.

5. This has been particularly the case with agriculture, where the EC's Common Agricultural Policy involves very high trade barriers in order to protect inefficient production in Europe.

6. Whether the North American bloc could in fact effectively use its negotiation muscle is open to question, as the member countries (unlike those in the EC) continue to form their trade policies independently of one another.

## The Costs of Free Trade

*Andrew Stritch*

During the 1992 U.S. presidential election campaign, independent candidate Ross Perot attacked the proposed extension of the North American Free Trade Agreement to include Mexico because he said he could hear a "giant sucking sound" of jobs and investment being transferred south of the border. In a characteristically blunt and graphic style he highlighted one of the central issues in the whole debate over continental free trade, namely the potential effect on the movement of industries and jobs.

This concern is a relatively new one for the United States, but for Canadians it has been on the political agenda periodically throughout the nation's history. However, from a Canadian perspective it is the United States that has been doing the sucking. In the election of 1911, for example, it was an issue, along with national sovereignty, when Canada considered (and rejected) a "free trade" deal with its southern neighbour. Before that, Sir John A. Macdonald's National Policy tariffs of 1879 had long been defended as an instrument of nation-building, encouraging the location of production in Canada rather than in the United States. Trade and tariff policy has thus always had much broader political and economic ramifications for Canada, and there has been a perennial fear that close economic integration with the United States would sooner or later lead to political integration and loss of sovereignty. This fear is no less apparent today in the continuing debate over the Canada–U.S. Free Trade Agreement and NAFTA.

Despite the efforts of proponents to portray this policy as being simply about trade and nothing else,[1] these agreements go well beyond explicit trade and tariff issues to deal with such things as investment, energy pricing, regulatory policy, government procurement, technical standards, and the overall role of government in the economy. Beyond this, there are wider implications for many areas of Canadian life and public policy including industrial relocation, tax policy, social programs, government incentives, public ownership, the power of business, labour relations, regional integration, and federal–provincial relations. In fact, it is hard to think of many areas where free trade will *not* have some effect.

Underlying this whole movement toward continental free trade has been a resurgent faith in the virtues of *laissez-faire* economics over industrial planning, which has been a feature of the rightward swing in North American politics in the 1980s. This faith in free markets reached triumphalist proportions with the collapse of the Soviet Union, which had for a long time been seen as living proof of the vicissitudes of state intervention. Now that the Soviet Union is dead, and the Russian Republic has discovered new and different vicissitudes, it has become harder to find convenient examples of economies victimized by government planning. In the new world order, the United States is no longer battling the Soviet Union, but waging an economic battle against countries such as Japan and Germany where active government intervention is an accepted part of economic life. Against these economies the United States is having a tougher time, and the supposed advantages of laissez-faire over a planned industrial policy are less clear.

In the industrial development of North America the principles of laissez-faire have been more apparent in ideology than in practice. In both Canada and the United States, governments at all levels have been very active in shaping the course of national economic history through a variety of interventionist policies such as protective tariffs, government procurement, labour market regulation, business subsidies, market development policies, and the provision of a transportation infrastructure.

In Canada, the role of government in modifying market forces has been especially pronounced. With a small population, a huge area, a tough climate, and severe physical and cultural barriers to nation-building, Canada has not emerged as a prosperous industrial country by letting nature take its course. In the words of one of Canada's greatest economic historians, W.A. Mackintosh, "Canada is a nation created in defiance of geography."[2] It has also been created in defiance of the United States. Historically, Canada has had to expand its economy and defend its sovereignty in the face of aggressive and sometimes predatory competition from its very proximate neighbour. This "defensive expansionism" has required an active role by the federal government in carving out a separate Canadian identity and containing American political and economic influence.[3] In this respect the last ten years have marked an important watershed in Canadian history. We have turned away from defensive expansionism and economic nationalism, and have embraced continentalism and closer integration with the United States.

Locking ourselves into a North American free trade arrangement has been portrayed as the abandonment of narrow nationalism, and as something in line with the inevitable march of globalization in the world economy. In reality, we have increasingly turned away from the rest of the world and have retreated into a continental trading bloc dominated by the United States. The proportion of Canada's trade with countries other than the United States has diminished over the last ten years, with exports to the rest of the world falling from 27.1 percent of the total in 1983 to 22.7 percent in 1992.[4] Such bloc formation is not globalism; it is actually a process of deglobalization and regional parochialism. This is all the more worrying because at this point in history American industrial hegemony is in decline, and we may therefore be tying ourselves, almost completely, to an economic regime that is in the process of being eclipsed.

Aside from these general concerns, Canada's formal accession to continental free trade has a number of worrying implications—not just in terms of economic consequences, but with regard to the political and social impact as well. In many respects these problems are intertwined, but I will try to isolate what I consider to be the most significant aspects in the analysis that follows.

# INDUSTRIAL RELOCATION

One of the main problems of continental free trade is that it is likely to have a significant effect on where businesses choose to locate their production facilities. If businesses believe that they have open access to all markets throughout North America without the prospect of border tariffs or other barriers, then they have a much freer hand in deciding where to set up their factories and plants. Once the financial penalty for shipping goods across national borders is removed on a stable basis, then businesses have less to fear from "cross-border hopping," and are freer to make locational decisions based on factors such as relative production costs in different countries. Obviously, this has an impact on where jobs are created or lost.

This is a serious problem for Canada in relation to the United States, and is likely to become more serious as free trade is extended to Mexico. It is not just a matter of traditional cost disadvantages associated with climate, distance, transportation, etc., but also involves a whole range of other costs related to the nature of public policies in different places. Significant issues here are such things as levels of corporate taxation; the extent of payroll levies such as employee pensions, unemployment insurance, and workers' compensation; and the burden of government regulation on business. Other things being equal, businesses will move to geographic locations where these costs are lower. With free trade removing barriers to mobility, and with taxes, employee benefits, and government regulation generally lower in the United States than in Canada (and lower still in Mexico), the "call of the south" has become hard to resist for many Canadian companies.

In addition to these attractions, labour costs are a major factor in encouraging business mobility. Many U.S. states, particularly in the South, have very low minimum wage laws or have abolished the minimum wage altogether. A large number have passed "right-to-work" legislation that undermines union organization, while American labour laws generally offer much less protection for unions and workers' rights than in Canada. This is reflected in differential rates of unionization. In Canada, 34.7 percent of the work force is unionized, whereas in the United States the figure is 16.1 percent.[5] As a result, it is easier for businesses to keep wages down, control working conditions, and prevent strikes. While this increases business profits, the implications for workers are lower standards of living, fewer employment rights, and greater vulnerability in the workplace. This is particularly apparent in Mexico where wages can be lower than $1 per hour and independent unions are suppressed, making it even more attractive for business.

Labour costs are certainly not the only factor considered by business in making locational decisions, nor are they even necessarily the most important consideration. However, when labour cost advantages are added to other policy and geographic benefits, then the whole package can be decisive in prompting relocation outside of Canada. This is further encouraged by American state and local governments that aggressively "target" Canadian and other foreign companies by offering them a variety of incentives to locate in their jurisdiction. For example, South Carolina recently attracted a major BMW plant by offering to train BMW's entire work force at state expense, as well as providing 1,000 acres of land at a lease of $1 a year. Canadian steelmakers Dofasco and Co-Steel were persuaded to locate a new joint-venture mill in Kentucky by state incentives that included $140 million in tax credits, $4 million in water treatment facilities, and a $132,000 worker training grant.[6]

The most vulnerable groups of workers to such out-migration of industry are those employed in relatively low-skilled, labour-intensive occupations such as the clothing industry or component assembly operations. Where labour is a big component of total business costs, then the lure of cheap labour areas is greater, especially where companies are already under pressure from lower-cost foreign competitors. These lower-skilled workers, when abandoned in Canada, will have the hardest time finding new jobs, thus raising the prospect of persistent long-term unemployment with strains on social services and an erosion of Canada's tax base. Consequently, it will be more difficult to solve chronic problems of government debt and budget deficits.

It might be argued that these sorts of problems would be likely to emerge in any case even without agreements on continental free trade— as trade barriers have come down globally in the postwar period, so the impediments to business mobility have diminished. While this is true, the impact of a formal North American arrangement is that it will provide a greater degree of certainty for businesses seeking to restructure their operations on a continental basis. Locational decisions are some of the most important ones facing corporate decision-makers, and there is always a fear that moving abroad will be a costly mistake if the domestic governments decide to re-establish protectionist policies at some time in the future. The existence of a formal continental agreement reduces this possibility and removes an important restraint on "footloose" companies.

## CANADA'S COMPETITIVE ENVIRONMENT

Part of the rationale for North American free trade is that it is supposed to open up new competitive opportunities for Canadian companies in the United States and Mexico. Supposedly, it will also force Canadian companies to be more competitive at home in the face of new challenges from south of the border. This rosy scenario is based on an assumption that Canadian business is well poised to respond to these challenges, and will be able to "gear up" to take advantage of this less protected environment.

The problem with this scenario is that it makes unrealistic assumptions about the level of competitiveness of the Canadian economy, particularly in the manufacturing sector. Most recent studies point to a number of serious deficiencies that need to be addressed if Canada is to escape from a long-term competitive decline—let alone pull ahead of its major trading partners. These are exemplified in reports by the Organization for Economic Cooperation and Development and by Harvard competitiveness "guru" Michael Porter.[7] The major areas of concern are (a) low productivity growth and high unit labour costs, (b) continued resource dependency and weakness of the manufacturing sector, and (c) inadequate levels of technological research and skills development.

Productivity growth is one of the principal indicators of national competitiveness, and in this regard Canada has been worse than most other industrialized countries. Between 1979 and 1990 Canada experienced zero growth in total factor productivity, well behind the OECD average.[8] The situation has been particularly acute in manufacturing where the labour productivity gap between Canada and the United States jumped from 24 percent to 45 percent in the course of the 1980s.[9] In this decade unit labour costs in manufacturing increased faster than most of our industrial competitors, and twice as fast as in the United States.[10]

The weakness of Canadian manufacturing has gone hand-in-hand with a historical dependency on the extraction and export of natural resources. Canadian emphasis has been on the exploitation of raw or semi-finished products, which are then exported without much further processing. We have failed to develop the secondary processing of our own resources within Canada, and we have suffered from a relatively stunted manufacturing base. Only 17 percent of Canadian output is in manufacturing, which is substantially below the G-7 average.[11] Consequently, the production of high-value, high-technology manufactured goods is diminished, and we are forced to import many of our finished products. Coupled with a concomitant lack of competitiveness in services, we have also encountered growing trade deficits in nonresource sectors, which is a important sign of competitive problems.[12]

Part of the problem with Canadian manufacturing is the low level of aggregate spending on research and development. Despite considerable government incentives, private sector research and development is seriously deficient. Our innovative capacity is lagging behind most of the G-7 group, and we are not developing the high technologies necessary to sustain the high-paying jobs of the future. In Japan, Germany, and the United States, the private sector spends a sum roughly equivalent to 2 percent of national GDP on research and development. In Canada, the figure is less than 0.75 percent of GDP.[13]

Another crucial factor is the low priority that the Canadian education system gives to the development of technological and scientific skills. Despite enormous expenditures, Canada has a poor overall level of educational attainment and a notable weakness in vocational training. We have relatively few scientists and engineers, with low and declining interest in these subjects by most students. Roughly 90 percent of our high-school students are enrolled in nonvocational programs; we have an overall dropout rate of approximately 30 percent; an illiteracy rate of 24 percent; and little on-the-job training provided by industry.[14] As the world's leading economies move increasingly toward high-value, knowledge-based production, Canada must address these educational deficiencies if it is to compete successfully.

None of this is currently very encouraging for Canada's future competitive prospects, and it undermines optimistic claims that Canada is well positioned to do battle in the new competitive environment once the shackles of protectionism have been removed. Free trade is typically a philosophy of the strong—when one country is more competitive than another then a free market will allow that advantage to be felt. However, when a country has serious competitive problems, as Canada does, then increased exposure is likely to leave the economy in a very vulnerable position.

# INDUSTRIAL STRATEGY

It is naive to assume that Canada's serious structural economic problems will be self-correcting, or that government can simply stand by and do nothing while market forces run their course. The problems are too deep, and the Canadian public is too demanding. What is needed is a coordinated industrial strategy aimed at restoring the long-run competitiveness of the Canadian economy and addressing the structural weakness of Canada's industrial base. There is nothing particularly radical about this—long-term strategic planning is not some deviant practice of foreign governments, but is undertaken by every large and successful private sector corporation. Yet this is just the sort of strategy that is made more difficult for government by free trade.

The continental agreements in which Canada has become embroiled essentially reflect a dominant ideological strain in the United States where government is viewed with suspicion and public authority is seen as a menace to the private sector. This ideology of nonintervention, which is out of step with most of the world's other industrialized economies, is inimical to planned industrial strategies, and it ties the hands of the Canadian government at a time when there is a pressing need for concerted action. By adopting this shaky American vision, we are abdicating responsibility for our own economic fate and reducing our industrial policy options in a way that most other successful economies do not.

In particular, we have given up any realistic prospect of controlling the extensive American ownership of the Canadian economy. Rules on national treatment for foreign investment open up even more sections of Canadian industry to the threat of American corporate takeover, with serious implications for Canada's economic future. Direct foreign ownership of Canadian industry amounted to over $136 billion at the end of 1992, with the United States accounting for 64 percent of this total. Approximately 47 percent of assets in Canadian manufacturing are foreign owned, and in 1992 Canada paid out over $4.5 billion in interest and dividends to direct foreign investors.[15]

One of the main problems here is that foreign-owned branch plants do not conduct much R&D in Canada. As Michael Porter has noted, parent companies tend to concentrate their research and development in their "home base." This is where most of the innovation takes place, and where the high-value products and high-paying jobs are created.[16] Canada is being marginalized to the status of a spectator in the international technology race, which is all the more worrying because technological and scientific knowledge are playing an increasing role in determining national competitiveness. The free trade agreements, which make it harder to regulate foreign ownership, undermine any realistic prospect of reversing this situation and stimulating our own indigenous techno-logical capacities.

Free trade also constrains other elements of Canadian industrial policy. For instance, the creation of crown corporations becomes more difficult as Canada has obligated itself to compensate U.S. companies for the potential loss of future profits. This might restrain such things as public auto insurance in Ontario, which would be prohibitively expensive if American insurance companies had to be compensated. Energy policy is also curtailed—we cannot regulate the price of our energy in order to favour domestic industries without granting the same concessions to American industries. Incentive programs, subsidies, performance requirements, and traditional trade policy instruments have all been subjected to new restrictions on government action. Canada's industrial house needs fixing, but the free trade agreement has thrown away the industrial policy toolbox. This may satisfy laissez-faire ideologues, but it is not going to solve Canada's entrenched industrial problems. If you applied the same philosophy to gardening, for example, you would end up with nothing but weeds.

## POLICY HARMONIZATION

Free trade has placed restrictions on the industrial policy options available to the Canadian government and in so doing has pushed Canada closer to an American conception of what is appropriate in this field. It is a form of policy harmonization in which Canadian industrial strategy is diminished to a point where it increasingly resembles that of the United States. This is significant by itself, but it is only one part of a more pervasive network of pressures for the harmonization between the United States and Canada across a spectrum of policy areas. Although these pressures have always existed, they have become intensified as a result of free trade, and this is necessarily troubling for Canadians who do not want to follow American directions in regulatory policy, health care, welfare, labour law, the environment, etc.

Essentially, pressure for harmonization is coming from business groups in Canada. In an environment that is open to more intense continental competition, it is no surprise that corporations in Canada have become especially sensitive to anything that gives their American counterparts an advantage. Whether it is lower minimum wage laws, or lower tax rates, or the existence of "right-to-work" anti-union legislation, or weaker enforcement of occupational safety and health laws, or a variety of other policy distinctions, Canadian businesses want a "level playing field" because of competitive pressure. With Mexico included in NAFTA, this pressure will get worse as Canadian companies find themselves in competition with producers in a jurisdiction where social policies and regulatory enforcement are even more minimal.

It has occasionally been argued that business will not seek such a harmonization of social policies because business is itself a beneficiary of these policies.[17] This view rests on the assumption that businesses would have to provide employer-based social benefits as a result of collective bargaining if state programs were not available. The problem with this argument is that it overestimates the current power of labour unions to extract concessions from employers. With little more than a third of the Canadian labour force belonging to a union, and with a rate of unemployment around 11 percent, the ability of workers to exert this sort of leverage is severely diminished.

Certainly, business groups themselves are not great advocates of increased social spending by government, and most see cutbacks as desirable. Governments could of course simply resist these demands and maintain Canada's social safety net regardless of business opposition, but this is now harder to do in a continental market characterized by high mobility of capital and few barriers to the movement of goods, services, or investments. If governments in Canada do not respond favourably to business demands, then business can always move south—as many are already doing. With the prospect of an eroding tax base, Canadian governments will face enormous financial pressures to "equalize" the policy environment and remove some of the incentive for business flight. We will thus have a harmonization of policy on terms dictated by mobile business.

# REGIONAL FRAGMENTATION

Throughout its history Canada has struggled to establish and maintain a viable economic linkage among disparate regions spread along a 3,000-mile east-west axis. Links of trade, commerce, and transportation have played a vital role in preserving a tenuous political unity in the face of Canada's many centrifugal forces. Today, strong economic ties are even more crucial as Canada tries to cope with heightened regional disaffection, resurgent Quebec nationalism, a fragmented national party system, the declining financial capacity of the federal government, and problems of maintaining a distinct national identity in an increasingly multicultural society.

Commercial bonds within Canada need to be strengthened, yet internal barriers still block the movement of goods and people. For example, Quebec's construction industry regulations have discriminated against out-of-province workers, provoking reciprocal retaliatory measures in 1993 from New Brunswick and Ontario. Regulatory and procurement policies have too frequently been used as trade barriers against other provinces, and while provincial markets across Canada are being thrown open to American producers, they can remain relatively closed to Canadian companies in other regions of the country.

Continental free trade has exacerbated this trend by encouraging a pattern of trading relations that increasingly run on north–south lines rather than east–west ones. The effect has been a further erosion of Canada's economic and political integration at a time when national unity is already threatened. This disintegrating impact of the FTA has been well recognized by Parti Québécois leader Jacques Parizeau who supported the deal largely because he saw it as conducive to Quebec's separation from the rest of Canada.[18] With Mexico included, the lines of trade will be pushed even further along a north–south axis, and the forces of regional fragmentation would receive yet another boost.

The free trade agreement also has a disintegrating effect because of its differential impact on federal and provincial levels of government. As Richard Simeon has pointed out, the FTA puts constraints on the federal government's main industrial policy instruments without imposing the same level of restrictions on the provinces. The result is a further decentralization of Canadian public policy.[19] What Canada needs is a national strategy to reduce interprovincial trade barriers and promote economic linkages among the provinces. It does not need a continental trade agreement that encourages regional fragmentation and puts new restraints on the power of the federal government.

# CONCLUSION

The costs of continental free trade could thus be very heavy for Canada. We have locked ourselves into an agreement that makes it easier for industries to relocate outside of the country. Businesses can take advantage of lower costs in the southern United States or Mexico and will be able to supply the North American market from these locations with little fear of Canadian border measures. Business support for the FTA and NAFTA is understandable—it increases the freedom of corporations to move production to sunnier financial climates without having to pay a price when they ship their products back to Canada.

It also enhances the power of business over both government and labour. It is easier to negotiate contract concessions or favourable government policies if the threat of "moving out" is a realistic one—and these trade agreements certainly make it more realistic. We thus face the prospect of seeing significant elements of our tax base departing over the southern horizon. This reality of business flight is in stark contrast to the optimistic economic forecasts of how many extra jobs would be created by the FTA. Jobs have been lost, not gained, as many companies begin to restructure (and relocate) their Canadian operations for the continental market. As Cedric Ritchie, the Chairman of the Bank of Nova Scotia, has put it: "There is no doubt that Canadian firms are adjusting to the Free Trade Agreement. The problem is that too many are adjusting by leaving Canada."[20]

Not only are we losing domestic industries, but we may be losing investment from outside of North America as well. The same logic applies just as well for foreign firms as for domestic ones—Canada can now be supplied from lower cost, less unionized, less regulated southern locations with few impediments. Mikio Kawamura, Mitsubishi Corporation's director of the Americas, stated the situation plainly: "If we invest in America we can have Canada as well. Logically, it is better for us to invest in the States, as long as other conditions are the same."[21]

Canada's increased vulnerability to the dictates of mobile business comes at a point in history when both the economy and the political system are under strain. Our weak competitive structure, low productivity growth, and lagging technological development provide little grounds for optimism on the new continental battlefield. At the same time, we have restricted the sorts of industrial policy tools we can use to solve these problems in order to conform to an eroding American ideological vision. We have moved away from the possibility of a coherent industrial strategy toward a policy framework that will increasingly resemble that of the United States, and we have prioritized north–south linkages at the expense of our own national economic integration.

## NOTES

1. Canadian Alliance for Trade and Job Opportunities, *The Globe and Mail*, November 3, 1988, p. A10.

2. W.A. Mackintosh, "Economic Factors in Canadian History," in W.T. Easterbrook and M.H. Watkins, eds., *Approaches to Canadian Economic History* (Ottawa: Carleton University Press, 1986), p. 15.

3. H.G. Aitken, "Defensive Expansion: The State and Economic Growth in Canada," in Easterbrook and Watkins, ibid., p. 221.

4. Statistics Canada, 65–202.

5. Figures are for 1991; Statistics Canada (71–202) and Statistical Abstract of the United States, 1992.

6. *Business Week*, September 27, 1993, p. 101, and *The Globe and Mail*, July 20, 1993, p. B1.

7. Organization for Economic Cooperation and Development, *OECD Economic Surveys: Canada* (Paris: OECD, 1992); and Michael E. Porter, *Canada at the Crossroads: The Reality of a New Competitive Environment* (Business Council on National Issues and Minister of Supply and Services Canada, 1991).

8. Porter, *Canada at the Crossroads*, p. 7; and OECD, *Economic Surveys: Canada*, p. 56.

9. OECD, *Economic Surveys: Canada*, p. 53.

10. Porter, *Canada at the Crossroads*, pp. 7–8.

11. OECD, *Economic Surveys: Canada*, p. 53.

12. Porter, *Canada at the Crossroads*, p. 18.

13. OECD, *Economic Surveys: Canada*, pp. 70–71.

14. Economic Council of Canada, *Pulling Together: Productivity, Innovation and Trade* (Ottawa: Minister of Supply and Services Canada, 1992), p. 35; Canada, House of Commons, Standing Committee on Industry, Science and Technology, Regional and Northern Development, *Canada Must Compete* (December 1990), pp. 7–8; Economic Council of Canada, *A Lot to Learn: Education and Training in Canada, A Summary* (Economic Council of Canada, 1992), p. 29; Porter, *Canada at the Crossroads*, p. 49.

15. Statistics Canada, 67–001 and 67–202.

16. Porter, *Canada at the Crossroads*, p. 6.

17. Thomas J. Courchene, "Social Policy and Regional Development," in John Crispo, ed., *Free Trade: The Real Story* (Toronto: Gage, 1988), p. 136.

18. *The Gazette* (Montreal), January 21, 1988, p. 1.

19. Richard Simeon, "Federalism and Free Trade," in Peter M. Leslie, ed., *Canada: The State of the Federation 1986* (Kingston, Ont.: Queen's University, Institute of Intergovernmental Relations, 1986), p. 210.

20. *Maclean's*, March 18, 1991, p. 36.

21. *The Globe and Mail*, May 28, 1991, p. B8.

# POSTSCRIPT

Wooton outlines the theoretical argument for free trade, and does so convincingly. The problem, though, is that practice does not always follow theory. He admits that free trade will produce losers in Canada, but contends that the latter can be compensated through the gains made possible by free trade. However, the limited experience with the FTA suggests that the compensation is meagre, and that those who are thrown out of work by the FTA are often left to their own devices; on this point, see Daniel Schwanen, "Were the Optimists Wrong on Free Trade? A Canadian Perspective," *Commentary* (C.D. Howe Institute), no. 37 (October 1992). The fact that NAFTA is almost certain to produce job losses in the low-skill areas of manufacturing indicates that the need to address the problem of compensation—say, for example, in the form of job retraining—remains important.

Wooton also states that the continental free trade agreement enhances security of access to lucrative American markets. But does it? Since the implementation of the FTA, Canada and the United States have been involved in some serious trade disputes. Some argue that the mechanisms set up to resolve disputes and thereby ensure security of access are functioning in a less than optimal manner. Finally, Wooton says very little about the implications of continental free trade for Canada's sovereignty. He seems to assume that what is good *economically* for Canada is also good *politically*. This is a debatable assumption.

Like Wooton, Stritch makes some good points, but he also offers some arguments that appear to clash with reality. Stritch believes that Canadian industries will be unable to compete under the FTA, but preliminary studies of the agreement suggest otherwise. The aforementioned paper by Daniel Schwanen reports that many sectors of the Canadian economy—crucial sectors—have done quite well. Stritch also worries that the continental trade agreements may have tied Canada to a tired, worn-out American economy, and that more attractive markets located elsewhere have been forsaken. But Wooton argues that the fear of the world forming regional trading blocs might stimulate a movement to multilateral trade arrangements. More generally, one may note that the pursuit of bilateral and multilateral trade agreements respectively need not be mutually exclusive.

Free trade between Canada and the United States (and now Mexico) is an extremely complicated subject. Students should prepare to examine this issue by first gaining an appreciation of the relevant history. Jack Granatstein's article "Free Trade Between Canada and the United States: The Issue That Will Not Go Away," in Denis Stairs and Gilbert R. Winham, eds., *The Politics of Canada's Economic Relationship with the United States* (Toronto: University of Toronto Press, 1985) does a good job of offering the necessary historical background.

A number of books and articles on both the economics and politics of the FTA have been written, including: Robert M. Campbell and Leslie A. Pal, *The Real Worlds of Canadian Politics*, 2nd ed. (Peterborough: Broadview Press, 1991), ch. 3; G. Bruce Doern and Brian W. Tomlin, *Faith and Fear: The Free Trade Story* (Toronto: Stoddart, 1991); John Crispo, ed., *Free Trade: The Real Story* (Toronto: Gage, 1988); Gilbert R. Winham, *Trading With Canada: The Canada–U.S. Free Trade Agreement* (New York: Priority Press, 1988); Duncan Cameron, ed., *The Free Trade Deal* (Toronto: James Lorimer, 1988); and Marc Gold and David Leyton-Brown, eds., *Trade-Offs on Free Trade: The Canada–U.S. Free Trade Agreement* (Toronto: Carswell, 1988).

Though NAFTA is a more recent development than the FTA, it too has attracted the attention of scholars. Two texts that address NAFTA are Stephen J. Randall, ed., *North America Without Borders? Integrating Canada, the United States, and Mexico* (Calgary: University of Calgary Press, 1992), and Steven Globerman and Michael Walker, eds., *Assessing NAFTA: A Trinational Analysis* (Vancouver: Fraser Institute, 1993). For brief—and largely positive—assessments of NAFTA, one might turn to Richard Lipsey, Daniel Schwanen, and Ronald J. Wonnacott, "Inside or Outside the NAFTA? The Consequences of Canada's Choice," *Commentary* (C.D. Howe Institute), no. 48 (June 1993), and William G. Watson, "North American Free Trade: Lessons from the Trade Data," *Canadian Public Policy* vol. 18, no. 1 (March 1992). For a critical perspective on NAFTA, consult Maude Barlow and Bruce Campbell, *Take Back the Nation 2*, rev. ed. (Key Porter: Toronto, 1993).

# APPENDIX

## How to Write an Argumentative Essay

*Lucille Charlton*

Argumentative essays are written to convince or persuade readers of a particular point or opinion. Whether that point is to change the public's mind on a political issue or to persuade a person to stop smoking, all argumentative essays have common elements: a well-defined, convincing argument, credible evidence, and a rebuttal of criticism. While most points of general essay writing apply to argumentative essays, there are several special guidelines the writer of a good persuasive essay must consider. The following sections introduce students to six basic steps in writing an argumentative or persuasive essay.

## STEP 1: DEFINE THE ARGUMENT

It is very easy to point out that there are two sides to every discussion; however, it is difficult to define precisely one's own opinion on a subject and write about it. First, the writer must be certain that there is, in fact, something to disagree about. For example, Brian Mulroney was a Canadian prime minister; no one can dispute that fact. However, if I claim in my essay that Mulroney was Canada's greatest prime minister, many people would disagree with me. There must be room for disagreement with whatever position is taken, so an argumentative essay must be more than an affirmation of acknowledged facts. In this way, argumentative writing differs from descriptive or journalistic writing. Also, the writer must state the entire argument in a precise thesis statement that will act as a controlling idea for the entire essay. All ideas expressed in the essay must relate to the thesis statement.

Second, an argumentative essay is more than a restatement of the two sides of the question. A simple recounting of opposing arguments does not give the reader any clear indication of how the writer feels about the subject, and is not really a persuasive statement. For example, a court reporter records every word spoken by the witnesses at a trial. These statements are entered as evidence in the court, but it is up to the lawyers for both sides to interpret the evidence and present it in a persuasive manner to the jury, leaving no doubt about which side they are on. In the same way, the writer first carefully defines the subject, examines the evidence, and then interprets that evidence by writing a precise opinion. An argumentative essay takes one side of a controversial issue; there should be no doubt in the reader's mind where the writer stands on that issue.

## STEP 2: GATHER THE EVIDENCE

Arguments need credible supporting evidence, and good persuasive writers assemble a variety of information from different sources. This evidence can be found in statements from authorities, statistics, personal experience, or can be interpreted from laws or philosophic statements. The authors found in this book have chosen one or more of these types of evidence to support their positions. David Kilgour, John Kirsner, and Kenneth McConnell (Issue 11) use voting statistics from both the United States and Canada as evidence for their views on party discipline. Personal experience is effectively used by both Flora MacDonald and Don Page, who draw on their experience in government to comment on the civil service (Issue 10). Philip Bryden and Robert Martin (Issue 6) draw on both concrete examples and broader philosophical arguments in discussing the impact of the Charter of Rights and Freedoms. These four types of evidence can also be used by student writers in their argumentative essays.

When researching evidence to support a particular position, the writer needs to keep the four *R*'s in mind: *reliable, relevant, recent,* and *referenced.* First, all authorities used for supporting evidence need to be reliable—that means an acknowledged authority published in a recognized source. Evidence can be suspect if it is published only in unreliable sources. A good writer recognizes acceptable sources and is knowledgeable of the biases normally found in newspapers, magazines, and journals. Reference librarians can assist students in finding a variety of trustworthy sources for essays. Using suspect sources will damage the credibility of the writer and create immediate suspicion on the part of the reader. A variety of reliable sources adds credibility to the writer's statements.

Second, sources need to be relevant; that is, they have something to contribute on the immediate topic. The Economic Council of Canada has expertise in the area of the Canadian economy, but scholars know that it would not be a source for comments on the consequences of the power struggle in Russia. Writers can easily lose unity in their essays by adding irrelevant quotes or paraphrases just to sound authoritative.

Third, a good writer looks for updated information on the topic. Using outdated information could affect the outcome of the argument. For example, if I were arguing for increased subsidization of child-care spaces, I would not base my essay on statistics from 1980, when fewer women were in the work force. The writer should be familiar with the effects of recent changes on the topic: politicians can reverse their positions, new statistics can change the writer's perspective, and new research can add to the evidence. However, a writer must also know how much background research needs to be done to introduce the topic to the reader. If background information is necessary, the writer may need to research how things have changed over the last number of years. Don Page responds to Flora MacDonald by putting her experience in the historical context of the time and then examines more recent examples that refute her contentions (Issue 10).

Finally, all sources need to be carefully quoted and referenced in an acceptable citation form. There are a few basic rules to follow when using someone else's material:

1. Quotations are the exact words of the original author. They must always be referenced. Consult one of the reference books listed at the end of this article for correct formats. If you are unsure how to reference a particular or unusual source, consult with your instructor or a reference librarian.

2. Paraphrases are your restatement of the original author's ideas. Paraphrases keep the same idea, but are restated in your own words. All paraphrases must be referenced. See Charlton's paraphrasing of Boyer's arguments in Issue 16 as an example.

3. Do not take either quotations or paraphrases out of context, thereby misquoting a source. I could quote Jeffrey Simpson on pollsters as saying "their craft, with all its scientific splendours, represents the purest form of democracy," but when the entire document is examined, Simpson really comes out strongly against governments relying on the polls for advice (Issue 14 ).

4. Give credit whenever using information that did not originate with you, except for general information or well- known facts. For example, you do not need to acknowledge that Brian Mulroney was prime minister of Canada from 1984 to 1993. However, you must acknowledge statistical data taken from census or research reports, for example, that is used to support your arguments. All of the contributors

to this volume have acknowledged their sources at the end of their articles in notes or references.

In gathering the evidence, keep careful notes and records of all your sources. Make sure to acknowledge all of your sources. The reference manuals listed at the end of this article have helpful information on deciding how to cite your sources. Avoid plagiarism. If you are not certain what constitutes plagiarism, ask your instructor for assistance and consult your institution's policy on plagiarism. All colleges and universities have serious penalties for plagiarism.

## STEP 3: REFUTE THE OPPOSITION

In order to be convincing, writers have to support their argument while defusing criticism of the position taken. When researching the arguments, the writer also anticipates opposing viewpoints, researches them thoroughly, and is ready to refute them in the essay. Casting doubt on other writers' positions or reasoning can clinch your support. This can be done in several ways. First, the writer can cite authorities who hold opposing views, then refute their arguments by quoting other sources or different statistics. For an example of this method, see Issue 16, where Charlton states eight points that Boyer makes, and then refutes each one. Second, rebuttals of arguments can be constructed through differing personal experiences (Issue 10). Another method frequently used is that of attacking the opposition's interpretation of documents and facts. Michael Adams effectively challenges Jeffrey Simpson's interpretations of the meaning and use of polls in Issue 14.

Another tactic Adams uses is conceding some of the arguments and agreeing with his opponent on a couple of points. Conceding part of the argument and finding common ground with an opponent makes the writer seem to be a reasonable person. Concessions should be included early in the argument, so that the writer can finish on a strong point. Whatever the method, it is essential to refute or to concede opposing arguments in order to be effective. Avoiding all mention of the opposing position is not a good strategy.

Whether building support for their own arguments or refuting criticism of their positions, writers must be careful to avoid argumentative fallacies, or mistakes in reasoning or argument. The most common fallacies that appear in essays are overgeneralization, faulty cause and effect, and misrepresentation of the opposition. For a complete discussion of argumentative fallacies, see Fowler et al., *The Little, Brown Handbook*, 1st Can. ed. (Toronto: Gage, 1991).

# STEP 4: OUTLINE YOUR ESSAY

Good essay writers start with an outline that incorporates their key ideas into the body of the essay. All argumentative essays begin with an attention-getter; the writer quotes an interesting fact, makes a dramatic statement, or even illustrates with the opposite opinion (see Jack Roberts in Issue 19). Once the reader is hooked into reading the essay, the writer continues with a thesis statement and proceeds with the arguments.

The body of an argumentative essay can be organized in two ways:

**Pattern I**

Introduction
Thesis Statement
Background (if needed)
Listing of all your arguments with supporting evidence
A refutation of your opponent's points
A reminder of your strongest arguments
Conclusion, including a strong opinion statement

**Pattern II**

Introduction
Thesis Statement
Background (if needed)
Statement of your opponent's first argument, with concession or refutation
Statement of your opponent's second argument, with concession and refutation
Continue refuting your opponent's arguments in order
Conclusion, with a strong statement of your own opinion

Most of the contributors to this volume follow Pattern II, which is more effective for longer essays. Pattern I is acceptable for shorter essays with fewer points of supporting evidence, because the reader will not get lost following the train of thought from argument to refutation. In both patterns, concessions are made early in the argument, and a strong opinion statement concludes the essay.

# STEP 5: DECIDE TONE AND STYLE

The tone and style of your essay will depend on your audience. Most writers assume that they are writing for an intelligent audience with open minds on the topic. Therefore, the tone of the essay cannot be insulting or pejorative. Treat your opposition with respect.

Examples:

*Wrong*: As every intelligent person knows …
*Better*:  Many people believe …

*Wrong*: Only children would assume that …
*Better*:  I do not agree with those who take the position …

The essay must also be readable. Using language that is either hard to understand or too casual for the audience will not win converts to your point of view. The language used in an essay must be clear, direct, understandable, and free of gender or racial biases.

Examples:

*Wrong*: Legitimized concerns on this matter were postponed by the committee.
*Better*:  The committee delayed discussion.

*Wrong*: Those guys really messed up on this one.
*Better*:  The politicians made mistakes in their analysis.

*Wrong*: A cabinet minister is accountable for his decisions.
*Better*:  Cabinet ministers are accountable for their decisions.

Most academic essays are written in a formal tone, making minimal use of the pronoun "I." However, be sure to know what your audience expects. Sometimes persuasive essays or speeches are directed at a particular group, and the writer can then use a less formal style of presentation.

# STEP 6: CHECK AND DOUBLE-CHECK

After writing a draft of an essay, follow this basic checklist of items. By working through the list, you can catch errors in your essay.

Argumentative essay checklist:

1. Have I defined the argument?

2. Do I have a well-stated opinion on the topic?

3. Is my thesis statement clear? Does it have sufficient support?

4. Is my essay unified? Do all parts of the essay relate to the thesis statement?

5. Have I avoided argumentative fallacies?

6. Are my tone and style consistent?

7. Have I varied my sentence structure and vocabulary?

8. Have I concluded with a strong statement?

9. Does the opening paragraph grab the reader's attention?

10. Have I checked for spelling errors and misused words and expressions?

11. Have I cited all sources in an acceptable style?

12. Have I correctly punctuated my sentences?

## SOURCES TO CONSULT ON ESSAY WRITING

Buckley, Joanne. *Fit to Print: The Canadian Student's Guide to Essay Writing*, 2nd ed. Toronto: Harcourt Brace Jovanovich, 1991.

Fowler, H. Ramsey, Jane Aaron, Deane E.D. Downey, and Barbara H. Pell. *The Little, Brown Handbook*, 1st Can. ed. Toronto: Gage, 1991.

Gibaldi, Joseph, and Walter S. Achtert. *MLA Handbook for Writers of Research Papers*, 3rd. ed. New York: Modern Language Association, 1988.

Hacker, Diana. *A Canadian Writer's Reference.* Toronto: Nelson, 1990.

Northey, Margot. *Making Sense*, 3rd ed. Toronto: Oxford University Press, 1993.

**For ESL students:**

Levy, April Lambert. *Writing College English.* Toronto: Harcourt Brace Jovanovich, 1988.

# CNTRIBUTORS

**Michael Adams** is president of Environics Research Group Limited.

**Carol Agócs** is a professor at the Centre for Administrative and Information Studies, University of Western Ontario. She is the co-author (with Catherine Burr and Felicity Somerset) of *Employment Equity: Cooperative Strategies for Organizational Change.*

**Janet Ajzenstat** is a professor of political science at McMaster University.

**Taylor Alexander** is president of Alexa Health Consulting in Ottawa. Dr. Alexander is a specialist in health policy, and also teaches in the Master of Health Administration Program, Faculty of Administration, University of Ottawa.

**Reginald W. Bibby** is a professor of sociology at the University of Lethbridge. He has published numerous works, including *Mosaic Madness: The Poverty and Potential of Life in Canada* and *Fragmented Gods: the Poverty and Potential of Religion in Canada.*

**Benoît Bouchard** is a former minister in the Conservative government of Brian Mulroney.

**Lucien Bouchard** is the leader of the Bloc Québécois.

**Patrick Boyer** was a Conservative Member of Parliament from 1984 to 1993. He has published a number of books, including *The People's Mandate: Referendums and a More Democratic Canada* and *Direct Democracy: The History and Future of Referendums.*

**Ed Broadbrent**, leader of the New Democratic Party between 1975 and 1990, is president of the International Centre for Human Rights and Democratic Development.

**Philip L. Bryden** is Associate Dean of the Faculty of Law at the University of British Columbia.

**J.M.S. Careless** is a professor emeritus of history at the University of Toronto. His many books include *Canada: A Story of Challenge* and *The Growth of Canadian Institutions, 1841–1857.*

**William D. Coleman** is a professor of political science at McMaster University. He is author of *Business and Politics: A Study of Collective Action, the Independence Movement in Quebec, 1945–80,* and *The State, Business and Industrial Change in Canada* (with Michael Atkinson).

**Paul Conlin** is a political science student at Carleton University.

**David Elton** is a professor of political science at the University of Lethbridge and president of the Canada West Foundation. He has written extensively on western alienation.

**Thomas Flanagan** is a professor of political science at the University of Calgary. He has written widely on native issues in Canada and is the co-author of *An Introduction to Government and Politics: A Conceptual Approach* (with Mark Dickerson) and *Human Rights and Social Technology: The New War on Discrimination* (with Rainer Knopff).

**Augie Fleras** is a professor of sociology at the University of Waterloo. He has published a number of books on multiculturalism and native issues, including *Multiculturalism in Canada: The Challenge of Diversity* and *Nations Within: Aboriginal–State Relations in Canada, the United States, and New Zealand.*

**H. Patrick Glenn** is Peter M. Laing Professor of Law at McGill University.

**Leo Groarke** is a professor of philosophy at Wilfrid Laurier University and is author of *Greek Scepticism: Anti-Realist Trends in Greek Philosophy.*

**John Hiemstra** is a professor of political science at The King's University College, Edmonton, Alberta.

**R. Brian Howe** is a professor of political science at the University College of Cape Breton.

**Robert J. Jackson** is a professor of political science at Carleton University and is co-author of *Politics in Canada: Culture, Institutions, Behaviour and Public Policy, Contemporary Government and Politics: Democracy and Authoritarianism,* and *Stand Up for Canada.*

**David Kilgour** is a Liberal Member of Parliament for Edmonton Southeast and author of *Uneasy Patriots—Western Canada in Confederation.*

**Ronald G. Landes** is chairperson and professor of political science at Saint Mary's University (Halifax, Nova Scotia). He is author of the popular textbook *The Canadian Polity: A Comparative Perspective* and editor of *Canadian Politics: A Comparative Reader.*

**Flora MacDonald** is a former Conservative cabinet member in the Clark and Mulroney governments.

**Paul Marshall** is a professor of political theory at the Institute for Christian Studies, Toronto. He has co-authored a number of books, including *Servant or Tyrant? The Task and Limits of Government.*

**Robert Martin** is a professor of law at the University of Western Ontario. He is author of *The Philosopher's Dictionary* and co-author of *A Sourcebook of Canadian Media Law.*

**Douglas J. McCready** teaches economics at Wilfrid Laurier University. He has written numerous articles on health policy and public finance, and is the author of *The Canadian Public Sector.*

**John Meisel** is a professor of political science at Queen's University and former chairperson of the Canadian Radio-Television and Telecommunications Commission.

**F.L. Morton** is a professor of political science at the University of Calgary, and the author of *Morgentaler v. Borowski: Abortion, the Charter, and the Courts* and co-author (with Rainer Knopff) of *Charter Politics.*

**Brian Mulroney** is a former prime minister of Canada.

**Michael Nolan**, a professor of journalism at the University of Western Ontario, has authored books and articles on the media and politics, including *Michael Blackburn: A Man For All Media.*

**John A. Olthuis** is a lawyer who has acted as legal counsel to various First Nations on land claims, aboriginal rights, and constitutional issues.

**Don Page** is vice-president for academic affairs at Trinity Western University. He spent sixteen years as senior historian, policy analyst, and speech writer in the Department of External Affairs and International Trade Canada, and has written numerous articles on Canadian foreign policy.

**Jack Roberts** is a professor of law at the University of Western Ontario.

**Jeffrey Simpson** is a national affairs columnist for *The Globe and Mail.* He has published many books on Canadian politics, including *Discipline of Power: The Conservative Interlude and the Liberal Restoration* and *Spoils of Power: The Politics of Patronage.*

**Denis Smith** is a professor of political science at the University of Western Ontario. His publications include *Gentle Patriot: A Political Biography* *of Walter Gordon, Diplomacy of Fear: Canada and the Cold War, 1941–1948,* and a forthcoming biography of John Diefenbaker.

**W.T. Stanbury** is a professor of regulation and competition policy in the Faculty of Commerce and Business Administration at the University of British Columbia. He is author of *Business–Government Relations in Canada: Influencing Public Policy,* and has written numerous articles on matters relating to business and government.

**Andrew Stritch** is a professor of political science at Bishop's University. He is co-author of *Business and Government in Canada* (with Stephan Brooks).

**David Taras** is director of the Canadian Studies Program at the University of Calgary. He is co-editor of *Prime Ministers and Premiers: Political Leadership and Public Policy in Canada* (with Leslie Pal) and author of *The Newsmakers: The Media's Influence on Canadian Politics.*

**William Thorsell** is editor-in-chief of *The Globe and Mail.*

**Roger Townshend** is a lawyer specializing in native issues. He was senior researcher at the Treaty and Aboriginal Rights Research Centre (Manitoba).

**Pierre Trudeau** is a former prime minister of Canada.

**William Watson** is a professor of economics at McGill University and social sciences editor at McGill-Queen's University Press.

**Joseph Wearing** is a professor of political science at Trent University. He is author of *The L-shaped Party: The Liberal Party of Canada, 1958–1980, Strained Relations: Canada's Parties and Voters,* and editor of *The Ballot and Its Message: Voting in Canada.*

**M.W. Westmacott** is a professor of political science at the University of Western Ontario. He has written many articles on the subject of Canadian federalism and is the co-editor (with R.D. Olling) of *Perspectives on Canadian Federalism.*

**Geoff Wilson** is a former Conservative Member of Parliament for Swift Current–Maple Creek, Saskatchewan.

**Ian Wooton** is a professor of economics at the University of Western Ontario.

**R.A. Young** is a professor of political science at the University of Western Ontario. He has authored numerous articles on various aspects of Canadian politics, and is the editor of *Confederation in Crisis.*

# CONTRIBUTORS ACKNOWLEDGMENTS

Permission to reprint copyrighted material is gratefully acknowledged. Information that will enable the publisher to rectify any error or omission will be welcomed.

**Issue 1**
Prime Minister Brian Mulroney (speaker), "Dualism in Canada," House of Commons, *Debates*, February 15, 1990, pp. 8400–8405. Reprinted by permission of the House of Commons.

William Thorsell, "Let Us Compare Mythologies," reprinted from *Report on Business* 6, no. 11 (May 1990):105–107, 110–111, by permission of *The Globe and Mail*.

**Issue 2**
Reginald Bibby, "Is Multiculturalism Tearing Us Apart?" reprinted from *Compass: A Jezuit Journal* (Toronto: Jezuits of Upper Canada Province, Society of Jesus, 1992), pp. 26–28, by permission of the Jezuits of Upper Canada Province, Society of Jesus and the author.

Augie Fleras, "Multiculturalism as Society-Building: Doing What is Necessary, Workable and Fair," © Nelson Canada 1994.

**Issue 3**
David Elton, "The West Wants In," adapted from "Federalism and the Canadian West," in R.D. Olling and M.W. Westmacott, eds., *Perspective on Canadian Federalism* (Toronto: Prentice-Hall Canada, 1988), pp. 348–351, by permission of Prentice-Hall and the author.

J.M.S. Careless, "The Myth of the Downtrodden West," reprinted from *Saturday Night* 96, no. 5 (May 1981):30–36, by permission of the author.

**Issue 4**
John Olthuis and Roger Townshend, "The Case for Native Sovereignty," © Nelson Canada 1994.

Don Page, "Ministers and Mandarins: Ministers Must Lead," © Nelson Canada 1994.

## Issue 11

David Kilgour, John Kirsner, and Kenneth McConnell, "Discipline versus Democracy: Party Discipline in Canadian Politics," © Nelson Canada 1994.

Robert J. Jackson and Paul Conlin, "The Imperative of Party Discipline in the Canadian Political System," © Nelson Canada 1994.

## Issue 12

F.L. Morton, "Why the Judicial Appointment Process Must Be Reformed," © Nelson Canada 1994.

H. Patrick Glenn, " Parliamentary Hearings for Supreme Court of Canada Appointments," © Nelson Canada 1994.

## Issue 13

John Meisel, "The Decline of Parties," reprinted from "The Decline of Party in Canada," in Hugh Thorburn, ed., *Party Politics in Canada*, 5th ed. (Scarborough, Ont.: Prentice-Hall Canada), pp. 98–108, by permission of Prentice-Hall Canada.

Ronald Landes, "In Defence of Canadian Political Parties," © Nelson Canada 1994.

## Issue 14

Jeffrey Simpson, "Pollstruck," reprinted from *Policy Options* 8, no. 2 (March 1987):3–7, by permission of the Institute for Research on Public Policy.

Michael Adams, "Pro Polling," reprinted from *Policy Options* 8, no. 6 (July 1987):28–30, by permission of the Institute for Research on Public Policy.

## Issue 15

John Hiemstra, "Getting What You Vote For," © Nelson Canada 1994.

Paul Barker, "Voting for Trouble," © Nelson Canada 1994.

## Issue 16

Patrick Boyer, "Our Democratic Reformation." from *Direct Democracy in Canada: the History and Future of Referendums* (Toronto: Dundurn Press).

Mark Charlton, "The Limits of Direct Democracy," © Nelson Canada 1994.

## Issue 17

William Coleman, "One Step Ahead: Business in the Policy Process in Canada," © Nelson Canada 1994.

William Stanbury, "Assessing the Political Power of Business Interests," © Nelson Canada 1994.

**Issue 18**
David Taras, "Bad habits and Broken Promises: The Media and Election Campaigns,"© Nelson Canada 1994.

Michael Nolan, "Don't Shoot the Messenger: The Media and Election Campaigns," © Nelson Canada 1994.

**Issue 19**
Carol Agócs, "Employment Equity: Is It Needed? Is It Fair?" reprinted by permission of the author.

Jack Roberts, "Employment Equity—Unfair," © Nelson Canada 1994.

**Issue 20**
Leo Groake, "Pornography: From Liberalism to Censorship," reprinted from *Queen's Quarterly* 90, no. 4 (Winter 1983):1108–1120, by permission of the author.

William Watson, "Pornography and Liberalism," reprinted from *Policy Options* (June 1985):18–21, by permission of the Institute for Research on Public Policy.

**Issue 21**
Geoff Wilson, "The Case for Capital Punishment," House of Commons, *Debates,* June 22, 1987, pp. 7421–7423. Reprinted by permission of the House of Commons.

Ed Broadbent, "The Case Against Capital Punishment," House of Commons, *Debates,* April 27, 1987, pp. 5219–5222. Reprinted by permission of the House of Commons.

**Issue 22**
Taylor Alexander, "Universal Medicare: Can We Afford to Lose It?" © Nelson Canada 1994.

Douglas, McCready, "Social Justice: Universality and Health Care in Canada," © Nelson Canada 1994.

**Issue 23**
Brian Howe, "The Case for a Canadian Social Charter," © Nelson Canada 1994.

Janet Ajzenstat, "A Social Charter Eh? Thanks, But No Thanks," © Nelson Canada 1994.

**Issue 24**
Ian Wooton, "The Case for a More Liberal Trade Regime," © Nelson Canada 1994.

Andrew Stritch, "The Costs of Free Trade," © Nelson Canada 1994.

## To the owner of this book

We hope that you have enjoyed *Crosscurrents: Contemporary Political Issues* and we would like to know as much about your experiences with it as you would care to offer. Only through your comments and those of others can we learn how to make this a better text for future readers.

School _____ Your instructor's name _____

Course _____ Was the text required? _____ Recommended? _____

**1.** What did you like the most about *Crossscurrents: Contemporary Political Issues?*

_____

_____

_____

**2.** How useful was this text for your course?

_____

_____

_____

**3.** Do you have any recommendations for ways to improve the next edition of this text?

_____

_____

_____

**4.** In the space below or in a separate letter, please write any other comments you have about the book. (For example, please feel free to comment on reading level, writing style, terminology, design features, and learning aids.)

_____

_____

_____

## Optional

Your
name _____ Date _____

May Nelson Canada quote you, either in promotion for *Crosscurrents: Contemporary Political Issues* or in future publishing ventures?

Yes _____ No _____

*Thanks!*

- - - - - - - - - - - - - - - - - - - - - - - - - - - FOLD HERE - - - - - - - - - - - - - - - - - - - - - - - - - -

**MAIL** ⮞**POSTE**

Canada Post Corporation / Société canadienne des postes

| **Postage paid** if mailed in Canada | **Port payé** si posté au Canada |
| --- | --- |
| **Business Reply** | **Réponse d'affaires** |
| 0107077099 | 01 |

**Nelson**

TAPE SHUT

0107077099-M1K5G4-BR01

**Nelson Canada**
College Editorial Department
1120 Birchmount Rd.
Scarborough, ON  M1K 9Z9

PLEASE TAPE SHUT. DO NOT STAPLE.